THE LAW OF THE SEA

Ocean Law and Policy

Thomas A. Clingan, Jr.

Austin & Winfield, Publishers
Lanham · New York · Oxford

Austin & Winfield, Publishers
4720 Boston Way
Lanham, Maryland 20706

12 Hid's Copse Rd.
Cumnor Hill, Oxford OX2 9JJ

Printed in the United States of America
ritish Library Cataloging in Publication Information Available

Library of Congress Cataloging-in-Publication Data

Clingan, Thomas A.
Law of the Sea: Ocean Law and Policy / Thomas A. Clingan, Jr.
p. cm
Includes bibliographical references and index.
1. Maritime law. I. Title.
JX4411.C56 1993 341.4'5—dc20 93-3931 CIP

ISBN 1-880921-28-6 (pbk. : alk. ppr.)

The paper used in this publication meets the minimum requirements of American National Standard for Information Sciences—Permanence of Paper for Printed Library Materials, ANSI Z39.48—1984

FOREWORD

This book has been written primarily for classroom use, although some of the materials included in this work also serve as reference materials. The book contains the most recent materials available on the law of the sea. It was designed not only to provide current materials, but also those materials necessary to show the evolutionary development of the doctrines over many years, because an understanding of that evolution, it is believed, leads to a greater insight into understanding the current state of the law.

While emphasis has been given to the international law of the sea, some materials contained herein deal with the law of the United States on particular subjects, so that the reader can gain some insight into how U.S. courts and the Congress play a role in setting law of the sea policy for the United States, and for comparative purposes. For example, the Fishery Conservation and Management Act of 1976 has been included to show the way the United States manages its fishery resources and invites the reader to compare it with international rules.

The law of the sea is a rapidly developing field. The 1982 United Nations Convention on the Law of the Sea, a major consideration in this book, was designed to provide global stability to the rules of international law on the subject. However, the reader must be aware that it is really the starting point, rather than the ending. Much remains to be done to expand upon and clarify the rules contained in that treaty. The law of the sea, thus, remains a viable subject for study for many years to come.

I would like to give credit, and thanks, to Dean Mary Doyle of the University of Miami School of Law for her support for this project in the form of research assistance and research grants. I must also give thanks to the staff of the law school for their support in terms of computer and other services, and Michael Cover for his valuable research assistance. Finally, I should like to thank my wife, Nancy, for her support and encouragement throughout the process.

T. A. Clingan, Jr.
Coral Gables, FL

January, 1993

CONTENTS

Introduction to the Law of the Sea.......I

Chapter 1: The United Nations and the Law of the Sea.......1

A. The Structure of the Conference.......1

B. The Rules of Procedure.......3

C. How Substantive Negotiations were Conducted.......5

D. The Drafting Committee.......8

Chapter 2: Freedom of the High Seas.......10

A. Introduction.......10

B. The Origins and Evolution of the Doctrine.......10

1. Early History

2. Hugo Grotius and Mare Liberum.......12

3. John Selden and Mare Clausum.......18

C. Treaty Elaboration of the Doctrine.......21

D. The Exclusive Economic Zone.......24

E. The "Presential Sea".......27

F. The Problem of Enclosed and Semi-Enclosed Seas.......41

H. Treaty Rules Governing the High Seas.......49

I. Collision Jurisdiction.......56

J. Slavery.......57

K. Piracy.......58

L. Narcotic Drugs.......61

M. Hot Pursuit.......62

Chapter 3: Internal Waters and the Territorial Sea.......75

A. Introduction.......75

B. Internal Waters.......75

1. Definition....75

2. Access to Internal Waters....76

3. The Application of Coastal State Authority over Vessels in Internal Waters

a. Warships....79

b. Criminal Jurisdiction over a Commercial Vessel while in Port....80

C. The Territorial Sea....81

1. Origins of the Concept of the Legal Regime of the Territorial Sea....81

2. The Breadth of the Territorial Sea....85

a. The First and Second United Nations Conference on the Law of the Sea....86

b. The Third United Nations Conference....97

3. Passage of Vessels through Jurisdictional Zones

a. The Concept of Innocent Passage through the Territorial Sea....98

i. Generally

ii. Innocent Passage of Warships....101

iii. Innocent Passage under the 1982 Convention....105

b. Passage through Straits used for International Navigation....110

c. Archipelagic Sealanes Passage....121

Chapter 4: Contiguous Zones....125

A. Introduction....125

B. Development of the Concept 125

C. Contiguous Zones in Law and State Practice 127

1. Customs Zones 127

2. Neutrality Zones 130

3. The Article 24 Contiguous Zone 134

4. Pirate Broadcasting 137

5. Environmental Protection 139

Chapter 5: Baselines 144

A. Introduction 144

B. The Normal Baselines 145

C. Islands and their Baselines 147

D. Special Cases 151

1. The Straight Baseline 151

2. Bays 160

a. Juridical Bays 160

b. Historic Bays 162

c. Bays Bounded by Two or more States 172

3. Permanent Harbor Works 173

4. Roadsteads 173

5. Low Tide Elevations 174

6. Rivers Emptying into the Sea 175

Chapter 6: The Continental Shelf 177

A. Introduction 177

B. Geology of the Continental Shelf 177

C. Resources of the Shelf 179

D. Oil and Gas Technology 181

E. Evolution of the Doctrine....183

F. The Continental Shelf Regime....189

1. Introduction....189

2. Rights Exercisable and Resources Included under the Continental Shelf Concept....190

3. Seaward Extent....200

G. Structures Permitted on the Continental Shelf....208

H. Federalism and the Continental Shelf....213

Chapter 7: Delimitation and Apportionment....216

A. Delimitation of Ocean Boundaries....216

B. Apportionment of Ocean Space Between States whose Coasts are Opposite or Adjacent....216

1. The Territorial Sea....216

2. The Continental Shelf....218

3. Exclusive Economic Zone....220

C. Case Studies in Delimitation of Maritime Boundaries....222

D. Problems of Islands....260

Chapter 8: The Deep Ocean Floor: The "Seabed" Question....264

A. Introduction....264

B. Some Marine Geology and Seabed Mining Technology....264

C. The "Seabed" Question in the United Nations....269

1. Early Proceedings: The Seabed Committee....269

a. Background....269

b. At the United Nations....273

2. The "Moratorium" and "Principles" Resolutions....275

a. The Moratorium....275

b. The Principles 278

D. The Third United Nations Conference on the Law of the Sea 280

E. The New Regime 282

1. Principles Governing the Area 282

2. Policies Relating to Mining 282

3. General Structure and Establishment of the International Seabed Authority 283

4. Composition, Powers and Decision-Making in the Authority 285

a. The Assembly 285

b. The Council 287

c. Subsidiary Organs 292

5. The System of Access 296

a. The Parallel System 296

b. The Banking System 296

6. Plans of Work 297

a. Requirements for Plans of Work 297

b. Qualifications of Applicants 298

c. Size of Areas 299

d. Flow of Contract Approval 299

7. Production Authorizations 301

8. Production Limitations 302

9. Financial Implications 304

a. Financing the International Seabed Authority 304

b. Financing the Enterprise 305

c. Financial Terms of Mining Contracts 307

10. Transfer of Technololgy 309

11. Review Conference 311

12. Amendments to the Treaty other than by Review Conference 313

13. Entry into Force of Amendments 314

14. Investment Protection 315

F. Related Documents 321

Chapter 9: Exploitation of Living Resources 359

A. Introduction 359

B. Objectives of Fishery Management 359

C. Alternatives for Management 361

1. Limited Entry 363

D. Management of International Fisheries 367

1. Bilateral Agreements 368

2. Multilateral Agreements 373

E. Exclusive Fishing Zones 387

1. Fishing in the Exclusive Economic Zone: The Convention 387

2. Domestic Fisheries Management 395

Chapter 10: Marine Scientific Research 435

A. Introduction 435

B. Goals of Marine Scientific Research 435

C. The Conduct of Marine Scientific Research under the Convention 442

D. International Cooperation in Marine Scientific Research 452

E. Transfer of Marine Technology 460

Chapter 11: Protection and Preservation of the Marine Environment 466

A. The Nature of the Problem: Sources of Pollution 466

B. Responsibility and Liability....471

1. Responsibility....471

a. General Principles of International Liability....471

b. Responsibility under Treaty Law....473

C. Vessel Source Pollution....478

D. Ocean Dumping....504

E. United Nations Conference on the Environment and Development (UNCED)....515

Chapter 12: Dispute Settlement....517

A. Introduction....517

B. Dispute Settlement Procedures....527

Chapter 13: Military Use of the Marine Environment....560

A. Introduction....560

B. Military Use of the Seabed....561

1. Denuclearization....561

2. Anti-Submarine Warfare....566

C. Problems of Naval Mobility....568

1. Generally....568

2. Territorial Sea Breadth....576

3. Passage Through Straits....577

4. Zones of Peace and Security....577

5. The "High Seas" Status of the Exclusive Economic Zone....579

D. National Security, Generally....579

Chapter 14: United States Ocean Policy....586

Annex A: Convention on the High Seas....607

Annex B: Convention on the Territorial Sea and the Contiguous Zone....615

Annex C: Convention on the Continental Shelf 623

Annex D: Convention on Fishing and Conservation

of the Living Resources of the High Seas 627

Annex E: Optional Protocol of Signature 633

INTRODUCTION TO THE LAW OF THE SEA

Before embarking upon our study, the student should have some idea of the extent and nature of the important uses of the seas and their beds, and the traditional concepts and definitions that apply. We shall examine how ocean space has in the past been divided, and for what reasons.

The oceans, constituting approximately 72 percent of the earth's surface area, are clearly among civilization's greatest and most important resources. Recognition of this fact has made the law of the sea a major component of public international law for some time. It is especially so today as an examination of any major international law textbook will reveal. The importance of the oceans to society lies in their uses. Basically, these uses can be classified as resource and non-resource issues.

It is these uses that have, over the centuries, generated a zonal approach to ocean regulation. Logically, this should not be so. The oceans constitute a great, constantly flowing fluid body, and one of its most important resource contributions, living marine resources, are mobile in nature, respecting no artificial boundaries. Nor does it make sense to regulate marine scientific research, which requires a global rather than local effort, by local rules. Nonetheless, humans tend to develop rules regarding new situations with reference to past experience. Thus it is not surprising to find, as the law of the sea evolved, heavy reliance was placed on prior land-based experience. On land, governance has traditionally been based on divisions and subdivisions of property, called by different names: nations, states, counties, cities, towns, etc., with each discrete unit developing rules applicable to its own particular needs and aspirations.

Although the sea has no natural boundaries for subdivision, such as rivers on land, usage has developed that dictates that jurisdictional lines be drawn, much as on the land. Natural submerged features and resources have traditionally dominated the way in which these lines have been established.

The major jurisdictional concepts, which will be treated individually in subsequent chapters of this book, are, moving seaward from the land on the surface of the water, the territorial sea, the contiguous zone, the exclusive economic zone, and the high seas. On the seabed, the major jurisdictional zones are the continental shelf and the deep seabed. These zones are illustrated in graphic form on the diagram at the end of this introduction.

Each of these jurisdictional zones was established in response to specific needs. The territorial sea, as we will see in more detail later, was a concept created primarily in response to a need for national security, and a need to protect local fishing industries. The contiguous zone was created as a buffer, or transition zone, between the almost complete sovereignty within the territorial sea, on the one hand, and the complete freedom of the high seas, on the other. The continental shelf theory evolved in response to the exploitation of minerals, primarily oil and gas, from the submerged lands adjacent to the major continents. The deep seabed regime was created to regulate a much more recent resource, polymetallic nodules. The newly created exclusive economic zone was a response to the fact that the territorial sea proved inadequate to afford protection for fisheries in today's modern world. And so on.

The first thing you have probably noticed is that the oceans, for purpose of the law of the sea, are divided both horizontally and vertically. Vertical subdivision is necessary because of the completely different nature, and therefore management problems, of the water column and the bottom of the sea.

Horizontal subdivision is necessitated by the different uses, to which the sea traditionally has been put.

The distinction between the continental shelf and the deep seabed area has been drawn primarily on the basis of geology. As we will develop later, the geology of the continental shelf is similar to that of the adjoining land mass, and thus we might expect, and indeed do find, that resources found on the adjacent dry land mass, such as oil and gas, are frequently found on the submerged lands of the continental shelf as well. But the geology of the deep seabed, basically basaltic rock overlain with a thin veneer of sediment in places, is entirely different, and does not lend itself to the creation of petroleum development. Thus the seabeds beyond the continental shelf are important, so far as is known today, only for the development of a different set of resources, primarily the polymentallic nodule containing commercial quantities of many minerals, the most important of which are manganese, nickel, copper, and cobalt. As you can imagine, the difference between the available resources, such as fish, petroleum and hard minerals, and the difference between the manner in which they are reduced to possession, makes necessary disparate regimes for their management. The rules relating to the management of fisheries, for example, bear no resemblance to those for the extraction of oil and gas. We shall examine all of these regimes during the course of study of these materials.

A word needs to be said about the process of evolution of the law of the sea. The most significant landmark in this process of evolution was the period in the fifteenth and sixteenth centuries notable for the works of Hugo Grotius, the great international jurist. For this was the period when the basic doctrine of the freedom of the high seas was for the first time clearly articulated and generally accepted. That doctrine was based upon the then already accepted international legal norm that stated that the freedom of communication, the right to trade, between nations was a fundamental right enshrined in the law of nations. From this concept, the freedom of navigation upon the high seas was spawned. Matters during that early period were simply perceived, because the needs were simple. The oceans were seen primarily as a medium for international trade and for the extraction of their living resources. The vastness of the areas involved, and the unsophisticated technologies required for shipping and fishing, required no elaborate controls or regulations. The seas were simply deemed free for all to use, wherever and whenever desired.

Over the centuries, this picture changed slowly but definitely. As new technologies evolved, new uses of ocean space came upon the scene. Even the traditional uses of navigation and fishing became more problematic. The revolutionary advent of steam power for ships increased immensely the volume of trade. Traditional trade routes became more crowded, as did traditional fishing grounds. As this occurred, conflicts inevitably arose, and it became clear that some rules were needed to reduce their frequency and severity.

At first, the rules were but of a general nature. The 1958 Convention on the High Seas, for example, illustrates the general principle of accomodation of users. It created a legal obligation upon the various users of ocean space to respect the rights of other users and encoded the principle of reasonable use.

As time passed, this rule of reasonableness was found not to be sufficient. Nations began a cooperative effort to develop rather detailed rules to respond to problems as they arose. For example, the crowding of sea lanes led to the creation of rules regarding how navigation should be conducted, and the result of those efforts was a code of rules of the road governing such things as the right of way as between vessels meeting or overtaking on the high seas. Increased communications made nations aware of marine disasters as well. While such occurences had always been a product of maritime trade, the new awareness of the magnitude of the problem, and the increased fequency of occurrences due in part to the presence of larger and faster ships, called for a set of rules regarding the safety of life at sea, and such a code was developed. Along with a growing awareness that the seas were no longer as vast, in terms of ability to transverse them, as was thought in earlier days, there was also a growing awareness that new technologies had some unwanted effects, such as the pollution of the marine environment from ships. Accordingly, rules were developed with regard to the discharge of oil and oily substances from ships. These are a few examples of international responses to perceived needs for regulation. No longer, therefore, were nations entirely free to use the seas in any way they saw fit. The doctrine of the freedom of the seas was still firmly entrenched in jurisprudence, but the way that such freedom was exercised was being increasingly subjected to detailed regulation.

In the first half of the present century, new technologies led to exploitation of resources in dramatically new ways. When one thinks of resources, one necessarily begins to think in terms of ownership and property. This is true of the resources of the oceans as much as those on land. Again, the response to these new sets of problems was the creation of rules addressing a large set of questions. Who, if anyone, owns the resources in place? If no one, at what point can a property interest be acquired in them and through what mechanisms? How valid is the concept of the freedom of the high seas with respect to resource acquisition, and with what consequences? Such questions led to an increased recognition that there was an inherent conflict, at least potentially, between the use of the oceans for transportation, and their uses for resource extraction and the principles of property.

As we reach, and examine, the 1982 United Nations Convention on the Law of the Sea, we will be seeing the first substantial effort to deal with these potentially conflicting policies. Concepts of property rights and freedom of navigation were addressed and a solution of accomodation sought, however imperfect.

Most of the readers of these materials are already familiar with the processes of the development of international law, such as the interplay between law developed by custom and that developed or codified by international treaty. In these materials, this parallel set of processes will be apparent, and it will be necessary, from time to time, to consider such questions as which particular treaty provisions, if any, represent the progressive development of new rules of international law, and which are merely codifications of previously existing customary international law. As you are undoubtedly aware, the distinction is important in considering the globally binding effect of rules of the law of the sea. As an example, the United States is a party to the 1958 Convention on the High Seas, but is not even a signatory to the new 1982 United Nations Convention. The degree to which the United States, then, is entitled to any rights articulated in the latter convention, depends in large part whether those rights are also contained in the earlier one, or, alternatively, whether they are simply codified versions of a rule of customary internaitonal law. The distinction, then, is relevant to deciding the scope of the binding force of certain rules, and a comprehension of who is bound by them and who is not. It is a complicated process that cannot always be resolved with any satisfying degree of clarity. And yet we must make the attempt.

As a final consideration, the ensuing materials must be viewed not only as elucidating rules of law, but as the result of an astounding process. The Third United Nations Conference on the Law of the Sea was an amazing exercise in international diplomacy, and we can learn much about large international conferences and their management through the medium of understanding how that conference did its work. Understanding the process is not merely an examination of procedural matters. The procedures adopted to facilitate the creation of a new treaty had real impacts upon the substance that emerged. We shall consider those procedures in connection with these materials. Suffice it to say at this point that this was the largest international conference that has ever been held with the announced purpose of creating a globally binding international treaty. Since more than 150 nations and other internationally recognized entities participated in the decision-making leading to the treaty, the dynamics of negotiation were necessarily complex on the one hand, and extremely tenuous on the other. This was necessitated by the fact that early in the process the conference took the decision that there would be no votes taken on any substantive issue until all efforts at consensus were exhausted. In other words, the objective was the adopting of a large, complex treaty by consensus. The situation that faced nations at the opening of the conference can thus be likened to taking 150 guests to a restaurant, giving them a menu which listed two or three hundred entrees, and then telling them they could have anything they wanted to eat, so long as they all agreed on what that item would be. For a better understanding of these dynamics, the next chapter, before embarking upon substantive considerations, will sketch out the mechanisms, formal and informal, by which the conference accomplished its objectives.

Related to this complexity are two factors worthy of mention. The first is the impact of the development of technology. Clearly new technologies impact upon the need for new rules and the need to change or modify old ones that are too simplistic to provide solutions to new complexities. For example, prior to the Second World War, offshore production of oil and gas was virtually unknown. Subsequently, experimental drilling on submerged lands began but was extremely primitive. Drilling was done in very shallow water using the technologies developed on land by placing such drilling rigs on barges. As more sophisticated methods were developed, drilling moved further seaward into deeper waters. As drilling approached the limits of the territorial sea, it was perceived that a different kind of legal regime would be needed to assure potential drillers that their investments would be protected.

Accordingly, in 1949, President Truman issued a proclamation claiming the exclusive jurisdiction over submerged lands adjacent to the United States. This led to many similar claims by other countries. The legal concept now known as the continental shelf was incorporated, in crude form, into the 1958 Convention on the Continental Shelf. But that convention was very vague concerning the legal outer limit of the shelf. Development of even newer technologies in the 1970's made drilling in even deeper waters possible, and, as a result, an even more precise definition of the outer limit was negotiated into the 1982 United Nations Convention on the Law of the Sea.

This is but one example of the impact of the evolution of sophisticated technologies has had an impact on the evolution of the law as well. New technologies with respect to fisheries has had a similar impact. Faster, more powerful fishing vessels with longer ranges, and new techniques for catching fish began to bring about severe shortages in certain stocks of fish, and conflicts over the right to fish, on the one hand, with the right to regulate fishing on the other. We shall examine these developments in more detail in this text. These introductory comments are made to alert the reader, at the outset, to be sensitive to the driving forces that create new law as each topic is being considered.

Technology was not the only force impacting on the development of the law of the sea, however, particularly in more recent years. When the 1958 Geneva conventions were adopted, most of the nations that participated were developed, mainly western European countries. Africa and other parts of the world were made up in large part of European colonies. The collapse of colonialism around the world led to a spate of new, independent nations that had no part in forging the rules incorporated by treaty into the law of the sea. So it was that when the most recent negotiations began leading to the 1982 treaty, the majority of nations participating were smaller developing countries with entirely different political orientation and economic needs than the major "western" powers. Their sheer numbers gave them tremendous negotiating power, and since they had the votes to block any results they did not like, they had an immense impact on the shape and content of the emerging treaty.

Nowhere is this more apparent than in the provisions relating to deep seabed mining. This activity, as we shall examine in detail, takes place in very deep water beyond the limits of the jurisdiction of any nation, however defined. The developing countries were determined to block any possibility of establishing western domination over the deep seabeds, which would represent, in their view, a form of neo-colonialism. Thus they pressed for, and were successful in obtaining, the incorporation into the new treaty of a declaration that the seabeds beyond national jurisdiction were not to be subjected to the sovereignty of any State, but were rather to be the "common heritage of mankind". Keeping in mind that many of these countries, in a political sense, leaned toward one or another form of a centralized, controlled economy, one can easily ascertain a corresponding political bent to the deep seabeds provisions of the treaty, as opposed to a free market approach.

It will be interesting to note, and consider, with the breakup of the former Soviet Union, and its attempts to shift its economy to the western-style free market approach, how this will impact on the law of the sea for the future.

These, then, are the multi-faceted features that create the framework for our study of the law of the sea. In succeeding chapters, we shall see how they play out. Before considering our first set of substantive issues, however, the student should have some idea how major international treaties, particularly the new law of the sea convention, are negotiated. An understanding of large international negotiations helps to explain the existence of otherwise seemingly incomprehensible solutions to rather obviously simple problems in the provisions of the resulting treaty.

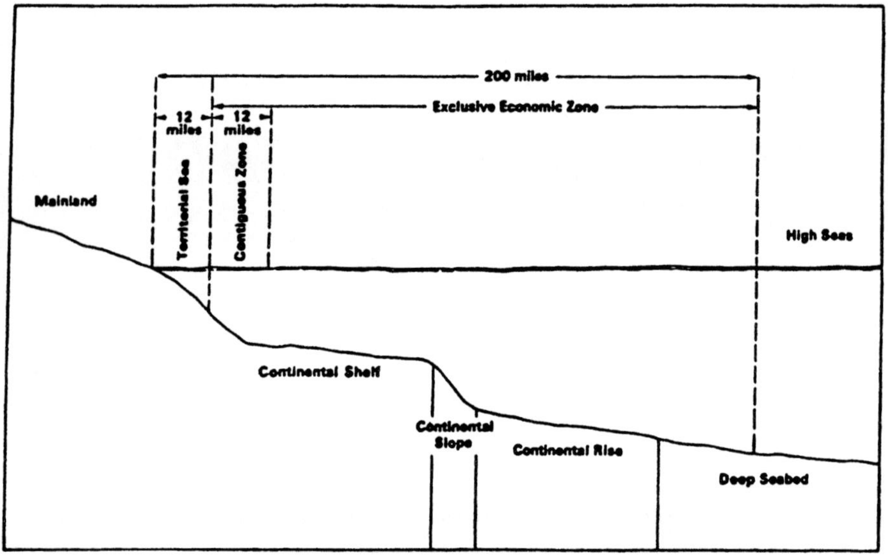
200 miles
Exclusive Economic Zone
12 miles
12 miles
Territorial Sea
Contiguous Zone
Mainland
High Seas
Continental Shelf
Continental Slope
Continental Rise
Deep Seabed

CHAPTER 1

THE UNITED NATIONS AND THE LAW OF THE SEA

The United Nations is responsible for three separate law of the sea conferences. The first took place in 1958 and resulted in the four Geneva Conventions on law of the sea. The second took place in 1960 with the sole agenda of seeking agreement on the legal breadth of the territorial sea, an endeavor that failed. The third, and most comprehensive conference began in 1974 after some years of intensive preparatory work done in the United Nations.

The 1958 conference differed substantially in the way in which it achieved its results than the methods utilized in the more recent one. Prior to 1958, the United Nations requested the International Law Commission, a body of independent legal experts, to study the subject and to prepare draft conventions. After several years of work, those drafts were laid before a conference of plenipotentiaries meeting in Geneva, which adopted almost all of the proposed provisions without change.

The latest conference was much different. The matter, being viewed as having a high political as well as legal content, was not referred to the ILC. Instead, the General Assembly decided to refer all issues to a full plenipotentiary conference where the political implications, as well as the legal doctrine, could be taken fully into account. Thus the first session of the Third United Nations Conference on the Law of the Sea was convened in Caracas, Venezuela, in 1974. It had no draft treaty before it. The sole official document before it was a list of important issues on which treaty provisions should be developed that had been sent to it by the General Assembly. That list became the agenda for the conference's work.

The conference was the largest and most complex international conference ever held. It was necessary to develop very special rules of procedure to ensure its success. The structure of the conference, in both its formal and informal variations, and the rules utilized are the subject matter of this chapter.

A. THE STRUCTURE OF THE CONFERENCE

As is traditional with most international conferences, the main decision-making body was the plenary, in which every participating entity sat and had one vote. Since the list of issues was long and omplex, and since it would be too unwieldy to seek to resolve all of the issues in such a large group, the conference, which had to develop its own organization and rules of procedure, began by splitting the issues into three groups. Each related group of issues was assigned to a separate committee of the conference. Again, each State participating had a seat on each of the committees. A glance at the treaty itself will inform you how the issues were grouped. Basically, all matters pertaining to the major new issue to be dealt with, the exploration and exploitation of the deep seabed beyond national jurisdiction, were assigned to the First Committee. The Third Committee was asked to prepare treaty texts dealing with the conduct of marine scientific research, transfer of marine technology, and protection of the marine environment. The remaining issues, quite numerous but mostly more traditional ones, were assigned to the Second Committee for resolution. The conference also created a General Committee, a Credentials Committee, and a Drafting Committee as part of its formal organization. The plenary, the decision-making body of the conference, was chaired by the conference President who was, as were other officers of the conference, elected by the conference itself.

The officers of the conference, as provided for in rule 6 of the rules of procedure, consisted of the President, 31 Vice-Presidents, a Rapporteur-General, and the chairmen of the three main committees and the chairman of the Drafting Committee. These officers, when sitting together, formed the General Committee. The General Committee, being broadly representative of all interests in the conference, was used as a "sounding board" by the President. He would air proposals of a procedural nature he intended to place before the plenary in the General Committee as a preliminary matter to test the general acceptability of the proposal before taking it to the full plenary. By utilizing this device, he was able to make changes to accomodate expected objections from the floor.

The Credentials Committee had the responsibility of verifying the credentials of those delegates appearing before any session of the conference, and for recommending ways to resolve any disputes concerning any delegation's make-up or legitimacy. The Three main committees were the primary negotiating committees in the conference, although they had no power to give final approval to any provisions they drafted. That task was assigned to the plenary, to whom the three committees submitted their reports. The Drafting Committee, which had no substantive role in the conference, had as its responsibility the "cleaning up" of the texts by making necessary grammatical and clarifying changes in the texts (again, to be approved in plenary) without altering their substance. Its job was essentially a bifurcated one. First, it had the task, a difficult one, of assuring that the treaty read juridically the same in all six official languages: Arabic, Chinese, English, French, Spanish, and Russian. Second, it had the job of making necessary drafting changes in all of the official languages of the texts. How it went about this difficult task is described in a subsequent section, below.

The main committees of the conference met in two modes, formal and informal. Formal meetings of the committees were held in open session and on the record. These meetings provided the opportunity in public meetings to exchange views on the variety of interests under discussion, and to set forth national positions. Negotiations were not, in the normal sense, carried on in these formal sessions. Usually the committees would meet in this mode at the beginning and at the end of each negotiating session, and, occasionally, during the session.

Most of the committee meetings were conducted in their informal mode. Informal committee meetings were conducted in closed session with the public excluded, and no record was kept. The reason for this secrecy was to allow delegates more flexibility in exchanging frank views without the concern of being publicly quoted. The more relaxed atmosphere was seen as being an enhancement to making progress. The problem with this procedure from a purely academic perspective is that, unlike the 1958 conference, little of the record exists. This is a problem in seeking to interpret various provisions of the treaty, since little is readily available to give the interpreter any insight into what the delegates thought they were saying, or what they thought any particular substantive rule meant. In other words, there is a very skimpy "legislative history" of this conference.

Thus, the work of the conference proceeded as follows. Treaty provisions were negotiated in the main committees, although the general provisions and dispute settlement procedures were negotiated in plenary. The proposed articles were transmitted by the Chairman of each main committee to the President of the Conference, who, in due course, would place them before the plenary for approval. More will be said about this later. Parallel to this process, the Drafting Committee proceeded along similar lines, submitting all proposed drafting changes (of which there were hundreds) to the plenary for approval.

B. THE RULES OF PROCEDURE.

Crucial to the success of the conference was the development of an effective set of procedural rules. The rules, as adopted, embody two very basic but critically important concepts. First, the conference was determined from the outset to avoid the result, as in 1958, of a series of discreet conventions on separate topics. This was so for two reasons. First, there was general recognition that almost all aspects of ocean uses are interrelated, and therefor should not be negotiated as though they existed in a vacuum. Secondly, developing a series, rather than one, treaty enabled countries to pick and choose, becoming parties to the conventions they like and rejecting those that they do not. From an international stability point of view, this has not proved desirable. The conference, therefor, decided to negotiate a single universal convention on the law of the sea that incorporated all aspects of ocean use and related topics.

The second basic concept was presented to the conference by the General Assembly in a principle known as the "Gentlemen's Agreement", which read as follows: "The Conference should make every effort to reach agreement on substantive matters by way of consensus and there should be no voting on such matters until all efforts at consensus have been exhausted." This obviously was directed at an effort to create a universal and globally binding agreement. It directed the conference to avoid divisiveness and it had the effect of avoiding the adoption of provisions which were narrowly adopted. It also had the effect of forcing nations to view the emerging document as a whole and evaluate it in that perspective. Thus a country may find parts of the document objectionable, or even totally unacceptable, from the perspective of its national interests, but yet be willing to go along with them because the treaty as a whole represented a net gain.

These concepts came to be referred to as "consensus" and the "package deal". At the end, each nation would have to accept the treaty as a whole, or reject it completely. No reservations were to be permitted. The following are the key rules of procedure that put these principles into effect.

DECISION-MAKING

Requirements for voting

Rule 37

1. Before a matter of substance is put to the vote, a determination that all efforts at reaching general agreement have been exhausted shall be made by the majority specified in paragraph 1 of rule 39.

2. Prior to making such a determination the following procedures may be invoked:

(a) When a matter of substance comes up for voting for the first time, the President may, and shall if requested by at least 15 representatives, defer the question of taking a vote on such matter for a period not exceeding 10 calendar days. The provisions of this sub-paragraph may be applied only once on the matter.

(b) At any time the Conference, upon a proposal by the President or upon the motion by any representative, may decide, by a majority of the representatives present and voting, to defer the question of taking a vote on any matter of substance for a specified period of time.

(c) During any period of deferment, the President shall make every effort, with the assistance as appropriate of the General Committee, to facilitate the achievement of general agreement, having regard to the over-all progress made on all matters of substance which are closely related, and a report shall be made to the Conference by the President prior to the end of the period.

(d) If by the end of a specified period of deferment the Conference has not reached agreement and if the question of taking a vote is not further deferred in accordance with subparagraph (b) of this paragraph, the determination that all efforts at reaching general agreement have been exhausted shall be made in accordance with paragraph 1 of this rule.

(e) If the Conference has not determined that all efforts at reaching agreement had been exhausted, the President may propose or any representative may move, nothwithstanding rule 36, after the end of a period of no less than five calendar days from the last prior vote on such a determination, that such a determination be made in accordance with paragraph 1 of this rule; the requirement of five days' delay shall not apply during the last two weeks of a session.

3. No vote shall be taken on any matter of substance less than two working days after an announcement that the Conference is to proceed to vote on the matter has been made, during which period the announcement shall be published in the Journal at the first opportunity.

Voting rights

Rule 38

Each State represented at the Conference shall have one vote.

Required majority

Rule 39

1. Decisions of the Conference on all matters of substance, including the adoption of the text of the Convention on the Law of the Sea as a whole, shall be taken by a two-thirds majority of the representatives present and voting, provided that such majority shall include at least a majority of the States participating in that session of the Conference.

2. Rule 37 shall not apply to the adoption of the text of the Convention as a whole. However, the Convention shall not be put to the vote less than four working days after the adoption of its last article.

3. Except as otherwise specified in these rules, decisions by the Conference on all matters of procedure shall be taken by a majority of the representatives present and voting.

4. If the question arises whether a matter is one of procedure or of substance, the President shall rule on the question. An appeal against this ruling shall immediately be put to the vote and the President's ruling shall stand unless the appeal is approved by a majority of the representatives present and voting.

Meaning of the phrase "representatives present and voting" and of the term "States participating"

Rule 40

1. For the purpose of these rules, the phrase "representatives present and voting" means representatives present and casting an affirmative or negative vote; representatives who abstain from voting shall be considered as not voting.

2. Subject to the provisions of rules 1 and 5 and without prejudice to the powers and functions of the Credentials Committee, the term "States participating" in relation to any particular session of the Conference means any State whose representatives have registered with the Secretariat of the Conference as participating in that session and which has not subsequently notified the Secretariat of its withdrawal from that session or a part of it. The Secretariat shall keep a Register for this purpose.

Method of voting

Rule 41

1. The Conference shall normally vote by show of hands or by standing, but any representative may request a roll-call. The roll-call shall be taken in the English alphabetical order of the names of the States participating in the Conference, beginning with the delegation whose name is drawn by lot by the President.

2. When the Conference votes by mechanical means, a non-recorded vote shall replace a vote by show of hands or by standing and recorded vote shall replace a roll-call vote. Any representative may request a recorded vote. In the case of a recorded vote, the Conference shall, unless a representative requests otherwise, dispense with the procedure of calling out the names of the States; nevertheless, the results of the voting shall be inserted in the record in the same manner as that of a roll-call vote.

* * * * * *

You can see from the structure of the rules, voting was perceived as possibly necessary, but by the combination of majorities and built-in delays, it was made quite difficult. In point of fact, only one substantive vote was taken at all, and that was on the adoption of the text as a whole. The few other votes taken were all of a procedural nature. All delegates were quite sensitive to the fact that if voting were to begin on even a single article, the entire package deal could become unraveled and in that case the conference would in all likelihood collapse. While on occasion a delegation might threaten to go to a substantive vote, perhaps out of frustration, it did not happen. Only one vote taken prior to the end of the conference that was arguably a matter of substance, but a ruling from the President that it was of a procedural nature was left unchallenged.

C. HOW SUBSTANTIVE NEGOTIATIONS WERE CONDUCTED.

Substantive negotiations were carried out differently in each main committee and at different stages of the conference. The Second Committee, under the chairmanship of Ambassador Andres Aguilar, will be used as an example.

As previously noted, the Second Committee was assigned a long list of subjects from the list of issues. These, for the most part, dealt with the more traditional uses of the seas: navigation, fishing, the continental shelf, regime of islands, etc. Many were uncontroversial and were already covered by treaty provisions in the 1958 conventions, thus were easily transferred to the new document. Other items, such as the concept of the exclusive economic zone, were not so easily resolved. Before trying to achieve resolution of such issues, it was necessary that all delegations be aware of the range of possibile solutions, and the strength and variety of various national positions. For this reason, a rather lengthy initial "education" period was required. This was accomplished in large part by the chairman, during the first session, by asking all delegations who had strong feelings on any of the issues on the list to submit proposed draft articles that they thought resolved the issue most to their satisfaction.

The result of this initial exercise was that some issues had almost no proposals, but many had a large number of proposals. All of these proposals were then considered in the Second Committee one by one during a "second reading". Each delegation was free to comment on every proposed draft. Thus some delegations supported one or another proposal, some rejected proposed solutions, and still others would support a particular proposal if it were amended in some way. As can be imagined, this was a tedious and extremely complex way to proceed, and could not succeed in reaching, much less approaching, consensus. But it served the useful purpose of allowing the delegations, and hence the chairman, to understand the range of views and to begin to think about possible ways to strike acceptable compromises.

Upon completion of the first working session of the conference, the chairman, on his own initiative, prepared a working document to lay before the committee at its second session. Essentially, after studying all of the proposals, he selected (or drafted if none existed) one proposal at each end of the range of proposals (at each extreme), and one proposal he thought was middle ground. These three drafted positions then represented the entire range of the discussions, and they reduced the number of pieces of paper to a manageable number. It was then possible for delegations to focus upon proposing changes to one or another of these positions to satisfy their national interests. The second session of the conference was spent in receiving such comments.

At the completion of the second session, the conference took the decision that the chairmen of the three main committees should undertake to prepare a single document for each committee. The document, prepared by the chairman on the basis of the discussions, was known as the "Single Negotiating Text". The SNT for the Second Committee contained one article for each issue. It was made perfectly clear that the document was a negotiating document only, to be used for more focused negotiations. It bound no delegation, and all delegations were free to make new proposals for consideration. While delegations were free to offer substitute proposals, most attempted to deal with the issues by offering amendments to the draft.

This process was repeated several times. The second version was known as the RSNT (Revised Single Negotiating Text). After the RSNT had been thoroughly discussed, the President of the Conference took it upon himself to combine the three separate committee texts into a single document, the Integrated Composite Negotiating Text (ICNT). The ICNT itself was subjected to three more revisions, each revision becoming more and more refined in the hope that the process was leading toward a consensus. In 1981, a last revision was denominated as a Draft Convention, although its formal status was no different than any of the previous drafts. By the time the Draft Convention was issued, it was apparent that many of the issues had been essentially resolved and that the conference was approaching as close to a consensus as would ever be achieved. The final step, of course, was the formal adoption of the treaty in the fall of 1981.

The term "consensus" is no where defined in the rules of procedure. In practice, consensus seemed to mean that there had been no formal objection by any country having a significant interest in the issue under discussion. Thus a consensus could exist even if there was widespread criticism of a draft, if that criticism did not rise to the level of a formal objection. And objections of States having no identifiable national interest in the subject could often be overlooked. But if even one country having such a significant and strong national interest at stake objected, the article could not move into the text. So, for example, if a country like Japan had an objection to a draft article dealing with salmon fishing, that article could not move forward. Japan had a significant interest in fishing for salmon.

Obviously, negotiating in the full committees can, because of the numbers, be only partially effective. As a result, a vast "shadow" structure developed during the course of the conference, with special groups forming and desolving as needed. The objective of these groups was to seek to consolidate positions where possible, giving additional impact to proposals that might be developed. There were various kinds of groups that formed. One very common type of informal group consisted of States having, if not similar positions, similar interests. For example, one informal group consisted of those States having the largest continental margins. They met regularly to negotiate among themselves common proposals or responses to other proposals. In that way they could present a coordinated position to the conference or in committee. Similar type groups formed consisting of the major maritime powers and the most industrialized countries. Some were geographically oriented, such as the Coastal States Group and the Land-locked and Geographically Disadvantaged Group. The largest and most influential such group was politically oriented. This was the Group of 77, which in fact consisted of more than one hundred developing countries. This group was a power to be acknowledged and negotiated with in matters related to deep seabed mining.

An entirely different kind of group was often referred to as a "contact" group. Frequently, the chairman of a committee found it useful to convene, informally, a smaller body of countries with representative views to try to find solutions to knotty problems that could not be resolved in the full committee. One of the most successful of these groups was the so-called Evensen Group, named for its chairman, Ambassador Jens Evensen of Norway. This group's first effort was directed at producing a paper containing draft articles with regard to fishing in the exclusive economic zone. The group, like so many of its kind, consisted of important countries on both sides of the issue, with a sprinkling of "expediters" -- countries having no strong interest in the subject but with the capability of trying to formulate compromise positions. Such groups, when successful, normally produced a paper containing any possible compromises, or as close to a compromise as the group was able to reach. The chairman of the group would then submit the paper to the appropriate chairman who would then distribute it to the full committee in the form of an "anonymous" proposal. If the group had been carefully selected, the chances that its proposals would be generally acceptable was greatly enhanced.

There were also formal geographical groups, patterned after the usual United Nations practice. These consisted of the Latin American, African, Asian, Eastern European groups plus a kind of catch-all group called the Western Europeans and Others. Because these groups all contained nations of very diverse national interests, they were rarely able to take substantive common positions. But they were quite useful in discussing procedural matters referred to them by the President.

Other groups of importance during the conference were the groups of EEC States, the Organization of African Unity, and the so-called Group of Five. This latter group was a coordinating group consisting of France, the United Kingdom, Japan, the United States and the then Soviet Union. The political power potential of this group must be obvious.

All of these groups, plus many others from time to time served important objectives in accelerating the negotiating process. But in the long run, much of the work was done by delegations meeting privately in the halls to try to work out differences in their views. For example, the United States met often with the Japanese to try to work out a common salmon article, even though the U.S. interest was that of a State of origin in whose waters salmon spawned, while the Japanese interest was that of a fishing State with an interest in catching U.S.-spawned salmon. Eventually they agreed, and then the U.S. put together a broader group of interested States to obtain approval of the bilateral draft, as slightly amended to take into account the interests of this broader group.

The United States delegation was one of the more agressive delegations in the conference, and hence, in many ways, one of the most successful. It had the internal organization and resources to take the initiative in pushing draft proposals through this complicated process. It had the manpower to keep its finger on the pulse of the conference and to sense changes in attitudes and directions. This is not to say that others were not agressive as well. It is simply to note that the U.S. probably had the greatest resources available to it, including much backup expertise in Washington which it could call upon as needed.

The above is a thumbnail sketch of the negotiating process. We will have occasion to refer to this material from time to time as we discuss the evolution of particular treaty articles.

D. THE DRAFTING COMMITTEE.

The Law of the Sea Convention is written in six equally authentic official languages: Arabic, Chinese, English, French, Russian and Spanish. Since the texts have equal legal authority, the work of the drafting committee was critical. The committee consisted of the representatives of twenty-one countries. As mentioned previously, it had as its task the cleaning up of the drafts of the treaty in the various languages without changing any matter of substance that had been negotiated in the main committees, and making sure that recurring words and phrases were consistent throughout. In addition, a much more difficult task, the committee was to make sure that the text in each official language was juridically identical to each of the others. Because of the structures of the various languages, it was not possible to make the six texts literally the same. But it was essential that they all conveyed exactly the same meaning.

The process by which this was done is unique, and had never been tried before. In order to approach the problem, and recognizing the above factors, the committee decided, although there was no mention of it in the rules of procedure, to establish six language groups, one for each of the official languages, to be chaired by a coordinator elected by the committee. These groups were open-ended, that is, the meetings of the groups were open to any delegate that wished to participate. The largest of these groups, by far, was the English Language Group, chaired by the United States. Participants did not function, however, as representatives of their countries, *per se*, but rather in their capacity as legal experts.

The procedure was as follows. As agreed texts emerged from the main committees, they were translated into the official languages by the Secretariat staff, and transmitted to the appropriate language group. That group then examined each and every article in the treaty text, one by one. As an individual article came up for discussion, the participants were invited to submit, in writing, proposed drafting changes. These proposals were then discussed, primarily to determine their acceptability to the group and to ascertain that they were in fact only drafting suggestions not affecting the substantive meaning of the article under discussion. If any member of the drafting group objected to making any proposed change within that group, the proposal was rejected, unless the proponent of the change could persuade the objector to the contrary.

If that were all that the groups had to do, it would have been a comparatively simple job. But the task was complicated by the fact that each change proposed in each group also had to meet the approval of every other language group. Thus, for example, every change approved in the English Language Group was then transmitted to the other groups. The other groups would then review it to ascertain whether there were any objections to its being made in the English text. By this method, comparability of texts in all languages was attempted. The exact form in which the proposed changes were made and transmitted between groups was determined by the Secretariat. Basically, if the translators ascertained that the change affected the English text only, and required no corresponding changes in other languages, the proposal was transmitted in English only. If, however, corresponding changes were necessary in other languages as a result of the English proposal, the proposal would be transmitted in English and all affected languages. Thus, if a change in language in English also called for a change in the French text, the transmittal document contained the change as it would appear in both the English and French languages.

Thus, the language groups had responsibility not only for proposing their own drafting changes, but for reviewing and accepting or rejecting changes in any of the other languages as well. After each group had discussed the changes proposed to a given treaty article in all of the languages, the six coordinators would meet, in open session, with the Chairman of the Drafting Committee. It was at these sessions, usually weekly, that the coordinators would have the opportunity to make objections to changes proposed in other languages. If any coordinator objected, and if the appropriate coordinator proposing the change could not explain the change to the satisfaction of the challenger, the change was not made. This, then, constituted the second level of review. But it did not end there.

Once the coordinators agreed to a change, that change then went to the full Drafting Committee, where the process was repeated. If any member of the committee made an objection which was not subsequently withdrawn, then, again, the proposed change went no further. When the full Drafting Committee agreed on changes, then the changes went to the Conference Plenary for the final review. This was necessary because most of the countries in the plenary were not also members of the Drafting Committee. Each change was again brought up for a final review in the plenary. Those that received no objections were adopted into the final text.

Given the many layers of the decision-making process, and the requirement that drafting changes be adopted by consensus, it is surprising that any changes survived. In point of fact, however, hundreds of drafting changes were adopted. Those who are conversant with several languages will undoubtedly still find discrepancies among the various texts, but this truly unique process has to be considered to have been a substantial success and perhaps a model for future multilateral negotiations.

* * * * * *

The foregoing material is but a brief outline of how the law of the sea conference accomplished its astonishing work. This is said without comment on the correctness of its decisions. Those issues will be discussed in relationship with the substantive materials to follow in this book. A basic understanding of the process, however, is deemed to be somewhat helpful in understanding why some provisions in the treaty are purposely vague, and why some are clearly compromises.

We shall now begin our examination of the substantive issues of the law of the sea. We begin that examination with the most fundamental and ancient doctrines of the law of the sea: the doctrine of the freedom of the high seas.

CHAPTER 2

FREEDOM OF THE HIGH SEAS

A. INTRODUCTION.

The doctrine of the freedom of the high seas is the most fundamental doctrine in the law of the sea. Because of that, it is the first topic for our consideration. In this chapter you will be exposed to the historical underpinnings of the doctrine -- why and how it came about, and then we shall move to a consideration of the primary rules applicable to that area that we refer to as the high seas. As previously noted, the doctrine has undergone much change over a period of more than 300 years. As in the case of other areas of international law, law of the sea doctrine has had to respond to changes in ocean usage. What was logical in the time of Hugo Grotius may not be as viable today. However, the fundamental idea that the high seas are free to open use by all, and not subject to appropriation by any, is still a viable concept.

As we shall note, the idea of free use of the high seas has come into conflict with the need to be able to have assured access to resources, and the need to conserve them. The doctrine has evolved accordingly.

The need to achieve that balance brought about the creation of a new concept, that of the exclusive economic zone, in the 1992 United Nations Convention on the Law of the Sea. This concept does not fit neatly into either of the traditional categories of territorial sea or high seas. But it is more closely related to the high seas concept, so those provisions that establish the juridical nature of the zone are considered in this chapter, while specific rules relating to fisheries, the protection and preservation of the marine environment, and the conduct of marine scientific research will be studied in separate chapters to come.

We will begin with the historical evolution of the doctrine of the freedom of the high seas.

B. THE ORIGINS AND EVOLUTION OF THE DOCTRINE.

1. EARLY HISTORY.

Pardo, THE LAW OF THE SEA ITS PAST AND ITS FUTURE, 63 Ore.L.Rev. 7- (1984)[1]

We can trace the origins of present law of the sea to Roman times. The earliest formal pronouncements on the subject appear to go back to the second-century jurist Marcianus, who, in one of his decisions, declared that the sea and the fish in the sea were *communis omnium naturali jure* (common or open to all men by the operation of natural law). The Romans did not claim jurisdiction over the sea (not even within a three mile limit) which was measured not from the low water mark along the coast, but from the high water mark at flood tide. These customs were later incorporated into the Code of Justinian in 529 A.D.

---

1. Reprinted by permission Copyright c 1984 by University of Oregon.

At the time of the Roman emporers, however, the principle of common or free use of the sea and its products was not formal international law -- because there were no States in the Mediterranean basin independent of the Roman Empire -- but rather basic public policy of the Roman State. Since the Mediterranean was a Roman lake completely controlled by the Roman navy, there was no need to assert explicit dominion. Nor was there any need to restrict access to living resources, for the problems of overfishing and depletion of sea resources had not yet emerged.

The collapse of the Roman Empire resulted in the fragmentation of western Europe and of the Mediterranean basin. A variety of large and small States competed for supremacy over both land and water. The seas washing the coasts of European States became the object of conflicting claims variously founded upon the desire for exclusive control over trade routes, rich fishing grounds, or increased revenues by taxation of foreign shipping. Also, in many cases the claims of coastal States were rooted in the general insecurity of the times, and on the need to police adjacent seas. It was during this period -- the thirteenth and fourteenth centuries -- that jurists began to recognize that coastal States had jurisdiction over waters more or less adjacent to their coasts.

In the fifteenth century when the Portuguese, under Prince Henry the Navigator, began systematically to explore the west coast of Africa, Pope Nicholas V encouraged the Portuguese by granting them in the bull *Romanus Pontifex*, exclusive and permanent rights to the lands of Africa from Ceuta to Guinea and "beyond, towards that southern shore."

Forty years later, in the bull *Inter caetera* of May 3, 1493, Alexander VI assigned to Spain all lands discovered, or to be discovered, in her name. The bull included a clause safeguarding the grants already made to Portugal. On May 4, 1493, Pope Alexander issued a second bull *Inter caetera*. This bull granted to Spain the exclusive right to all newly discovered lands, not possessed by a Christian king prior to December 24, 1492, that lay west of a demarcation line drawn from the North Pole to the South Pole, one hundred leagues west of the Azores and the Cape Verde islands. The bull prohibited everyone, upon pain of excommunication, from traveling west of the demarcation line, "for the purpose of trade or any other reason to the islands or mainlands, found or to be found," without prior permission from Spain.

The bulls were followed by direct negotiations between Spain and Portugal which resulted in the Treaty of Tordesillas in June 1494. Under this treaty the demarcation line between the possessions of Spain and those of Portugual was moved to 370 leagues west of the Cape Verde islands: all lands east of the line were to be Portuguese and all lands west of the line were to be Spanish. The language of the treaty strongly implied that the two sovereigns owned the seas within their respective spheres; however, since Spanish ships had to cross Portuguese waters to reach the Americas, the Spaniards were permitted "to sail...freely, securely, and peacefully, over the said seas of the said King of Portugal, and within the said line...They shall take their courses direct to the desired region...and shall not leave their course, unless compelled to do so by contrary weather." These phrases are similar to those now used to define innocent passage in the territorial sea.

Thus, over a period of one thousand years, the Western world passed from a policy of total freedom of the sea to the principle of legal division of the entire ocean. International law, however, does not exist in a vacuum. Instead, it rather closely reflects the beliefs, needs and perceived interests at any point in time of the predominant classes of most influential States within the international community. The seas might have continued to be divided between Spain and Portugal but for a series of events which together brought about a revolution in the law.

At the close of the fifteenth century, Europe was on the verge of a triple revolution which eventually ushered in the modern age. The Protestant revolution, by repudiating the spiritual and temporal authority of the Pope, implicitly questioned the validity of the "grants" obtained by Spain and Portugal. Luther nailed his 95 theses to the cathedral door of the Schlosskirche in Wittenberg scarcely a century after the Treaty of Tordesillas. The Protestant revolution was successful particularly in those States of northwestern Europe which were destined to hold the dominion of the sea for the next three centuries.

The Protestant revolution accelerated the end of the feudal age in much of northwestern Europe. Thus the second revolution was a social revolution, and its effects were particularly far-reaching in those countries that were achieving naval ascendancy. At the end of the sixteenth century, throughout much of northwestern Europe the feudal aristocracy had been replaced as the leading political class by a merchant aristocracy.

Third, Europe experienced a political revolution. Spain and Portugal, by becoming militant defenders of the religious status quo and by overexpanding in Africa, the Indies and the Americas fatally weakened themselves. The union of Spain and Portugal and the defeat of the Spanish Armada, were the Churchillian hinge of fate which marked both the high point and the beginning of the end of Spanish domination over the seas. The decline of Spanish naval power was accompanied by a progressive decline in the capacity of Spain to enforce its exclusive rights over the sea.

The life of Hugo Grotius, the Dutch scholar and lawyer, is an example of these new religious, political and social forces. As a Protestant, Grotius could not endorse the papal bull forbidding navigation to Portuguese and Spanish territories. "Trade with the East Indies," he proclaimed, "does not belong to the Portuguese by virtue of title based on the Papal Donation....For no one can give away what he does not himself possess...." As a legal representative of the merchant aristocracy, he had to reject in principle all foreign claims to closed seas and trade monopolies. As a patriotic Dutchman, Grotius could not but oppose the exclusion of the Netherlands from the East Indian trade.

* * * * * *

2. HUGO GROTIUS AND MARE LIBERUM.

Hugo Grotius was one of the most influential lawyers in international law. In fact, he is often referred to as "the father of international law" because of his work *De Jure Belli ac Pacis* (On the Law of War and Peace) written in 1625, which is considered to be the first systematic treatment of the subject. Grotius was a prodigy. He composed latin verse at age 9, entered the university at 12, and edited an encyclopedia at 15. While we know him best as a lawyer, he was also a diplomat, philosopher, theologian and historian.

For our purposes, however, another of Grotius' works, *Mare Liberum,* which appeared as Chapter XII of his *De Iure Praeda* (Commentary on the Law of Prize and Booty), is of great significance. This work, written in 1609 in support of the right of the Dutch to participate in the East Indian trade, was the first organized set of arguments that gave rise to the doctrine of the freedom of the high seas. We will first examine his arguments, and in this chapter (as well as the rest of the book) we will have occasion to examine and question how much of the doctrine remains and whether his underlying arguments remain valid. We will see that the doctrine has certainly changed, and that even if his arguments are no longer as valid as they once were, the doctrine is so widely ingrained in international law that it no longer needs such supporting arguments.

Grotius, THE FREEDOM OF THE SEAS OR THE RIGHT WHICH BELONGS TO THE DUTCH TO TAKE PART IN THE EAST INDIAN TRADE[2]

CHAPTER I

By the Law of Nations navigation is free to all persons whatsoever

My intention is to demonstrate briefly and clearly that the Dutch -- that is to say, the subjects of the Netherlands -- have the right to sail to the East Indies, as they are now doing, and to engage in trade with the people there. I shall base my argument on the following and most specific and unimpeachable axiom of the Law of Nations, called a primary rule or first principle, the spirit of which is self-evident and immutable, to wit: Every nation is free to travel to every other nation, and to trade with it.

God Himself says this speaking through the voice of nature; and inasmuch as it is not His will to have Nature supply every place with all the necessaries of life, He ordains that some nations excel in one art and others in another. Why is this His will, except it be that He wished human freindships to be engendered by mutual needs and resources, lest individuals deeming themselves entirely sufficient unto themselves should for that very reason be rendered unsociable? So by the decree of divine justice it was brought about that one people should supply the needs of another, in order, as Pliny the Roman writer says, that in this way, whatever has been produced anywhere should seem to have been destined for all.... Those who deny this law, destroy this most praiseworthy bond of human fellowship, remove the opportunities for doing mutual service, in a word do violence to Nature herself. For do not the oceans, navigable in every direction with which God has encompassed all the earth, and the regular and occasional winds which blow now from one quarter and now from another, offer sufficient proof that Nature has given to all peoples a right of access to all other peoples? Seneca thinks this is Nature's greatest service, that by the wind she united the widely scattered peoples, and yet did so distribute all her products over the earth that commercial intercourse was a necessity to mankind. Indeed the most famous jurists extent its application so far as to deny that any state or any ruler can debar foreigners from having access to their subjects and trading with them.... We know that certain wars have arisen

It follows therefore that the Portuguese, even if they had been sovereigns in those parts to which the Dutch make voyages, would nevertheless be doing them an injury if they should forbid them access to those places and from trading there.

Is it not an incalculably greater injury for nations which desire reciprocal commercial relations to be debarred therefrom by the acts of those who are sovereigns over which their connecting high road runs? Is not that the very cause which for the most part prompts us to execrate robbers and pirates, namely, that they beset and infest our trade routes?

---

2. Reprinted by permission of the Oxford University Press.

CHAPTER II

The Portuguese have no right by title of discovery to sovereignty over the East Indies to which the Dutch make voyages

The Portuguese are not sovereigns of those parts of the East Indies to which the Dutch sail, that is to say, Java, Ceylon, and the many of the Moluccas. This I prove by the incontrovertible argument that no one is sovereign of a thing which he himself has never possessed, and which no one else has ever held in his name. These islands of which we speak, now have and always have had their own kings, their own government, and their own laws, and their own legal systems. The inhabitants allow the Portuguese to trade with them, just as they allow other nations the same privilege. Therefore, inasmuch as the Portuguese pay tolls, and obtain leave to trade from the rulers there, they thereby give sufficient proof that they do not go there as sovereigns but as foreigners....

First of all, if they say that those lands have come under their jurisdiction as the reward of discovery, THEY LIE, both in law and in fact. For to discover a thing is not to seize it with the eyes but to take real possession thereof, as Gordian points out in one of his letters. For that the Grammarians give the same signification to the expressions `to find' or `to discover' and `to take possession of' or `to occupy'; and all the Latin with which I am acquainted tells us that the opposite of `to find' is `to lose'. However, natural reason itself, the precise words of the law, and the interpretation of the more learned men all show clearly that the act of discovery is sufficient to give a clear title of sovereignty only when it is accompanied by actual possession. And this only applies of course to movables or such immovables as are actually inclosed within fixed bounds and guarded. No such claim can be established in the present case, because the Portuguese maintain no garrisons in these regions....

But in addition to all this, discovery *per se* gives no legal rights over things unless before the alleged discovery they were *res nullius.*

CHAPTER V

Neither the Indian Ocean nor the right of navigation thereon belongs to the Portuguese by title of occupation

If therefore the Portuguese acquired no legal right over the nations of the East Indies, and their territory and sovereignty, let us consider whether they have been able to obtain exclusive jurisdiction over the sea and its navigation or over trade. Let us consider the case of the sea.

Now, in the legal phraseology of the Law of Nations, the sea is called indifferently the property of no one (*res nullius*), or a common possession *(res communis)*, or public property *(res publica)*. it will be most convenient to explain the signification of these terms if we follow the practice of all poets since Hesiod, of the philosophers and jurists of the past, and distinguish certain epochs, the divisions of which are marked off perhaps not so much by intervals of time as by obvious logic and essential character. And we ought not to be criticised if in our explanation of a law deriving from nature, we use the authority and definition of those whose natural judgment admittedly is held in the highest esteem.

It is therefore necessary to explain that in the earliest stages of human existence both sovereignty and common possession had meanings other than which they bear at the present time. For nowadays sovereignty means a particular kind of proprietorship, such in fact that it absolutely excludes like possession by any one else. On the other hand, we call a thing `common' when its ownership or possession is held by several persons jointly according to a kind of partnership or mutual agreement from which all other persons are excluded. Poverty of language compels the use of some words for things that are not the same. And so because of a certain similarity and likeness, our modern nomenclature is applied to that state of primitive law. Now, in ancient times, `common' meant simply the opposite of `particular'; and `sovereignty' or `ownership', meant the privilege of lawfully using common property..... According to [Seneca's] reasoning there was a kind of sovereignty, but it was universal and unlimited. For God had not given all things to this individual or to that, but to the entire human race, and thus a number of persons, as it were *en masse*, were not debarred from being substantially sovereigns or owners of the same thing, which is quite contrary to our modern meaning of sovereignty. For it now implies particular or private ownership, a thing which no one then had....

It seems that the transition to the present distinction of ownership did not come violently, but gradually, nature herself pointing out the way. For since there are some things, the use of which consists in their being used up, either because of having become part of the very substance of the user they can never be used again, or because by use they become less fit for future use, it has become apparent, especially in dealing with the first category, such things as food and drink for example, that a certain kind of ownership is inseparable from use. For `own' implies that a thing belongs to one and the same person, in such a way that it cannot belong to any other person. By the process of reasoning this was next extended to things of the second category, such as clothes and movables and even some living things.

. . . .

When property or ownership was invented, the law of property was established to immitate nature. For as that use began in connection with bodily needs, from which we have said property first arose, so by a similar connection it was decided that things were the property of individuals. This is called `occupation', a word most appropriate to those things which in former times had been held in common....

This occupation or possession, however, in the case of things which resist seizure, like wild animals for example, must be uninterrupted or perpetually maintained, but in the case of other things it is sufficient after physical possession is once taken the intention to possess is maintained. Possession of movables implies seizure, and possession of immovables either the erection of buildings or some determination of boundaries, such as fencing in.....

Two conclusions can be drawn from what has thus far been said. The first is, that that which cannot be occupied, or which has never been occupied, cannot be the property of any one, because all property has arisen from occupation. The second is, that all that which has been so constituted by nature that although serving some one person it still suffices for the common use of all persons, is today and ought in perpetuity to remain in the same condition as when it was first created by nature....

. . . .

The air belongs to this class of things for two reasons. First, it is not susceptible of occupation; and second its common use is destined for all men. For the same reasons the sea is common to all, because it is so limitless that it cannot be the possession of any one, and because it is adapted for the use of all, whether we consider it from the point of view of navigation or of fisheries. Now, the same right which applies to the sea applies also to the things which the sea has carried away from other uses and made its own, such for example as the sands of the sea, of which the portion of the land is called the coast or the shore.....

These things therefore are what the Romans call `common' to all men by natural law, or as we have said, `public' according to the law of nations; and indeed they call their use sometimes common, sometimes public. Nevertheless, although those things are with reason said to be *res nullius,* so far as private ownership is concerned, still they differ very much from those things which, though also *res nullius,* have not been marked out for common use, such for example as wild animals, fish and birds. For if any one seizes these things and assumes possession of them, they can become objects of private ownership, but the things in the former category by consensus of opinion of all mankind are forever exempt from such private ownership on account of their susceptibility to universal use; and as they belong to all they cannot be taken away from all by any one person any more than what is mine can be taken away from me by you....

Therefore the sea can in no way become the private property of any one, because nature not only allows but enjoins its common use.....

We have now shown that whatever by occupation can become private property can also become public property, that is, the private property of a whole nation. And Celsus considered the shore included within the limits of the Roman Empire to be the property of the Roman people. There is not therefore the least reason for surprise that the Roman people through their emporers or praetors was able to grant its subjects the right of occupying the shore. This public occupation, however, no less than private occupation, was subject to the restriction that it should not infringe on international rights. Therefore the Roman people could not forbid any one from having access to the seashore, and from spreading his fishing nets there to dry, and from doing other things which all men long ago decided were always permissible.

The nature of the sea, however, differs from that of the shore, because the sea, except for a very restricted space, can neither easily be built upon, nor enclosed; if the contrary were true yet this could hardly happen without hindrance to the general use. Nevertheless, if any small portion of the sea can thus be occupied, the occupation is recognized....

Now Celsus holds that piles driven into the sea belong to the man who drove them. But such an act is not permissible if the use of the sea be thereby impaired. And Ulpian says that whoever builds a breakwater must see to it that it is not prejudicial to the interests of any one; for if this construction is likely to work an injury to any one, the injunction `Nothing may be built on public property' would apply....

Now, the same principle which applies to navigation applies also to fishing, namely, that it remains free and open to all. Nevertheless there shall be no prejudice if any one shall by fencing off with stakes an inlet of the sea make a fish pond for himself, and so establish a private preserve...

. . . .

...[T]he sea is one of those things which is not an article of merchandise, and which cannot become private property. Hence it follows, to speak strictly, that no part of the sea can be considered the property of any people whatsoever....

. . . .

CHAPTER VIII

By the Law of Nations trade is free to all persons whatsoever

If however the Portugues claim that they have an exclusive right to trade with the East Indies, their claim will be refuted by practically all the same arguments which already have been brought forward. Nevertheless I shall repeat them briefly, and apply them to this particular claim.

By the law of nations the principle was introduced that the opportunity to engage in trade, of which no one can be deprived, should be free to all men. This principle, inasmuch as its application was continually necessary after the distinctions of private ownerships were made, can therefore be seen to have a very remote origin. Aristotle, in a very clever phrase, in his work entitled the Politics, has said that the art of exchange is a completion of the independence which Nature requires. Therefore trade ought to be common to all according to the law of nations, not only in a negative but also in a positive, or as the jurists say, affirmative sense. The things that come under the former category are subject to change, those of the latter category are not. This statement can be explained in the following way.

Nature had given all things to all men. But since men were prevented from using many things which were desirable in every day life because they lived so far apart, and because, as we have said above, everything was not found everywhere, it was necessary to transport things from one place to another; not that there was yet an interchange of commodities, but that people were accustomed to make reciprocal use of things found in one another's territory according to their own judgment. They say that trade arose among the Chinese in about this way. Things were deposited at places out in the desert and left to the good faith and conscience of those who exchanged things of their own for what they took.

But when movables passed into private ownership (a change brought about by necessity, as has been explained above), straightway there arose a method of exchange by which the lack of one person was supplemented by that of which another person had an over supply. Hence commerce was born out of necessity for the commodities of life, as Pliny shows by a citation from Homer. But after immovables also began to be recognized as private property, the consequent annhilation of universal community of use made commerce a necessity not only between men who were neighbors; and in order that trade might be carried on more easily, somewhat later they invented money, which, as the derivation of the word shows, is a civic institution.

Thereafter the universal basis of all contracts, namely exchange, is derived from nature; but some particular kinds of exchange, and the money payment itself, are derived from law; although the older commentators on the law have not made this distinction sufficiently clear. Nevertheless all authorities agree that the ownership of things, particularly of movables, arises out of the primary law of nations, and that all contracts in which a price is not mentioned, are derived from the same source. The philosophers distinguish two kinds of exchange using Greek words which we shall take the liberty to translate as `wholesale' and `retail' trade. The former, as the Greek word shows, signifies trade or exchange between two widely separated nations, and it ranks first in the order of Nature as shown in Plato's Republic. The latter seems to be the same kind of exchange that Aristotle calls by another Greek word which means retail or shop trade between citizens. Aristotle makes a further division of wholesale trade into overland and overseas trade. But of the two, retail trade is the more petty and sordid, and wholesale the more honorable; but most honorable of all is the wholesale overseas trade, because it makes so many people sharers in so many things.

Hence Ulpian says that the maintenance of ships is the highest duty of a state, because it is an absolutely natural necessity, but that the maintenance of hucksters has not the same value. In another place Aristotle says: "For the art of exchange extends to all possessions, and it arises at first in a natural manner from the circumstance that some have too little, others too much." And Seneca is also to be cited in this connection for he has said that buying and selling is the law of nations.

Therefore freedom of trade is based on a primitive right of nations which has a natural and permanent cause; and that right cannot be destroyed, or at all events it may not be destroyed except by the consent of all nations. So far is that from being the case, that any nation may justly oppose in any way, any other two nations that desire to enter into a mutual and exclusive contractual relation.

NOTES

1. The above excerpts show that Grotius relied on many different sources in support of his arguments -- lawyers, philosophers, and even religion. It is easy to see, however, that he relied heavily upon natural law. In particular he stresses the fundamental right of trade and commerce as being essential to international law. His other arguments against the Portuguese include the fact that the seas are so vast that they cannot be appropriated, and the fact that the resources of the seas are inexhaustible, thus there is enough for everyone. The question is today whether either of these facts are as true as they were then. If not, how should we structure a legal order for the high seas today?

2. His appropriation argument seems to be based on the concept of *res publicus,* while the inexhaustibility argument sounds more like *res communis.* Was it necessary to do this? Is there any other sound theoretical basis for the freedom of the high seas?

3. JOHN SELDEN AND MARE CLAUSUM.

The Grotian argument did not please all nations. Of particular interest in this regard is the reaction of the English, who read the arguments of Grotius as an attack upon the exclusiveness of British fishing grounds. The principle English respondents to Grotius were William Wellwood and John Selden. In this section we will consider Selden's response.

Newton, INEXHAUSTIBILITY AS A LAW OF THE SEA DETERMINANT, 16 Tex. Int'l L.J. 369, 387-91 (1981)[3]

Selden wrote in response to Grotius' *Mare Liberum*, but because his arguments are largely historical it will serve continuity to start with Selden's views. His work, *Mare Clausum*, is divided into two main arguments: first, that the oceans may be subjected to dominion and second, that England has in fact exercised dominion over the surrounding seas. For purposes of this study the first argument is of greater interest.

Both Selden's first and second arguments draw heavily on history. There are several reasons for such reliance on historical evidence. First, the Royal mandate presupposed a search of historical records for proof of the English position -- and Selden was well disposed toward Royal mandates. Nor was this appoach patently erroneous. International law from whatever source, was still in its formative stages. In the past, an historical approach to the relations of states had been the only perspective used. While it is something of an oversimplification, it is generally accurate to say that in the early seventeenth century, norms of state practice were based on historical precedent. Even a people less fond of history than the English might well have chosen to rely heavily on history. Moreover, as Selden's work amply demonstrates, a great deal of history supported his arguments. Those who review past confrontations of ideas may confront the same problem of perspective familiar to lawyers reviewing cases that proved pivotal to particular rules of law. If one approaches the initial arguments knowing which argument prevailed and having lived with its consequences, then unless the prevailing view is woefully inadequate, one tends to view countervailing approaches with a predisposition toward rejection. In a system which emphasizes precedent, a leading case is often one that most observers at the time felt was a sure victory for the party which in fact failed. Because international law as an ordering of interstate relations was at a nascent stage, and history was and had been the touchstone of the legitimacy of state activity, most observers at the time of the Selden-Grotius controversy probably would have predicted a victory for Selden's historical arguments.

Selden's first general argument is that the oceans may be subjected to dominion. Selden is aware that the objections to this proposition are largely normative. He classifies the objections under the headings of the natural law of nations, the physical nature of the sea, and various learned opinions. The first heading encompasses opponents' claims that ancient law recognized certain things, including air and water, to be communal in nature. Selden argues that this theoretical proposition is not supported by the customary practice of nations which shows a consistent pattern allowing dominion of the oceans. Therefore, dominion is not contrary to the law of nations or the law of nature as exemplified by the law of nations.

Selden next turns his attention to the physical nature of the ocean. Oceans are by physical nature fluid and boundless and thus incapable of effective occupation, according to the critics of dominion of the oceans. Selden answers that all bodies of water are fluid and yet rivers and lakes are appropriable, and that the oceans are not unbounded -- every ocean has shore or islands by which they may be measured. Furthermore, argues Selden, nautical science enables limits to be fixed in the open sea. Moreover, the rationale used for rivers and lakes applies to the seas as well. Rivers and lakes are exhaustible resources and thus not practically subject to being treated as communal in nature. Selden argues that the seas are also exhaustible.

Lastly, that which is objected, touching the vast magnitude of the Sea, and its inexhaustible abundance, is of very little weight here. Suppose it to be inexhaustible, so that he which shall appropriate it to himself, can receive no damage by other men's using it, what more prejudice is this to the right of ownership or dominion, than it is to the owner of a Fire or Candle, that another man's should be lighted by his? Is he therefore less Master of his own fire or candle? But truly we often see, that the sea itself, by reason of other men's Fishing, Navigation, and Commerce, becomes the worse for him that owns it, and others that enjoy it in his right; So that less profit ariseth, than might otherwise be received thereby....

. . . .

It is obvious therefore to every man, that the gain of such a Voyage...may be lessened, and that the abundance either of pearles themselves, or of those shell-fishes, which produce them, may through a promiscuous and common use of the Sea, be diminished in any Sea whatsoever. Where then is that inexhaustible abundance of Commodities in the Sea, which cannot be impaired? There is truly the same reason also, touching on every kind of fishing.

Selden's argument that the seas are exhaustible is composed of two elements. First, he argues that unrestricted navigation, commerce and fishing diminish the right of the owner by reducing his profit. This argument presupposes that of the propriety of a property right in the sea. It assumes a static or fixed value for ocean uses; mutual expansion could not work to the advantage of all concerned. This area was of great importance in the formulation of the doctrine of the freedom of the sea and Selden's arguments on this point were unconvincing and largely rejected. His second argument that the seas are exhaustible was that overpearling or overfishing could deplete the stocks and thus demonstrate physical exhaustibility. The pearls would simply be "used up." Selden was correct, at least with respect to shellfish and fish. However, at that time not all agreed with Selden and, in any event, the arguments relating to commerce and navigation received most attention.

Selden makes extensive use of authority throughout his work, distinguishing or criticizing statements of his peers and predecessors. He amasses considerable writing in support of his position but unfortunately ignores material, strains the interpretation of other material, and tends to rely so heavily on volume of detailed historical recitation that his work sinks under its own weight. Selden's second argument that the "Sea of England" has in fact been subjected to dominion by the British, while interesting politically, is of less significance for the law of the sea. Selden made it clear that the maritime sovereignty claimed by England was of the most abolute kind in the same terms of sovereignty over the land.

. . . .

NOTES

1. From the works of Selden and Grotius, we can see the beginnings of tensions that exist to the present day. One set of tensions is that between navigation and resource management. The other set is between the need to have free commerce over the seas with the need for coastal States to be able to protect their national interests near their shores. The first, we will see, gave impetus to the creation of the exclusive economic zone, while the second to the concept of the territorial sea. The victory of Grotius set in motion another force the impact of which was felt strongly at the Third United Nations Conference on the Law of the Sea. Increased freedom of trade led almost inexorably to increased colonialism. Thus it was that at the most recent conference, relatively new, ex-colonial States tended to equate the freedom of the seas with exploitation and colonial domination.

2. As noted by Newton, Selden was right as to the exhaustibility of living resources, at least in the long run. But was not Grotius equally correct given the conditions existing at the time of these writings? Would one not conclude, therefore, that the best claim that Selden could make is that someday in the future, there may be a need to assign jurisdiction to a belt of water near the coast to the coastal State?

3. Both of these scholars placed emphasis upon navigation and fishing, as these were the most important uses of the high seas at the time. Clearly, they were not the only conceivable uses. Thus these early writings should not be read as excluding other freedoms of the high seas as new technologies developed and the needs of nations changed. We will see, for example, that the 1958 Conventions incorporate other freedoms, based upon the practice of States. But the scope of the doctrine remains in debate even today. Deep seabed mining was not even contemplated until recently. It was certainly not an issue in 1958. Should it nonetheless be considered a freedom of the high seas today? In answering that question, one faces much the same kind of debate that we see in regard to the Constitution of the United States. I refer to the "original intent" versus the "living document" perceptions.

4. During these early developmental years, there were many other scholars who entered the debate. However, Selden and Grotius were the most important. Over the next two centuries, the doctrine of the freedom of the high seas was defined mostly by reference to what States were actually doing. Thus the doctrine evolved through customary international law. This was a confusing period, because there was such a variety of national claims. Eventually, there evolved a recognition that there was a need for a codification of the rules to give them more universality. Also, as time passed, and shipping technology evolved, it became clear that the freedom of the high seas could no longer be excercised by States in complete disregard of the rights of other States to do the same. Inability to appropriate areas of the seas was not as clear as it used to be. Despite the need for a law of the sea code, there was no successful effort to codify the customary rules until 1958. We shall now shift to an examination of the juridical nature of various zones, and the doctrine of freedom of the high seas as codified in the 1958 and 1982 Conventions on the Law of the Sea.

* * * * *

C. TREATY ELABORATION OF THE DOCTRINE

In this section, we examine the codification of the freedom of the high seas (without dealing with the boundaries of those seas) in the 1958 and 1982 treaties. The purpose is to understand what, if any, difference do these documents incorporate from the doctrine as propounded by Grotius, and to explore the differences in language between the two treaties.

CONVENTION ON THE HIGH SEAS

Article 1

The term "high seas" means all parts of the sea that are not included in the territorial sea or in the internal waters of a State.

Article 2

The high seas being open to all nations, no State may validly purport to subject any part of them to its sovereignty. Freedom of the high seas is exercised under the conditions laid down by these articles and by the other rules of international law. It comprises, inter alia, both for coastal and non-coastal States:

(1) Freedom of navigation;

(2) Freedom of fishing;

(3) Freedom to lay submarine cables and pipelines;

(4) Freedom to fly over the high seas.

These freedoms, and others which are recognized by the general principles of international law, shall be exercised by all States with reasonable regard to the interests of other States in their exercise of the freedom of the high seas.

INTERNATIONAL LAW COMMISSION, Draft Articles on the Law of the Sea, 1956 Commentary

Commentary to Article 26

Some large stretches of water, entirely surrounded by dry land, are known as "lakes", others as "seas". The latter constitute internal seas, to which the regime of high seas is not applicable. Where such stretches of water communicate with the high seas by a strait or arm of the sea, they are considered as "internal seas" if the coasts, including those of the waterway giving access to the high seas, belong to a single State. If that is not the case, they are considered as high seas. These rules may, however, be modified for historical reasons or by international agreement.

Commentary to Article 27

The principle generally accepted in international law that the high seas are open to all nations governs the whole regulation of the subject. No State may subject any part of the high seas to sovereignty; hence no State may exercise jurisdiction over any such stretch of water. States are bound to refrain from any acts which might adversely affect the use of the high seas by nationals of other States. Freedom to fly over the high seas is expressly mentioned in this article because the Commission considers that it follows directly from the principle of the freedom of the sea;....

The list of freedoms of the high seas...is not restrictive. The Commission has merely specified four of the main freedoms, but is aware that there are other freedoms, such as freedom to undertake scientific research on the high seas -- a freedom limited only by the general principle stated in the third sentence of [the preceding] paragraph...

[T]he Commission [did not] make any express pronouncement on the freedom to undertake nuclear weapons tests on the high seas. In this connexion the general principle enunciated in the third sentence [referred to above]...is applicable.

The term "submarine cables" applies not only to telegraph and telephone cables, but also to high-voltage power cables.

Any freedom that is to be exercised in the interests of all entitled to enjoy it, must be regulated. Hence, the law of the high seas contains certain rules, most of them already recognized in positive international law, which are designed, not to limit or restrict the freedom of the high seas, but to safe-guard its exercise in the interests of the entire international community. These rules concern particularly:

(i) The right of States to exercise their sovereignty on board ships flying their flag;

(ii) The exercise of certain policing rights;

(iii) The rights of States relative to the conservation of the living resources of the high seas;

(iv) The institution by a coastal State of a zone contiguous to its coast for the purpose of exercising certain well-defined rights;

(v) The rights of coastal States with regard to the continental shelf.

These matters form the subject of the present articles.

1982 UNITED NATIONS CONVENTION ON THE LAW OF THE SEA

PART VII

SECTION 1. GENERAL PROVISIONS

Article 86

Application of the provisions of this Part

The provisions of this Part apply to all parts of the sea that are not included in the exclusive economic zone, in the territorial sea or in the internal waters of a State, or in the archipelagic waters of an archipelagic State. This article does not entail any abridgment of the freedoms enjoyed by all States in the exclusive economic zone in accordance with article 58.

Article 87

Freedom of the high seas

1. The high seas are open to all States, whether coastal or land-locked. Freedom of the high seas is exercised by the conditions laid down by this Convention and by other rules of international law. It comprises, *inter alia*, both for coastal and land-locked States:

(a) freedom of navigation;

(b) freedom of overflight;

(c) freedom to lay submarine cables and pipelines, subject to Part VI;

(d) freedom to construct artificial islands and other installations permitted under international law, subject to Part VI;

(e) freedom of fishing, subject to the conditions laid down in section 2;

(f) freedom of scientific research, subject to Parts VI and XIII.

2. These freedoms shall be exercised by all States with due regard to the interests of other States in their exercise of the freedom of the high seas, and also with due regard for the rights under this Convention with respect to activities in the Area.

Article 88

Reservation of the high seas for peaceful purposes

The high seas shall be reserved for peaceful purposes.

Article 89

Individual claims of sovereignty over the high seas

No State may validly purport to subject any part of the high seas to its sovereignty.

NOTES

1. The 1958 Convention, you will note, places certain restrictions on the exercise of the freedom of the high seas. The most important of these is the duty not to restrict the right of other States to exercise their freedom of the high seas. This "reasonable use" concept was not a part of the Grotian doctrine.

2. While the concept of freedom of the high seas was carried forward to the 1982 Convention, you can see that there were several changes in language and structure. Any time a lawyer notes changes of this kind, he or she should certainly inquire why that was done. Why, for example, was the restriction on sovereignty removed from the body of the article and placed in a separate new article 89? And why does Article 1 of the 1958 Convention begin with the words "The term `high seas' means..." while the new Convention begins with "The provisions of this Part apply..."? We shall gain some insight to these questions in the next part.

D. THE EXCLUSIVE ECONOMIC ZONE

Reference is made, in Article 86 of the 1982 Convention, to the Exclusive Economic Zone, or the EEZ. As we shall see, this new zone extends seaward from the coasts as far as 200 nautical miles. As such, it covers an area that was mostly considered to be high seas in the 1958 Convention. We shall deal with specific rules concerning the jurisdiction of the coastal State later, particularly with respect to fisheries, the conduct of marine scientific research, and the protection and preservation of the marine environment. Here, however, we are mostly concerned with the juridical status of the EEZ. Is its outer part still high seas, is it a zone of national jurisdiction, or is it something entirely different?

1982 UNITED NATIONS CONVENTION ON THE LAW OF THE SEA

PART V

EXCLUSIVE ECONOMIC ZONE

Article 55

Specific legal regime of the exclusive economic zone

The exclusive economic zone is an area beyond and adjacent to the territorial sea, subject to the specific legal regime established in this Part, under which the rights and jurisdiction of the coastal State and the rights and freedoms of other States are governed by the relevant provisions of this Convention.

Article 56

Rights, jurisdiction and duties of the coastal State in the exclusive economic zone

1. In the exclusive economic zone, the coastal State has:

(a) sovereign rights for the purpose of exploring and exploiting, conserving and managing the natural resources, whether living or non-living, of the waters superjacent to the sea-bed and of the seabed and its subsoil, and with regard to other activities for the economic exploitation and exploration of the zone, such as the production of energy from the water, currents and winds;

(b) jurisdiction as provided for in the relevant provisions of this Convention with regard to:

(i) the establishment and use of artificial islands, installations and structures;

(ii) marine scientific research;

(iii) the protection and preservation of the marine environment;

(c) other rights and duties provided for in this Convention.

2. In exercising its rights and performing its duties under this Convention in the exclusive economic zone, the coastal State shall have due regard to the rights and duties of other States and shall act in a manner compatible with the provisions of this Convention.

3. The rights set out in this article with respect to the sea-bed and subsoil shall be exercised in accordance with Part VI.

Article 57

Breadth of the exclusive economic zone

The exclusive economic zone shall not extend beyond 200 nautical miles from the baselines from which the breadth of the territorial sea is measured.

Article 58

Rights and duties of other States in the exclusive economic zone

1. In the exclusive economic zone, all States, whether coastal or land-locked, enjoy, subject to the relevant provisions of this Convention, the freedoms referred to in article 87 of navigation and overflight and of the laying of submarine cables and pipelines, and other internationally lawful uses of the sea related to these freedoms, such as those associated with the operation of ships, aircraft and submarine cables and pipelines, and compatible with the other provisions of this Convention.

2. Articles 88 to 115 and other pertinent rules of international law apply to the exclusive economic zone in so far as they are not incompatible with this Part.

3. In exercising their rights and performing their duties under this Convention in the exclusive economic zone, States shall have due regard to the rights and duties of the coastal State and shall comply with the laws and regulations adopted by the coastal State in accordance with the provisions of this Convention and other rules of international law in so far as they are not incompatible with this Part.

Article 59

Basis for the resolution of conflicts regarding the attribution of rights and jurisdiction in the exclusive economic zone

In cases where this Convention does not attribute rights or jurisdiction to the coastal State or to other States within the exclusive economic zone, and a conflict arises between the interests of the coastal State and any other State or States, the conflict should be resolved on the basis of equity and in the light of all of the relevant circumstances, taking into account the respective importance of the interests involved to the parties as well as to the entire international community as a whole.

NOTES

1. During the conference that led to the adoption of the 1982 Convention, the new concept of the exclusive economic zone emerged to satisfy the interests of coastal States regarding their offshore natural resources -- primarily fisheries. But the idea of the creation of such a new zone precipitated a long and intense battle as to the juridical nature of the zone. On the one hand, the coastal States, particularly those coastal States which at that time were claiming territorial seas of 200 nautical miles, were urging that the zone be seen as a zone of national jurisdiction. Under their theory, other States would in the zone enjoy the rights of navigation, overflight and laying of submarine cables and pipelines. All other rights and jurisdictions would accrue to the coastal States. If that theory had been accepted, the zone would closely resemble a territorial sea.

This was totally unacceptable to the maritime powers, mainly because of national security concerns. Those States, with the United States and the former Soviet Union very much in prominence, wanted to classify the zone as high seas, meaning that all rights other than resource rights would be enjoyed by all States in the zone. The articles that resulted from those negotiations appear above. Notice that no where is the zone categorized either as high seas or a zone of national jurisdiction.

2. After careful examination of the language, do you understand the significance of the language in article 58 that begins "other internationally lawful uses of the sea related to these freedoms"?

3. What is the reason paragraph 2 of article 58 incorporates articles 88 to 115 by reference, but not article 87? Why are the cross-referenced articles incorporated only to the extent that they "are not incompatible with this Part?

4. Since the rights of coastal States are spelled out in article 56 and those of other States in 58, what is the purpose of article 59?

E. THE "PRESENTIAL SEA"

Very recently, a new concept has arisen and been promoted having an impact on the regime for the high seas. The following articles give some insight into the nature of this concept, however vague, and the problems some see with its possible implementation.

Orrego, TOWARDS AN EFFECTIVE MANAGEMENT OF HIGH SEAS FISHERIES AND THE SETTLEMENT OF THE PENDING ISSUES OF THE LAW OF THE SEA[4]

Consolidation and Uncertainties of the Law of the Sea.

A recent study on the effect of the Exclusive Economic Zones and Exclusive Fishery Zones on world fisheries shows in a conclusively that developing countries have fared rather well in terms of the increase in their catches. In fact, 53 developing countries that have enacted such zones of maritime jurisdiction have increased the tonnage caught, out of 63 countries that have made gains. On the other hand, only 20 developing countries have experienced decreases in their catches after these enactments, out of a total of 30 countries showing losses. Two developing countries have not shown changes.

Among the most important winners there are Chile, China, Republic of Korea, Indonesia, Ecuador, Mexico, Turkey and India. Among the greatest losses where those expereinced by Peru, Angola and Vietnam, and most of these decreases are attributable to internal political strife or the application of wrong policies rather than to the operation of the Law of the Sea. In 1987, deveoping countries reached a share of 25.08% of world catch, up from 17.2% in 1970. The largest participations in this share were those of Chile (24.44%), Thailand (10.83%), Indonesia (9.27%), India (8.72%), D.R. Korea (8.10%), Philipines (7%), and Mexico (5.67%). Developed countries increased their catch in the same period from 51.44% to 52.38%. The increase in the value of the catch has also been significant in many cases.

It should also be noted that among the top twenty fishing nations of the world several developing countries figure quite prominently: Chile (4), Peru (6), ROK (7), Thailand (9), Indonesia (10), India (12), Korea (R.D.) (13), Philippines (16), Mexico (18), Ecuador (20). The Republic of Korea and Taiwan operate important distant water fishing fleets, an activity which Chile is also beginning to undertake.

These figures, positive as they are, also indicate the existence of some important problems in relation to the exploitation of the living resources of the sea. The first is that not all developing countries have been able to benefit from the new rules of the law of the sea, partly because of differing natural conditions but also because of the inabilitoy to adopt appropriate management measures for the Exclusive Economic Zone and related areas. This question will be addressed further below.

---

4. Delivered at the Twenty-Third Annual Law of the Sea Institute at Genoa, Italy, June 24, 1992. Reprinted by permission of the Law of the Sea Institute.

The second problem evidenced by these figures is that the main fishing nations of the world, with few exceptions, have not substantially diminished their share of the world catch. This phenomenon is explained by the intensification of the fishing effort in areas adjacent to those countries, by the increase in the number of agreements granting access to the fishing zones of developing countries, and by the intenstification of high seas fisheries, which gives rise to a considerable set of new issues. Not least of these, illegal fishing has also increased.

From the above discussion one can also draw an interesting legal implication as to the characteristics of world practice on the law of the sea during the past decade: while the law and practice relating to areas under national jurisdiction have been fairly stable and consolidated during this period, the law and practice relating to areas beyond national jurisdiction -- both the high seas and the seabed area -- have remained uncertain and in a state of flux, and this unstable condition is leading to new concepts and legal approaches. While briefly examining the main trends as to the first aspect, this article will concentrate on the pending issues of the Law of the Sea, with particular reference to the question of high seas fisheries.

The Law of the Sea in Areas under National Jurisdiction

[In this section, the author discusses how well national policies within areas of coastal State jurisdiction have been harmonized with the treaty]

Economic foundations of Fisheries Policy

As mentioned above, not all developing countries have successfully taken advantage of the Exclusive Economic Zone in terms of the exploitation of its living resources. Technical and scientific shortcomings, the lack of a comprehensive fisheries policy, international agreements granting access to third countries, or joint-venture arrangments that are not always advantageous to the coastal State, have all been factors indluencing this situation. Further, inefficient mechanisms for international fisheries cooperation have not been helpful on many occasions.

The underlaying problem affecting the full utilization of the Exclusive Economic Zone is not so much of a legal or technical nature as an economic one. Policies allowing for a free access to the living resources of the sea have resulted in a well-known phenomenon of economic inefficiency, overcapitalization, overexploitation and depletion of resources. Traditional regulatory instruments calling for various forms of state intervention, which have been frequently applied by most developing countries, have generally not proven successful. In the light of this experience an entirely new approach, based on individual transferrable quotas, is being implemented in a number of countries -- including Chile as one developing country -- with the specific characteristic of recognizing individual fishing rights by an innovative mechanism of privatization and market-oriented regulations.

The advantages of this new approach have proven to be considerable, not only in overcoming the problems of inefficiency but also in providing a useful tool for the full utilization of the resources of the Exclusive Economic Zone. However, difficult problems of implementation have also been encountered, particularly at the stage of allocation of the fishing rights. This option, as well as the trend to adopt self-regulation as a mechanism for fisheries management, should be closely considered in the case of developing counties and other groups.

These experiences clearly point to the need for reevaluating fisheries policies and the objectives that have been traditionally followed by many developing countries, contemplating new criteria for fisheries legislation and its institutional framework and the availability of information, training and research.

Coastal States' Interests in High Seas Fisheries

If the law and practice relating to maritime areas under national jurisdiction has been moving towards greater consolidation and harmonization with the 1982 Law of the Sea Convention, the same cannot always be said of the situation today characterizing high seas fisheries. In fact, since the Convention was opened for signature a number of new problems have emerged in relation to the conservation and utilization of the living resources of the high seas, an area being subjected to increasing pressures.

The current search for new legal solutions has been occasionally interpreted as an effort directed to enlarge national jurisdiction in a spatial sense beyond the 200-mile limit. The emerging trend, however, responds to an entirely different reasoning based on the recognition of the oceans as an integrated ecosystem and the fact that the coastal State cannot be indifferent to what happens in areas of the high seas closely related to the areas under national jurisdiction. The concept of ecosystem management is leading to a greater emphasis on rational management of the living resources. While this is true in a broad sense within the Exclusive Economic Zone, it has become more evident and pressing in relation to the high seas, where generally there is no regulatory authority whatsoeve. Furthermore, conservation of resources in the Exclusive Economic Zone has become mandatory under the 1982 Law of the Sea Convention, while the high seas follow looser conservation arrangements. It follows that a new special interest is being expressed in this new context, which is related specifically to recent issues affecting the high seas.

The paramount cases in which coastal state rights, duties and interests regarding high seas fisheries have been recognized under international law are those concerning straddling stocks, highly migratory species, marine mammals, anadromous stocks, and catadromous species. There is, however, a more general proposition that needs to be examined. It is quite clear that states can adopt conservation measures for their nationals and vessesls in the high seas and that they must ensure cooperation with other States by means of the appropriate organization in order to apply common restrictions. The issue is whether this can be done without the participation of the relevant coastal State as the traditional law of high seas fisheries would suggest. In the light of the close interrelationship existing between the high seas and the Exclusive Economic Zone, both in terms of biological and ecological interactions, it is submitted that such a divorce is no longer possible and that consequently conservation measures in the high seas need to ensure the participation of the relevant coastal state as a condition of their effectiveness. This trend in no way diminishes the validity of cooperation and binding dispute settlement as the preferred alternative, but it ensures that if all such mechanisms should fail or prove to be ineffective the interest of the coastal state will not be ignored.

Highly Migratory Species and the Prevalence of Coastal States interests

Highly migratory species provide one important case where there is a very close interaction between the high seas and the Exclusive Economic Zone. The 1982 Law of the Sea Convention clearly recognizes this reality in Article 64, which calls for arrangements on cooperation. The long-standing position of the United States, claiming that highly migratory species could be managed only through international arrangements and that no coastal State jurisdiction should intervene in the Exclusive Economic Zone or otherwise, gradually began to change in the light of the specific problems that have to be addressed in practice. This was firstly and indirectly done by means of the 1987 Treaty on Fisheries between a group of Pacific Island States and the United States, and next in a direct manner 1990 when the United States began claiming jurisdiction over highly migratory species within its Exclusive Economic Zone.

The interpretation upheld in this matter by a number of developing countries proved warranted, although regretably Latin American initiatives in this field did not contribute to a positive solution. Indeed, neither the 1983 Agreement and Protocol on tuna fishing between Costa Rica, Panama and the United States, nor the Agreement of 1989 establishing the Eastern Pacific Tuna Fishing Organization seem to coincide with the balanced approach sought by the 1982 Convention, since, as concluded by one author, "they do not appear to meet the conditions required to assure an ample participation of interested States". In the first case the approach is somewhat distorted to the detriment of the interest of the coastal state since its role is minimized in the Exclusive Economic Zone, a situation that basically responded to the views of the United States at that time. In the second case the approach is somewhat distorted to the detriment of the interest of other states in high seas fisheries, which is not appropriately taken into account in a scheme controlled entirely by a group of coastal States. Future negotiations will have to be undertaken on different bases responding to the present state of understanding and cooperation which characterizes the issue of highly migratory species elsewhere in the world.

Marine mammals constitute, of course, a different category of highly migratory species, being governed in part by the International Convention on the Regulation of Whaling and the work of the International Whaling Commission and in part by the more stringent provisions of Article 65 of the 1982 Law of the Sea Convention, which is applicable both within and beyond the Exclusive Economic Zone as a further recnition of the intrinsic unity of ocean space.

Straddling Stocks

A second situtsation in which there is a very close interaction between the Exclusive Economic Zone and the High Seas is that relating to straddling stocks. This has become a pressing question, affecting, among other situations, the interests of Canada, the United States, New Zealand, Mexico, Central America, Argentina, Chile and Peru. The current discussion of this question clearly shows that the underlying issue is the expression of interest of coastal states in fisheries beyond the Exclusive Economic Zone where the fisheries' stocks are inseparable from the Exclusive Economic Zone in terms of management and conservation. Various countries concerned elaborated on this interest in the Conference on Conservation and Management of the high seas living resources held in St. John, Terranova, in 1990. There the adoption of measures to avoid adverse effects of high seas fisheries on living resource under coastal state jurisdiction was emphasized, together with the concept that management of straddling stocks in the high seas must be consistent with the management regime applied in the Exclusive Economic Zone. The new approach underlying this policy does not involve at all an issue of creeping jurisdiction of the coastal state, and it is conceived within the framework of the 1982 Law of the Sea Convention, subject to perfecting the meaning and extent of some of its provisions. Furthermore, this approach can be understood as preventing a kind of reverse creeping jurisdiction in vavor of distant-water fishing states.

This process of elaboration was taken a step further by means of a meeting of experts from Canada, Chile, and New Zealand, which met in Santiago on 17 May 1991, followed by a larger gathering that met in New York on 26 July 1991 with the participation of Argentina, Australia, Barbados, Brazil, Canada, Chile, New Zealand, and the Forum Fisheries Agency. The scope of these discussions was broader since they addressed the whole range of issues relating to the conservation and management of living resources of the high seas and not only the question of straddling stocks. The issue has also been discussed in the context of the work of the 1992 United Nations Convention on Environment and Development.

Anadromous and Catadromous Species

Another area where special interests in the high seas haven been duly recognized under international law is that related to anadroumous stocks. In accordance to Article 66 of the 1982 Law of the Sea Convention the states in whose rivers these stocks originate shall have the "primary interest in and responsibility for such stocks", a provision which extends to the management of salmon in the high seas with only minor restrictions relating to the cooperation with other States concerned.

Significant legal changes have been prompted by the special characteristics of the salmon fisheries and the need to introduce effective conservation measures. The important development of ocean ranching has also contributed to this change in the legal approach.

Catadromous species are one further example of coastal states' special interest extending to fisheries and conservation in the high seas.

Other Expressions of Coastal State Interest in the High Seas

Various other developments of interest in relation to the high seas fisheries should be mentioned. One such development is the emerging trend of approaching marine affairs in terms of "large marine ecosystems", which promotes a focus upon conservation, development, and research, not within the limited bounds of traditional jurisdictional areas, but in the light of broad geographical and biological realities. Large marine ecosystems often extend beyond national jurisdictional areas, not to claim jurisdiction but to ensure an appropriate management within the perspective of environmentally sustainable activities. It should be pointed out in this regard that the concept of large marine ecosystems is not related to questions of exercise of jurisdiction in a juridical sense, but to the rational management of biological realities, a distinction that has not always been clear and that many times has conduced to unecessary difficulties in the negotiations on marine affairs. While many large marine ecosystems extend along the continents, a number of others involve large ocean expanses extending into the high seas.

Another development of importance relates to the practice of boarding and inspection of foreign vessels in the high seas in order to prevent illegal catching of salmon, particularly in the context of the use of driftnets or as an incidental catch. The United States has been developing this practice in the North Pacific in relation to Korea and Taiwan under bilateral agreements and in relation to Japan under the International North Pacific Fisheries Commission and other arrangement, having the Soviet Union followed a similar albeit more limited practice. It would not be surprising if the same right of boarding and inspectiion is claimed in the near future in relation to other species or situations where conservation is seriously affected by unregulated high seas operations. The same policy of boarding and inspection has been followed by the United States in relation to the ships suspected of engaging in narcotic drugs traffic.

A third development of importance in state practice relates to the regulation of certain types of high seas fishing operations, with particular reference to the issue of driftnets, again on the ground of the need to ensure conservation and avoid indiscriminated catches. The Convention for the Prevention of Fishing with Long Driftnets in the South Pacific, and the passing of the United Nations General Assembly Resolution 44/225 on Large-Scale Pelagic Driftnet Fishing, are all recent examples of initiatives aimed at the regulation of high seas fisheries in situations where they are clearly at odds with conservation criteria. The control of transshipment of driftnetting catches and reflagging of vessels are other practices where the role of coastal States will be increasingly felt in the near future.

The whole issue of environmental protection of the seas and oceans is of course leading to the adoption of measures in the high seas, including eventually coastal state action in given instances. The long-term implication of this policy is more complex since it refers to the question of whether fisheries management will be introduced in the high seas in a manner comparable to what is now done within the Exclusive Economic Zone. Given the fact that conservation problems are not intrinsically different in such areas it can be expected that this development will take place in the future. In this regard Article 116 of the Convention has become particularly pertinent in relating the freedom of fishing to the rights and duties as well as the interests of coastal states.

The Presential Sea

A high-ranking Chilean naval officer has recently put forward the concept of a "Presential Sea", a concept which has been received with great interest in Chile and other countries and which has also raised questions about its compatibility with international law in some European capitals and other quarters. The meaning and extent of the "Presential Sea" can well be explained in the light of the development explained since it closely responds to the expression of a special interest of the coastal state -- in this instance Chile -- but it can also be applied to many other geographical situations throughout the world. To this extent the new concept can well serve the needs of many countries throughout the world, although of course in given narrow geographical situations it may be more difficult to implement.

The presential sea involves, first, the participation in and surveilance of the activities undertaken by other states in the high seas of particular interest for the coastal state. In this regard it is not a question of excluding any state from such areas, but, on the contrary, of ensuring the active inclusion of the coastal state concerned. There is no question of exclusive coastal state rights involved in this concept, or the drawing of new maritime boundaries in a legal sense; neither should participation in such activities be understood as a kind of compulsory intervention by the coastal state in the activities undertaken there by other countries, but only as ensuring its own right to operate actively in the area. The concept expressly safeguards the legal status of the high seas established by the 1982 United Nations Convention on the Law of the Sea and does not purport to disavow the high seas as such. It follows that the approach has been conceived of in a manner entirely consistent with the current status of the international law of the sea.

Next, the presential sea concept encourages the coastal state to undertake economic activities in the high seas in order to promote national economic development and to ensure that other activities therein are conducted in such a way as to avoid direct or indirect harmful effects upon this development. This element involves the undertaking of legitimate forms of competition, while at the same time it requires the development of more active forms of cooperation and other measures in order to prevent adverse effects upon the interest of the coastal state. This type of situation has already been recognized in relation to issues such as straddling stocks, highly migratory species, salmon ranching and salmon natural stocks, marine pollution, and a number of other matters which have been mentioned, and that will probably be perfected in a variety of ways in the near future. Again here there is consistency with the current and evolving status of international law. The concept does not have as such a jurisdictional content or claim to the area of the presential sea, but it can eventually have jursdictional implications if mechanisms for international cooperation or nonexistent or ineffective. This would be the case, for example, if the coastal state has to introduce conservation measures in areas of the high seas in the absence of any other regulatory authority while negotiations conduce to a solution.

Thirdly, the concept of a presential sea is related to a broad view of national security, understood not in a strict military sense but in terms of protection of the national interest, including the economic dimension mentioned above, with particular reference to the Exclusive Economic Zone and the territorial sea. The same interest will of course be present in relation to the continental shelf areas and eventually in relation to the seabed beyond the limits of national jurisdiction, not to the detriment of whatever international regime might be brought into force but in order to ensure that the interest of the coastal state will be expressed in the latter framework in an appropriate manner.

Geographically the presential sea area of interest for Chile has been defined as the high seas beyond the Exclusive Economic Zone and located opposite to the continent, Antarctica, and Easter Island, in the broad quadrangle of the Southeast Pacific. A similar definition is contained in the Chilean fisheries law passed in 1991. After the passing of this law the concept acquired a legal status in Chile, thus also becoming an official government policy. The geographical extent of application of the presential sea may of course vary from case to case, taking into account different national and regional realities. Since such a concept does not involve a jurisdictional claim over the high seas it can well be adapted to such different realities.

The presential sea is a concept where all the trends, issues and concerns described converge within a framework which, while fully consistent with present international law, is at the same time opening new frontiers for its development in the light of the changing reality of ocean management. It can therefore be expected that such a concept will lead to a number of changes in the law of high seas fisheries in the years ahead, not only because it represents the expression of interest of many developing countries but also because it responds to the pressing and potential needs of developed countries as well. Just as it happened with the Exclusive Economic Zone, this new concept has the potential of evolving into customary international law, reflecting both the interest of the coastal states and those of the international community. In fact, to a meaningful extent the coastal state will be acting on behalf of the international community in the Presential sea as long as the international community will not ensure adequate conservation in the high seas.

Renewed Efforts for Seabed Mining Joint Ventures

The law related to the seabed beyond the limits of national jurisdiction is also in a state of uncertainty as a result of the stagnation affecting Part XI of the 1982 Law of the Sea Convention. This is not the occasion to repeat the debate surrounding this matter, the work of the Preparatory Commission or the conversations convened by the United Nations secretary general, but only to reiterate the views expressed elsewhere regarding a new effort to organize a joint-venture system.

[In this section, the author summarizes views not relevant to the present problem.]

. . . .

Reordering High Seas Fisheries

The decade that has lapsed since the signature of the 1982 Law of the Sea Convention has been enormously rich in terms of the development of law and practice relating to the implementation of the Convention. A process of consolidation and harmonization is well under way as far as domestic legislation and the areas subject to national jurisdiction are concerned. Developing and developed countries alike have had a most important role in this process.

The characteristics of the next decade of development in the Law of the Sea have already emerged quite clearly in that a similar process of consolidation will take place in relation to areas beyond the limits of national jurisdiction, most particularly the reordering of high seas fisheries. The presential sea will become in this context an influential concept for such purposes. Developing coutries had not normally been actively concerned about high seas fisheries, which many times were beyond their capabilities. This is the fundamental point that has now changed, because developing countries are today in the position of both competing in terms of high seas fishing and ensuring that such activities do not result in adversely affecting the resources in areas under national jurisdiction. It is this new interest that is gradually being recognized under international law and which will inspire the pending issues of the Law of the Sea. The conference on high seas fisheries convened by the United Nations for 1993 will mark the beginning of this process of redefinition and clarification.

ED. NOTE: The above paper was delivered before a knowledgable audience, and it evoked lively response, much of it negative. While the author denies that this new concept has jurisdictional implications, do you believe that is the case? Recall that Chile was one of the nations pressing for the extended jursdiction that eventually became the EEZ. Some observers were additionally disturbed by the fact that Canada is an active participant in the development of the concept, a country also active in seeking ways to extend control over fisheries beyond the EEZ, and by the fact that the idea was said to have been originated by a "high ranking naval officer".

Additionally, how relevant are the examples that he gives to support the foundations of the new proposal?

Peru, as well, has made some ambiguous statements concerning its maritime areas. Consider the following.

DECLARATION BY PERU IN ADHERING TO THE UNITED NATIONS CONVENTION ON THE LAW OF THE SEA

In adhering to the United Nations Convention on the Law of the Sea the Government of Peru, in conformity with provisions of article 310 of the Convention, places on record the present declaration to be incorporated in the registry of the instrument of adhesion:

Paragraph one: The Republic of Peru shall maintain unchanged the definitions concerning its territorial, maritime and aerial dominions contained in article 97, 98 and 99 of the Political Constitution of the State, which reads as follows:

"Article 97: The territory of the Republic is inviolable. It includes the soil, the subsoil, the maritime dominion and the superjacent air space".

"Article 98: The maritime dominion of the State comprehends the sea adjacent to its coasts, as well as its soil and subsoil, up to the distance of two hundred nautical miles, measured from the baselines established by law. In its maritime dominion, Peru exercises sovereignty and jurisdiction, without prejudice to the international freedoms of communication, in accordance with the law and the international conventions ratified by the Republic".

"Article 99: The State exercises sovereignty and jurisdiction over the air space which covers the territory and adjacent sea up to the limit of two hundred miles, in accordance with the law and the international conventions ratified by the Republic".

Paragraph two: Peru shall also retain other pertinent instruments of its internal legislation and, subject to agreement among Parties, the conventions celebrated with other States concerning their respective maritime zones.

Paragraph three: In conformity with provisions of articles 98 and 99 of its Constitution, while being a Party to the Convention, Peru shall exercise its sovereignty and jurisdiction in the maritime dominion of the State and in the superjacent air space, in a manner compatible with the provisions of the Convention concerning the territorial sea, the contiguous zone, the exclusive economic zone and the continental shelf.

Paragraph four: As soon as the Convention enters into force and while being a Party to it, Peru shall apply its provisions with respect to other States on the basis of reciprocity.

Paragraph five: In conformity with provisions of article 310, this declaration intends to apply the relevant legislation of the Peruvian State in a manner compatible with the provisions of the Convention, and does not preclude or modify the legal effect of such provisions in its application to Peru and other States Parties.

MAR PRESENCIAL (THE PRESENTIAL SEA): DEJA VU ALL OVER AGAIN?[5]

Thomas A. Clingan, Jr.

Professor of Law

University of Miami School of Law

This essay is in response to the concepts contained in the accompanying paper by Francisco Orrego Vicuna.[6] It is not a detailed response to points made by him, which are clearly and expertly put forward, but rather to the general theme; in particular the exposition of the doctrine which has been named the Mar Presencial or Presential Sea.[7] It represents an attempt by me to understand the doctrine's objective and purposes, and more importantly, the possible consequences of its implementation for the future law of the sea.

I begin with the source of my concern, which leads me to seek clarification of this new doctrine. Chile, along with other Latin American coastal States have a history of looking seaward. There are good and sufficient reasons for this. Certainly, Chile is geographically somewhat isolated, located as it is on the southwestern tip of South America. In addition, its land territory constitutes a relatively narrow strip along the coast. There is literally very little interior to look to, and it is only natural that Chile should look primarily seaward. Secondly, the history of the country shows its vulnerability over the years to privations from other countries, both militarily and economically (primarily with regard to fisheries). Third, Chile, being relatively advanced in its economy and with regard to its small but sophisticated navy, might well regard itself as being poised on the brink of a

---

[5]. Reprinted by permission. Copyright c 1984 by University of Oregon. .

[6]. Towards an Effective Management of High Seas Fisheries and the Settlement of the Pending Issues of the Law of the Sea, originally presented at the recent meeting of the Law of the Sea Institute in Genoa, Italy. Reprinted by permission of the Law of the Sea Institute.

[7]. Roughly translated to "to see and be seen."

significant leadership role in the area, and is looking to the sea as a mechanism to advance its national security, social and economic goals.

Accordingly, at the Third United Nations Law of the Sea Conference, at which Professor Orrego was extremely active and influential, it was not surprising to see Chile among that group of nations championing what was first the patrimonial sea, and later emerging in the form of the now well-accepted concept of the exclusive economic zone, or EEZ. In a real sense, Chile could not truly have been viewed among several other States as being a "territorialist" or an advocate of a 200 mile territorial sea. Although it was not entirely clear, one can conclude from earlier positions that Chile did not ever, in fact, advocate a broad territorial sea as a solution to issues affecting its coastal interests. In 1947, the president of Chile, by proclamation, claimed a 200-mile limit. However, this proclamation stated expressly that the declaration of sovereignty did not affect the freedoms of navigation recognized by international law.[8] In 1952, Chile joined Ecuador and Peru in the Santiago Declaration. That declaration stated that the three governments "possesses sole sovereignty and jurisdiction over the area of sea adjacent to the coast of its own country and extending not less than 200 nautical miles from the said coast." But it also stated that "This declaration shall not be construed as disregarding the necessary restrictions on the exercise of sovereignty and jurisdiction imposed by international law to permit the innocent and inoffensive passage of vessels of all nations through the zone aforesaid."[9] While not a model of clarity, it is clear that these claims were something less than a full claim to territorial sovereignty.

Nonetheless, the seaward-looking attitude of Chile over the years has been consistent and has been constantly expanding in the direction, toward rather than away, from the concept of territorial sovereignty. This fact causes me to be concerned by the adoption of the Presential Sea by Chile, and this concern is bolstered by its lack of clarity on many points. The concern is not alleviated by the fact that its major proponent was not a member of the political branch of government, but rather Admiral Jorge Martinez Busch, Commander in Chief of the Chilean navy. Obviously, I am not suggesting that this necessarily means a military motivation. However, Chile must accept the fact that since the statement of the concept is far from clear, acceptance on an international level must rest in part upon perceptions of the international community, and perceptions are fed by historical context and by the nature of the advocacy.

Let us look at the concept from the standpoint of its content and its scope. The first observation relates to size. The declared Mar Provencial is enormous. It is located in the high seas between the outer limit of Chile's EEZ and the meridian passing through the western edge of the continental shelf of Easter Island, and it extends southward to the South Pole, covering about 19,967,337 square kilometers.[10] If we, for the moment, simply characterize the area as a zone of influence, however defined, it constitutes one of the largest areas of hegemony in existence. This intensifies the need to understand clearly how Chile views its roll in this zone, and the extent of its exertion of influence.

---

8. See The Exclusive Economic Zone, A Latin American Perspective, Orrego Ed., 1984, at 20.

9. Id, at 22.

10. For this information, I am relying on the translations contained in The Chilean Mar Presential: A Harmless Concept or a Dangerous Precedent?, a paper submitted by Jane G. Dalton in partial fulfillment of the requirements toward the LLM degree at the University of Virginia.

The Chilean justification for its declaration is set forth in several areas. But major stress, as is evident in Professor Orrego's paper, is placed upon fisheries. Reference is made, for example, to the idea of ecosystem management, as was discussed at the U.N. Conference on the Environment and Development. His excellent exposition draws our attention to the intimate relationship between the management of the resources within the economic zone and the exploitation of high seas living resources in the area adjacent to that zone. This observation is undeniable. The fact that high seas fishing has or could have an impact on stocks of fish within the EEZ is clear, and was addressed in the United Nations Convention on the Law of the Sea,[11] although it is clear that Professor Orrego is not satisfied that the convention adequately protects the coastal State interest.

The point must be conceded. Article 63 of the Convention addresses the problem of "straddling stocks". Paragraph 2 requires coastal States and States fishing stocks that occur both within the economic zone and the area immediately adjacent to "seek...to agree upon the measures necessary for the conservation of these stocks in the adjacent area". In addition, Article 116 proclaims that all States have the right to fish on the high seas, subject to "the rights and duties as well as the interests of coastal States provided for, inter alia, in article 63, paragraph 2, and aricles 64 to 67". Thus it is clear that coastal States have a strong, if not preferential, interest in the conservation of high seas stocks adjacent to their economic zones. The treaty requires good faith negotiation of conservation measures among the affected parties, and, in case of disagreement, the concerned parties may resort to the dispute settlement mechanism provided for elsewhere in the Convention.[12] But the problem, as the United States itself has discovered, is really one of enforcement. The problem occurs when a fishing State either refuses to negotiate conservation measures or, if negotiated, fails to abide by them. For the United States, the problem is exemplified in the so-called "Doughnut Hole" in the central Bering Sea, where fishing fleets, primarily Japanese, have been fishing heavily in an area outside the economic zones of the United States and Russia. The problem has been severe enough that pressure groups within the U.S. have been lobbying Congress to extend the jurisdiction of the United States further seaward, or advocating other forms of unilateral action.[13] Thus the concerns voiced by Professor Orrego are legitimate.

Professor Orrego also points to the management of highly migratory species, or lack thereof, as a futher example of the failure to adequately take into account the special interest of the affected coastal States. But the primary barrier to an effective regional management system over the past decade has been the long-standing position of the United States (now abandoned) that tuna can only be appropriately managed by an international mechanism, and that the coastal State, therefore, should not have management jurisdiction over them even within their own EEZ. But the barrier has now been removed, with the U.S. now claiming jurisdiction to manage tuna within its zone. Thus the way is open for new, more effective agreements, and these should be crafted expeditiously.

---

11. See, for example, Article 63(2), the provision dealing with the so-called "straddling stocks" problem, which says that in such a case, the States affected "shall seek, either directly or through appropriate subregional or regional organizations, to agree upon the measures necessary for the conservation of these stocks in the adjacent area " This is to be read in the light of Article 116, which states that all States have the right to fish on the high seas, subject to "the rights and duties as well as the interests of coastal States provided for, inter alia, in article 63, paragraph 2..." It is of note that this obligation, since it does not appear in articles with respect to the EEZ, but rather in the section on the high seas, is not subject to the extremely restrictive and limited sort of dispute settlement (conciliation) for fisheries disputes in that zone.

12. Part XV, United Nations Convention on the Law of the Sea

13. Miles and Burke, Pressures on the United Nations Convention on the Law of the Sea of 1982 Arising from New Fisheries Conflicts: The Problem of Straddling Stocks, 20 J.O.D.I L. 343, 348-49 (1989).

With respect to anadromous species, such as salmon, Professor Orrego notes that the U.S. protects its interest by enforcement on the high seas. Once again, however, this is done within the scheme provided for in the Convention. Unfortunately, as noted, the Convention provides no similar scheme for the high seas fisheries.

Professor Orrego is careful to explain that the Presential Sea doctrine is not a claim to extended coastal State jurisdiction. But, he warns, "it can eventually have jurisdictional implications if mechanisms for international cooperation are nonexistent or ineffectual". He goes on to comment upon the security interest of the coastal State, without defining precisely the dimensions of that interest. And he speaks vaguely of Chile conducting activities in that sea in order to ensure that other activities (presumeably foreign) in the area will not have harmful effects on Chile. He notes that the concept of the presential sea, like the exclusive economic zone, might someday evolve into customary international law. All of these things taken together suggest to me that the Chilean effort not only has jurisdictional implications for the future, but has such implications today. How will the principle, for example, evolve into customary international law? Presumeably through State practice. What practices will Chile utilize? And how can it be that Chile will be "acting on behalf of the international community"?

Turning to national security, it seems probable that Admiral Martinez's suggestions to enhance it is designed to encourage Chile to build an ocean-going naval fleet that can and would be used to effectively patrol the new area with a view to countering any possible threats to security. This, of course, is a laudable goal. But Chile's position on some matters of security has not always been consistent with the new Convention. For example, while the Convention clearly mandates that all vessels are entitled to innocent passage in the territorial sea, Chile requires prior notification by warships for entry into its territorial waters.[14] Presumeably, they may not enter without prior permission. This and other provisions are inconsistent with Article 19 and Article 21 of the Convention. One must recall, also, that Chile was a supporter of the effort in the last days of the U.N. Conference on the Law of the Sea to amend Article 33 governing contiguous zones to add security to the list of purposes for which such zones could be created.[15] Chile has also taken a restrictive view of navigation in the Drake Passage. It is interesting that Chile should maintain these positions while its chief naval officer promotes a greater high seas role for its fleet.

It is impossible to understand, at the present stage, the full implications of the Chilean Mar Presencial. The discussions on this subject are too vague and lacking in specific content. Taken in its worse light, that is, to imagine that the Chilean navy might take an agressive posture to protect perceived national interests in economic, social and security matters within the zone. An agressive posture of this nature would be in clear conflict with and in violation of the Law of the Sea Convention. Presence in the zone is one thing. But presence is permitted under international law today. Certainly, the United States understands this and has been a major participant in building a global naval presence, but always consistent with traditional rules of the law of the sea. If this is what Chile wishes to emulate, then there is no need for the Presential Sea. If there is a perceived need for the zone, at least one implication is that Chile has intentions to exert more influence in the zone than is now possible under traditional high seas concepts. On the bright side, however, one must conclude that Chile can in fact act in a manner that is fully consistent with present rules. Professor Orrego has stated that this is the national intent. If so, then there is no problem. However, in light of some of the factors I have discussed, and the admitted jurisdictional implications for the future, the whole idea is troublesome to me. It bears close watching.

---

14. Supreme Decree No. 1385 of Oct. 18, 1951, as modified by Supreme Decree No 2623 of Sept. 16, 1955.

15. A/CONF.62/L.117

Professor Orrego has laid some stress on analogy to large marine ecosystems in support of what Chile wishes to accomplish. Certainly, the concept is gaining strength. Large marine ecosystem management is fine, if, and only if, it is carried out through international agreement. It is not alright if it simply is a mechanism for arguing for extended national jurisdictions.

At the heart of my concern is the fact that all of the stated objectives in Professor Oreggo's paper can, and should be achieved through appropriate international arrangements, freely agreed to by all participants. One must hope that the Presential Sea is no more than a declaration by Chile of its wish to become a major participant in a global effort to fill the gaps that remain after the entry into force of the Law of the Sea Convention, and nothing more than that. In other words, one must hope that Chile is making no more than a declaration of national aspirations in the international area. But as in the past, the participation of coastal States in solving regional problems, can and should be done cooperatively under the umbrella of an agreed international regime.

F. THE PROBLEM OF ENCLOSED AND SEMI-ENCLOSED SEAS

As the following materials will illustrate, enclosed and semi-enclosed seas posed a special problem for nations which bordered them. As could be expected, such States wished a special regime to apply in those areas, giving the littoral States much more control over activities, including navigation, in those seas. This, naturally, was resisted by the maritime powers. The following excerpt from the summary records of the conference illustrates the difference of views. At the same time, it was generally recognized that enclosed and semi-enclosed seas had special problems not in common with the oceans in general. Part IX attempts to deal with these problems without creating special powers for littoral States.

PROVISIONAL SUMMARY RECORD

THIRD U.N. CONFERENCE ON THE LAW OF THE SEA

SECOND COMMITTEE, THIRTY-EIGTH MEETING (13 August 1974)

Mr. KAZEMI (Iran) said that the particular cases of enclosed and semi-enclosed seas raised difficult problems which could not be solved within the framework of regional or bilateral agreements. Semi-enclosed seas were distributed all along the margin of the continents at varying distances from the major oceanic basin, which was why they were often called the marginal seas. There were between 40 and 50 such seas like the Baltic, the Black Sea and the Persian Gulf that fell into a special category because of the small volume of their waters and their single outlet to the ocean.

The problems raised by the semi-enclosed seas with regard to the management of their resources, international navigation and the preservation of the marine environment justified granting them a particular status constituting an exception to the general rule. When worked out on a regional basis, that status would obviously have to take account of the needs and interests of all the coastal States of the region.

As to the management of resources, the fact that the total area of the semi-enclosed seas lay above the continental shelf of the coastal States justified the working out of a special regime. In that connexion, the delimitation of the various areas of jurisdiction would present problems which were peculiar to semi-enclosed seas and which would have to be solved on the basis of principles of justice, equity and equidistance....

Apart from the problems of delimitation, the exploitation of exclusive fishery zones in semi-enclosed seas raised a number of questions with regard to the preservation of the species, and solutions would have to be tailored to fit the particular situation of those seas.

With regard to international navigation in semi-enclosed seas, there was of course a marked difference between the coastal States of those seas, on the one hand, for which freedom of passage through straits connecting those seas to the oceans was vital to their trade and communications, and on the other hand all other States. Such freedom of passage must be fully guaranteed for the former category of States. However, a different regime should apply to navigation of the other States whose ships could pass through the straits connecting the oceans with semi-enclosed seas only for the purpose of calling at one of the ports of the semi-enclosed sea.

The semi-enclosed seas were highly vulnerable to pollution owing to the small volume of their waters, which lowered their capacity for absorption, and the absence of currents to change the waters. A number of semi-enclosed seas like the Persian Gulf were the scene of intensive petroleum production and heavy tanker traffic, which increased the threat of pollution.

....

With regard to scientific research, semi-enclosed seas were not of great interest since the geomorphological structure of their basins was quite uncomplicated and had already been studied by numerous scientific expeditions.

Mr. QUENEUDEC (France) said that the expression "enclosed or semi-enclosed seas" was not a traditional concept of international law. The notion of "enclosed seas" seemed rather to be a purely geographical one; the legal rules applicable to them were not part of international public maritime law and the Conference should not concern itself with them. The idea of "semi-enclosed seas" was extremely vague. The inclusion of the item in the agenda tended to give an ambiguous formula legal status.

Undoubtedly, the geographical situation of the coastal States of a semi-enclosed sea obliged them, in certain circumstances, to become aware of the links that bound them to or to consider themselves coastal States in relation to a sort of interior sea. However, to make those maritime spaces subject to special rules would resuscitate the Roman formula of mare nostrum, with the consequent risk of establishing a mare clausum. What, in any case, was the purpose of the exercise?

It was inconceivable that the idea was to restrict the freedom of navigation and overflight in areas considered to be semi-enclosed seas. The institution of a 200-mile economic zone would place all the renewable and non-renewable resources of the maritime areas concerned under the jurisdiction of the coastal States and there was thus no need for those coastal States to demand special provisions for semi-enclosed seas in the Convention; regional arrangements should suffice. As far as the preservation of the marine environment was concerned, the maritime areas in question were, like necessary in certain special circumstances, such as those recognized in a number of international conventions. There, too, there was no need to estabish a new legal category to solve the problems that might arise.

For the reasons stated, his delegation felt that there would be more disadvantages than advantages in introducing into the law of the sea a concept that was ambiguous and was not in conformity with the interests of the international community.

Mr. BARABOLYA (Union of Soviet Socialist Republics) said he wished to draw attention to certain peculiarities of the problem under discussion. Firstly, a clear distinction must be made between enclosed and semi-enclosed seas. From a juridical point of view, enclosed seas were comparativley small, had no outlet to the ocean, and did not serve as international shipping routes in the broadest sense. Such seas should be subject to specific regimes established by existing international agreements and international custom.

Semi-enclosed seas, on the other hand, were large bodies of water with several outlets through which passed international waterways. They had never been subject to any special regime. Almost any sea could be called semi-enclosed, and it would be quite unjustified to compare such seas with enclosed seas. His country could not accept the establishment of a special regime benefiting any given country in waters that had traditionally been used by all countries for international shipping on a basis of equality. The question of enclosed seas had both a geographical and juridical aspect. Was the Mediterranean, for example, an enclosed or semi-enclosed sea? He would say that it was neither. It contained many other seas and could be compared to an ocean. It was an immense body of water used as a high sea by all countries for international shipping.

Another peculiarity of the issue was that the Geneva Conferences had not laid down principles for enclosed seas, although the International Law Commission had confirmed the usefulness of extending a special regime to some seas. No specific proposals had been put forward in the Sea-Bed Committee with the exception of a proposal submitted by Turkey; so there was only one chapter heading for the issue in the Committee's report. Nevertheless, the question had been raised, mainly in connexion with the problem of the delimitation of maritime areas. The question had recently become of some current interest as a result of the prospect of establishing economic zones of a breadth up to 200 miles. Although the question of economic zones would cause no problems where the coastlines faced the open sea, it would create a number of problems in enclosed or semi-enclosed seas, as the representative of Turkey had pointed out, particularly in connexion with the delimitation of sea areas between States.

The point at issue was not a regime for enclosed seas, but the possibility of taking a regional approach to certain questions in specific marine areas where the application of certain provisions of international maritime law by one State might affect the rights and interests of other States. His country's position was that in those specific regions regional decisions on questions of sea law could be taken only within the framework of the international convention to be adopted by the Conference. Solutions to problems must be arrived at by agreement between the coastal States concerned, without prejudice to the legitimate interests of other countries of the world.

1982 UNITED NATIONS CONVENTION ON THE LAW OF THE SEA

PART IX

ENCLOSED OR SEMI-ENCLOSED SEAS

Article 122

Definition

For the purposes of this Convention, "enclosed or semi-enclosed sea" means a gulf, basin or sea surrounded by two or more States and connected to another sea or the ocean by a narrow outlet or consisting entirely of or primarily of the territorial seas and exclusive economic zones of two or more States.

Article 123

Co-operation of States bordering enclosed or semi-enclosed seas

States bordering on an enclosed or semi-enclosed sea should co-operate with each other in the exercise of their rights and in the performance of their duties under this Convention. To this end they shall endeavour, directly or through an appropriate regional organization:

(a) to co-ordinate the management, conservation, exploration and exploitation of the living resources of the sea;

(b) to co-ordinate the implementation of their rights and duties with respect to the protection and preservation of the marine environment;

(c) to co-ordinate their scientific research policies and undertake where appropriate joint programmes of scientific research in the area;

(d) to invite, as appropriate, other interested States or international organizations to co-operate with them in furtherance of the provisions of this article.

NOTE

You will observe that the articles are quite weak. Two things are unclear. The first is the extent of legal duty placed upon the littoral States. Most international legal provisions imposing duties use strong words, such as "shall" when imposing a duty. This article uses words like "endeavour" and "co-operate". Second, the definition is unclear. Certain bodies of water such as the Persian Gulf clearly fit the definition. But others, such as the Bering Sea may or may not fit the description.

G. LANDLOCKED STATES

Another specialized problem related to the overall question of the freedom to navigate the high seas was the question of guaranteed access to those seas. Clearly, a landlocked State has no access for its ships to the high seas other than any that might be accorded to it by its coastal neighbors. Landlocked States insisted that the Convention deal with this problem. The following materials show the nature of the problem and how it was dealt with in the 1958 Conventions and in the 1982 Convention. Other problems related to the access of landlocked States to marine resources will be dealt with later.

Sinjela, FREEDOM OF TRANSIT AND THE RIGHT OF ACCESS FOR LAND LOCKED STATES: THE EVOLUTION OF PRINCIPLE AND LAW, 12 Ga. J.I.& C.L. 31-35 (1982)[16]

States having no direct access to and from the sea are described as land-locked, a geographic status which places these countries at a severe disadvantage relative to their coastal counterparts. For land-locked nations, access to the sea is dependent upon their ability to pass through one or more countries of transit. The availability of suitable transport facilities normally is subject to little or no control by the land-locked State, and countries of transit sometimes have used their strategic position as an economic or political lever against land-locked neighbors. Occasionally, transit has been denied altogether, thereby forcing the land-locked country to try to seek alternate routes or means for the transport of its goods to and from the sea. Sometimes, goods in transit of land-locked countries have been subject to seizures for the satisfaction of orders issued in States of transit, and routine impositions on the external trade of land-locked countries include the levy of heavy customs duties for simple movement of goods through territory of the transit State, as well as cumbersome and costly formalities of procedure.

These burdens are a principal cause of land-locked countries relative poverty. As a recent report concludes:

> Land-locked developing countries are generally among the very poorest of the developing countries... Their lack of territorial access to the sea, aggravated by remoteness and isolation from world markets and the greater difficulties and costs of international transport services, appears to be one of the major causes of their relative poverty, and a serious constraint to their further economic and social development.

Given these facts, the essential legal issue is whether land-locked countries have a *right* of access to and from the sea, or whether such access is merely a *privilege*, i.e., contingent upon terms and conditions unilaterally imposed by countries of transit.

. . . .

The claims of land-locked States were originally founded on principles of natural law. It was argued that the right of free transit was conferred on every land-locked country by its very sovereignty, a necessary corollary to accepted notions of freedom of the high seas. This view maintained that, because the oceans are open to all nations, littoral and land-locked alike, the latter must be entitled to free transit in exercise of their equal rights within the *res communis*.

Another theory supporting this right is derived from the Roman concept of "servitude", a limited right of ownership. Under Roman law the owner of a piece of land had the right to use it any way he chose, so long as that use did not infringe on the rights of his neighbor. If A's land were located in such a way that it was necessary to cross B's land before he could enjoy his own land, A was said to have a natural servitude across B's property. From this it may be argued that land-locked States have a similar servitude to traverse neighboring States, a logical and necessary extension of the sovereignty they exercise over their own territory. As Claus has stated:

---

16. Reprinted by permission of the Georgia Journal of International Law and Commerce.

> It cannot be denied that there are in international law relationships which present an analogy to praedial servitudes of the Roman law or to easements of the common law almost amounting to identify, namely those relationships in which a part of the whole of the territory of one State is made to serve the economic needs of another.

In recent years, this argument of fundamental necessity has grown steadily more compelling. Oceans have always provided the most economical means of transporting goods among world markets, and, as States become increasingly dependent on this international commerce, it is obvious that no country can remain isolated without suffering economic stagnation. Even where transit historically has been allowed on an ad hoc bilateral basis, risks of disruption inherent in the absence of a legal guarantee inject added insecurity to investment and development plans. For these reasons alone, advocates have maintained that a right of passage must be recognized, provided only that its exercise cause no damage to interests of the transit State.

Lauterpacht has summarized the prerequisites to legal recognition of the right of free access to a land-locked State in two basic conditions. First, the State claiming the right must be able to justify it under considerations of necessity or convenience; second, the exercise of the right must cause no harm or prejudice to the transit state. The former inquiry is a limited one, however, for:

> [i]t is doubtful whether it is important to justify or define the requirement of `necessity'.... The concept of `necessity' here envisaged by writers such as Grotius, Pufendorf and Vatel is a wider and more flexible notion than necessity in the sense of immediate or overwhelming urgency. Rather, it is indistinguishable from the idea of `convenience' concieved as the existence of a bona fide and legitimate interest. It is not an element in this definition that the route sought is the only route available. Clearly, if it is the only route, the claim becomes stronger.

The established principle of innocent passage through the territorial sea of coastal States also has been cited in support of an analogous right of transit for land-locked States. Some writers have maintained that:

> the right of land-locked States to free transit over land is the same as recognized in territorial waters of innocent passage. Indeed, both land and territorial waters are the property of the coastal State and the right of innocent passage over land as well as water in favour of one State and its nationals to use land, sea and air of another State for passage. The reason for the existence of innocent passage in international law is the same as in civil law.

The cogency of these arguments has increased as other rights of land-locked States have been articulated at the Third United Nations Conference on the Law of the Sea, particularly where it has recognized their right to participate in resources of the exclusive economic zone and the deep seabed.

....

The major obstacle to development of a guaranteed right of access to the sea for land-locked countries has been the claim of territorial sovereignty by coastal States. These nations have consistently argued that principles of state sovereignty allow them to approve or disallow all transit through their territories. Their position is that rights of access for land-locked countries are not properly resolved through a single international rule, but are instead a matter for bilateral or regional arrangements. Countries of transit argue that sovereign jurisdiction over all activities within their territories includes the prerogative of denying the traffic of land-locked countries as a matter of security. Furthermore, some have contended that rights of transit need be granted and enforced only on a reciprocal basis.

. . . .

CONVENTION ON THE TERRITORIAL SEA AND THE CONTIGUOUS ZONE

Article 14

1. Subject to the provisions of these articles, ships of all States, whether coastal or not, shall enjoy the right of innocent passage through the territorial sea.

CONVENTION ON THE HIGH SEAS

Article 2

...Freedom of the high seas...comprises, inter alia, both for coastal and non-coastal States:

(1) Freedom of navigation;

. . . .

Article 3

1. In order to enjoy the freedom of the seas on equal terms with coastal States, States having no sea-coast should have free access to the sea. To this end States situated between the sea and a State having no sea-coast shall by common agreement with the latter and in conformity with existing international law accord:

(a) To the State having no sea-coast, on a basis of reciprocity, free transit through their territory; and

(b) To ships flying the flag of that State treatment equal to that accorded their own ships, or to the ships of any other States, as regards access to seaports and the use of such ports.

2. States situated between the sea and a State having no sea-coast shall settle, by mutual agreement with the latter, and taking into account the rights of the coastal State or State of transit and the special conditions of the State having no sea-coast, all matters relating to freedom of transit and equal treatment in ports, in case such States are not already parties to existing international conventions.

Article 4

Every State, whether coastal or not, has the right to sail ships under its flag on the high seas.

1982 UNITED NATIONS CONVENTION ON THE LAW OF THE SEA

PART X

RIGHT OF ACCESS OF LAND-LOCKED STATES TO AND FROM THE SEA AND FREEDOM OF TRANSIT

Article 124

Use of terms

1. For the purposes of this Convention:

(a) "land-locked State" means a State which has no sea-coast;

(b) "transit State" means a State, with or without a sea-coast, situated between a land-locked State and the sea, through whose territory traffic in transit passes;

(c) "traffic in transit" means transit of persons, baggage, goods and means of transport across the territory of one or more transit States, when the passage across such territory, with or without trans-shipment, warehousing, breaking bulk or change in the mode of transport, is only a portion of a complete journey which begins or terminates within the territory of the land-locked State;

(d) "means of transport" means:

(i) railway rolling stock, sea, lake and river craft and road vehicles;

(ii) where local conditions so require, porters and pack animals.

2. Land-locked States and transit States may, by agreement between them, include as means of transport pipelines and gas lines and means of transport other than those included in paragraph 1.

Article 125

Right of access to and from the sea and freedom of transit

1. Land-locked States shall have the right of access to and from the sea for the purposes of exercising the rights provided for in this Convention including those relating to the freedom of the high seas and the common heritage of mankind. To this end, land-locked States shall enjoy freedom of transit through the territory of transit States by all means of transport.

2. The terms and modalities for exercising freedom of transit shall be agreed betwwen the land-locked States and transit States concerned through bilateral, subregional or regional agreements.

3. Transit States, in the exercise of their full sovereignty over their territory, shall have the right to take all measures necessary to ensure that the rights and facilities provided for in this Part for land-locked States shall in no way infringe their legitimate interests.

Article 126

Exclusion of application of the most-favoured-nation clause

The provisions of this Convention, as well as special agreements relating to the exercise of the right of access to and from the sea, establishing rights and facilities on account of the special geographical position of land-locked States, are excluded from the application of the most-favoured-nation clause.

Article 127

Customs duties, taxes and other charges

1. Traffic in transit shall not be subject to any customs duties, taxes or other charges except charges levied for specific services rendered in connection with such traffic.

2. Means of transport in transit and other facilities provided for and used by land-locked States shall not be subject to taxes or charges higher than those levied for the use of means of transport of the transit State.

Article 128

Free zones and other customs facilities

For the convenience of traffic in transit, free zones or other customs facilities may be provided at ports of entry and exit in the transit States, by agreement between those States and the land-locked States.

Article 129

Co-operation in the construction and improvement of means of transport

Where there are no means of transport in transit States to give effect to the freedom of transit or where the existing means, including the port installations and equipment, are inadequate in any respect, the transit States and land-locked States may co-operate in constructing or improving them.

Article 130

Measures to avoid or eliminate delays or other difficulties of a technical nature in traffic in transit

1. Transit States shall take all appropriate measures to avoid delays or other difficulties of a technical nature in traffic in transit.

2. Should such delays or difficulties occur, the competent authorities of the transit States and land-locked States concerned shall co-operate towards their expeditious elimination.

Article 131

Equal treatment in maritime ports

Ships flying the flag of land-locked States shall enjoy treatment equal to that accorded to other foreign ships in maritime ports.

Article 132

Grant of greater transit facilities

This Convention does not entail in any way the withdrawal of transit facilities which are greater than those provided in this Convention or granted by a State Party. This Convention also does not preclude such grant of greater facilities in the future.

H. TREATY RULES GOVERNING THE HIGH SEAS

1. RULES PERTAINING TO FLAGS AND NATIONALITY OF SHIPS

A persistent problem in the law of the sea is that arising from what is characterized as "flags of convenience". For various reasons, as outlined in the excerpt below, many shipowners have preferred to register their ships in countries other than their own, sailing them under foreign flags. This can lead to difficulties in seeking to enforce stringent regulations regarding safety features and the training of their crews. Such matters are controlled by the State of registry. If registry States seek to entice shipping to register with them, the temptation can be great to lower standards. The following excerpt describes the motivation for registering under flags of convenience.

McConnell, "...DARKENING CONFUSION MOUNTED UPON DARKENING CONFUSION: THE SEARCH FOR THE ELUSIVE GENUINE LINK", 16 J. Mar. L. & Commerce (1985) 365, 367-368[17]

Colorful though the history of open registry practice is, it is not necessary for purposes of this discussion to do more than briefly outline it. The practice of "flagging out", that is, registering vessels in states with more convenient laws or policies, is not new. For example during the 17th century the French Flag was used by English fishermen in Newfoundland. In the 19th century British fishermen registered vessels in Norway to avoid fishing restrictions. It is important, as pointed out by Boczek to distinguish between the reasons why ships leave their own countries and what governs choice of a particular registry facility. The reasons for leaving have varied with the times and international situations. For example, during World War II many shipowners in combatant states re-registered under neutral flags to avoid becoming enmeshed in the events of war. In the case of American shipowners it was to avoid obvious infringment of American neutrality policy. For other shipowners, such as nationals of Israel or South Africa, it was, and is, to avoid flag discrimination. The use of alternative registries by American shipowners was encouraged by the American government as a means of maintaining a merchant fleet under American control without requiring public taxation to subsidize it. In addition, American owned open registry fleets formed a component of the American defense strategy.

Avoiding taxation, unions or vessel safety standards are most often cited by opponents as reasons for the use of open registry facilities. However, recent studies suggest that,

> In many instances the home governments have offered taxation concession grants and subsidies of such magnitude in order to `compete' with open registry countries -- that, as far as taxation is concerned, a shipowner might be just as well off operating under his national flag.

---

[17]. Reprinted by permission of the Journal of Maritime Law and Commerce.

Similarly, the avoiding of unions per se is not a primary aim: reduction in direct operating costs is. The fact of several major oil spills involving open registry vessels has provided a basis for the argument that open registry facilities were used to avoid more stringent safety standards required by other registries. While this may be the case for some shipowners it is, as pointed out by Professor Edgar Gold, becoming increasingly difficult to generalize. Many open registry fleets are composed of modern, well maintained vessels. In addition many ofthe open registry states have begun to enforce safety standards and inspections in compliance with IMO and ILO conventions. Given that the reasons for moving to an open registry will vary for each owner, it is possible to point to a common element: the desire for freedom from burdensome regulation and allowance of maximum operating flexibility. This enables the shipowner to operate in the most profitable manner possible. (This presupposes a free market economy).

* * * *

The rules appertaining to registry and flags were first codified in 1958.

CONVENTION ON THE HIGH SEAS

Article 4

Every State, whether coastal or not, has the right to sail its ships under its flag on the high seas.

Article 5

1. Each State shall fix the conditions for the grant of its nationality to ships, for the registration of ships in its territory, and for the right to fly its flag. Ships have the nationality of the State whose flag they are entitled to fly. There must be a genuine link between the State and the ship; in particular, the State must effectively exercise its jurisdiction and control in administrative, technical and social matters over ships flying its flag.

2. Each State shall issue to ships in which it has granted the right to fly its flag documents to that effect.

Article 6

1. Ships shall sail under the flag of one State only and, save in exceptional cases expressly provided for in international treaties or in these articles, shall be subject to its exclusive jurisdiction on the high seas. A ship may not change its flag during a voyage or while in a port of call, save in the case of a real transfer of ownership or change of registry.

2. A ship which sails under the flags of two or more States, using them according to convenience, may not claim any of the nationalities in question with respect to any other State, and may be assimilated to a ship without nationality.

Article 7

The provisions of the preceding articles do not prejudice the question of ships employed on the official service of an international organization flying the flag of the operation.

INTERNATIONAL LAW COMMISSION

1956 COMMENTARY

DRAFT ARTICLE 29

Each State lays down the conditions on which ships may fly its flag. Obviously the State enjoys complete liberty in the case of ships owned by it or ships which are the property of a nationalized company. With regard to other ships, the State must accept certain restrictions. As in the case of the grant of nationality of persons, national legislation on the subject must not depart too far from the principles adopted by the majority of States, which may regarded as forming part of international law. Only on that condition will the freedom granted to States not give rise to abuse and to friction with other States. With regard to the national element required for permission to fly the flag, a great many systems are possible, but there must be a minimum national element.

On this principle, the Institute of International Law, as long ago as 1896, adopted certain rules governing the permission to fly the flag. At its seventh session the Commission deemed these rules acceptable in slightly amended form, while realizing that, if the practical ends in view were to be achieved, States would have to work out more detailed provisions when incorporating these rules in their legislation.

At its eighth session, the Commission, after examining the comments of Governments, felt obliged to abandon this viewpoint. It came to the conclusion that the criteria it had formulated could not fulfill the aim it had set for itself. Existing practice in the various States is too divergent to be governed by a few criteria adopted by the Commission. Regulations of this kind would be bound to leave a large number of problems unsolved and could not prevent abuse. The Commission accordingly thought it best to confine itself to enunciating the guiding principle that, before the grant of nationality is generally recognized, there must be a genuine link between the ship and the State granting permission to fly its flag. The Commission does not consider it possible to state in any greater detail what form this link should take. The lack of precision made inserting such a stipulation impractical. But the majority of the Commission preferred a vague criterion to no criterion at all. While leaving States a wide latitude in this respect, the Commission wished to make it clear that the grant of its flag to a ship cannot be a mere administrative formality, with no accompanying guarantee that the ship possess a real link with the new State. The jurisdiction of the State over ships, and the control it should exercise in conformity with article 34 of these articles, can only be effective where there exists in fact a relationship between the State and the ship other than mere registration or a mere grant of a certificate of registry.

* * * * *

As the foregoing commentary reflects, there was little agreement and much confusion concerning the meaning of the "genuine link" requirement. The Restatement of the Law: The Foreign Relations Law of the United States (Third) elaborates somewhat.

501. Nationality of Ships

A ship has the nationality of the State that registered it and authorized it to fly the state's flag, but a state may properly register a ship and authorize it to fly the state's flag only if there is a genuine link between the state and the ship.

Comment:

. . . .

b."Genuine link." In general, a state has a "genuine link" entitling it to register a ship and to authorize the ship to use its flag if the ship is owned by nationals of the state, whether natural or juridical persons, and the state exercises effective control over the ship. In most cases a ship is owned by a corporation created by the state of registry. However, in determining whether a "genuine link" with the state of registry exists, the following additional factors are to be taken into account: whether the company owning the ship is owned by nationals of the state; whether the officers and crew of the ship are nationals of the state; how often the ship stops in ports of the state; and how extensive and effective is the control that the state exercises over the ship.

* * * *

ED. NOTE: The 1982 United Nations Convention on the Law of the Sea contains provisions (90-93) essentially identical to Articles 4-7 of the Convention on the High Seas. Article 91, however, omits the language used in Article 5 with respect to the maintenance of control over administrative, technical and social matters. That language, in the new Convention, is found in Article 94 which deals with the duties of the flag State. Sorensen has said that this language meant that a genuine link is related not only to the quality of ownership, but also the ability to maintain this control. In view of that, does the transposition of the language into a different article mean that control, while a duty of the flag State, is no longer a requirement to be fulfilled before there can be said to be a genuine link? Article 94 follows.

1982 UNITED NATIONS CONVENTION ON THE LAW OF THE SEA

Article 94

Duties of the flag State

1. Every State shall effectively exercise its jurisdiction and control in administrative, technical and social matters over ships flying its flag.

2. In particular every State shall:

(a) maintain a register of ships containing the names and particulars of ships flying its flag, except those which are excluded from generally accepted international regulations on account of their small size; and

(b) assume jurisdiction under its internal law over each ship flying its flag and its master, officers and crew in respect of administrative, technical and social matters concerning the ship.

3. Every State shall take such measures for ships flying its flag as are necessary to ensure safety at sea with regard, *inter alia*, to:

(a) the construction, equipment and seaworthiness of ships;

(b) the manning of ships, labour conditions and the training of crews, taking into account applicable international instruments;

(c) the use of signals, the maintenance of communications and the prevention of collisions.

(4) Such measures shall include those necessary to ensure:

(a) that each ship, before registration and thereafter at appropriate intervals, is surveyed by a qualified surveyor of ships, and has on board such charts, nautical publications and navigational equipment and instruments as are appropriate for the safe navigation of the ship;

(b) that each ship is in charge of a master and officers who possess appropriate qualifications, in particular in seamanship, navigation, communications and marine engineering, and that the crew is appropriate in qualification and numbers for the type, size, machinery and equipment of the ship.

(c) that the master, officers and, to the extent appropriate, the crew are fully conversant with and required to observe that the applicable international regulations concerning the safety of life at sea, the prevention of collisions, the prevention, reduction and control of marine pollution, and the maintenance of communications by radio.

5. In taking the measures called for in paragraphs 3 and 4 each State is required to conform to generally accepted international regulations, procedures and practices and to take any steps which may be necessary to secure their observance.

6. A State which has clear grounds to believe that proper jurisdiction with respect to a ship have not been exercised may report the facts to the flag State. Upon receiving such a report, the flag State shall investigate the matter and, if appropriate, take any steps which may be necessary to remedy the situation.

7. Each State shall cause an inquiry to be held before a suitably qualified person or persons into every marine casualty or incident of nagivation on the high seas involving a ship flying its flag and causing loss of life or serious injury to nationals of another State or serious damage to ships or installations of another State or to the marine environment. The flag State and the other State shall co-operate in the conduct of any inquiry held by that other State into any such marine casualty or incident of navigation.

ED. NOTE: Paragraph 6 of Article 94 was included to deal in part with the fact that it was well settled that no State could refuse to recognize a flag flown by a vessel on the ground that no genuine link in fact existed. The paragraph places at least some obligation on the flag State to respond to a report from another State that that State considers a genuine link to be lacking.

In U.S. law, the question of flags frequently is litigated. The cause for this litigation most often is in cases involving searches of vessels upon the high seas for illegal substances such as narcotic drugs. Article 6(2) of the Convention on the High Seas (Article 97(2) of the 1982 Convention) makes clear that if a ship attempts to fly more than one flag, according to its convenience, that ship may be considered as stateless. The result is that the vessel involved is no longer considered to be under the exclusive jurisdiction and protection of any State, and thus can be boarded and inspected freely upon the high seas. Thus the issue in such cases is usually one of fact. Did or did not the master of the ship appear to switch flags at sea in order to deceive patrols.

While the Article speaks of flying two or more flags, jurisprudence on the subject shows that that requirement is not taken literally. Thus a vessel can be considered stateless and boarded if the ship shows one home port in one country on its stern, but the master produces registration papers of another country, or if he switches home ports on the stern during the course of a voyage without having a legitimate change of registry.

One American case, U.S. v. Postal, 589 F.2d 743 (1985) involved a situation where the U.S. Coast Guard boarded a vessel on the high seas, without permission, even though the ship carried a legitimate single registration. This was a clear violation of the Convention on the High Seas. In subsequent litigation, however, the U.S. court upheld the boarding on the ground that Article 6 was not self-executing and thus did not override existing U.S. law that would permit the boarding. This case has been severely criticized, and the Coast Guard has ceased such boardings, thus mooting the question.

2. IMMUNITIES OF VESSELS UNDER INTERNATIONAL LAW

Obviously, there are many different kinds of ships plying the oceans. Most are privately owned. But many are owned by States. The most obvious of the latter class are warships. But some States also own merchant vessels as part of a State enterprise. As shall be seen, warships are considered to be immune from the exercise of jurisdiction by any State other than the flag State. The reason for this rule should be obvious. Warships cannot carry out their traditional role if they are to be subject to arrest by another State for some offense committed against that other State. We will now examine the international law on this subject.

CONVENTION ON THE HIGH SEAS

Article 8

1. Warships on the high seas have complete immunity from the jurisdiction of any State other than the flag State.

2. For the purposes of these articles, the term "warship" means a ship belonging to the naval forces of a State and bearing the external marking distinguishing warships of its nationality, under the command of an officer duly commissioned by the government and whose name appears in the Navy list, and manned by a crew who are under naval discipline.

Article 9

Ships owned or operated by a State and used only on government non-commercial service shall, on the high seas, have complete immunity from the jurisdiction of any State other than the flag State.

ED. NOTE: Article 8 appears in the 1982 Convention as Article 95. The second paragraph defining warships, however, has been removed and made a separate provision in Article 29, which is identical to Article 8 except that the references to "navy" have been changed to "armed forces". This was merely a clarifying change to indicate that certain law enforcement vessels, such as U.S. Coast Guard vessels, have the status of warships in international law. This was always assumed to be so, but the change in language makes it clear. Article 9 of the Convention on the High Seas now appears as Article 96 of the 1982 treaty.

The principle issue addressed by Article 9 concerns the status (with regard to immunity) of government owned vessels that are not warships. The I.L.C. draft article which was the precedent for Article 9 of the Convention read as follows:

"For all purposes connected with the exercise of power on the high seas by States other than the flag State, ships owned or operated by a State and used only on government service, whether commercial or non-commercial, shall be assimilated to and shall have the same immunity as warships."

In the relevant commentary, the I.L.C. noted that:

"The Commission discussed the question whether ships used on commercial government service on the high seas could claim the same immunity as warships with respect to the exercise of powers by other States, and answered this question in the affirmative. Although aware of objections to the granting of immunity to merchant ships used on government service, which led to the denial of this right in the International Convention for the Unification of Certain Rules relating to the Immunity of State-Owned Vessels, signed at Brussels on 10 April 1926, the Commission held that, as regards navigation on the high seas, there were no sufficient grounds for not granting the same immunity as other State ships. The Commission thinks it worth pointing out that the assimilation referred to in article 33 concerns only the immunity of ships for the purpose of the exercise of powers by other States, so that there is no question of granting to ships that are not warships policing rights over other ships, exercisable under international law by warships."

The United States proposed an amendment to the draft article submitted by the I.L.C. (A/CONF.13/C.2/L.76, IV Official Records at 135) which provided that "[s]hips owned or operated by a State and used only on government non-commercial service shall, when on the high seas, have complete immunity from the jurisdiction of any State other than the flag State." The United States added a comment to its proposal which provided in part that:

"...the International Law Commission's commentary indicates that it was not intended that government-owned ships other than warships should have policing rights on the high seas. As drafted, the article might be interpreted as meaning that other government-owned ships have such rights. The proposal clarifies the article to conform to the intent of the International Law Commission.

"The United States delegation believes that the immunity of vessels owned or operated by a State should be based on the purpose of its service."

ED. NOTE: During the debates concerning the I.L.C. draft at the Conference resulting in the 1958 treaties, the idea of extending immunity to all government-owned vessels, be they commercial or non-commercial, was strongly supported by the then U.S.S.R. Had they been successful in this debate, the consequences would be far-reaching, considering that all vessels of the Soviet Union were State-owned. This would mean that no such vessel on merchant service could be arrested for any civil liability incurred by it.

The United States strongly attacked this provision. At the conclusion of the debate, the U.S. proposal was adopted by 46 votes to 9, with two abstentions. As a result of the adoption of the U.S. amendment the following Parties to the Convention filed reservations: Albania, Bulgaria, Byelorussian S.S.R., Czechoslovakia, Hungary, Mexico, Poland, Romania, Ukrainian S.S.R. and the Soviet Union. The language of these reservations were in line of that of the Soviet reservation:

> "The Government of the Union of Soviet Socialist Republics considers that the principle of international law according to which a ship on the high seas is not subject to any jurisdiction

except that of the flag State applies without restriction to all government ships."

All of the reservations were objected to by the Netherlands, the United Kingdom and the United States; Australia objected to all except that made by Mexico which had not been published at the time of Australia's objection. Portugal objected to the Mexican reservation.

The soveriegn immunity provisions of Articles 8 and 9 are carried forward in the 1992 Convention as Articles 95 and 96. Sovereign immunity issues in U.S. Courts are governed by the Foreign Sovereign Immunities Act of 1976, which exempts from sovereign immunity in U.S. courts a wide range of activities, including actions based on commercial activities carried on in the United States by a foreign State and actions based on rights in propery taken in violation of international law.

I. COLLISION JURISDICTION

1982 UNITED NATIONS CONVENTION ON THE LAW OF THE SEA

Article 97

Penal jurisdiction in matters of collision or any other incident of navigation

1. In the event of a collision or any other incident of navigation concerning a ship on the high seas, involving the penal or disciplinary responsibility of the master or of any other person in the service of the ship, no penal or disciplinary proceedings may be instituted against such person except before the judicial or administrative authorities either of the flag State or of the State of which such person is a national.

2. In disciplinary matters, the State which has issued a master's certificate or a certificate of competence or license shall alone be competent, after due legal process, to pronounce the withdrawal of such certificates, even if the holder is not a national of the State which issued them.

3. No arrest or detention of the ship, even as a measure of investigation, shall be ordered by any authorities other than those of the flag State.

Article 98

Duty to render assistance

1. Every State shall require the master of a ship flying its flag, in so far as he can do so without serious danger to the ship, the crew or its passengers:

(a) to render assistance to any person found at sea in danger of being lost;

(b) to proceed with all possible speed to the rescue of persons in distress, if informed of their need for assistance, in so far as such action may reasonably be expected of him;

(c) after a collision, to render assistance to the other ship, its crew and passengers and, where possible, to inform the other ship of the name of its own ship, its port of registry and the nearest port at which it will call.

2. Every coastal State shall promote the establishment, operation and maintenance of an adequate and effective search and rescue service regarding safety on and over the sea and, where circumstances so require, by way of mutual regional arrangements co-operate with neighbouring States for this purpose.

ED. NOTE: In its commentaries to its draft article on this subject, the I.L.C. noted:

"The commission thought that no account should be taken for the moment of private international law problems arising out of the question of collision, but considered it essential to determine what tribunal was competent to deal with any penal proceedings arising out of a collision. In view of the judgment rendered by the Permanent Court of International Justice on 7 September 1927 in the "Lotus" case, the Commission felt obliged to take a decision on the subject. This judgment, which was carried by the President's casting vote after an equal vote of six to six, was very stronly criticized and caused serious disquiet in international maritime circles. A diplomatic conference held at Brussels in 1952 disagreed with the conclusions of the judgment. The Commission concurred with the decisions of the conference, which were embodied in the International Convention for the Unification of Certain Rules relating to Penal Jurisdiction in matters of Collisions and Other Incidents of Navigation, signed at Brussels on 10 May 1952. It did so with the object of protecting ships and their crews from the risk of penal proceedings in foreign courts in the event of collisions on the high seas, since such proceedings may constitute an intolerable interference with international navigation. In such a case, proceedings may take place only before the judicial or administrative authorities of the State whose flag was flown by the ship on which the persons in question were serving or of the State of which they are nationals. In making this latter addition, the Commission adopted the findings of the Brussels Conference in order to enable States to take penal or disciplinary measures against their nationals serving on board foreign vesels who are accused of causing collisions, since in such cases some States wish to be able to prosecute their nationals with a view to withdrawing certificates issued to them. The power to withdraw certificates rests solely with the State which has issued them."

In the Lotus case, P.C.I.L. Ser. A. No. 10 (1927), the Court held that "there is no rule of international law in regard to collision cases to the effect that the criminal proceedings are exclusively within the jurisdiction of the state whose flag is flown."

J. SLAVERY

While in modern days, slavery is not nearly so common as it was in earlier years, it persists sufficiently to warrant the law of the sea in doing its part to suppress it. While slavery was not always condemned by everyone, it is now considered to be an offense of universal jurisdiction. This means, according to the Restatement of the Foreign Relations Law of the United States, that any State may apply its laws to punish these offenses even though the State has no links of territory with the offense, or nationality of the offender or victim. The new treaty copies Article 13 of the Convention on the high seas with regard to slavery aboard ships.

1982 UNITED NATIONS CONVENTION ON THE LAW OF THE SEA

Article 99

Prohibition of transport of slaves

Every State shall adopt effective measures to prevent and punish the transport of slaves in ships authorized to fly its flag, and to prevent the unlawful use of its flag for that purpose. Any slave taking refuge on board any ship, whatever its flag, shall ipso facto be free.

NOTE: Section 522 of the Restatement explains this provision. In the Reporters Notes to that section, we find:

2. SLAVE TRADE.

. . . .

Apart from special treaty authorization, a ship suspected of slave trade may be visited and inspected by foreign law enforcement ships on the high seas for the purpose of verifying the ship's right to fly its flag, but it cannot be seized. It is the flag state that has the duty to take effective measures to prevent an punish the transport of slaves in ships authorized to fly its flag and to prevent the unlawful use of its flag for this purpose....

The Comment to this section adds the following:

"However, since slave trade has now been recognized as an offence subject to universal jurisdiction..., the state that approached and boarded the vessel could try members of the crew if the flag state consented, and any state could try them later if it obtained jurisdiction over them."

K. PIRACY

Unlike slavery, piracy is still rampant in many parts of the world. The basis for jurisdiction as set forth in the Convention is the common interest of all States in protecting commerce and navigation on the high seas. The international law is quite clear on this subject, but it is necessary to understand clearly what constitutes piracy and what does not. The following articles of the 1982 Convention, except for the relevant cross-reference numbers, track articles 14-21 of the Convention on the High Seas.

1982 UNITED NATIONS CONVENTION ON THE LAW OF THE SEA

Article 100

Duty to co-operate in the repression of piracy

All States shall co-operate in the repression of piracy on the high seas or in any other place outside the jurisdiction of any State.

Article 101

Definition of piracy

Piracy consists of any of the following acts:

(a) any illegal acts of violence or detention, or of any act of depredation, committed for private ends by the crew or passengers of a private ship or aircraft, and directed:

(i) on the high seas, against another ship or aircraft, or against the persons or property on board such ship or aircraft;

(ii) against any ship, aircraft, person or property in a place outside the jurisdiction of any State;

(b) any act of voluntary participation in the operation of a ship or of an aircraft with knowledge of facts making it a pirate ship or aircraft;

(c) any act of inciting or intentionally facilitating an act described in sub-paragraph (a) or (b).

Article 102

Piracy by a warship, government ship or government aircraft whose crew has mutinied

The acts of piracy, as defined in article 101, committed by a warship, government ship or government aircraft whose crew has mutinied and taken control of the ship or aircraft are assimilated to acts committed by a private ship or aircraft.

Article 103

Definition of a pirate ship or aircraft

A ship or aircraft is considered a pirate ship or aircraft if it is intended by the persons in dominant control to be used for the purpose of committing one of the acts referred to in article 101. The same applies if the ship or aircraft has been used to commit any such act, so long as it remains under the control of the persons guilty of that act.

Article 104

Retention or loss of nationality of a pirate ship or aircraft

A ship or aircraft may retain its nationality although it has become a pirate ship or aircraft. The retention or loss of nationality is determined by the law of the State from which the nationality was derived.

Article 105

Seizure of a pirate ship or aircraft

On the high seas, or in any other place outside the jurisdiction of any State, every State may seize a pirate ship or aircraft, or a ship or aircraft taken by piracy and under the control of pirates, and arrest the persons and seize the property on board. The courts of the State which carried out the seizure may decide upon the penalties to be imposed, and may also determine the action to be taken with regard to the ships, aircraft or property, subject to the rights of third parties acting in good faith.

Article 106

Liability for seizure without adequate grounds

Where the seizure of a ship or aircraft on suspicion of piracy has been affected without adequate grounds, the State making the seizure shall be liable to the State the nationality of which is possessed by the ship or aircraft for any loss or damage caused by the seizure.

QUESTIONS

After reading the above provisions, can you answer the following questions?

1. What is meant by "a place outside the jurisdiction of any State"?

2. What is the difference, if any, between mutiny and piracy? Does your answer have significance as to who may try the offenders?

3. Assume that several persons alleged to be members of the Palestinian Liberation Organization board a ship as passengers. When the ship is upon the high seas, these persons arm themselves and take control of the ship. Subsequently, they kill an American citizen, and, later board and seize another vessel. If apprehended, can these persons be treated as pirates for either offense? If not, why not?

This last question, of course, is directed to the question of terrorism. Recognizing that there has been a world wide escalation of terrorism, and recognizing also the weakness of the traditional piracy rules, or at least uncertainties about them, a new Convention was negotiated on 10 March 1988. That Convention is the Convention for the Suppression of Unlawful Acts against the Safety of Maritime Navigation, IMO Doc. SUA/CONF/15/Rev.1, 10 March 1988. No attempt was made to make terrorism a universal crime. What this Convention did was define acts of terrorism at sea and places upon each State Party a legal obligation to take measures to define jurisdiction over offences on board their ships, in their territory, or committed by their nationals. It also has provisions dealing with the extradition of terrorists seized in the territory of any State Party, and the responsibility of that State Party, if it does not extradite, to punish the offenders according to their own law.

* * * *

The following article is relevant to the subject of piracy and slavery:

Article 110

Right of visit

1. Except where acts of interference derive from powers conferred by treaty, a warship which encounters on the high seas a foreign ship, other than a ship entitled to complete immunity in accorance with articles 95 and 96, is not justified in boarding it unless there is reasonable ground for suspecting that:

(a) the ship is engaged in piracy;

(b) the ship is engaged in the slave trade;

(c) the ship is engaged in unauthorized broadcasting and the flag State of the warship has jurisdiction under article 109;

(d) the ship is without nationality; or

(e) though flying a foreign flag or refusing to show its flag, the ship is, in reality, of the same nationality of the warship.

2. In the cases provided for in paragraph 1, the warship may proceed to verify the ship's right to fly its flag. To this end, it may send a boat under the command of an officer to the suspected ship. If suspicion remains after the documents have been checked, it may proceed to a further examination on board the ship, which must be carried out with all possible consideration.

3. If the suspicions prove to be unfounded, and provided the ship boarded has not committed any act justifying them, it shall be compensated for any loss or damage that may have been sustained.

4. These provisions apply *mutatis mutandis* to military aircraft.

5. These provisions also apply to other duly authorized ships or aircraft clearly marked and being on government service.

ED. NOTE: Article 110 also, as previously mentioned, has relevance for drug interdiction on the high seas. Note that the article does not refer to ships carrying illegal narcotic drugs. Thus if boarding is to be carried out on the high seas, it must be under the terms of a treaty between the boarding State and the flag State, or it must be done with the consent of the flag State, except where the boarding State suspects the other vessel, although showing or claiming a foreign registration, is actually registered in the State of the boarding vessel, or it has no valid registration at all. If the boarding vessel is a U.S. warship or its equivalent, and the boarded vessel is actually a U.S. vessel, then U.S. law, including the fourth Amendment to the U.S. Constitution regarding searches and seizures applies. For the intricacies of this problem, consult U.S. jurisprudence.

L. NARCOTIC DRUGS

Because of the severity of the problem with respect to the smuggling of narcotic drugs by sea, an attempt was made by several nations during the Third United Nations Conference on the Law of the Sea to negotiate stringent new rules, perhaps modeled after the piracy articles, creating universal jurisdiction for the offense. For many reasons, a number of countries resisted this attempt, and the following indicates the best that could be agreed upon:

1982 UNITED NATIONS CONVENTION ON THE LAW OF THE SEA

Article 108

Illicit traffic in narcotic drugs or psychotropic substances

1. All States shall co-operate in the suppression of illicit traffic in narcotic drugs and psychotropic substances engaged in by ships on the high seas contrary to international conventions.

2. Any State which has reasonable grounds for believing that a ship flying its flag is engaged in illicit traffic in narcotic drugs or psychotropic substances may request the co-operation of other States to suppress such traffic.

M. HOT PURSUIT

This is a topic that forms a link between the high seas and the territorial sea and contiguous zones, to be considered subsequently. As we will see, a coastal State enjoys almost total sovereignty in its territorial sea and can apply all of its laws in that zone. In the contiguous zone, that State also enjoys jurisdictions, but of much more limited extent. Absent any special powers, a coastal State would be helpless against vessels committing offenses against their laws within their jurisdiction, but which escape from that jurisdiction onto the high seas before they can be apprehended. The doctrine of hot pursuit is at least a partial answer to that problem. It permits, under certain restrictions, law enforcement vessels to pursue vessels committing offenses within their jurisdiction on to the high seas.

CONVENTION ON THE HIGH SEAS

Article 23

1. The hot pursuit of a foreign ship may be undertaken when the competent authorities of the coastal State have good reason to believe that the ship has violated the laws and regulations of that State. Such pursuit must be commenced when the foreign ship or one of its boats is within the internal waters or the territorial sea or the contiguous zone of the pursuing State, and may only be continued outside the territorial sea or the contiguous zone if the pursuit has not been interrupted. It is not necessary that, at the time when the foreign ship within the territorial sea or the contiguous zone receives the order to stop, the ship giving the order should likewise be within the territorial sea or the contiguous zone. If the foreign ship is within the contiguous zone, as defined in article 24 of the Convention on the Territorial Sea and the Contiguous Zone, the pursuit may only be undertaken if there has been a violation of the rights for the protection of which the zone was established.

2. The right of hot pursuit ceases as soon as the ship pursued enters the territorial sea of its own country or a third State.

3. Hot pursuit is not deemed to have begun unless the pursuing ship has satisfied itself by such practicable means as may be available that the ship pursued or one of its boats or other craft working as a team and using the ship pursued as a mother ship are within the limits of the territorial sea, or as the case may be within the contiguous zone. The pursuit may only be commenced after a visual or auditory signal to stop has been given at a distance which enables it to be seen or heard by the foreign ship.

4. The right of hot pursuit may be exercised only by warships or military aircraft, or other ships or aircraft on government service specially authorized to that effect.

5. Where hot pursuit is effected by aircraft:

(a) The provisions of paragraphs 1 to 3 of this article shall apply mutatis mutandis;

(b) The aircraft giving the order to stop must itself actively pursue the ship until another ship or aircraft of the coastal State, summoned by the aircraft, arrives to take over the pursuit, unless the aircraft itself is able to arrest the ship. It does not suffice to justify an arrest on the high seas that the ship was merely sighted by the aircraft as an offender or suspected offender, if it was not both ordered to stop and pursued by the aircraft itself or other aircraft or ships which continue the pursuit without interruption.

6. The release of a ship arrested within the jurisdiction of a State and escorted to a port of that State for purposes of an inquiry before competent authorities may not be claimed solely on the ground that the ship, in the course of its voyage, was escorted across a portion of the high seas, if circumstances rendered this necessary.

7. Where a ship has been stopped or arrested on the high seas in circumstances which do not justify the exercise of the rights of hot pursuit, it shall be compensated for any loss or damage that may have been thereby sustained.

INTERNATIONAL LAW COMMISSION, 1956 COMMENTARY

DRAFT ARTICLE 47

(1) In the main, this article is taken from article 11 of the regulations adopted by the Second Committee of the Hague Codification Conference in 1930. The right concerned is not contested in international law. Only certain details as to the exercise of the right call for comment.

(i) It is not necessary that, at the time when the foreign ship within the territorial sea receives the order to stop, the ship giving the order should likewise be within the territorial sea. This rule applies in practice in the case of patrol vessels cruising for police purposes just outside the territorial sea. The essential point is that the ship committing the infringement must be in the territorial sea when the pursuit begins.

(ii) Hot pursuit must be continuous. Once broken off it cannot be resumed. The right of hot pursuit in any case ceases as soon as the ship pursued enters the territorial sea of its own country or of a third State.

(iii) Hot pursuit cannot be considered to have begun until the pursuing vessel has spotted the foreign ship in the territorial sea and has ordered it to stop by giving the prescribed signal. To prevent abuse, the Commission declined to admit orders given by wireless, as these could be given at any distance; the words "visual or auditory signal" exclude signals given at a great distance and transmitted by wireless.

(iv) The article also applies to ships which lie outside the territorial sea and cause their boats to commit unlawful acts in that sea. The Commission, however, refused to assimilate to such cases that of a ship staying outside the territorial sea and using not its own boats, but other craft.

(2) The rules laid down by the above are all in conformity with those adopted by the Hague Conference. The article adopted by the Commission differs from that of 1930 on two points only:

(a) The majority of the Commission was of the opinion that the right of hot pursuit should also be recognized when the ship is in a zone contiguous to the territorial sea, provided such pursuit is undertaken on the ground of violation of rights for the protection of which the zone was established. Thus, a State which has established a contiguous zone for the purposes of customs control cannot commence hot pursuit of a fishing boat accused of unlawfully fishing in the territorial sea if the fishing boat is within the contiguous zone. Some members of the Commission were of the opinion that since the coastal State does not exercise sovereignty in the contiguous zone, no pursuit commenced when the ship is already in the contiguous zone can be recognized. The majority of the Commission did not share that opinion. It admitted, however, that the offenses giving rise to hot pursuit must always have been committed in internal waters or in the territorial sea: acts committed in the contiguous zone cannot confer upon the coastal State a right of hot pursuit.

(b) The Commission wished to make it clear that the right of hot pursuit may be exercised only by warships and ships on government service specially authorized by the flag State to that effect. It is quite natural that customs and police vessels should be able to exercise the right of hot pursuit, but there can be no question of government ships on commercial service, for example, claiming that right.

(c) The ship finally arresting the ship pursued need not necessarily be the same as the one which began the pursuit, provided that it has joined in the pursuit and has not merely effected an interception.

(d) The Commission also dealt with the right of hot pursuit of a ship by aircraft. In spite of the dissenting opinion of some of its members, it felt able to recognize the lawfulness of such a practice, provided it is exercised in accordance with the principles governing its exercise by ships. It accordingly made the exercise of an aircraft's right to pursue a ship on the high seas and to arrest it -- if necessary in co-operation with a ship -- subject to the conditions laid down in paragraph 5. It is essential for the purposes of the proper exercise of the right of hot pursuit that the ship pursued should have been ordered to stop while it was still in the territorial sea or the contiguous zone. The aircraft must be in a position to give a visible and comprehensible signal to that effect; signals by wireless are barred in the case of aircraft also.

(e) It is recommended that the ship or aircraft should establish the position of the ship pursued at the moment when hot pursuit commences; it must wherever possible mark the position by physical means, for example, by dropping a buoy.

(f) The Commission included in this article a case which presents some analogy with the right of hot pursuit and which gave rise to differences of opinion, since it arose after the 1930 Conference. The question was whether a ship pursued and stopped in the territorial sea can be escorted to a port of the State of the pursuing vessel across the high seas, where there is no choice but to pass through the high seas. The Commission considered that it would be illogical to recognize the right of the pursuing vessel to seize a ship on the high seas and escort it to port across the high seas, while at the same time refusing to the government ship, in respect of a ship already apprehended in the territorial sea, the right to escort it to port across the high seas in cases where special circumstances forced it to leave the territorial sea in order to reach port.

RESTATEMENT OF THE LAW, THIRD

FOREIGN RELATIONS LAW OF THE UNITED STATES

[Sec.] 513

Comment:

. . . .

g. Hot pursuit. International law permits a coastal state to engage in hot pursuit of a foreign ship beyond the state's territorial sea if the state has good reason to believe that the ship had violated the state's laws or regulations within its internal waters or its territorial sea. Hot pursuit may begin in the contiguous zone for violation of those regulations for which the zone was designed; it may begin in the exclusive economic zone or over the continental shelf for violations of economic rights of the coastal state committed in that zone or on that shelf. Hot pursuit may be exercised only by a warship, a military aircraft, or a duly authorized ship or aircraft clearly identifiable as being on government service. The right of hot pursuit may be continued only if it has not been interrupted, and ceases as soon as the ship pursued enters the territorial sea of its own state or of a third state....

ED. NOTE: The above information, while seemingly clear, has given rise to some questions. Most of these concern the contiguous zone. Article 33 of the 1982 Convention states that contiguous zones may be established for the prevention of violation of four types of regulations: customs, fiscal immigration or sanitary. Is this list exclusive? What about fisheries? Does the term "sanitation" include pollution? What if a government ship observes, within a contigous zone, a violation of regulations for which that zone is established? May the government ship commence hot pursuit from that zone? Consider these questions in reading the following cases.

THE I'M ALONE

II Hackworth, Digest of International Law, 703-708 (1941)

"On March 22, 1929, the *I'm Alone,* a rum-runner of Canadian registry, was sunk on the high seas about 200 miles south of the Louisiana coast in the Gulf of Mexico by the United States revenue cutter *Dexter*. Inquiry as to the facts having been made by the Canadian Minister in Washington, the Department of State, on March 28 following, transmitted a note to him in which the facts were stated as follows:

On March 20, 1929, the *I'm Alone* was sighted by the United States Coast Guard vessel *Wolcott* northwest of Trinity Shoal, within approximately ten and one half miles of the coast of the United States. The *Wolcott* ordered the *I'm Alone* to heave to for boarding and examination, but this order was ignored; whereupon the *Wolcott* fired a warning shot across the bow of the *I'm Alone* and repeated its command for the vessel to heave to. When the second command was not complied with, the *Wolcott* fired through the sails and rigging of the vessel. The *I'm Alone* was proceeding seaward and the Wolcott took up the chase. The *Wolcott's* gun jammed and it could not therefore stop the *I'm Alone* but it kept in close chase and reported the incident to the Commanding Officer of the Coast Guard Base at Pascagoula, Mississippi, who dispatched the vessels *Dexter* and *Dallas* to assist the *Wolcott*.

"The *Wolcott* continued the pursuit of the *I'm Alone* and, according to statements of the appropriate authorities, was at all times in sight of it. The Coast Guard vessel *Dexter* overhauled the *Wolcott* close up with the *I'm Alone* about eight a.m. on March 22, with the latter vessel headed toward Yucatan. The Commander of the *Dexter* ordered the *I'm Alone* to heave to but the master of the latter vessel refused saying that he would rather sink than stop. The commanding officer of the *Dexter* then spoke with the master of the *I'm Alone* through a megaphone and informed him that the *I'm Alone* would be sunk unless it obeyed the command to stop. Warning shots were fired ahead, and, when the vessel did not stop, the *Dexter* fired through the rigging and later put about a dozen shots into the hull of the *I'm Alone*. It is stated that the sea was too rough to permit the *I'm Alone* to be boarded and seized by force and that furthermore the master of the *I'm Alone* waved a revolver in a threatening manner indicating that he would resist forcibly any attempt to board his vessel.

"The *I'm Alone* sank about 9:05 a.m. on March 22 in latitude 25° 41' and longitude 90° 45'. The Coast Guard vessels picked up the members of the crew of the *I'm Alone* with the exception of one person who was drowned...."

In its reply, the Canadian Legation stated that, according to the master of the vessel, the *I'm Alone* was anchored at a point not less than fourteen and one half miles off the coast of the United States; that even if the vessel was within approximately ten and one half miles, as contended by the the Government of the United States, "she was then beyond an hour's sailing distance from the shore"; that the convention between the United States and Great Britain concluded on January 23, 1924, regarding the smuggling of intoxicating liquors (43 Stat. 1761), conferred rights of search and seizure, to be exercised at a distance not greater, from the United States coast, than could be traversed in one hour by the suspected vessel, or by any other vessel in which the liquor was to be conveyed to the shore; that on the evidence available, the pursuit and sinking of the vessel appeared not to have been authorized by the terms of the convention of 1924 or by international law; and that:

"...It has been intimated that pursuit and seizure on the high seas might be justified on ground of hot and continous pursuit. It is agreed that international law recognizes that pursuit within the territorial waters may be continued on the high seas, if immediate and continuous. It does not, however, appear to apply to the present case. The pursuit did not begin within the territorial 3-mile limit, which is an essential factor....

"It is further to be noted that the cutter which sank the schooner had not participated in the original pursuit, but had come up from an entirely different direction two days later. Under these circumstances, the most essential elments of justification under the doctrine of hot pursuit appear to be lacking."

To this the Department of State replied, on April 17, 1929, inter alia:

"It is the contention of this Government that the *I'm Alone* was sighted and commanded to heave to at a point not more than 10.8 miles from the coast of the United States; that this distance is less than the distance which could be traversed by the vessel in one hour,....and that under the doctrine of "hot pursuit," the Coast Guard vessels possessed authority to follow the *I'm Alone* beyond the distance of one hour's sailing stipulated in the treaty between the United States and Great Britain of January 23, 1924, and compel it to comply with the orders of the Coast Guard officers to stop.

"....

"In the estimation of this Government, the correct principle underlying the doctrine of hot pursuit is that if the arrest would have been valid when the vessel was first hailed, but was made impossible through the illegal action of the pursued vessel in failing to stop when ordered to do so, then hot pursuit is justified and the locus of the arrest and the distance of the pursuit is immaterial provided:

(1) That it is without the territorial waters of any other state;

(2) that the pursuit had been hot and continous.

"With regard to the duration of pursuit I may state that it is the view of this Government that this is unimportant, provided the other elements of hot pursuit are always present...

"....

"With regard to the fact that the arrest of the *I'm Alone* was performed not by the original pursuing vessel but by another which had been called for assistance, I desire to present the following considerations.

"It is submitted that so long as the *Wolcott* was present at all times and was actually cooperating with the *Dexter* in a joint endeavor to make the *I'm Alone* stop, the requirements of the doctrine of "hot pursuit" were met and the additional factor that the *Dexter* joined in the chase does not invalidate the legality of the action of the American authorities."

The dispute was submitted to two commissioners, the Right Honorable Lyman Poore Duff, appointed by Canada, and the Honorable Willis Van Devanter, appointed by the United States.

In a joint interim report, dated June 30, 1933, the commissioners stated that they were "not in agreement...nor have they reached a final disagreement" as to whether the United States, under the convention of 1924, had the right of hot pursuit where the offending vessel was within an hour's sailing distance of the shore at the commencement of the pursuit and beyond that distance at its termination. The commissioners further stated that "based upon the *assumption* [italics added] that the United States Government had the right of hot pursuit in the circumstances and was entitled to exercise the rights under article 2 of the Convention at the time when the *Dexter* joined the *Wolcott* in the pursuit of the *I'm Alone* and upon the assumption that the averments set forth in paragraph 8 of the answer of the United States are true (these related particularly to the manner and extent of the use of force), "the admittedly intentional sinking of the vessel was not justified by anything in the Convention. The Commissioners now add that it could not be justified by any principal of international law." In view of the fact that the *I'm Alone*, although of Canadian registry, was "*de facto* owned, controlled, and at the critical times, managed, and her movements directed and her cargo disposed of, by a group of persons acting in concert who were entirely, or nearly so, citizens of the United States," the commissioners considered that no compensation ought to be paid for the loss of the ship or cargo. In view of the fact, however, that the "act of sinking the ship,...by officers of the United States Coast Guard, was...an unlawful act," the commisioners considered that the United States ought formally to acknowledge its illegality and apologize to His Majesty's Canadian Government, and to pay $25,000 to the Government "in respect of the wrong." The commissioners recommended that $25,666.50 should be paid to the captain and members of the crew, "none of whom was a party to the illegal conspiracy to smuggle liquor into the United States and sell the same there." On January 19, 1935 the United States after pointing out that although the commissioners found that "the mission and use of the vessel at the time of its sinking were unlawful" and that nevertheless they also found that "its sinking by the United States was unlawful," tendered to His Majesty's Canadian Government an apology for the sinking of the vessel. On November 7, 1935, a check in the amount of $50,666.50 in full settlement of all claims resulting from the sinking of the vessel was transmitted to the Charge d'Affairs ad interim of Canada by the Department of State.

GILLAM v. UNITED STATES

27 F.2d 296 (4th. Cir. 1928)

[This case involved the seizure of a vessel sighted 7 1/2 miles from the coast of the United States, but apprehended after a chase at a distance of 12 3/4 miles from the coast. The vessel was found to be carrying a cargo of liquor and, according to the court, she was bound illegally for a U.S. port. The court said the following about the legality of the seizure:]

On this question, the contention on behalf of the vessel is (1) that, as she was admittedly beyond the 3-mile limit at all times, she had not committed a crime within the territorial limits of the United States, and was therefore not subject to seizure, and (2) under the Treaty with Great Britain of May 22, 1924, 43 Stat. 1761, seizure is authorized only when it appears that the vessel is within one hour's sailing distance of shore and has committed or is attempting to commit an offense against the laws of the United States, which prohibit the importation of alcoholic beverages. No point is made that the vessel was actually overhauled and the seizure actually made beyond one hour's sailing distance and beyond the 12-mile limit, if she was within those limits when signaled; and we think it is clear, under the "hot pursuit" doctrine, that if the right of seizure existed at the time the vessel was signaled, the right was not lost because she had succeeded in getting farther from shore in her attempt to run away...

While it is true, as contended, that the vessel never came within the 3-mile territorial waters of the United States, we think that, as she was bound for the United States with an unmanifested cargo and came within 12 miles, or 4 marine leagues, of the coast, her seizure was justified under the revenue statutes of the United States, and that these statutes constitute a valid exercise of the sovereign power of the government.

UNITED STATES v. F/V TAIYO MARU

395 F.Supp. 413 (1975)

These proceedings arise from the seizure of a Japanese fishing vessel, the F/V TAIYO MARU 28, by the United States Coast Guard for violation of a United States fisheries law. On September 5, 1974, the Coast Guard sighted the TAIYO MARU 28 fishing at Latitude 43-35.9 North, Longitude 69-20 West. That point is approximately 16.25 miles off the coast of the State of Maine and approximately 10.5 miles from Monhegan Island. It is conceded to be within the contiguous fisheries zone of the United States.... The Coast Guard signalled the TAIYO MARU 28 to stop, but the vessel attempted to escape by accelerating toward the high seas. The Coast Guard immediately pursued and seized the vessel on the high seas at Latitude 42-58 North, Longitude 68-24 West, a point approximately 67.9 miles at sea from the mainland of the continental United States.

Defendant asserts that Article 23 of the Convention on the High Seas must be read in conjunction with Article 24 of the Convention on the Territorial Sea and the Contiguous Zone. The argument is that since article 24 only authorizes the establishment of a contiguous zone for the purposes of enforcing the coastal State's customs, fiscal, immigration or sanitary regulations, and since Article 23 permits hot pursuit of a foreign ship from such a contiguous zone only for the four purposes listed in Article 24, the United States was without authority to commence hot pursuit of the TAIYO MARU 28 from within the contiguous fisheries zone for the purpose of enforcing fisheries regulations.

....

Both parties recognize that the general rule of law is that the power of the government to enforce a forfeiture or prosecute a defendant is not impaired by the illegality of the method by which it acquired control over the property of the defendant.... Defendant relies upon the exception to this general rule established in Cook v. United States, 288 U.S. 102, 53 S.Ct. 305, 77 L.Ed. 641 (1933). In *Cook*, the United States Coast Guard seized a British vessel, the *Mazel Tov*, caught in rum-running, on the high seas outside American jursidictional limits set by a British-American treaty covering the apprehension of prohibition law violators. The Supreme Court held that the United States "lacking power to seize, lacked power, because of the Treaty, to subject the vessel to our laws. To hold that adjudication may follow a wrongful seizure would go far to nullify the purpose and effect of the Treaty."...

Mr. Justice Brandeis made clear, however, that the exception to the general rule recognized in *Cook* covers the particular situation where the United States has by treaty "imposed a territorial limitation upon its own authority."... As stated in Autry v. Wiley, the *Cook* doctrine is a "narrow" exception to the general rule; it "applies only to violation of a specific territorial jurisdictional circumscription set by treaty."

Defendant strenuously argues that the *Cook* exception destroys the jurisdiction of this Court in these proceedings because by Article 23 of the Convention on the High Seas, read together with Article 24 of the Convention on the Territorial Sea and the Contiguous Zone, the United States has undertaken a specific obligation not to institute hot pursuit of a foreign ship from the contiguous fisheries zone for violation of its fisheries law. Defendant's position is that Article 23 limits the government's right of hot pursuit from a contiguous zone to the four purposes for which Article 24 authorizes the establishment of such a zone, and the enforcement of domestic fisheries law is not one of the purposes recognized by Article 24. The Court is persuaded, however, that neither the language nor the history of the Conventions shows that the signatory powers intended to limit the right of a coastal State to exercise exclusive fishery jurisdiction within 12 miles from its coast, to establish a contiguous zone for such a purpose, or to conduct hot pursuit from such a zone.

Analysis of the text of Article 23 of the Convention on the High Seas shows that the Article provides general authority to undertake hot pursuit from a contiguous zone when the authorities of the coastal State have good reason to believe that a foreign vessel has violated the coastal State's laws and regulations. It is true that Article 23 permits hot pursuit from a contiguous zone, created for one of the four purposes enumerated in Article 24 of the Convention on the Territorial Sea and the Contiguous Zone, only if there has been a violation of the rights for the protection of which the zone was established. But Article 23 does not in terms deny a coastal State to commence hot pursuit from a contiguous zone established for a purpose other than one of those specified in the Article. The language of Article 24, relating to the purposes for which a contiguous zone may be established, is permissive, rather than restrictive. It provides that a coastal State "may" establish a contiguous zone for the purposes of enforcing its customs, fiscal, immigration or sanitary regulations. Although Article 24 only affirmatively recognizes the right of a coastal State to establish a contiguous zone for one of the four enumerated purposes, nothing in the Article precludes the establishment of such a zone for other purposes, including the enforcement of domestic fisheries laws. In short, unlike the British-American treaty in *Cook*, the Conventions in the case at bar contain no specific undertaking by the United States not to conduct hot pursuit from a contiguous fisheries zone extending 12 miles from its coast. The *Cook* excption, therefore, is not applicable, because the United States has not by treaty "imposed a territorial limitation upon its own authority."

The history of the 1958 Conventions confirms the conclusion that the United States did not specifically undertake to limit its authority to exercise exclusive fisheries jurisdiction within 12 miles of its coast, to establish a contiguous zone for such a purpose, or to conduct hot pursuit from such a zone. The Convention on the High Seas and the Convention on the Territorial Sea and the Contiguous Zone were the product of the Conference on the Law of the Sea convened at Geneva in 1958 pursuant to Resolution 1105 of the General Assembly of the United Nations.... Although the Conference was convened to resolve a variety of matters pertaining to the codification of the Law of the Sea, most commentators agree that the two principal issues presented for the Conference's consideration were the question of the breadth of the territorial sea, and the closely-related question of whether there should be an additional contiguous zone in which the coastal States could exercise exclusive jurisdiction over fishing.... The 1958 Geneva Conference was unable to achieve agreement on either issue, primarily because of the volatile political ramifications involved in setting a limit to the territorial sea. In recommending that the Senate give its advice and consent to the ratification of the Conventions, the Senate Report from the Committee on Foreign Relations made clear that the Convention on the Territorial Sea and the Contiguous Zone did not define the width of the territorial sea, or circumscribe the right of a coastal State to assert exclusive fisheries jurisdiction:

> "This convention does not fix the breadth of the territorial sea. This subject and the closely related one of the extent to which the coastal State should have exclusive fishing rights in the sea off its coast were hotly debated without any conclusion being reached."

It is clear from the foregoing history that, in becoming a signatory to the 1958 Conventions, the United States could not have intended to accept any limitation on its right to conduct hot pursuit for violations of exclusive fishery rights occurring within 12 miles of its coast, since the Geneva Conference could not agree as to whether a contiguous zone could be established for the purpose of enforcing domestic fisheries law.

It is apparent that Congress was well aware of the obligations under the 1958 Conventions when the 1966 Contiguous Fisheries Zone Act was enacted, and that Congress perceived no conflict between the Act and the treaty provisions. This is evident from the House Report, which discusses the Conventions and their relationship to the proposed legislation:

> "In 1958, and again in 1960, the Law of the Sea Conferences held in Geneva, Switzerland, left unresolved the twin questions of the width of the territorial sea and to the extent to which a coastal state could claim exclusive fishing rights in the high seas off its coast. At the second conference in 1960, the United States and Canada put forth a compromise proposal for a 6-mile territorial sea, plus a 6-mile exclusive fisheries zone (12 miles of exclusive jurisdiction in all) subject to the continuation for 10 years of traditional fishing by other states in the outer 6 miles. This compromise proposal failed by one vote to obtain the two-thirds vote necessary for adoption.
>
> Since the 1958 Law of the Sea Conference, there has been a trend toward the establishment of a 12-mile fisheries rule in international practice. Thirty-nine countries acting individually or in concert with other countries have extended their fisheries limits to 12 miles since 1958."

The Report also notes that, as of July 1, 1966, of the 99 United Nations coastal states, slightly more than 60 countries asserted a 12-mile exclusive fishery zone, either as a territorial sea or as territorial sea plus a contiguous zone.

Since the seizure of the TAIYO MARU 28 on the high seas following hot pursuit from the contiguous zone was not in violation of Article 23 of the Convention on the High Seas, and, moreover, was sanctioned by domestic law and in conformity with the prevailing consensus of international law and practice, this Court has jursidction to decide the present proceedings on their merits. Defendant's motion to dismiss for lack of jurisdiction is therefore denied.

ED. NOTE: How persuasive is the foregoing opinion? Does the fact that so many nations were claiming such zones have significance for the interpretation of the treaties, or does that fact have a different significance? Does a conclusion that the nations assembled at the conference intended flexibility in the establishment of different kinds of zones necessarily follow from the fact that they could not agree?

1982 UNITED NATIONS CONVENTION ON THE LAW OF THE SEA

Article 111

Right of hot pursuit

....

2. The right of hot pursuit shall apply *mutatis mutandis* in the exclusive economic zone or on the continental shelf, including safety zones around continental shelf installations, of the laws and regulations of the coastal State applicable in accordance with this Convention to the exclusive economic zone or the continental shelf, including safety zones.

....

N. USE OF THE BED OF THE HIGH SEAS FOR SUBMARINE CABLES AND PIPELINES.

CONVENTION ON THE HIGH SEAS

Article 2

....Freedom of the high seas...comprises, *inter alia*....

....

(3) Freedom to lay submarine cables and pipelines;

....

Article 26

1. All States shall be entitled to lay submarine cables and pipelines on the bed of the high seas.

2. Subject to its right to take reasonable measures for the exploration of the continental shelf and the exploitation of its natural resources, the coastal State may not impede the laying or maintenance of such cables or pipelines.

3. When laying such cables or pipelines the State in question shall pay due regard to cables or pipelines already in position on the seabed. In particular, possibilities of repairing existing cables or pipelines shall not be prejudiced.

INTERNATIONAL LAW COMMISSION, 1956 Commentary

Article 27

Every State shall take necessary legislative measures to provide that the breaking or injury by a ship flying its flag or by a person subject to its jurisdiction of a submarine cable beneath the high seas done wilfully or through culpable negligence, in such a manner as to be liable to interrupt or obstruct telegraphic or telephonic communications, and similarly the breaking or injury of a submarine pipeline or high-voltage power cable shall be a punishable offense. This provision shall not apply to any break or injury caused by persons who acted merely with the legitimate object of saving their lives or their ships, after having taken all necessary precautions to avoid such break or injury.

Article 28

Every State shall take the necessary legislative measures to provide that, if persons subject to its jurisdiction who are owners of a cable or a pipeline beneath the high seas, in laying or reparing that cable or pipeline, cause a break or injury to another cable or pipeline, they shall bear the cost of the repairs.

Article 29

Every State shall take the necessary legislative measures to insure that the owners of ships who can prove that they have sacrificed an anchor, a net or any other fishing gear, in order to avoid injuring a submarine cable or pipeline, shall be indemnified by the owner of the cable or pipeline, provided that the owner of the ship has taken all reasonable precautionay measures beforehand.

CONVENTION ON THE CONTINENTAL SHELF

Article 4

Subject to its right to take reasonable measures for the exploration of the continental shelf and the exploitation of its natural resources, the coastal State may not impede the laying of submarine cables or pipelines on the continental shelf.

INTERNATIONAL LAW COMMISSION

1956 Commentary

DRAFT ARTICLE 70

(1) The coastal State is required to permit the laying of submarine cables on the seabed of its continental shelf, but in order to avoid unjustified interference with the exploitation of the natural resources of the seabed and subsoil, it may impose conditions concerning the route to be followed.

(2) The Commission considered whether this provision should not be extended to pipelines. In principle, the answer must be in the affirmative. The question, however, is complicated by the fact that it would often be necessary to install pumping stations at certain points which might hinder th exploitation of the soil more than cables. It follows that the coastal State might be less liberal in this matter than in the use of cables. As the question does not yet seem to be of practical importance, the Commission has not expressly referred to pipelines in the present article.

ED. NOTE: The 1982 Convention also provides for the right to lay submarine cables and pipelines, in substantially the same form, as the following articles illustrate.

1982 UNITED NATIONS CONVENTION ON THE LAW OF THE SEA

Article 112

Right to lay submarine cables and pipelines

1. All States are entitled to lay submarine cables and pipelines on the bed of the high seas beyond the continental shelf.

2. Article 79, paragraph 5, applies to such cables and pipelines.

Article 113

Breaking or injury of a submarine cable or pipeline

Every State shall adopt laws and regulations necessary to provide that the breaking or injury by a ship flying its flag or by a person subject to its jurisdiction of a submarine cable beneath the high seas done wilfully or through culpable negligence, in such a manner as to be liable to interrupt or obstruct telegraphic or telephonic communications, and similarly the breaking or injury of a submarine pipeline or high-voltage power cable, shall be a punishable offense. This provision shall apply also to conduct calculated or likely to result in such breaking and injury. However, it shall not apply to any break or injury caused by persons who acted merely with the legitimate object of saving their lives or their ships, after having taken all necessary precautions to avoid such break or injury.

Article 114

Breaking or injury by owners of a submarine cable or pipeline of another submarine cable or pipeline

Every State shall adopt laws and regulations necessary to provide that, if persons subject to its jurisdiction who are owners of a submarine cable or pipeline beneath the high seas, in laying or repairing that cable or pipeline, cause a break or injury to another cable or pipeline, they shall bear the cost of repairs.

Article 115

Indemnity for loss incurred in avoiding injury to a submarine cable or pipeline

Every State shall adopt laws and regulations necessary to ensure that the owners of ships who can prove that they have sacrificed an anchor, a net or any other fishing gear, in order to avoid injuring a submarine cable or pipeline, shall be indemnified by the owner of the cable or pipeline, provided that the owner of the ship has taken all reasonable precautionary measures beforehand.

CHAPTER 3

INTERNAL WATERS AND THE TERRITORIAL SEA

A. INTRODUCTION

Having considered the most basic and fundamental doctrine of the law of the sea, from which most other rules have evolved, we now turn to consideration of internal waters and the territorial sea. While the doctrine of the freedom of the high seas was, and is, important in the global scheme of the use of the oceans, it should be equally apparent that nations also have vital coastal interests to be protected, and that the freedom of the seas, if total and unregulated, could threaten those vital interests. Thus it was natural that the international community would come to accept that within a certain belt of water adjacent to its coasts, a nation should have considerable regulatory jurisdiction; hence the concepts of internal waters and the territorial sea.

Perhaps the most important of these interests is national security. But there are others as well. The need for food caused many coastal nations to turn to fisheries, with the corresponding desire to reserve coastal fisheries to their own fishermen. And all manner of coastal State laws could not be effective unless they can also be applied in the marginal belt of their seas. Such laws include customs and immigration laws, pollution control laws, shipping regulations, and the like. All of these important needs require a degree of coastal State jurisdiction over the adjoining belt of the oceans.

There is an obvious conflict between the need, on the one hand, for maximum freedom to navigate, and, on the other, the natural desire of coastal States to exert their influence farther and farther seaward from their coasts. Thus one could expect, and find, a difference in attitude between those States that are primarily coastal, with little or no navies or long-distance fishing fleets and those States that could be considered as maritime powers, either in the military or commercial shipping or fisheries contexts. For some States, the problem is complex. The United States, for example, is a major maritime power, but it also has, collectively, one of the longest coastlines of the world. Thus it is faced with having to reconcile the often conflicting views of the military, the fishermen, the oil companies, the marine scientists, and many others. Thus the formation of overall law of the sea policy for the United States is a difficult and time-consuming process.

In this chapter, we shall begin with the concept of internal waters and then move to the examination of the territorial sea. Our consideration of internal waters will be limited to views as to the jurisdiction of the coastal State in those waters. Our consideration of the territorial sea will begin with some historical materials, and then we shall move to other aspects such as the extent of coastal State jurisdiction, the breadth of the territorial sea, and the concept of innocent passage. Since there is a need to consider related concepts, such as that of transit passage in international straits and archipelagic sealanes passage, we will examine them as well, although they are technically distinct concepts. By this device we can compare these concepts with that of innocent passage and note their similarities and differences.

B. INTERNAL WATERS

1. DEFINITION

Sholowitz, SHORE AND SEA BOUNDARIES

311. Inland Waters

The inland or internal waters include all bodies of water within the land territory, such as rivers and lakes, as well as bodies of water which open on the coast and fall within the category of "true" bays.

Churchill and Lowe, THE LAW OF THE SEA, 45 (1983)[1]

Internal, or national, or interior, waters are those waters which lie on the landward side of the baseline from which the territorial sea and other maritime zones are measured.... Thus,...internal waters of a maritime character mostly comprise bays, estuaries and ports....

2. ACCESS TO INTERNAL WATERS

The question here examined is when, and under what conditions, may a vessel demand access to the ports of a coastal State. Views have varied over the years. In practice, States have in fact often restricted access to certain ports by certain vessels. Hugo Grotius, for example, took the position that no sovereign could bar foreigners from having access to its ports. On the other hand, it is frequently asserted that a State exercises the same sovereignty over its internal waters as it does over its land territory. Were that completely true, it would lead to the conclusion that a State has the right to close its internal waters to foreign shipping just as it has the right to close its land border. Probably the best exposition of the most widely accepted view is contained in the following excerpt.

ED. NOTE: Colombos took the view that a coastal State does not have an unlimited right to prohibit a vessel from entering its ports. The basic principle, he said, was that in time of peace commercial ports must be left open to international traffic. Nor can any port be shut to a vessel in distress. However, he goes on to say that a military port may be closed both to warships and commercial vessels on grounds of "jusifiable precaution". And, he pointed out, commercial ports may impose certain restrictions or conditions on the entry of military vessels into their waters. Colombos, "International Law of the Sea", Longmans, 1961, at 150.

RESTATEMENT, FOREIGN RELATIONS LAW, THIRD

Reporters notes to section 512

3. Access to ports. It has been said that, as no civilized state has "the right to isolate itself wholly from the outside world," there is "a corresponding obligation imposed upon each maritime power not to deprive foreign vessels of commerce of access to all of its ports."... The LOS Convention does not mention a right of access of ships to foreign ports, but the customary law of the subject, as reflected in a number of international agreements, has been confirmed by at least one international decision. Thus, the Statute on the International Regime of Maritime Ports of 1923, confirmed the freedom of access to maritime ports by foreign vessels on condition of reciprocity; but it allows the coastal state "in exceptional cases, and for as short a period as possible," to deviate from this provision by measures that a state "is obliged to take in case of an emergency affecting the safety of the state or the vital interest of the country."... Although this Statute has been ratified by less than 30 states and the United States is not a party to it, the Statute has been accepted as reflecting a customary rule of international law. An arbitral tribunal, relying on this Statute, stated that "[a]ccording to a great principle of international law, ports of every State must be open to foreign merchant vessels and can only be closed when the vital interests of the State so require." [citing the Aramco dispute].

The Institute of International Law has considered this issue in 1898, 1928, and 1957, and each time, after a heated discussion, it affirmed the right of access to ports, subject to various conditions. In

---

1. Reprinted by permission of Manchester University Press.

1898, the Institute agreed that, as a general rule, access to ports "is presumed to be free to foreign ships," except when a state, "for reasons of which it is the sole judge," declares its ports, or some of them, closed "when the safety of the State or the interest of public health justifies the order," or when it refuses entrance to ships of a particular nation "as an act of reprisal."... In 1928, the Institute stated that, as a general rule, access to ports "is open to foreign vessels," but, as an exception and for a term limited as possible, "a state may suspend this access by particular or general measures which it is obliged to take in case of serious events touching the safety of the state or the public health"; it also confirmed the exception in case of reprisals..... In 1957, the Institute distinguished between internal waters and ports, and pointed out that a coastal state may deny access to internal waters, "[s]ubject to the rights of passage sanctioned either by usage or by treaty," but should abstain from denying such access to foreign commercial vessels "save where in exceptional cases this denial of access is imposed by imperative reasons." On the other hand, the Institute declared that "it is consistent with the general practice of States to permit free access to ports and harbors by such vessels....

ED. NOTE: There is no real case law on access to ports. But in a single arbitration award, the Saudi Arabia/ARAMCO dispute, the question was addressed. At issue was an agreement between Saudi Arabia and Aristotle Onassis for the carriage of Saudi oil. Aramco contended that its prior concession agreement with Saudi Arabia gave Aramco control over who carried Saudi oil. The tribunal found that every state must open its ports to foreign vessels, closing them only when vital interests are engaged. One special case of access to ports, however, should be given consideration. This is the question of distress, usually referred to as the doctrine of force majeur. This has been described by Professors McDougal and Burke as follows:

"The one customary right of access, quite universally accepted, arises from the humanitarian obligation to admit vessels in distress because of the weather or damage to the vessel. A threat to the safety of the vessel, or persons aboard, is generally considered to require the suspension of coastal laws prohibiting or serverely penalizing entry into port without coastal consent."

RESTATEMENT OF THE LAW, SECOND, FOREIGN RELATIONS LAW OF THE UNITED STATES

SECTION 48

(1) A foreign vessel or aircraft has the right to enter the territory of a state when such entry is necessary for the safety of the vessel, aircraft or persons aboard, and to leave the territory once the conditions that made the entry necessary have ceased to exist.

(2) The territorial state may not exercise its jurisdiction under the rule stated in [sec.] 20 to enforce rules prescribed by it with respect to

(a) acts aboard a foreign vessel or aircraft necessary to effectuate entry in distress,

(b) the possession or carriage of property aboard a foreign vessel or aircraft entering in distress, bona fide and without intent to evade the customs and anti-smuggling laws of the coastal state, except in so far as such regulation may reasonably be necessary for reasons of health and safety of the coastal state.

UNITED STATES v. MEXICO (Kate A. Hoff Claim). CLAIMS COMMISSION, UNITED STATES AND MEXICO, APRIL 2, 1919

[The American schooner Rebecca bound for Tampico, Mexico, from Morgan City, Louisiana, had on board goods destined for Brazos Santiago, Texas, but before being able to deliver them was forced by high winds and rough seas to a point off Tampico where she was disabled and in an unsafe condition. The Rebecca put into the port of Tampico because of the dangerous condition of the vessel. Mexican officials seized the merchandise originally destined for Texas and charged the master with smuggling. A claim was filed which alleged that because the vessel entered in distress, it should have been immune from local customs laws.]

It is of course well established that, when a merchant vessel belonging to one nation enters the territorial waters of another nation, it becomes amenable to the jurisdiction of the latter and subject to its laws, except in so far as treaty stipulations may relieve the vessel from the operation of local laws. On the other hand, there appears to be general recognition among the nations of the world of what may doubtless be considered to be an exception, or perhaps it may be said two exceptions, to this general, fundamental rule of subjection to local jurisdiction over vessels in ports.

Recognition has been given to the so-called right of "innocent passage" for vessels through the maritime belt in so far as it forms a part of the high seas for international traffic. Similarly, recognition has also been given -- perhaps it may be said in a more concrete and emphatic manner -- to the immunity of a ship whose presence in territorial waters is due to a superior force. The principles with regard to the status of a vessel in "distress" find recognition in both domestic laws and in international law....

Domestic courts have frequently considered pleas of distress in connection with charges of infringement of customs laws. Interesting cases in which pleas of distress were raised came before American courts in the cases of vessels charged with violation of the interesting American so-called "non-intercourse" acts forbidding trade with French and British possessions.... In these cases it was endeavored in behalf of the vessels to seek immunity from prosecution under these laws by alleging that the vessels had entered forbidden waters as a result of *vis major*....

The enlightened principle of comity which exempts a merchant vessel, at least to a certain extent, from the operation of local laws has been generally stated to apply to vessels forced into port by storm, or compelled to seek refuge for vital repairs or for provisioning, or carried into port by mutineers. It has also been asserted in defense of a charge of attempted breech of blocade... In the instant case we are concerned simply with distress said to have been occasioned by violent weather.

While recognizing the general principle of immunity of vessels in distress, domestic courts and international courts have frequently given consideration to the degree of necessity prompting vessels to seek refuge. It has been said that the necessity must be urgent. It seems possible to formulate certain reasonably concrete criteria applicable and controlling in the instant case. Assuredly, a ship floundering in distress, resulting either from the weather or from other causes affecting the management of the vessel, need not be in such condition that it is dashed helplessly on the shore or against rocks before a claim of distress can properly be invoked on its behalf. The fact that it may be able to come into port under its own power can obviously not be cited as delaying seeking refuge until his ship was wrecked, obviously he would not be using his best judgment with a view to the preservation of the ship, the cargo and the lives of the people on board. Clearly an important consideration may be determination of the question whether there is evidence in a given case of a fraudulent attempt to circumvent local laws. And even in the absence of any such attempt, it can probably be correctly said that a matter of mere convenience in making repairs or in avoiding a measure of difficulty of navigation can not justify a disregard of local laws.

....

ED. NOTE: The above materials sketch out the general right of entry under conditions of distress. A few points need some elaboration. The immunity from local laws referred to is not a general immunity. It is only immunity from local laws involving the act of entry (such as pilotage requirements) and laws relating to the carriage or possession of prohibited or regulated cargo. Persons on board are not immune from laws relating to crimes. Second, the claim, obviously, must be made in good faith. The question of good faith is a question of fact, to be decided in the first instance by the local authorities. Likewise, the claim to enter may not be made, or need not be recognized, if the act of entry creates a danger to the local port. Finally, as noted above, the right to enter under force majeur extends only for the length of time necessary to affect necessary repairs.

3. THE APPLICATION OF COASTAL STATE AUTHORITY OVER VESSELS IN INTERNAL WATERS

a. WARSHIPS

Obviously, warships in the internal waters of a foreign State are a different case than commercial vessels. This is due to their nature. On the one hand, the port State has an interest in protecting its inhabitants from acts done by warships or their crews, or resulting from their presence. On the other hand, the flag State has an interest to exercise exclusive control over its military vessels.

Coastal States may place any conditions they might wish on the entry of warships, such as time limitations and health or safety regulations. Other than that, the general policy is that which is reflected in The Schooner Exchange, 11 U.S. 116 (1812). The Court there said that the warship

"...constitutes a part of the military force of her nation; acts under the immediate and first command of the sovereign; is employed by him in national objects. He has many and powerful motives for preventing those objects from being defeated by the interference of a foreign state. Such interference cannot take place without affecting his power and dignity. The implied license, therefore, under which such vessel enters a friendly port, may reasonably be construed, and it seems to the court, ought to be construed, as containing an exemption from the jurisdiction of the sovereign within whose territory she claims the rites of hospitality.

"Upon these principles, by the unanimous consent of nations, a foreigner is amenable to the laws of the place; but certainly in practice, nations have not yet asserted their jurisdiction over the public armed ships of a foreign sovereign entering a port open for their reception."

RESTATEMENT OF THE LAW, SECOND, FOREIGN RELATIONS LAW OF THE UNITED STATES

Sec. 49

Except as otherwise expressly indicated by the coastal state, its consent to the entry of a foreign naval or other military vessel into its internal waters implies that the coastal state

(a) waives the right to exercise aboard the vessel its enforcement jurisdiction...except to the extent necessary to prevent imminent injury to persons or property not involved in the operation of the vessel, and

(b) consents to the exercise by the foreign state of such of its enforcement jurisdiction...as is necessary for the internal management and discipline of the vessel.

ED. NOTE: It is customary for warships planning a visit to a foreign port to give advance notification of its intent to enter the port. It is not necessary that the port State reply. If it does not object to the visit after such notification, the vessel may assume it is cleared to enter.

The Restatement makes clear that everyday disciplinary matters are left to the commanding officer of the visiting ship. However, the port State may take jurisdiction over crimes committed on the ship which cause injuries ashore (throwing a grenade over the side). The jurisdiction of the vessel to deal with disciplinary matters does not extend to the conduct of personnel of that vessel while on shore. Furthermore, the enforcement jurisdiction of the State of the vessel is limited to detention, the inflicting of minor punishment, or the holding of courts martial. It does not include the inflicting of major punishment, such as the death penalty, so long as the vessel remains in port.

b. CRIMINAL JURISDICTION OVER A COMMERCIAL VESSEL WHILE IN PORT

WILDENHUS'S CASE, 120 U.S. 1 (1888)

[In this case, one Belgian crewman killed another on a Belgian ship while anchored in a New Jersey Port. The question before the court was whether the state of New Jersey had jurisdiction over that crime.]

"...it was found long ago that it would be beneficial to commerce if the local government would abstain from interfering with the internal discipline of the ship, and the general regulation of the rights and duties of the officers and crew towards the vessel or among themselves. And so by comity it came to be generally understood among civilized nations that all matters of discipline and all things done on board which affected only the vessel or those belonging to her, and did not involve the peace or dignity of the country or the tranquility of the port, should be left by the local government to be dealt with by the authorities of the nation to which the vessel belonged as the laws of that nation or the interests of its commerce should require. But if crimes are committed on board of a character to disturb the peace and tranquility of the country to which the vessel has been brought, the offenders have never by comity or usage been entitled to any exemption from the operation of the local laws for their punishment, if the local tribunals see fit to assert their authority.

[The court went on to describe the appropriate test to be applied]

"If that [the act] is of a character to awaken public interest when it becomes known, it is a `disorder' the nature of which is to affect the community at large, and consequently to invoke the power of the local government whose people have been disturbed by what was done. The very nature of such an act is to disturb the quiet of a peaceful community..."

[The court upheld the jurisdiction of the port State.]

ED. NOTE: As the above case illustrates, it is possible for both the flag State and the port State to exercise jurisdiction over criminal acts committed by a person on board a commercial vessel while in a foreign port. There have been cases where the U.S. has asserted jurisdiction over crimes committed on U.S. vessels in foreign ports. In U.S. v. Flores, 289 U.S. 137 (1933), for example, the court upheld U.S. jurisdiction over a crime committed on board a U.S. vessel 250 miles up the Congo River. Do you think that a person should be punished twice for the same crime, once by the flag State and again by the port State?

C. THE TERRITORIAL SEA

1. ORIGINS OF THE CONCEPT OF THE LEGAL REGIME OF THE TERRITORIAL SEA

Churchill and Lowe, THE LAW OF THE SEA, 53-57 (1983)[2]

Although the recent legislation of several States, such as Guyana, Pakistan and the Seychelles, declares that the State's soveriegnty `extends and has always extended' to its territorial sea, such statements are historically incorrect; the true picture of the development of the concept is rather more complex.

Since the replacement of the Holy Roman Empire by a system of independent sovereign States having definite boundaries -- what has been termed the `birth of territoriality', in the sixteenth century -- it has been generally accepted that coastal States enjoy some rights to regulate in their own interests activities in the sea adjoining their coasts. Even during the great debates in the seventeenth century between Grotius, as advocate of the freedom of the seas, and the proponents of `closed seas",...this much was agreed. Grotius, for example, did not claim that all the seas were open to use by all men. Borrowing a distinction drawn by the Italian civil lawyer Baldus in the fourteenth century, between rights of property (*dominium*) and rights of jurisdiction or control (*imperium*) in the sea, Grotius argued that there could be no property rights in the high seas but seems to have admitted the existence of jurisdiction without property rights in coastal waters which could be effectively controlled from the land.

Grotius' position was developed during the seventeenth century by writers such as Pontanus in Holland, Wellwood in Scotland, and Meadows in England, who abandoned his distiction between property rights and the existence of jurisdiction for their protection and that the right to exclude, for example, foreign fishermen by the exercise of jurisdiction is tantamount to the existence of property rights, the idea gained ground of a simple distinction between high seas, free and open to all, and coastal waters susceptible to appropriation by the adjacent State. By the end of that century this idea was well established: for instance, the influential work by Bynkershoek, *De domino maris dissertatio*, published in 1702, was based upon the twin pillars of the freedom of the high seas and the `sovereignty' of the coastal State over its adjacent sea.

Although Bynkershoek himself regarded this `sovereignty' as complete, and as including the right to deny foreign ships passage through the territorial sea, his view was not generally shared and was not to survive. Vattel, whose treatise *Le droit des gens* was published in 1758, took the part of earlier writers such as Grotius and Gentilis, and declared that ships of all States enjoyed a right of innocent passage through the territorial sea. While the exact scope of this right has been questioned in several respects, such as its extension to warships, its existence has not been seriously challenged since the early nineteenth century.

As the distinction between high seas and the territorial sea (or `territorial waters', as it was,

---

2. Reprinted by permission of Manchester University Press.

and is, commonly known) crystallised, two matters remained unresolved: first, the question of the width of those waters...and, secondly, the question of the precise juridical nature of coastal States' rights over the territorial sea. Some writers claimed that coastal States either had proprietorial rights in their territorial seas, or at least enjoyed sovereignty or plenary jurisdiction over them. The practice of many States supported this view: for example, by the early nineteenth century British and American jurisdictional claims were premised upon the existence of a belt of maritime territory surrounding a State, and the civil codes adopted in the middle of that century by several Latin American States treated territorial seas as integral parts of the State. On the other hand, States such as France and Spain did not claim ownership or sovereignty over the territorial sea, but merely jurisdictional competence over adjacent waters for specific purposes -- notably defence and the regulation of customs and fishing. These claims had not then been consolidated into a single claim to maritime territory -- indeed the distances over which jurisdiction was claimed often varied according to the subject matter of the regulation.... This approach was more easily reconciled with the existence of a right of innocent passage than the sovereignty doctrine, and found some enthusiastic advocates. The theory was expounded in various forms -- neatly summarised, along with other theories, in Fauchille's *Traite de droit international public* (1925) -- but found its classic exposition in an article by La Pradelle in 1898. He argued that States enjoy a `bundle of servitudes'...over coastal waters permitting them to exercise jurisdiction in the measure necessary for the protection of their interests, and accepted the corollary that if the existence of a right of jurisdiction were to be questioned the burden lay upon the coastal State to prove that it did exist -- quite the opposite of the presumption flowing from the `sovereignty' doctrine.

These two broad approaches coexisted for several decades. They were considered by the English Court for Crown Cases Reserved in the *Franconia* case..., in which the question of the status of the territorial sea arose. Keyn was the commander of the German ship *Franconia*, which collided with the British ship *Strathclyde* two and a half miles off Dover beach, causing the death of thirty-eight of the *Stranthclyde's* passengers. Keyn was prosecuted for manslaughter and convicted by an English court. He appealed on the ground that the court lacked jurisdiction to try him, because he was a foreigner and at the material time sailing on a foreign ship on the high seas. The Crown maintained that the collision, having occurred within three miles of the shore, had occurred within the realm and so within British jurisdiction. After an extensive review of the conflicting authorities, contained in a set of judgments of great learning, the Court for Crown Cases Reserved decided by a majority of seven to six...to allow the appeal. The common thread running through the majority judgments was the view that even though Great Britain might be entitled to claim a territorial sea, it had not expressly done so, and until legislation repaired the omission British jurisdiction did not extend to foreigners and foreign ships beyond British shores. Some judges went further and argued that Britain could not, consistently with international law, apply the whole of its criminal law to foreigners in the territorial sea.

The *Franconia* decision was clearly not expected by the British government, and two years later English law was brought back into line with the view of international law which Great Britain had taken throughout the nineteenth century, by the enactment of the Territorial Waters Jurisdiction Act, 1878. That Act reaffirmed the `rightful jurisdiction' of the Crown over territorial waters, which were `deemed by international law to be within the territorial sovereignty of Her Majesty'. This position has been consistently adhered to ever since, although, as will be seen, the Act was the subject of much critical comment, and there were occasional doubts on the question expressed privately within the British government.

Doubts concerning the juridical nature of the territorial sea survived into the present century. States such as France, Italy, Russia and the Ottoman Empire continued to claim separate jurisdictional zones for various purposes, rather than sovereignty and plenary jurisdiction over a belt of maritime territory as was claimed, for example, by the countries of the British Empire (which had agreed upon a single three-mile limit for all jurisdictional purposes at the 1923 Imperial Conference), the United

States, the Netherlands and the Scandinavian States. Jurists were similarly divided in their views, as is evident, for instance, from the debates of the International Law Association and the Committee of Experts preparing for the Hague Codification Conference, both in the 1920s. With hindsight it is possible to see that the trend in doctrine and State practice was steadily towards recognition of coastal States' sovereignty over their territorial seas. Governments had repeatedly had the question of the juridical status of those waters put before them directly, in the context of various diplomatic exchanges from the early nineteenth century onwards, and indirectly through the deliberations of influential bodies such as the Institute of International Law. And in the twenty years preceding the 1930 Hague Conference the question had arisen in several connections -- notably in relation to the limits of neutrality and naval warfare during World War I; the work of the 1919 Conference on Aerial Navigation...; the dispute over the application of the United States' liquor laws to foreign ships...; and the preparation for the Hague Conference itself. In each case, it was evident that support for the principle of coastal State sovereignty over the territorial sea was growing.

The replies of governments to the Schedule of Points circulated before the Hague Conference showed that most respondents preferred the sovereignty doctrine. Some, such as France and Poland, considered the juridical state of the territorial sea as unsettled; and other States which had not replied to the Schedule, such as Greece and Czechoslovakia, argued at the conference against the ascription of sovereignty to the coastal State. But it was clear that, despite some reluctance to use a word so burdened with implications and overtones deriving from its use in connection with land territory, there was general agreement that the principle of coastal sovereignty should be included in any draft treaty. The final text forwarded to the conference by its Territorial Waters Committee accordingly provided that:

> The territory of a State includes a belt of sea described in this Convention as the territorial sea. Sovereignty in this belt is exercised subject to the conditions prescribed by the present Convention and other rules of international law.

The text was not adopted as a convention, mainly because of a failure to agree on the vital question of the breadth of the territorial sea. Nonetheless, there has been no serious challenge to the principle of coastal sovereignty over the territorial sea since the Hague Conference, and the 1930 conference may fairly be regarded as the occasion when the doubts over the sea's juridical status which had persisted right up to the preceding decade, were finally dispelled.

In the years following the Hague Conference, the few States which had not espoused the sovereignty doctrine came to do so, as did States gaining their independence. That is not to say that the municipal law of every State treats the sea in the same way as the land, so that, for example, municipal laws automatically apply there. Thus British territorial waters remain outside the `realm', and British laws apply therein only to the extent specifically provided. But for the purposes of international law, States have sovereignty and the plenary jurisdiction which is its concomitant, over the territorial sea. This principle was sufficiently well established in State practice for Francois to adopt it in his report to the ILC in 1950, and for it to survive, almost unquestioned, throughout the ILC debates and the 1958 Geneva Conference. Such discussion as there was centered upon the relationship between coastal State sovereignty and the right of innocent passage.... In order to emphasise that the right of innocent passage rendered coastal States' rights less extensive than those over their land territory, the Hague formula was amended to provide that:

> (1) The sovereigny of a State extends, beyond its land territory and its internal waters, to a belt of sea adjacent to its coast, described as the territorial sea.
>
> (2) This sovereignty is excercised subject to the provisions of these articles and to other rules of international law.

A substantially similar provision, in which there has been inserted a reference to archipelagic waters after that to internal waters, appears in the Law of the Sea Convention [of 1982].

ED. NOTE: The above discussion of "sovereignty" over the territorial sea seems to suggest that, apart from the doctrine of force majeure, the major difference from sovereignty over the land is the doctrine of innocent passage, to be discussed in detail subsequently. Thus it follows that the jurisdiction of a coastal State extends not only on the surface of the water, but to the airspace above, the water column itself, and to the submerged lands below the territorial sea.

The first formal position taken by the United States with respect to its territorial sea is reflected in the following note.

NOTE FROM SECRETARY OF STATE THOMAS JEFFERSON TO THE BRITISH MINISTER, MR. HAMMOND, NOVEMBER 8, 1793, 1 Moore, International Law Digest 702-703 (1926)

The President of the United States, thinking that, before it shall be finally decided to what distance from our seashores the territorial protection of the United States should be exercised, it will be proper to enter into friendly conferences and explanations with the powers chiefly interested in the navigation of the seas on our coasts, and relying that convenient occasions may be taken for these hereafter, finds it necessary in the meantime to fix provisionally on some distance for the present government of these questions. You are sensible that very different opinions and claims have been heretofore advanced on this subject. The greatest distance to which any respectable assent among nations has been at any time given, has been the extent of human sight, estimated at upwards of twenty miles, and the smallest distance, I believe, claimed by any nation whatever, is the utmost range of a cannon ball, usually stated at one sea league. Some intermediate distances have also been insisted on, and that of three sea leagues has some authority in its favor. The character of our coast, remarkable in considerable parts of it for admitting no vessels of size to pass near the shores, would entitle us, in reason, to as broad a margin of protected navigation as any nation whatever. Reserving, however, the ultimate extent of this for future deliberation, the President gives instructions to the officers acting under his authority to consider those heretofore given them as restrained for the present to the distance of one sea league or three geographical miles from the seashores. This distance can admit of no opposition, as it is recognized by treaties between some of the powers with whom we are connected in commerce and navigation, and is as little, or less, than is claimed by any of them on their own coasts.

For the jurisdiction of the rivers and bays of the United States, the laws of the several States are understood to have made provision, and they are, moreover, as being landlocked, within the body of the United States.

ED. NOTE: In 1923, the Supreme Court of the United States added its voice to the debate. In Cunard v. Mellon, 262 U.S. 101 (1923), a case in which the United States applied its National Prohibition Act against a British vessel within the territorial sea, the Court said, in part:

> It is now settled in the United States and recognized elsewhere that the territory subject to its jurisdiction includes the land areas under its dominion and control, the ports, harbors, bays and other enclosed arms of the sea along its coasts and a marginal belt of the sea extending from the coastline outward a marine league, or three geographical miles.... This, we hold, is the territory which the [18th] Amendment designates as its field of operation and the

designation is not of a part of this territory but of "all" of it.

2. THE BREADTH OF THE TERRITORIAL SEA

Again, as the above excerpts show, there was no agreement among nations with regard to the breadth of the territorial sea. But there had been a growing correspondence of claims. By 1900 the 3 mile limit had been adopted or acknowledged by 20 of 21 States claiming a territorial sea. By the time of the Hague Conference in 1930, only a small part of the coastal States attending claimed more than 3 miles. However, the conference was unable to adopt any provision on the breadth in international law.

It was estimated that 20 of the 38 States attending that conference would have accepted the three mile limit, or three miles of territorial sea with a contiguous zone. The merchant tonnage of the nations supporting that limit at the time was more than 70% of the world total. The question, then, was the breadth of the territorial sea, and not the right of a coastal State to claim one. In 1951, this right was clearly spelled out by the International Court, subject to the limitations placed upon the coastal State by international law. In the Anglo-Norwegian fisheries case, the Court said:

> "The delimitation of sea areas has always an international aspect; it cannot be dependent merely upon the will of the coastal State as expressed in its municipal law. Although it is true that the act of delimitation is necessarily a unilateral act, because only the coastal State is competent to undertake it, the validity of the delimitation with regard to other States depends upon international law."

Between 1930 and 1958, several significant events took place influencing the future of negotiations on the breadth of the territorial sea. Some of these are referred to here.

Before listing them, it should be understood that there was constant pressure upon States, internally and externally, to extend their jurisdiction further seaward. The main pressure upon States was not simple greed. It was the need to protect their coastal fisheries, which by that time had begun to be depleted by foreign fleets. The simplest, but not the best, way to do this is by making claims to extended territorial seas.

In 1947, for example, Chile issued a presidential proclamation aimed primarily at the continental shelf. But in its terms, the proclamation asserted "protection and control" over the seas between the coast and a distance of 200 nautical miles. This declaration, however specifically protected the right of free navigation on the high seas.

This was followed by a similar declaration by Peru in that same year. Peru declared "national sovereignty and jurisdiction" to a distance of 200 nautical miles. This declaration, also, protected navigation.

In 1951, Chile, Ecuador and Peru issued a document known as the Santiago Declaration proclaiming "as a rule of their international maritime policy, the exclusive sovereignty and jurisdiction corresponding to each of them over the ocean adjacent to the coasts of their respective countries up to a minimum distance of 200 marine miles." This language, of course, was much stronger, and the United States filed a protest with each of them.

The maritime powers were, of course, growing uneasy with this turn of events. But in a sense, the action of these Latin American States had in fact been triggered by the United States. As we will discuss later, in 1945, then President Harry Truman issued a proclamation declaring the continental shelf adjacent to U.S. coasts to appertain to the United States and to be subject to its jurisdiction and control. The Latin States cited this unilateral action as a basis for their own extended claims. If the United States can unilaterally lay claim to vast areas of submerged lands to assume control over its hydrocarbon resources, they argued, why is it not acceptable for them to do the same to protect their living resources from exploitation by others?

At any rate, the United States and other maritime powers had other interests that were threatened by extended claims to territorial sea jurisdiction. Foremost among these was national security. The United States relied heavily for its defense upon the growing power of its navy. To the extent that extended coastal State claims carved large areas from the high seas, and territorialized them in one form or another, the mobility of navies was reduced. Thus we can see the beginning of a long struggle between these competing interests: national security and resource jurisdiction.

This, then, was the situation leading up to the 1958 Geneva Conference. We shall examine, first, the preparatory work of the International Law Commission, then the Conference itself. We next turn to the next attempt at agreement, the Second United Nations Conference on the Law of the Sea in 1960. We will end our investigation with a discussion of the provisions of the Third United Nations Conference on the Law of the Sea and the provisions of the 1982 United Nations Convention on the Law of the Sea.

a. THE FIRST AND SECOND UNITED NATIONS CONFERENCES ON THE LAW OF THE SEA (1958 and 1960)

We should first note that the 1958 convention avoided the question of the breadth of the territorial sea.

CONVENTION ON THE TERRITORIAL SEA AND THE CONTIGUOUS ZONE

Article 1

1. The sovereignty of a State extends, beyond its land territory and its internal waters, to a belt of sea adjacent to its coast, described as the territorial sea.

2. This sovereignty is exercised subject to the provisions of these articles and to other rules of international law.

. . . .

Article 6

The outer limit of the territorial sea is the line every point of which is at a distance from the nearest point of the baseline equal to the breadth of the territorial sea.

* * * * *

The records of the preliminary work of the International Law Commission indicates the nature of the disagreements and different points of view that prevented a specific distance from appearing in the convention.

INTERNATIONAL LAW COMMISSION, 1956 Commentary

Draft Article 3

1. The Commission recognizes that international practice is not uniform as regards the delimitation of the territorial sea.

2. The Commission considers that international law does not permit an extension of the territorial sea beyond twelve miles.

3. The Commission, without taking any decision as to the breadth of the territorial sea up to that limit, notes, on the one hand, that many States have fixed a breadth greater than three miles and, on the other hand, that many States do not recognize such a breadth when their own territorial sea is less.

Commentary

(1) At its seventh session the Commissionn had adopted certain guiding principles concerning the limits of the territorial sea, but before drafting the final text of an article on this subject, it had wished to see the comments of governments.

(2) First of all, the Commission had recognized that international practice was not uniform as regards the traditional limitation of the territorial sea to three miles. In the opinion of the Commission, that was an incontrovertible fact.

(3) Next the Commission had stated that international law did not justify an extension of the territorial sea beyond twelve miles. In its opinion, such an extension infringed upon the principle of the freedom of the seas, and was therefore contrary to international law.

(4) Finally, the Commission had stated that it took no decision as to the breadth of the territorial sea up to the limit of twelve 12 miles. Some members held that as the rule fixing the breadth of the territorial sea at three miles had been widely applied in the past and was still maintained by a number of important maritime States, it should, in the absence of any other rule of equal authority, be regarded as recognized by international law and binding on all States. That view was not supported by the majority of the Commission; at its seventh session, however, the Commission did not succeed in reaching agreement on any other limit. The extension by a State of its territorial sea to a breadth of between three and twelve miles was not characterized by the Commission as a breach of international law. Such an extension would be valid for any other State which did not object to it, and a fortiori for any State which recognized it tacitly or by treaty, or was a party to a judicial or arbitral decision recognizing the extension. A claim to a territorial sea not exceeding 12 miles in breadth could be sustained erga omnes by any State, if based on historic rights. But subject to such cases, the Commission by a small majority declined to question the right of other States not to recognize an extension of the territorial sea beyond the three-mile limit.

(5) At its eighth session the Commission resumed its study of this problem in the light of the comments by Governments. Those comments showed a wide diversity of opinion, and the same diversity was noted within the Commission. Several proposals were made. They are referred to below in the order in which they were put to the vote. Some members were of the opinion that it was for each coastal State, in the exercise of its sovereign powers, to fix the breadth of its territorial sea. They considered that in all cases where the delimitation of the territorial sea was justified by the real needs of the coastal State, the breadth of the territorial sea was in conformity with international law; this would cover the case of those States which had fixed the breadth at between three and twelve miles.

Another opinion was that the Commission should recognize that international practice was not uniform as regards limitation of the territorial sea at three miles, but would not authorize an extension of the territorial sea beyond twelve miles. A third opinion was that the Commission should recognize that every coastal State was entitled to a territorial sea of a breadth of at least three, but not exceeding twelve, miles. If, within those limits, the breadth was not determined by long usage, it should not exceed what was necessary for satisfying the justifiable interests of the State, taking into account also the interests of other States in maintaining the freedom of the high seas and the breadth generally applied in the region. In the case of a dispute, the question should, at the request of either of the parties, be referred to the International Court of Justice. A fourth opinion was reflected in a proposal to state that the breadth of the territorial sea could be determined by the coastal State in accordance with its economic and strategic needs within the limits of three and twelve miles, subject to recognition by States maintaining a narrower belt. According to a fifth opinion and proposal, the breadth of the territorial sea would be three miles, but a greater breadth should be recognized if based on customary law. Furthermore, any State might fix the breadth of its territorial sea at a higher figure than three miles, but such an extension could not be claimed against States which had not recognized it or had not adopted an equal or greater breadth. In no case could the breadth of the territorial sea exceed twelve miles.

(6) None of these proposals managed to secure a majority in the Commission, which, while recognizing that it differs from the final articles, finally accepted, by a majority vote, the text included in this draft as article 3.

(7) The Commission noted that the right to fix the limit of the territorial sea at three miles was not disputed. It states that international law does not permit that limit to be extended beyond twelve miles. As regards this right to fix the limit between three and twelve miles, the Commission was obliged to note that international practice was far from uniform. Since several States have established a breadth of between three and twelve miles, while others are not prepared to recognize such extensions, the Commission was unable to take a decision on the subject, and expressed the opinion that the question should be decided by an international conference of plenipotentiaries.

(8) It follows from the foregoing that the Commission came out against claims to extend the territorial sea to a breadth which, in its view, jeopardizes the principle that has governed maritime law since Grotius, namely, the freedom of the high seas. On the other hand, the Commission did not succeed in fixing the limit between three and twelve miles.

(9) The Commission considered the possibility of adopting a rule that all disputes concerning the breadth of the territorial sea should be submitted to the compulsory jurisdiction of the International Court of Justice. The majority of the Commission, however, were unwilling to ask the Court to undertake the settlement of disputes on a subject regarding which the international community had not yet succeeded in formulating a rule of law. It did not wish to delegate and essentially legislative function to a juridical organ which, moreover, cannot render decisions binding on States other than the parties. For these reasons it considered that the question should be referred to the proposed conference.

RESOLUTION ADOPTED BY THE 1958 UNITED NATIONS CONFERENCE ON THE LAW OF THE SEA (A/CONF.13/L.56, No. VIII), April 27, 1958

The United Nations Conference on the Law of the Sea,

Considering that, on the basis of the report prepared by the International Law Commission, it has approved agreements and other instruments on the regime applicable to fishing and the conservation of the living resources of the high seas, the exploration of the continental shelf and the exploitation of its natural resources and other matters pertaining to the general regime of the high seas and to the free access of land-locked States to the sea,

Considering that it has not been able to reach agreement on the breadth of the territorial sea and some other matters which were discussed in connexion with this problem,

Recognizing that, although agreements have been reached on the regime applicable to fishing and the conservation of the living resources of the high seas, it has not been possible, in those agreements, to settle certain aspects of a number of inherently complex questions.

Recognizing the desirability of making further efforts at an appropriate time to reach agreement on questions of the international law of the sea, which have been left unsettled,

Resolves to request the General Assembly of the United Nations to study, at its thirteenth session, the advisability of convening a second international conference of plenipotentiaries for further consideration of the questions left unsettled by the present Conference.

ED. NOTE: In 1960, the conference referred to in that resolution was in fact convened. Despite concentrated effort, this second conference was unable to resolve the question of the breadth of the territorial sea. The following article by Arthur Dean, head of the U.S. delegation to that conference, sheds light on the difficulties involved and the reasons for failure.

Arthur H. Dean, THE SECOND GENEVA CONFERENCE ON THE LAW OF THE SEA: THE FIGHT FOR FREEDOM OF THE SEAS
54 A.J.I.L 751, 772-782 (1960)[3]

The second Conference, like the first Conference, was governed by the procedural rules adopted at the Conference and resembling United Nations rules in voting procedure. A Committee of the Whole was formed by all the states present for the purpose of discussing and debating the various proposals on the territorial sea and the contiguous fishing zone. This committee by a simple majority vote could adopt a report which would include proposals to the Plenary Session of the Conference, where an official convention could be adopted by the same delegates upon the affirmative vote of two-thirds of the states present and voting and not abstaining.

The concept of the fishing zone as originally proposed by Canada at the first Conference was formulated to permit coastal states to establish in the high seas exclusive coastal fishing jurisdiction without qualification in a zone out to 12 nautical miles from their coasts. At first the Canadians proposed that the territorial sea should remain at 3 miles, but after the United Kingdom and the United States shifted their support to a 6-mile territorial sea as a compromise, the Canadians adopted the same limit for the territorial sea with the fishing zone remaining at 12 miles. At the beginning of the second Conference the Canadians reintroduced this proposal, which granted the coastal state in the outer 6-mile zone "the same rights in respect of fishing and the exploitation of the living resources of the sea as it has in its territorial sea." Thus, in this zone, the coastal state allegedly would be free from any restrictions or conservation limitations which could otherwise become applicable to fishing in the

3. Reprinted with permission from 54 A.J.I.L. 772-782 (1960), published by the American Society of International Law.

high seas when invoked by other nations.

At the first Conference the United States had sponsored a proposal for a 6-mile fishing zone beyond a 6-mile territorial sea, subject to "historic" fishing rights in the outer 6 miles for vessels of states which could prove a practice of fishing in the area during a five-year period of time referred to as the "base period." Unless modified by subsequently negotiated agreements, these "historic" rights were to be perpetual. It was for this reason that Canada refused its support. A similar United States proposal early in the second Conference included a limitation that such historic rights would only permit fishing

> "for the same groups of species as were taken therein during the base period to an extent not exceeding in any year the annual average level of fishing carried on in the outer zone during the said period."

The concept of unlimited historic rights in the outer 6-mile fishing zone had divided Canada and the United States, but after extended negotiations between the chairmen of the two delegations during the conference, an agreement was reached on a compromise fishing proposal of April 8, 1960. This U.S.-Canadian compromise proposal was framed so as to suspend in favor of historic rights the exclusive coastal fishing jurisdiction during an interim "period of ten years from October 31, 1960." The vessels of those states which could now show that their fishing boats had made a "practice of fishing in the outer six miles of fishing zone" for the five-year base period January 1, 1953, to January 1, 1958, could continue to fish for the further ten year period indicated. After that period vessels of foreign nationals could not continue to have the right to fish even in the outer 6-mile zone without being expressly granted such rights in bilateral treaties with the coastal state. When no practice of fishing could be proved, the coastal state immediately could claim a 12-mile fishing jurisdiction.

A Soviet proposal at the beginning of the Conference would have left the question open by a purported flexible rule permitting each state to choose for itself any limit to the territorial sea from 3 to 12 miles and an exclusive fishing zone out to 12 miles. Of course, this proposal would result, in practice, in great pressure for extension of territorial sea limits to 12 miles in many critical areas of the world. For example, if states A and B have a common boundary and state A claimed a territorial sea of 12 miles and state B one of three miles, then the nationals of state B could not fish in state A's outer nine miles, but the nationals of state A could fish in state B's outer nine miles. Thus state B would be at a disadvantage unless it also extended its territorial sea or fishing zone to 12 miles.

A grave threat was presented by the so-called "18-Power" proposal of April 11, 1960, sponsored by Mexico, Indonesia, the Philippines, Ethiopia, Ghana, Guinea, Iraq, Iran, Jordon, Lebanon, Libya, Morocco, Saudi Arabia, Sudan, Tunisia, the U.A.R., Venezuela and Yemen, for a flexible territorial sea of 3 to 12 miles and an exclusive fishing zone of 12 miles. This proposal provided that any state which

> "has fixed the breadth of the territorial sea or contiguous fishing zone at less than 12 nautical miles, is entitled vis a vis any other State with a wider delimitation thereof, to exercise the same sovereignty or the rights in respect of fishing and the exploitation of the living resources of the sea as it has in its territorial sea] up to a limit equal to the limits fixed by that other State."

This "18-Power" proposal was substantially similar to an earlier "16-Power" proposal but with the added suppport of Mexico and Venezuela, and was realistically a replacement for the U.S.S.R. proposal, although the Soviets avoided official sponsorship and thereby defeat.

The "18-Power" proposal was put forward technically as the revision of the original Mexican proposal at the beginning of the Conference, which had provided a sliding scale of fishing-zone bonuses for territorial sea claims out to, but less than 12 miles. That is, the Mexican proposal would have permitted extension of the fishing zone to the following limits:

(a) Where the breadth of the territorial sea is from 3 to 6 miles, up to a limit of 18 miles;

(b) Where the breadth of the territorial sea is from 7 to 9 miles, up to a limit of 15 miles;

(c) Where the breadth of the territorial sea is from 10 to 11 miles, up to a limit of twelve miles.

Thus, a state would have an incentive to curtail its territorial sea if it wished to extend its fishing zone.

The U.S.-Canadian compromise "joint proposal" was sincerely designed to find a rule acceptable to the Conference, though admittedly at considerable expense to U.S. fishing interests. In the absence of treaty rights, it would necessitate immediately giving up the right to fish off foreign coasts within 6 miles, and between 6 and 12 miles except where the practice of fishing during the 5-year base period could be proved; it would necessitate giving up fishing rights within 12 miles everywhere after 10 years unless bilateral treaties with respect to such rights could be negotiated in the interim. Per contra, in the absence of any agreement, as nations unilaterally extend the breadths of their territorial seas and attempt to prevent foreign fishing therein, the fishing rights of American vessels might be gradually whittled away so that continued operation would be uneconomic. The sacrifice inherent in the joint proposal was offered in the hope of achieving agreement at the Conference on a territorial sea limited to 6 miles without increasing the contiguous fishing zone beyond 12 miles, while protecting American fishing vessels against unilateral claims for at least 10 years. Thus, it is not correct to say that security interests overrode all consideration of American fishing interests; it was a question of timing and balance.

The joint proposal was favorably received in the Committee of the Whole and was adopted by a vote of 43 in favor to 33 against, with 12 abstentions, out of a total of 76 nations voting. The proposal thus obtained more than the simple majority of votes required in the Committee of the Whole and became its proposal in its Report to the Plenary Session. Subsequently, this U.S.-Canadian joint proposal, embodied in the Report of the Committee of the Whole, after being amended, received support in the Plenary Session from 54 nations in favor, to 28 against, with a total of 82 nations voting and 5 abstentions. Thus, this proposal was only one negative vote short of a two-thirds majority as required in Plenary Session under the rules adopted by the Conference.

The support for this joint proposal as amended in Plenary Session compares favorably with the lack of support for the "10-Power" proposal, sponsored by Mexico, Venezuela, Indonesia, and the Arab states of Iraq, Lebanon, Morocco, Saudi Arabia, Sudan, U.A.R. and Yemen, provided that "all States participants in this Conference which had declared their independence prior to 24 October 1945" (the date the United Nations Charter entered into force) should "abstain from extending the present breadth of their territorial sea pending the consideration of this question" by the General Assembly or by another conference which might be called in the futures; in the meantime, however, the 12-mile fishing zone was to be recognized. Futhermore, those states coming into being after October 24, 1945, apparently could extend their territorial seas without limit.

This "10-Power" proposal was supported by the Soviet Union after its proposal was withdrawn. However, the active support of Ethiopia, Ghana, Iran, Jordan, Libya, the Philippines and Tunisia had been lost since the defeat of the "18-Power" proposal in the Committee of the Whole. The "10-Power" proposal fell 8 votes short of even simple majority when it received only 32 votes in favor, to 39 votes opposed, with 17 abstentions. Thus, this proposal, which would have permitted a chaos of extended territorial sea claims, received 22 votes less than the 54 votes received by the 6-mile territorial sea, 6-mile fishing zone joint proposal as amended.

In the Committee of the Whole, Argentina proposed an amendment to the U.S.-Canadian joint proposal that would have given to coastal states the right to claim preferential fishing rights in the high seas off its coasts beyond 12 miles, without the necessity of notifying fishing states in advance or sustaining the burden of proof before an impartial international commission:

> "In any area of the high seas adjacent to its exclusive fishing zone the coastal state shall have a preferential right of fishing, expecially if its economic development or the feeding of its population depends on that activity."

Proposals similar to this Argentine amendment had been submitted earlier by Peru, Cuba and Iceland.

In the Committee of the Whole, the Soviet bloc abstained on these proposed preferential right amendments, apparently because they are building huge fishing fleets which are intended to operate all over the world and invade the traditional fishing areas of other states on the high seas and close to other nations' shores. Naturally, the U.S.S.R. opposed proposals, such as the Cuban proposal, to give any preferential rights to coastal states. However, after losing their attempt to defeat the U.S. Canadian joint proposal in the Committee of the Whole, it understood that Soviet approaches were made to the Argentine Delegation to the effect that if the Argentinians would re-introduce their preferential coastal fishing proposal in Plenary Session the Soviet bloc and the Arab bloc would vote in its favor. This action was, of course, an attempt to defeat Canada, the United States, the Western European fishing states and Japan, in the knowledge that this proposal to give preferential fishing rights to coastal states beyond a 6-mile territorial sea and 6-mile contiguous fishing zone could not be acceptable to them.

To meet sincere desires of the Latin American states for such preferential rights and avoid the threat of Soviet obstructionist tactics, the United States met with Canada and the Western European and Latin American countries involved. At the meeting the United States offered support for an amendment to the joint proposal embodied in the Report of the Committee of the Whole to the following effect: (a) that the procedure of settlement under the auspices of an International Commission set up by Article 9 of the 1958 Convention on Fishing and Conservation of the Living Resources of the High Seas should apply to claims by the coastal state to preferential right in the high seas; and (b) that the Commission should hear evidence on both sides as to the scientific proof justifying preferential fishing rights for the coastal state in the high seas beyond the 12-mile limit before making its decision.

Subject to the approval of their respective foreign ministries, the proposed amendment appeared to be acceptable to Argentina, Cuba, Guatemala, El Salvador, Chile and Ecuador. With this amendment El Salvador and Ecuador agreed to abstain, and the others appeared disposed to vote in favor of the thus amended joint proposal embodied in the Report of the Committee of the Whole. Brazil, Colombia, Dominican Republic, Honduras and Costa Rica were already in favor of the U.S.-Canadian proposal. Venezuela and Panama were opposed and so remained.

Consequently, Brazil, Cuba, and Uruguay sponsored an "amendment" to the joint proposal as adopted by the Committee of the Whole, providing that

> "the coastal State has the faculty of claiming preferential fishing rights in any area of the high

seas adjacent to its exclusive fishing zone when it is scientifically established that a special situation or condition makes the exploitation of the living resources of the high seas in that area of fundamental importance to the economic development of the coastal State or the feeding of its population."

In such a case, however, "any other State concerned may request that any claim be determined by the special Commission" under Article 9 of the Convention in order to

> "determine on the basis of scientific criteria whether special conditions exist, after a hearing at which both the coastal State and the fishing State concerned shall have the right to present all relevant evidence, technical, geographical, biological, and economic."

The Brazil-Cuba-Uruguay amendment also provided that the provisions on historic fishing rights and the 10-year phasing out period "shall not apply or may be varied between States which enter into bilateral, multilateral or regional agreements" relating to fishing. This provision had been requested by Italy and Korea as being essential to obtain their favorable votes because of disputes with Yogoslavia and Japan, respectively.

The Brazil-Cuba-Uruguay amendments were put to the vote in Plenary Session all together as an "amendment" to the joint proposal "as adopted by the Committee of the Whole." As a separate issue, this Brazil-Cuba-Uruguay amendment received over a two-thirds' majority of the votes with 58 in favor, to 19 opposed, with 10 abstentions. It should be noted that this was also a two-thirds' majority of the nations present.

Thereupon, Japan, which had previously advised the writer that it would vote in favor of the joint proposal, stated that she would have to abstain because of objections from their fishing interests to the Brazil-Cuba-Uruguay amendment. Japan is the most important fishing state in the world, with an annual fish catch reported at over 5-1/2 million metric tons live weight, more than twice that of the United States. Japan advocates unrestricted right to fish up to 3 miles off the coasts of other countries, and, therefore, in the first place had only agreed reluctantly to the U.S.-Canadian 6-mile territorial sea plus a 6-mile fishing zone proposal.

Naturally, many of the new Southeast Asia States, such as India, Burma, Laos, Cambodia and Viet-Nam wished to prevent other countries from fishing within 12 miles of their coasts, or in the perimeters of their archipelagos in the case of the Philippines and Indonesia. Nevertheless, Laos and Viet-Nam voted in favor of the amended joint proposal and Cambodia abstained.

A special problem arose with regard to Ecuador, which had enforced its claim to an exclusive fishing zone of 200 miles by seizing American fishing vessels operating within those limits off its coasts. Ecuador also asserted a claim to a 12-mile territorial sea. Ecuador argued that there could be no valid acquisition of historical fishing rights during any base period by any vessel of foreign nationals in the outer 6-mile zone off its coasts, because rights of this nature could not be obtained in the face of its domestic laws establishing the territorial sea and fishing zones in the high seas. They insisted that these Ecuadorian laws were valid even though not recognized by other nations.

This Ecuadorian thesis was destructive of the whole theory of the U.S.-Canadian compromise that states which had made a practice of fishing in the outer 6-mile zone off any coastal state in the base period of 1953 to 1958 could continue thus to fish for a further ten years. Naturally the Ecuadorian thesis was not acceptable to many distant-water fishing nations, which were already making a tremendous sacrifice in accepting the 10-year phase out period of fishing rights in the outer 6-mile zone in the high seas. These rights were regarded by these fishing nations as perpetual, as in the case of fishing rights in other parts of the high seas.

Fortunately, it developed after investigation that U.S. vessels were the only ones which could prove a practice of fishing in the base period in the outer 6-mile zone off the coast of Ecuador. Therefore, after consulting with our fishery advisers and the Department of State, the writer was able to propose to Ecuador that the United States would agree to refrain from taking the necessary evidentiary steps to perfect its rights to prove that a practice of fishing had existed during the period of 1953 to 1958 within 12 miles of Ecuador's coast. The practical effect of that offer was to assure Ecuador that, without regard to the validity of their municipal legislation, their exclusive fishing jurisdiction for 12 miles could be recognized immediately. The text of this proposed agreement appeared to be acceptable to Ecuador, and it was understood by the U.S. Delegation that Ecuador would abstain on the joint proposal adopted by the Committee of the Whole as modified by the Brazil-Cuba-Uruguay amendment in view of the proposed U.S. agreement.

However, a few days later, Ecuador insisted that the proposed U.S.-Ecuadorian agreement should apply to the past as well as the future, and that the writer, as Chairman of the United States Delegation, should sign a release on behalf of the United States and all U.S. nationals as to any claim for reimbursement of fines paid to Ecuador or for damages for losses and injuries sustained in the past seizures of American fishing vessels. It was explained to the representatives of Ecuador that a representative of the Executive Branch of the United States Government could not change or waive rights or obligations conferred or imposed by legislation passed by the Congress of the United States of America and lacked authority to waive private claims of U.S. nationals, and if such an agreement were made, it would be void. The evening before the final voting in Plenary Session it was understood that Ecuador had accepted this statement and would abstain on the joint proposal as modified by the Brazil-Cuba-Uruguay amendment in view of the proposed U.S. agreement.

The voting started in Plenary Session on the morning of April 26, and, once the voting started, it could not be interrupted as decreed in Rules 38 and 49 of the Conference Rules of Procedure. It was at that point that the Ecuador Delegation advised the Chairman of the U.S. Delegation that, unless a release as to all claims of the United States and its nationals was received immediately, Ecuador would not abstain, as had been understood, but would vote against the amended joint proposal.

There still would have been a two-thirds' majority if it had not been for the fact that Chile, which had previously indicated it would be free to vote for the joint proposal after adoption of the Brazil-Cuba-Uruguay amendment, subsequently stated that this was not possible. The Chilean delegate explained that Chile could not obtain from Peru a satisfactory written release from the obligations imposed under the 1952 Declaration on the Maritime Zone, to which Chile, Ecuador and Peru were parties, although Chile had previously understood that such a written release from Peru would be forthcoming. An agreement of 1954, supplementing the 1952 Declaration, had provided that each of the parties "undertake not to enter into any agreements, arrangements, or conventions which imploy a diminution of the sovereignty of the said zone [of 200 miles]."

Had either Chile or Ecuador merely abstained, there would have been 54 affirmative votes to 27 negative votes, with 6 abstentions, or a two-thirds' majority for the compromise proposal which had resulted from patient negotiations and sacrifices of many nations. Thus the success which could have been achieved at the Conference evaporated at the very last minute.

ED. NOTE: As can be seen in the above materials, the problem lurking behind the inability to reach agreement on the breadth of the territorial sea was primarily fishing. Coastal States in parts of the world where substantial fisheries were conducted quite naturally wished to have control over that fishing, in one way or another. The United States faced a number of problems in developing its own national policy regarding fishing. In the first place, the U.S. Government has always been suspicious of any attempts to broaden coastal State jurisdiction in any form. The concern was basically military in nature. The Defense Department feared that jurisdiction for any reason, in the adjacent belt of water, has a tendency to become jurisdiction for all purposes. This concept was sometimes referred to as "creeping jurisdiction". A claim to fishing jurisdiction to 200 nautical miles was seen, if accepted, to be an invitation to a 200 mile territorial sea at some subsequent point. If that were to occur, then many critical areas of oceans might be closed to the nation's naval vessels.

In addition to this concern, the establishment of a coherent fisheries policy in the United States is complicated by the fact that the U.S. is both a fisheries nation and a coastal State. Furthermore, there exists in the United States both a distant-water fishing industry, and a coastal fishing industry. The latter, obviously, would prefer broad coastal State jurisdiction in order to reserve the coastal fisheries to the U.S. fishing industry. On the other hand, the distant-water fishermen, such as those who fish for tuna off foreign coasts, would much prefer a narrow belt of coastal State jurisdiction. The 1960 effort was apparently an exercise in seeking to try to accomodate these conflicting needs, while at the same time protecting our national security interests.

But considering the fact that it is almost impossible to develop and apply rational conservation measures for fisheries in a belt as narrow as 12 miles, the 6 and 6 proposal of 1960 would probably have failed as a measure designed to conserve the fisheries, even though it addressed the military issue.

As the United States prepared for the Third United Nations Conference on the Law of the Sea, it was quite clear that the fisheries issue would have to be addressed in a different way than simply expanding the territorial sea. Mention was made in the last chapter concerning the concept known as the exclusive economic zone. This is a new concept that was crafted to deal with the problem. The materials that follow give an indication of some of the earlier approaches to the problem of the breadth of the territorial sea. Detailed analysis of how the fisheries are regulated in the EEZ will be deferred until a later chapter.

DRAFT ARTICLES ON THE BREADTH OF THE TERRITORIAL SEA, STRAITS, AND FISHERIES SUBMITTED BY THE UNITED STATES

U.N. Doc. A/AC.138/SC.ii/l.4
July 1971

Article I

1. Each state shall have the right, subject to the provisions of Article II [dealing with passage through straits used for international navigation], to establish the breadth of the territorial sea within limits of no more than 12 nautical miles, measured in accordance with the provisions of th 1958 Geneva Convention on the Territorial Sea and the Contiguous Zone.

ED. NOTE: Notice the reference to international straits in that draft article. The United States, while apparently willing to consider uniform agreement on a 12 mile territorial sea, was concerned with the fact that in enlarging the territorial sea from 3 to 12 miles through international agreement, would bring many important international straits which under a 3 mile limit would contain a high seas corridor within those straits, under the jurisdiction of one or more coastal States if the distance between the coasts were to be less than 24 miles. For that reason, U.S. acceptance of a 12 mile distance was linked to the necessity to have a special navigational regime for international straits, a subject that will be dealt with later in this chapter. The following excerpt by John R. Stevenson, the first head of the U.S. Delegation to the Law of the Sea Conference, makes allusion to that need.

John R. Stevenson, INTERNATIONAL LAW AND THE OCEANS
62 Dep't State Bull 339 (1970)

It appears that there is widespread support for fixing the breadth of the territorial sea and 12 nautical miles. However, the extension of the territorial sea to 12 miles would place many important international straits, which with a 3-mile limit have high seas running through them, within the territorial sea of the coastal state. This would mean that vessels could only traverse these straits in innocent passage; furthermore, there is no established right of innocent passage for aircraft in the airspace over straits within territorial waters. In the view of many countries this is not a satisfactory situation. The freedom of the seas would have a far more restrictive meaning indeed if rights to traverse straits are not clear and secure. A significant number of nations agree that this problem requires solution if a 12-mile territorial sea is to be accepted.

ED. NOTE: In addition to the problem cited above, Ambassador Stevenson also noted that there is another side to the equation as well. While maritime powers would not be likely to agree to the proposed extension unless the straits problem were addressed, coastal States who might view 12 miles as a limitation rather than extension of their competence would not be likely to accept that number unless their fisheries concerns were also addressed. Those concerns led to some extreme proposals early in the conference. An example follows.

ECUADOR: PROPOSAL ON THE TERRITORIAL SEA
U.N. Doc. A/CONF.62/C.2/L.10
16 July 1974

Article 1

1. The sovereignty of a coastal State extends beyond its coast and internal or archipelagic waters to an adjacent zone described as the territorial sea.

2. The sovereignty extends also to the sea-bed and subsoil of the territorial sea as well as to the corresponding air space.

3. Each State has the right to establish the breadth of the territorial sea up to a distance not exceeding 200 nautical miles, measured from the applicable baseline.

Article 2

The coastal State exercises its sovereignty over the territorial sea subject to the provisions of this Convention.

ED. NOTE: In introducing the above proposal, the delegate from Ecuador stated that this concept was based upon other declarations, such as the Santiago Declaration of 1952 (which was less than clear on the extent of coastal State sovereignty). In addition, he made clear that the extension he proposed was based upon economic reasons, and that while the reference was made to the territorial sea, it was not a reference to the "traditional" notion of sovereignty, but to a new notion that would be subject to certain norms yet to be worked out. He appeared to be trying to do two things at once. First, he had to take account of the fact that the territorial sea was viewed in his country as an important political issue. But second, he seemed to be hinting that Ecuador was willing to accept something less than full sovereignty if the zone was broad.

Brazil had a somewhat different problem. While it could be argued that Ecuador's vague claim to 200 miles was something less than full sovereignty (indeed, they recognized the usual high seas right to navigation), Brazil had formally claimed a full 200 mile territorial sea. Nonetheless, on the day following the Ecuadorian proposal, Brazil supported the Ecuadorian explanation, but still insisted that there should only be two zones: a national sea and, beyond that, an international sea. Clearly, countries such as these were struggling to rationalize and integrate the concepts referred to as the territorial sea and the exclusive economic zone, and to rationalize them with their own domestic laws.

As is shown in the following articles, the 12 mile territorial sea was eventually adopted in the new treaty. But keep in mind that the 12 mile limit was only acceptable to the degree that there were also acceptable provisions on straits and fisheries.

b. THE THIRD UNITED NATIONS CONFERENCE

1982 UNITED NATIONS CONVENTION ON THE LAW OF THE SEA

Article 3

Breadth of the territorial sea

Every State has the right to establish the breadth of the territorial sea up to a limit not exceeding 12 nautical miltes, measured from the baselines determined in accordance with this Convention.

Article 4

Outer limit of the territorial sea

The outer limit of the territorial sea is the line every point of which is at a distance from the nearest point of the baseline equal to the breadth of the territorial sea.

* * * * *

The following proclamation shows present U.S. policy on the breadth of the territorial sea.

December 28, 1988

BY THE PRESIDENT OF THE UNITED STATES OF AMERICA

A PROCLAMATION

International law recognizes that coastal nations may exercise sovereignty and jurisdiction over their territorial sea.

The territorial sea of the United States is a maritime zone extending beyond the land territory and internal waters of the United States over which the United States exercises sovereignty and jurisdiction over the territorial sea, as well as to its bed and subsoil.

Extension of the territorial sea by the United States to the limits permitted by international law will advance the national security and other significant interests of the United States.

NOW THEREFORE, I, RONALD REAGAN, by the authority vested in me as President by the Constitution of the United States of America, and in accordance with international law, do hereby proclaim the extension of the territorial sea of the United States of America, the Commonwealth of Puerto Rico, Guam, American Samoa, the United States Virgin Islands, and any other territory or possession over which the United States exercises sovereignty.

The territorial sea of the United States henceforth extends to 12 nautical miles from the baselines of the United States as determined in accordance with international law.

In accordance with international law, as reflected in the applicable provisions of the 1982 United Nations Convention on the Law of the Sea, within the territorial sea of the United States, the ships of all countries enjoy the right of innocent passage and the ships and aircraft of all countries enjoy the right of transit passage through international straits.

Nothing in this proclamation:

(a) extends or otherwise alters existing Federal or State law or any jurisdiction, rights, legal interests, or obligations derived therefrom; or

(b) impairs the determination in accordance with international law, of any maritime boundary of the United States with a foreign jurisdiction.

* * * *

3. PASSAGE OF VESSELS THROUGH JURISDICTIONAL ZONES

a. THE CONCEPT OF INNOCENT PASSAGE THROUGH THE TERRITORIAL SEA

i. GENERALLY

CONVENTION ON THE TERRITORIAL SEA AND THE CONTIGUOUS ZONE

Section III. Right of Innocent Passage

Sub-Section A. Rules applicable to all ships

Article 14

1. Subject to the provisions of these articles, ships of all States, whether coastal or not, shall enjoy the right of innocent passage through the territorial sea.

2. Passage means navigation through the territorial sea for the purpose either of traversing that sea without entering internal waters, or of proceeding to internal waters, or of making for the high seas from internal waters.

3. Passage includes stopping or anchoring, but only in so far as the same are incidental to

ordinary navigation or are rendered necessary for force majeure or by distress.

4. A passage is innocent so long as it is not prejudicial to the peace, good order or security of the coastal State. Such passage shall take place in conformity with these articles and with other rules of international law.

5. Passage of foreign fishing vessels shall not be considered innocent if they do not observe such laws and regulations as the coastal State may make and publish in order to prevent these vessels from fishing in the territorial sea.

6. Submarines are required to navigate on the surface and to show their flag.

Article 15

1. The coastal State must not hamper innocent passage through the territorial sea.

2. The coastal State is required to give appropriate publicity to any dangers to navigation, of which it has knowledge, within its territorial sea.

Article 16

1. The coastal State may take the necessary steps in its territorial sea to prevent passage which is not innocent.

2. In the case of ships proceeding to internal waters, the coastal State shall also have the right to take the necessary steps to prevent any breach of the conditions to which admission of those ships to those waters is subject.

3. Subject to the provisions of paragraph 4, the coastal State may, without discrimination amongst foreign ships, suspend temporarily in specified areas of its territorial sea the innocent passage of foreign ships if such suspension is essential for the protection of its security. Such suspension shall take effect only after having been duly published.

....

Article 17

Foreign ships exercising the right of innocent passage shall comply with the laws and regulations enacted by the coastal State in conformity with these articles and other rules of international law and, in particular, with such laws and regulations relating to transport and navigation.

ED. NOTE: The right of innocent passage does not extend to aircraft flying over the territorial sea. Air rights are covered by another convention.

In interpreting the 1958 provisions on innocent passage, the question necessarily becomes one of definition. How does one put content into "peace, good order and security"? Only by defining that phrase, however, can one decide whether a vessel's passage is "innocent". Does it refer to the manner of passage? The motive? Is the cargo on board a vessel relevant to the question?

In the deliberations leading to the adoption of the Convention, the United States took a very restrictive view. It thought that innocent passage should be limited to that which is not prejudicial to the security of the coastal State, meaning that there should be no military or other threat to its sovereignty. Other States tended to give the coastal State wide discretion in defining innocence. For example, it was proposed that passage is not innocent if it affects the "interests" of the coastal State. As a compromise between these two poles, India proposed adding the words "peace" and "good order". While these terms were not defined, it is clear that the interests being protected by their use fell somewhere between the two extremes.

Consider the following examples and identify which would, in your judgment, be justified under the 1958 provisions.

U.S. TEMPORARY SUSPENSION OF RIGHT OF INNOCENT PASSAGE NEAR AMCHITKA
65 Dept. State Bull. 599 (1971)

Following are notices by the Government of the United States of temporary suspension of right of innocent passage through territorial waters surrounding Amchitka Island.

FIRST NOTICE, NOVEMBER 1

Press relased 252 dated November 1

Pursuant to Article 15 of the 1958 Geneva Convention on the Territorial Sea and Contiguous Zone, the right of innocent passsage within three nautical miles of Amchitka Island...is suspended temporarily from 0001 X November 2, 1971 to 2400 X November 4, 1971, inclusive, Bering Sea Daylight time due to U.S. Atomic Energy Commission experiment.

SECOND NOTICE, NOVEMBER 4

Pursuant to Article 15 of the 1958 Convention on the Territorial Sea and the Contiguous Zone, the right of innocent passage within three nautical miles of Amchitka Island is suspended temporarily from 0001 X November 5, 1971, to 2400 X November 7, 1971, inclusive, Bering Sea Daylight time due to U.S. Atomic Energy Commission experiment.

* * * *

NIGERIAN PORTS AUTHORITY

HARBOUR MASTER'S NOTICE NO. 124 OF 1947

NOTICE OF PROHIBITED ZONE
6 International Legal Materials 682 (1967)[4]

Notice is hereby given that a Prohibited zone to all shipping including fishing boats has been established as follows:

[4]. Reprinted with permission from 6 I.L.M. 682 (1967), published by the American Society of International Law.

"East of a line...and a line parallel at a distance of twelve nautical miles from the coast of Nigeria until the international waters of the Republic of Cameroun are reached off the Calabar River."

* * * *

VIETNAM DECREE ON SEA SURVEILLANCE COMMUNIQUE OF THE MINISTRY OF FOREIGN AFFAIRS
REPUBLIC OF VIET NAM, APRIL 27, 1965
4 International Legal Materials 461 (1965)[5]

Due to the fact of a constant increasing infiltration by sea into the Republic of Viet Nam of Viet Cong personnel, arms, ammunition and various war supplies,

the Prime Minister has signed Decree No. 81/NG of the 27th of April 1965, by which the following measures have been decided upon to ensure the security and defense of the territorial waters of Viet-Nam:

I. - The territorial waters up to the three mile limit is declared a defensive sea area. The passage of vessels through the territorial sea of the Republic of Viet Nam which is prejudicial to the peace, good order or security of the Republic of Viet Nam is not considered as innocent passage and is forbidden by the law of the Republic of Viet Nam. Ships of any country operating within the territorial sea of the Republic of Viet Nam which are not clearly engaged in innocent passage are subject to visit and search, and may be subject to arrest and disposition, as provided by the law of the Republic of Viet Nam in conformity with accepted principles of international law.

Cargoes will be considered suspect unless it can be clearly established that they are destined for a port outside of the Republic of Viet Nam or a legitimate recipient in the Republic of Viet Nam. Cargoes will be considered particularly suspect if containing any of the items listed below.

1-) Weapons, ammunition, electrical and communications equipment.

2-) Primer, mine, gunpowder and other explosives.

3-) Chemical products which can serve military purposes.

4-) Medical supplies of Communist North Vietnam, Communist China or Soviet Bloc origin.

5-) Foodstuffs of Communist North Vietnam, China or Soviet Bloc origin.

i. INNOCENT PASSAGE OF WARSHIPS

There is no doubt that the concept of innocent passage applies to commercial vessels. It has not, over the years, been so clear that warships are entitled to innocent passage as well. As can be seen by the excerpts below, scholars were split on the issue. During the most recent conference, there were many debates on the issue with the maritime powers asserting that warships have always been so entitled, and many coastal States asserting the opposite or seeking to insert language in the new treaty to require warships to give prior notification and obtain prior consent before entering territorial waters.

---

5. Reprinted with permission from 4 I.L.M. 461 (1965), published by the American Society of International Law.

In this subsection we shall examine the 1958 convention on the topic, and in the next, consider the new treaty.

ED. NOTE: Hall, in his book on international law, takes the position that innocent passage does not extend to vessels of war. It is his view that the concept was designed to enhance commerce. Not being a commercial vessel, the risks, he says, of allowing free access by warships to the territorial waters of another State are not compensated by any general benefit to any but a few maritime States. Thus, he concludes, a coastal State has the right to refuse access to its territorial waters by such vessels. Hall, International Law (8th ed., by Higgins, 1924) at 198. This, of course, is not the view of the United States today.

Colombos has noted that the question of innocent passage of warships is controversial. He thinks, however, that the better view appears to be "that such user should not be denied in time of peace when the territorial waters are so placed that passage through them is necessary for international traffic." This intermediate posisition is contrary to the position of the United States that warships enjoy an unqualified right of innocent passage through the territorial sea. Colombos, "International Law of the Sea", Longmans, 1961, at 114.

REPORT OF THE INTERNATIONAL LAW COMMISSION, 1954

Article 26

Passage

1. Save in exceptional circumstances, warships shall have the right of innocent passage through the territorial sea without previous authorization or notification.

2. the coastal State has the right to regulate the conditions of such passage. It may prohibit such passage in the circumstances envisaged in article 20.

3. Submarines shall navigate on the surface.

4. There must be no interference with the passage of warships through straits used for international navigation between two parts of the high seas.

NOTE: This language did not survive, however, and the article the Commission finally submitted to the Conference read as follows:

Article 24

The coastal State may make the passage of warships through the territorial sea subject to previous authorization or notification. Normally it shall grant innocent passage subject to their observance of the provisions of articles 17 and 18.

This version of "passage" failed, during the Conference, to obtain the two thirds majority needed for passage, and only article 23, below, received the necessary majority. But in its commentary to draft article 24, the ILC indicated that the rules of innocent passage set forth in subsection A (Rules applicable to all ships) were in fact applicable to warships. Since article 24 was not adopted, the situation was left confused.

CONVENTION ON THE TERRITORIAL SEA AND THE CONTIGUOUS ZONE

Article 23

If any warship does not comply with the regulations of the coastal State concerning passsage through the territorial sea and disregards any request for compliance which is made to it, the coastal State may require the warship to leave the territorial sea.

ED. NOTE: The structure of the treaty lends support in favor of innocent passage for warships. Section III of the treaty deals with innocent passage. Subsection A contains the rules for *all* ships. In this subsection we find the rule that requires submarines to navigate on the surface. It is the same subsection that grants the right of innocent passage. Since at that time the only submarines were military vessels, the implication is that warships are entitled to innocent passage. Subsection C contains the "Rule applicable to warships". But the only rule is that contained in article 23. It can be argued that this rule does not preclude a warship from innocent passage, but only provides for a coastal State remedy if a warship does not comply with regulations the coastal State clearly has the power to impose. It makes clear that, because of the special considerations due to warships, the only measure the coastal State may take is to require the warship to leave.

Regardless of such arguments, States continued to enact laws regarding the passage of warships through their territorial waters, such as the following.

THE SUDAN TERRITORIAL WATERS AND CONTINENTAL SHELF ACT, 1970
(1970 Act No. 106)

Chapter II, Art. 8(3)

The passage of military vessels in the territorial waters shall be subject to previous permission and the Government may take all necessary action against ships committing any breach, and submarines shall navigate on the surface and show the flag of the nation to which they belong.

NOTE: No agreement could be reached on different language in the 1982 Convention. See articles 30, 31 and 32. The debate concerning warships raged throughout the Third United Nations Conference on the Law of the Sea, without reaching any satisfactory resolution of the issue. Both sides remained adamant and refused to compromise. At the end of the Conference, several amendments were offered up. An amendment proposed by Gabon (A/CONF.62/L.97) would have added language to article 21 (Laws and regulations of the coastal State relating to innocent passage) to permit the coastal State to adopt laws and regulations in respect of "navigation of warships, including the right to require prior authorization and notification for passage through the territorial sea." This proposal, of course, was strenuously opposed by the maritime powers. It appeared that the issue would go to the vote. But in the final moments, Gabon agreed to withdraw the amendment on the promise that the President of the Conference would read the following statement into the record, which he did.

> "Although the sponsors of the amendment...had proposed the amendment with a view to clarifying the text of the Convention, in response to the President's appeal they have agreed not to press it to a vote. They would, however, like to reaffirm that their decision is without prejudice to the rights of coastal States to adopt measures to safeguard their security interests, in accordance with articles 19 and 25 of the Convention."

Since the articles referred to had already been agreed to, the maritime States felt that this statement added nothing to the law. Among most States, this statement is construed as allowing innocent passage of warships. Nonetheless, since the completion of the treaty, States have continued to enact laws requiring prior authorization or notification or both. While some States may continue to dispute the issue under international law, U.S. law is clear on the subject.

UNITED STATES v. CONROY
589 F.2d 1258 (5th Cir. 1979)

[This case involved the seizure of a vessel by the U.S. Coast Guard, with Haiti's oral consent, within Haitian territorial waters. On the applicable international law, the court made the following comments.]

Our statutory interpretation of the Coast Guard authority, premised on the concurring opinion of Mr. Justice Brandeis in Maul, is implicity supported by principals of international law that justify law enforcement activities of the Coast Guard in foreign waters. International law is part of our domestic law.... The possible application of the law of nations to supplement the statute is consistent with the statement in the House of Representatives report, "The powers conferred by this act are not to be construed to affect any other powers conferred by existing law."...

The law of nations classifies Coast Guard vessels as warships. Such vessels belong to the State, are under the direction of a military commander and manned by a military crew, and legally bear the ensign of the national navy....

Early interpretations of the law of nations denied the right of innocent passage of warships; it was thought that armed vessels did not "enjoy an absolute legal right to pass through a state's territorial waters any more than an army may cross the land territory," P. Jessup, The Law of the Territorial Waters and Maritime Jurisdiction 120 (1927), and prior permission had to be obtained. Until 1959, a regulation issued by the United States Office of the Chief of Naval Operations provided "Naval vessels should not be navigated in or near such claimed territorial waters without having obtained prior authorization from higher authority." 4 Whiteman's Digest of International Law 417 (1965).

The United States sponsored Convention on the Territorial Sea and the Contiguous Zone entered into force in 1964; the United States Senate had previously ratified the Convention in 1960, and the United States had signed it in 1961. 15 U.S.T. 1606, T.I.A.S. No. 5639 (1958). Haiti is also a party to the Convention. Thus the Convention represents existing U.S. policy, at least with respect to other party nations.

After much debate, the draftsmen of the multilateral treaty rejected any requirement of previous authorization by a coastal state for the entry of a warship into its territorial waters.... Article 14(1) of the Convention on the Territorial Sea and the Contiguous Zone states simply, "Subject to the provisions of these articles, ships of all States, whether coastal or not, shall enjoy the right of innocent passage through the territorial sea.".... Article 16(1) provides that the coastal State may take "the necessary measures in its territorial sea to prevent passage which is not innocent." No distinction is made between warships and other vessels.

At least between the parties to the Convention, such as the United States and Haiti, a warship of one nation may enter the territorial waters of another without first giving notification and receiving authorization. Ratification of the Convention by the United States manifests implicit authorization for its warships to do what the warships of other nations do. The DAUNTLESS was not, of course, on a hostile mission. Indeed, it bears emphasis that, despite the fact that presumeably no consent by

Haitian authority was required under the terms of the treaty, permission was in fact obtained. Therefore, in the ensuing search, there was a conjunction of implicit recognition by the United States Government of the power of its warship to make the search, and explicit approval by the Haitian Government

....

iii. INNOCENT PASSAGE UNDER THE 1982 CONVENTION

1982 UNITED NATIONS CONVENTION ON THE LAW OF THE SEA

PART II

TERRITORIAL SEA AND CONTIGUOUS ZONE

SECTION 3

INNOCENT PASSAGE IN THE TERRITORIAL SEA

Subsection A. Rules applicable to all ships

Article 17

Right of innocent passage

Subject to this Convention, ships of all States, whether coastal or land-locked, enjoy the right of innocent passage through the territorial sea.

Article 18

Meaning of Passage

1. Passage means navigation through the territorial sea for the purpose of:

(a) traversing that sea without entering internal waters or calling at a roadstead or port facility outside internal waters;

(b) proceeding to or from internal waters or a call at such roadstead or port facility.

2. Passage shall be continuous and expeditious. However, passage includes stopping and anchoring but only in so far as the same are incidental to ordinary navigation or are rendered necessary by force majeure or distress or for the purpose of rendering assistance to persons, ships or aircraft in danger of distress.

Article 19

Meaning of innocent passage

1. Passage is innocent so long as it is not prejudicial to the peace, good order or security of the coastal State. Such passage shall take place in conformity with this Convention and with other rules of

international law.

2. Passage of a foreign ship shall be considered prejudicial to the peace, good order or security of the coastal State if in the territorial sea it engages in any of the following activities:

(a) any threat or use of force against the sovereignty, territorial integrity or political independence of the coastal State, or in any manner in violation of the principles of international law embodied in the Charter of the United Nations;

(b) any exercise or practice with weapons of any kind;

(c) any act aimed at collecting information to the prejudice of the defence or security of the coastal State;

(d) any act of propaganda aimed at affecting the defence or security of the coastal State;

(e) the landing, launching or taking on board of any military device;

(g) the loading or unloading of any commodity, currency or person contrary to the customs, fiscal, immigration or sanitary laws and regulations of the coastal State;

(h) any act of wilful and serious pollution contrary to this Convention;

(i) any fishing ativities;

(j) the carrying out of research or survey activities;

(k) any act aimed at interfering with any systems of communication or any other facilities or installation of the coastal State;

(l) any other activity not having a direct bearing on passage.

Article 20

Submarines and other underwater vehicles

In the territorial sea, submarines and other underwater vehicles are required to navigate on the surface and show their flag.

Article 21

Laws and regulations of the coastal State relating to innocent passage

1. The coastal State may adopt laws and regulations, in conformity with the provisions of this Convention and other rules of international law, relating to innocent passage through the territorial sea, in respect of all or any of the following:

(a) the safety of navigation and the regulation of maritime traffic;

(b) the protection of navigational aids and facilities and other facilities or installations;

(c) the protection of cables and pipelines;

(d) the conservation of the living resources of the sea;

(e) the prevention of infringement of the fisheries laws and regulations of the coastal State;

(f) the preservation of the environment of the coastal State and the prevention, reduction and control of pollution thereof;

(g) marine scientific research and hydrographic surveys;

(h) the prevention of the infringement of the customs, fiscal, immigration or sanitary laws or regulations of the coastal State;

2. Such laws and regulations shall not apply to the design, construction, manning or equipment of foreign ships unless they are giving effect to generally accepted international rules or standards.

3. The coastal State shall give due publicity to all such laws and regulations.

4. Foreign ships exercising the right of innocent passage through the territorial sea shall comply with all such laws and regulations and all generally accepted international regulations relating to the prevention of collisions at sea.

Article 22

Sea lanes and traffic separation schemes

1. The coastal State may, where necessary having regard to the safety of navigation, require foreign ships exercising the right of innocent passage through their territorial sea to use such sea lanes and traffic separation schemes as it may designate or prescribe for the regulation of the passage of ships.

2. In particular, tankers, nuclear-powered ships and ships carrying nuclear or other inherently dangerous or noxious substances or materials may be required to confine their passage to such sea lanes.

3. In the designation of sea lanes and traffic separation schemes under this article, the coastal State shall take into account:

(a) the recommendations of the competent international organization;

(b) any channels customarily used for international navigation;

(c) the specific characteristics of particular ships and channels; and

(d) the density of traffic.

4. The coastal State shall clearly indicate such sea lanes and traffic separation schemes on charts to which due publicity shall be given.

Article 23

Foreign nuclear-powered ships and ships carrying nuclear or other inherently dangerous or noxious substances

Foreign nuclear-powered ships and ships carrying nuclear or other inherently dangerous or noxious substances shall, when exercising the right of innocent passage through the territorial sea, carry documents and observe special precautionary measures established for such ships by international agreements.

Article 24

Duties of the coastal State

1. The coastal State shall not hamper the innocent passage of foreign ships through the territorial sea except in accordance with this Convention. In particular, in the application of this Convention or of any laws or regulations adopted in conformity with this Convention, the coastal State shall not:

(a) impose requirements on foreign ships which have the practical effect of denying or impairing the right of innocent passage; or

(b) discriminate in form or in fact against ships of any State or against ships carrying cargoes to, from or on behalf of any State.

2. The coastal State shall give appropriate publicity to any danger to navigation, of which it has knowledge, within its territorial sea.

Article 25

Rights of protection of the coastal State

1. The coastal State may take the necessary steps in its territorial sea to prevent passage which is not innocent.

2. In the case of ships proceeding to internal waters or a call at a port facility outside territorial waters, the coastal State also has the right to take the necessary steps to prevent any breach of the conditions to which admission of those ships to internal waters or a call is subject.

3. The coastal State may, without discrimination in form or fact among foreign ships, suspend temporarily in specific areas of its territorial sea the innocent passage of foreign ships if such suspension is essential for the protection of its security, including weapons exercises. Such suspension shall take effect only after having been duly published.

Article 26

Charges which may be levied upon foreign ships

1. No charge may be levied upon foreign ships by reason only of their passage through the territorial sea.

2. Charges may be levied upon a foreign ship passing through the territorial sea as payment

only for specific services rendered the ship. These charges shall be levied without discrimination.

SUBSECTION B. RULES APPLICABLE TO MERCHANT SHIPS AND GOVERNMENT SHIPS OPERATED FOR COMMERCIAL PURPOSES

Article 27

Criminal jurisdiction on board a foreign ship

1. The criminal jurisdiction of a coastal State should not be exercised on board a foreign ship passing through the territorial sea to arrest any person or to conduct any investigation in connection with any crime committed on board the ship during its passage, save only in the following cases:

(a) if the consequences of the crime extend to the coastal State;

(b) if the crime is of the kind to disturb the peace of the country or the good order of the territorial sea;

(c) if the assistance of local authorities has been requested by the master of the ship or by a diplomatic agent or consular officer of the flag State; or

(d) if such measures are necessary for the suppression of illicit traffic in narcotic drugs or psychotropic substances.

2. The above provisions do not affect the right of the coastal State to take any steps authorized by its law for the purpose of an arrest or investigation on board a foreign ship passing through the territorial sea after leaving internal waters.

3. In the cases provided for in paragraphs 1 and 2, the coastal State shall, if the master so requests, notify a diplomatic agent or consular officer of the flag State before taking any steps, and shall facilitate contact between such agent or officer and the ship's crew. In cases of emergency this notification may be communicated while the measures are being taken.

4. In considering whether or in what manner an arrest should be made, the local authorities shall have due regard to the interests of navigation.

5. Except as provided in Part XII or with respect of violations of laws and regulations adopted in accordance with Part V, the coastal State may not take any steps on board a foreign ship passing through the territorial sea to arrest any person or to conduct any investigation in connection with any crime committed before the ship entered the territorial sea, if the ship, proceeding from a foreign port, is only passing through the territorial sea without entering internal waters.

Article 28

Civil jurisdiction in relation to foreign ships

1. The coastal State should not stop or divert a foreign ship passing through the territorial sea for the purpose of exercising civil jurisdiction in relation to a person on board the ship.

2. The coastal State may not levy execution against or arrest the ship for the purpose of any civil proceedings, save only in respect of obligations or liabilities assumed or incurred by the ship itself in the course of or for the purpose of its voyage through the waters of the coastal State.

3. Paragraph 2 is without prejudice to the right of the coastal State, in accordance with its laws, to levy execution against or arrest, for the purpose of any civil proceedings, a foreign ship lying in the territorial sea, or passing through the territorial sea after leaving internal waters.

b. PASSAGE THROUGH STRAITS USED FOR INTERNATIONAL NAVIGATION

Having considered the regime for innocent passage through the territorial sea, there are two more passage regimes in the new Convention that require some comparative analysis. The first, transit passage in international straits, will be considered next, followed by consideration of archipelagic sealanes passage.

The chapter in the treaty dealing with international straits is a new one. It was necessary to develop a more particular regime for transit through straits because of the adoption of a clear 12-mile limit to the territorial sea. Arguably, the breadth of the territorial sea had been 3 miles, at least that is the limit that had been recognized by the United States. By expanding the breadth of the territorial sea to the new limit, many important international straits that had previously had high seas corridors through them no longer would have one. Instead, the route through the strait would fall inside someone's territorial sea. This was an unacceptable situation to the major maritime powers because a route that had previously been governed by the freedom of the high seas would now be within the rules for innocent passage. Overflight would no longer be permitted and submarines would be required to navigate on the surface.

A strait is defined, loosely, as a narrow passage of water joining two larger bodies of water. Some of these straits are of considerable strategic importance to the maritime powers for economic and military reasons -- Gibralter, Hormuz, Bab el Mandeb, Malacca, for example. Thus the issue of naval mobility in these important lifelines was of critical importance to the maritimes. Coastal States that border on these and other straits also had concerns to be accomodated. Obviously, the passage of foreign warships so close to their coasts engaged their important national interests. And, because of the proximity of vessels to their shores, they were legitimately concerned about the threat of pollution. In reading these materials, consider how these polarized interests were accomodated by the treaty.

Before looking at the treaty provisions on this subject, consider the state of the law prior to the recent conference, as reflected in the following ICJ opinion and the single provision of the 1958 Convention on the Territorial Sea and the Contituous Zone.

CORFU CHANNEL CASE
1949 [I.C.J.] 4, 25-81

[This case dealt with, among other issues, the question concerning the right of passage of warships in time of peace through an international strait. At the heart of the case was the fact that British warships had been damaged by striking mines placed by Albania in the Corfu Channel off its coast. The Albanians contended that Britain violated Albanian sovereignty by sending her warships through the channel without Albania's consent.]

It is, in the opinion of the Court, generally recognized and in accordance with international custom that States in time of peace have the right to send their warships through straits used for international navigation between two parts of the high seas without the previous authorization of a coastal State, provided that passage is innocent. Unless otherwise prescribed in an international convention, there is no right for a coastal State to prohibit such passage through straits in time of peace.

The Albanian Government does not dispute that the North Corfu Channel is a strait in the geographical sense, but it denies that this Channel belongs to the class of international highways through which a right of passage exists, on the grounds that it is only of secondary importance and not even a necessary route between two parts of the high seas, and that it is used almost exclusively for local traffic to and from the ports of Corfu and Saranda.

It may be asked whether the test is to be found in the volume of traffic passing through the Strait or in its greater or lesser importance for international navigation. But in the opinion of the Court the decisive criterion is rather its geographical situation as connecting two parts of the high seas and the fact of its being used for international navigation. Nor can it be decisive that this Strait is not a necessary route between two parts of the high seas, but only an alternative passage between the Aegean and the Adriatic seas. It has nevertheless been a useful route for international maritime traffic. In this respect, the Agent for the United Kingdom Government gave the Court the following information relating to the period from April 1st, 1936, to December 31st, 1937: "The following is the total number of ships putting in at the Port of Corfu after passing through or just before passing through the Channel. During the period of one year nine months, the total number of ships was 2,884. The flags of the ships are Greek, Italian, Roumanian, Yugoslav, French, Albanian and British. Clearly, very small vessels were included, as the entries for Albanian vessels were high, and of course one vessel may make several journies, but 2,884 ships for a period of one year nine months is quite a large figure. These figures relate to vessels visited by the Customs at Corfu and so do not include the large number of vessels that went through without calling at Corfu at all." There were also regular sailings through the Strait by Greek vessels three times weekly, by a British ship fortnightly, and by two Yugoslav vessels weekly and by two other fortnightly. The Court is further informed that the British Navy has regularly used this Channel for eighty years or more, and that it has also been used by the navies of other States.

One fact of particular importance is that the North Corfu Channel constitutes a frontier between Albania and Greece, that a part of it is wholly within the territorial waters of those States, and that the Strait is of special importance to Greece by reason of the traffic to and from the port of Corfu.

Having regard to these various considerations, the Court has arrived at the conclusion that the North Corfu Channel should be considered as belonging to the class of international highways through which passage cannot be prohibitied by a coastal State in time of peace.

On the other hand, it is a fact that the two coastal States did not maintain normal relations, that Greece had made territorial claims precisely with regard to a part of Albanian territory bordering on the Channel, that Greece had declared that she considered herself techinically in a state of war with Albania, and that Albania, invoking the danger of Greek incursions, had considered it necessary to take certain measures of vigilance in this region. The Court is of the opinion that Albania, in view of these exceptional circumstances, would have been justified in issuing regulations in respect of the passage of warships through the Strait, but not in prohibiting such passage or subjecting it to the requirement of special authorization.

For these reasons the Court is unable to accept the Albanian contention that the Government of the United Kingdom has violated Albanian sovereignty by sending warships through the Strait without having obtained the previous authorization of the Albanian Government.

....

The Albanian Government has further contended that the sovereignty of Albania was violated because the passage of the British warships on October 22nd, 1946, was not an innocent passage. The reasons advanced in support of this contention may be summed up as follows: The passage was not an ordinary passage, but a political mission; the ships were manoevering and sailing in diamond combat formation with soldiers on board; the position of the guns was not consistent with innocent passage; the vessels passed with crews at action stations; the number of ships and their armament surpassed what was necessary in order to attain their object and showed an intention to intimidate and not merely to pass; the ships had received orders to observe and report upon the coastal defences and this order was carried out.

It is shown by the Admiralty telegram of September 21st, cited above, and admitted by the United Kingdom agent, that the object of sending the warships through the Strait was not only to carry out a passage for purposes of navigation, but also to test Albania's attitude. As mentioned above, the Albanian Government, on May 15th, 1946, tried to impose by means of gunfire its view with regard to the passage. As the exchange of diplomatic notes did not lead to any clarification, the Government of the United Kingdom wanted to ascertain whether the Albanian Government would maintain its illegal attitude and impose its views by firing at passing ships. The legality of this measure taken by the Government of the United Kingdom cannot be disputed, provided that it was carried out in a manner consistent with the requirements of international law. The Government of the United Kingdom was not bound to abstain from exercising its right of passage, which the Albanian Government illegally denied.

It remains, therefore, to consider whether the manner in which the passage was carried out was consistent with the principle of innocent passage and to examine the various contentions of the Albanian Government in so far as they appear to be relevant.

When the Albanian coastguards at St. George's Monastery reported that the British warships were sailing in combat formation and were manoevering, they must have been under a misapprehension. It is shown by the evidence that they were not manoevering until after the first explosion. Their movements thereafter were due to the explosions and were made necessary in order to save human life and the mined ships. It is shown by the evidence of witnesses that the contention that the soldiers were on board must be due to a misunderstanding probably arising from the fact that the two cruisers carried their usual detachment of marines.

It is known from the above-mentioned order issued by the British Admiralty on August 10th, 1946, that ships, when using the North Corfu Strait, must pass with armaments in the fore and aft position. That this order was carried out during the passage of October 22nd is stated by Commander-in-Chief, Mediterranean, in a telegram of October 26th to the Admiralty. The guns were, he reported, "trained fore and aft, which is their normal position at sea in peace time, and were not loaded". It is confirmed by the commanders of Saumarez and Volage that the guns were in this position before the explosions. The navigating officer on board Mauritius explained that all guns in that cruiser were in their normal stowage position. The main guns were in the line of the ship, and the antiaircraft guns were pointed outwards and up into the air, which is the normal position of these guns on a cruiser both in harbour and at sea. In the light of this evidence, the Court cannot accept the Albanian contention that the position of the guns was inconsistent with the rules of innocent passage.

In the above-mentioned telegram of October 26th, the Commander-in-Chief reported that the passage "was made with ships at action stations in order that they might be able to retaliate quickly if fired upon again". In view of the firing from the Albanian battery on May 15th, this measure of precaution cannot, in itself, be regarded as unreasonable. But four warships -- two cruisers and two destroyers -- passed in this manner, with crews at action stations, ready to retaliate quickly if fired upon. They passed one after another through this narrow channel, close to the Albanian coast, at a time of political tension in this region. The intention must have been, not only to test Albania's attitude, but at the same time to demonstrate such force that she would abstain from firing again on passing ships. Having regard, however, to all the circumstances of the case, as described above, the Court is unable to characterize these measures taken by the United Kingdom authorities as a violation of Albania's sovereignty.

CONVENTION ON THE TERRITORIAL SEA AND THE CONTIGUOUS ZONE

Article 16

....

3. Subject to the provisions of paragraph 4, the coastal State may, without discrimination amongst foreign ships, suspend temporarily the innocent passage of foreign ships if such suspension is essential for the protection of its security. Such suspension shall take effect only after having been duly published.

4. There shall be no suspension of the innocent passage of foreign ships though straits which are used for international navigation between one part of the high seas and another part of the high seas or through the territorial sea of a foreign State.

ED. NOTE: One way to deal with problems related to the passage of vessels through international straits is for the affected nations to get together and agree on an appropriate set of rules for those straits. Thus, over the years, there have been individual agreements regarding specific straits. See "Guide to Instruments Affecting the Legal Status of Straits," U.N. Doc. A/CONF.13/14 (12 November 1957). Perhaps the best known such arrangement concerns passage though the Dardanelles. Excerpts from this treaty follow.

CONVENTION CONCERNING THE REGIME OF STRAITS -- DARDANELLES AND BOSPHORUS

(MONTREUX, JULY 20, 1936)
173 League of Nations Treaty Series 213
In force November 9, 1936

Article 1. The High Contracting Parties recognize and affirm the principle of freedom of transit and navigation by sea in the Straits.

The exercise of this freedom shall henceforth be regulated by the provisions of the present Convention.

Article 2. In time of peace, merchant vessels shall enjoy complete freedom of transit and navigation in the Straits, by day and by night, under any flag and with any kind of cargo, without any formalities, except as provided in article 3 below. No taxes or charges other than those authorized by Annex I to the present Convention shall be levied by the Turkish authorities on these vessels when passing in transit without calling at a port in the Straits.

In order to facilitate the collection of these taxes or charges merchant vessels passing through the Straits shall communicate to the officials at the stations referred to in article 3 their name, nationality, tonnage, destination and last port of call (provenance)....

Article 4. In time of war, Turkey not being belligerent, merchant vessels, under any flag or with any kind of cargo, shall enjoy freedom of transit and navigation in the Straits subject to the provisions of articles 2 and 3....

Article 5. In time of war, Turkey being belligerent, merchant vessels not belonging to a country at war with Turkey shall enjoy freedom of transit and navigation in the Straits on condition that they do not in any way assist the enemy....

[The convention also contains detailed provisions concerning the passage of warships. Parties are Bulgaria, France, the United Kingdom, India, Greece, Japan, Romania, Turkey, the Soviet Union,and Yugoslavia. Note that this is the type of treaty that bestows rights upon nations that are not parties to the agreement. Other States, then, may claim the right of transit, if they do not reject the provisions benefitting them.]

We now turn to the regime for international straits contained in the 1982 Convention. Agreement to these articles was, as mentioned before, was part of the package deal, and were important to the major maritime powers. It is unlikely that any of those powers would have agreed to a treaty not having this or a similar regime for transit passage.

1982 UNITED NATIONS CONVENTION ON THE LAW OF THE SEA

PART III

STRAITS USED FOR INTERNATIONAL NAVIGATION

SECTION 1. GENERAL PROVISIONS

Article 34

Legal status of waters forming straits used for international navigation

1. The regime of passage through straits used for international navigation established in this Part shall not in other respects affect the legal status of waters forming such straits or the exercise by States bordering the straits of their sovereignty or jurisdiction over such waters and their air space, bed and subsoil.

2. The sovereignty or jurisdiction of the States bordering the straits is exercised subject to this Part and to other rules of international law.

Article 35

Scope of this Part

Nothing in the Part affects:

(a) any areas of internal waters within a strait, except where the establishment of straight baselines in accordance with the method set forth in article 7 has the effect of enclosing as internal waters areas which had not previously been considered as such;

(b) the legal status of waters beyond the territorial sea of States bordering straits as exclusive economic zones or high seas; or

(c) the legal regime in straits in which passage is regulated in whole or in part by long-standing international conventions in force specifically relating to such straits.

Article 36

High seas route or routes through exclusive economic zones through straits used for international navigation

This Part does not apply to a strait used for international navigation if there exists through the strait a route through the high seas or through an exclusive economic zone of similar convenience with respect to navigational and hydrographical characteristics; in such routes, the other relevant Parts of this Convention, including the provisions regarding the freedoms of navigation and overflight, apply.

SECTION 2. TRANSIT PASSAGE

Article 37

Scope of this section

This section applies to straits which are used for international navigation between one part of the high seas or an exclusive economic zone and another part of the high seas or an exclusive economic zone.

Article 38

Right of transit passage

1. In straits referred to in article 37, all ships and aircraft enjoy the right of transit passage, which shall not be impeded; except that, if the strait is formed by an island of a State bordering the strait and its mainland, transit passage shall not apply if there exists seaward of the island a route through the high seas or through an exclusive economic zone of similar convenience with respect to navigational and hydrographical characteristics.

2. Transit passage means the exercise in accordance with this Part of the freedom of navigation and overflight solely for the purpose of continuous and expeditious transit of the strait between one part of the high seas or an exclusive economic zone and another part of the high seas or an exclusive economic zone. However, the requirement of continuous and expeditious transit does not preclude passage through the strait for the purpose of entering, leaving or returning from a State bordering the strait, subject to the conditions of entry to that State.

3. Any activity which is not an exercise of the right of transit passage through a strait remains subject to the other applicable provisions of this Convention.

Article 39

Duties of ships and aircraft during transit passage

1. Ships and aircraft, while exercising the right of transit passage, shall:

(a) proceed without delay through or over the strait;

(b) refrain from any threat or use of force against the sovereignty, territorial integrity or political independence of States bordering the strait, or in any manner in violation of the principles of international law embodied in the Charter of the United Nations;

(c) refrain from any activities other than those incident to their normal modes of continuous and expeditious transit unless rendered necessary by *force majeure* or distress.

2. Ships in transit passage shall:

(a) comply with generally accepted international regulations, procedures and practices for safety at sea, including the International Regulations for Preventing Collisions at Sea;

(b) comply with generally accepted international regulations, procedures and practices for the prevention, reduction and control of pollution from ships.

3. Aircraft in transit passage shall:

(a) observe the Rules of the Air established by the International Civil Aviation Organization as they apply to civil aircraft; state aircraft will normally comply with such safety measures and will at all times operate with due regard for the safety of navigation;

(b) at all times monitor the radio frequency assigned by the competent international organization or the appropriate international distress frequency.

Article 40

Research and survey activities

During transit passage, foreign ships, including marine scientific and hydrographic survey ships, may not carry out any research or survey activities without the prior authorization of the States bordering the straits.

Article 41

Sea lanes and traffic separation schemes

1. In conformity with this Part, States bordering straits may designate sea lanes and prescribe traffic separation schemes for navigation in straits where necessary to promote the safe passage of ships.

2. Such States may, when circumstances require, and after giving due publicity thereto, substitute other sea lanes or traffic separation schemes for any sea lanes or traffic separation schemes previously designated or prescribed by them.

3. Such sea lanes and traffic separation schemes shall conform to generally accepted international regulations.

4. Before designating or substituting sea lanes or prescribing or substituting traffic separation schemes, States bordering straits shall refer proposals to the competent international organization with a view to their adoption. The organization may adopt only such sea lanes and traffic separation schemes as may be agreed with the States bordering the straits, after which the States may designate, prescribe or substitute them.

5. In respect of a strait where sea lanes or traffic separation schemes through the waters of two or more States bordering the strait are proposed, the States concerned shall co-operate in formulating proposals in consultation with the competent international organization.

6. States bordering straits shall clearly indicate all sea lanes and traffic separation schemes designated or prescribed by them on charts to which due publicity shall be given.

7. Ships in transit passage shall respect applicable sea lanes and traffic separation schemes established in accordance with this article.

Article 42

Laws and regulations of States bordering straits relating to transit passage

1. Subject to the provisions of this section, States bordering straits may adopt laws and regulations relating to transit passage through straits, in respect of all or any of the following:

(a) the safety of navigation and the regulation of maritime traffic as provided for in article 41;

(b) the prevention, reduction and control of pollution by giving effect to applicable international regulations regarding the discharge of oil, oily wastes and other noxious substances in the strait;

(c) with respect to fishing vessels, the prevention of fishing including the stowage of fishing gear;

(d) the loading or unloading of any commodity, currency or person in contravention of the customs, fiscal, immigration or sanitary laws and regulations of States bordering straits.

2. Such laws and regulations shall not discriminate in form or in fact among foreign ships or in their application have the practical effect of denying, hampering or impairing the right of transit passage as defined in this section.

3. States bordering straits shall give due publicity to all such laws and regulations.

4. Foreign ships exercising the right of transit passage shall comply with such laws and regulations.

5. The flag State of a ship or the State of registry of an aircraft entitled to sovereign immunity which acts in a manner contrary to such laws and regulations or other provisions of this Part shall bear international responsibility for any loss or damage which results to States bordering straits.

Article 43

Navigational and safety aids and other improvements and the prevention, reduction and control of pollution

User States and States bordering a strait should by agreement co-operate:

(a) in the establishment and maintenance in a strait of navigational and safety aids or other improvements in aid of international navigation; and

(b) for the prevention, reduction and control of pollution from ships.

Article 44

Duties of States bordering straits

States bordering straits shall not hamper transit passage and shall give appropriate publicity to any danger to navigation or overflight within or over the straits of which they have knowledge. There shall be no suspension of transit passage.

SECTION 3. INNOCENT PASSAGE

Article 45

Innocent passage

1. The regime of innocent passage, in accordance with Part II, section 3, shall apply in straits used for international navigation:

(a) excluded from the application of the regime of transit passage under article 38, paragraph 1; or

(b) between a part of the high seas or an exclusive economic zone and the territorial sea of a foreign State.

2. There shall be no suspension of innocent passage through such straits.

* * * *

ED. NOTE: Recently, the International Court of Justice was called upon to resolve a problem not anticipated during the negotiations of the straits provisions: obstructing bridges across straits. The problem was resolved by negotiation before the Court had time to rule. However, the following excerpts show that new problems have a habit of emerging that were not explicity covered by the treaty.

Wolfrum, BRIDGES OVER STRAITS[6]

The entrance from the North Sea to the Baltic consists of three straits, properly speaking the Little Belt, the Sound and the Great Belt. The passage of the Little Belt, being part of Danish internal waters, is situated between Jutland and Fyn and has a length of 68 miles and a minimum depth of 11.8 meters. The width of the Little Belt varies between 700 meters and 27.5 kilometers. In May, 1935, a bridge opened over the Little Belt connecting the Jutland peninsula with the island of Fyn. The Sound, being the easternmost of the three entrances from the Kattegat to the Baltic, is situated between Sjaeland and the southwest coast of Sweden. The Sound is divided at its northern part into an eastern and a western channel by the island of Ven. Although the Sound is the shortest route between the eastern Baltic and the North Sea, the passage is limited by its minimum depth of 7.7 meters in the

6. Paper delivered at the annual meeting of the Law of the Sea Institute, Genoa, Italy, June 1992. Reprinted by permission of the Law of the Sea Institute.

channel on the Danish (Drogden) side and 7.1 meters on the Swedish side. In 1991 the Danish and the Swedish Governments agreed in principle to establish a fixed link across the Sound. However, the project provides for the building of a tunnel under Drogden, hence this project is not expected to affect the passage of ships. The Great Belt is situated between the Danish islands of Fyn and Langeland in the west and Sjaeland and Lolland in the east. It is divided by the island of Sprogo into a western and eastern channel. The depth of the Great Belt varies between 20 and 25 meters.

Traditionally the Sound was the shortest and busiest passage between the Baltic Sea and the Kattegat, but with the increasing size of ships the East Channel of the Great Belt has become the most frequently used route for the passage of large vessels.

According to IMO Resolution A.339 (IX) of November 1975 the Danish authorities established a transit route passing through the East Channel of the Great Belt with an official depth of 17 meters, the effective depth being 15 meters. The Danish Government plans a crossing of the Great Belt by a fixed link consisting of a 6.6 kilometer road and a rail bridge spanning the Western channel. This bridge will have a navigational clearance of 18 meters. The crossing of the East Channel will be accomplished by a railway tunnel and a high-level road bridge having a clearance of 65 meters. The project has already been started and the bridge across the East Channel is expected to be opened to traffic during 1994. The Government of Finland maintains that the clearance of the bridge crossing the East Channel impedes the freedom of navigation through the Great Belt since ships and oil rigs built in Finland have a height exceeding the clearance and a draught in excess of that of the Sound. The Finnish Government maintains that international law guarantees the right of free passage of ships, including oil rigs and drill ships, through the Great Belt and that there is no justification for Denmark to unilaterally limit that right.

Schachte, INTERNATIONAL STRAITS AND NAVIGATIONAL FREEDOMS[7]

The problem a bridge poses is obvious -- it can impede, if not stop, navigation. If it is a non-fixed span, such as a drawbridge, and the width of the non-fixed span is of sufficient width, the problem is greatly reduced, assuming, of course, that the main channel is under the non-fixed span and is of sufficient depth to allow deep draught vessels to pass. In important straits of restricted width and congested traffic, a single movable span would also cause problems if its width were not sufficient to allow sufficiently broad traffic separation schemes for traffic to pass in both directions. Even if these criteria are satisfied, problems with the strait's hydrographic characteristics, such as severe tides and currents, and perhaps even habitually occurring strong winds, may effectively negate an otherwise acceptable design.

Another issue which is squarely joined in the Danish Bridge case currently before the Court is how "high is high enough," i.e. how much vertical clearance must there be under a fixed span in the main channel. Should it be of sufficient height to allow all existing ships to pass through, or enough to permit all ships presently under construction or planned for construction, or even more than that so as to allow for as yet uncontemplated designs to pass through? As was the case in balancing user and coastal State interests in formulating the Convention, the United States believes the correct response is between the two extremes. An acceptable fixed span bridge should clearly accomodate ship designs which are reasonably foreseeable.

Part and parcel of this question is what constitutes a "ship," again an issue which clearly will

7. Paper delivered at the annual meeting of the Law of the Sea Institute, Genoa, Italy, June 1992. Reprinted by permission of the Law of the Sea Institute.

have to be addressed on the merits. It is the view of the United States that a ship in this context includes any sea-going vessel which is designed for and is capable of self-propulsion and such propulsion is incident to the primary purpose for which it is normally used. Thus a drilling rig which is self-propelled and such means of propulsion is normally used for transporting it and positioning it in place for exploitation would be a ship. A corollary of this view, of course, is that an object being towed would enjoy the same rights of navigation provided that it did not exceed the same height criterion.

[The author then traces the U.S. interpretation of the law concerning innocent passage and transit passage. He concludes, with reference to the 1982 Convention, that the Great Belt strait is an article 35(c) strait, that is, one covered by a long-standing agreement, in this case the Treaty for the Redemption of Sound Dues of 1857.]

....

The Treaty for the Redemption of the Sound Dues of 14 March 1857 and the parallel Convention for the Discontinuance of the Sound Dues between Denmark and the United States of 11 April 1857, among others, recognized "entire freedom of the navigation of the Sound and the Belts" (Article I) and "free and unencumbered navigation" (Article II). Although only surface navigation and neither overflight nor submerged transit was in the contemplation of the parties in 1857, one cannot reasonably maintain that they are ipso facto excluded from the central intent of the agreement i.e. transit rights free from dues and interference. In a similar vein, as the regime established was ostensibly as broad a regime as it was possible to grant, subsequent developments in customary international law would be a legitimate means of interpreting its continued significance. The regime would preclude the Danes from applying their domestic laws to foreign ships transiting the straits except as recognized under modern international law (LOS Convention) and preclude them from applying their internal 1976 Ordinance to foreign warships.

ED. NOTE: The case before the Court raised a number of interesting issues. Finland was faced with a real problem. In its pleadings, Finland alleged that for at least six out of twenty-three offshore drilling platforms built between 1974 and 1990, the Great Belt was the only available passageway and that their height exceeded 65 meters. Further, larger units are planned. The Court would have to have decided whether these, as Admiral Schachte points out, are "ships" within the meaning of the relevant treaty. In addition, it would have to decide whether Denmark, if it must accommodate Finland, must anticipate larger "ships" for the future in addition to those already in existence.

Finland, apparently, was also alleging that Denmark's failure to accomodate Finland's needs would constitute an "abuse of rights". While these waters are not high seas, the claim to their use is a claim for the exercise of high seas rights. Treaty law on the subject clearly requires users of high seas to act reasonably in accomodating, or at least not interfering with, the legitimate use of the high seas by other.

For its part, Denmark was, inter alia, arguing that since Finland had known of its plans to build as early as 1948, and did nothing to protest until now, it had, in the eyes of the law "acquiesced" in those plans and cannot now be heard to complain.

* * * *

Subsequent to the above comments, on Sept. 10, 1992, the International Court of Justice issued an order dismissing the case filed by Finland. Finland and Denmark reached a friendly settlement involving the payment by Denmark to Finland of $16 million and agreement to explore ways to utilize an alternative but shallower strait through the Sound.

c. ARCHIPELAGIC SEA LANES PASSAGE

For some considerable period prior to the recent conference, several States that consisted of groups of islands had sought preferential treatment, because of their geographical situation. They argued that they should be permitted under international law to draw an envelope of straight lines around their outer perimeter, establishing for them sovereignty in the enclosed envelope. Obviously, the maritime powers would oppose such a concept, particularly since some States, such as Indonesia, are very large, and the application of the concept would cut off large areas of the high seas. The subject was broached at the Conference, and, after considerable negotiation, a compromise was reached. It was agreed to establish a legal regime for archipelagic States in the treaty in exchange for the establishment of a right of passage by ships through those waters. This right is called archipelagic sealanes passage. Because of the similarity of this concept with that of transit passage, it is considered here in the form of the treaty articles agreed to.

1982 UNITED NATIONS CONVENTION ON THE LAW OF THE SEA

PART IV

ARCHIPELAGIC STATES

Article 46

Use of terms

For the purposes of this Convention:

(a) "archipelagic State" means a State constituted wholly by one or more archipelagos and may include other islands;

(b) "archipelago" means a group of islands, including parts of islands, interconnecting waters and other natural features which are so closely interrelated that such islands, waters and other natural features form an intrinsic geographical, economic and political entity, or which historically have been regarded as such.

Article 47

Archipelagic baselines

1. An archipelagic State may draw straight baselines joining the outermost islands and drying reefs of the archipelago provided that within such baselines are included the main islands and an area in which the ratio of the area of water to the area of the land, including atolls, is between 1 to 1 and 9 to 1.

2. The length of such baselines shall not exceed 100 nautical miles, except that up to 3 per cent of the total number of baselines enclosing any archipelago may exceed that length, up to a maximum of 125 nautical miles.

3. The drawing of such baselines shall not depart to any appreciable extent from the general

configuration of the archipelago.

4. Such baselines shall not be drawn to or from low-tide elevations unless lighthouses or similar installations which are permanently above sea level have been built on them or where a low-tide elevation is situated wholly or partly at a distance not exceeding the breadth of the territorial sea from the nearest island.

5. The system of such baselines shall not be applied by and archipelagic State in such a manner as to cut off from the high seas or the exclusive economic zone the territorial sea of another State.

6. If a part of the archipelagic waters of an archipelagic State lies between two parts of an immediately adjacent neighboring State, existing rights and all other legitimate interests which the latter State traditionally exercised in such waters and all rights stipulated by agreement between those States shall continue and be respected.

7. For the purpose of computing the ratio of water to land under paragraph 1, land areas may include waters lying within the fringing reefs of islands and atolls, including that part of a steep-sided oceanic plateau which is enclosed or nearly enclosed by a chain of limestone islands and drying reefs lying on the perimeter of the plateau.

8. The baselines drawn in accordance with this article shall be shown on charts of a scale or scales adequate for ascertaining their position. Alternatively, lists of geographical co-ordinates of points, specifying the geodetic datum, may be substituted.

9. The archipelagic State shall give due publicity to such charts or lists of geographical co-ordinates and shall deposit a copy of each such chart or list with the Secretary-General of the United Nations.

Article 48

Measurement of the breadth of the territorial sea, the contiguous zone, the exclusive economic zone and the continental shelf

The breadth of the territorial sea, the contiguous zone, the exclusive economic zone and the continental shelf shall be measured from the archipelagic baselines drawn in accordance with article 47.

Article 49

Legal status of arcipelagic waters, of the air space over archipelagic waters and of their bed and subsoil

1. The sovereignty of an archipelagic State extends to the waters enclosed by the archipelagic baseline drawn in accordance with article 47, regardless of their depth or distance from the coast.

2. This sovereignty extends to the air space over the archipelagic waters, as well as to their bed and subsoil, and of the resources contained therein.

3. This sovereignty is exercised subject to this Part.

4. The regime of archipelagic sea lanes passage, established in this Part shall not in other resepcts affect the status of the archipelagic waters, including the sea lanes, or the exercise by the archipelagic State of its sovereignty over such waters and their air space, bed and subsoil, and the

resources contained therein.

Article 50

Delimitation of internal waters

Within its archipelagic waters, the archipelagic State may draw closing lines for the delimitation of its internal waters, in accordance with articles 9, 10 and 11.

Article 51

Existing agreements, traditional fishing rights and existing submarine cables

1. Without prejudice to article 49, an archipelagic State shall respect existing agreements with other States and shall recognize traditional fishing rights and other legitimate activities of the immediately adjacent neighbouring States in certain areas falling within archipelagic waters. The terms and conditions for the exercise of such rights and activities, including the nature, the extent and the areas to which they apply, shall, at the request of any of the States concerned, be regulated by bilateral agreements between them. Such rights shall not be transferred or shared with third States or their nationals.

2. An archipelagic State shall respect existing submarine cables laid by other States and passing through its waters without making a landfall. An archipelagic State shall permit maintenance and replacement of such cables upon receiving due notice of their location and the intention to repair or replace them.

Article 52

Right of innocent passage

1. Subject to article 53 and without prejudice to article 50, ships of all States enjoy the right of innocent passage through archipelagic waters, in accordance with Part II, section 3.

2. The archipelagic State may, without discrimination in form or in fact among foreign ships, suspend temporarily in specified areas of its archipelago the innocent passage of foreign ships if such suspension is essential for the protection of its security. Such suspension shall take effect only after having been duly published.

Article 53

Right of archipelagic sea lanes passage

1. An archipelagic State may designate sea lanes and air routes thereabove, suitable for the continuous and expeditious passage of foreign ships and aircraft through or over its archipelatic waters and the adjacent territorial sea.

2. All ships and aircraft enjoy the right of archipelagic sea lanes passage in such sea lanes or air routes.

3. Archipelagic sea lanes passage means the exercise in accordance with this Convention the rights of navigation and overflight in the normal mode for the purpose of continuous, expeditious and unobstructed transit between one part of the high seas or exclusive economic zone and another part of

the high seas or exclusive economic zone.

4. Such sea lanes and air routes shall traverse the archipelagic waters and shall include all normal passage routes used as routes for international navigation or overflight through ore over archipelagic waters and, within such routes, so far as ships are concerned, all normal navigational channels, provided that duplication of routes of similar convenience between the same entry and exit points shall not be necessary.

5. Such sea lanes and air routes shall be defined by a series of continuous axis lines from the entry points of passage routes to the exit points. Ships and aircraft in archipelagic sea lanes passage shall not deviate more than 25 nautical miles to either side of such axis lines during passage, provided that such ships and aircraft do not navigate closer to the coasts than 10 per cent of the distance between the nearest points on islands bordering the sea lane.

6. An archipelagic State which designates sea lanes under this article may also prescribe traffic separation schemes for the safe passage of ships through narrow channels in such sea lanes.

7. An archipelagic State may, when circumstances require, after giving due publicity thereto, substitute other sea lanes or traffic separation schemes for any sea lanes or traffic separation schemes previously designated or prescribed by it.

8. Such sea lanes and traffic separation schemes shall conform to generally accepted international regulations.

9. In designating or substituting sea lanes or prescribing or substituting traffic separation schemes, an archipelagic State shall refer proposals to the competent international organization with a view to their adoption. The organization may adopt only such sea lanes and traffic separation schemes as may be agreed with the archipelagic State, after which the archipelagic State may designate, prescribe or substitute them.

10. The archipelagic State shall clearly indicate the axis of the sea lanes and traffic separation schemes designated or prescribed by it on charts to which due publicity shall be given.

11. Ships in archipelagic sea lanes passage shall respect applicable sea lanes and traffic separation schemes established in accordance with this article.

12. If an archipelagic State does not designate sea lanes or air routes, the right of archipelagic sea lanes passage may be exercised through the routes normally used for international navigation.

Article 54

Duties of ships and aircraft during their passage, research and survey activities, duties of the archipelagic State and laws and regulations of the archipelagic State relating to archipelagic sea lanes passage

Article 38, 40, 42 and 44 apply *mutatis mutandis* to archipelagic sea lanes passage.

CHAPTER 4

CONTIGUOUS ZONES

A. INTRODUCTION

In previous chapters, we considered the regimes for the territorial sea and the high seas. If it were possible to constrain coastal State authority strictly within the territorial sea, and leave the area seaward of that completely subject to the freedoms of the high seas, the law of the sea would be greatly simplified. In practice, however, this is simply not practicable. We must recognize that there is an area beyond the territorial sea where it is essential for a coastal State to exercise some limited exercises of authority, simply to protect its legitimate national interests.

This thought, as we have seen, is also reflected in the doctrine of hot pursuit. Now we are going to take a look at the right of a coastal State to establish certain, limited zones adjacent to their territorial sea for the enforcement of certain laws and regulations. These zones are normally referred to in international law as "contiguous zones". As we will sea, the classic statement of the law on this subject limits these zones to the enforcement of customs, immigration, fiscal and sanitary laws. But the State practice on this subject goes far beyond. In one sense, the exclusive economic zone is a kind of contiguous zone, although, as we now know, it has a completely different juridical base.

We need to know, therefore, what kinds of claims of special authority in these areas are likely to receive international approbation, and we need to know how far seaward these competences can be extended. These are questions we shall address in this chapter. First, however, we need to take a look at the development of the concept in international law. The following excerpt does this nicely.

B. DEVELOPMENT OF THE CONCEPT

Churchill and Lowe, THE LAW OF THE SEA 101-104 (1983)[1]

The contiguous zone is a zone of sea contiguous to and beyond the territorial sea in which States have limited powers for the enforcement of customs, fiscal, sanitary and immigration laws. It has its origins in the eighteenth century `Hovering Acts' enacted by Great Britain against foreign smuggling ships hovering within distances up to eight leagues (i.e. twenty-four miles) from the shore. These Acts, which had effect from 1736 until their repeal by the 1876 Customs Consolidation Act, were at the time regarded as permitted by `the common courtesy of nations for their convenience', as Lord Stowall put it in the case of Le Louis in 1817. However, this was at a time when practice had not yet given the three-mile limit for the territorial sea the force of a rule of law.

A dispute with Spain in the early years of the nineteenth century over seizures of British ships within the six-mile Spanish customs zone, among other incidents, focussed attention on the extent of maritime claims. By mid-century the three mile limit for the territorial sea, combined with the exclusivity of flag State jurisdiction on the high seas beyond, was well established in Anglo-American practice and served well the interests of free navigation. Great Britain recognised that its wider customs zones were inconsistent with the three-mile rule. The seizure of the French ship the Petit Jules twenty-three miles off the Isle of Wight in 1850 was the last occasion on which the Hovering Acts were enforced against a foreign ship beyond the marine league. Indeed, the British Law Officers advised that the seizure was impermissible under international law, and the one member of the crew who had been captured was set free. From then on, the three-mile rule was applied in Britain and its

1. Reprinted by permission of Manchester University Press

dominions and colonies. But this rule was subject to two qualifications allowing the exercise of jurisdiction against foreign vessels at greater distances from shore.

First, according to the doctrine of constructive presence, where a ship beyond the marine league sent its boats within that limit, such as occurred for the purpose of illegal fishing in the case of the Araunah (1888) and for the purpose of releasing prisoners in Australia in the Catalpa incident (1877), no distinction was drawn between the ship and its boats, and the ship was liable to be seized for the violation of the local law. According to later refinements of the doctrine, illustrated, for example, by some of the diplomatic exchanges concerning the seizure of the Henry L. Marshall for violation of the American liquor laws in 1922 and by the Italian case of the Sito in 1957, it had no application where a foreign ship communicated with the shore not by means of its own boats but by means of boats sent out from the shore. Here the exclusive jursidiction of the flag State over its ships on the high seas remained intact. The second exception was the doctrine of hot pursuit. This provides that when a ship was found within the territorial sea of a State, and there was good reason to believe that it had violated the local law, it could be pursued and arrested on the high seas.... What is important for present purposes is the fact that it, like the doctrine of constructive presence, allowed a measure of enforcement jurisdiction beyond the three-mile limit, which was otherwise adhered to more or less strictly.

Other States adopted different approaches. Several, mostly in Europe, did not claim united territorial seas as such but...claimed a variety of jurisdictional zones. The width of the zones was fixed at whatever distance the State concerned thought was necessitated by the purpose for which the zone was established. For example, France maintained three-mile zones for fishery and general policing purposes, but a six-mile neutrality zone and a twenty-kilometre customs zone. Belgium, Italy, Greece and Spain and, outside Europe, Cuba and Turkey were among other States adopting this position. While exact widths varied from State to State, customs and security zones were usually more extensive than other zones.

The practice of a third group of States was much closer to the concept of the contiguous zone as it is recognised today. Several Latin American States claimed a one-league belt as the public property of the State, and beyond that zone of sovereignty a second zone, of a further three leagues, in which the State enjoyed the right of policing for customs and security purposes only....

Thus by the early part of the twentieth century there were three main approaches to the question of jurisdiction beyond the three-mile limit. First, States which denied that such jurisdiction existed, except where given by treaty or under the doctrines of hot pursuit and constructive presence.... Second, States which claimed a variety of jurisdictional zones; and, third, States which claimed a jurisdictional zone, usually for customs and security purposes, which was clearly distinct from the territorial sea.

The idea of using the contiguous zone beyond a narrow territorial sea as a basis for compromise between such groups of States and for resolving the question of the breadth of the territorial sea, had been put forward by Renault during the discussion of neutrality zones by the Institute of International Law in 1894. The idea was taken up more generally by the learned societies in the years before the Hague Conference, but despite considerable interest shown in proposals to include a zone of extended customs, sanitary and security jurisdiction in the Hague conference text, none was in fact agreed upon, doubtless largely as a result of the same failure to agree upon the width of the territorial sea which prevented the text from being adopted as a treaty.

In the years between the Hague and Geneva conferences, State practice remained divided between those States...which did not recognize the validity of contiguous zone claims, and the increasing number of States which made such claims. During this period the notion of a territorial sea distinct from other jurisdictional zones became generally accepted, although a few States...still kept to the idea of a `territorial sea' whose width varied according to the purpose for which the jurisdiction was exercised. But most States claimed special customs and security, and sometimes sanitary and immigration zones, on the high seas contiguous to their territorial sea. Claims to fishery zones also became commonplace, and State practice does not seem to have distinguished between the legal character of these zones and that of other contiguous zones. However, Gidel did distinguish between them, requiring the establishment of fishery zones by treaty while admitting of the legality of unilateral claims to other contiguous zones....

C. CONTIGUOUS ZONES IN LAW AND STATE PRACTICE

1. CUSTOMS ZONES

As noted in the above excerpt, there were differing notions of the right of a coastal State to enforce its laws beyond the territorial sea. One method for resolving these differences was to enter into a treaty with one or more States to settle the question of the jurisdiction of the coastal State to enforce its laws in a particular area. The following, relating to customs enforcement, is an example.

This treaty resulted from the objections by the British, and others, to United States enforcement of its liquor laws.

CONVENTION BETWEEN THE UNITED STATES AND GREAT BRITAIN FOR PREVENTION OF SMUGGLING OF INTOXICATING LIQUORS

(Signed January 23, 1924, in force for the United States May 22, 1924)
[43 Stat. 1761; U.S.T.S. 685; IV Trenwith, Treaties, etc. (1938) 4225; 27 L.N.T.S. 182]

The High Contracting Parties declare that it is their firm intention to uphold the principle that 3 marine miles extending from the coastline outwards and measured from the low-water mark constitute the proper limits of territorial waters.

(1) His Britannic Majesty agrees that he will raise no objection to the boarding of vessels under the British flag outside the limits of territorial waters by the authorities of the United States, its territories or possessions in order that enquiries may be addressed to those on board and an examination be made of the ship's papers for the purpose of ascertaining whether the vessel or those on board are endeavouring to import or have imported alcoholic beverages into the United States, its territories or possessions in violation of the laws there in force. When such enquiries and examination show a reasonable ground for suspicion, a search of the vessel may be instituted.

(2) If there is reasonable cause for belief that the vessel has committed or is committing or attempting to commit an offense against the laws of the United States, its territories or possessions prohibiting the importation of alcoholic beverages, the vessel may be seized and taken into a port of the United States, its territories or possessions for adjudication in accordance with such laws.

(3) The rights conferred by this article shall not be exercised at a greater distance from the coast of the United States, its territories or possessions than can be traversed in one hour by the vessel suspected of endeavoring to commit the offense. In cases, however, in which the liquor is intended to be conveyed to the United States, its territories or possessions by a vessel other than the one boarded and searched, it shall be the speed of such other vessel and not the speed of the vessel boarded, which shall determine the distance from the coast at which the right under this article can be exercised.

ED. NOTE: In 1933 the Supreme Court of the United States was faced with the task of interpreting and applying this treaty. Mazel Tov [Cook v. United States, 288 U.S. 102 (1933)] At issue in that case was a seizure occuring behond the one hour sailing distance, and the validity of the subsequent adjudication. In examining the validity of the adjudication, Mr. Justice Brandeis said:

> The treaty fixes the conditions under which a "vessel may be seized and taken into a port of the United States, its territories or possessions for adjudication in accordance with" the applicable laws. Thereby, Great Britain agreed that adjudication may follow a rightful seizure. Our Government, lacking power to seize, lacked power, because of the Treaty, to subject the vessel to our laws. To hold that adjudication may follow a wrongful seizure would go far to nullify the purpose and effect of the Treaty.

He also found the treaty to be self-executing, in that no legislation was needed to authorize executive action in pursuance of its provisions.

In addition to creating customs zones by treaty, the United States has also, on occasion, acted unilaterally. The following statute is an example. Notice its scope

.

ANTI-SMUGGLING ACT OF 1935

49 Stat. 517; 19 U.S.C. 1701-1711

Sec. 1701

(a) Whenever the President finds that at any place or within any area on the high seas adjacent to but outside customs waters any vessels hover or are being kept off the coast of the United States and that, by virtue of the presence of any such vessel or vessels at such place or within such area, the unlawful introduction or removal into the United States of any merchandise or person is being or may be occasioned, promoted, or threatened, the place or area so found and declared shall constitute a customs-enforcement area for the purposes of this chapter. Only such waters on the high seas shall be within a customs-enforcement area as the President finds and declares are in such proximity to such vessel or vessels that such unlawful introduction or removal of merchandise or persons may be carried on by or to from such vessel or vessels. No customs-enforcement area shall include any waters more than one hundred nautical miles from the place or immediate area where the President declares such vessel or vessels are hovering or are being kept and, notwithstanding the foregoing provision, shall not include any waters more than fifty nautical miles outwards from the limits of customs waters. Whenever the President finds that, within any customs-enforcement area, the circumstances no longer exist which gave rise to the declaration of such area, he shall so declare, and thereafter, and until a further finding and declaration is made under this subsection with respect to waters within such area, no waters within such area shall constitute part of such customs-enforcement area. The provisions of law applying to the highs seas adjacent to customs waters of the United States shall be enforced in a customs-enforcement area upon any vessel, merchandise or person found therein.

(b) At any place within a customs-enforcement area the several officers of the customs may go on board any vessel and examine the vessel and any merchandise or person on board, and bring the same into port, and, subject to regulations of the Secretary of the Treasury, it shall be their duty to pursue and seize or arrest and otherwise enforce upon such vessel, merchandise or person, the provisions of law which are made effective thereto in pursuance of subsection (a) of this section in the same manner as such officers are or may be authorized or required to do in like case at any place in the United States by virtue of any law respecting the revenue: Provided, That nothing maintained in this section or in any other provision of law respecting the revenue shall be construed to authorize or to require any officer of the United States to enforce any law thereof upon the high seas upon a foreign vessel in contravention of any treaty with a foreign government enabling or permitting the authorities of the United States to board, examine, search, seize, or otherwise enforce upon such vessel upon the high seas the laws of the United States except as such authorities are or may otherwise be enabled or permitted under special arrangement with such foreign government. Provided further, That none of the provisions of this chapter shall be construed to relieve the Secretary of Commerce of any authority, responsibility, or jurisdiction now vested in or imposed on that officer.

* * * *

The above legislation goes far beyond the traditional view of a customs contiguous zone to a distance of perhaps one marine league beyond the territorial sea. This unilateral action was not popularly received on the international level. The following exchange of correspondence explains.

4 Whiteman, DIGEST OF INTERNATIONAL LAW (1965) pp. 490-492

At a time when the Anti-Smuggling Bill, approved August 5, 1935, was pending before the Senate of the United States, the British Ambassador to the United States, Lord Lindsay, on June 17, 1935, addressed the following communication to the Secretary of State:

"Consequent upon a preliminary examination by the competent authorities in London of the Anti-Smuggling Bill (H.R. 7980) which has passed the House and is now before the Senate, I have been instructed by His Majesty's Principal Secretary of State for Foreign Affairs to make the following communication.

"As is well known it is the view of His Majesty's Government in the United Kingdom that under international law a country has no right to interfere with foreign ships outside of the limits of territorial waters except in so far as such a right is granted by treaty with regard to the ships of a particular foreign country. The United States Government will be aware that His Majesty's Government do not admit that under international law a state has the right to fix by municipal legislation an extended limit (whether it be the twelve mile limit provided for by this and previous United States legislation or the customs enforcement area mentioned in the present Bill), within which it shall exercise jurisdiction over foreign vessels for the protection of its customs and revenue law. Consequently His Majesty's Government would be obliged to protest against any interference with British ships outside the three mile limit except in those cases where interference could be justified under the provisions of the Liquor Convention.

"In connection with Sections 1 to 3 and in connection also with the second subparagrah (m) of Section 201 of the present Bill, His Majesty's Government in the United Kingdom wish to emphasize that the foregoing considerations apply in respect of a vessel of British registry, whatever her ownership and control."

On June 22, following, Assistant Secretary of State Moore replied:

"Your note expressed the view of your Government that under international law a country has no right to interfere with foreign ships outside the limits of territorial waters, except in so far as such a right is granted by treaties with regard to the ships of a particular foreign country. In this regard may I invite your attention to the fact that the pending Anti-Smuggling Bill in Section 1(b), which relates to customs enforcement areas, contains the following language:

"Provided, that nothing contained in this section or in any other provision of law respecting the revenue shall be construed to authorize or to require any officer of the United States to enforce any law thereof upon the high seas upon a foreign vessel in contravention of any treaty with a foreign government enabling or permitting the authorities of the United States to board, examine, search, seize or otherwise enforce upon such vessel upon the high seas the laws of the United States except as such authorities are or may otherwise be enabled or permitted under special arrangement with such foreign government."

> "A similar proviso is contained in Section 202(h) of the same Bill relating to the boarding of vessels."

Subsequently, on August 6, 1935, Lord Lindsay explained he was instructed by the British Secretary of State for Foreign Affairs, Sir Samuel Hoare, to make "a semi-official communication" to the Secretary of State in the following terms:

> "His Majesty's Government in the United Kingdom appreciate the courtesy of the United States Government in furnishing the information contained in the Secretary of State's letters of June 22nd and July 9th. In connection with the former note His Majesty's Government were fully aware that care had been taken in the Anti-Smuggling Bill to ensure that no provisions should be construed as authorizing the enforcement of the law on the high seas in contravention of any international treaty, such as the Liquor Convention between the United States and the United Kingdom. But the Bill appears to confer the faculty to enforce the law upon the high seas in any case where there is no treaty whose provisions would be inconsistent with such enforcement. What His Majesty's Government are concerned to maintain is the general principle that in no cases where there is no treaty or arrangement between the United States and the appropriate foreign Government the ordinary rules of international law must apply, and the United States cannot be held in international law to have the right, by virtue of municipal legislation, to extend beyond the three mile limit, as is done in the present Bill, the area within which jurisdiction may be exercised over foreign vessels. In the view of His Majesty's Government such extension could only be recognized when agreed upon by means of an international treaty. His Majesty's Government assume it to be clearly understood that they would be obliged to protest against interference with a British ship outside the United States territorial waters except in those cases where interference could be justified by the provisions of the Liquor Convention."

ED. NOTE: Only five customs-enforcement zones were established and they were discontinued in 1946. [1948-1949] U.S. Naval War College, International Legal Documents 176-80. The U.S. Supreme Court upheld the right of a coastal State to exercise jursidiction beyond the territorial sea to prevent violation of its laws in Church v. Hubbart, 6 U.S. (2 Cranch) 186 (1809).

2. NEUTRALITY AND SECURITY ZONES

While zones for the protection of neutrality or security are not among those mentioned in the treaty, there has been some State practice in this regard. This section explores some of the views on this subject.

ED. NOTE: Philip C. Jessup, in his earlier classic on the territorial sea and contiguous zones, noted a number of scholars that took the position that security and neutrality zones were based upon the principle of self-defense. See Jessup, "The Law of Territorial Waters and Maritime Jurisdiction, Jennings Co. 1927, pp. 96-97. A proposal to include within the contiguous zone concept a security zone was considered by the International Law Commission at its final session in 1956. The Commission ruled against its inclusion because: (a) it was so vague as to invite abuse, and; (b) the right of self defense was adequate to provide a basis for a State taking action if protective measures are warranted. As to efforts to make reference to security zones during the Third United Nations Conference on the Law of the Sea, see Chapter 3. Some examples of attempts to create neutrality or national security zones follow.

FINAL ACT OF THE CONSULTATIVE MEETING OF FOREIGN MINISTERS OF THE AMERICAN REPUBLICS [1 Dept. State Bull. 321, 331-333 (1939)]

XIV

"Declaration of Panama"

The Governments of the American Republics meeting at Panama, have solemnly ratified their neutral status in the conflict which is disrupting the peace of Europe [World War II], but the present war may lead to unexpected results which may affect the fundamental interests of America and there can be no justification for the interests of the belligerents to prevail over the rights of neutrals causing disturbances and suffering to nations which by their neutrality in the conflict and because of their distance from the scene of events, should not be burdened with its fatal and painful consequences.

During the World War of 1914-1918 the Governments of Argentina, Brazil, Chile, Colombia, Ecuador and Peru advanced, or supported, individual proposals providing in principle a declaration by the American Republics that the belligerent nations must refrain from committing hostile acts within a reasonable distance from their shores.

The nature of the present conflagration, in spite of its already lamentable proportions, would not justify any obstruction to inter-American communications, which, engendered by important interests, call for adequate protection. This fact requires the demarcation of a zone of security including all the normal maritime routes of communication and trade between the countries of America.

To this end it is essential as a measure of necessity to adopt immediately provisions based on the above-mentioned precedents for the safeguarding of such interests, in order to avoid a repetition of the damages and sufferings sustained by the American nations and by their citizens during the war of 1914-1918.

There is no doubt that the Governments of the American Republics must foresee those dangers and as a measure of self-protection insist that the waters to a reasonable distance from their coasts shall remain free from the commission of hostile acts or from the undertaking of belligerent activities by nations engaged in a war in which said governments are not involved.

For these reasons the Governments of the American Republics Resolve and Hereby Declare:

1. As a measure of continental self-protection, the American Republics, so long as they maintain their neutrality, are as of inherent right entitled to have those waters adjacent to the American continent, which they regard as of primary concern and direct utility in their relations, free from the commission of any hostile act by any non-American belligerent nations, whether such hostile act be attempted or made from land, sea or air.

Such waters shall be defined as follows. All waters comprised within the limits set forth hereafter except the territorial waters of Canada and of the undisputed colonies and possessions of European countries within these limits: [There follows a listing of coordinates describing an area extending as far as three hundred miles to sea.]

....

2. The Governments of the American Republics agree that they will endeavor, through joint representation to such belligerents as may now or in the future be engaged in such hostilities, to secure the compliance by them with the provisions of this declaration without prejudice to the exercise of the individual rights of each State inherent in their sovereignty.

3. The Governments of the American Republics further declare that whenever they consider it necessary they will consult together to determine upon the measures which they may individually or collectively undertake in order to secure the observance of the provisions of this Declaration

4. The American Republics, during the existence of a state of war in which they themselves are not involved, may undertake, whenever they may determine that the need therefor exists, to patrol, either individually or collectively, as may be agreed upon by common consent, and in so far as the means and measures of each may permit, the waters adjacent to their coasts within the area above defined. (Approved, October 3, 1939.)

REPLY OF THE UNITED KINGDOM TO THE PROTEST OF AMERICAN REPUBLICS CONCERNING VIOLATION OF THE NEUTRALITY ZONE [2 Dept. State Bull. 199-201 (1940)]

His Majesty's Government in the United Kingdom have devoted most careful consideration to the communication agreed upon unanimously by the 21 American Republics, the text of which was telegraphed to His Majesty the King by the Acting President of Panama on December 23rd last. In that communication reference was made, among other matters, to the recent naval action between British and German warshps in the South Atlantic, and to the maritime security zone described in the Declaration of Panama of October 3rd, 1939.

His Majesty's Government, who themselves so long strove to prevent war, fully appreciate the desire of the American Republics to keep the war away from the shores of the American Continent. It was therefore not merely with interest but with understanding that His Majesty's Government learned of the maritime security zone proposal. His Majesty's Government noted with satisfaction from the Declaration of Panama itself that the attempt would be made to base the observance of its provisions upon the consent of the belligerents. This fresh expression of adherence to the idea of solving international difficulties by mutual discussion, which has always been upheld by the American Republics, confirmed His Majesty's Government's belief that these Powers would not attempt to enforce observance of the zone by unilateral action and encouraged their hope that it would be possible to give effect by means of negotiation to the intentions which inspired it.

It was in this spirit that His Majesty's Government were examining the proposal of the Conference of Panama at the time when the communication of December 23rd was received. In view of this communication His Majesty's Government desire to draw attention of the American Republics to the following consideration:

It will be apparent, in the first place, that the proposal, involving as it does the abandonment by the belligerents of certain legitimate belligerent rights, is not one which on any basis of international law can be imposed upon them by unilateral action, and that its adoption requires their specific assent.

The acceptance by His Majesty's Government of the suggestion that the belligerents should forego their rights in the zone must clearly be dependent upon their being assured that the adoption of the zone proposal would not provide German warships and supply ships with a vast sanctuary from which they could emerge and attack Allied and neutral shipping, to which they could return to avoid being brought to action, and in which some un-neutral service might be performed by non-German ships, for example by the use of wireless communications. It would also be necessary to ensure that German warships and supply ships would not be enabled to pass with impunity from one ocean to another through the zone, or German merchant ships to take part in inter-American trade and earn foreign exchange, which might be used in attempts to promote subversion and sabotage abroad and to procure supplies for the prolongation of the war, thus depriving the Allies of the fruits of their superiority at sea. Moreover, the acceptance of the zone proposals would have to be on the basis that it should not constitute a precedent for a far-reaching altercation in the existing laws of maritime neutrality.

Unless these points are adequately safeguarded, the zone proposals might only lead to the accumulation of belligerent ships in the zone. This in turn might well bring the risk of war nearer to the American States and lead to friction between on the one hand the Allies, pursuing their legitimate belligerent activities, and on the other hand the American Republics, endeavouring to make this new policy prevail.

The risk of such friction, which His Majesty's Government would be the first to deplore, would be increased by the application of sanctions. His Majesty's Government must emphatically repudiate any suggestion that His Majesty's Ships have acted, or would act, in any way that would justify the adoption of neutrals of punitive measures which do not spring from the accepted canons of neutral rights and obligations. If, therefore, the American States were to adopt a scheme of sanctions for the enforcement of the zone proposal, they would, in effect, be offering sanctuary to German warships, within which His Majesty's Ships would be confronted with the invidiuous choice of having either to refrain from engaging their enemy or laying themselves open to penalties in American ports and waters.

Up to the present it does not appear that means have been found by which the disadvantages of the zone proposal could be eliminated. That this is the case was shown by the operations in the zone of the warship Admiral Graf Spee and the supply ship Tacoma.

With regard to the specific incidents of which mention is made in the communication under reply, His Majesty's Government must observe that the legitimate activities of His Majesty's Ships can in no way imperil, but must rather contribute to the security of the American Continent, the protection of which was the object of the framers of the Declaration of Panama. His Majesty's Government cannot admit that there is any foundation for a claim that such activities have in any way exposed them to justifiable reproach, seeing that the zone proposal has not been made effective and belligerent assent has not yet been given to the operation.

In view of the difficulties described above, it appears to His Majesty's Government that the only effective method of achieving the American object of preventing belligerent acts within the zone would be, firstly, to ensure that the German Government would send no more warships into it. Secondly, there are obvious difficulties in applying the zone proposal at this stage of the war when so much German shipping has already taken refuge in American waters. If the Allies are to be asked to forego the opportunity of capturing those vessels, it would also seem to be necessary that they should be laid up under Pan-American control for the duration of the war.

In the view of His Majesty's Government it would only be by means such as those indicated that the wish of the American Governments to keep war away from their coasts could be realised in a truly effective and equitable manner. Until His Majesty's Government are able to feel assured that the scheme will operate satisfactorily, they must, anxious as they are for the fulfillment of American hopes, necessarily reserve their full belligerent rights in order to fight the menace presented by German action and policy and to defend that conception of law and that way of life, which they believe to be as dear to the peoples and Governments of America as they are to the peoples and Governments of the British Commonwealth of Nations.

ED. NOTE: Although not dealing with the surface of the oceans, the United States has taken control of the air space above it. By regulations pursuant to 49 U.S.C. 1348(a) and 1510, rules have been developed for operating civil aircraft in a defense area, or into or out of the United States. These regulations [14 CFR Part 99] call for the establishment of air defense identification zones (ADIZ's) which are defined as "areas of airspace over land or water in which the ready identification, location, and control of civil aircraft is required in the interest of national security".

In addition to requiring civil aircraft in an ADIZ to have a functioning two-way radio and to file a flight plan, the regulations require pilots of civil aircraft to report to an appropriate facility the time, position and altitude at which the aircraft passed the last reporting point before entering the zone. This report must be made when the aircraft is between one hour and two hours cruising distance from the United States, and, failure to do so precludes the aircraft from entering the United States through a coastal ADIZ.

With respect to the jurisdictional implications of these regulations, the Restatement of the Foreign Relations Law of the United States, in its comment on Sec. 21, observes:

"Regulations of a state applying to vessels and aircraft proposing to enter its territory may require them to comply, within designated zones beyond the limit of the territorial sea, with certain procedures intended to insure the security of the territory. The jurisdiction of a state in establishing such zones is not based on the rule stated in this Section [Section 21 restates the rule contained in article 24 of the Convention on the Territorial Sea and the Contiguous Zone regarding the establishment of contiguous zones]. The requirement of compliance with the procedures is a condition to entry; the act of entry is subject to the state's jurisdiction to prescribe under the rule stated in Sec. 17(a) [A state has juridiction to prescribe a rule of law...attaching consequences to conduct that occurs within its territory whether or not such consequences are determined by the effects of the conduct outside the territory...]. If the requirement is not complied with, its violation may be punished by enforcement actions taken by the state after the offending vessel or aircraft has come into the territory. Whether on the ground of self defense, a state may enforce compliance with the procedures in such zones by vessels or aircraft not entering the territory is beyond the scope of the Restatement on this subject."

The last sentence leaves open the question whether an aircraft entering an ADIZ without complying with the conditions imposed could be forced out of the zone. Presumeably, if real self defense was involved, it could. Lesser threats would be more questionable under international law.

3. THE ARTICLE 24 CONTIGUOUS ZONE

We now turn to a consideration of the interpretation of Article 24 of the Convention on the Territorial Sea and the Contiguous zone, which is replicated with one change in the Third United Nations Convention on the Law of the Sea in Article 33:

CONVENTION ON THE TERRITORIAL SEA AND THE CONTIGUOUS ZONE

Article 24

1. In a zone of the high seas contiguous to its territorial sea, the coastal State may exercise the control necessary to:

(a) Prevent infringement of its customs, fiscal, immigration or sanitary regulations within its territory or territorial sea;

(b) Punish infringement of the above regulations committed within its territory or territorial sea.

2. The contiguous zone may not extend beyond twelve miles from the baseline from which the breadth of the territorial sea is measured.

3. Where the coasts of two States are opposite or adjacent to each other, neither of the two States is entitled, failing agreement between them to the contrary, to extend its contiguous zone beyond the median line every point of which is equidistance from the nearest points on the baselines from which the breadth of the territorial seas of the two States is measured.

INTERNATIONAL LAW COMMISSION
1956 Commentary

(1) International law accords States the right to excercise preventive or protective control for certain purposes over a belt of the high seas contiguous to their territorial sea. It is, of course, understood that this power of control does not change the legal status of the waters over which it is exercised. These waters are and remain a part of the high seas and are not subject to the sovereignty of the coastal State, which can exercise over them only such rights as are conferred on it by the present draft or are derived from international treaties.

(2) Many States have adopted the principle that in the contiguous zone the coastal State may exercise customs control in order to prevent attempted infringements of its customs and fiscal regulations within its territory or territorial sea, and to punish infringements of those regulations committed within its territory or territorial sea. The Commission considered that it would be impossible to deny to States the exercise of such rights.

(3) Although the number of States which claim rights over the contiguous zone for the purpose of applying sanitary regulations is fairly small, the Commission considers that, in view of the connexion between customs and sanitary regulations, such rights should also be recognized for sanitary regulations.

(4) The Commission did not recognize special security rights in the contiguous zone. It considered that the extreme vagueness of the term "security" would open the way for abuses and that granting of such rights was not necessary. The enforcement of customs and sanitary regulations will be sufficient in most cases to safeguard the security of the State. In so far as measures of self-defense against an imminent and direct threat to the security of the State concerned, the Commission refers to the general principles of international law and the Charter of the United Nations.

(5) Nor was the Commission willing to recognize any exclusive right of the coastal State to engage in fishing in the contiguous zone. The Preparatory Committee of the Hague Codification

Conference found, in 1930, that the replies from Governments offered no prospect of an agreement to extend exclusive fishing rights of the coastal State beyond the territorial sea. The Commission considered that in that respect the position has not changed.

(6) The Commission examined the question whether the same attitude should be adopted with regard to proposals to grant the coastal State the right to take whatever measures it considered necessary for the conservation of living resources of the sea in the contiguous zone. The majority of the Commission were unwilling to accept such a claim. They argued, first, that measures of this kind applying only to the relatively small area of the contiguous zone would be of little practical value and, secondly, that having provided for the regulation of the conservation of living resources in a special part of the present draft, it would be inadvisable to open the way for duplication of these rules by different provisions designed to regulate the same matters in the contiguous zone only. Since the contiguous zone is a part of the high seas, the rules concerning conservation of living resources of the sea apply to it.

(7) The Commission did not maintain its previous decision to grant the coastal State, within the contiguous zone, a right of control in respect of immigration. In its report on the work of its fifth session the Commission commented on this provision as follows:

> "It is understood that the term `customs regulations' as used in the article refers not only to regulations concerning the import and export of goods. In addition, the Commission thought it necessary to amplify the formulation previously adopted by referring expressly to immigration, a term which is also intended to include emigration."

Reconsidering this decision, the majority of the Commission took the view that the interests of the coastal State do not require an extension of the right to control immigration and emigration. It considered that such control could be exercised in the territory of the coastal State and that there was no need to grant it special rights for this purpose in the contiguous zone.

(8) The Commission considered the case of areas of the sea situated off the junction of two or more adjacent States, where the exercise of rights in the contiguos zone by one State would not leave any free access to the ports of another State except through that zone. The Commission, recognizing that in such cases the exercise of rights in the contiguous zone by one State may unjustifiably obstruct traffic to and from a port of another State, considered that in the case referred to it would be necessary for the two States to include a prior agreement on the exercise of rights in the contiguous zone. In view of the exceptional nature of the case, however, the Commission did not consider it necessary to include a formal rule to this effect.

(9) The Commission considers the breadth of the contiguous zone cannot exceed twelve miles from the coast, the figure adopted by the Preparatory Committee of the Hague Codification Conference (1930). Until such time as there is unanimity in regard to the breadth of the territorial sea, the zone should be measured from the coast and not from the outer limit of the territorial sea. States who have claimed extensive territorial waters have in fact less need for a contiguous zone than those which have been more modest in their delimitation.

(10) The Commission thought it advisable to clarify the expression "from the coast" by stating that the zone is measured from the baseline from which the breadth of the territorial sea is measured.

(11) The exercise by the coastal State of the rights enunciated in this article does not affect the legal status of the air space above the contiguous zone. The question whether the establishment of such an air control zone could be contemplated is outside the scope of these rules of the law of the sea.

ED. NOTE: As the prior materials, as well as those to follow, show, article 24 is not an accurate description of State practice with regard to contiguous zones. In two respects, State practice differs. First, States have not restricted themselves to establishing contiguous zones only for the purpose of protecting their customs, fiscal, immigration and sanitary interests. Fisheries zones, for example, have been quite common, as have security or neutrality zones. Second, the breadth of a maximum of twelve nautical miles has not been universally adhered to. Examples to the contrary are the U.S. customs-enforcement area, the Korean fifty mile security zone, and the Canadian 100 mile pollution control zone. These facts illustrate that article 24 is simply too restrictive. No State may be expected to restrict its right to protect interests of vital importance that may not be covered by article 24, but may arise in the future. The key to the validity of a proposed zone, then, would seem to lie in its acceptance by the international community. U.S. courts, clearly, have recognized this general principle.

The 1982 Convention, however, did little to amend the 1958 rule, except to broaden permissible zones in response to the establishment of a 12 mile territorial sea. Arguably, if one assumes the 12 mile limit for contiguous zones to have been valid, there would have been no need to continue the concept at all after the breadth of the territorial sea was settled at 12 nautical miles. In addition, the adoption of the 200 mile exclusive economic zone giving the coastal States broad new powers weakens the need for contiguous zones further. While the Commission noted that the waters within a contiguous zone remained high seas, under the new Convention, they would be exclusive economic zone. However, as before, the high seas freedoms still exist in the contiguous zone, except for resource matters.

1982 UNITED NATIONS CONVENTION ON THE LAW OF THE SEA

Article 33

Contiguous zone

1. In a zone contiguous to its territorial sea, described as the contiguous zone, the coastal State may exercise the control necessary to:

(a) prevent infringement of its customs, fiscal, immigration or sanitary laws or regulations within its territory or territorial sea;

(b) punish infringement of the above laws and regulations committed within its territory or territorial sea.

2. The contiguous zone may not extend beyond 24 nautical miles from the baselines from which the breadth of the territorial sea is measured.

4. PIRATE BROADCASTING

Churchill and Lowe, THE LAW OF THE SEA (1983) 149-150[2]

....

[2]. Reprinted by permission of Manchester University Press

In the early 1960's a number of ships anchored in the North Sea and began broadcasting, for profit, without a license from the States where the transmissions were received. Since these `pirate' radio stations were based on foreign ships on the high seas, the view was taken that coastal States had no jurisdiction over them. Under the European Agreement for the Prevention of Broacasting transmitted from Stations outside National Territories, signed in 1965, several European States agreed to punish their nationals engaged in or assisting unauthorized broadcasting, as well as anyone, of whatever nationality, on ships flying their flag from which unauthorized broadcasts were being made. This forced most stations to close down. Thus far, action against pirate broadcasting had not exceeded the general principle of exclusive flag State jurisdiction. But the Law of the Sea Convention has gone further, allowing States where unauthorized transmissions either are received or result in interference with authorized radio communication to exercise jurisdiction over unauthorized broadcasters; flag States and national States of broadcasters retain a concurrent jurisdiction.

Rights of visiting and boarding, and of seizing ships, and arresting and prosecuting persons on board, are vested in those Sttes which have jurisdiction over unauthorized broadcasting, and are exercised under the condition described...in relation to piracy.

In the case of piracy and unauthorized broadcasting, States other than the flag State are given under the Convention both legislative jurisdiction and enforcement jurisdiction over ships on the high seas (which exist anyway as a matter of customary international law in the case of piracy). In a number of other cases States enjoy extended enforcement jurisdiction over foreign ships on the high seas, unaccompanied by a right to prescribe rules which they are obliged to obey.

1982 UNITED NATIONS CONVENTION ON THE LAW OF THE SEA

Article 109

Unauthorized broadcasting from the high seas

1. All States shall co-operate in the suppression of unauthorized broadcasting from the high seas.

2. For the purposes of this Convention, "unauthorized broadcasting" means the transmission of sound, radio or television broadcasts from a ship or installation on the high seas intended for reception by the general public contrary to international regulations, but excluding the transmission of distress calls.

3. Any person engaged in unauthorized broadcasting may be prosecuted before a court of:

(a) the flag State of the ship;
(b) the State of registry of the installation;
(c) the State of which the person is a national;
(d) the State where the transmissions can be received; or
(e) any State where authorized radio communication is suffering interference.

4. On the high seas, a State having jurisdiction in accordance with paragraph 3 may, in conformity with article 110, arrest any person or ship engaged in unauthorized broadcasting and seize the broadcasting apparatus.

5. ENVIRONMENTAL PROTECTION

It is obvious that coastal States have a direct interest in protecting their coastlines from environmental degradation. Because States have jurisdiction over their territorial seas, they can exercise whatever protective control methods they may choose in that zone. But it is just as obvious that the desired result cannot be adequately achieved if enforcement activity is restricted to the territorial sea. A coastal State may, therefore, seek to establish a special contiguous zone for that purpose. Canada took such a step regarding the prevention of oil pollution from ships, as the following materials illustrate.

U.S. OPPOSES UNILATERAL EXTENSION BY CANADA OF HIGH SEAS JURISDICTION

Department of State Press Release 121, April 15, 1970
62 Dept. State Bull. (1970)

Last week the Canadian Government introduced in the House of Commons two bills dealing with pollution in the Arctic, fisheries, and the limits of the territorial sea. The enactment and implementation of these measures would affect the exercise by the United States and other countries of the right to the freedom of the high seas in large areas of the high seas and would adversely affect our efforts to reach international agreement on the use of the seas.

The bills seek to establish pollution zones in Arctic waters up to 100 miles from every point of Canadian coastal territory above the 60th parallel. Within these zones, Canada would assert the right to control all shipping, to prescribe standards of vessel construction, navigation, and operation, and to prohibit, if Canada deemed it necessary, the free passage of vessels in those waters. Additionally, the legislation seeks to authorize the establishment of exclusive Canadian fisheries in areas of the high seas beyond 12 miles, such as the Gulf of St. Lawrence and the Bay of Fundy, and a 12-mile territorial sea off Canada's coasts.

International law provides no basis for these proposed unilateral extensions of jurisdiction on the high seas, and the United States can neither accept nor acquiesce in the assertion of such jurisdiction.

We are concerned that this action by Canada, if not opposed by us, would be taken as precedent in other parts of the world for other unilateral infringements of the freedom of the seas. If Canada had the right to claim and exercise exclusive pollution and resources jurisdiction on the high seas, other countries could assert the right to exercise jurisdiction for other purposes, some reasonable and some not, but all equally invalid according to international law. Merchant shipping would be severely restricted, and naval mobility would be seriously jeopardized. The potential for serious international dispute and conflict is obvious.

The United States has long sought international solutions rather than national approaches to problems involving the high seas. We are working for appropriate actions within the United Nations framework toward the conclusion of a new international treaty dealing with the limit of the territorial sea, guaranteeing freedom of transit through and over international straits, and defining preferential fishing rights for coastal states on the high seas.

We are also seeking new international means for controlling pollution on the high seas. Last fall 47 countries, including the United States and Canada, participated in the preparation of two international conventions establishing the right of a coastal state to take certain limited antipollution measures against vessels on the high seas and also imposing strict liability upon the owners of vessels responsible for pollution.

These conventions, which the United States has recently signed, were concluded under U.N. auspices at Brussels. Other international approaches to control of pollution are underway at NATO and the U.N.. Moreover, the United States is acutely aware of the peculiar ecological nature of the Arctic region and the potential dangers of oil pollution in that area. The Arctic is a region important to all nations in its unique environment and its increasing significance as a world trade route and as a source of natural resources. We believe that the Arctic beyond national jurisdiction should be subject to internationally agreed rules protecting its assets, both living and nonliving, and have noted with pleasure the Canadian Prime Minister's public statement that Canada would be prepared to enter into multilateral efforts to develop agreed rules of environmental protection. To this end, we intend shortly to ask other countries to join in an international conference designed to establish rules for the Arctic beyond national jurisdiction by international agreement. We would be pleased if Canada were to join us in organizing such a conference.

We regret that the Canadian Government, while not excluding these cooperative international approaches to our mutual problems involving the oceans, now proposes to take unilateral action to assert its own jurisdiction and establish its own rules pending the conclusion of international agreements satisfactory to it. For the reasons indicated earlier, the United States cannot accept these unilateral jurisdictional assertions, and we have urged the Canadian Government to defer making them effective while cooperating in efforts promptly to reach internationally agreed solutions.

If, however, the Canadian Government is unwilling to await international agreement, we have urged that in the interest of avoiding a continuing dispute and undermining our efforts to achieve international agreement we submit our differences regarding pollution and exclusive fisheries jurisdiction beyond 12 miles to the International Court of Justice, the forum where disputes of this nature should rightfully be settled. Canada's action last week excluded such disputes from its acceptance of the International Court's compulsory jurisdiction. However, such action only prevents Canada from being forced into the Court. It does not preclude Canada from voluntarily joining with us in submitting these disputes to the Court or to an appropriate chamber of the Court.

With respect to the 12-mile limit on the territorial sea, we have publicly indicated our willingness to accept such limit, but only as a part of an agreed international treaty also providing for freedom of passage through and over international straits.

The history of U.S.-Canadian relations is unique in world affairs for its closeness and cooperation. We are confident that, in this spirit, our two countries will continue to resolve our differences amicably and with mutual understanding.

SUMMARY OF CANADIAN NOTE OF APRIL 16, 1970, TABLED BY THE SECRETARY OF STATE FOR EXTERNAL AFFAIRS IN THE HOUSE, APRIL 17, 1970

The Canadian Government is unable to accept the views of the United States Government concerning the Arctic Waters Pollution Prevention Bill and the amendments to the Territorial Sea and Fishing Zones Act, and regrets that the United States is not prepared to acquiesce in them. The Canadian Government cannot accept in particular the view that international law provides no basis for the proposed measures. For many years, large numbers of states have asserted various forms of limited jursidiction beyond their territorial sea over marine areas adjacent to their coasts. The position of the United States Government is that the waters beyond a three-mile limit are high seas and that no state has a right to exercise exclusive pollution or resources jurisdiction on the high seas beyond a three-mile territorial sea. The Canadian Government does not accept this view which indeed the

United States itself does not adhere to in practice. For example, as early as 1790, at a time when the international norm for the breadth of the territorial sea was without question three miles, the United States claimed jurisdiction up to twelve miles for customs purposes and enacted appropriate enforcement legislation, which is still in force. Since 1935 the United States has claimed the authority to extend customs enforcement activities as far out to sea as 62 miles, in clear contradiction of applicable international law. In 1966, the United States established exclusive fisheries jursidiction beyond its three-mile territorial sea extending out to twelve miles from shore, and the United States has just passed analogous legislation asserting exclusive pollution control jurisdiction beyond its three-mile territorial sea and up to twelve miles. Canada reserves to itself the same rights as the United States has asserted to determine for itself how best to protect the vital interests, including in particular its national security. It is the further view of the Canadian Government that a danger to the environment constitutes a threat to its security. Thus the proposed Canadian Arctic Waters Pollution Prevention Legislation constitutes a lawful extension of a limited form of jurisdiction to meet particular dangers, and is of a different order from unilateral interferences with the freedom of the high seas such as, for example, the atomic tests carried out by the United States and other states which, however necessary they may be, have appropriated to their own use vast areas of the high seas and constituted grave perils to those who would wish to utilize those areas during the period of the test blast. The most recent example of such a test by the United States and its consequences for the freedom of the high seas, as was pointed out by some governments at that time, occurred in October 1969 when the United States warned away shipping within a 50-mile radius of the test it was conducting at Amchitka Island. The proposed anti-pollution legislation, proposed fisheries protection legislation and the proposed 12-mile territorial sea constitute a threat to no state and a peril to no one.

It is a well-established principle of international law that customary international law is developed by state practice. Recent and important instances of such state practice on the law of the sea are, for example, the Truman Proclamation of 1945 proclaiming United States jurisdiction over the continental shelf and the unilateral establishment in 1966 by the United States of exclusive fishing zones. Overwhelming evidence that international law can be and is developed by state practice lies in the fact that in 1958, at the time of the first of recent failures of the international community to reach agreement on the breadth of the territorial sea, some 14 states claimed a 12-mile territorial sea, whereas by 1970 some 45 states have established a 12-mile territorial sea and 57 states have established a territorial sea of 12 miles or more. Indeed, the three-mile territorial sea, now claimed by only 24 countries, was itself established by state practice.

....

The Canadian Government has long been concerned about the inadequacies of international law in failing to give the necessary protection to the marine environment and to ensure the conservation of fisheries resources. The proposed anti-pollution legislation is based on the overriding right of self-defense of coastal states to protect themselves against grave threats to their environment. Traditional principles of international law concerning pollution of the sea are based in the main on ensuring freedom of navigation of shipping states, which are now engaged in the large scale carriage of oil and other potential pollutants. Such traditional concepts are of little or no relevance anywhere in the world if they can be cited as precluding a coastal state to protect this environment. Such concepts are particularly relevant, however, to an area having the unique characteristics of the Arctic, where there is an intimate relationship between the sea, the ice and the land, and where the permanent defilement of the environment could occur and result in the destruction of whole species. It is idle, moreover, to talk of freedom of the high seas with respect to an area, large parts of which are covered with ice throughout each year, and where local inhabitants use the frozen area as an extension of the land to travel over it by dogsled and snowmobile far more than they can use it as water. While the Canadian Government is determined to open up the Northwest Passage to safe navigation, it cannot accept the suggestion that the Northwest Passage constitutes high seas.

ED. NOTE: An activity related to oil pollution is the disposal of wastes, some toxic and some not. Waste disposal in waters adjacent to the territorial sea has raised the same kind of questions as other uses of these waters. Is it legal for a coastal State to designate special contiguous zones either for the disposal of waste or for its regulation?

McDougal and Burke, THE PUBLIC ORDER OF THE OCEANS (1965) 861-862[3]

There is practically unanimous agreement that uninhibited or unrestrained disposal of wastes is not desirable and perhaps it is not too much to infer that such disposal would be regarded as unlawful. There seems to be, for example, general -- if tacit -- agreement that high level wastes ought not to be placed intentionally in the ocean as a part of a waste disposal program and unless new persuasive considerations are introduced it would not be surprising if disposal of these wastes came generally to be regarded as unlawful.

There are, of course, ample doctrinal propositions available to justify exclusive prescriptions seeking to prevent disposal in certain high seas areas. As discussed previously, all states may claim, under customary international law, to exercise certain authority in the ocean areas contiguous to their territorial sea. But whether coastal states are authorized to prohibit disposal activities in a contiguous area in a particular instance depends here, as in other instances, on appraisal of what is reasonable in the particular context. it is possible that in some circumstances disposal is a reasonable use of the site concerned, being limited in area and in amount deposited, and, expecially, offering little threat to other uses. On the other hand, preclusion of disposal in other areas might be entirely reasonable, as where highly valuable fishing grounds would no longer be useful or where apprehension in the coastal populace threatened to work a drastic reductionin the recreational possibilities of the area.

ED. NOTE: There are many examples of U.S. domestic legislation that establish for the United States certain competences regarding the environment in areas beyond the territorial sea. For example, the Marine Protection, Research and Sanctuaries Act of 1972 authorizes the Secretary of Commerce, after consultation with other affected agencies, to establish by designation marine sanctuaries in the ocean as far seaward as the edge of the continental shelf for purposes of conservation and the preservation of recreational, ecological or esthetic values.

This legislation calls for negotiations with foreign governments for the purpose of achieving agreements furthering the objectives of the act. Regulations concerning a marine sanctuary, absent agreement with affected foreign States, may not be imposed upon non-citizens from those States.

Sanctuaries have been designated under this legislation, one of them in Biscayne Bay. Another, designated in 1975, is the Monitor Marine Sanctuary, the purpose of which is to preserve the Civil War ironclad warship "Monitor". This sanctuary consists of a vertical water column in the Atlantic Ocean one mile in diameter extending from the seabed to the surface, the center of which is about 18 miles from Cape Hatteras, North Carolina. Among the prohibited activities are anchoring, conducting any salvage operations, diving, seabed drilling or coring, and trawling.

Another example of extended U.S. jurisdiction for environmental reasons is the Federal Water Pollution Control Act [now the Clean Water Act]. Section 1321 of that Act declares it to be the policy of the United States that there should be no discharges of oil or hazardous substances into or upon the

---

3. Reprinted by permission of New Haven Press

navigable waters of the United States, including into the contiguous zone as defined by the 1958 Convention. And the Oil Pollution Act of 1990 provides for liability for oil discharges into navigable waters, and, by definition, this includes the exclusive economic zone. These are but a few examples. Are any of them arguably justifiable in international law?

CHAPTER 5

BASELINES

A. INTRODUCTION

In previous chapters we have studied various zones of the sea, such as internal waters and the territorial sea from a juridical point of view. In several instances we have encountered such language as "the baselines from which the breadth of the territorial sea is measured." These baselines, then, are important to coastal States in setting forth accurately the limits of their various zones of jurisdiction. It is important, too, for other States whose vessels may utilize these zones. We have seen, for example, that the baseline separates internal waters from the territorial sea, and that the competence of the coastal State is quite different in each of these zones or areas. Thus, again, it is important that the users know clearly where one zone begins and another ends in order to know what their responsibilities are to the coastal State at any time.

In addition, in a subsequent chapter we shall consider the delimitation of maritime boundaries between States. This is a critical operation often leading to disputes involving vast amounts of resources or of extremely important political impact. As we will see, many of these cases have gone to international tribunals for resolution. Here, again, baselines play an important, sometimes critical role.

It is for this reason that in this chapter we will learn about the normal ways baselines are drawn on charts, as well as examine some exceptional cases requiring special rules, such as juridical or historic bays.

States often use the method by which they draw their baselines to, in effect, lay claim to large amounts of water. It is important for that reason as well to know what the rules of international law are in the process of evaluating those claims.

Delimitation of the maritime boundaries of a State is, of course, a task that only the coastal State itself can undertake. But the validity of those lines is subject to scrutiny by the international community, and it depends upon their acceptance. As the International Court of Justice observed in the Anglo-Norwegian Fisheries Case (to be examined later):

> "The delimitation of sea areas has always an international aspect; it cannot be dependent merely upon the will of the coastal State as expressed in its municipal law. Although it is true that the act of delimitation is necessarily a unilateral act, because only the coastal State is competent to undertake it, the validity of the delimitation with regard to other States depends upon international law."

With this in mind, let us examine the rules.

B. THE NORMAL BASELINE: MAINLANDS

CONVENTION ON THE TERRITORIAL SEA AND THE CONTIGUOUS ZONE

Article 3

Except where otherwise provided in these articles, the normal baseline for measuring the breadth of the territorial sea is the low-water line along the coasts as marked on large-scale charts officially recognized by the coastal State.

* * * *

Article 5 of the 1982 United Nations Convention on the Law of the Sea is identical. Before we can fully understand what these articles mean, it is first necessary to understand what the low-water mark really is, and what is meant by large-scale charts.

As to the latter question, Shalowitz had this to say.

Shalowitz, SHORE AND SEA BOUNDARIES (Vol. 1, 1962) at 274

Although "large scale" is a relative term and is not defined in the convention, a scale of 1/80,000 (approximately 1 nautical mile to the inch) would probably be the upper limit of such classification

* * * *

In his second volume, Shalowitz give his opinion that scales up to and including 1/20,000 would be considered large scales, those between 1/20,000 and 1/80,000 would be intermediate scales, and those smaller than 1/80,000 would be small scale.

To put this in better perspective, a scale of 1/80,000 means that one inch on the chart represents 80,000 inches, or 1.11 miles, on the surface of the earth, while on a scale of 1/20,000 one inch on the chart represents .278 miles on the surface of the earth. Obviously, the latter chart shows more detail.

In addressing the first question, we must understand first of all that some level of water must be selected as the standard, or "tidal datum plane" before a baseline may be drawn on a chart. Obviously, the line representing the coastline on a chart would be placed differently if it represented the high tide mark rather than the low tide mark. Since charts are used mainly for navigation, it is best to select the tidal datum plane least misleading to the navigator. If the high tide mark were used, and all the depths appearing on the chart represented high tide, the navigator might be lulled into a false sense of security. If there is a large tidal range in the area, there may be in fact a dangerously low depth of water at low tide. Thus chart makers have chosen to use low water, and the navigator may consider, for the most part, that there will normally be more water below the keel than that shown on the chart.

But note that it is not just low water that is spoken of in the conventions. It is the low water mark as indicated on large scale charts. That language is deliberately selected because not all charts use precisely the same datum plane. The reason for this is that the tidal cycles are not precisely the same in all locations or at all times during the day. These daily variations are known as diurnal inequality. Shalowitz describes the phenomenon as follows.

Shalowitz, SHORE AND SEA BOUNDARIES (Vol. I, 1962) 84-90

621. Diurnal Inequalitiy

Along the Pacific Coast of the United States [see Fig. 5-1 at the end of the chapter], the mixed type of tide is the predominant one -- two high and two low waters occur each tidal day, with marked differences between the morning and afternoon tides. This difference is called diurnal inequaltiy and varies with the changing declination of the moon during a lunar month. In general, the inequality tends to increase with an increasing declination, either north or south, and to diminish as the moon approaches the equator.

The existence of diurnal inequality is an important factor in the determination of the various vertical datums based on tidal definition, and makes necessary the distinction between the two high waters and the two low waters of a day. Thus, of the former the higher is called "higher high water" and the lower the "lower high water." Similarly, of the two low waters, the lower is called "lower low water" and the higher the "higher low water".

* * * *

Note that on Figure 5-1 at the end of the chapter, there are different tidal patterns at differing places in the United States. The east coast pattern has much less variation than the west coast pattern, and the gulf coast pattern is entirely different from either of them.

In addition to diurnal inequalities, there are other fluctuations in tidal cycles that must be taken into account in drawing the coastline. Shalowitz goes on to describe them.

622. Spring and Neap Tides

Another variation in the rise and fall of the tide is related to the different phases through which the moon passes during a lunar, or synodic, month of approximately 29 1/2 days. At new moon the sun and moon are in line on the same side of the earth. The tidal forces are then in the same phase and work in conjunction to strenthen each other and bring about large tides which have been designated "spring tides." At such times high water rises higher and low water falls lower than at other times. At the end of 7 1/2 days the moon has passed through one-quarter of its journey and has reached quadrature. The tidal forces of sun and moon then act at right angles on the waters of the earth and are in opposition to each other, or in opposite phase. Each force tends to minimize the force of the other body. The tide therefore does not rise as high nor fall as low as on the average. Because of their small range they have been designated as "neap tides."

After another 7 1/2 days, the sun and moon are again in line but on opposite sides of the earth. The moon is then in its "full" phase and the tidal forces act the same as during new moon and spring tides again occur. At the end of another period of 7 1/2 days, the moon has arrived at the third quarter of its course and is again in quadrature. The tidal forces act in opposition as in the first quarter and neap tides result. At the end of a further period of 7 1/2 days, the sun and moon are again in line and on the same side of the earth and another cycle begins.

ED. NOTE: In deciding on a tidal datum plane, a period of 19 years is used to obtain the average. This is because the more important of the periodic tidal variations due to astronomic causes will have gone through complete cycles. In Borax Consolidated v. City of Los Angeles, 296 U.S. 10 (1935), the court adopted this period. At issue there was the computation of mean high tide, since this line is used by many, but not all, states to demark the dividing line between state and private ownership. In adopting the same period, the court noted:

"The view of the definition of the mean high tide, as given by the United States Coast and Geodetic Survey, that `Mean high water at any place is the average of all the high waters at that place over a considerable period of time,' and the further observation that `from theoretical considerations of an astronomical character' there should be `a periodic variation in the rise of water above sea level having a period of 18.6 years,' the Court of Appeals directed that in order to ascertain the mean high-tide line with requisite certainty in fixing the boundary of valuable tidelands, such as those here in question appear to be, an average of 18.6 years should be determined as near as possible.' We find no error in that instruction."

C. ISLANDS AND THEIR BASELINES

Before discussing where baselines should be drawn about islands, it is necessary to consider what an island is in the legal sense. Oviously, some isolated bits of land are so insignificant that they probably should have no legal effect. But which ones?

CONVENTION ON THE TERRITORIAL SEA AND THE CONTIGUOUS ZONE

Article 10(1)

An island is a naturally formed area of land, surrounded by water, which is above water at high tide.

* * * *

But what does "naturally formed" mean? And are their specific obj[illegible] excluded from the definition? With regard to the latter, the ILC explained.

INTERNATIONAL LAW COMMISSION, 1956 Commentary

Draft Article 10, Comment (2)

(2) An island is understood to be any area of land surrounded by water which, except in abnormal circumstances, is permanently above high-water mark. Consequently, the following are not considered islands and have no territorial sea:

(i) Elevations which are above water at low tide only. Even if an installation is built on such an elevation and is itself permanently above water -- a lighthouse, for example -- the elevation is not an "island" as understood in this article;

(ii) Technical installations built on the seabed, such as installations used for the exploitation of the continental shelf... The Commission nevertheless proposed that a safety zone around such installations should be recognized in view of their extreme vulnerability. It does not consider that a similar measure is required in the case of lighthouses.

* * * *

The question of what constitutes a "naturally formed" island is more complex. Shalowitz has his own explanation.

Shalowitz, SHORE AND SEA BOUNDARIES (Vol. II, 1962) 225-227

D. ISLANDS AND LOW-TIDE ELEVATIONS

Another important factor in the process of delimiting the territorial sea is the treatment of islands and low-tide elevations. An island, whether within or without the territorial sea, carries its own belt of territorial waters, whereas a low-tide elevation generates such a belt only if it lies wholly or partly within the territorial sea. It therefore becomes necessary to be clear as to the meaning of these terms in the technical sense.

(a) *Definition of Island.* -- Article 10 of the convention defines an island as "a naturally-formed area of land, surrounded by water, which above water at high-tide." The definition is essentially the same as that recommended by the International Law Commission but with one important difference -- where the ILC definition left open the question whether artifically formed islands, such as spoil banks resulting from dredging operations, fall within the scope of the draft rules, the Geneva convention definitely excludes such formmations.

To fall within the definition, the land must be surrounded by water and must be above water at high tide. On the face of it, this would seem to raise the question whether it must be surrounded by water at high tide only or also at low tide. But a little reflection will show that insofar as the territorial sea is concerned it must be surrounded by water at all stages of the tide. Although not specifically provided for, it must be assumed that neither habitability, shape, area, nor texture is a necessary ingredient of an island for the purpose of delimiting the territorial sea.

Islands have been considered in other contexts and may be defined somewhat differently from that adopted by the Geneva Conference. For example, for the purpose of determining the ownership of new islands formed in a navigable stream, it has been held that land surrounded by water only in times of high water is not an island within the rule that the state takes title to such lands.

For mapping and charting purposes, the following definition has been used: A body of land extending above and completely surrounded by water at the mean high-water stage; an area of dry land entirely surrounded by water or a swamp; an area of swamp entirely surrounded by open water.

ED. NOTE: We will come back to the issue of habitability when we look at the provision in the new convention. At least one court has agreed with Shalowitz on the issue of texture being irrelevant. In The Anna, 5 Rob. 373 (1805) a British court was faced with a case where an American ship was seized by a British privateer in the Gulf of Mexico in a place more than 3 miles from the U.S. mainland, but approximately 2 miles from small mud islands composed of earth and driftwood off the mouth of the Mississippi River. It was held that they were natural appendages to the coast and "whether they are composed of earth or solid rock, will not vary the right of dominion, for the right of dominion does not depend upon the texture of the soil," even though it was contended that they were not inhabited and used only for shooting birds.

The question left unanswered by Shalowitz is whether an area of spoil or a dumping area, which according to him, is not naturally formed and thus not an island can subsequently become an island. This could be an important question because if it is an island it has consequences for how much territorial sea can be claimed at that point. Dr. Robert Hodgson, former State Department Geographer discusses this problem.

Hodgson, ISLANDS: NORMAL AND SPECIAL CIRCUMSTANCES (Research Study, Bureau of Intelligence and Research, U.S. Department of State, December 10, 1973)

The use of "formed" rather than "created" raises distinct or potential questions of interpretation. Obviously, the island must be composed of land-dirt, rock, organic matter, or a combination thereof. Its formation may be assisted, however, by man's efforts. To maintain navigation channels, states and individuals dredge certain earth materials from the subsoil of rivers, harbors, and other coastal areas. Such material, or spoil, creates problems of disposal, and dredgers, motivated by cost factors, seek a local place in which to dump the spoil. Nearby shallows often furnish the site.

Currents, tides, and other natural forces act upon these manmade dumps of earth. When dumping ceases, most often they disappear, transported and redistributed by the relentless environment of coastal waters over the bottom from which they were dredged. Occasionally these spoil dumps remain above sea level, but their external shapes and dimensions are altered markedly or "formed" by actions of tides, waves, currents, and wind. Thus a "naturally formed island" is born. Should it be considered an island under the terms of the Convention?

The language of the Convention and the labors of the legal and techical experts who assisted in its preliminary drafts emphasize chart representation of geographic features -- the external, two-dimensional forms. Genesis of landforms, difficult and expensive to establish or prove, was not a major factor in the proceedings. Charted forms dominate in the geographical-legal definitions of bays, river mouths, etc. As a consequence, man-created spoil banks may become, through the forces of nature, islands in the legal-political as well as the geographical, sense of the Convention. It should be noted, however, that the effects of such islands on the extension of the territorial sea normally are limited since the islands, to survive, must be in relatively shallow water close to land.

However, if dumping of spoil at a site continues, the artificial nature of the spoil bank will be maintained. The shape of the "island" will continue to be artifically formed and the definition in the Convention will be negated. This fact would be reinforced if the coastal state continued to mark the "island" as "spoil" on official charts. The "island" would then remain "an artificially formed" node above sea level and should have no effect on the extension of the teritorial sea. Geographically an island, the spoil bank would not exist legally as a basepoint.

* * * *

ED. NOTE: Other questions have arisen, platforms and installations aside, regarding the deliberate construction of islands. Some years ago, for example, the Dutch did a study on the feasibility of using large quantities of dredge fill obtained from the deepening of the channel into Rotterdam so that the port could accomodate supertankers, to form an artificial island to be used as an industrial park. The legal questions studied included whether the Netherlands could build such an island outside of their territorial waters, whether the island could have its own territorial sea, and whether the Netherlands could apply its own civil and criminal laws to workers on the island regardless of their nationality. What is your view of the appropriate answers to these questions?

The above materials make reference to the effect of the existence of islands on zones of jurisdiction of the coastal State.

CONVENTION ON THE TERRITORIAL SEA AND THE CONTIGUOUS ZONE

Article 10(2)

The territorial sea of an island is measured in accordance with the provisions of these articles.

INTERNATIONAL LAW COMMISSION, 1956 Commentary

(1) This article applies both to islands situated in the high seas and to islands in the territorial sea. In the case of the latter, their own territorial sea will partly coincide with the territorial sea of the mainland. The presence of the island will create a bulge in the outer limit of the territorial sea of the mainland. The same idea can be expressed in the following form: islands, wholly or partly situated in the territorial sea, shall be taken into consideration in determining the outer limit of the territorial sea.

CONVENTION ON THE CONTINENTAL SHELF

Article 5(2), (4)

2. ...the coastal State is entitled to construct and maintain or operate on the continental shelf installations and other devices necessary for its exploration and the exploitation of its natural resources....

....

4. Such installations and devices, though under the jurisdiction of the coastal State, do not possess the status of islands. They have no territorial sea of their own, and their presence does not affect the delimitation of the territorial sea of the coastal State.

1982 UNITED NATIONS CONVENTION ON THE LAW OF THE SEA

Article 121

Regime of islands

1. An island is a naturally formed area of land, surrounded by water, which is above water at high tide.

2. Except as provided for in paragraph 3, the territorial sea, the contiguous zone, the exclusive economic zone and the continental shelf of an island are determined in accordance with the provisions of this Convention applicable to other land territory.

3. Rocks which cannot sustain human habitation or economic life of their own shall have no exclusive economic zone or continental shelf.

* * * *

ED. NOTE: Notice that a new paragraph 3 has been added to the 1958 provisions. It refers to rocks that cannot sustain human habitation or economic life of their own. Can you think of any reason why this was added? Further, what do the terms "human habitation" and "economic life" possibly mean? Does it mean, for example that the "rock" must have a permanent population? Does it mean that it does not sustain such habitation if there is no water supply?

D. SPECIAL CASES

1. THE STRAIGHT BASELINE

In certain limited special cases, States may depart from the use of the normal baseline when specific conditions exist. There is both customary and conventional law on the subject. The customary rules are contained in the Anglo-Norwegian Fisheries case, below. As to conventional rules and the actual practice of States, see the following.

Churchill and Lowe, THE LAW OF THE SEA (1983) 28-30[1]

Conventional rules. At the time it was given, the Court's [ICJ] judgment was widely regarded as a piece of "judicial legislation". However, the rules enunciated by the Court were taken up by the ILC and eventually incorporated in the Territorial Sea Convention (art.4), which closely follows the language of the Court's judgment. While the Court suggests that straight baselinses are simply a special application of the low-water mark principle of constructing the baseline, the Territorial Sea and Law of the Sea Conventions more realistically recognise straight baselines as a distinct method of construction.

....

State practice. Although both the International Court of Justice in the *Anglo-Norwegian Fisheries* case and the Territorial Sea and Law of the Sea Conventions regard the use of straight baselines as being limited to exceptional geographical circumstances, and although few States have a coastline that is anywhere near as indented or fringed with islands as that of Norway, about half the world's coastal States have in fact drawn straight baselines along all or part of their coasts. As we have seen, the rules governing the use of straight baselines laid down in customary and conventional law are relatively imprecise, and thus allow States a considerable latitude in the way they draw straight baselines. Some States, however, do appear to have gone beyond the spirit and the vague wording of these rules. Of the forty straight baseline systems so far analysed by the Geographer of the US Department of State in the Limits in the Seas series, no fewer than twenty-five (e.g. those of Mexico, Madagascar and Thailand) are considered in one way or another not to comply with the rules (although three of these cases -- the Faroes, Indonesia and the Philippines -- are better regarded as the justifiable use of acrchipelagic baselines. Perhaps the most extreme system is that of Burma, one of whose straight baselines is 222 miles long and at one point seventy-five miles from the nearest land.

The effect of drawing straight baselines, even strictly in accord with the rules, is often to enclose considerable bodies of sea as internal waters: for example, the whole of the Minches, lying between the Inner and Outer Hebrides of the west coast of Scotland, is enclosed by straight baselines and thus is internal waters.

[1]. Reprinted by permission of the Manchester University Press

FISHERIES CASE
(UNITED KINGDOM v. NORWAY [1951] I.C.J. Rep. 116)

[In 1935, by Royal Decree, Norway constructed a system of straight baselines (as illustrated by Fig. 5-4 at the end of this chapter) in order to reserve fishing rights to themselves in the area known as the "skjaergaard". The English, who had been fishing in those waters prior to the decree, and would now be exluded, challenged Norway in the ICJ. At issue was the validity under international law of Norway's claim to the right to draw these baselines. In question was the validity of 47 baselines totalling about 600 miles in length established by a Norwegian Royal Decree in 1935. The breadth of the territorial sea was not in issue. The baselines in question varied in length from 100 yards to 44 miles. Twenty-five of them exceeded 10 miles in length and eight were longer than 20 miles in length.]

....

The Application asked the Court

"(a) to declare the principles of international law to be applied in defining the baselines, by reference to which the Norwegian Government is entitled to delimit a fisheries zone, extending to seaward 4 sea miles from those lines and exclusively reserved to its own nationals, in the light of the arguments of the Parties, in order to avoid further legal differences between them;

(b) to award damages to the Government of the United Kingdom in respect of all interferences by the Norwegian authorities with British fishing vessels outside the zone which, in accordance with the Court's decision under (a), the Norwegian Government is entitled to reserve for its nationals."

....

Although the Decree of July 12th, 1935, refers to the Norwegian fisheries zone and does not specifically mention the territorial sea, there can be no doubt that the zone delimited by this Decree is none other than the sea area which Norway considers to be her territorial sea. That is how the Parties argued the question and that is the way in which they submitted it to the Court for decision.

....

The claim of the United Kingdom is founded on what it regards as the general international law applicable to the delimitation of the Norwegian fisheries zone.

The Norwegian Government does not deny that there exist rules of international law to which this delimitation must conform. It contends that the propositions formulated by the United Kingdom Government in its "Conclusions" do not possess the character attributed to them by that Government. It further relies on its own system of delimitation which it asserts to be in every respect in conformity with the requirements of international law.

....

The coastal zone concerned in the dispute is of considerable length. It lies...north of the Arctic Circle, and it includes the coast of the mainland of Norway and all of the islands, islets, rocks and reefs, known by the name of "skjaergaard" (literally, rock rampart), together with all Norwegian internal and territorial waters. The coast of the mainland, without taking into account of fjords, bays and minor indentations, is over 1,500 kilometers in length, is of a very distinctive configuration. Very broken along its whole length, it constantly opens out into indentations penetrating for great distances inland: the Porsanderfjord, for instance, penetrates 75 sea miles inland. To the west, the land configuration stretches out into the sea: the large and small islands, mountainous in character, the islets, rocks and reefs, some always above water, others emerging only at low tide, are in truth but an extension of the Norwegian mainland. The number of insular formations, large and small, which make up the "skjaergaard", is estimated by the Norwegian Government to be one hundred and twenty thousand. From the southern extremity of the disputed area to the North Cape, the "skjaergaard" lies along the whole coast of the mainland; east of the North Cape, the "skjaergaard" ends, but the coast line continues to be broken by large and deeply indented fjords.

Within the "skjaergaard", almost every island has its large and small bays; countless arms of the sea, straits, channels and mere waterways serve as a means of communication for the local population which inhabits the islands as it does the mainland. The coast of the mainland does not constitute, as it does in practically all other countries, a clear dividing line between the land and sea. What matters, what really constitutes the Norwegian coast, is the outer limit of the "sjaergaard".

The whole of the region is mountainous. The North Cape, a sheer rock little more than 300 metres high, can be seen from a considerable distance; there are other summits rising to over a thousand metres, so that the Norwegian coast, mainland, and "skjaergaard", is visible from far off.

Along the coast are situated comparatively shallow banks, veritable under-water terraces which constitute fishing grounds where fish are particularly abundant; these grounds were known to Norwegian fishermen and exploited by them from time immemorial. Since these banks lay within the range of vision, the most desirable fishing grounds were always located and identified by means of the method of alignments ("meds"), at points where two lines drawn between points selected on the coast or islands intersected.

In these barren regions the inhabitants of the coastal zone derive their livelihood essentially from fishing.

Such are the realities which must be borne in mind in appraising the validity of the United Kingdom contention that the limits of the Norwegian fisheries zone laid down at the 1935 Decree are contrary to international law.

The Parties being in agreement on the figure of 4 miles for the breadth of the territorial sea, the problem which arises is from what baseline this breadth is to be reckoned. The Conclusions of the United Kingdom are explicit on this point: the baseline must be the low-water mark on permanently dry land which is a part of Norwegian territory, or the proper closing line of Norwegian internal waters.

The Court has no difficulty in finding that, for the purpose of measuring the breadth of the territorial sea, it is the low-water mark as opposed to the high-water mark, or the mean between the two tides, which has generally been adopted in the practice of States.

....

The Court finds itself obliged to decide whether the relevant low-water mark is that of the mainland or of the "skjaergaard". Since the mainland is bordered in its western sector by the "skjaergaard", which constitutes a whole with the mainland, it is the outer line of the "skjaergaard" which must be taken into account in delimiting the belt of Norwegian territorial waters. This solution is dictated by geographic realities.

Three methods have been contemplated to effect the application of the low-water mark rule. The simplest would appear to be the method of the trace parallele, which consists of drawing the outer limit of the belt of the territorial waters by following the coast in all its sinuosities....

In the present case this method of trace parallele, which was invoked against Norway in the Memorial was abandoned in the written Reply, and later in the oral argument of the Agent of the United Kingdom Government. Consequently, it is no longer relevant to the case. "On the other hand", it said in the Reply, it is the courbe tangente -- or, in English, "envelopes of arcs of circles" -- method which the United Kingdom considers to be the correct one.

In the arcs of circles method, which is constantly used for determining the position of a point or object at sea, is a new technique in so far as it is a method for delimiting the territorial sea. This technique was proposed by the United States delegation at the 1930 Conference for the codification of international law. Its purpose is to secure the application of the principle that the belt of territorial waters must follow the line of the coast. It is not obligatory by law, as was admitted by Counsel for the United Kingdom Government in his oral reply. In these circumstances, and although certain of the Conclusions of the United Kingdom are founded on the application of the arcs of circles method, the Court considers that it need not deal with these Conclusions in so far as they are based on this method.

The principle that the belt of territorial waters must follow the general direction of the coast makes it possible to fix certain criteria valid for any delimitation of the territorial sea; these criteria will be elucidated later. The Court will confine itself at this state to noting that, in order to apply this principle, several States have deemed it necessary to follow the straight baselines method and that they have not encountered objections of principle by other States. This method consists of selecting appropriate points on the low-water mark and drawing straight baselines between them. This has been done, not only in the case of well-defined bays, but also in cases of minor curvatures of the coast line where it was solely a question of giving a simpler form to the belt of territorial waters.

....

The Court now comes to the question of the length of the baselines drawn across the waters lying between the various formations of the "skjaergaard". Basing itself on the analogy with the alleged general rule of ten miles relating to bays, the United Kingdom Government still maintains on this point that the length of straight baselines must not exceed ten miles.

In this connection, the practice of States does not justify the formulation of any general rule of law. The attempts that have been made to subject groups of islands or coastal archipelagoes to conditions analogous to the limitations concerning bays (distance between the islands not exceeding twice the breadth of the territorial waters, or ten or twelve sea miles), have not got beyond the state of proposals.

Furthermore, apart from any question of limiting the lines to ten miles, it may be that several lines can be envisaged. In such cases the coastal State would seem to be in the best position to appraise the local conditions dictating the selection.

Consequently, the Court is unable to share in the view of the United Kingdom Government, that "Norway, in the matter of baselines, now claims recognition of an exceptional system". As will be shown later, all that the Court can see therein is the application of general international law to a specific case.

The Conclusions of the United Kingdom, points 5 and 9 to 11, refer to waters situated between the baselines and the Norwegian mainland. The Court is asked to hold that on historic grounds these waters belong to Norway, but that they are divided into two categories: territorial and internal waters, in accordance with two criteria which the Conclusions regard as well founded in international law, the waters falling within the conception of a bay being deemed to be internal waters, and those having the character of legal straits being deemed to be territorial waters.

As has been conceded by the United Kingdom, the "skjaergaard" constitutes a whole with the Norwegian mainland; the waters between the baselines of the belt of territorial waters and the mainland are internal waters. However, according to the argument of the United Kingdom a portion of these waters constitutes territorial waters. There are inter alia the waters followed by the navigational route known as the Indreleia. It is contended that since these waters have this character, certain consequences arise with regard to the determination of the territorial waters at the end of this waterway considered as a maritime strait.

The Court is bound to observe that the Indreleia is not a strait at all, but rather a navigational route prepared as such by means of artificial aids to navigation provided by Norway. In these circumstance the Court is unable to accept the view that the Indreleia, for the purposes of the present case, has a status different from that of the other waters included in the "skjaergaard".

Thus the Court, confining itself for the moment to the Conclusions of the United Kingdom, finds that the Norwegian Government in fixing the baselines for the delimitation of the Norwegian fisheries zone by the 1935 Decree has not violated international law.

It does not at all follow that, in absence of rules having the technically precise character alleged by the United Kingdom Government, the delimitation undertaken by the Norwegian Government in 1935 is not subject to certain principles which make it possible to judge as to its validity under international law. The delimitation of sea areas has always an international aspect; it cannot be dependent merely upon the will of the coastal State as expressed in its municipal law. Although it is true that the act of delimitation is necessarily a unilateral act, because only the coastal State is competent to undertake it, the validity of the delimitation with regard to other States depends upon international law.

In this connection, certain basic considerations inherent in the nature of the territorial sea, bring to light certain criteria which, though not entirely precise, can provide courts with an adequate basis for their decisions, which can be adapted to the diverse facts in question.

Among these considerations, some reference must be made to the close dependence of the territorial sea upon the land domain. It is the land which confers upon the coastal State a right to the waters off its coasts. If follows that while such a State must be allowed the latitude necessary in order to be able to adapt its delimitation to practical needs and local requirements, the drawing of baselines must not depart to any appreciable extent from the general direction of the coast.

Another fundamental consideration, of particular importance in this case, is the more or less close relationship between certain sea areas and the land formations which divide or surround them. The real question raised in the choice of baselines is in effect whether certain sea areas lying within these lines are sufficiently closely linked to the land domain to be subject to the regime of internal waters. This idea, which is at the basis of the determination of rules relating to bays, should be liberally applied in the case of a coast, the geographical configuration of which is as unusual as that of Norway.

Finally, there is one consideration not to be overlooked, the scope of which extends beyond purely geographical factors: that of certain economic interests peculiar to a region, the reality and importance of which are clearly evidenced by long usage.

....

The Court, having...established the existence and constituent elements of the Norwegian system of delimitation, further finds that this system was consistently applied by the Norwegian authorities and that it encountered no opposition on the part of other States.

In the light of these considerations, and in the absence of convincing evidence to the contrary, the Court is bound to hold that the Norwegian authorities applied the system of delimitation consistently and uninterruptedly from 1869 until the time of the dispute arose.
From the standpoint of international law, it is now necessary to consider whether the application of the Norwegian system encountered any opposition from foreign States.

....

The general toleration of foreign States with regard to the Norwegian practice is an unchallenged fact. For a period of more than sixty years the United Kingdom Government itself in no way contested it....

The United Kingdom Government has argued that the Norwegian system of delimitation was not known to it and that the system therefore lacked the notoriety essential to prove the basis of an historic title enforceable against it. The Court is unable to accept this view. As a coastal State on the North Sea, greatly interested in the fisheries in this area, as a maritime Power traditionally concerned with the law of the sea and concerned particularly to defend the freedom of the seas, the United Kingdom could not have been ignorant of the Decree of 1869 which had at once provoked a request for explanations from the French Government. Nor, knowing of it, could it have been under any misapprehension as to the significance of its terms, which clearly described it as constituting the application of a system.

This Court is thus led to conclude that the method of straight baselines, established in the Norwegian system, was imposed by the peculiar geography of the Norwegian coast; that even before the dispute arose, this method had been consolidated by a constant and sufficiently long practice, in the face of which the attitude of governments bear witness to the fact that they did not consider it to be contrary to international law.

....

For these reasons, the Court, rejecting all submissions to the contrary, finds by ten votes to two, that the method employed for the delimitation of the fisheries zone by the Royal Norwegian Decree of July 12th, 1935, is not contrary to international law, and by eight votes to four, that the baselines fixed by the said Decree in application of this method are not contrary to international law.

CONVENTION ON THE TERRITORIAL SEA AND THE CONTIGUOUS ZONE

Article 4

1. In localities where the coastline is deeply indented and cut into, or if there is a fringe of islands along the coast in its immediate vicinity, the method of straight baselines joining appropriate points may be employed in drawing the baselines from which the breadth of the territorial sea is measured.

2. The drawing of such baselines must not depart to any appreciable extent from the general direction of the coast, and the sea areas lying within the lines must be sufficiently closely linked to the land domain to be subject to the regime of internal waters.

3. Baselines shall not be drawn to and from low-tide elevations, unless lighthouses or similar installations which are permanently above sea level have been built on them.

4. Where the method of straight baselines is applicable under the provisions of paragraph 1, account may be taken, in determining particular baselines, of economic interests peculiar to the region concerned, the reality and importance of which are clearly evidenced by a long usage.

5. The system of straight baselines may not be applied by a State in such a manner as to cut off from the high seas the territorial sea of another State.

6. The coastal State must clearly indicate straight baselines on charts, to which due publicity must be given.

Article 5

1. Waters on the landward side of the baseline of the territorial sea form part of the internal waters of the State.

2. Where the establishment of straight baselines in accordance with Article 4 has the effect of enclosing as internal waters areas which previously had been considered as part of the territorial sea or of the high seas, a right of innocent passage as provided in articles 14 to 23, shall exist in those waters.

ED. NOTE: In the opinion in the Fisheries Case, the Court itself notes that the criteria it had laid out were imprecise. The opinion left open many questions. What, for example, did the Court have in mind when it limited these systems to coasts "deeply indented" or if there is a "fringe of islands"? Precisely what do these terms mean? In addition, the Court gave no guidance as to the maximum allowable length for a straight baseline. And how does one determine the general direction of the coast? Over what segments, or is it the entire coast?

It appears that the Court recognized that each case would be somewhat unique with its own specific facts, thus it did not wish to promulgate rules to be applicable to every case in detail. Perhaps it would be impossible to do so. The Court thus left the application of the facts in future cases to be utilized in order to satisfy the general criteria it had set forth.

On August 31, 1987, the Department of State published, under its "Limits in the Seas" series, issue number 106 entitled "Developing Standard Guidelines for Evaluating Straight Baselines". In this publication an attempt was made to provide more precise methodologies for answering such questions as put above. For example, as to criteria for deeply indented coastlines, the publication set out three criteria which must be fulfilled:

"(1) Within the particular locality being considered, baseline segments accounting for at least 70% of the total length of the relevant baselines should each have at least a 6:10 ratio of coastal penetration to segment length;

"(2) A coastline must have at least three significant indentations in any given locality;

"(3) No individual straight baseline segment should exceed 48 nautical miles in length."

Similar tests were provided for the other terms used in the convention. While this publication provides helpful and logical rules, and is excellent guidance for use within the Department when it is evaluating particular baseline claims, it must be emphasized that these tests are not based on any statement of international law on the subject, though over time they may become widely recognized and applied.

The use of straight baselines, as noted before, can lend itself to abuse. While normal baselines are necessarily fixed by geography, straight baselines are a more artificial concept and can be manipulated to meet the desires of the coastal State.

For example, the State Department has rejected the Ecuadorian Supreme Decree No. 959-A of June 28, 1971, by which Ecuador established straight baselines for its mainland coast and around the Galapagos Islands (see figures 5-5 and 5-6 at the end of this chapter).

In its International Boundary Study No. 42, the Geographer of the State Department concluded as follows:

"The entire system of Ecuadorian straight baselines is questionable, based upon accepted international legal practices and on criteria established at the 1958 Geneva Law of the Sea Conference. The mainland coast is not `deeply indented and cut into,' and it is not an accepted principle of customary international law that baselines can be constructed around archipelagos.

"

The foregoing analysis points out that Ecuador has no right to construct the mainland baselines as it has, because the system deviates from the `general direction of the coast.'

Of the 12 segments of the Ecuadorian straight baselines, all but one exceed the length of the longest baseline approved by the International Court of Justice (ICJ) in the Anglo-Norwegian Fisheries Case. The ICJ, on December 18, 1951, approved a Norwegian straight baseline 44 miles in length. However, the length of the Norwegian baseline was directly related to the decision that much of the water enclosed by the baselines was indeed Norwegian historic waters. The issue of historic waters is relevant when considering the Ecuadorian straight baselines, as the coastal waters are not viewed to be historically within the domain of Ecuador because of long usage of the coastal regime."

The 1982 United Nations Convention on the Law of the Sea tracks the language used in the 1958 Convention with two exceptions. First, in Article 7(4) speaking of the drawing of straight baselines to or from low-tide elevations, new language was added to the exception based on lighthouses that reads "...or except in instances where the drawing of baselines to or from such elevations has received general international recognition." This language was added at the request of India, who argued that developing countries that could not afford to build lighthouses or other structures should not be penalized. The second change was to add a new paragraph 2, as follows:

"2. Where because of the presence of a delta and other natural conditions the coastline is highly unstable, the appropriate points may be selected along the furthest seaward extent of the low-water line and, notwithstanding subsequent regression of the low-water line, the straight baselines shall remain effective until changed by the coastal State in accordance with this Convention."

This new language was in response to Bangladesh, whose coastline qualifies under that paragraph. Bangladesh had made a proposal during the Third United Nations Conference, opposed by the United States and others, as follows:

"INFORMAL SUGGESTION BY BANGLADESH

"Article 7, Paragraph 2: Baselines

"Where most part of a coastline of a State is constituted by a continuous process of sedimentation and fluvial deposits rendering the low-water line highly unstable, the method of straight baselines joining appropriate points may be employed along the furthest seaward extent of sedimentary delta in drawing the baseline from which the breadth of the territorial sea is measured."

The opposition to this proposal arose from the uncertainty involved. The baselines would be constantly shifting as the submerged delta accreted or eroded. In addition, the proposal would have given Bangladesh a baseline in places more than 100 miles at sea. It was felt that the change that was adopted to Article 7 was a sufficient solution to the problem posed by Bangladesh.

The issue has come up in U.S. law as well. Consider the following brief excerpts.

UNITED STATES v. CALIFORNIA, 381 U.S. 139 (1964)

California argues that because the Convention permits a nation to use the straight baseline method for determining its seaward boundaries if its "coastline is deeply indented or cut into, or if there is a fringe of islands along the coast in its immediate vicinity," California is therefore free to use such boundary lines across the openings of its bays and around its islands. We agree with the United States that the Convention recognizes the validity of straight-baselines used by other countries, Norway for instance, and would permit the United States to use such base lines if it chose, but California may not use such base lines to extend our international boundaries beyond their traditional international limits against the expressed opposition of the United States. The national responsibility for conducting our international relations obviously must be accomodated with the legitimate interest of the States in the territory over which they are sovereign. Thus a contraction of a State's recognized territory imposed by the Federal Government in the name of foreign policy would be highly questionable. But an extension of state sovereignty to an international area by claiming it as inland water would necessarily also extend national sovereignty, and unless the Federal Government's responsibility for questions of external sovereignty is hollow, it must have the power to prevent States from so enlarging themselves. We conclude that the choice under the Convention to use the straight-base-line method for determining inland waters claimed against other nations is one that rests with the Federal Government, not with the individual States.

California relies upon Manchester v. Massachussetts, 139 U.S. 240, for the proposition that a state may draw its boundaries as it pleases within limits recognized by the law of nations regardless of the position taken by the United States. Although some dicta in the case may be read to support that view, we do not so interpret the opinion. The case involved neither the expansion of our traditional international boundary nor opposition by the United States to the position taken by the State.

UNITED STATES v. LOUISIANA, 394 U.S. 11 (1969)

In United States v. California...we held that "the choice under the Convention to use the straight-base-line method for determining inland waters against other nations is one that rests with the Federal Government, and not with the individual States". Since the United States asserts that it has not drawn and does not want to draw straight baselines along the Louisiana coast, that disclaimer would, under the California decision, be conclusive of the matter. Louisiana argues, however, that because the Louisiana coast is so perfectly suited to the straight baseline method, and because it is clear that the United States would employ it in the conduct of international affairs were it not for this lawsuit, the Court should reconsider its holding in California and itself draw appropriate baselines. While we agree that the straight baseline method was designed for precisely such coasts as the Mississippi River Delta area, we adhere to the position that the selection of this optional method of establishing boundaries should be left to the branches of Government responsible for the formulation and implementation of foreign policy. It would be inappropriate for this Court to review or overturn the considered decision of the United States, albeit partially motivated by domestic concerns, not to extend its borders to the furthest extent consonant with international law.

2. BAYS

Bays represent a special case in international law. Because they are bodies of water that fall "within the jaws" of the land the coastal State arguably has a greater interest in them than even their territorial sea. International law recognizes that interest, but the question remains as to the extent that the coastal State may exercise special jurisdiction with respect to them. In the law of the sea, two kinds of bays are recognized: juridical bays and historic bays. In this section we take a look at the rules regarding each.

a. JURIDICAL BAYS

CONVENTION ON THE TERRITORIAL SEA AND THE CONTIGUOUS ZONE

Article 7

1. This article relates only to bays the coasts of which belong to a single State.

2. For the purposes of these articles, a bay is a well-marked indentation whose penetration is in such proportion to the width of its mouth as to contain certain landlocked waters and constitute more than a mere curvature of the coast. An indentation shall not, however, be regarded as a bay unless the area is as large as, or larger than, that of the semi-circle whose diameter is a line drawn across the mouth of that indentation.

3. For the purpose of measurement, the area of an indentation is that lying between the low-water mark around the shore of the indentation and a line joining the low-water mark of its natural entrance points. Where, because of the presence of islands, an indentation has more than one mouth, the semi-circle shall be drawn on a line as long as the sum total of the lengths of the lines across the different mouths. Islands within an indentation shall be included as if they were part of the water area of the indentation.

4. If the distance between the low-water marks of the natural entrance points of a bay does not exceed twenty-four miles, a closing line may be drawn between these two low-water marks, and the waters enclosed thereby shall be considered as internal waters.

5. Where the distance between the low-water marks of the natural entrance points of a bay exceeds twenty-four miles, a straight baseline of twenty-four miles shall be drawn within the bay in such a manner as to enclose the maximum area of water that is possible with a line of that length.

6. The foregoing provisions shall not apply to so-called "historic" bays, or in any case where the straight baseline system provided for in article 4.

ED. NOTE: The appropriate reference to the 1982 Convention is article 10. That article is identical to the above, except that the cross-reference in paragraph 6 is to article 7 of the new Convention. As the following indicates, Shalowitz has recognized some ambiguities and gives reasons for their resolution. In particular, he explains the reason for the multi-mouth bay rule, and the relationship between the semi-circle test and the closing line.

Shalowitz, SHORE AND SEA BOUNDARIES, Vol. 1 222-224

[Referring to the multi-mouth bay rule] This is not free of ambiguity and raises the question whether the sum of the widths of the several entrances may exceed the length of the closing line, or whether it must be kept within that limit [24 miles].

For an answer to this question, it is appropriate to examine the basis for the rule in the report of the International Law Commission. In commentary (2) of Article 7, it is stated that the Commission's intention in using the total length of the lines across the different mouths "was to indicate that the presence of islands at the mouth of an indentation tends to link it more closely to the mainland, and this consideration may justify some alteration in the ratio between the width and the penetration of the indentation." In such a case, the Commission notes, an indentation which, if it had no islands at its mouth, would not fulfill the necessary conditions, is to be recognized as a bay. Clearly, this indicates an intent to liberalize the rule for bays in such situations. This liberalization is accomplished by not using the full width of the bay, for purposes of applying the semicircular rule, but only the water distances across the several entrances, omitting the island expanses. The semicircle in such cases would be drawn on a diameter no greater than the closing line for bays, thus reducing the diameter of the semicircle and altering the ratio of width to penetration so as to result in an indentation becoming a bay that might not meet the test if the full width from headland to headland were to be used. Under this interpretation, no opening could exceed 24 miles..., nor could the sum of all openings exceed such distance. If it did, the indentation could not qualify as a bay on the basis of islands at the entrance but would have to be tested by the rule for indentations wider than the closing line.

....

The purpose of the rule [Art. 7, para. 5] seems simple enough, but its application to an indentation raises an important question of interpretation -- that is, whether the semicicular rule is to be applied to the whole indentation only, to the portion enclosed by the closing line, or to both.

As paragraph 5 is worded, the inference could be drawn that the semicircular rule is first applied to the whole indentation; if it becomes a true bay by the test, the 24-mile line is then drawn within the bay without any further application of the semicircular rule. There is a measure of logic in this interpretation, since the semicircular rule is geometric in concept whereas a closing line limitation is arbitrary in nature, and it could be reasoned that once an indentation has met the semicircle test it should suffice. But the difficulty with this interpretation is that if the situation were reversed and the whole indentation did not satisfy the test, it could automatically exclude an area within the 24-mile line from becoming inland waters even though it qualified as a bay. This would not seem reasonable.

The more reasonable interpretation of paragraph 5 would be that only the portion of the indentation enclosed by the closing line must satisfy the semicircle test. The basis for this is that where an indentation has a greater width at the entrance than the permissible closing line, the question of its status does not arise until the limiting line is drawn. That this was also the thinking of the committee of experts, is borne out by the definition it adopted for a bay and by the 10-mile limitation it recommended. In its definition, it stated: "A bay is a bay in the juridical sense," and in adopting the 10-mile limitation, it stated: "The closing line across a (juridical) bay should not exceed 10 miles in width." Identifying the term bay with the word "juridical" in the last sentence indicates that the portion of the indentation across which the closing line will be placed must satisfy the legal fiction of a true bay, that is, satisfying the semicircular rule, otherwise it would not be a bay in the legal sense.

b. HISTORIC BAYS

The system of juridical bays is designed to meet normal circumstances. But international law of the sea has long recognized that there are some exceptional cases where bodies of water do not qualify as a juridical bay, but where the affected coastal State has a strong and traditional interest in exercising some modicum of jurisdiction over those waters with the acquiescence of other members of the international community. At the same time it is necessary to create a doctrine with regard to these "historic" bays that places some limitation on coastal States because these bays take from the rest of the international community areas of water that previously had been mostly high seas. Recall that article 10 of the 1982 Convention, as did the 1958 Convention, specifically does not apply to this category of bays. In this section we shall examine the generally accepted elements of law relating to the validity of a claim to historic waters.

Pharand, CANADA'S ARCTIC WATERS IN INTERNATIONAL LAW (1988) 91-105[2]

5.1 Origin and recognition of historic waters

The doctrine of historic waters developed from that of historic bays which had emerged during the 19th century for the protection of certain large bays closely linked to the surrounding land area and traditionally considered by claiming States as part of their national territory. Those bays were often expressed to be of vital importance from the economic and national security standpoints. As rules relating to the delimitation of maritime areas developed, the idea of claiming bays on the basis of an historic title was extended to other areas of the sea adjacent to the coast.

---

2. Reprinted by permission of the Press Syndicate of the University of Cambridge

The nature of historic waters in international law was never spelled out in any convention. In 1958, it was the view of the International Law Commission's Special Rapporteur on the Law of the Sea, Mr. Francois, that the Commission did not have sufficient material at its disposal to formulate principles on the matter. Safeguard provisions, however, were inserted in the Convention on the Territorial Sea, thus recognizing the legitimacy of both historic bays and historic waters. Provisions for both cases, however, were formulated as exceptions to the general rules for drawing territorial waters. It was specified that the rules relating to the maximum 24-mile closing line for bays "...do not apply to so-called `historic bays'". In the same way, the equidistance rule governing the delimitation of the territorial sea between States with opposite or adjacent coasts was said not to apply "where it is necessary by reason of historic title...to delimit the territorial sea of the two States in a way which is at variance therewith".

After the 1958 Conference, the Secretariate of the United Nations prepared a document on the "Juridical Regime of Historic Waters, including Historic Bays", which, along with the 1957 Secretariate document on historic bays, constitutes a good summary of the status of those two documents. However, the matter was not pursued by the International Law Commission and the Third Law of the Sea Conference did not address those questions. Consequently, the Convention on the Law of the Sea of 1982 merely reproduced the 1958 provisions without clafifying the legal status of historic waters.

5.2 Legal status of historic waters

It is now generally accepted that historic waters have the status of internal waters. Even in 1923, when Sir Cecil Hurst made his study on `The Territoriality of Bays', he concluded that `...all the waters lying inwards from this baseline are national waters, and form part of national territory'. He specified that `...they stand in all respects on precisely the same footing as the national territory'.

In 1951, the same conclusion was reached by the International Court in the *Fisheries Case* with respect to historic waters generally. The United Kingdom had argued that, although Norway was entitled on historic grounds to claim certain fjords and sounds as internal waters, it was only entitled to claim as territorial waters certain other fjords and sounds which had the character of legal straits. Addressing itself to this argument, the Court began by formulating the principle that `by "historic waters" are usually meant waters which are treated as *internal waters* but which would not have that character were it not for the existence of an historic title'. At the end of its judgment, it concluded that all of the waters enclosed by straight baselines, including those where an historic title had been established, had the status of internal waters. The Court held specifically that `...the waters of the Vestfjord, as indeed the waters of all other Norwegian fjords, can only be regarded as internal waters'.

As for the 1958 Convention on the Territorial Sea, it dealt with the legal status of historic bays and historic waters in an indirect way only. It provided that the waters enclosed by the 24-mile closing line for bays `shall be considered as internal waters' and that the 24-mile rule did not apply to historic bays. The implication is clear that the waters of historic bays are also to be considered as internal waters. And, since no special provision was inserted on historic waters generally, the same legal status must have been intended. In the words of Professor O'Connell, `It is...clear that Article 7(6) should not be interpreted as restricting the category of historic waters to that of historic bays. The latter is but an instance of the former, although, for obvious reasons, the number of claims to bays is greater than to other maritime areas'.

The common provision in the 1958 and 1982 Conventions, touching on historic waters, stipulates that the equidistance rule for the delimitation of the territorial waters between opposite and adjacent coasts is not to apply `where it is necessary by reason of historic title to use another mode of delimitation'. Since the article deals only with the outer limit of the territorial sea between coasts for which it adopts the equidistance rule, an exception to that rule because of an historic title would simply extend that limit. Consequently, the Conventions would seem to envisage the possibility of an historic title to water areas, aside from bays, resulting only in a status of territorial waters rather than internal waters.

That possibility was also envisaged by the United Nations Secretariate in its study of 1962 when it concluded that the legal status of historic waters `would in principle depend on whether the sovereignty exercised in the particular case over the area of the claiming State and forming a basis for the claim, was sovereignty as over internal waters or sovereignty as over the territorial sea'. In other words, the exact legal status of historic waters would depend on whether the right of innocent passage has been recognized in those waters. If the claimant State did not allow such passage, the result would be internal waters whereas, if it did, the result would be territorial waters.

As was seen, such an interpretation is possible under both the 1958 and 1982 Conventions. However, it is strongly suggested that, in customary law as interpreted and applied by the International Court in the *Fisheries Case* of 1951, an historic title results in internal waters, whether or not these waters have the configuration of bays. The status of internal waters means that the sovereignty of the coastal State is complete. Those waters have exactly the same status as `inland waters' and generally refer to lakes, canals, rivers, ports and harbours. As emphasized by Professor Gidel, the coastal State is no longer obliged to recognize the innocent passage of foreign ships in internal waters. The coastal State may, if it wishes, permit such innocent passage, but is under no legal obligation to do so. If it does, the foreign ship is then exercising a privilege granted by the coastal State, rather than a right recognized by the international community.

Even if such historic waters are enclosed by straight baselines, the right of innocent passage would not exist under the Territorial Sea Convention since those waters would not have been considered part of the territorial sea or of the high seas before their enclosure. In other words, the status of internal waters would not result from the drawing of straight baselines, but rather from the proof of historic title. This was the opinion expressed by Judge Hackworth in the *Fisheries Case* in the following declaration:

> Judge Hackworth declares that he concurs in the operative part of the judgment but desires to emphasize that he does so for the reason that he considers that the Norwegian Government has proved the existence of an *historical title* to the disputed areas of water.

It would appear that Judge Hackworth did not believe that the disputed areas could be considered as internal waters because of the drawing of straight baselines, but rather because an historic title had been established.

....

Requirements of historic waters

....

6.1 Exclusive exercise of State authority

Since a claim to historic waters is one over a maritime area which the coastal State considers as an integral part of its national territory, the type of jurisdiction exercised over that area should be essentially the same as that being exercised on the rest of the territory. More precisely, the coastal State must exercise an effective control over the maritime area being claimed to the exclusion of all other States. Naturally, the extent of control will vary depending on a number of factors such as the size of the maritime area, its remoteness and the degree of its usability. The actual control might be limited, but yet sufficient, in remote areas. In the words of Professor O'Connell, `just as in the case of remote and little used seas, very little in the way of effective exercise of sovereignty need be required', to show that a State took whatever action was necessary to assert and maintain its authority and control over the area in question.

As to the type of manifestation of sovereignty which must be adduced, Professor Gidel states that `[t]he exclusion from these areas of foreign vessels or their subjection to rules imposed by the coastal State, which exceed the usual scope of regulations made in the interests of navigation, would obviously be acts affording convincing evidence of the State's intent'. The learned author is careful to point out, however, that those are not the only acts of authority which constitute evidence of the exercise of authority by the coastal State. Normally, the physical act of excluding foreign vessels is preceded by national legislation which forbids the entry of foreign ships and subjects them to certain conditions. As an example, Professor Bourquin states, in respect of a bay, that `the State which forbids foreign ships to penetrate the bay or to fish therein indisputably demonstrates by such action its desire to act as the sovereign'. The same author emphasizes, however, that the intent or desire of the State must be expressed by deeds and not merely by proclamations. This being admitted, if the laws and regulations of the coastal State are never challenged, very little action is necessary to maintain the effective and exclusive control needed to support a claim of sovereignty.

6.2 Long usage and passage of time

`Historic titles must enjoy respect and be preserved as they have always been by long usage', said the International Court in 1982. How much passage of time must take place before a sufficiently long usage is attained cannot be determined in the abstract. Somewhat as for the formation of a custom, it is impossible to determine in advance how long the effective control must last before it materializes into an historic title. A great variety of terms is employed to describe the length of time required for a usage to have legal effect. The more common expressions used are `well-established usage', `continuous usage of long standing', `continued and well-established usage', `immemorial usage', and usage `from time immemorial'.

The length of time required will depend on a number of factors such as the degree of change being effected, the attitute of other States and the political strength of the claimant State.... What is certain is that the longer the effective control endures, the firmer the legal title becomes, resulting in a virtual presumption of acquiescence.

6.3 Acquiescence by foreign States

Everybody agrees that the attitude of foreign States is important, particularly on the part of States primarily affected by the usage in question, and that some form of acquiescence is necessary before an historic title can arise. However, there is some disagreement as to the precise form which the acquiescence should take. The opinions seem to be divided into two groups. Those who consider historic waters as an exception to the general rules relating to the acquisition of maritime sovereignty take a stricter view of acquiescence. They seem to consider acquiescence as a form of consent or recognition of the sovereignty of the coastal State over certain maritime areas, and this recognition or consent must come from those States that are affected by the claim in question. The other group maintains that silence or the absence of protest on the part of the other States is sufficient for the exercise of sovereignty by the claimant state to result in an historic title. The first group, represented by Fitzmaurice, admits that acquiescence need not take the form of a positive act on the part of the foreign States and that the role of the theory of historic rights is to create `a presumption of acquiescence arising from the facts of the case and from the inaction and toleration of States'. The other group, represented by Professor Bourquin, maintains that while it is false to say that the acquiescence of these States is reuired, it is true that if their reactions intefere with the peaceful and continous exercise of sovereignty no historic title can be formed.

The difference in approach as to the exact form which the reaction of foreign States should take was evident in the Fisheries Case of 1951. While admitting that the reaction of foreign States constitutes a very important element in the formation of an historic title, even taken in the special sense of consolidation of title, the Norwegian Government rejected the view of the United Kingdom.... The Norwegian Government went on to say that it considered the absence of reaction on the part of foreign States as being sufficient to confirm the peaceful and continuous character of the usage.

The Court seemed to accept the Norwegian argument when it stated that `the general toleration of foreign States with regard to the Norwegian Practice is an unchallenged fact'. Having found as a fact that the Norwegian straight baseline system had met with the general toleration of foreign States, the Court went on to hold that Norway was entitled to enforce her system against the United Kingdom. The Court stated in particular:

> The notoriety of the facts, the general toleration of the international community, Great Britain's position in the North Sea, her own interest in the question, and her prolonged abstention would in any case warrant Norway's enforcement of her system against the United Kingdom.

It thus appears from the judgment of the Court that a general toleration or absence of protest on the part of foreign States suffices for a consolidation of title to materialize. But would it suffice to create an historic title as an exception to the general rules relating to the acquisition of sovereignty? This is doubtful, because the general toleration involved in the Fisheries Case was towards the straight baseline system which was found to be, not in derogation of, but rather in accordance with, the general rules for the delimitation of maritime jurisdiction. Consequently, the general toleration resulted in an historical consolidation of title rather than in the actual creation of an historical title. In the words of the Court, `it is indeed this system (of straight baselines) itself which would reap the benefit of general toleration, the basis of an historical consolidation which would make it enforceable against all States'. If history had been the sole basis for the claim that enclosed waters were subject to Norway's sovereignty, a more positive form of acquiescence would probably have been necessary. Professor O'Connell puts it as follows:

In the case of historic waters, what has to be established is the virtually total toleration of those nations whose interests are clearly affected, because the situation, having its origins in an illegal act which time and absence of opposition alone can validate, is analogous to the subversion of a neighbouring title on land by adverse occupation'.

Presuming that there exists that kind of acquiescence or total toleration, an historic title to sea areas might well arise. But what if, on the contrary, there have been protests?

....

ED. NOTE: The author goes on to point out that the protest must be real and it must be followed on by some forceful action on the part of the protesting State. By that he does not mean the use of force, but rather by prosecution of the objection by diplomatic negotiation, or perhaps by some form of dispute settlement. He notes that the vital interests of the claimant State may play a role, but only in making a general appraisal of the basic requirements. Finally he notes that when historic title is the sole basis for the claim, a special burden of proof rests on the claimant State.

In connection with a recent declaration which appeared, at least in part, to be based upon a historic claim, in October, 1973, Libya laid claim to the whole of the Gulf of Sirte, a large expanse of water. Libya declared that no private vessels could enter without their permission and claimed full rights of ownership as in any other parts of the country. This claim was rejected by the maritime powers as not fulfilling the requirements for a claim to historic waters, and that a closing line across its mouth would far exceed the 24-mile rule. The U.S. Navy subsequently sought to exercise its rights under international law by sailing a fleet toward the Gulf of Sirte. Libya resisted by putting fighters into the air. In a subsequent confrontation, Navy planes shot down one of the Libyan craft.

The next case shows how historic rights claims are viewed in the domestic law of the United States.

UNITED STATES v. ALASKA, 422 U.S. 184 (1975)

The issue here is whether the body of water known as Cook Inlet is a historic bay....

I

In early 1967 the State of Alaska offered 2,500 acres of submerged lands in lower Cook Inlet for a competitive oil and gas lease sale. The tract in question is more than three geographical miles from the shore of the inlet and is seaward more than three miles from a line across the inlet at Kalgin Island, where the headlands are about 24 miles apart, as contrasted with 47 miles at the natural entrance of Cape Douglas. In the view of the United States, contending that the lower inlet constitutes high seas, brought suit in the United States District Court for the District of Alaska to quiet title and for injunctive relief against the State. Alaska defended on the ground that the inlet, in its entirety, was within the accepted definition of a "historic bay" and thus constituted inland waters properly subject to state sovereignty. Alaska prevailed in the District Court. 352 F.Supp. 815 (1972). The United States Court of Appeals for the Ninth Circuit affirmed with a *per curiam* opinion. 497 F.2d 1155 (1974). We granted certiorari because the case presented a substantial question concerning the proof necessary to establish a body of water as a historic bay. 419 U.S. 1045 (1974).

II

...Since the distance between the natural entrance points to Cook Inlet is greatly in excess of 24 miles, the parties agree that Alaska must demonstrate that the inlet is a historic bay in order to successfully claim sovereignty over its lower waters and the land beneath those waters.

The term "historic bay" is not defined in the Convention. The Court, however, has stated that in order to establish that a body of water is a historic bay, a coastal nation must have "traditionally asserted and maintained dominion with the acquiescence of foreign nations." *United States v. California*, 381 U.S., at 172. Furthermore, the Court appears to have accepted the general view that at least three factors are significant in the determination of historic bay status: (1) the claiming nation must have exercised authority over the area; (2) that exercise must have been continuous; and (3) foreign states must have acquiesced in the exercise of authority. *Louisiana Boundary Case*, 394 U.S. at 75 and 23-24, n.27. These were the general guidelines for the District Court and the Court of Appeals in this case.

The District Court divided its findings on the exercise of authority over lower Cook Inlet into three time periods, namely, that of Russian sovereignty, that of United States sovereignty, and that of Alaskan statehood. We discuss these in turn.

A

The evidence that Russia exercised authority over lower Cook Inlet as inland waters is understandably sparse. The District Court, nonetheless, concluded that "Russia exercised sovereignty over the disputed area of Cook Inlet." The court based this conclusion on three findings. First, by the early 1800's there were four Russian settlements on the shores of Cook Inlet. Second, about 1786, an attempt by an English vessel to enter the inlet drew a volley of cannon fire from a Russian fur trader in the vicinity of Port Graham. Third, in 1821, Tsar Alexander I issued a ukase that perported to exclude all foreign vessels from the western waters within 100 miles of the Alaska coast....

We feel that none of these facts, as found by the District Court, demonstrate the exercise of authority essential to the establishment of a historic bay. The presence of the early Russian settlements on the shores of Cook Inlet certainly demonstrates the existence of a claim to the land, but it gives little indication of the authority Russia may have exerted over the vast expanse of waters that constitutes the inlet. The incident of the fur trader's firing on an English vessel near Port Graham might be some evidence of a claim of sovereignty over the waters involved, but the act appears to be that of a private citizen rather than of a government official. In the absence of some evidence that the trader was acting with governmental authority, the incident is entitled to little legal significance. Moreover, under the then-common Cannon Shot Rule, the firing of cannon from shore was wholly consistent with the present position of the United States that the inland waters of Alaska near Port Graham are to be measured by the three-mile limit. Finally, the imperial ukase of 1821 is clearly inadequate as a demonstration of Russian authority over the waters of Cook Inlet because shortly after it had been issued the ukase was unequivocally withdrawn in the face of vigorous protests from the United States and England.

B

In reviewing the period of United States sovereignty over the Territory of Alaska, the District Court found that there had been five separate instances in which the Federal Government had exercised authority over all the waters of Cook Inlet. [The Court then reviewed the facts pertaining to the five instances]...

Based on the facts summarized above, the District Court concluded that the United States had exercised authority over the waters of lower Cook Inlet continuously from the Treaty of Cession in 1867 until Alaska statehood. The District Court, of course, was correct insofar as it found that the United States had exercised jurisdiction over lower Cook Inlet during the territorial period *for the purpose of fish and wildlife management*. It is far from clear, however, that the District Court was correct in concluding that the fact of enforcement of fish and wildlife regulations was legally sufficient to demonstrate the type of authority that must be exercised to establish title to a historic bay.

In determining whether the enforcement of fishery and wildlife management regulations in Cook Inlet was an exercise of authority sufficient to establish title to that body of water as a historic bay, it is necessary to recall the threefold division of the sea recognized in international law. As the Court said in the *Louisiana Boundary Case*:

> "Under generally accepted principles of international law, the navigable sea is divided into three zones, distinguished by the nature of the control over them. Nearest to the nation's shores are its inland, or internal waters. These are subject to the complete sovereignty of the nation, as much as if they were a part of its land territory, and the coastal nation has the privilege even to exclude foreign vessels altogether. Beyond the inland waters, and measured from their seaward edge, is a belt known as the marginal, or territorial sea. Within it the coastal nation may exercise extensive control but cannot deny the right of innocent passage to foreign nations. Outside the territorial sea are the high seas, which are international waters not subject to the dominion of any single nation." 394 U.S., at 22-23 (footnotes omitted).

We also recognized in the *Louisiana Boundary Case* that the exercise of authority necessary to establish historic title must be commensurate in scope with the nature of the title claimed. There the state of Louisiana argued that the exercise of jurisdiction over certain coastal waters for the purposes of regulating navigation had given rise to historic title over the waters in question as inland waters. Since the navigation rules in question had allowed the innocent passage of foreign vessels, a characteristic of territorial seas rather than inland waters, the Court concluded that the exercise of authority was not sufficient in scope to establish historic title to Cook Inlet as inland waters.

As has been noted, and as the parties agree, Alaska, in order to prevail in this case, must establish historic title to Cook Inlet as inland waters. For this showing, the exercise of sovereignty must have been, historically, an assertion of power to exclude all foreign vessels and navigation. The enforcement of fishing and wildlife regulations, as found and relied upon by the District Court, was patently insufficient to establish historic title to Cook Inlet as historic waters.

Only one of the fishing regulations relied upon by the court, the Alien Fishing Act, treated foreign vessels any differently than it did American vessels. That Act, however, did not purport to apply beyond the three-mile limit in Cook Inlet. It simply applied to "the waters of Alaska under the jurisdiction of the United States."... The meaning of that general statutory phrase, as applied to Cook Inlet, can only be surmised, since there was not a single instance of enforcement to suggest that the Act was applicable to foreign vessels in the waters beyond the three-mile limit in lower Cook inlet. The remainder of the fish and wildlife regulations relied upon by the District Court clearly were enforced throughout lower Cook Inlet for at least much of the territorial period, but these regulations were not commensurate in scope with the claim of exclusive dominion essential to historic title over the inland waters. Each afforded foreign vessels the same rights as were enjoyed by American ships. To be sure, there were instances of enforcement in the lower inlet, but in each case the vessels involved were American. These incidents prove very little, for the United States can and does enforce fishing and wildlife regulations against its own nationals, even on the high seas.

Our conclusion that the fact of enforcement of game and fish regulations in Cook Inlet is inadequate, as a matter of law, to establish historic title to the inlet as inland waters is not based on mere technicality. The assertion of fisheries management frequently differs in geographical extent from the boundaries claimed as inland or even territorial waters.... This limited circumscription of the traditional freedom of fishing on the high seas is based, in part, on a recognition of the special interest that a coastal state has in the preservation of the living resources in the high seas adjacent to its territorial sea....

Even a casual examination of the facts relied upon by the District Court in this case reveals that the geographic scope of the fish and wildlife enforcement efforts was determined primarily, if not exclusively, by the needs of effective management of the fish and game population involved....

Even if we could agree that the boundaries selected for purposes of enforcing fish and wildlife regulations coincided with an intended assertion of territorial sovereignty over Cook Inlet as inland waters, we would still disagree with the District Court's conclusion that historic title was established in the territorial period. The court found that the third essential element of historic title, acquiescence by foreign nations, was satisfied by the failure of any foreign nation to protest. Scholarly comment is divided over whether the mere absence of opposition suffices to establish title.... In this case, we feel that something more than mere failure to object must be shown. The failure of other countries to protest is meaningless unless it is shown that the governments of those countries knew or reasonably should have known of the authority being asserted. Many assertions of authority are such clear expressions of exclusive sovereignty that they cannot be mistaken by other governments. Other expressions of exclusive authority, however, may not be so clear. One scholar notes: "thus, the placing of lights or beacons may sometimes appear to be an act of sovereignty, while in other circumstances it may have no such significance.".... We believe that the routine enforcement of domestic game and fish regulations in Cook Inlet in the territorial period failed to inform foreign governments of any claim of dominion. In the absence of any awareness on the part of foreign governments of a claimed territorial sovereignty over lower Cook Inlet, the failure of those governments to protest is inadequate proof of the acquiescence to historic title.

C

The District Court stresses two facts as evidence that Alaska had exercised sovereignty over all the waters of Cook Inlet in the recent period of Alaska statehood. First, the court found that since statehood Alaska had enforced fishing regulations in basically the same fashion as had the United States during the territorial period. Second, the court found that in 1962 Alaska had arrested two vessels of a Japanese fishing fleet in the Shelikof Strait. Since we have concluded that the general enforcement of fishing regulations by the United States in the territorial period was insufficient to demonstrate sovereignty over Cook Inlet as inland waters, we must also conclude that Alaska's following the same basic pattern of enforcement is insufficient to give rise to the historic title now claimed. The Shelikof Strait incident, however, deserves scrutiny because the seizure of a foreign vessel more than three miles from shore manifests an assertion of sovereignty to exclude foreign vessels altogether.

The facts of the incident, for the most part, are undisputed. In early 1962 a private commercial fishing enterprise in Japan, Eastern Pacific Fisheries Company, publicly announced its intention to send a fishing fleet into the waters of Cook Inlet and Shelikof Strait. Alaska officials learned of the plan through newspaper accounts and requested action by the Federal Government to prevent entry of the fleet into the inlet and the strait. The Federal Government, although thus forewarned of the intrusion, significantly took no action. In March 1962, the mothership Banshu Maru 31 and five other vessels arrived at the Kodiak fishing grounds. On April 5, the six vessels sailed north of the Barren Islands into the lower portion of Cook Inlet. The vessels left the inlet the next day and sailed southwest into the Shelikof Strait. The vessels fished in the Strait for approximately ten days undisturbed. Then, on April 15, Alaska law enforcement officials boarded two of the vessels in the Shelikof Strait. At the time, at least one of the ships was more than three miles from shore. The officials arrested three of the fleet's captains and charged them with violating the state fishing regulations applicable to the strait. On April 19, Eastern Pacific Fisheries Company and the State of Alaska entered into an agreement whereby the State released the company's employees and ships in return for a promise from the company that it would not fish in the inlet or in the strait pending judicial resolution of the State's jurisdiction to enforce fishing regulations therein.... The Japanese Government did not participate in, or approve of, the agreement between the company and Alaska. Instead, shortly after the agreement was executed, Japan formally protested to the United States Government. Our Government declined to take an official position on the matter pending completion of the judicial proceedings. Ultimately, the judicial proceedings were dismissed without reaching any conclusion on the on the extent of Alaskan jurisdiction over the strait. The Federal Government took no formal position on the issue after the dismissal of the proceedings.

To the extent that the Shelikof Strait incident reveals a determination on the part of Alaska to exclude all foreign vessels, it must be viewed, to be sure, as an exercise of authority over the waters in question as inland waters. Nevertheless, for several reasons, we find the incident inadequate to establish historic title to Cook Inlet as inland waters. First, the incident was an exercise of sovereignty, if at all, only over the waters of Shelikof Strait. The vessels were boarded in the strait, some 75 miles southwest from the nearest portion of the inlet. Although Alaska officials knew of the fleet's earlier entry into Cook Inlet, no action was taken to force the vessels to leave the inlet, and no charges were filed for the intrusion into those waters. Second, even if the events in Shelikof Strait could constitute an assertion of authority over the waters of Cook Inlet as well as those of the strait, we are not satisfied that the exercise of authority was sufficiently unambiguous to serve as the basis of historic title to the inland waters. The adequacy of a claim to historic title, even in a dispute between a State and the United States, is measured primarily in international, rather than a purely domestic claim.... Viewed from the standpoint of the Japanese Government, the import of the incident in the strait is far from clear. Alaska clearly claimed the waters in question as inland waters, but the United States Government neither supported nor disclaimed the State's position. Given the ambiguity of the Federal Government's position, we cannot agree that the assertion of sovereignty possessed the clarity essential to a claim of historic title over inland waters. Finally, regardless of how one views the Shelikof Strait incident, it is impossible to conclude that the exercise of sovereignty was acquiesced in by the Japanese Government. Japan immediately protested the incident and has never acceded to the position taken by Alaska. Admittedly, the Eastern Pacific Fisheries Company formally and tentatively agreed to respect the jurisdiction claimed by Alaska but, as we have already noted, the acts of a private citizen cannot be considered representative of a government's position in the absence of some official license or other governmental authority.

In sum, we hold that the District Court's conclusion that Cook Inlest is a historic bay was based on an erroneous asessment of the legal significance of the facts it had found. The judgment of the Court of Appeals, accordingly, is reversed and the case is remanded for further proceedings consistent with this opinion.

ED. NOTE: Two things should be noted about the above case. First, without a great deal of discussion the Court was applying the rule that in a dispute between a state and the United States, the evidence will be evaluated as though the United States was making a claim of historic title against foreign States. Second, as we have seen and shall see again, this case reflects the general hostility of the Court to claims to extended jurisdiction by states of the union against the United States, particularly where oil and gas revenues are concerned.

c. BAYS BOUNDED BY TWO OR MORE STATES

As we have already noted, the Convention's rules regarding juridical bays do not apply to historic bays, although by implication such bodies of water are recognized. In addition, the conventional rules do not apply except where the bay in question is bounded entirely by a single State. Here we examine whether, and under what theory or theories, two or more States may claim joint jurisdiction over a common bay.

Churchill and Lowe, THE LAW OF THE SEA (1983), at 33[3]

As with historic bays, bays which are bordered by more than one State are not dealt with by either the Territorial Sea Convention or the Law of the Sea Convention. There are over forty such bays in the world. Examples include Lough Foyle (bordered by Ireland and the United Kingdom), the Bay of Figuier (France and Spain) and Passamaquoddy Bay (Canada and the USA). The normal rule of customary international law in relation to such bays would appear to be that, unlike bays covered by article 7 of the Territorial Sea Convention and article 10 of the Law of the Sea Convention, or historic bays, they cannot be closed by a line across their mouth. Instead the baseline is constituted by the low-water mark around the shores of the bay. The matter, however, is not free from controversy. Exceptionally it may be possible for the riparian States to show that the position is different by reason of historic title. Such is the case with the Gulf of Fonseca, bordered by El Salvador, Honduras and Nicaragua. in *El Salvador v. Nicaragua* (1917) the now defunct Central American Court of Justice held that the Gulf was an historic bay, thus having the character of internal waters, and that the three riparian States were co-owners of its waters except for the innermost three miles which was the exclusive property of each.

ED. NOTE: The opinion, unique in its nature, of the Central American Court of Justice in Republic of El Salvador v. Nicaragua, 1911, concerning the Gulf of Fonseca, can be found in 11 A.J.I.L. 674-730 (1911).

Like the Gulf of Fonseca, the Gulf of Aqaba presents an interesting case. That gulf represents Israel's only access to the Red Sea and onward. It has been an important issue in the on-going disputes between Israel and its arab neighbors for decades. Israel claims the right to freely navigate the gulf. The arab countries in the region have frequently claimed the gulf to be a closed sea, and that Israel, occupying the gulf port of Elath illegally (they claim) by reason of the violation of a peace treaty, has no rights of navigation.

---

3. Reprinted by permission of the Manchester University Press

3. PERMANENT HARBOR WORKS

CONVENTION ON THE TERRITORIAL SEA AND THE CONTIGUOUS ZONE

Article 8

For the purpose of delimiting the territorial sea, the outermost permanent harbour works which form an integral part of the harbour system shall be regarded as forming part of the coast.

INTERNATIONAL LAW COMMISSION, 1956 Commentary, Draft Article 8

(1) The waters of a port up to a line drawn between the outermost installations form part of the internal waters of the coastal State. No rules for ports have been included in this draft, which is exclusively concerned with the territorial sea and the high seas.(2) Permanent structures erected on the coast and jutting out to sea (such as jetties and coast protective works) are assimilated to harbour works.

(3) Where such structures are of excessive length (for instance, a jetty extending several kilometers into the sea), it may be asked whether the article could still be applied or whether it would not be necessary, in such cases, to adopt the system of safety zones provided for in article 71 for installations on the continental shelf. As such cases are very rare, the Commission, while wishing to draw attention to the matter, did not deem it necessary to state an opinion.

ED. NOTE: Article 8 of the Convention on the Territorial Sea and the Contiguous Zone has been carried forward as article 11 of the 1982 Convention, except that a new sentence has been added which reads: "Off-shore installations and artificial islands shall not be considered as permanent harbour works". This addition helps to clarify the article by indicating that in order to qualify as a basepoint, the permanent works must be attached to the coast. Presumably, any kind of installation not so connected would not fall within the scope of this provision. This is in keeping with the holding of the U.S. Supreme Court in United States v. California, 381 U.S. 139 (1965), where the Court, putting emphasis on the fact that these features must be an "integral part" of the harbour system, refused to include anchorages within the category "harbour works."Under U.S. law, it would not be possible for a state to construct harbor works, such as jetties, for the purpose of extending their inland waters. This is so, as a practical matter, because under 33 U.S.C. 403, no such structures may be built in the waters of the United States without the approval of the Corps of Engineers.

4. ROADSTEADS

CONVENTION ON THE TERRITORIAL SEA AND THE CONTIGUOUS ZONE

Article 9

Roadsteads which are normally used for loading, unloading and anchoring of ships, and which would otherwise be situated wholly or partly outside the outer limits of the territorial sea, are included in the territorial sea. The coastal State must clearly demarcate such roadsteads and indicate them on charts together with their boundaries, to which due publicity must be given.

ED. NOTE: Article 12 of the 1982 Convention tracks the above article, except that the last sentence has been eliminated because the matter of indicating such features on charts has now been covered in a general fashion by article 16.In its 1959 commentary, the ILC discusses its reasons for assimilating roadsteads to the territorial sea rather than to internal waters. The latter, it said, would be too restrictive in that innocent passage in roadsteads would be eliminated, and that the coastal State would have adequate regulatory powers in the territorial sea. In this respect, roadsteads are treated differently from ports, which are internal waters.

The roadstead issue came up during Congressional hearings leading to the adoption of the Deepwater Port Act. The Act stipulates that the laws of the adjacent U.S. state apply to deepwater ports (artificial structures for offloading oil) even though they may be located beyond the limits of the territorial sea. Discussion centered on the method by which this could be done without violating international law. One suggestion was that these ports could be assimilated to roadsteads, thus applying territorial sea doctrine to them. But this was rejected because it was felt that roadsteads were an entirely different creature of the law, and did not encompass such things as these "ports".

Congress eventually solved the problem by inserting section 1528(c) into title 33 of the U.S. Code. That provision reads as follows:

> (c) Except in a situation involving force majeure, a licensee of a deepwater port shall not permit a vessel, registered in or flying the flag of a foreign state, to call at, or otherwise utilize a deepwater port licensed under this chapter unless (1) the foreign state involved, by specific agreement with the United States, has agreed to recognize the jurisdiction of the United States over the vessel and its personnel, in accordance with the provisions of this chapter, while the vessel is located within the safety zone, and (2) the vessel owner or operator has designated an agent in the United States for receipt of service of process in the event of any claim or legal proceeding resulting from activities of the vessel or its personnel while located within such a safety zone.

5. LOW TIDE ELEVATIONS

Low tide elevations come into consideration in two respects. First, they may have significance regarding the extent of the outer limit of the territorial sea, and, second, in limited cases, they may be used as basepoints for the drawing of straight baselines.

CONVENTION ON THE TERRITORIAL SEA AND THE CONTIGUOUS ZONE

Article 11

1. A low-tide elevation is a naturally formed area of land which is surrounded by and above water at low-tide but submerged at high tide. Where a low-tide elevation is situated wholly or partly at a distance not exceeding the breadth of the territorial sea from the mainland or an island, the low-water line on that elevation may be used as the baseline for measuring the breadth of the territorial sea.

2. Where a low-tide elevation is wholly situated at a distance exceeding the breadth of the territorial sea from the mainland or an island, it has no territorial sea of its own.

ED. NOTE: It is apparent from the above (article 13 of the 1982 Convention is identical) that when a low tide elevation exists wholly or partly within the territorial sea, it is treated juridically as if it was an island. But the case is the opposite if it is wholly outside the territorial sea; it has no territorial sea of its own.

As to base points for the drawing of straight baselines, you may recall that low tide elevations may not be used unless they have lighthouses or other permanent installations on them or unless they have traditionally been viewed as appropriate for baseline construction.

In a contemporary case in U.S. law, United States v. Louisiana, 394 U.S. 11 (1969), a question was raised concerning what was meant by the phrase "from the mainland". At stake was the extent of Louisiana's claim to jurisdiction over submerged lands adjacent to its coast. The Submerged Lands Act granted Louisiana, along with several other states, jurisdiction to three miles. Louisiana drew a straight baseline across a bay. The low-tide elevation in question was more than three miles from the coast, but less than three miles from the baseline. Thus if Louisiana could use the baseline as the legal equivalent of the "mainland", the LTE in question would have the legal status of an island and could be used to extend jurisdiction.

The United States took a literal reading of the term, contending that it did not include baselines. The Court disagreed. It noted that the underlying principle of article 11 was that while an LTE within the territorial sea could be assimilated to an island, the resulting territorial sea extension could not be used to confer island status on another LTE which, before the extension, had lain wholly outside the territorial sea. In other words, one could not "leapfrog" from one LTE to another. It concluded that the ILC had intended to include baselines within the meaning of the word "mainland".

6. RIVERS EMPTYING INTO THE SEA

CONVENTION ON THE TERRITORIAL SEA AND THE CONTIGUOUS ZONE

Article 13

If a river flows directly into the sea, the baselines shall be a straight baseline across the mouth of the river between points on the low-tide line of its banks.

Churchill and Lowe, THE LAW OF THE SEA (1983) 33,34[4]

Article 13 of the Territorial Sea Convention and article 9 of the Law of the Sea Convention provided in almost identical wording that:

If a river flows into the sea, the baseline shall be a straight line across the mouth of the river between points on the low-water line of its banks.

No limit is placed on the length of such a river closing line. The provision, in the absence of any qualification to the contrary, would appear to apply to both rivers with a single riparian State as well as rivers with two riparian States, although the latter application is apparently not accepted by some States, such as the USA.

---

4. Reprinted by permission of the Manchester University Press

...It should be noted that articles 13 and 9 apply only to rivers that flow `directly' into the sea. Most large rivers do not flow directly into the sea, but enter it via estuaries. In such cases the question of the baseline should be governed by the provisions concerning bays... The original ILC draft did in fact contain a specific provision in this regard, but it was deleted at UNCLOS I because of the difficulty of defining an estuary.

It may not always be easy to distinguish between a river entering the sea directly and one entering the sea via an estuary, and in any case the distinction is open to abuse. An example of this problem can be seen in the action of Argentina and Uruguay in 1961 in drawing a line 120 miles in length across the mouth of the River Plate between Punta del Este in Uruguay and Cabe San Antonio in Argentina. This action, which has met with protests by a number of States, including the United Kingdom and the USA, is said by Argentina and Uruguay to be based on article 13, although few cartographers would be likely to choose the location of the above line as the mouth of the River Plate or indeed say that the river entered the sea `directly': furthermore, the River Plate estuary has in the past been claimed, inconsistently with the present claim, as an historic bay.

ED. NOTE: With regard to the River de la Plata problem, the Office of the Geographer, Department of State noted:

> "The Rio de la Plata, as stated before, does not fulfill the geographic requirement for a river in spite of its generic designation in Spanish. The Rio is an estuary or a type of geographic gulf or bay as a consequence of its configuration and dimensions. The closing line delimited in the declaration measures approximately 120 nautical miles.... Were the water body to be considered a juridical bay or estuary, the closing line would exceed the maximum length permitted by the Convention. In contrast, the Convention does not prescribe a maximum limit for a river closing line. The Plata estuary, however, does not conform to the geomorphic concepts of a river. As a resut, the provisions of the Convention's article 7 on historic bays would presume to apply.

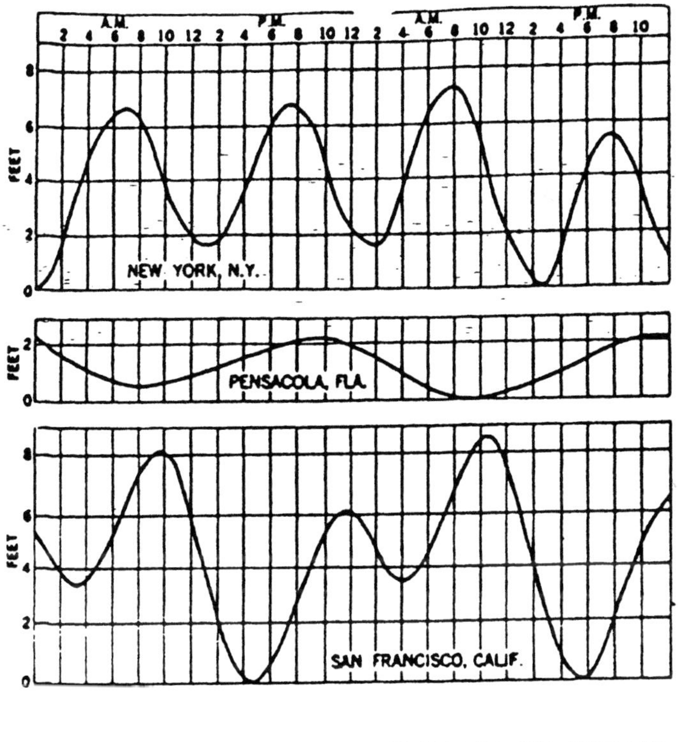

[from Shalowitz, SHORE AND SEA BOUNDARIES, (Vol. 1, 1962) at 83].

Fig. 5-1

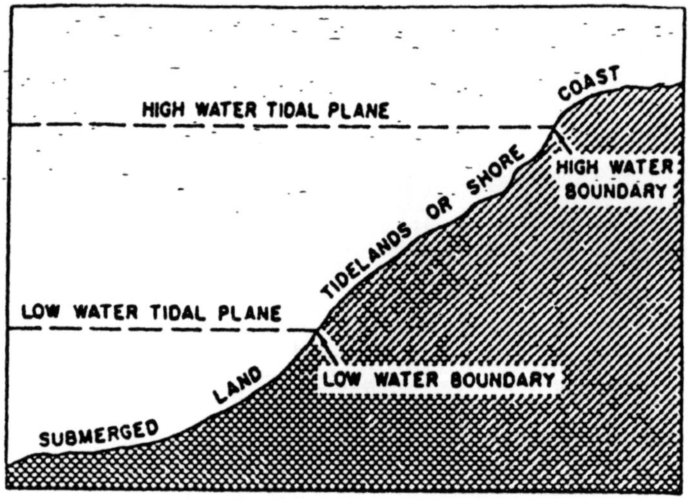

[from Shalowitz, SHORE AND SEA BOUNDARIES (Vol. 1, 1962) 90].

Fig. 5-2

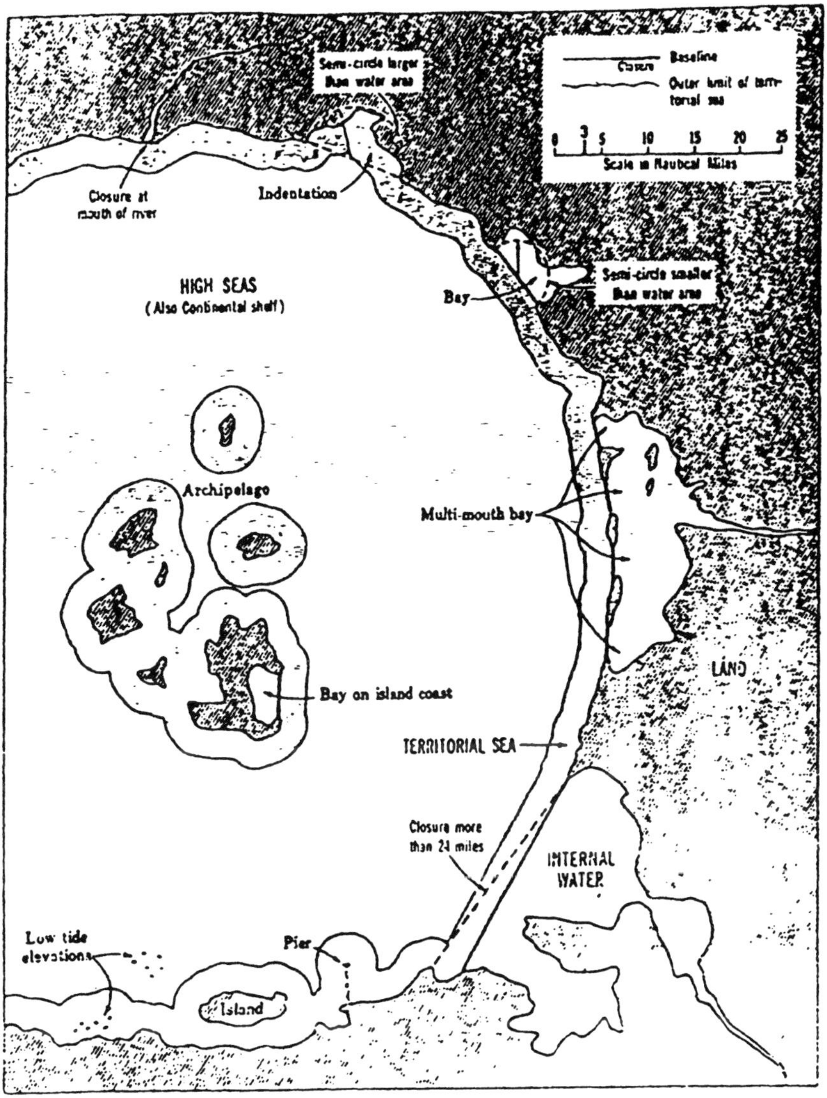

[From Sovereignty of the Sea, Geographic Bulletin No. 3, Department of State; revised, October, 1969.]

Fig. 5-3

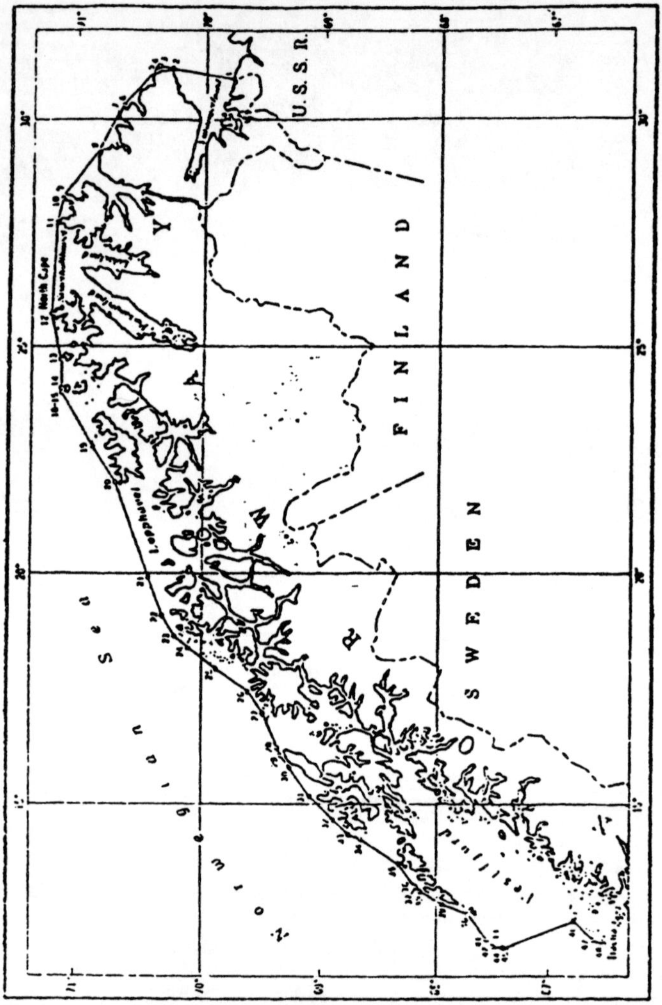

[From Shalowitz, Shore and Sea Boundaries, Vol. 1 (1962) at 69.]

Fig. 5-4

CHAPTER 6

THE CONTINENTAL SHELF

A. INTRODUCTION

In this chapter we examine the legal regime for the continental shelf. We need to understand several important concepts bearing on the question of the outer limit of the continental shelf, the nature of coastal State rights on the shelf, and the relationship of the continental shelf to the exclusive economic zone and to the deep seabed.

To this end, we shall compare the 1958 approach to the problem with that contained in the 1982 United Nations Law of the Sea Convention. We shall see significant changes. These changes were necessitated by the creation, in the new Convention, of the regime for deep seabed mining beyond the limits of national jurisdiction. Because of this new regime, it was necessary to define the limits of national jurisdiction more precisely, particularly with regard to the shelf, because in many areas the shelf extends beyond the 200 nautical mile limit of the exclusive economic zone.

But before looking at those problems, it would be helpful to have some understanding of the geology of the shelf and related subjects.

B. GEOLOGY OF THE CONTINENTAL SHELF.

Knight, "THE DRAFT UNITED NATIONS CONVENTION ON THE INTERNATIONAL SEABED AREA: BACKGROUND, DESCRIPTION, AND SOME PRELIMINARY THOUGHTS, 8 San Diego Law Review 459, 463-470 (1971)[1]

a. The Continental Shelf. The continental shelf is the seaward portion of the extension of the continental land mass which begins with the upland coastal plain and extends seaward until a marked increase in slope occurs. Although the continental shelf actually consists of the entire continental structure beginning at approximately the 600 foot contour above sea level, only the submerged portion is of interest to those concerned with marine resources, and the term has come generally to refer only to that submerged portion. The average water depth at the break in slope was traditionally considered to be 200 meters although in fact this average depth is approximately 72 fathoms or 130-140 meters. This average figure may be somewhat misleading, however, since there are few places in the world where the 72 fathom or 130-140 meter isobath actually coincides with the shelf edge. Rather, the shelf edge varies from water depths of 20 to 550 meters. The average slope of the shelf is given as 0° 07', or about ten feet per mile, and the average water depth over continental shelves as 30 fathoms. The width of the continental shelf also varies substantially, ranging from virtually zero breadth off the western coast of South America to 800 miles or more beneath the Bering Sea, averaging approximately 40 miles in width world-wide. In the United States, shelf width varies from as little as one mile off portions of California, to 100-150 miles off the Gulf coast, to over 200 miles off New England. The area of the world continental shelves, based on a 200 meter isobath shelf edge, is generally given as 7.5-7.6 percent of the ocean floor area. Classification of continental shelf types and descriptions of their origins are beyond the scope of this review, but may be found elsewhere. The surface of the shelf shows some degree of topographical relief, including canyons (extending from the coast seaward) and parallel trenches. Most shelf areas are covered by a relatively thick layer of various types of

---

unconsolidated sediment reaching depths of five kilometers, although areas exist without sediment. According to K. O. Emery, "[c]ontinental shelves are characterized by structure and stratigraphy that are similar to, or are natural continuations of, the structure and stratigraphy of the adjacent land." It is therefore not surprising that some mineral deposits found in upland locations are also found on and beneath the continental shelves. Some of the resources, such as fish and manganese nodules are, of course, unique to the shelf environment (vis-a-vis the upland), but large deposits of petroleum and natural gas are also present beneath shelves underlain by consolidated sedimentary strata. This area is also exploited to a lesser extent for sand and gravel, ilmenite, rutile, zircon, tin, monazite, iron, gold, and diamonds.

b. The Continental Slope. The continental slope lies seaward of the continental shelf and has recently been the object of a great deal of scientific and political speculation as a result of proposals to extend exclusive coastal state jurisdiction over seabed resources to the outer edge of the slope or continental margin. The term "continental margin" refers generally to the area of the seabed including a seaward portion of the shelf, all of the slope, and a landward portion of the continental rise, excluding the ocean basin. The continental slope may be defined as the area of seabed extending from the outer margin of the continental shelf to, in the absence of a continental rise, the oceanic abyss. It has been described as:

> {T]he greatest topographic feature on the face of the earth an escarpment 3-1/2 km. high and over 350,000 km. in length, which is in turn the surface expression of the greatest structural discontinuity on the earth's surface, the transition from continental to oceanic crust.

The seaward limit of the slope is ill-defined, but is conventionally taken as the point where the change in gradient from the steep banked slope to the ocean floor is less than 1:40. The water depth at the seaward extent averages 2500 meters, the range running from less than 1,000 meters to more than 4,000 meters. As a result of an average declivity of 4° 07', the width of the continental slope extends from 15 to 50 kilometers. The area of the slope has been placed at 8.5 percent of the area beneath the oceans. Slopes, like shelves, are overlain by unconsolidated sedimentary deposits composed principally of mud, sand, and gravel, with the mud/sand ratio being higher than on shelves. Attempting to characterize slope types would also be beyond the scope of this brief summary and it should suffice to note that although slopes, like shelves, contain irregularities, slopes are continuous between the shelf and the deep ocean floor with the exception of intermediate terraces or series of basings and ridges. These intermediate terraces are commonly referred to as continental borderlands or plateaus, the most notable of the United States coast being the Blake Plateau from which manganese nodules have recently been recovered, which lies at depths of 500-1,100 meters, and which has an area of approximately 200,000 square kilometers. There is growing evidence that many natural resources, including hydrocarbons and surficial hard mineral deposits, occur on portions of the slope in quantities comparable to those occurring on the shelf. The potential of continental borderlands and plateaus especially for economic hydrocarbon and hard mineral recovery in the relatively near future has enhanced the feeling of urgency surrounding efforts to secure adoption of a legal-economic regime to govern exploitation of such resources in the interests of all mankind as opposed to extension of exclusive coastal state jurisdiction to cover these areas.

c. The Continental Rise. The continental rise exists in situations where the steep portion of the continental slope is terminated on its seward edge by a gentle slope which may extend for substantial distances into the deep-ocean basins. This sedimental structure creates a significant problem in some instances in locating the actual edge of the continental formation since it may overlie deep ocean structures at its seaward edge. Accordingly, determination of the "edge of the continental margin" is more difficult to ascertain than the edge of the continental shelf, these being the two boundaries utilized in the regime proposed for the Draft Convention. The rise occurs on the landward side in water depths ranging from 1,200 meters to 3,500 meters and on the seaward side from 3,500 meters to 5,500 meters. The area of the continental rise is about 5 percent of the total ocean bottom, has an average slope of approximately one-half degree, and may extend to a width of 1,000 kilometers. Detailed discussions of the characteristics of the rise may be found elsewhere but for purposes of this paper it will be sufficient to note that the sedimentary nature of the formation, its overlap of the actual boundary between the continental land mass and the oceanic crust, and the fact that hydrocarbons may be found in the area.

C. RESOURCES OF THE SHELF

While there are a variety of minerals that can be exploited from the continental shelf, the most important by far are oil and gas. In the United States in 1960, production of oil onshore in millions of barrels was 2790.4. The corresponding offshore production was 116.8, or 4 percent of total U.S. oil production. By 1971, the offshore production had risen to 13.4 of total production. For natural gas, the proportion was 3 percent of total production in 1961, and 15.2 percent in 1971. On a worldwide scale, in 1971, about 12 percent of total production of oil came from offshore wells, and figure for natural gas was about 14.4 percent.

While these figures appear to show promise for offshore oil and gas, consider the following article.

Jones, OUTER CONTINENTAL SHELD PETROLEUM RESOURCES AND THE NATION'S FUTURE ENERGY NEEDS, 15 Syr. J. Int'l Law and Commerce 305-13 (1989)[2]

The United States and other oil consuming nations are enjoying abundant supplies of energy at relatively low prices. Oil prices fell precipitously during early 1986 producing a flood of crude oil on world markets. Lower oil prices and complacency with the current world oil surplus is disguising an important fact: the United States faces the serious theat of a repeat of the energy crisis of the 1970s.

While the drop in oil prices brought good economic news for consumers and the economy in general, it has accelerated the rate at which the United States is becoming dependent on oil imports. Net imports of crude oil have risen from twenty-seven percent of consumption in 1985 to over forty percent in 1980. This is comparable to the level of imports when the 1970s oil crisis occurred. If United States dependence on foreign oil continues at this level, imports are expected to supply about two-thirds of United States oil needs by the end of this century at an estimated cost of $150 to $200 billion. Thus, although the current oil surplus and drop in petroleum prices have lessened concern about the availability of energy supplies in future years, "supply and demand trends indicate potential domestic (shortages) and rising oil imports by the end of the century."

More importantly, with the dramatic drop in oil prices, drilling and exploration activity have been drastically curtailed, domestic reserves and production have declined, the United States oil and gas service industry has been devastated, and the productive capacity of the petroleum industry is being seriously threatened....

The Reagan administration recognized that the United States was over-dependent on foreign oil, and that the Nation could not "afford to become dangerously dependent upon other nations -- sometimes unstable nations -- for essential elements of our economy." It maintained, however, that conservation and renewable energy resources would not significantly relieve this dependence. The Reagan administration believed that the United States could produce enough energy domestically so that it would not be vulnerable to supply disruption, unreasonable price increases, or political pressures

---

[2]. Reprinted by permission of the Syracuse J. Intl Law and Commerce.

by major oil producing countries or the Organization of Petroleum Exporting Countries (OPEC). It was the policy of the Reagan administration, therefore, to increase domestic energy production by authorizing increased exploration on public lands, with particular reliance upon an accelerated outer continental shelf (OCS) leasing program.

OCS oil and gas production represented twelve percent of domestic oil production and twenty-four percent of natural gas production in 1986. However, OCS oil and gas production as a percentage of total United States production has remained constant since 1970. Moreover, the Mineral Management Service (MMS) recently lowered the estimates of undiscovered recoverable OCS oil and natural gas as a result of unsuccessful exploration in the Alaska and Atlantic OCS regions. The downgraded resource estimates raise major questions about the Nation's potential oil and gas supply and the government's reliance upon the OCS as the major element of its national energy policy. Outside of the Gulf of Mexico and California nearshore areas, OCS exploration has added very little to proven domestic petroleum reserves. Furthermore, offshore oil and gas exploration and production is a long term business. An offshore project can take up to ten years from preliminary geological work to production. In Alaska, it may require fifteen or more years before production can commence.

The United States is, and for many years will continue to be, heavily dependent upon foreign oil. Domestic production from OCS fields can help relieve this dependence, but it is not the whole or immediate answer. What the United States desparately needs and has been sorely lacking is a coherent national energy policy. In order to effectively plan for future energy requirements the Nation must reevaluate the role and resource potential of its OCS areas.

....

[T]he percentage of United States oil production coming from OCS areas has increased from .1 percent in 1954 to twelve percent in 1986. However, OCS production as a percentage of total United States production has remained rather constant since 1970, between ten and twelve percent. For natural gas, the contribution from the OCS has increased steadily from less than one percent in 1954, to four percent in 1965, seventeen percent in 1975, and twenty-four percent in 1989. Like OCS oil production, natural gas production has stabilized between twenty-two and twenty-five percent for the period 1978-86.

The prospects for oil and gas in the United States OCS regions are good. However, energy experts agree that there is a possibility that only an insignificant amount of economically recoverable oil and gas may be discovered. In fact, the Point Arguello Field, off southern California's shore, is the only major OCS field discovered since 1970 that significantly increased domestic petroleum reserves. Furthermore, the history of petroleum exploration demonstrates that large fields are generally discovered early in the exploration cycle, and that substantial exploration has already occurred in some OCS frontier regions, such as the Gulf of Alaska and Atlantic regions.

Current energy forecasts demonstrate the uncertainty of the petroleum reserves of the federal OCS as a potential energy resource to lessen United States dependence on foreign sources of oil. In 1981, the United States Geological Survey (USGS) estimated that the undiscovered economically recoverable oil and gas resources of the OCS totalled twenty-seven billion barrels of oil and 162.7 trillion cubic feet of gas. A more recent study in 1985 by the Minerals Management Service (MMS) revised these figures downward by fifty-five percent for oil reserves, to 12.2 billion barrels and by forty-four percent for natural gas resources, to 90.5 trillion cubic feet. The resource estimates were lowered largely as a result of unsuccessful exploratory drilling in the Atlantic and Alaskan OCS regions, and particularly from new estimating procedures. In comparison, "the [N]ation's largest offshore field, Prudhoe Bay, is a ten billion barrel field." If the MMS estimates are correct, the entire OCS may contain only slightly more petroleum than Prudhoe Bay.

Despite the lower OCS oil and gas estimates, the Reagan administration still supported OCS leasing as a significant element of the Nation's energy policy. The administration maintained that the history of the search for petroleum contains numerous examples of major discoveries in regions with little evidence of hydrocarbons or areas where previous exploratory drilling has been unsuccessful. Prudhoe Bay in Alaska, the East Texas Field, the North Sea, and the Monterey formation offshore California are examples of this drilling scenario. Offshore drilling in the region will also provide industry with geographical data to guide future searches for petroleum reservoirs and may change the relative potential of different OCS areas....

....

D. OIL AND GAS TECHNOLOGY

COMMISSION ON MARINE SCIENCE, ENGINEERING AND RESOURCES, Report of the Panel on Marine Engineering and Technology (1969) VI-1, VI-164-169

III. Offshore Oil and Gas

....

C. Exploration

1. Geophysical Surveys and Geological Analysis

Exploration encompasses the broad reconnaissance surveys followed by more detailed surveys that actually delineate (i.e., exploration activities involve locating promising areas for drilling activities). Exploration begins with geologists making a general study of the structure of the earth to select an area with characteristics possibly favorable for oil or gas recovery.

After selecting a promising area, tests pinpoint the site to probe further for possible reserves. These can be simple magnetometer readings taken from an airplane or a ship. By showing a variation in the earth's magnetic field, the tests indicate geologic structures below the ocean floor. In addition, towed marine gravimeters can determine very small variations in the earth's gravity field. Both types of geophyisical surveys can be made in any depth of water and at any distance from land. However, in themselves, they usually do not provide information of sufficient accuracy to permit siting an exploratory well.

The most successful technique to locate test drilling sites is seismic profiling. Such surveys require much more expensive equipment but because of the high speed at which the surveys can be conducted, the actual cost per mile is about one-third as much as on land. A sound pulse is generated, a portion of which is reflected from the layers of sediment and rock under the ocean floor. The reflections when received at the surface are recorded on a graph showing an approximation of the depth and characteristics of underlying geological structures. In earlier surveys black powder or dynamite was used to generate the sound pulse. Today, electrical sparking systems, air guns, contained-gas explosions, mechanical boomers, and other nonexplosive energy sources are used. Seismic data are recorded routinely on magnetic tape and processed by digital computers, enhancing quality and reliability.

The above-mentioned geophysical techniques are indirect methods for examining structures under our continental margins. The most satisfactory method to date for obtaining geologic samples of rock on or at shallow depths under the sea floor has been with small coring devices operated from a surface ship. These devices drill a hole several hundred feet into the sea floor and recover samples of rock for further study. Similar holes have been drilled in the U.S. continental margin beyond the shelves to 5,000 feet deep. Coring in such depths has been accomplished from floating, dynamically positioned vessels. As long ago as 1961, several experimental core holes were drilled in 11,700 feet of water as part of the early phase of Project Mohole.

Exploration technology has made rapid strides in new seismic energy sources and receiving systems. Computers permit analysis of data while under way at sea. The Navy Navigation Satellite System will permit seismic teams to determine more accurately survey locations in remote areas.

2. Exploratory Drilling

Determining the presence of oil or gas requires full scale drilling operations at the site, a much more difficult and expensive task than drilling shallow core holes....

While the types of platforms used to support the drilling rigs vary greatly, the rigs are fairly standardized. They consist of: (1) a tall steel tower to hoist the bit, pipe, and other equipment in and out of the hole, (2) a system to rotate the pipe and bit, and (3) a system to circulate fluid to the bottom of the hole.

Fixed platforms supported by pilings were constructed in shallow offshore waters as the drillers followed the seaward extension of oil fields. As the industry moved into deeper waters, it continued using this type of foundation for exploitation drilling. However, for exploratory drilling, where the incidence of dry holes is inherently higher, fixed platforms soon became too costly.

The industry then began to develop mobile drilling platforms. This minimized the capital investment chargeable to each well site. The first mobile platforms were submersible barges for operation in 20 to 40 feet of water and evolved from the barge-mounted driling rigs used in southern Louisiana marshlands. Later, jack-up rigs were developed for greater water depths.

...There are three general types of mobile platforms--submersible, jack-up, and floating.

The jack-up rig is mounted on a buoyant hull to which extendable legs are attached. The legs are raised for moving the rig and lowered to the floor to lift the platform above the ocean waves during drilling operations....

The advantage of a jack-up and submersible rig is that they rest on the bottom while the platform stands clear of the highest waves, enabling them to operate in rough seas. The jack-up rig has more depth flexibility and capability while the submersible rig, a monolithic structure, can be towed more readily from one location to another.

While floating platforms lack the stability of the bottom support type, they are not as restricted to a given depth of water and are cost-competitive at 200 feet or more. The floating platform includes two major categories: semi-submersibles and the ship-shaped type.

The semi-submersibles are floating platforms supported on tall columns which rise from buoyant barge-like hulls or cylindrical torpedo-shaped tubes.... Upon arrival on location they are ballasted so that approximately one-half the unit is below water. Their advantage over drilling ships or barges is that the major structure is located above or below the region of most severe wave action. This configuration provides improved stability by its large inertia, and by having a vertical natural frequency of movement which is affected little by wave forces.

The semi-submersibles can be raised by pumping ballast water from the tubes and columns. Finally, they can be used to drill while resting on the sea floor if in sufficiently shallow water.

Ship-shaped platforms consist of a drilling rig supported on a barge or self-propelled ship. A barge, because it is not self-propelled, must be moved by tugs to new assignments, but it has the advantage of low initial cost. The ship-shaped platform can transit at higher speeds and at less expense. A disadvantage of the ship-shaped vessel platforms is that much drilling time can be lost in bad weather due to vessel motion; however, this may not be an important consideration in protected drilling locations....

E. EVOLUTION OF THE DOCTRINE

The continental shelf, as a legal concept, is of relatively recent origin. While the idea of the shelf as a physical feature had been known for some considerable amount of time, it was not until its potential for resource development became known and appreciated did the need for a regime of legal rights emerge. The traditional doctrine of the freedom of the high seas was perfectly adequate to assure a petroleum developer's right to utilize that space beyond the limits of the territorial sea. But that doctrine provided no protection for the developer from encroachment on his claim. But, nonetheless, no such doctrine existed, as far at the United States was concerned, until the middle of the 20th century, as is reflected by the following correspondence.

LETTER FROM SECOND ASSISTANT SECRETARY OF STATE (ADEE) TO MR. FRANK R. NEWTON, September 10, 1918, MS. Department of State, file 312.11/8645, 2 Hackworth, Digest of International Law 697-670 (1940)

The Department is in receipt of your letter of August 20, 1918, concerning the alleged discovery of a large pool of oil in the Gulf of Mexico about 40 miles from land on a reef where the water is less than 100 feet deep. With regard to this matter, you ask on behalf of yourself and other interested parties whether it would be possible to acquire property or leasehold rights to this tract of ocean bottom so as to be protected in an effort to obtain oil from this pool. You suggest that an artificial island might be erected and inquire whether such island could be brought under the jurisdiction of the United States and whether it could protect your rights by giving you a lease to the property. You further suggest that, if protective rights could not be acquired by individuals, you would be willing to turn your discovery over to the Government for a consideration and allow the United States to operate the oil well.

In reply, the Department informs you that the United States has no jurisdiction over the ocean bottom of the Gulf of Mexico beyond the territorial waters adjacent to the coast. Therefore, it does not appear feasible for the United States to grant to you the leasehold or other property rights in the ocean bottom which you desire.

The Department further informs you that, unless the erection of an artificial island interfered with rights of the United States or its citizens, or formed the subject of a complaint made upon apparently good grounds, it is not likely that this Government would object to the erection by American citizens of such an island as you suggest. The Department is not in a position to procure information from other nations as to their attitude toward such a project, but it would seem that no foreign government would interfere with the erection of an artificial island in the Gulf of Mexico unless its interests or the rights of its citizens were injuriously affected thereby.

It may also be observed, although the Department can give no assurances on the subject, that it would seem possible that, if an island were constructed 40 miles from the coast of the United States by the efforts of American citizens and inhabited and controlled by them in the name of the United States, this Government would assume some sort of control over the island. However, it would seem that some special action by the President and Congress would be necessary to this end. If the island were erected, and if the United States assumed control over it, it would then be possible to take such steps as were necessary to protect the rights of the occupants.

* * * *

ED. NOTE: One of the early harbingers of coastal State jurisdiction over submerged lands involved the Gulf of Paria. In 1942 the United Kingdom and Venezuela concluded a treaty relating to the submarine areas of the Gulf of Paria which provided for the division of such areas between the United Kingdom and Venezuela (Trinidad, which is situated between the Gulf and the open sea, was then a British possession). "Submarine areas" was defined to mean the seabed and subsoil outside of the territorial waters of the parties. Subsequently, an Order of Council of the United Kingdom was passed which provided in part that:

> "As from the date of this Order all of the submarine areas in the Gulf of Paria [defined as the seabed and subsoil situated beneath the waters, excluding territorial waters, described in the Order]...shall be annexed to and form a part of His Majesty's dominion...." I United Kingdom, Statutory Rules and Order, August 6, 1942, at 919.

The Order was not a general claim to continental shelf lands, but related exclusively to the Gulf of Paria continental shelf. Although not the first general claim, the most significant claim was the proclamation of President Truman made on September 28, 1945.

PRESIDENTIAL PROCLAMATION NO. 2667 (SEPTEMBER 28, 1945), 3 C.F.R., 1943-1948 Comp., p. 67, 13 State Dep't Bull 485 (1945)

"Policy of the United States with Respect to the Natural Resources of the Subsoil and Sea Bed of the Continental Shelf"

WHEREAS the Government of the United States of America, aware of the long range world-wide need for new sources of petroleum and other minerals, holds the view that efforts to discover and make available new supplies of these resources should be encouraged; and

WHEREAS its competent experts are of the opinion that such resources underlie many parts of the continental shelf off the coasts of the United States of America, and that with modern technological progress their utilization is already practicable or will become so at an early date; and

WHEREAS recoginized jurisdiction over these resources is required in the interest of their conservation and prudent utilizationn when and as development is undertaken; and

WHEREAS it is the view of the Government of the United States that the exercise of jurisdiction over the natural resources of the subsoil and sea bed of the continental shelf by the contiguous nation is reasonable and just, since the effectiveness of measures to utilize or conserve these resources would be contingent upon cooperation and protection from shore, since the continental shelf may be regarded as an extension of the land mass of the coastal nation and thus naturally appurtenant to it, since these resources frequently form a seaward extension of a pool or deposit lying within the territory, and since self-protection compels the coastal nation to keep close watch over activities off its shores which are of their nature necessary for utilization of these resources;

NOW, THEREFORE I, HARRY S. TRUMAN, President of the United States of America, do hereby proclaim the following policy of the United States of America with respect to the natural resources of the subsoil and sea bed of the continental shelf.

Having concern for the urgency of conserving and prudently utilizing its natural resources, the Government of the United States regards the natural resources of the subsoil and sea bed of the continental shelf beneath the high seas but contiguous to the coasts of the United States as appertaining to the United States, subject to its jurisdiction and control. In cases where the continental shelf extends to the shores of another State, or is shared with an adjacent State, the boundary shall be determined by the United States and the State concerned in accordance with equitable principles. The character as high seas of the waters above the continental shelf and the right to their free and unimpeded navigation are no way thus affected.

WHITE HOUSE PRESS RELEASE, September 28, 1945, 13 State Dep't Bull. 484-485 (1945)

"Proclamations Concerning United States Jurisdiction Over Natural Resources in Coastal Areas and the High Seas"

....

The Policy proclaimed by the President in regard to jurisdiction over the continental shelf does not touch upon the question of Federal versus State control. It is concerned solely with establishing the jurisdiction of the United States from an international standpoint. It will, however, make possible the orderly development of an underwater area 750,000 square miles in extent. Generally, submerged land which is contiguous to the continent and which is covered by no more than 100 fathoms (600 feet) of water is considered as the continental shelf.

Petroleum geologists believe that portions of the continental shelf beyond the three-mile limit contain valuable oil deposits. The study of sub-surface structures associated with oil deposits which have been discovered along the Gulf coast of Texas, for instance, indicates that corresponding deposits may underlie the offshore, or submerged land. The trend of oil-productive salt domes extends directly into the Gulf of Mexico off the Texas coast. Oil is also being taken at present from wells within the three mile limit off the coast of California. It is quite possible, geologists say, that the oil deposits extend beyond this traditional limit of national jurisdiction.

Valuable deposits of minerals other than oil may also be expected to be found in these submerged areas. Ore mines now extend under the sea from the coasts of England, Chile, and other countries.

While asserting jurisdiction and control of the United States over the mineral resources of the continental shelf, the proclamation in no wise abridges the right of free and unimpeded navigation of waters of the character of high seas above the shelf, nor does it extend the present limits of the territorial waters of the United States.

The advance of technology prior to the present war had already made possible the exploitation of a limited amount of minerals from submerged lands within the three-mile limit. The rapid development of technical knowledge and equipment occasioned by the war now makes possible the determination of the resources of the submerged lands outside of the three-mile limit. With the need for the discovery of additional resources of petroleum and other minerals, it became advisable for the

United States to make possible orderly development of these resources. The proclamation of the President is designed to serve this purpose.

ED. NOTE ON SUBSEQUENT CONTINENTAL SHELF CLAIMS.

Between the Gulf of Paria Order in Council and the Truman Proclamation, the Republic of Argentina issued Decree No. 1,386 deisgnating as "temporary zones of mineral reserves" the area, inter alia, of the epicontinental sea of Argentina. Thereafter virtually every coastal nation in the world issued decrees, proclamations or claims relating to the continental shelf or the mineral resources thereof, or ratified the 1958 Convention on the Continental Shelf.

As might have been expected, the Truman Proclamation unleashed a raft of national claims regarding jurisdiction over the adjacent continental shelf. But international law was slow to fully embrace the doctrine, as the following case shows.

PETROLEUM DEVELOPMENT LTD. vs. SHEIKH OF ABU DHABI
(Lord Asquith of Bishopstone, Umpire; 1951)

[Petroleum Development (Trucial Coast) Ltd. ("Company") secured a concession from the Ruler of Abu Dhabi ("Ruler") in 1939 providing for the exclusive right to explore for and exploit petroleum within an area specified in the concession as follows:

> "Article 2. The area included in this Agreement is the whole of the lands which belong to the rule of the Ruler of Abu Dhabi and its dependencies and all the islands and the sea waters which belong to that area...."

A dispute arose as to the rights of the Company in petroleum deposits situated in submerged lands off the coast of Abu Dhabi. The Company claimed that the concession applied to submerged lands beneath the Ruler's territorial sea and beyond that to areas beneath the high seas to which the Ruler's jurisdiction might extend (i.e., the continental shelf). The specific question presented was whether, *at the time of the agreement,* the Ruler owned the mineral rights in submerged lands beneath Abu Dhabi's territorial sea and/or continental shelf and, if so, whether the same were conveyed by the terms of the concession. Lord Asquith of Bishopstone delivered the award.]

I should certainly in 1939 have read the expression "the sea waters which belong to that area" not only as including, but as *limited* to, the territorial belt and its subsoil. At that time neither contracting party had ever heard of the doctrine of the Continental Shelf, which as a legal doctrine did not then exist. No thought of it entered their heads. None such entered that of the most sophisticated jurisconsult, let alone the "understanding" perhaps strong but "simple and unschooled" of Trucial Sheikhs.

Directed, as I apprehend I am, to apply a simple and broad jurisprudence to the construction of this contract, it seems to me that it would be a most artificial refinement to read back into the contract the implications of a doctrine not mooted till seven years later, and, if the view which I am about to express is sound, not even today admitted to the canon of international law. However, the time has now come to consider this doctrine more narrowly.

<u>The doctrine of the Continental Shelf, its substance and history</u>: The expression "Continental Shelf" was first used by a geographer in 1898. The legal doctrine which later gathered round this geographical term was possibly foreshadowed when in 1942 England and Venezuela concluded a treaty about the Gulf of Paria providing for spheres of influence in respect of areas covered by the high seas and followed by certain annexations coincident with these spheres. The doctrine was perhaps first explicitly asserted as a legal doctrine (in very exaggerated form) in a proclamation by the Argentine

Republic in 1944, but its classical enunciation in the form in which it has mainly to be considered in this case was the well-known proclamation by President Truman of September 28, 1945.

Is the doctrine in any of its forms part and parcel of international law?: The preceding section calls attention not only to the recent origin of the doctrine but to the great variety of forms which in its short life it has assumed. Some States claim sovereignty over the Shelf. Others pointedly avoid doing so, claiming only "jurisdiction" or "control," "appurtenance" and the like. Whatever the scope of those rights claimed, some States assert those right by declaratory proclamations implying their pre-existence; others issue proclamations which on the face of them are a new departure and designed to be constitutive of title. What is the seaward limit of the Shelf? Here again the answers differ. Some States say, "its geological or geographic limit, its `edge' or its `drop'." Others (whether because their particular Shelf has got no edge and has got no drop, or for other reasons), say, "the point at which the sea becomes 100 fathoms or 200 metres deep"; while yet others say, "a line drawn parallel to the coast of the contiguous power and 200 nautical miles from it." The 200-mile claim seems to be more or less universally discredited. The other two criteria seem on their face much more reasonable. But what is the position where as in the Persian Gulf itself, both of these more reasonable criteria fail us, because the Shelf not only has no edge,but extends continuously across a sea whose waters never attain a depth of as much as 100 fathoms? Is it to extend outwards to a "reasonable distance" from the coast--the expression used in the recital of the Abu Dhabi proclamation? If so, what is a "reasonable distance"? Where States are grouped, as in this case, round a more or less cylindrical gulf, is the principle "*usque ad medium filum*" applicable? How could it possibly be applied in the case of comparably shallow seas of completely irregular configuration, such as the North Sea? Again how are rights of whatever character to the subsoil of the Shelf acquired? Can they indeed be acquired at all? Or would their existence inevitably conflict with the "freedom" of the high seas? Before the doctrine of the Shelf was promulgated I think the general answer might well have been that they cannot be acquired at all -- that the Shelf is a inappropriable as the high seas that roll or repose above it: Subject to this reservation, that the sea-bed (not the subsoil) of the submarine area is, in certain rare cases, subject to a customary right vested in certain States to conduct "sedentary" fisheries in such sea-bed. For instance, the right to fish for sponges, coral, oysters, pearls and chank. Indeed, the shallow seas of the Persian Gulf are subject to mutual pearling rights by subjects of the various littoral States. If, however, the submarine area is capable not merely of being the subject-matter of these limited occupational rights over the sea-bed, and *pro tanto* a "*res nullius*," is its subsoil as a whole *res nullius*? That is to say, something in which rights can be acquired, but only by effective occupation? Or is the position, as the claimants' main argument maintains, that the rights in the subsoil of the Shelf adhere (and must be taken always to have adhered) *ipso jure* -- occupation or no occupation -- to the contiguous coastal Power? Or failing that, if occupation be indeed necessary; in cases where it is most impracticable, may proclamations, or similar acts be treated as a constructive or symbolic or inchoate occupation (the claimants' alternative contention under this head)?

Conclusion as to doctrine of the Continental Shelf: Neither the practice of nations nor the pronouncements of learned jurists give any certain or consistent answer to many -- perhaps most -- of these questions. I am of opinion that there are in this field so many ragged ends and unfilled blanks, so much that is merely tentative and exploratory, that in no form can the doctrine claim as yet to have assumed hitherto the hard lineaments or the definitive status of an established rule of international law.

Whether there *ought* to exist a rule giving effect to the doctrine in one or other and, if so, which of its forms is another question and one which, if I had to answer it, I should answer in the affirmative. There seems to me much cogency on the arguments of those who advocate the *ipso jure* variant of the doctrine. In particular: (1) it is extremely desirable that someone, in what threatens to become an oil-starved world, should have the right to exploit the subsoil of the submarine area outside of the territorial limit; (2) the contiguous coastal Power seems the most appropriate and convenient agency for this purpose. It is in the best position to exercise effective control, and the alternatives teem with disadvantages; (3) there is no reason in principle why the subsoil of the high seas should, like the high seas themselves, be incapable of being the subject of exclusive rights in any one. The main reasons why this status is attributed to the high seas is (i) that they are the great highways between nations and navigation on these highways should be unobstructed. (ii) that fishing in the high seas should be unrestricted (a policy approved by this country ever since Magna Carta abolished "several" fisheries). The subsoil, however, of the submarine area is not a highway between nations and the installations necessary to exploit it (even though sunk from the surface into the subsoil rather than tunnelled laterally) need hardly constitute an appreciable obstacle to free navigation; nor does the subsoil contain fish. (4) To treat this subsoil as *res nullius* -- "fair game" for the first occupier -- entails obvious and grave dangers so far as occupation is possible at all. It invites a perilous scramble. The doctrine that occupation is vital in the case of a *res nullius* has in any case worn thin since the East Greenland Arbitration and more especially since that relating to Clipperton Island. But leaving that aside, it is difficult to imagine any arrangement more calculated to produce international friction than one which entitles nation A, it may be thousands of miles from nation B, to stake out claims on the Continental Shelf contiguous to nation B by "squatting" on B's doorstep -- at some point just outside B's territorial water limit.

* * * *

ED. NOTE: As the following document indicates, a small effort was made at the First U.N. Conference on the Law of the Sea to suggest an a+lternative to coastal state jurisdiction over the resources of the continental shelf. The proposal met with no success. However, the German position should be borne in mind when, in the next chapter, materials are presented relating to the legal regime to govern non-living resource extractive activities beyond the limits of national jurisdiction.

FEDERAL REPUBLIC OF GERMANY: MEMORANDUM CONCERNING DRAFT ARTICLES 67 TO 73. VI Official Records 125-126 (1958), U.N. Doc. A/CONF.13/C.4/L.1, 4 March 1958

....

With regard to the continental shelf in particular, the delegation of the Federal Republic of Germany considers...that, in view of the growing importance of the wealth of the subsoil of the high seas, it is necessary, in the interests of the international community, to establish certain rules which will neither hamper the systematic exploration and exploitation of the subsoil of the sea nor unduly restrict the other freedoms of the high seas.

....

According to the international law in force, the coastal State has no rights over the continental shelf beyond the outer limit of its territorial sea. Accordingly, anyone is free to explore and exploit the subsoil of the sea outside the territorial sea, provided that such activity does not unduly hamper the other activities on the high seas which under international law are open to all....

Now, if this freedom is to be regulated in the interests of the international community, it would be both logical and sufficient to agree on self-executing rules governing the exploration and exploitation of the subsoil of the sea. The international community has set the example in this respect, for a number of multinational conventions have been entered into which govern other activities on the high seas (safety of navigation, sea-borne traffic, regulations concerning the police of fisheries, whaling, conservation of marine species, protection of cables, pollution of the seas)....

* * * *

NORTH SEA CONTINENTAL SHELF CASES, [1969] I.C.J. 3, Paras. 19,63

[T]he Court entertains no doubt [that] the most fundamental of all the rules of law relating to the continental shelf, enshrined in Article 2 of the 1958 Geneva Convention, though quite independent of it, [is] that the rights of the coastal State in respect of the area of the continental shelf that constitutes a natural prolongation of its land territory into and under the sea exist *ipso facto* and *ab initio*, by virtue of its sovereignty over the land, and as an extension of it in an exercise of sovereign rights for the purpose of exploring the seabed and exploiting its natural resources. In short, there is here an inherent right. In order to exercise it, no special legal process has to be gone through, nor have any special legal acts to be performed. Its existence can be declared (and many States have done this) but does not need to be constituted. Furthermore, the right does not depend upon its being exercised. To echo the language of the Geneva Convention, it is "exclusive" in the sense that if the coastal State does not choose to explore or exploit the areas of the shelf appertaining to it, that is its own affair, but no one else may do so without its express consent.

....

[Articles 1 to 3 of the Continental Shelf Convention], it is clear, were then [1958] regarded as reflecting, or as crystallizing, received or at least emergent rules of customary international law relative to the continental shelf, amongst them the question of the seaward extent of the shelf; the juridical character of the coastal State's entitlement; the nature of the rights exercisable; the kind of natural resources to which these relate; and the preservation intact of the legal status of the high seas of the waters over the shelf, and of the superjacent air space.

F. THE CONTINENTAL SHELF REGIME

1. INTRODUCTION.

In this section we shall examine the nature of the legal regime of the continental shelf concerning both the question of the extent of coastal State jurisdiction seaward, and the question of the content of that jurisdiction. In the process, we will compare the regime established under the 1958 Convention on the Continental Shelf with the relevant provisions of the 1982 United Nations Convention on the Law of the Sea. In studying these materials, you should investigate whether the new convention rules are legally the same as those in the 1958 convention, or whether an entirely different regime has been created. The answer to this is important to States, such as the United States, who have not signed the new convention, and who have declared their intent not to become parties to it. The United States, as a party to the 1958 convention must assume the obligations and claim the rights thereunder. Can it also, on the basis of customary law, claim the rights specified in the new treaty? Could the United States, for example, submit its continental shelf limits to the boundary review commission created by it? We will have occasion in class to address these and other questions of the same kind.

In addition to looking at the legal regime of the continental shelf, we shall address related questions, such as the rules for installations placed upon the shelf. While there is extensive statutory and case law dealing with U.S. continental shelf matters, we can only, because of time restraints, consider the basics. Two problems only will be addressed. The first relates to the identification of the kinds of regulation the Congress of the United States can impose on the U.S. continental shelf. The second relates to the way in which the United States, being a federal system, has chosen to share the resources of its shelf with the individual states of the union.

2. RIGHTS EXERCISABLE AND RESOURCES INCLUDED UNDER THE CONTINENTAL SHELF CONCEPT.

CONVENTION ON THE CONTINENTAL SHELF

Article 2

1. The coastal State exercises over the continental shelf sovereign rights for the purpose of exploring it and exploiting its natural resources.

2. The rights referred to in paragraph 1 of this article are exclusive in the sense that if the coastal State does not explore the continental shelf or exploit its natural resources, no one may undertake these activities, or make a claim to the continental shelf, without the express consent of the coastal State.

3. The rights of the coastal State over the continental shelf do not depend on occupation, effective or notional, or on any express proclamation.

4. The natural resources referred to in these articles consist of the mineral and other non-living resources of the seabed and subsoil together with living organisms belonging to sedentary species, that is to say, organisms which, at the harvestable stage, either are immobile on or under the seabed or are unable to move except in constant physical contact with the seabed or the subsoil.

INTERNATIONAL LAW COMMISSION, 1956 Commentary

Draft Article 68

(1) While this article, as provisionally formulated in 1951 (article 2 of the draft), referred to the continental shelf as "subject to the exercise by the coastal State of control and jurisdiction for the purpose of exploring it and exploiting its natural resources," the article as now formulated lays down that "the coastal State exercises over the continental shelf sovereign rights for the purpose of exploring and exploiting its natural resources."

(2) The Commission desired to avoid language lending itself to interpretations alien to an object which the Commission considers to be of decisive importance, namely, the safeguarding of the principle of the full freedom of the superjacent sea and the air space above it. Hence it was unwilling to accept the sovereignty of the coastal State over the seabed and subsoil of the continental shelf. On the other hand, the text as now adopted leaves no doubt that the rights conferred upon the coastal State cover all rights necessary for and connected with the exploration and exploitation of the natural resources of the continental shelf. Such rights include jurisdiction in connexion with the prevention and punishment of violations of the law. The rights of the coastal State are exclusive in the sense that, if it

does not exploit the continental shelf, it is only with its consent that anyone else may do so.

(3) At its fifth session, the Commission decided after long discussion to retain the term "natural resources," as distinct from the more limited term "mineral resources." In its previous draft the Commission had only dealt with "mineral resources" and some members proposed adhering to that course. The Commission, however, came to the conclusion that the products of "sedentary" fisheries, in particular to the extent that they were natural resources permanently attached to the bed of the sea should not be left outside the scope of the regime adopted, and that this aim acould be achieved by using the term "natural resources." it is clearly understood that the rights in question do not cover so-called bottom fish and other fish which, although living in the sea, occassionally have their habitat at the bottom of the sea or are bred there.

(4) At the eighth session it was proposed that the condition of permanent attachment to the seabed should be mentioned in the article itself. At the same time the opinion was expressed that the marine fauna and flora in question should live in constant physical and biological relationship with the seabed and the continental shelf; examination of the scientific aspects of that question should be left to the experts. The Commission however decided to leave the text of the article and of the commentary as it stood.

(5) It is clearly understood that the rights in question do not cover objects such as wrecked ships and their cargoes (including bullion) lying on the seabed or covered by the sand of the subsoil.

(6) In the view of the Commission, the coastal State, when exercising its exclusive rights, must also respect the existing rights of nationals of other States. Any interference with such rights, when unavoidably necessitated by the requirements of exploration and exploitation of natural resources, is subject to the rules of international law concerning respect for the rights of aliens. However, apart from the case of acquired rights, the sovereign rights of the coastal State over its continental shelf also cover "sedentary" fisheries in the sense indicated above. As regards fisheries which are also sometimes described as "sedentary" because they are conducted by means of equipment fixed in the sea, but which are not concerned with natural resources attached to the seabed, the Commission refers to article 60 of these rules.

(7) The rights of the coastal State over the continental shelf do not depend on occupation, effective or notional, or on any express proclamation.

(8) The Commission does not deem it necssary to expatiate on the question of the nature and legal basis of the sovereign rights attributed to the coastal State. The considerations relevant to this matter cannot be reduced to a single factor. In particular, it is not possible to base the sovereign rights of the coastal State exclusively on recent practice, for there is no question in the present case of giving the authority of a legal rule to a unilateral practice resting solely upon the will of the States concerned. However, that practice itself is considered by the Commission to be supported by considerations of law and of fact. In particular, once the seabed and subsoil have become an object of active interest to coastal States with a view to the exploration and exploitaton of their resources, they cannot be considered as *res nullius*, i.e., capable of being appropriated by the first occupier. It is natural that coastal States should resist any such solution. Moreover, in most cases the effective exploitation of natural resources must presuppose the existence of installations on the territory of the coastal State. Neither is it possible to disregard the geographical phenomenon whatever the term -- propinquity, contiguity, geographical continuity, appurtenance or identity -- used to define the relationship between the submarine areas in question and the adjacent non-submerged land. All these considerations of general utility provide a sufficient basis for the principle of the sovereign rights of the coastal State as now formulated by the Commission. As already stated, that principle, which is based on general principles corresponding the present needs of the international community, is in no way incompatible

with the principle of the freedom of the seas.

1982 UNITED NATIONS CONVENTION ON THE LAW OF THE SEA

Article 77

Rights of the coastal State over the continental shelf

1. The coastal State exercises over the continental shelf sovereign rights for the purpose of exploring it and exploiting its natural resources.

2. The rights referred to in paragraph 1 are exclusive in the sense that if the coastal State does not explore the continental shelf or exploit is natural resources, no one may undertake these activities without the express consent of the coastal State.

3. The rights of the coastal State over the continental shelf do not depend on occupation, effective or notional, or on any express proclamation.

4. The natural resources referred to in this Part consist of the mineral and other non-living resources of the sea-bed and subsoil together with living organisms belonging to sedentary species, that is to say, organisms which, at the harvestable stage, either are immobile on or under the sea-bed or are unable to move except in constant physical contact with the sea-bed or the subsoil.

Article 78

Legal status of the superjacent waters and air space and the rights and freedoms of other States

1. The rights of the coastal State over the continental shelf do not affect the legal status of the superjacent waters or of the air space above those waters.

2. The exercise of the rights of the coastal State over the continental shelf must not infringe, or result in any unjustifiable interference with navigation and other rights and freedoms of other States as provided for in this Convention.

....

Article 81

Drilling on the continental shelf

The coastal State shall have the exclusive right to authorize and regulate drilling on the continental shelf for all purposes.

....

Article 85

Tunnelling

This Part does not prejudice the right of the coastal State to exploit the subsoil by means of tunnelling, irrespective of the depth of water above the subsoil.

* * * *

The following two cases illustrate the view of U.S. courts with respect to the resources protected under continental shelf doctrine.

TREASURE SALVORS v. UNIDENTIFIED WRECK, ETC.

569 F.2d 330 (5th Cir. 1978)

Treasure Salvors, Inc., and Armada Research Corp., Florida corporations, sued for possession of and confirmation of title to an unidentified wrecked and abandoned vessel thought to be the *Nuestra Senora de Atocha*. The *Atocha* sank in the sea off the Marquesas Keys in 1662 while enroute to Spain. The United States intervened, answered, and counterclaimed, asserting title to the vessel. Summary judgment was entered for the plaintiffs, 408 F.Supp. 907 (S.D.Fla.1976), and the government appealed.

....

The Antiquities Act

The Antiquities Act authorizes executive designation of historic landmarks, historic and prehistoric structures, and objects of historic or scientific interests situated upon lands owned or controlled by the United States as national monuments. Permission to examine ruins, excavate archeological sites, and gather objects of antiquity must be sought from the secretary of the department exercising jurisdiction over such lands. As the district court noted, the Antiquities Act applies by its terms only to *lands owned or controlled by the Government of the United States*. The wreck of the *Atocha* rests on the continental shelf, outside the territorial waters of the United States.

The government asserts that the Outer Continental Shelf Lands Act (OCSLA), 43 U.S.C. [sec.] 1331 et seq., demonstrates Congressional intent to extend the jurisdiction and control of the United States to the outer continental shelf. OCSLA was passed, along with the Submerged Lands Act, 43 U.S.C. [sec.] 1301 et seq., to clarify the respective interests of coastal states and the United States in the natural resources of the subsoil and seabed of the continental shelf. A look at the background and interpretation of OCSLA is necessary to determine its scope.

The Truman proclamation of September 28, 1945, spurred national and international interest in exploitation of the mineral wealth of the oceans. The proclamation asserted the jurisdiction and control of the United States over the mineral resources of the continental shelf, but was not intended to abridge the right of free and unimpeded navigation of waters above the shelf, nor to extend the limits of American territorial waters. See 13 Dep't State Bull. 485 (Sept. 30, 1945). The Convention on the Continental Shelf, written thirteen years later, assured to each coastal nation the exclusive right to explore and exploit the resources of the seabed and subsoil, not only of its territorial sea, but also of the adjacent continental shelf beyond the terrirorial sea. See Master's Report, *supra* n.14, at 69.

During the years following the Truman proclamation, intense interest in exploiting ocean resources resulted in disputes between the United States and coastal states asserting jurisdiction over territorial waters. In *United States v. California*, 332 U.S. 19, 67 S.Ct. 1658, 91 L.Ed. 1889 (1947), and its progeny, the United States was held to have rights in the offshore seabed superior to and exclusive of the states. The political reaction to these decisions led to passage of the Submerged Lands Act in May 1953 and the Outer Continental Shelf Lands Act a few months later. See 15 Va. J. Int'l L. 1009, 1011 (1975). By enactement of the Submerged Lands Act, Congress recognized the coastal states' title to and ownership of the lands and natural resources beneath navigable waters within the territorial sea. See *United States v. Maine*, 420 U.S. 515, 95 S.Ct. 1155, 43 L.Ed.2d 363, 370-71 (1975). In the Outer Continental Shelf Lands Act, "Congress emphatically implemented its view that the United States has paramount rights to the seabed beyond the three-mile limit." Id. at 526, 95 S.Ct. at 1161, 43 L.Ed.2d at 371.

The superiority of the federal claim to resources on the outer continental shelf to the claims of states was clearly established in 1975 in *United States v. Maine*, supra. The United States asserted in its complaint in *Maine* only "...sovereign rights over the seabed and subsoil underlying the Atlantic Ocean, lying more than three geographic miles seaward from the coastline to the outer edge of the continental shelf for the purpose of exploring the area and exploiting its natural resources...." Master's Report, *supra* n.14 at 3. The special master found the "basic question involved" in the litigation to be "whether the right to explore and exploit the natural resources of the seabed and subsoil of that portion of the continental shelf...belongs to the United States or to the defendant States or any of them." Id. at 1. After *Maine*, the primacy of federal over state interests in the natural resources of the continental shelf cannot be doubted. But the decision in Maine did not address the extent of control by the United States of the shelf in all circumstances.

43 U.S.C. [sec.] 1332(a) declares the policy of the United States to be "that the subsoil and seabed of the outer Continental Shelf appertain to the United States and are subject to its jurisdiction, control, and power of disposition as provided in this subchapter." Certain language in the Conference Committee report on the bill supports the view that Congress intended to extend the jursidiction and control of the United States to both the seabed and subsoil. However, this language must be taken in the context of the bill's stated purpose "...to amend the Submerged Lands Act in order that the area in the outer Continental Shelf beyond boundaries of the States may be leased and developed by the Federal Government...."

This court held in *Guess v. Read*, 290 F.2d 622, 625 (1961), *cert. denied*, 386 U.S. 957, 82 S.Ct. 394, 7 L.Ed.2d 388 (1962), that "[t]he Continental Shelf Act was enacted for the purpose, primarily, of asserting ownership of and jurisdiction over the minerals in and under the Continental Shelf." The structure of the Act itself, which is basically a guide to the administration and leasing of offshore mineral-producing properties, reinforces this conclusion. The Act consists almost exclusively of specific measures to facilitate exploitation of the natural resources on the continental shelf. In addition, 43 U.S.C. [sec.] 1332(b) provides the Act "shall be construed in such manner that the character as high seas of the waters above the outer Continental Shelf and the right to navigation and fishing therein shall not be affected." As the court below noted, an extension of jurisdiction for purposes of controlling the exploitation of the natural resources of the continental shelf is not necessarily an extension of sovereignty.

We believe that a limited construction of the Act comports with the primary purpose of resolving competing claims to ownership of the natural resources of the offshore seabed and subsoil. So read, the Act is consistent with Article 2 of the Convention on the Continental Shelf:

1. The coastal state [nation] exercises over the continental shelf sovereign rights for the purpose of exploring it and exploiting its natural resources.

The Convention on the Continental Shelf was a product of the United Nations Conference on the Law of the Sea convened at Geneva in 1958. It was the result of eight years' work by the International Law Commission. See generally Neblett, The 1958 Conference on the Law of the Sea: What Was Accomplished, in the Law of the Sea (L. Alexander ed. 1967). The Convention on the Continental Shelf became effective as law in the United States eleven years after passage of the Outer Continental Shelf Lands Act and superseded any incompatible terminology in the domestic statute. United States v. Ray, 423 F.2d 16, 21 (5th Cir. 1970), See Cook v. United States, 288 U.S. 102, 118-19, 53 S.Ct. 305, 311, 77 L.Ed. 641, 649-50 (1932).

Interpretations of the Convention and the Act by legal scholars have, with remarkable accord, reached the same conclusion regarding the nature of control of the United States over the continental shelf. The most compelling explication of the Convention regarding national control over non-resource-related material in the shelf is contained in the comments of the International Law Commission:

> It is clearly understood that the rights in question do not cover objects such as wrecked ships and their cargoes (including bullion) lying on the seabed or covered by the sand of the subsoil.

This comment is consistent with the Commission's general perception of national jurisdiction over the continental shelf:

> [The Commission] was unwilling to accept the sovereignty of the coastal State over the seabed and subsoil of the continental shelf....the text as now adopted leaves no doubt that the rights conferred upon the coastal state cover all rights necessary for and connected with the exploration and exploitation of the natural resources of the continental shelf.

We have demonstrated the limited scope of American control over the wreck site. We conclude that the remains of the Atocha are not situated on lands owned or controlled by the United States under the provisions of the Antiquities Act.

....

The judgment is modified and as modified AFFIRMED.

ED. NOTE: In 1960 President Eisenhower issued Presidential Procalmation No. 3339 [3 C.F.R., 1959-1963 Comp., p. 71 (1960); 25 Fed. Reg. 2352] which designated certain submerged lands off the coast of Florida as the Key Largo Coral Reef Preserve. Regulations were subsequently issued protecting that natural resource. See also Order No. 2978 of the Secretary of the Interior [40 Fed. Reg. 42039 (September 10, 1975)] which effectuates a program designed to conserve and prevent the waste of the coral reefs located on the outer continental shelf of the United States.

Were these two actions compatible with United States international obligations concerning the continental shelf? How do they differ from the *Treasure Salvors* case? What would have happened if, prior to Order No. 2978, an entrepreneur wished to construct an offshore resort hotel on a coral reef?

UNITED STATES v. RAY

423 F.2d 16 (1970)

The United States brought this action for injunctive relief against Louis M. Ray and Acme General Contractors, Inc. alleging interference with the rights of the United States on coral reefs located on its Continental Shelf on two grounds. In the first count the Government alleged that the activities of these defendants in building caissons on the reefs, dredging material from the seabed and depositing that material within the caissons was causing irreparable injury to the reefs which are subject to the control of the United States, and that these activities constituted trespass. The second count alleged that these activities were being unlawfully conducted without the required authorization of the Secretary of the Army. See 33 U.S.C. [sec.] 1333(f). A preliminary injunction was granted against defendants. Thereafter Atlantis Development Corporation, Ltd., which was also contemplating commercial development of the reefs, was allowed by this Court to intervene in the proceedings. Intervenor filed a cross claim, alleging its superior title to the property by virtue of discovery of the reefs by its predecessor. After an extensive nonjury trial, at which numerous witnesses, lay and expert, testified and at which voluminous exhibits were introduced, the District Court adopted all of the facts stipulated by the parties and further found:

> "1. Triumph and Long Reefs are a part of the Continental Shelf extending seaward from the East Coast of Florida, and all waters overlying the reefs do not exceed one hundred fathoms in depth.
>
> "2. Triumph and Long Reefs are completely submerged at all times, except when their highest projections are fleetingly visible while awash at mean low water. Accordingly, Triumph and Long Reefs are part of the `seabed' and `subsoil' of the Outer Continental Shelf within the Outer Continental Shelf Lands Act of 1953....
>
> "3. These reefs, together with the organisms attached thereto, are `natural resources' within the Outer Continental Shelf Lands Act, and the Geneva Convention on the Continental Shelf.
>
> "4. The caissons positioned by Ray and the jack platform construction or `boathouses' built on pilings proposed by Atlantis constitute `artificial islands and fixed structures...erected...for the purpose of...developing' the reefs, within the Outer Continental Shelf Lands Act."

The District Court denied all claims of defendants and intervenor, but denied the Government's claim of trespass under the first count. In doing so, the District Court recognized the sovereign rights of the United States, but concluded that those rights are limited as the claimed interest of the United States is something less than a property right, consisting of neither ownership nor possession, and subsequently not supporting a common law action for trespass *quare clausum fregit*.

All parties have appealed. The Government's appeal is limited to the Court's denial of an injunction on count one of the amended complaint. We affirm the District Court's factual findings and its grant of injunctive relief under the Government's second count. However, we reverse the Court's denial of injunctive relief on the first count of the Government's amended complaint.

....

It is clear that the reefs in question are within the area designated as the Continental Shelf by both national (Outer Continental Shelf Lands Act, supra) and international (Geneva Convention on the Continental Shelf...) law.

The Outer Continental Shelf Lands Act, 43 U.S.C. [sec.] 1331(a), in pertinent part provides:

"The term `outer Continental Shelf' means all submerged lands lying seaward and outside of the area of lands beneath navigable waters as defined in section 1301 of this title, and of which the subsoil and seabed appertain to the United States and are subject to its jurisdiction and control."

Article 1 of the international Convention on the Continental Shelf similarly reads:

"For the purpose of these articles, the term `continental shelf' is used as referring (a) to the seabed and subsoil of the submarine areas adjacent to the coast but outside the area of the territorial sea, to a depth of 200 metres or, beyond that limit, to where the depth of the superjacent waters admits of the exploitation of the natural resources of he said areas;...." 15 U.S.T. 473.

The evidence shows that the reefs are completely submerged at mean high water, and as the Court specifically found, "at all times, except when their highest projections are fleetingly visible while awash at mean low water." Thus the reefs are contemplated within the definition of the Outer Continental Shelf Lands Act and the Geneva Convention on the Continental Shelf, if they meet the definition of "seabed" as "lands underlying the sea." The evidence establishes that the term "seabed" is commonly understood to be any terrain below the high water line. The federal and common law comports with this understanding in defining the "bed" of a body of water as lands below the ordinary high water mark.... The record shows that on the death of the coral, which has a natural predilection for cementing itself onto preexisting rocky structures, its skeletal remains become part of the seabed of the Continental Shelf. The District Court's finding that the reefs are part of the "seabed" of the Shelf is fully supported by substantial evidence of record.

The same national and international laws (The Outer Continental Shelf Lands Act and the Geneva Convention on the Continental Shelf) explicitly recognize the sovereign rights of the United States to explore the Shelf and exploit its resources.

The Outer Continental Shelf Lands Act (43 U.S.C. [sec.] 1332(a) states:

"It is declared to be the policy of the United States that the subsoil and the seabed of the outer Continental Shelf appertain to the United States and are subject to its jurisdiction, control, and power of disposition as provided in this subchapter."

To the extent that any of the terms of the Act are inconsistent with the later adopted Geneva Convention on the Continental Shelf, they should be considered superseded.... But there is nothing in the pertinent language of the Geneva Convention on the Continental Shelf which detracts from or is inconsistent with the Outer Continental Shelf Lands Act. To the contrary, the Geneva Convention confirms and crystallizes the exclusiveness of those rights, particularly with reference to the natural resources of the Shelf.

....

It is unnecessary for us to decide whether the Outer Continental Shelf Lands Act, Section 1332(a), supra (which does not limit the nation's "jurisdiction, control, and power of disposition" to the natural resources of the Shelf), alone confers rights sufficient to authorize the injunctive relief sought. The right of the United States to control those resources is implicit in Article 23, paragraphs 1, 2 and 3, supra, of the Geneva Convention on the Continental Shelf, and explicitly recognized in the Submerged Lands Act, 43 U.S.C. [sec.] 1301 et seq. This Act further provides (43 U.S.C. [sec.] 1302) the definition of "natural resources" of the Continental Shelf:

> "Nothing in this chapter shall be deemed to affect in any wise the rights of the United States to the natural resources of that portion of the subsoil and seabed of the Continental Shelf lying seaward and outside the area of lands beneath the navigable waters, as defined in Section 1301 of this title, all of which natural resources appertain to the United States, and the jurisdiction and control of which by the United States is confirmed."

Section 1301, referred to within the above-quoted section, defines "natural resources" as including "*without limiting the generality thereof*, oil, gas, and all other minerals, and *fish*, shrimp, oysters, clams, crabs, lobsters, sponges, kelp, *and other marine animal* and plant *life*...." (Emphasis supplied.) 43 U.S.C. [sec.] 1301(e).

Article 2, paragraph 4, of the Geneva Convention on the Continental Shelf includes in its definition of "natural resources" both living and non-living resources, for it defines the term as consisting of "...mineral and other non-living resources of the seabed and subsoil together with living resources of the sedentary species...."

Although the complaint is inaccurately framed in terms of trespass in count one, the Government repeatedly stresses that it is not claiming ownership of the reefs. We do not question the District Court's conclusion that the Government's interest, being something less than fee simple, cannot support a common law action for trespass quare clausum fregit. But we do not understand that claim to seek such a remedy, despite the language in which the petition is couched. Damages, an inseparable element in the common law action for trespass, are not sought here, and the only relief requested is restraint from interference with rights to an area which appertains to the United States and which under national and international law is subject not only to its jurisdiction but its control as well. It is in this light that we consider the allegations of amended count one.

Neither ownership nor possession is, however, a necessary requisite for the granting of injunctive relief. This principle is implicit in the companion decisions of the Supreme Court, United States v. Louisiana, 339 U.S. 699, 70 S.Ct. 914, 94 L.Ed. 1216 (1950); United States v. State of Texas, 339 U.S. 707, 70 S.Ct. 918, 94 L.Ed. 1221 (1950), in which injunctive relief was granted to protect "paramount rights" of the United States beyond the territorial limits of Louisiana and Texas, to distances farther out in international waters than that involved here and at a time when those rights had not yet been statutorily established.

In United States v. Republic Steel Corp., 362 U.S. 482, 80 S.Ct.884, 4 L.Ed.2d 903 (1960), the Supreme Court did not consider lack of specific statutory authority a bar to injunctive relief in an action alleging activities which resulted in obstruction to commerce in a navigable river. The test for such relief, the Court said, citing United States v. San Jacinto Tin Co., 125 U.S. 273, 8 S.Ct. 850, 31 L.Ed. 747, was "whether the United States had an interest to protect or defend." 362 U.S. at 494, 80 S.Ct.at 890....

The evidence overwhelmingly shows that the Government has a vital interest, from a practical as well as an aesthetic viewpoint, in preserving the reefs for public use and enjoyment.

The protective underwater crannies of the reef serve as a haven and spawning ground for myriad species of tropical and game fish. The unique and spectactular formations of the submerned coral deposits attract scores of water sports enthusiasts, skin divers, nature students, and marine researchers. Certain organisms living on the reefs contain substances useful in pharmacology. The reefs protect the inland waters from the heavy wave action of the open sea, thus making the area conducive to boating and other water sports. Congress, intent on conserving the value and natural beauty of the area, recently enacted the Biscayne Monument Bill establishing the area, which includes both Triumph and Long Reefs, as a national monument. The reefs are a part of the series of coral reefs which dot the coastal and international waters extending out from southeastern Florida. Slightly to the south and west of the Triumph and Long Reefs, and straddling the three-mile dividing line between federal and state waters, is the huge federal-approved John Pennekamp Coral Reef State Park, also known as Key Largo Coral Reef Preserve. The fact that the area is worthy of preservation is abundantly demonstrated by the evidence. But more importantly, the evidence shows that protective action by the Government to prevent despoilation of these unique natural resources is of tantamount importance. There was convincing evidence that the activities of the defendants in dredging and filling the reefs has and would continue to kill the sensitive corals by smothering them; that the construction would constitute a navigational hazard to pleasure craft, and would destroy a very productive marine area and other natural resources. Obviously the United States has an important interest to protect in preventing the establishment of a new sovereign nation within four and one-half miles of the Florida Coast, whether it be the Grand Capri Republic or Atlantis, Isle of Gold.

The rights of the United States in and to the reefs and vital interest which the Government has in preserving the area require full and permanent injunctive relief against any interference with those rights by defendants and intervenor.

We find without merit the additional errors alleged, particularly the challenge to the District Court's jurisdiction. The District Court held, and we agree, that jurisdiction lies under 28 U.S.C. [sec.] 1345 (an action by the United States); under 28 U.S.C. [sec.] 1331 (a case or controversly arising under the Constitution, laws or treaties of the United States involving more than [10,000 dollars]); under the Court's general equity and ancillary jursdiction; and under 43 U.S.C. [sec.] 1333(b) (The Outer Continental Shelf Lands Act)....

ED NOTE: The authority of the United States to take steps to conserve coral reefs is limited, however. In *U.S. v. Alexander*, 602 F.2d 1228 (5th Cir. 1979), the Secretary of the Interior had issued a regulation stating that "[n]o person shall engage in any operation which directly causes damage or injury to a viable coral community that is located on the Outer Continental Shelf without having obtained a permit for said operations." As authority for issuing this regulation, he cited a provision of the Outer Continental Shelf Lands Act which authorized him to prescribe rules "necessary" to "provide for...the conservation of the natural resources of the outer Continental Shelf." Criminal liability attaches for violation of the regulation.

Alexander, not having obtained a permit, was convicted for a violation of the regulation arising out of his having damaged a coral reef while carrying out vessel salvage operations. On appeal, his conviction was reversed. The Court held that the jurisdiction of the United States over the continental shelf extended only to activities related to the exploration and exploitation of the natural resources of the shelf. Hence, the Secretary could promulgate regulations prohibiting the damaging of coral by OCS lessees or others engaged in operations substantially related to mineral activities, but not with respect to other activities, such as Alexander's salvage operations that have nothing to do with mineral leases. The regulation was invalid.

3. SEAWARD EXTENT

CONVENTION ON THE CONTINENTAL SHELF

Article 1

For the purpose of these articles, the term "continental shelf" is used as referring (a) to the seabed and subsoil of the submarine areas adjacent to the coast but outside the area of the territorial sea, to a depth of 200 metres or, beyond that limit, to where the depth of the superjacent waters admits of the exploitation of the natural resources of the said areas; (b) to the seabed and subsoil of similar submarine areas adjacent to the coasts of islands.

....

Article 7

The provisions of these articles shall not prejudice the right of the coastal State to exploit the subsoil by means of tunnelling irrespective of the depth of water above the subsoil.

* * * *

INTERNATIONAL LAW COMMISSION, 1956 Commentary, Draft Article 67

....

(4) [T]he Inter-American Specialized Conference on "Conservation of Natural Resources: Continental Shelf and Oceanic Waters", held at Ciudad Trujillo (Dominican Republic) in March 1956, had arrived at the conclusion that the right of the coastal State should be extended beyond the limit of 200 metres, "to where the depth of the superjacent waters admits of the exploitation of the natural resources of the seabed and subsoil." Certain members thought that the article adopted in 1953 should be modified. While agreeing that in present circumstances the limit adopted is in keeping with practical needs, they disapproved of a provision prohibiting exploitation of the continental shelf at a depth greater than 200 metres even if such exploitation was a practical possibility. They thought that in the latter case, the right to exploit should not be made subject to prior alteration of the limit adopted. While maintaining the limit of 200 metres in this article as the normal limit corresponding to present needs, they wished to recognize forthwith the right to exceed that limit if exploitation of the seabed or subsoil at a depth greater than 200 metres proved technically possible. It was therefore proposed that the following words should be added to the article, "or, beyond that limit, to where the depth of the superjacent waters admits of the exploitation of the natural resources of the said areas." In the opinion of certain members this addition would also have the advantage of not encouraging the belief that up to 200 metres depth there is a fixed zone where rights of sovereignty other than those stated in article 68 below can be exercised. Other members contested the usefulness of the addition, which in their opinion unjustifiably and dangerously impaired the stability of the limit adopted. The majority of the Commission nevertheless decided in favour of the addition.

(5) The sense in which the term "continental shelf" is used departs to some extent from the geological concept of the term. The varied use of the term by scientists is in itself an obstacle to the adoption of the geological concept as a basis for legal regulation of this problem.

(6) There was yet another reason why the Commission decided not to adhere strictly to the

geological concept of the continental shelf. The mere fact that the existence of the continental shelf in the geological sense might be questioned in regard to submarine areas where the depth of the sea would nevertheless permit of exploitation of the subsoil in the same way as if there were a continental shelf, could not justify the application of a discriminatory legal regime to these regions.

(7) While adopting, to a certain extent, the geographical test for the "continental shelf" as the basis of the juridical definition of the term, the Commission therefore in no way holds that the existence of a continental shelf, in the geographical sense as generally understood, is essential for the exercise of the rights of the coastal State as defined in these articles. Thus, if, as is the case in the Persian Gulf, the submarine areas never reach the depth of 200 metres, the fact is irrelevant for the purposes of the present article. Again, exploitation of a submarine area at a depth not exceeding 200 metres is not contrary to the present rules, merely because the area is not a continental shelf in the geological sense.

....

(9) Noting that it was departing from the strictly geological concept of the term, inter alia, in view of the inclusion of exploitable areas beyond the depth of 200 metres, the Commission considered the possibilty of adopting a term other than "continental shelf". It considered whether it would not be better, in conformity with the usage employed in certain scientific works and also in some national laws and international instruments, to call these regions "submarine areas." The majority of the Commission decided to retain the term "continental shelf" because it is in current use and because the term "submarine areas" used without further explanation would not give a sufficient indication of the nature of the areas in question. The Commission considered that some departure from the geological meaning of the term "continental shelf" was justified, provided that the meaning of the term for the purpose of these articles was clearly defined. It has stated this meaning of the term in the present article.

(10) The term "continental shelf" does not imply that it refers exclusively to continents in the current connotation of that word. It also covers submarine areas contiguous to islands.

(11) Lastly the Commission points out that it does not intend limiting the exploitation of the subsoil of the high seas by means of tunnels, cuttings or wells dug from terra firma. Such exploitation of the subsoil of the high seas by a coastal State is not subject to any legal limitation by reference to the depth of the superjacent waters.

STUDY PREPARED BY THE SECRETARIATE OF THE UNITED NATIONS FOR THE AD HOC COMMITTEE TO STUDY THE PEACEFUL USES OF THE SEA-BED AND THE OCEAN FLOOR BEYOND THE LIMITS OF NATIONAL JURISDICTION, U.N. Doc. A/AC.135/19, Paragraphs 24-26, 28-34, June 21, 1968

(a) <u>Question whether the whole submarine areas of the high seas can become part of the continental shelf</u>.

It has been contended that article 1 of the Convention could be interpreted as causing all the submerged areas in the oceans and seas to become part of the continental shelf if technology should advance to the point where all such areas are exploitable. The ground advanced for this interpretation is the language of the definition which, referring to "the seabed and subsoil of the submarine areas adjacent to the coast", extends the continental shelf "to where the depth of the superjacent waters admits of the exploitation of the resources of the said areas." From this language, it is inferred that as technical capability develops, a coastal State may extend its jurisdiction across the deep sea floor until it encounters the limit of the similarly extended jurisdiction of the coastal State opposite, in accordance with rules for the delimitation of boundaries of the continental shelf contained in article 6 of the Convention.

Opponents of this interpretation have argued that it ignores the element in the definition of the continental shelf requiring that such areas be "adjacent to the coast." On the basis of the language of article 1 of the Continental Shelf Convention, this requirement applies whether the sea-bed is less than 200 metres or whether it is deeper, but admits of exploitation. Although the concept of adjacency may not be very precise, it would, it is argued, prevent extending the continental shelf to the middle of the ocean. It has also been argued against that interpretation that the term "continental shelf" was deliberately retained by both the International Law Commission and the Geneva Conference. The International Law Commission said in its report on the eighth session (1956) that it decided to retain the term "because the term `submarine areas' used without further explanation would not give sufficient indication of the nature of the areas in question." The Commission also said in the same report that it was not possible "to disregard the geographical phenomenon whatever the term -- propinquity, contiguity, geographical continuity, appurtenance or identity -- used to define the relationship between the submarine areas in question and the adjacent non-submerged land." Likewise several of the representatives in the Fourth Committee of the 1958 Geneva Conference referred to the fact that the continental shelf was a prolongation of the mainland as the basis for extending the rights of the coastal State over it. Moreover, it is pointed out that the Commission, in the commentary on article 27 of its final draft (later article 2 of the Convention on the High Seas) said:

> "The Commission has not made specific mention of the freedom to explore or exploit the subsoil of the high seas. It considered that apart from the case of the exploitation or exploration of the soil or subsoil of a continental shelf...such exploitation had not yet assumed sufficient practical importance to justify special regulation."

It thus appears that the Commission's intention was not to deal with the "freedom to explore or exploit the subsoil of the high seas" (an expression which in itself differentiates such areas from the continental shelf), and that the Commission did not consider that the question of the regime of such areas would be automatically settled by the gradual extension of the continental shelf as the result of developing technology of exploitation. Finally, it is argued that if the International Law Commission and the Geneva Conference had had in mind the possibility of such a radical extension of national jurisdiction they would have undoubtedly made this clear.

The Government of France has formally adhered to the restrictive interpretation of the concept of adjacency by declaring in its instrument of accession to the Convention that with respect to article 1 "in the view of the Government of the French Republic, the expression `adjacent' areas implies a notion of geophysical, geological and geographical dependence which *ipso facto* rules out an unlimited extension of the continental shelf." Two of the parties to the Convention [United Kingdom and the United States] have reserved their position as regards the declaration of the French Government concerning article 1. No party has specifically objected to it.

(b) The question of the relation between the criterion of depth and the criterion of exploitability.

....

According to the definition in article 1 of the Convention on the Continental Shelf, the continental shelf means "the seabed and subsoil of the submarine areas adjacent to the coast but outside the area of the territorial sea, to a depth of 200 metres, or beyond that limit, to where the depth of the superjacent waters admits of the exploitation of the natural resources of the said areas." There has been considerable discussion of the mutual relationship between the two criteria of depth and exploitability set forth in the foregoing definition.

Some have considered that the two criteria were completely independent of each other, and have even stated that they were mutually incompatible. On this view, the result would tend to be that only the criterion of exploitability would have a real effect. Others find no incompatibility between the two criteria, but consider that they are complementary, so that all coastal States would automatically acquire rights up to a depth of 200 metres, but beyond that point they would do so only through actual increase of exploitability.

Another view is that the criterion of exploitability has a supplementary and subordinate function, and was intended to permit a coastal State to exercise rights over activities carried out on the continental slopes and in the continental border land in continuation of activities begun, or in connexion with those carried out, in zones with a depth of less than 200 metres. This view, however, recognizes that the development of technology might bring about the unexpected result that the criterion of exploitability, though originally intended to be ancillary, might come in practice to supplant the criterion of 200-metre depth.

Finally, the view has also been advanced that each criterion applies to a separate category of States; the criterion of 200 metres depth would apply to States bounded by a continental shelf, while the criterion of exploitability would apply to States having no true continental shelf.

(c) The question of the meaning of the criterion of exploitability.

The part of the definition in article 1 of the Convention on the Continental Shelf which reads "...or beyond that limit, to where the depth of the superjacent waters admits of the exploitation of the natural resources of the said areas" has given rise to a number of questions. In the first place, there is a question whether, in order for a State to exercise rights in the continental shelf beyond a depth of 200 metres, there must be actual recovery of a natural resource, or whether it is sufficient simply that a possibility of exploitation exists. The language of article 1, "admits of exploitation", would seem to favour the latter interpretation. It may also be recalled that paragraph 2 of article 2 of the Convention makes it clear that the coastal State has exclusive rights even if it does not explore the continental shelf or exploit its natural resources. Paragraph 3 of article 2 of the Convention provides that "The rights of the coastal State over the continental shelf do not depend upon occupation, effective or notional...." At the 1958 Conference some delegations spoke in favour of the view that a State would have rights in the continental shelf whether or not it was itself actually able to exploit the natural resources contained therein.

In the second place, questions have been raised as to the meaning of exploitability. Is the phrase "admits of exploitation" to be understood as requiring that there be a possiblity of real economic benefit, or does a mere scientific and technical possibility of carrying on activities on the sea-bed and in the subsoil suffice? If one State, without motives of profit, carries on purely scientific activities involving, for instance, drilling in an area of sea-bed which is more than 200 metres deep, does it thereby extend its rights and those of other States in the continental shelf? If a State's activity consists simply of picking up from the sea-bed some relatively easily available natural resources such as manganese nodules, does this activity give the State rights over the resources of the subsoil, which are not exploitable by present technology? Does simple exploration constitute exloitation? If not, will lack of security of rights and of sanctions before the time when exploitaton has been clearly proved possible?

Moreeover, it has been pointed out that although article 1 of the Convention says "...to where the depth of the superjacent waters admits of...exploitation", there may be difficulties of exploitation from other causes than simple depth, so that even if the depth offers no obstacle, exploitation may still be impossible. In any even, it is claimed, it may be very difficult to prove that the depth permits exploitation by any other means than actual exploitation.

QUESTIONS

(1) Would exploitation by one nation at a depth in excess of 200 meters automatically extend continental shelf jursidiction for all coastal nations?

(2) Would exploitation of sedentary species of living resources at 330 meters water depth automatically extend continental shelf jursidiction for petroleum and natural gas to the same depth?

(3) Is the achievement of commercial production of petroleum or natural gas in 500 meters of relatively calm Gulf of Mexico waters indicative of technological capability to produce those resources from 500 meters water depth of the coast of Alaska with its severe weather and great tide ranges?

* * * *

ED. NOTE: The above materials illustrate the approach taken in defining the outer limit of the continental shelf in the 1958 Convention, based on the dual criteria of depth and exploitability. The questions indicate the vagueness of this approach. As the ILC's explanations suggest, no one at the time anticipated that there actually would ever be exploitation beyond 200 meters, and thus the Commission was not concerned about the lack of clarity with regard to exploitation in deeper waters. But in a very short time the eventuality they provided for actually occurred.

In the 1982 Convention, we see an entirely different approach to defining the outer limit of the continental shelf and the allocation of resources. As mentioned previously, the creation of the International Seabed Authority, having jurisdiction over submerged lands beyond the limits of national jurisdiction made it essential to have a more precise definition of the outer limit of the continental shelf. The definition agreed to is as follows.

1982 UNITED NATIONS CONVENTION ON THE LAW OF THE SEA

Article 76

Definition of the continental shelf

1. The continental shelf of a coastal State comprises the sea-bed and subsoil of the submarine areas that extend beyond its territorial sea throughout the natural prolongation of its land territory to the outer edge of the continental margin, or to a distance of 200 nautical miles from the baselines from which the breadth of the territorial sea is measured where the outer edge of the continental margin does not extend up to that distance.

2. The continental shelf shall not extend beyond the limits provided for in paragraphs 4 to 6.

3. The continental margin comprises the submerged prolongation of the land mass of the coastal State, and consists of the sea-bed and subsoil of the shelf, the slope and the rise. It does not include the deep ocean floor with its oceanic ridges or the subsoil thereof.

4. (a) For the purposes of this Convention, the coastal State shall establish the outer edge of the continental margin wherever the margin extends beyond 200 nautical miles from the baselines from which the territorial sea is measured, by either:

(i) a line delineated in accordance with paragraph 7 by reference to the outermost fixed points at each of which the thickness of sedimentary rocks is at least 1 per cent of the shortest distance from such point to the foot of the continental slope; or

(ii) a line delineated in accordance with paragraph 7 by reference to fixed points not more than 60 miles from the foot of the continental slope.

(b) In the absence of evidence to the contrary, the foot of the continental slope shall be determined as the point of maximum change in the gradient at its base.

5. The fixed points comprising the line of the outer limit of the continental shelf on the sea-bed drawn in accordance with paragraph 4(a)(i) and (ii), either shall not exceed 350 nautical miles from the baseline from which the breadth of the territorial sea is measured or shall not exceed 100 nautical miles from the 2,500 metre isobath, which is a line connecting the depth of 2,500 metres.

6. Notwithstanding the provisions of paragraph 5, on submarine ridges, the outer limit of the continental shelf shall not exceed 350 nautical miles from the baselines from which the breadth of the territorial sea is measured. This paragraph does not apply to submarine elevations that are natural components of the continental margin, such as its plateaux, rises, caps, banks and spurs.

7. The coastal State shall delineate the outer limits of the continental shelf where that shelf extends beyond 200 nautical miles from the baselines from which the breadth of the territorial sea is measured, by straight lines not exceeeding 60 nautical miles in length, connecting fixed points, defined by coordinates of latitude and longitude.

8. Information on the limits of the continental shelf beyond 200 nautical miles from the baselines from which the breadth of the territorial sea is measured shall be submitted by the coastal State to the Commission on the Limits of the Continental Shelf set up under Annex II on the basis of equitable geographical representation. The Commission shall make recommendations to coastal States on matters related to the establishment of the outer limits of the continental shelf. The limits of the shelf established by a coastal State on the basis of these recommendations shall be final and binding.

9. The coastal State shall deposit with the Secretary-General of the United Nations charts and relevant information, including geodetic data, permanently describing the outer limits of its continental shelf. The Secretary-General shall give due publicity thereto.

10. The provisions of this article are without prejudice to the question of delimitation of the continental shelf between States with opposite or adjacent coasts.

* * * *

Article 76 represents a fairly broad margin. In order to persuade other States, particularly the Land-Locked and Geographically Disadvantaged States, to accept such broad jurisdiction for the coastal State, it was necessary for coastal States to agree on the sharing of revenues from continental shelf exploitation beyond 200 miles. That agreement was incorporated into the following article.

Article 82

Payments and contributions with respect to the exploitation of the continental shelf beyond 200 nautical miles

1. The coastal State shall make payments or contributions in kind in respect of the exploitation of the non-living resources of the continental shelf beyond 200 nautical miles from the baselines from which the breadth of the territorial sea is measured.

2. The payments and contributions shall be made annually with respect to all production at a site after the first five years of production at that site. For the sixth year, the rate of payment or contributions shall be 1 per cent of the value or volume of production at the site. The rate shall increase by 1 per cent for each subsequent year until the twelfth year and shall remain at 7 per cent thereafter. Production does not include resources used in connection with exploitation.

3. A developing State which is a net importer of mineral resources produced from its continental shelf is exempt from making such payments or contributions in respect of that mineral resource.

4. The payments or contributions shall be made through the Authority which shall distribute them to States Parties to the Convention, on the basis of equitable sharing criteria, taking into account the interests and needs of developing States, particularly the least developed and the land-locked among them.

* * * *

The Commission referred to in paragraph 8 of Article 76 is to be set up and have the functions contained in the following Annex.

ANNEX II. COMMISSION ON THE LIMITS OF THE CONTINENTAL SHELF

Article 1

In accordance with the provisions of article 76, a Commission on the Limits of the Continental Shelf beyond 200 nautical miles shall be established in conformity with the following articles.

Article 2

1. The Commission shall consist of 21 members who shall be experts in the field of geology, geophysics or hydrography, elected by States Parties to this Convention from among their nationals, having due regard to the need to ensure equitable geographic representation, who shall serve in their personal capacities.

2. The initial election shall be held as soon as possible but in any case within 18 months after the date of entry into force of this Convention. At least three months before the date of the election, the Secretary-General of the United Nations shall address a letter to the States Parties, inviting the submission of nominations, after appropriate regional consultations, within three months. The Secretary-General shall prepare a list in alphabetical order of all persons thus nominated and shall submit it to all States Parties.

3. Elections of the members of the Commission shall be held at a meeting of States Parties convened by the Secretary-General at the United Nations Headquarters. At that meeting, for which two thirds of the States Parties shall constitute a quorum, the persons elected to the Commission shall be those nominees who obtain a two-thirds majority of the votes of the representatives present and voting. Not less that three members shall be elected from each geographical region.

4. The members of the Commission shall be elected for a term of five years. They shall be eligible for re-election.

5. The State Party which submitted the nomination of a member of the Commission shall defray the expenses of that member while in the performance of Commission duties. The coastal State concerned shall defray the expenses incurred in respect of the advice referred to in article 3, paragraph 1(b), of this Annex. The secretariate of the Commission shall be provided by the Secretary-General of the United Nations.

Article 3

1. The functions of the Commission shall be:

(a) to consider the data and other material submitted by coastal States concerning the outer limits of its continental shelf in areas where those limits extend beyond 200 nautical miles, and to make recommendations in accordance with article 76 and the Statement of Understanding adopted on 29 August 1980 by the Third United Nations Conference on the Law of the Sea;

(b) to provide scientific and technical advice, if requested by the coastal State concerned during the preparation of the data referrred to in paragraph (a).

2. The Commission may co-operate, to the extent considered necessary and useful, with the Intergovernmental Oceanographic Commission of UNESCO, the International Hydrographic Organization and other competent international organizations with a view to exchanging scientific and technical information which might be of assistance in discharging the Commission's responsibilities.

Article 4

Where a coastal State intends to establish, in accordance with article 76, the outer limits of its continental shelf beyond 200 nautical miles, it shall submit particulars of such limits to the Commission along with supporting scientific and technical data as soon as possible but in any case within 10 years of the entry into force of this Convention for that State. The coastal State shall at the same time give the names of any Commission members who have provided it with scientific and technical advice.

Article 5

Unless the Commission decides otherwise, the Commission shall function by way of sub-commissions composed of seven members, appointed in a balanced manner taking into account the specific elements of each submission of a coastal State. Nationals of the coastal State making the submission who are members of the Commission and any Commission member who has assisted a coastal State by providing scientific and technical advice with respect to the delineation shall not be a member of the sub-commission dealing with that submission but has the right to participate as a member in the proceedings of the Commission concerning the said submission. The coastal State which has made a submission to the Commission may send its representatives to participate in the relevant proceedings without the right to vote.

Article 6

1. The sub-commission shall submit its recommendations to the Commission.

2. Approval by the Commission of the recommendations of the sub-commission shall be by a majority of two-thirds of Commission members present and voting.

3. The recommendations of the Commission shall be submitted in writing to the coastal State which made the submission and to the Secretary-General of the United Nations.

Article 7

Coastal States shall establish the outer limits of the continental shelf in conformity with the provisions of article 76, paragraph 8, and in accordance with appropriate national procedures.

Article 8

In the case of disagreement by the coastal State with the recommendations of the Commission, the coastal State shall, within a reasonable time, make a revised or new submission to the Commission.

Article 9

The actions of the Commission shall not prejudice matters relating to delimitation of boundaries between States with opposite or adjacent coasts.

G. STRUCTURES PERMITTED ON THE CONTINENTAL SHELF

CONVENTION ON THE CONTINENTAL SHELF

Article 3

The rights of the coastal State over the continental shelf do not affect the legal status of the superjacent waters as high seas, or that of the air space above those waters.

Article 4

Subject to its right to take reasonable measures for the exploration of the continental shelf and the exploitation of its natural resources, the coastal State may not impede the laying or maintenance of submarine cables or pipelines on the continental shelf.

Article 5

1. The exploration of the continental shelf and the exploitation of its natural resources must not result in any unjustifiable interference with navigation, fishing or the conservation of the living resources of the sea, nor result in any interference with fundamental oceanographic or other scientific research carried out with the intention of open publication.

2. Subject to the provisions of paragraphs 1 and 6 of this article, the coastal State is entitled to construct and maintain or operate on the continental shelf installations and other devices necessary for its exploration and the exploitation of its natural resources, and to establish safety zones around such installations and devices and to take in those zones measures necessary for their protection.

3. The safety zones referred to in paragraph 2 of this article may extend to a distance of 500 metres around the installations and other devices which have been erected, measured from each point of their outer edge. Ships of all nationalities must respect these safety zones.

4. Such installations and devices, though under the jurisdiction of the coastal State, do not possess the status of islands. They have no territorial sea of their own, and their presence does not affect the delimitation of the territorial sea of the coastal State.

5. Due notice must be given of the construction of any such installations, and permanent means for giving warning of their presence must be maintained. Any installations which are abandoned or disused must be entirely removed.

6. Neither the installations or devices, nor the safety zones around them, may be established where interference may be caused to the use of recognized sea lanes essential to international navigation.

7. The coastal State is obliged to undertake, in the safety zones, all appropriate measures for the protection of the living resources of the sea from harmful agents.

....

INTERNATIONAL LAW COMMISSION, 1956 Commentary

Draft Articles 69, 70 and 71

Commentary on Draft Article 69

Article 69 is intended to ensure respect for the freedom of the seas in face of the sovereign rights of the coastal State over the continental shelf. It provides that the rights of the coastal State over the continental shelf do not affect the legal status of the superjacent waters as high seas or of the airspace above the superjacent waters. A claim to sovereign rights in the continental shelf can only extend to the seabed and subsoil and not to the superjacent waters; such a claim cannot confer any jursidiction or exclusive right over the superjacent waters, which are and remain a part of the high seas. The articles on the continental shelf are intended as laying down the regime of the continental shelf, only as subject to and within the orbit or the paramount principle of the freedom of the seas and of the airspace above them. No modification of or exceptions to that principle are admissible unless expressly provided for in the various articles.

Commentary on Draft Article 70

(1) The coastal State is required to permit the laying of submarine cables on the seabed of its continental shelf, but in order to avoid unjustified interference with the exploitation of the natural resources of the seabed and subsoil, it may impose conditions concerning the route to be followed.

(2) The Commission considered whether this provision should not be extended to pipelines. In principle, the answer must be in the affirmative. The question is, however, complicated by the fact that it would often be necessary to install pumping stations at certain points, which might hinder the exploitation of the soil more than cables. It follows that the coastal State might be less liberal in this matter than in the case of cables. As the question does not yet seem to be of practical importance, the Commission has not expressly referred to pipelines in the present article.

Commentary on Draft Article 71

(1) While article 69 lays down in general terms the basic principle of the unaltered legal status of the superjacent sea and the air above it, article 71 applies that basic principle to the main manefestations of the freedom of the seas, namely, freedom of navigation and of fishing. Paragraph 1 of this article lays down that the exploration of the continental shelf must not result in any unjustifiable interference with navigation, fishing or the conservation of the living resources of the sea. It will be noted, however, that what the article prohibits is not any kind of interference, but only unjustifiable intereference. The manner and the significance of that qualification were the subject of prolonged discussion in the Commission. The progressive development of international law, which takes place against the background of established rules, must often result in the modification of those rules by reference to new interests or needs. The extent of that modification must be determined by the relative importance of the needs and interests involved. To lay down, therefore, that the exploration and exploitation of the continental shelf may never result in any interference whatsoever with navigation and fishing might result in many cases in rendering somewhat nominal both the sovereign rights of exploration and exploitation and the very purpose of the articles as adopted. The case is clearly one of assessment of the relative importance of the interests involved. Interference, even if substantial, with navigation and fishing might, in some cases, be justified. On the other hand, interference even on an insignificant scale would be unjustified if unrelated to reasonably conceived requirements of exploration and exploitation of the continental shelf....

(2) With regard to the conservation of the living resources of the sea, everything possible should be done to prevent damage by exploitation of the subsoil, seismic exploration in connexion with oil prospecting, and leaks from pipelines.

(3) Paragraphs 2 to 5 relate to the installations necessary for the exploration and exploitation of the continental shelf, as well as to safety zones around such installations and the measures necessary to protect them. These provisions, too, are subject to the overriding prohibition of unjustified interference. Although the Commission did not consider it essential to specify the size of the safety zones, it believes that generally speaking a maximum radius of 500 metres is sufficient for the purpose.

(4) Interested parties, i.e., not only Governments but also groups interested in navigation and fishing, should be duly notified of the construction of installations, so that these may be marked on charts. In any case, the installations should be equipped with warning devices (lights, audible signals, radar, buoys, etc.).

(5) There is, in principle, no duty to disclose in advance plans relating to contemplated construction of installations. However, in cases where the actual construction of provisional installations is likely to interfere with navigation, due means of warning must be maintained, in the same way as in the case of installations already completed, and as far as possible due notice must be given. If installations are abandoned or disused they must be entirely removed.

(6) With regard to the general status of installations, it has been thought useful to lay down expressly in paragraph 3 of this article, that they do not possess the status of islands and that the coastal State is not entitled to claim for installations any territorial waters of their own or treat them as relevant for the delimitation of territorial waters. In particular, they cannot be taken into consideration for the purpose of determining the baseline. On the other hand, the installations are under the jursdiction of the coastal State for the purpose of maintaining order and of the civil and criminal competence of its courts.

(7) While, generally, the Commission, by formulating the test of unjustifiable interference, thought it advisable to eliminate any semblance of rigidity in adapting the existing principle of the

freedom of the sea to what is essentally a novel situation, it thought it desirable to rule out expressly any right of interference with navigation in certain areas of the sea. These areas are defined in paragraph 5 of this article as narrow channels or recognized sea lanes essential to international navigation. They are understood to include straits in the ordinary sense of the word. The importance of these areas for the purpose of international navigation is such as to preclude, in conformity with the test of equivalence and relative importance of the interests involved, the construction of installations or the maintenance of safety zones therein, even if such installations or zones are necessary for the exploration or exploitation of the continental shelf.

OUTER CONTINENTAL SHELF LANDS ACT

UNITED STATES OF AMERICA

67 Stat. 462; 43 U.S.C. [sec.] 1333(f)

....

(f) The authority of the Secretary of the Army to prevent obstruction to navigation in the navigable waters of the United States is extended to artificial islands and fixed structures located on the outer Continental Shelf.

ED. NOTE: The Secretary's authority, referred to in the above section, was contained in the Rivers and Harbors Act of 1899. That Act specifies that no structure posing a potential interference with navigation may be constructed in the navigable waters of the United States except upon the permission of the Secretary. This section does not declare that the ocean above the continental shelf is "navigable water of the United States," but simply extends the Secretary's authority to prevent obstructions to navigation to continental shelf structures. Thus, petroleum companies wishing to emplace a rig on the continental shelf for exploratory or production work must first secure a permit from the U.S. Army Corps of Engineers. Of course, such structures must also comply with regulations promulgated by the Coast Guard (for safety purposes) and other affected federal agencies.

1982 UNITED NATIONS CONVENTION ON THE LAW OF THE SEA

Article 79

Submarine cables and pipelines on the continental shelf

1. All States are entitled to lay submarine cables and pipelines on the continental shelf, in accordance with the provisions of this article.

2. Subject to its right to take reasonable measures for the exploration of the continental shelf, the exploitation of its natural resources and the prevention, reduction and control of pollution from the pipelines, the coastal State may not impede the laying or maintenance of such cables or pipelines.

3. The delineation of the course for the laying of such pipelines on the continental shelf is subject to the consent of the coastal State.

4. Nothing in this Part affects the right of the coastal State to establish conditions for cables and pipelines entering its territory or territorial sea, or its jurisdiction over cables and pipelines constructed or used in connexion with the exploration of its continental shelf or exploitation of its resources or the operations of artificial islands, installations and structures under its jurisdiction.

Article 80

Artificial islands, installations and structures on the continental shelf

Article 60 applies *mutatis mutandis* to artificial islands, installations and structures on the continental shelf.

....

Article 60

Artificial islands, installations and structures in the exclusive economic zone

1. In the exclusive economic zone, the coastal State shall have the exclusive right to construct and to authorize and regulate the construction, operation and use of:

(a) artificial islands;

(b) installations and structures for the purposes provided for in article 56 and other economic purposes;

(c) installations and structures which may interfere with the exercise of the rights of the coastal State in the zone.

2. The coastal State shall have exclusive jurisdiction over such artificial islands, installations and structures, including jurisdiction with regard to customs, fiscal, safety and immigration laws and regulations.

3. Due notice must be given of the construction of artificial islands, installatons and structures, and permanent means for giving warning of their presence must be maintained. Any installations or structures which are abandoned or disused shall be removed to ensure the safety of navigation, taking into account any generally accepted international standards established in this regard by the competent international organization. Such removal shall also have due regard to fishing, the protection of the marine environment and the rights and duties of other States. Appropriate publicity shall be given to the depth, position and dimensions of any installations or structures not entirely removed.

4. The coastal State may, where necessary, establish reasonable safety zones around artificial islands, installations and structures in which it may take appropriate measures to ensure the safety both of navigation and of the artificial islands, installations and structures.

5. The breadth of the safety zones shall be determined by the coastal State, taking into account applicable international standards. Such zones shall be designed to ensure that they are reasonably related to the nature and function of the artificial islands, installations or structures, and shall not exceed a distance of 500 metres around them, measured from each point of their outer edge, except as authorized by generally accepted international standards or as recommended by the competent international organization. Due notice shall be given of the extent of safety zones.

6. All ships must respect these safety zones and shall comply with generally accepted international standards regarding navigation in the vicinity of artificial islands, installations, structures and safety zones.

7. Artificial islands, installations and structures and the safety zones around them may not be established where interference may be caused to the use of recognized sea lanes essential to international navigation.

8. Artificial islands, installations and structures do not possess the status of islands. They have no territorial sea of their own, and their presence does not affect the delimitation of the territorial sea, the exclusive economic zone or the continental shelf.

H. FEDERALISM AND THE CONTINENTAL SHELF

Because of the federal system of government practiced in the United States, there is a history of tension between the coastal states of the U.S. and the federal government regarding revenues derived from oil and gas exploitation on the continental shelf. While this subject is only remotely related to the international law on the subject, it is worth a brief summary here.

The earliest Supreme Court case related to the rights of states regarding their coastlines was Martin v. Waddell, 16 Peters (U.S.) 367 (1842). The case involved tidal lands in New Jersey. While not submerged lands, as such, the important feature of the case was that the Court held that these tidelands appertained to the state as an incident of its sovereignty. Another early case that has relevance to the more recent ones was Pollard's Lessee v. Hagan, 3 Howard (U.S.) 212 (1845). In that case, Alabama, when it entered the Union, entered into a compact which stated that "all navigable waters shall forever remain public highways". At issue was whether this constituted a reservation of federal rights to the Union. In its negative holding, the Court pronounced that new states have the same right to public lands as the original states of the Union. This is usually referred to as the "equal footing" doctrine.

The first significant case involving the continental shelf was United States v. California, 332 U.S. 19 (1947). The U.S. alleged that since it was the fee simple owner of the lands under the Pacific Ocean seaward of the ordinary low water mark to a distance of three miles, the state of California should be enjoined from trespassing by leasing those lands for petroleum and gas extraction. California responded that the thirteen original states acquired title from England to all lands within their boundaries, including the three-mile belt, and since California was admitted on an "equal footing" with those states, it must have acquired the same rights.

The Court, however, denied that the original colonies had aquired such rights. In holding for the U.S., Mr. Justice Black said, in part:

> "The crucial question on the merits is not merely who owns the bare legal title to the lands under the marginal sea. The United States here asserts rights in two capacities transcending those of a mere property owner. In one capacity it asserts the right and responsibility to exercise whatever power and dominion are necessary to protect this country against dangers to the security and tranquility of its people incident to the fact that the United States is located immediately adjacent to the ocean. The Government also appears in its capacity as a member of the family of nations. In that capacity it is responsible for conducting United States relations with other nations. It asserts that proper exercise of these constitutional responsibilities requires that it have power, unencumbered by state commitments, always to determine what agreements will be made concerning the control and use of the marginal sea and the land under it. In the light of the foregoing, our question is whether the state or the Federal Government has the paramount right and power to determine in the first instance when, how, and by what agencies, foreign or domestic, the oil and other resources of the soil of the marginal sea, known or hereafter discovered, may be exploited."

Of particular interest was the dissent by Mr. Justice Frankfurter. Relying less on policy considerations and more on traditional legal concepts, he said:

> "To speak of `dominion' carries precisely those overtones in the law which relate to property and not to political authority. Dominion, from the Roman concept of *dominium*, was concerned with property and ownership, as against *imperium*, which related to political sovereignty. One may choose to say, for example, that the United States has `national dominion' over navigable streams. But the power to regulate commerce over these streams, and its continued exercise, do not change the imperium of the United States into dominium over the land below the waters. Of course the United States has `paramount rights' in the sea belt of California -- the rights that are implied by the power to regulate interstate and foreign commerce, the power of condemnation, the treaty-making power, the war power. We have not now before us the validity of the exercise of any of these paramount rights. Rights of ownership are here asserted -- and rights of ownership are something else. Ownership implies acquisition in the various ways in which land is acquired -- by conquest, by discovery and claim, by cession, by prescription. When and how did the United States acquire this land?
>
> "The fact that these oil deposits in the open sea may be vital to the national security, and important elements in the conduct of our foreign affairs, is no more relevant than is the existence of uranium deposits, wherever they may be, in determining questions of trespass to the land of which they form a part..."

and:

> "...there is a difference between *dominium* and *imperium*. The U.S. could retain imperium while not having property rights."

Three years later, on the strength of the California case, the Court rejected a claim by Louisiana to a belt of submerged lands extending 27 miles seaward. U.S. v. Louisiana, 339 U.S. 699 (1950). But that did not end the litigation. On the same day, the Court rejected a Texas claim as well. U.S. v. Texas, 339 U.S. 707 (1950). Unlike Louisiana, Texas was able to argue a special circumstance. Texas claimed that it should receive special consideration because of its pre-admission history. Prior to admission to the Union, Texas was an independent nation, thus it had both *dominium* and *imperium*. After listening to this argument, the Court responded:

> "If the property, whatever it may be, lies seaward of the low water mark, its use, disposition, management and control involve national intersts and national responsibilities. That is the source of national rights in it. Such is the rationale of the California decision, which we have applied in Louisiana's case. The same result must be reached here if `equal footing' with the various states is to be achieved. Unless any claim or title which the Republic of Texas had to the marginal sea is subordinated to this full paramount power of the United States on admission, there is or may be in practical effect a subtraction in favor of Texas from the national sovereignty of the United States. Yet neither the thirteen original states nor California nor Louisiana enjoys such an advantage. The `equal footing' clause prevents extension of the sovereignty of a state into a domain of political and sovereign power of the United States from which the other states have been excluded, just as it prevents a contraction of sovereignty which would produce inequality among the states. For equality of states means that they are not `less or greater, or different in dignity or power.'"

In dissent, Mr. Justice Frankfurter opined:

> "...the submerged lands now in controversy were part of the domain of Texas when

she was on her own. The Court now decides that when Texas entered the Union she lost what she had and the United States acquired it. How that shift came to pass remains for me a puzzle."

The states, understanding that they were not going to succeed before the Supreme Court, mounted heavy political pressure in the Congress of the United States for legislation that would accomplish what the Court was unwilling to do. The result was the passage of the Submerged Lands Act of 1953, granting part of the submerged lands to the states. The Act was challenged on constitutional grounds in Alabama v. Texas, 347 U.S. 272 (1954). The gist of that challenge was that while the Congress clearly has the constitutional power to dispose of property belonging to the United States, it had only paramount rights in these lands, and not property. The Court, in rejecting this argument and upholding the statute noted that if the Congress can dispose of public property, it could surely dispose of less.

The Submerged Lands Act, in 43 U.S.C. 1311, set forth the basic theme:

> "The United States hereby releases and relinquishes unto the said States and persons aforesaid except as otherwise reserved herein, all right, title, and interest of the United States, if any it has, in and to all said lands...[to three miles]"

But in an attempt to accomodate states such as Texas, section 1312 added:

> "...nothing in this Section is to be construed as questioning or in any manner prejudicing the existence of any State's seaward boundary beyond three geographical miles if it was so provided by its constitution or laws prior to or at the time such state became a member of the Union, or if it has been heretofore approved by Congress."

In subsequent litigation the Court ignored the apparently disjunctive "or" between the two tests. In U.S. v. Louisiana et al., 363 U.S. 1 (1960), the Court held that both tests must be satisfied. The states had argued that a mere showing of existing boundary claims at the time of entry into the Union should suffice to satisfy the statutory requirement. The Court noted that if that were the case, there would be no way to prevent exaggerated state claims to the detriment of the federal government. On the merits, however, the Court ruled that Texas had acquired congressional approval of a 3 league boundary (approximately 9 miles) on the basis of congressional acceptance of the Annexation Resolution of 1867. And, in 1960, Florida was allowed the same limit on its west coast only by reason of the Reconstruction Act of 1867.

The final case in this saga was U.S. v. Maine, 420 U.S. 515 (1975). This was a case brought by the Attorneys General of all of the east coast states, based upon alleged historical title. The Supreme Court, not surprisingly, refused to depart from his holding in the original California case, and denied these extended claims.

The remaining litigation, which still goes on, concerns the rules that could be used for establishing the baseline from which state claims could be measured.

Today, coastal states are still active politically to have more of a say in the administration of adjacent submerged lands, and more of a share in the revenues.

CHAPTER 7

DELIMITATION AND APPORTIONMENT

A. DELIMITATION OF OCEAN BOUNDARIES

In this chapter we deal with a problem that has significant current impacts. The problem is how States that are opposite or adjacent to one another are to establish their maritime boundaries. Since offshore areas near the coast may contain significant amounts of oil and gas, or important fisheries, it is natural to expect that a State will attempt to claim a mutual boundary that gives it the greatest advantage. But the other State will do so also, and the resulting dispute, often as not, cannot be resolved amicably by negotiations. When that occurs, it is necessary for the parties to the dispute to seek third party dispute settlement in an appropriate international tribunal. That tribunal could be the International Court of Justice, a special panel of that Court, or an arbitral tribunal agreed to by the parties.

Tribunals over the years have struggled to establish the appropriate legal criteria for the resolution of these disputes. It must be obvious, even before reading the cases in this chapter, that the circumstances surrounding each dispute are unique. No two areas are identical, and thus it is impossible to construct one legal rule of precision that could be successfully applied in every case to achieve a result that would be fair and equitable.

In addition, in some instances, the guidance to be found in international treaties has evolved and changed, and the evolution of new international concepts, such as the exclusive economic zone, have both increased what is at stake and cause the tribunals to seek new criteria for the resolution of boundary disputes.

In this chapter, we examine several of the more important cases involving this issue in our effort to understand both the evolution of the law and how the appropriate criteria may change depending upon what the court is being asked to do.

In preparation for this exercise, the pertinent provisions of the 1958 and 1982 Conventions are set out in the next section for reference.

B. APPORTIONMENT OF OCEAN SPACE BETWEEN STATES WHOSE COASTS ARE OPPOSITE OR ADJACENT.

1. THE TERRITORIAL SEA.

CONVENTION ON THE TERRITORIAL SEA AND THE CONTIGUOUS ZONE

Article 12

1. Where the coasts of two States are opposite or adjacent to each other, neither of the two States is entitled, failing agreement between them to the contrary, to extend its territorial sea beyond the median line every point of which is equidistant from the nearest points on the baselines from which the breadth of the territorial seas of each of the two States is measured. The provisions of this

paragraph shall not apply, however, where it is necessary by reason of historic title or other special circumstances to delimit the territorial seas of the two States in a way which is at variance with this provision.

2. The line of delimitation between the territorial seas of two States lying opposite to each other or adjacent to each other shall be marked on large-scale charts officially recognized by the coastal States.

INTERNATIONAL LAW COMMISSION, 1956 Commentary, Draft Article 12

(1) The 1955 draft contained an article (12) entitled "Delimitation of the territorial sea in straits", and another (14) entitled "Delimitation of the territorial sea of two States, the coasts of which are opposite each other." It was correctly pointed out that the text could be simplified by combining these two articles, since the delimitation of the territorial sea in straits did not present any different problem from that of the opposite coasts of two States generally. It is only the right of passage in straits that calls for special attention. The Commission has dealt with this in article 17, paragraph 4.

(2) The delimitation in case of disagreement between those States, of the territorial seas between two States the coasts of which are opposite each other, was one of the main tasks of the committee of experts which met at The Hague in April 1953 at the Commission's request. The Commission approved of the experts' proposals (A/CN.4/61/Add.1) and took them as a basis for this article. It considered, however, that it would be wrong to go into too much detail and that the rule should be fairly flexible. Consequently, it did not adopt certain points of detail laid down by the experts. Although the Commission noted that special circumstances would probably necessitate frequent departures from the mathematical median line, it thought it advisable to adopt, as a general rule, the system of the median line as a basis for delimitation.

(3) Under the term "baselines" at the end of paragraph 1 the Commission includes both normal baselines and those applied under any straight baseline system adopted for the coast in question.

....

(6) The Commission is aware that the rules it has formulated in paragraphs 2 and 3 cannot be applied in all circumstances. Cases may arise in which, either by reason of differences in customary law or by reason of international conventions, it is necessary to apply a different rule to the sea between the two coasts. It is not impossible that the area of sea between two coasts of the same State may have the character of an internal sea subject to special cases; it must confine itself to stating the principles which, in general, could serve as a point of departure for determining the legal status of the areas in question.

(7) The rule established by the present article does not provide any solution for cases in which the States opposite each other have adopted different breadths for their territorial seas. As long as no agreement is reached on the breadth of the territorial sea, disputes of this kind cannot be settled on the basis of legal rules; they must be settled by agreement between the parties.

NOTE: The U.S. State Department publishes, in its Limits in the Sea series, maps and descriptions of all territorial sea boundaries agreed to by the affected States. These pamphlets can be obtained from the Office of the Geographer. The series also covers continental shelf apportionment agreements, descriptions of important international straits, and the delimitation of straight baselines by coastal States.

For a description of methods for actually establishing a median line on charts, see Shalowitz, Shore and Sea Boundaries, Vol. 1 (1962) at 232-235. In practice today, however, this exercise is done by computer.

1982 UNITED NATIONS CONVENTION ON THE LAW OF THE SEA

Article 15

Delimitation of the territorial sea between States with opposite or adjacent coasts

Where the coasts of two States are opposite or adjacent to each other, neither of the two States is entitled, failing agreement between them to the contrary, to extend its territorial sea beyond the median line every point of which is equidistant from the nearest points on the baselines from which the breadth of the territorial seas of each of the two States is measured. The above provision does not apply, however, where it is necessary by reason of historic title or other special circumstances to delimit the territorial sea of the two States in a way which is at variance therewith.

ED. NOTE: As you can see, the provisions regarding the delimitation of the territorial seas is identical in the two treaties. The provisions that follow are not. The reason for keeping the old provision in the new treaty was that many of the disputes concerning the territorial sea boundaries had already been resolved by negotiations based upon the principles contained in the 1958 Convention, and to change the rule at this late date would be unecessarily disruptive and, perhaps, reopening some disputes that had been resolved.

Even so, the adoption of article 15 caused problems for some countries. This is because reservations were permitted to article 12 of the 1958 Convention. Thus countries that felt prejudiced by the wording of that article could remove themselves from its application by reserving to it. This is not true in the new Convention. No reservations are permitted. Thus, for example, Venezuela felt that it could not sign the new treaty because application of article 15 could prejudice its position in a long-standing territorial sea dispute with Colombia. Presumeably, if that dispute can be resolved, the barrier to Venezuela's accession would be removed.

Note that there are three elements to be taken into consideration. The first principle is that these disputes must be resolved by agreement. That is basic. It is only when good faith efforts at reaching agreement fail that the other two elements -- median line and special circumstances -- kick in. We shall learn more about how these two elements operate when we look at specific cases.

2. CONTINENTAL SHELF

In the previous chapter, we became acquainted with questions of coastal State jurisdiction over resources of the continental shelf, and the seaward extent of that shelf in international law. When States that are opposite or adjacent to each other share a common area of continental shelf, however, disputes can arise, and such disputes can be very bitter.

The following are the provisions of the two treaties concerning boundary delimitation on the continental shelf.

CONVENTION ON THE CONTINENTAL SHELF

Article 6

1. Where the same continental shelf is adjacent to the territories of two or more States whose coasts are opposite each other, the boundary of the continental shelf appertaining to such States shall be determined by agreement between them. In the absence of agreement, and unless another boundary line is justified by special circumstances, the boundary is the median line, every point of which is equidistant from the nearest points of the baselines from which the breadth of the territorial sea of each State is measured.

2. Where the same continental shelf is adjacent to the territories of two adjacent States, the boundary of the continental shelf shall be determined by agreement between them. In the absence of agreement, and unless another boundary line is justified by special circumstances, the boundary shall be determined by application of the principle of equidistance from the nearest points on the baselines from which the breadth of the territorial sea of each State is measured.

3. In delimiting the boundaries of the continental shelf, any lines which are drawn in accordance with the principles set out in paragraphs 1 and 2 of this article should be defined with reference to charts and geographical features as they exist at a particular date, and reference should be made to fixed permanent identifiable points on the land.

1982 UNITED NATIONS CONVENTION ON THE LAW OF THE SEA

Article 83

Delimitation of the continental shelf between States with opposite or adjacent coasts

1. The delimitation of the continental shelf between States with opposite or adjacent coasts shall be affected by agreement on the basis of international law, as referred to in Article 38 of the Statute of the International Court of Justice, in order to achieve an equitable solution.

2. If no agreement can be reached within a reasonable period of time, the States concerned shall resort to the procedures provided for in Part XV.

3. Pending agreement as provided for in paragraph 1, the States concerned, in a spirit of understanding and co-operation, shall make every effort to enter into provisional arrangements of a practical nature and, during this transitional period, not to jeopardize or hamper the reaching of final agreement. Such arrangements shall be without prejudice to the final delimitation.

4. Where there is an agreement in force between the States concerned, questions relating to the delimitation of the continental shelf shall be determined in accordance with the provisions of that agreement.

ED. NOTE: Both of the treaties rely, as is in the case of the territorial sea, on agreement as the basis for resolving disputes. But the new provision in the 1982 Convention differs markedly from that in the 1958 Convention. As you read through the following materials in this chapter, try to analyze why the change was made.

The new Convention provisions also contains paragraphs dealing with the failure to reach agreement and provisional measures to be taken during the period until the dispute is resolved.

3. EXCLUSIVE ECONOMIC ZONE

The provisions contained in article 74 concerning the delimitation of the exclusive economic zone are identical to those in article 83, except that the exclusive economic zone is substituted for the continental shelf.

ED. NOTE: Negotiations over articles 74 and 83 were extremely difficult. There were many States at the conference that had maritime boundary problems either at the time or anticipated them in the future. Because these are essentially bilateral disputes, and because the outcome of the negotiations could have prejudiced their positions in these disputes, no agreement could be reached that would give greater weight to one principle or method over another principle or method. Hence, the vague language of the first paragraph of these articles.

It is not always true that States are unable to reach agreement on their mutual maritime boundaries. Many have. Some of the agreements show considerable imagination and inventiveness. The following agreement is one of those.

MARITIME BOUNDARY: MEXICO - UNITED STATES

On November 23, 1970, the Governments of Mexico and the United States signed a treaty for the clarification of the Rio Grande boundary and the creation of maritime boundaries between the claimed 12-nautical-mile Mexican territorial sea and the territorial sea and contiguous zone of the United States. The treaty delimits, in principle, the lines of separation in the Gulf of Mexico and in the Pacific Ocean. The two governments then established the final lines which were represented, at reduced scales, on two maps affixed to the treaty....

Article V of the treaty, which delimited the maritime boundaries, states:

> The Contracting States agree to establish and recognize their maritime boundaries in the Gulf of Mexico and in the Pacific Ocean in accordance with the following provisions:
>
> A. The international maritime boundary in the Gulf of Mexico shall begin at the center of the Rio Grande, wherever it may be located; from there it shall run in a straight line to a fixed point, at 25° 57' 22.18" North latitude and 97° 8' 19.76" West longitude, situated approximately 2,000 feet seaward from the coast; from this point the maritime boundary shall continue seaward in a straight line the delineation of which represents a practical simplification of the line drawn in accordance with the principle of equidistance established in Articles 12 and 24 of the Geneva Convention on the Territorial Sea and the Contiguous Zone. This line shall extend into the Gulf of Mexico to a distance of 12 nautical miles from the baseline used for its delineation. The international boundary in the Gulf of Mexico shall be recognized in accordance with the map entitled International Maritime Boundary in the Gulf of Mexico, which the Commission shall prepare in conformity with the foregoing description and which, once approved by the Governments, shall be annexed to and form a part of this Treaty.

B. The international maritime boundary in the Pacific Ocean shall begin at the westernmost point of the mainland boundary; from there it shall run seaward along a line the delineation of which represents a practical simplification, through a series of straight lines, of the line drawn in accordance with the principle of equidistance established in Articles 12 and 24 of The Geneva Convention on the Territorial Sea and the Contiguous Zone. This line shall extend seaward to a distance of 12 nautical miles from the baseline used for its delineation along the coast of the mainland and the islands of the Contracting States. The international maritime boundary in the Pacific Ocean shall be recognized in accordance with the map entitled International Maritime Boundary in the Pacific Ocean, which the Commission shall prepare in conformity with the foregoing description and which, once approved by the Governments, shall be annexed to and form a part of this Treaty.

C. These maritime boundaries, as they are shown in maps of the Commission entitled International Maritime Boundary in the Gulf of Mexico and International Maritime Boundary in the Pacific Ocean, shall be recognized as of the date on which this Treaty enters into force. They shall permanently represent the maritime boundaries between the two Contracting States; on the south side of these boundaries the United States shall not, and on the north side of them Mexico shall not, for any purpose claim or exercise sovereignty, sovereign rights or jurisdiction over the waters, air space, or seabed and subsoil. Once recognized, these new boundaries shall supercede the provisional maritime boundaries referred to in the Commission's Minute No. 229.

D. The establishment of these new maritime boundaries shall not affect or prejudice in any manner the positions of either of the Contracting States with respect to the extent of internal waters, of the territorial sea, or of the sovereign rights or jurisdiction for any other purpose.

E. The Commission shall recommend the means of physically marking the maritime boundaries and of the division of work for construction and maintenance of the markers. When such recommendations have been approved by the two Governments the Commission shall construct and maintain the markers, the cost of which shall be equally divided between the Contracting States.

The treaty has been ratified by both states and ratifications were exchanged in Washington, D.C. April 18, 1972.

Analysis

The Gulf of Mexico sector of the maritime boundary offers a unique solution to the problems of maritime boundaries tied to ambulatory features. The Mexico-United States terrestrial boundary reaches the sea in the Rio Grande. The river, which is subject to wide fluctuations in level and in course, is particularly susceptible to changes at its mouth. Seeking a relative degree of permanence in the maritime boundary, the two countries agreed that the point of origin would be the center of the mouth of the river, wherever it may be. The second point would be situated 2,000 feet due east of the midpoint of the river mouth at the time of the treaty (in effect at the time of the mapping of the river immediately after the signature of the document). Point one may meander with the mouth but point two will remain constant as a hinge. As a consequence, the stability of most of the boundary is assured. Finally, an equidistance boundary was constructed from the mouth of the river to the twelve-nautical mile limit measured from the respective low-water baselines and this point of intersection was chosen as the terminal point of the maritime boundary. In fact, the equidistance line did not vary to a great degree from the straight line segment between points two and three.

The two governments, however, sought a simple limit which would be practical to administer and which would not cause difficulties for fishing craft operating with unsophisticated navigational gear. Provisions exist to establish two markers on the ground, one in each state, to assist in the visual determination of position relative to the maritime boundary. The final segment of the boundary is formed by the great circle connecting the two points. The values of the points, on the North American datum, are given on the attached maps of the boundary. The very nature of the coastline, which is smooth and gently arcuate, favored the simplification of the boundary.

The maritime boundary in the Pacific also followed the principle of equidistance but with a measure of simplification particularly near the continental shore. Full value, as basepoint, was given to the Mexican Islas los Coronados which were situated to the south of the terrestrial boundary. The maritime limit from the shore to the point where the islands began to affect the equidistant line was simplified by an equal exchange of territory. The recalculation of the "terminal" point on the line affected by the Coronados, i.e., the first point after leaving the land terminus, involved a transfer of 608,141 square meters from Mexico to the United States and 608,139 square meters from the United States to Mexico. The difference in transfers were a mere 2 square meters. (Note: The transfers, of course, apply only to the difference between the practical lateral line and he "simplified" line agreed upon in the treaty.)

The final segments of the boundary were constructed by equidistance on specially constructed large-scale charts and verified by "computer" calculations to eliminate problems due to projections and to mechanical deficiencies, e.g., width of line of chart, distortion due to instability of base map, if any, etc.

As in the Gulf of Mexico, the segments between turning points relate to the great circles which connect the points. The final point of the maritime boundary is precisely 12 nautical miles from a cape on the western side of Point Loma (California) and one on the northwest shore of the northern island of los Coronados.

ED. NOTE: The interpretation of the 1958 treaty language, and that of the 1982 convention and the evolution of the law in this area is extremely difficult to understand. In this section we will examine the opinions of the International Court of Justice and certain arbitral tribunals to try to ascertain what the law of delimitation is and what methodology should be utilized in resolving disputes between States. Where results seem inconsistent, you should try to understand whether the law has been changing over the years, or whether cases are simply factually distinguishable.

C. CASE STUDIES IN DELIMITATION OF MARITIME BOUNDARIES

In reading the following cases, keep in mind that each case is unique. No two areas of the world are like any other two areas of the world, so in each case the tribunal is faced with a particular set of facts like no other. The location and placement of the States involved are important. So is the character of the coastlines. It is also important whether the tribunal is deciding a case having an impact on the continental shelf as opposed to the exclusive economic zone, or both. Think of these things when examining the cases.

NORTH SEA CONTINENTAL SHELF CASES, [1969] I.C.J. 3

[Being unable to arrive at a negotiated settlement concerning their continental shelf boundaries, the nations of West Germany, Denmark, and the Netherlands agreed to submit the dispute to the International Court of Justice for guidance concerning appropriate delimitation procedures. Figure 6-3 (reproduced at the end of this chapter) indicates the nature of the dispute arising, principally, from the concave construction of West Germany's coastline. Relevant excerpts from the Court's opinion appear below.]

....

5. In addition to the partial boundary lines between Federal Republic/Denmark and Federal Republic/Netherlands, which...were respectively established by the agreements of 9 June 1965 and 1 December 1964, and which are shown as lines A-B and C-D on [Fig. 6-3], another line has been drawn in this area, namely that represented by line E-F on that map. This line, which divides areas respectively claimed (to the north of it) by Denmark, and (to the south of it) by the Netherlands, is the outcome of an agreement between those two countries dated 31 March 1966, reflecting the view taken by them as to what are the correct boundary lines between their respective continental shelf areas and that of the Federal Republic, beyond the partial boundaries A-B and C-D already drawn. These further and unagreed boundaries to seaward, are shown on [Fig. 6-3] by means of the dotted lines B-E and D-E. They are the lines, the correctness of which in law the Court is in effect, though indirectly, called upon to determine. Also shown on [Fig.6-3] are the two pecked lines B-F and D-F, representing approximately the boundaries which the Federal Republic would have wished to obtain in the course of negotiations that took place between the Federal Republic and the other two Parties prior to the submission of the matter to the Court....

[The Court then held that Article 6 of the Convention on the Continental Shelf was *per se* inapplicable to the controversy because West Germany had never ratified it. Finding also that Article 6 did not reflect a customary rule on the subject, the Court then elaborated the principles which it felt were applicable to the situation.]

42. There seems in consequence to be no necessary and certainly no complete, identity between the notions of adjacency and proximity; and therefore the question of which parts of the continental shelf "adjacent to" a coastline bordering more than one State fall within the appurtenance of which of them, remains to this extent an open one, not to be determined on the basis exclusively of proximity. Even if proximity may afford one of the tests to be applied and an important one in the right conditions, it may not necessarily be the only, nor in all circumstances, the most appropriate one. Hence it would seem that the notion of adjacency so constantly employed in continental shelf doctrine from the start, only implies proximity in a general sense, and does not imply any fundamental or inherent rule the ultimate effect of which would be to prohibit any State (otherwise than by agreement) from exercising continental shelf rights in respect of areas closer to the coast of another State.

43. More fundamental than the notion of proximity appears to be the principle -- constantly relied upon by all the Parties -- of the natural prolongation or continuation of the land territory or domain, or land sovereignty of the coastal State into and under the high seas via the bed of its territorial sea which is under the full sovereignty of that State. There are various ways of formulating this principle, but the underlying idea, namely of an extention of something already possessed, is the same, and it is this idea of extension which is, in the Court's opinion, dominant. Submarine areas do not really appertain to the coastal State because -- or not only because -- they are near it. They are near it, of course; but this would not suffice to confer title, any more than, according to a well-established principle of law recognized by both sides in the present case, mere proximity confers *per se* title to land territory. What confers the *ipso jure* title which international law attributes to the coastal State in respect of its continental shelf, is the fact that the submarine areas concerned may be deemed to be actually a part of the territory over which the coastal State already has dominion, -- in the sense that, although covered with water, they are a prolongation or continuation of that territory, an extension of it under the sea. From this it would follow that whenever a given submarine area does not

constitute a natural -- or the most natural -- extension of the land territory of a coastal State, even though the area may be closer to it than it is the territory of any other State, it cannot be regarded as appertaining to that State; -- or at least it cannot be so regarded in the face of a competing claim by a State whose land territory the submarine area concerned is to be regarded as a natural extension, even if it is less close to it.

....

85. It emerges from the history of the development of the legal regime of the continental shelf, which has been reviewed earlier, that the essential reason why the equidistance method is not to be regarded as a rule of law is that, if it were to be compulsorily applied in all situations, this would not be consonant with certain basic legal notions which...have from the beginning reflected the *opinio juris* in the matter of delimitation; those principles being that delimitation must be the subject of agreement between the States concerned, and that such agreement must be arrived at in accordance with equitable principles. On a foundation of very general precepts of justice and good faith, actual rules of law are here involved which govern the delimitation of adjacent continental shelves -- that is to say, rules binding upon States for all delimitations; -- in short, it is not a question of applying equity simply as a matter of abstract justice, but of applying a rule of law in accordance with the ideas which have always underlain the development of the legal regime of the continental shelf in this field, namely:

(a) the parties are under an obligation to enter into negotiations with a view to arriving at an agreement and not merely to go through a formal process of negotiation as a sort of prior condition for the automatic application of a certain method of delimitation in the absence of agreement; they are under an obligation to conduct themselves that the negotiations are meaningful, which will not be the case when either of them insists upon its own position without contemplating any modification of it;

(b) the parties are under an obligation to act in such a way that, in the particular case, and taking all the circumstances into account, equitable principles are applied, -- for this purpose the equidistance method can be used, but other methods exist and may be employed, alone or in combination, according to the areas involved;

(c) for the reasons given in paragraphs 43 and 44, the continental shelf of any State must be the natural prolongation of its land territory and must not encroach upon what is the natural prolongation of another State.

....

101. For these reasons,

THE COURT

by eleven votes to six,

finds that, in each case,

(A) the use of the equidistance method of delimitation not being obligatory as between the Parties; and

(B) there being no other single method of delimitation the use of which is in all circumstances obligatory;

(C) the principle and rules of international law applicable to the delimitation as between the

Parties of the areas of the continental shelf in the North Sea which appertain to each of them beyond the partial boundary determined by the agreements of 1 December 1964 and 9 June 1965, respectively, are as follows:

(1) delimitation is to be affected by agreement in accordance with equitable principles, and taking account of all the relevant circumstances, in such a way as to leave as much as possible to each Party all those parts of the continental shelf that constitute a natural prolongation of its land territory into and under the sea, without encroachment on the natural prolongation of the land territory of the other;

(2) if, in the application of the preceding sub-paragraph, the delimitation leaves to the Parties areas that overlap, these are to be divided between them in agreed proportions or, failing agreement, equally, unless they decide on a regime of joint jurisdiction, user, or exploitation for the zones of overlap or any part of them;

(D) in the course of the negotiations, the factors to be taken into account include:

(1) the general configuration of the coasts of the Parties, as well as the presence of any special or unusual features;

(2) so far as known or readily ascertainable, the physical and geological structure, and natural resources, of the continental shelf areas involved;

(3) the element of a reasonable degree of proportionality, which a delimitation carried out in accordance with equitable principles ought to bring about between the extent of the continental shelf areas appertaining to the coastal State and the length of its coast measured in the general direction of the coastline, account being taken for this purpose of the effects, actual or prospective, of any other continental shelf delimitations between adjacent States of the same region.

ED.NOTE: Following this decision, the affected nations resumed negotiations and ultimately reached a settlement depicted by the map shown at the end of this chapter. Assuming there are significant deposits of natural gas at points "A" and "B", and that the "panhandle" area is likely devoid of natural resources, why would the F.R.G. opt for the panhandle, giving Denmark and the Netherlands exclusive access to the resource deposits?

DELIMITATION OF THE CONTINENTAL SHELF

Court of Arbitration: United Kingdom and France, 30 June 1977

[The United Kingdom and France were unable to agree on a delimitation of the continental shelf between the two nations and so submitted the issue to a special Court of Arbitration. Although the Court addressed several issues in its decision, the excerpt below relates principally to the delimitation in the Atlantic Ocean area, beyond the English Channel and in the open sea. The United Kingdom had contended that the equidistance principle should be applied, considering that both it and France were parties to the Convention on the Continental Shelf and thus bound by Article 6 thereof. France argued that an inequity would be worked by strict application of the equidistance principle because of the relative locations of the Scilly Islands (U.K.) and Ushant Island (Fr.). The Court ultimately decided upon a variation from a strict equidistance line, but one which did use the principal of equidistance by "splitting the difference" between an equidistance line with the two sets of islands taken into consideration, on the one hand, and a similar line without reference to the islands, on the other.]

....

67. [I]n invoking the application of Article 6, paragraph 1, the United Kingdom claims that this paragraph places an onus of proof on the French Republic to show the existence of any "special circumstances" on which it relies and to show that these circumstances justify a boundary other than the median line as defined by the paragraph. The French Republic, on the other hand, in contesting the applicability of Article 6 and invoking the rules of customary law, claims the governing principle to be that delimitation must be equitable and the equidistance principle to be merely one of numerous "methods" which may in certain circumstances be used to produce an equitable delimitation. Neither of these views of the equidistance "principle" or "method," however, appears to the Court to place it in its true perspective.

68. Article 6, as both the United Kingdom and the French Republic stress in the pleadings, does not formulate the equidistance principle and "special circumstances" as two separate rules. The rule there stated in each of the two cases is a single one, a combined equidistance-special circumstances rule. This being so, it may be doubted whether, strictly speaking, there is any legal burden of proof in regard to the existence of special circumstances. The fact that the rule is a single rule means that the question whether "another boundary is justified by special circumstances" is an integral part of the rule providing for application of the equidistance principle. As such, although involving matters of fact, the question is, always one of law of which in case of submission to arbitration, the tribunal must itself, propio motu, take cognisance when applying Article 6.

69. It also follows that the relevance of "special circumstances" in the application of Article 6 does not depend on a claim to invoke special circumstances having been advanced by the interested State when ratifying or acceding to the Convention.... Clearly this feature of Article 6 further underlines the full liberty of the Court in appreciating the geographical and other circumstances relevant to the determination of the continental shelf boundary, and at the same time reduces the possibility of any difference in the appreciation of these circumstances under Article 6 and customary law.

70. The Court does not overlook that under Article 6 the equidistance principle ultimately possesses an obligatory force which it does not have in the same measure under the rules of customary law; for Article 6 makes the application of the equidistance principle a matter of treaty obligation for Parties to the Convention. But the combined character of the equidistance-special circumstances rule means that the obligation to apply the equidistance principle is always qualified by the condition "unless another boundary line is justified by special circumstances." Moreover, the *travaux preparatoires* of Article 6, in the International Law Commission and at the Geneva Conference of 1958, show that this condition was introduced into paragraphs 1 and 2 of the Article because it was recognized that, owing to particular geographical features or configurations, application of the equidistance principle might not infrequently result in an unreasonable or inequitable delimitation of the continental shelf. In short, the role of the "special circumstances" condition in Article 6 is to ensure an equitable delimitation; and the combined "equidistance-special circumstances rule," in effect, gives particular expression to a general norm that, failing agreement, the boundary between States abutting on the same continental shelf is to be determined by equitable principles. In addition, Article 6 neither defines "special circumstances" nor lays down the criterion by which it is to be assessed whether any given circumstances justify a boundary line other than the equidistance line. Consequently, even under Article 6 the question whether the use of the equidistance principle or some other method is appropriate for achieving an equitable delimitation is very much a matter of appreciation in the light of the geographical and other circumstances. In other words, even under Article 6 it is the geographical

and other circumstances of any given case which indicate and justify the use of the equidistance method as the means of achieving an equitable solution rather than the inherent quality of the method as a legal norm of delimitation.

....

75. [T]he Court considers that Article 6 is applicable, in principle, to the delimitation of the continental shelf as between the Parties under the Arbitration Agreement. This does not, however, mean that the Court considers the rules of customary law discussed in the judgment in the *North Sea Continental Shelf* cases to be inapplicable in the present case. As already pointed out, the provisions of Article 6 do not define the conditions for the application of the equidistance-special circumstances rule and the rules of customary law have the same object -- the delimitation of the boundary in accordance with equitable principles. In the view of this Court, therefore, the rules of customary law are a relevant and even essential means both for interpreting and completing the provisions of Article 6. Indeed, the Court observes that in the present case, whether discussing the applicability of Article 6 or the position under customary law, both Parties have had free recourse to pronouncements of the International Court of Justice regarding the rules of customary law applicable in the matter....

....

239. ...In a situation where the coasts of the two States are opposite each other, the median line will normally effect a broadly equal and equitable delimitation. But this is simply because of the geometrical effects of applying the equidistance principle to an area of continental shelf which, in fact, lies between coasts that, in fact, face each other across that continental shelf. In short, the equitable character of the delimitation results not from the *legal* designation or the situation as one of "opposite" States *but from its actual geographical character as such*. Similarly, in the case of "adjacent" States, it is the lateral geographical relation of the two coasts, when combined with a large extension of the continental shelf seawards from those coasts, which makes individual geographical features on either coast more prone to render the geometrical effects of applying the equidistance principle inequitable than in the case of "opposite" States. The greater risk in these cases that the equidistance method may produce an inequitable delimitation thus also results not from the *legal* designation of the situation as one of "adjacent" States *but from its actual geographical character as one involving laterally related coasts*.

....

244. The projection of the Cornish peninsula and the Isles of Scilly, further seawards into the Atlantic than Brittany peninsula and the island of Ushant, is a geographical fact, a fact of nature; and, as was observed in the *North Sea Continental Shelf* cases, there is no question of equity "completely refashioning nature" or "totally refashioning geography." It may also be urged that the very fact of the projection of the United Kingdom land mass further into the Atlantic region has the natural consequence of rendering greater areas of continental shelf appurtenant to it. Nevertheless, when account is taken of the fact that in other respects the two States abut on the same continental shelf with coasts not markedly different in extent and broadly similar in their relation to that shelf, a question arises as to whether giving full effect to the Scilly Isles in delimiting an equidistance boundary out to the 1,000-metre isobath may not distort the boundary and have disproportionate effects as between the two States. In the view of the Court, the further projection westward of the Scilly Isles, when superadded to the greater projection of the Cornish mainland westwards beyond Finistere, is of much the same nature for present purposes, and has much the same tendency to distortion of the equidistance line, as the projection of an exceptionally long promontory, which is generally recognized to be one of the potential forms of "special circumstance." In the present instance, the Court considers the additional projection of the Scilly Isles into the Atlantic region does constitute an element of distortion which is material enough to justify the delimitation of a boundary other than the strict

median line envisaged in Article 6, paragraph 1, of the Convention.

245. The Court thus recognized that the position of the Scilly Isles west-south-west of the Cornish peninsula constitutes a "special circumstance" justifying a boundary other than the strict median line. It does not, however, consider that the existence of this "special circumstance" in the Atlantic region gives it carte blanche to employ any method that it chooses in order to effect an equitable delimitation of the continental shelf. The French Republic, it is true, has impressed upon this Court certain observations in the Judgment in the *North Sea Continental Shelf* cases to the effect that, in order to achieve an equitable solution, "it is necessary to seek, not one method of delimitation but one goal," and that "there is no legal limit to the considerations which States may take account of for the purpose of making sure that they apply equitable procedures." But in those cases the Parties had retained the actual delimitation of the boundary in their own hands for further negotiation in the light of the principles and rules to be stated by the International Court of Justice; and in any event the observations invoked by the French Republic have to be read in the light of certain other observations of the International Court in the same Judgment. In these other observations, it was stressed that any recourse to equitable considerations must be to considerations "lying not outside but within the rules" of law, and that there is no question of any decision *ex aequo et bono*; and, as already noted, it was stressed that "there can never be any question of completely refashioning nature." Furthermore, at the outset of the Judgment it was underlined that delimitation of the continental shelf is not a process of dividing it up into equitable "shares" but of delimiting a boundary in areas which, in principle, are already appurtenant to one or other State; and that the notion of "the just and equitable share" is wholly at variance with the fundamental principle that the continental shelf appertains to the coastal State as the natural prolongation of its land territory.

246. The "equitable" method of delimitation which is advocated by the French Republic, and which invokes a median line of the Channel coasts of the two countries, does not appear to the Court to be one that is compatible with the legal regime of the continental shelf. It detaches the delimitation almost completely from the coasts which actually abut on the continental shelf of the Atlantic region, and is thus not easily reconciled with the fundamental principle that the continental shelf constitutes the natural prolongation of a State's territory under the sea. In so far as that method may have relation to the respective land masses of the Parties, it is not apparent why the general direction of their Channel coasts alone should be considered to represent either the totality or any particular part of their land masses. In addition, there appears to be a radical inconsistency in the French Republic's recourse to the general directions of the two Channel coasts as the criterion for delimiting the continental shelf of the Atlantic region. In the pleadings, the French Republic has insisted that the coasts of the two countries within the Channel are irrelevant for the purpose of determining whether the situation in the Atlantic region is one of "opposite" States, for which a median line delimitation is indicated both by Article 6, paragraph 1 of the Convention and by customary law unless another boundary is justified by special circumstances. It is not, therefore, obvious how or why the coasts within the Channel should, on the contrary, aquire an absolute relevance in determining the course of the boundary itself in the Atlantic region. Nor is this inconsistency removed by invoking an alleged principle of proportionality by reference to the length of the coastlines; for use of the Channel, rather than the Atlantic, coastlines is left unexplained. Moreover, as the court has already stated in paragraphs 95-98, "proportionality" is not in itself a source of title to the continental shelf, but is rather a criterion for evaluating the equities of certain geographical situations.

247. The Court, for the above reasons, finds itself unable to accept the prolongations of the general directions of the Channel coasts of the two countries as a relevant basis for determining the course of the boundary in the Atlantic region....

....

249. The Court notes that in a large proportion of the delimitations known to it, where a particular geographical feature has influenced the course of the continental shelf boundary, the method of delimitation adopted has been some modification or variant of the equidistance principle rather than its total rejection. In the present instance, the problem also arises precisely from the distorting effect of a geographical feature in circumstances in which the line equidistant from the coasts of the two States would otherwise constitute the appropriate boundary. Consequently, it seems to the Court to be in accord not only with State practice to seek the solution in a method modifying or varying the equidistance method rather than to have recourse to a wholly different criterion of delimitation. The appropriate method, in the opinion of the Court, is to take account of the Scilly Isles as part of the coastline of the United Kingdom but to give them less than full effect in applying the equidistance method. Just as it is not the function of equity in the delimitation of the continental shelf completely to refashion geography, so it is also not the function of equity to create a situation of complete equity where nature and geography have established an inequity. Equity does not, therefore call for coasts, the relation of which to the continental shelf is not equal, to be treated as having completely equal effects. What equity calls for is an appropriate abatement of the disproportionate effects of a considerable projection onto the Atlantic continental shelf of a somewhat attenuated portion of the coast of the United Kingdom.

....

[For an illustration of the result, see Fig. 6-5 at the end of this chapter.]

CASE CONCERNING THE CONTINENTAL SHELF: TUNISIA/LIBYA, The International Court of Justice (1982)

[The Court was requested to address the following question: "What are the principles and rules of international law which may be applied for the delimitation of the area of the continental shelf appertaining to the Republic of Tunisia and the area of the continental shelf appertaining to the Socialist People's Arab Jamahiriya and, in rendering its decision to take account of equitable principles and relevant circumstances which characterize the area, as well as the recent trends admitted at the Third Conference on the Law of the Sea." In addition, the Court was requested to specify precisely the practical way in which the principles and rules apply so as to enable experts to delimit the areas without difficulty.]

....

23. Under Article 1 of the Special Agreement the Court is required first to state "the principles and rules of international law [which] may be applied for the delimitation of the area of the continental shelf" appertaining to each of the two countries respectively. The Court is specifically called upon, in rendering its decision, to take account of the following three factors, expressly mentioned in the Special Agreement: (a) equitable principles; (b) the relevant circumstances which characterize the area; and (c) the new accepted trends in the United Nations Conference on the Law of the Sea. While the Court is, of course, bound to have regard to all the legal sources specified in Article 38, paragraph 1, of the Statute of the Court in determining the relevant principles and rules applicable to the delimitation, it is also bound in accordance with paragraph 1(a), of that Article, to apply the provisions of the Special Agreement. Two of the three factors referred to are, however, in complete harmony with the jurisprudence of the Court, as appears from its Judgment in the North Sea Continental Shelf cases, in which it held that international law required delimitation to be affected "in accordance with equitable principles, and taking into account all of the relevant circumstances".... With regard to the third, the "new accepted trends," the Court would recall what it had to say on the subject of the work of the Third United Nations Conference on the Law of the Sea in the Fisheries Jurisdiction cases.... It must

however take note that the law-making process in this respect has now progressed much further.

24. ...the Court would have had proprio motu to take account of the progress made by the conference even if the parties had not alluded to it in their Special Agreement; for it could not ignore any provision of the draft convention if it came to the conclusion that the content of such provision is binding upon all members of the international community because it embodies or crystallizes a pre-existing or emergent rule of customary law.

....

41. Both Parties consider that the "continental shelf" is an institution of international law which, while it remains linked to a physical fact, is not to be identified with the phenomenon designated by the same term -- "continental shelf" -- in other disciplines. It was the continental shelf as "an area physically extending the territory of most coastal States into a species of platform" which "attracted the attention first of geographers and hydrographers and then of jurists"; but the Court notes that at a very early stage in the development of the continental shelf as a concept of law, it acquired a more extensive connotation, so as eventually to embrace any sea-bed area possessing a particular relationship with the coastline of a neighboring State, whether or not such area presented the specific characteristics which a geographer would recognize as those of what he would classify as a "continental shelf". This widening of the concept for legal purposes, evident particularly in the use of the criterion of exploitability for determining the seaward extent of shelf rights, is clearly apparent in the records of the International Law Commission and other travaux preparatoires of the 1958 Geneva Convention on the Continental Shelf.

42. It will be recalled that the definition of the continental shelf in Article 1 of the 1958 Convention is as follows:

"For the purpose of these articles, the term `continental shelf' is used as referring (a) to the seabed and subsoil of the submarine areas adjacent to the coast but outside of the area of the territorial sea, to a depth of 200 metres or, beyond that limit, to where the depth of the superjacent waters admits of the exploitation of the natural resources of the said areas; (b) to the seabed and subsoil of similar submarine areas adjacent to the coasts of islands."

While the 200-metre limit was chosen partly as corresponding approximately to the normal outer limit of the shelf in the physical sense, the definition of the outer limit of the shelf by reference to the possibility of exploitation of the sea-bed is clearly open-ended, and emphasizes the lack of identity between the legal concept of the continental shelf and the physical phenomenon known to geographers by that name. This definition, which was according to its terms expressed to be for the purpose of a convention text, was considered by the Court in its 1969 judgment to have been one of those regarded in 1958 as "reflecting, or as crystallizing, received or at least emergent rules of customary law relative to the continental shelf"... The fact that the legal concept, while it derived from natural phenomenon, pursued its own development, is implicit in the whole discussion by the Court in that case of the legal rules and principles applicable to it.

43. It was the Court itself in its 1969 judgment which gave currency to the expression "natural prolongation" as part of the vocabulary of international law of the sea.

44. Both Parties to the present case have in effect based their argument upon the idea that because a delimitation should, in accordance with the judgment in the North Sea Continental Shelf cases, leave to each Party "all those parts of the continental shelf that constitute a natural prolongation of its land territory into and under the sea", therefore the determination of what constitutes such natural prolongation will produce a correct delimitation....

45. Since the Court gave judgment in the North Sea Continental Shelf cases, a period has elapsed during which there has been much State practice in this field of international law, and it has been under a very close review, particularly in the context of the Third United Nations Conference on the Law of the Sea. The term "natural prolongation" has now made its appearance in Article 76 of the draft convention on the Law of the Sea. At this point, the Court must thus turn to the question whether principles and rules of international law applicable to the delimitation may be derived from, or may be affected by, the "new accepted trends" which have emerged at the Third United Nations Conference on the Law of the Sea.

46. The Court takes note that the request contained in the Special Agreement for account to be taken of accepted trends is not considered by the Parties themselves as authorization to decide ex aequo et bono or, or to regard those trends as being necessarily principles and rules of general international law.

47. Article 76 and Article 83 of the draft convention are the provisions of the draft convention prepared by the Conference which may be relevant as incorporating new accepted trends to be taken into account in the present case. According to Article 76, paragraph 1,

"The continental shelf of a coastal State comprises the sea-bed and subsoil of the submarine areas that extend beyond its territorial sea throughout the natural prolongation of its land territory to the outer edge of the continental margin, or to a distance of 200 nautical miles from the baselines from which the breadth of the territorial sea is measured where the outer edge of the continental margin does not extend up to that distance."

Paragraphs 2 to 9 of the Article, which deal with details of the outer limits of the continental shelf, can be disregarded for the purposes of the present judgment. While paragraph 10 states that the provisions of the Article "are without prejudice to the question of delimitation of the continental shelf between States with opposite or adjacent coasts", the definition given in paragraph 1 cannot be ignored. That definition consists of two parts, employing different criteria. According to the first part of paragraph 1, the natural prolongation of the land territory is the main criterion. In the second part of the paragraph, the distance of 200 nautical miles is in certain circumstances the basis of the title of a coastal State. The legal concept of the continental shelf as based on the "species of platform" has thus been modified by this criterion. The definition in Article 76, paragraph 1, also discards the exploitability test which is an element in the definition of the Geneva Convention of 1958.

48. The principle that the natural prolongation of the coastal States is a basis of its legal title to continental shelf rights does not in the present case, as explained above, necessarily provide criteria applicable to the delimitation of the areas appertaining to adjacent States. In so far as Article 76, paragraph 1, of the draft convention repeats this principle, it introduces no new element and does not therefore call for further consideration. In so far however as the paragraph provides that in certain circumstances the distance from the baseline, measured on the surface of the sea, is the basis for title of the coastal State, it departs from the principle of natural prolongation which was the sole basis of the title. The question therefore arises whether the concept of the continental shelf as contained in the second part of the definition is relevant to the decision of the present case. It is only the legal basis of the title to continental shelf rights -- the mere distance from the coasts -- which can be taken into account as possibly having consequences for the claims of the Parties. Both Parties rely on the principle of natural prolongation: they have not advanced any argument based on the "trend" towards the distance principle. The definition in Article 76, paragraph 1, therefore affords no criterion for delimitation in the present case.

49. With regard to the delimitation of the continental shelf between States with opposite or

adjacent coasts, Article 83, paragraph 1...provides that:

"The delimitation of the continental shelf between States with opposite or adjacent coasts shall be effected by agreement in conformity with international law. Such an agreement shall be in accordance with equitable principles, employing the median or equidistance line, where appropriate, and taking into account of all circumstances prevailing in the area concerned."

But on 18 August 1981, the President of the Conference presented to the Conference in Geneva the following proposal to replace Article 83, paragraph 1:

"The delimitation of the continental shelf between States with opposite or adjacent coasts shall be affected by agreement on the basis of international law, as referred to in Article 38 of the Statute of the Court of International Justice, in order to achieve an equitable solution."

In accordance with the decision taken by the Conference, this proposal has now acquired the status of part of the official draft convention before the Conference.

50. In the new text, any indication of a specific criterion which could give guidance to the interested States in their effort to achieve an equitable solution has been excluded. The principles and rules applicable to the delimitation of continental shelf areas are those which are appropriate to bring about an equitable result; this is a matter which the Court will have to consider further at a later stage. For the present, the Court notes that the new text does not affect the role of the concept of natural prolongation in this domain.

[The Court, at this point, responding to the reliance of both Parties on the natural prolongation principle, proceeded to address arguments of each Party with respect to the geological and historical evidence with regard to the shelf. The Parties disagreed, on the basis of propounded detailed expert evidence, on the general direction of the prolongation of the shelf.]

....

61. The conclusion which, in the Court's view, has ineluctably to be drawn from this analysis is that, despite the confident assertions of the geologists on both sides that a given area is "an evident prolongation" or the "real prolongation" of the one or the other State, for legal purposes it is not possible to define the areas of continental shelf appertaining to Tunisia and Libya by reference solely or mainly to geological considerations. The function of the Court is to make use of geology only so far as required for the application of international law. It is of the view that what must be taken into account in the delimitation of shelf areas are the physical circumstances as they are today; that just as it is the geographical configuration of the present-day coasts, so also it is the present-day sea-bed which must be considered. It is the outcome, not the evolution in the long-distant past, which is of importance.

....

69. Both Parties have, in their argument before the Court, dealt with the meaning and significance of equitable principles...in close relationship with the principle of natural prolongation, and devoted less attention to the question of what are the equitable principles to be taken into account. For Tunisia, however, "`equitable principles' do not mean equity in the large sense, but an equitable delimitation which respects as far as may be the actual physical situation -- the natural prolongation from the actual coasts of each Party", and "the function of equity is to do equity in the particular geographical circumstances, and faithfully reflect them". In its Counter-Memorial Tunisia included an additional submission to the effect that

"The delimitation must also be effected in conformity with equitable principles and taking into account of all the relevant circumstances which characterize the case, it being understood that a balance must be established between the various circumstances, in order to arrive at an equitable result, without refashioning nature."

Libya's submission from the outset have included a paragraph to the effect that

"A delimitation which gives effect to the principle of natural prolongation is one which respects the inherent ipso jure rights of each State, and the assertion of such rights is...in accordance with equitable principles."....

70. Since the Court considers that it is bound to decide the case on the basis of equitable principles, it must first examine what such principles entail, divorced from the concept of natural prolongation which has been found not to be applied for purposes of delimitation in this case. The result of the application of equitable principles must be equitable.... It is...the result which is predominant; the principles are subordinate to the goal....

71. Equity as a legal concept is a direct emanation of the idea of justice. The Court whose task is by definition to administer justice is bound to apply it. In the course of the history of legal systems the term "equity" has been used to define various legal concepts. It was often contrasted with the rigid rules of positive law, the severity of which had to be mitigated in order to do justice. In general, this contrast has no parallel in the development of international law; the legal concept of equity is a general principle directly applicable as law. Moreover, when applying positive international law, a court may choose among several possible interpretations of the law as the one which appears, in the light of the circumstances of the case, to be closest to the requirements of justice. Application of equitable principles can be distinguished from a decision ex aequo et bono. The Court can take such a decision only on condition that the Parties agree...and the Court is then freed from the strict application of legal rules in order to bring about an appropriate settlement. The task of the Court in the present case is quite different: it is bound to apply equitable principles as part of international law, and to balance up the various considerations which it regards as relevant in order to produce an equitable result. While it is clear that no rigid rules exist as to the exact weight to be attached to each element in the case, this is very far from being an exercise of discretion or conciliation; nor is it an operation of distributive justice.

[The Court then turned to a consideration of special circumstances in the case.]

....

73. .... As has been explained in connection with the concept of natural prolongation, the coast of the territory of the State is the decisive factor for title to submarine areas adjacent to it. Adjacency of the sea-bed to the territory of the coastal State has been the paramount criterion for determining the legal status of the submerged areas, as distinct from their delimitation, without regard to the various elements which have become significant for the extension of these areas in the process of the legal evolution of the rules of international law.

74. The coast of each of the Parties, therefore, constitutes the starting line from which one has to set out in order to ascertain how far the submarine areas appertaining to each of them extend in a seaward direction, as well as in relation to neighbouring States situated either in an adjacent or opposite position. The only areas which can be relevant for the determination of claims of Libya and Tunisia to the continental shelf in front of their respective coasts are those which can be considered as lying either off the Tunisian or off the Libyan coast. These areas form together the area which is relevant to the decision of this dispute. The area in dispute, where one claim encroaches on the other,

is that part of this whole area which can be considered as lying both off the Libyan coast and off the Tunisian coast.

....

[After further consideration,the Court concluded that the only portions of the coasts between Ras Kaboudia and Ras Tajoura were relevant to the dispute. See map at end of chapter.]

....

76. While the initial part of the Tunisian coast, westwards from Ras Ajdir, runs for some distance in approximately the same direction as the Libyan coast, the most marked characteristic of the coast, discussed at length by the Parties, is that it subsequently changes direction, so as to run roughly southwest-northeast. This aspect of the geographical situation as it exists in the area relevant to the decision is legally significant, in the context of the present examination of the application of equitable principles, as one of the relevant circumstances which characterize the area. The change in direction may be said to modify the situation of lateral adjacency of the two States, even though it clearly does not go so far as to place them in a position of legally opposite States.

....

[Having noted this, the Court concluded that the presence of the Kerkannah Islands was also a circumstance to be taken into account. It also accepted the landward boundary between the two States as a starting point for the delimitation, but it rejected a contention that the land boundary simply be extended in the same direction seaward. The Court then examined in detail the historical usage of both States in the disputed area.]

....

111. .... The Libyan approach is first to define the area in which delimitation must be effected, and then to determine the relevant natural prolongation which...is for Libya the northward thrust or prolongation of the African landmass...The resulting line is indicated on Map No.2 appended hereto.

112. After reserving the area of "historic rights"...Tunisia has indicated methods of two kinds, which give rise in their application to the area in question to a "sheaf of lines" of delimitation, all running in the same general direction across the area of continental shelf (indicated on Map. No. 2 appended hereto). The first group of methods consists in defining the natural prolongation of the two States on the basis of geological, geographical and bathymetric data which, according to Tunisia...themselves define possible lines of delimitation. The second group of methods is geometrical based on the configurations of the coasts of the two Parties, with a view of implementing the concepts of coastal front and of proportionality, taking account of the relevant circumstances which characterize the area, and abiding by equitable principles. The second type of method produces results similar to those of the first....

113. The delimitation method proposed by Libya, on the basis of the northward direction of natural prolongation, clearly stands or falls with its basic contentions as to that direction; since the Court has been unable to uphold those contentions, no more need be said as to the Libyan method. The same is true of the Tunisian method of the first group, since geological, geophysical and bathymetric material advanced in support of them do not, in the Court's view, add up to "relevant circumstances" on which a delimitation of the kind proposed by Tunisia could be based. In addition, however, the methods proposed by both Parties give insufficient weight to one circumstance in particular, and this consideration constitutes an objection also to the Tunisian geometrical methods,

which in any event were advanced more as a reinforcement of the methods based on other criteria than as independent propositions. The Court will therefore indicate what this circumstance is, and how it serves, with the support of other circumstances which the Parties themselves have taken into account, to produce an equitable delimitation.

114. Any examination of methods, like the examination of applicable rules and principles, must take as starting-point the particular geographic situation. The Court has already explained what it considers to be the relevant area in the present case; the fact that the Court has found that it is necessary to define this single area does not, however, imply that the Court considers it to be an area featuring such geographical homogeneity as to justify the application of a single method of delimitation throughout its extent. On the contrary, in the view of the Court, the proper appreciation and taking into account of the "relevant circumstances which characterize the area" call for the area close to the coasts of the Parties to be treated differently from the areas further offshore. The Court will therefore deal with the area as divided into two sectors. It must, however, be emphasized that such difference of treatment is ultimately dictated by the primordial requirement of achieving an overall equitable result.

....

116. Since the continental shelf begins, for purposes of delimitation, from the outer limit of the territorial sea, the starting point for the line of delimitation in this case must be from the boundary of the territorial sea off Ras Adjir....

....

[To determine the direction of the first leg from this point, the Court found relevant the practice of the two States regarding the issuance of offshore leases. While there was no agreement between the two States, they had in practice respected a line between their respective concessions running approximately on a bearing of 26 degrees from the meridian. The Court, therefore, selects this angle.]

...

121. .... The 26 degree line therefore reflects all appropriate factors; as the line extends further seawards, however, certain other relevant factors come into play, and it is to consideration of such factors, and of their effect in determining how far the 26 degree line should extend, and what should be the method of delimitation thereafter, that the Court must now turn.

122. The most evident geographical feature of the coastlines fronting on the area of shelf relevant for the delimitation is the radical change in the general direction of the Tunisian coastline marked by the Gulf of Gabes; and clearly no delimitation of the continental shelf in front of the coasts of the Parties could be regarded as equitable which failed to take account of that feature....

123. ...[A] considerable amount of argument has been addressed by the Parties to the question of the point at which the change in direction of the Tunisian coastline may properly be said to occur. The Court does not consider that this is a question it is called upon to decide; the examination of the matter by the Parties seems to the Court rather to demonstrate that the point -- if point there be -- at which the coastline changes direction will not necessarily be the subject of agreement among geographers or cartographers, and in short cannot be objectively determined as a matter of fact. Accordingly, if the Court were merely to indicate, for purposes of delimitation, that the line should change direction in relation to the point at which the coastline changes direction, it would be leaving room for extensive disagreement between the experts of the Parties, which would not necessarily be capable of final resolution. This would not, it seems to the Court, be a proper discharge of its duty to

indicate the practical method of delimitation in such a way as to enable the experts to effect the delimitation "without any difficulties".

124. The change in direction of the coast is however a fact which must be taken into account, and the Court considers that an appropriate point on the coast to be employed as a reference-point for reflecting the change in the delimitation, and one which has the advantage of being susceptible of objective determination as a matter of geography, is the most westerly point of the Tunisian coastline between Ras Kaboudia and Ras Adjir, that is to say, the most westerly point on the shoreline...of the Gulf of Gabes. Again the precise co-ordinates of this point will be for the experts to determine, but it appears to the Court that it will be approximately 34 degrees 10 minutes 30 seconds north. The initial delimitation line...will therefore extend from the outer limit of the territorial sea until its intersection with the parallel of latitude of the point just mentioned on the coast of the Gulf of Gabes. That delimitation line will then give place to a line at a different bearing, of which The Court will now indicate the justification and the factors determining its angulation.

....

128. The general change in direction of the Tunisian coast may, in the view of the Court, be regarded as expressed in a line drawn from the most westerly point of the Gulf of Gabes...to Ras Kaboudia, and the Court notes that the bearing of this line is approximately 42 degrees to the meridian. To the east of this line, however, lie the Kerkennah Islands, surrounded by islets and low-tide elevations, and constituting by their size and position a circumstance relevant for the delimitation, and to which the Court must therefore attribute some effect.... It is not easy to define what would be the inclination of a line drawn from the most westerly point on the Gulf of Gabes to seaward of the Kerkennah Islands to as to take account of the low-tide elevations to seaward of them; but a line drawn from that point along the seaward coast of the actual islands would clearly run at a bearing of approximately 62 degrees to the meridian. However, the Court considers that to cause the delimitation line to veer as far as to 62 degrees, to run parallel to the island coastline, would, in the circumstances of the case, amount to giving excessive weight to the Kerkennahs.

129. .... Taking into account the position of the Kerkennah Islands, and the low-tide elevations around them, the Court considers that it should go so far as to attribute to the islands a "half-effect"... On this basis the delimitation line, seawards of the parallel of the most westerly point of the Gulf of Gabes, is to be a parallel to a line drawn from that point bisecting the angle between the line of the Tunisian coast (42 degrees) and the line along the seaward coast of the Kerkennah Islands (62 degrees), that is to say at an angle of 52 degrees to the meridian....

....

[Lastly, the Court tested the equitableness of its solution by seeing whether the ratio of the two submerged portions so divided bore a reasonable relation to the proportionality of the two coastlines. It concluded that it did.]

....

[The two separate opinions and the two dissenting opinions have been omitted.]

....

ED. NOTE: Before turning to the recent jurisprudence on the delimitation of maritime boundaries, brief mention should be made of two decisions that were handed down in 1985.

The first of these was a decision of an arbitral tribunal on Feb. 14, 1985, concerning a dispute over the maritime boundary between Guinea and Guinea-Bissau, on the west coast of Africa. This case was different from the Libya/Tunisia case in a number of respects. First, the Parties asked the Tribunal to determine the course of the single line delimiting their territorial waters, their exclusive economic zones and their continental shelves, while the Libya/Tunisia dispute concerned only the continental shelf. Interestingly enough, unlike the Gulf of Maine case, yet to be examined, the Tribunal attached no particular significance to this fact. Like the earlier case, the Tribunal attached particular significance to the general configuration and direction of the coastline. It noted that the coastlines of the two States were concave in their configuration. To use an equidistance line to solve the dispute, as Guinea/Bissau argued, would be to the disadvantage of Guinea, but to use an extension of the southern boundary, sought by Guinea, would disadvantage Guinea-Bissau. Neither solution satisfied the Tribunal.

To achieve a more equitable result, the Tribunal passed from an examination of the general direction of the short coastline to that of a longer coastline focussing upon the entire West African region, and drew a perpendicular to the general direction of this longer coastline to delimit the boundary, observing that this method would be adaptable not only to the present delimitation but to future delimitations in the area as well. This unique approach is of interest because it not only resolves the dispute between the two States before the Tribunal, but it sets a precedent for resolving any future disputes between other States of the West African region who were not parties to the present case. The Tribunal, as has been fairly consistently reflected in international law of maritime boundary delimitation, rejected arguments based upon economic factors, i.e., "They're rich and we're poor, so we should get a larger piece of the disputed maritime area".

The second case, decided on June 3, 1985, settled the maritime boundary between Libya and Malta. These States face each other, and clearly present the situation of opposite coasts. Furthermore, their coasts are less than 400 miles apart. For Libya, the legal basis of title to continental shelf rights was the natural prolongation of the land territory. For Malta, the legal basis was the concept of the distance from the coast.

The Court noted the dual bases for legal claim on the continental shelf in Article 76 of the Law of the Sea Treaty, as had been noted in Libya/Tunisia as well. Both the concepts of natural prolongation and distance are contained in paragraph 1 of that article. In addition, the new treaty contained the concept of the exclusive economic zone giving a coastal State resource jurisdiction to a distance of 200 nautical miles. The apparent view of the Court was that natural prolongation had relevance in continental shelf delimitation disputes, if at all, only in those cases where the shelves extended beyond 200 miles, and that within that limit, distance was the only relevant criterion. Based upon that, the Court concluded that an equidistance line, adjusted for special circumstances, and tested by the proportionality of the length of the two coastlines, was the appropriate method to use. In this case, as well as in the previous one, the Court refused to consider the relative economic situation of the two States.

THE GULF OF MAINE CASE (U.S. v. Canada)

[Having been unable to resolve their differences over the maritime boundary in the Gulf of Maine, the two States referred the dispute to a panel of the International Court of Justice, Canada being permitted to appoint an Ad Hoc Judge to account for the fact that there was an American judge sitting on the panel. The Panel was asked by the Parties to determine the course of a single maritime boundary that divides the continental shelf and the fisheries zones of Canada and the United States beginning at a point agreed to by the Parties and ending in a triangular area 200 miles seaward (see the map at the end of the chapter).]

....

79. As already stated,...the Special Agreement provides that "The Chamber is requested to decide [the question submitted to it] in accordance with the principles and rules of international law applicable in the matter between the Parties. The time has therefore come to begin consideration of the problem of ascertaining the rules of law, in the international legal order, which govern the matter at issue in the present case. In the Chamber's opinion, the association of the terms "rules" and "principles" is no more than the use of a dual expression to convey one and the same idea, since in this context "principles" clearly means principles of law, that is, it also includes rules of international law in whose case the use of the term "principles" may be justified because of their more general and more fundamental character.

....

[The Court then reviewed the provisions of the 1958 and 1982 Conventions regarding boundary delimitations, as well as the North Sea Continental Shelf case, the arbitration between the U.K. and France, and the Libya/Tunisia case to ascertain the development of the use of "equitable principles".]

....

98. While asserting that, unfortunately, the points on which they disagreed were more numerous than those on which they agreed, the Parties were at pains to state, while considering the "rules and principles of international law" which, they held, should govern maritime delimitations, that they were at one in believing the existence of a "fundamental norm" of international law. According to them, this norm must apply to any delimitation and, a fortiari, to the drawing of a single maritime boundary like that sought in the Gulf of Maine area.

99. According to Canada's definition, the "fundamental norm" in question requires that this course be "determined according to the applicable law, in conformity with equitable principles, having regard to all relevant circumstances, in order to achieve an equitable result". According to the United States definition, which recalls those in the Court's judgments of 1969 and 1982, "the delimitation of a single maritime boundary requires the application of equitable principles, taking into account of all circumstances prevailing in the area concerned, in order to achieve an equitable solution". ....

100. The common conclusion of the Parties as to the "fundamental norm" governing, in their opinion, the question of maritime delimitation seems, therefore, to be closely related to the conclusion reached by an analysis of international case law and also, in the end, to that arrived at by the Third Conference on the Law of the Sea.

101. However, if both Parties recognize the existence in international law of a "fundamental norm" governing maritime delimitations, that is as far as their agreement goes. There is no longer agreement when each of the Parties separately seeks to ascertain whether international law might also contain other rules, possibly accompanied by corollaries, of mandatory application in the same field.

102. In this connection Canada concentrated its efforts on deducing these other rules of maritime delimitation from the concept of geographical adjacency, since it was convinced that this concept constituted the "basis of the title" ;of the coastal State to the partial extension of its jurisdiction to the continental shelf and the waters of which it formed the bed.

103. This argument calls for several comments. Regarding adjacency the Chamber acknowledges that in most cases this concept can be credited with the ability to express, perhaps better than that of natural prolongation, the link between a State's territorial sovereignty and its sovereign rights to adjacent submerged land. It can also be acknowledged to express correctly the link between the State's territorial sovereignty and its sovereign rights over waters covering such submerged land. It should not be forgotten, however, that "legal title" to certain maritime or submarine areas is always and exclusively the effect of legal operation. The same is true of the boundary of the extent of the title. That boundary results from a rule of law, and not from any intrinsic merit in the purely physical fact. In the Chamber's opinion it is therefore correct to say that international law confers on the coastal State a legal title to an adjacent continental shelf or to a maritime zone adjacent to its coasts; it would not be correct to say that international law recognizes the title conferred on the State by the adjacency of that shelf or that zone, as if the mere natural fact of adjacency produced legal consequences.

104. It might be objected that these remarks are self-evident and that no one seeks to contradict them. The points concerned must, however, be clearly stated in order to show that there is a logical gulf between recognizing the precise and circumscribed legal realities just mentioned and the idea of constructing solely on that basis an alleged principle which is sometimes given the name of "adjacency", sometimes "proximity" and sometimes, more especially, "distance", which is, besides, quite another thing. This is so because it is from a principle thus established that Canada seeks to deduce the existence in customary international law of rules for the delimitation between States whose continental shelves or adjacent maritime zones overlap. Following this line enables the Party in question eventually to assert that international law enshrines a rule that would concretely determine which of the two neighbouring States whose claims are at variance is to be recognized as having a more valid claim than the other to the attribution of certain maritime or submarine areas. Under this rule the State any part of whose coasts is less distant from the zones than those of the other State would ipso jure be entitled to have the zones recognized as its own.

105. The Chamber need not comment on the assertion that such a rule exists since the Court refused in the North Sea Continental Shelf case to "imply any fundamental or inherent rule the ultimate effect of which would be to prohibit any State...from exercising continental shelf rights in respect of areas closer to the coast of another State".... At that time the Court wished to stress that the submarine areas appertaining to the coastal State were not always closest to its coasts.

106. With regard to the reasoning by which the Party concerned arrived at the conclusion mentioned above, the Chamber merely notes that it amounts to just one more, still unconvincing, endeavour to instill the idea that "equidistance" -- rather than distance -- is a concept endorsed by customary international law, since the objective is to assert that whatever lies less far from the coasts of one State than from those of another should automatically appertain to the former State. It is another attempt to turn equidistance into a genuine rule of law, one to which general international law has supposedly given expression while yet tempering it to take account of special circumstances, and thus into something other than it is in reality; a practical method that can be applied for the purposes of delimitation.

....

108. The United States, for its part, has not merely disputed the determining force in international law of any principle of adjacency, proximity or distance, or of any legal rule allegedly derived therefrom. It has sought support for its contentions in the distinction, which the Chamber has already called unacceptable both in geography and in law, between coasts defined as "primary", simply because they follow the general direction of the mainland coastline as a whole, or are parallel to it, and coasts defined as "secondary", simply because they deviate from that direction. Answering the

objection, made by reference to case-law, that the equality of all coasts must be measured "in the same plane", the United States argued that only "comparable" coasts are entitled to comparable treatment and that not all coasts are comparable. On this basis, therefore, which Canada has described as an "ad hoc construction", the United States has purported to establish the principle of the preferential nature of the relationship between "primary" coasts and the maritime and submarine situated frontally before them. In terms of practical consequences, this preferential relationship should allegedly prevail over the relationship of "secondary" coasts, even if these are closer. The "proximity" concept should therefore yield to that of the "geographical natural prolongation" of the principal coasts and that of the "extension of the coastal front" of the State to which they belong.

109. In the Chamber's opinion, the a priori nature of these premises and these deductions is as patent as that of the thesis elaborated by the other Party. In both cases the outcome of the Parties' efforts can be said to have been preconceived assertions rather than any convincing demonstration of the existence of the rules that each had hoped to find established by international law.

110. Each Party's reasoning is in fact based on a false premise. The error lies precisely in searching general international law for, as it were, a set of rules which are not there. This observation applies particularly to certain "principles" advanced by the Parties as constituting well-established rules of law, e.g., the idea advocated by Canada that a single maritime boundary should ensure the preservation of existing fishing patterns which are vital to the coastal communities concerned, or the idea advanced by the United States that such a boundary should make it possible to ensure the optimum conservation and management of living resources and at the same time reduce the potential for future disputes between the Parties. One could add to these ideas of "non-encroachment" upon the coasts of another State or of "no cutting-off" of the seaward projection of the coasts of another State, and others which the Parties put forward in turn, which may in given circumstances constitute equitable criteria, provided, however, that no attempt is made to raise them to the status of established rules endorsed by customary international law.

....

112. The Chamber therefore wishes to conclude this review of the rules of international law on the question to which the dispute between Canada and the United States relates by attempting a more complete and, in its opinion, more precise formulation of the "fundamental norm" already mentioned.... What general international law prescribes in every maritime delimitation between neighbouring States could therefore be defined as follows:

(1) No maritime delimitation between States with opposite or adjacent coasts may be effected unilaterally by one of those States. Such delimitation must be sought and affected by means of an agreement, following negotiations conducted in good faith and with genuine intention of achieving a positive result. Where, however, such agreement cannot be achieved, delimitation should be effected by recourse to a third party possessing the necessary competence.

(2) In either case, delimitation is to be effected by the application of equitable criteria and by the use of practical methods capable of ensuring, with regard to the geographic configuration of the area and other relevant circumstances, an equitable result.

[The Chamber then turned to an examination of the criteria and methods to be applied between the Parties in giving effect to this norm. The Chamber rejected those found in Article 6 of the Geneva Convention on the Continental Shelf, even though both States were Parties to that convention. It was of the view that those provisions applied only to the continental shelf and did not represent general principles of international law as between the Parties; they could not be used for the single maritime boundary sought here. The Chamber then discussed the argument related to estopell which have been omitted because they are not directly relevant to the main issue in this case.]

....

164. Bearing in mind the considerations set forth in the preceding section, the Chamber now proposes, before turning to the concluding phase of its work, to examine the respective criteria and methods whose application to the delimitation is proposed by each of the Parties, and to undertake a comparative analysis of the four lines resulting from the application by them of these criteria and methods.

....

166. The Chamber would first recall that the United States, whose particular interest in the "maritime" or "fisheries" aspect of the subject of the dispute it has already emphasized, originally proposed in 1976 the application of a criterion which, as appears particularly from the recent explanations given by that Party, accorded decisive importance for the purposes of delimitation, to natural factors, that is, geomorphological, and, indeed especially, the ecological aspects of the area. The method proposed by that Party for the practical implementation of this criterion amounted, therefore, to adopting a line which corresponded approximately to a line of greatest depths. The main objective thus pursued was to keep intact the unity of each of the various ecosystems which, according to that Party, were clearly distinguishable throughout the area to be delimited....

....

168. The possibility of applying this criterion, which was originally advocated by the United States and to which it is still, to a certain extent, attached, and especially of applying it to the present delimitation, prompts serious reservations.... [T]he criterion underlying the United States line of 1976 was too much geared to one aspect of the present problem for it to be capable of being considered equitable in relation to the characteristics of the case. This criterion may have been justified for a delimitation concerning the exclusive fishery zone alone, but less so for a "single" delimitation, in whose purpose the continental shelf and especially the resources of its subsoil also play a most important part. When such a delimitation is made it is just possible that the choice of a criterion and a practical method that are manifestly appropriate for fishery delimitation may be the right one for determining a particular segment of the line, were it to appear that, in the area delimited by that segment, the continental shelf is not of decisive importance. The exceptional aspect of such a solution must, however, be acknowledged, and it is obviously impossible to employ, for the determination of the entire length of a single delimitation line which, as in the present case, simultaneously concerns two distinct and important objects, a criterion and a method that would be suitable for delimiting the one but not for delimiting the other.

169. The new line proposed when the Memorial of the United States was filed in September 1982 seems, especially at first sight, to be based on an entirely different conception. This conception belongs to a more recent context, comprising the recent and important arbitral and judicial decisions of 1977 and 1982 on the delimitation of the continental shelf, together with important delimitations affected by agreement,...the adoption of the Third United Nations Conference on the Law of the Sea of the new codification convention which covers, and extends, the field of the 1958 Conventions, and departs substantially from them in the context of the relevant articles.

170. An effort was clearly made by the United States to remedy the earlier omission of other important geographical aspects, and a new approach to the problem which the other Party has criticized as macrogeography. The United States thus fixed its final position on the central idea of the

general direction of the coast, on which it has based a series of observations and distinctions which may be summarized as follows:

(a) Recognition of the priority to be given, in all respects, to consideration of the general south-west and north-east direction of the eastern seaboard of the American continent;

(b) A distinction - already mentioned above -- between "primary coasts" and "secondary coasts", according as they follow the general direction of the coasts or, on the contrary, deviate from it.

(c) The classification, inter alia, of the Atlantic coast of Nova Scotia abutting on the Gulf of Maine -- like the coast of Massachusets abutting on that Gulf -- as "secondary" coasts;

(d) A finding that the coast of Maine abutting on the Gulf follows a direction corresponding to the "general direction" and is, therefore, a "primary" coast, and that Georges Bank, situated off and opposite the coast of Maine, is oriented in the same direction.

The "equitable criterion" that must be applied in delimiting the single maritime boundary of the area becomes that of the projection or frontal extension of the primary coast front, which the United States identifies with that of natural prologation, not in the geological or geomorphological sense, but "in the geographical sense". As has also been pointed out, the United States puts forward as additional equitable criteria, those of avoidance of encroachment and cut-off and that of proportionality.

171. Using this set of criteria, the dominant one now being the frontal projection of the primary coastal front, the United States therefore proposes, as a method for delimiting the course of the boundary line, the vertical line, perpendicular to the general direction of the coast. To be consistent with the system, the perpendicular line would have to be drawn from the terminal point of the international boundary, thus being a perpendicular to the continuous horizontal line formed by the coasts designated as principle coasts of Maine and New Brunswick. This is impractical....

....

176. It is an essential condition for the use of such a method in a specific case that the boundary be drawn in the particular case should concern two countries whose territories lie successively along a more or less rectilinear coast, for a certain distance at least.... [I]t is hard to imagine a case less conducive to the application of this method of delimitation than the Gulf of Maine case....

....

178. The Chamber will now examine the lines proposed successively, at the end of 1976 and at the end of 1977, thus in quick succession, by Canada. The Chamber believes they can be considered together, since the two lines are essentially based on the same criterion and both purport to be the result of applying a single method. This criterion...has been defined as that of the equal division of the disputed areas, and the method is broadly described by the term "equidistance".

[The Chamber notes that it had already rejected the equidistance method as a mandatory norm. But it went on to say that while the method cannot be claimed as mandatory, that is not to say that it could not be used where appropriate, adjusted by special circumstances.]

....

190. The consideration...as regards the equitable criteria and practical methods applicable in the abstract to maritime delimitation, and the critical assessment...of the particular criteria and methods proposed by the Parties...will now serve the Chamber as a guide in approaching its task of carrying out that delimitation. The conclusion reached by the Chamber shows clearly that it must undertake this final stage of the task entrusted to it and formulate its own solution independently of the proposals made by the Parties.

191. That being so, the Chamber has evidently to keep in mind its obligation to comply with the fundamental norm provided by general international law where this subject-matter is concerned. In this final phase of the decision-making process, the Chamber must therefore arrive at the concrete determination of the delimitation line that it is required to draw (a) while basing itself for the purpose on the criteria which it finds most likely to prove equitable in relation to the relevant circumstances of the case and (b) while making use, in order to apply these criteria to the case, of the practical method or combination of methods which it deems most appropriate, all this with the final aim of reaching an equitable result in the above circumstances.

192. Hence as regards in the first place, the choice of the criteria on which the Chamber should base its decision, all the foregoing considerations point to the advisability of its formally precluding the application of any criteria, however apparently equitable in themselves, which can now be seen as inappropriate to the delimitation of one or other of the two objects that the Parties' Special Agreement requests it to delimit. In this connection, the Chamber must again stress the responsibility laid upon it by the fact that the delimitation that it is required to carry out is, for the first time in international judicial or arbitral practice, a delimitation of two distinct elements by means of a single line. This is an unprecedented aspect of the case which lends it its special character and accordingly differentiates it from those that were the subject of previous decisions. To note this fact does not of course in any way imply that the criteria applied in those decisions must ipso facto be held inapplicable to the present case; all that is meant is that the fact that the criteria in question were then found equitable and appropriate for the delimitation of the continental shelf does not imply that they must automatically possess the same properties in relation to the simultaneous delimitation of the continental shelf and the superjacent fishery zone. It is necessary that the adaptability of those criteria to this essentially different operation should first be verified in relation to its specific requirements.

193. In other words, the very fact that the delimitation has a twofold object constitutes a special aspect of the case which must be taken into consideration even before proceeding to examine the possible influence of other circumstances on the choice of applicable criteria. It follows that, whatever may have been held applicable in previous cases, it is necessary, in a case like the present one, to rule out the application of any criterion found to be typically and exclusively bound up with the particular characteristics of one alone of the two natural realities that have to be delimited in conjunction. In commenting on the delimitation criteria proposed by the Parties, the Chamber has already pointed out the difficulty, if not the impossibility, of adopting, for the purpose of such a dual delimitation, a criterion disclosed by objective analysis to be essentially ecological. It so described the criterion initially proposed by the United States, whereby it should take as its main guideline the idea of a correspondence between the line to be drawn and the natural separation of the various ecosystems formed by the aquatic fauna of the delimitation area. As the Chamber then observed, a criterion of this kind could scarcely be adapted to a delimitation which had not only to divide a volume of water but had also to effect a division of the underlying continental shelf, in respect of which the criterion in question could not be appropriate. Conversely, it may be remarked that, in a concrete situation where distinctive geological characteristics can be observed in the continental shelf, such as might have special effect in determining the division of that shelf and the resources of the subsoil, there would in all likelihood be no reason to extend the effect of those characteristics to the division of the superjacent

volume of water, in respect of which they would not be relevant. These are merely two of many examples that could be cited.

....

195. ... [I]t is, accordingly towards an application to the present case of criteria more especially derived from geography that it [the Chamber] feels bound to turn. What is here understood by geography is of course mainly the geography of the coasts, which has primarily a physical aspect, to which may be added, in the second place, a political aspect. Within this framework, it is inevitable that the Chamber's basic choice should favour a criterion long held to be equitable to the special circumstances of the case, one should aim at an equal division of areas where the maritime projections of the coasts of the States between which the delimitation is to be effected converge and overlap.

[The Chamber then noted certain auxiliary criteria that it though necessary to correct minor inequities. These criteria were identified as (a) the difference between the lengths of the respective coastlines, (b) avoiding cutting off one coastline and (c) the effect of the presence of islands.]

198. The equitable nature of the criteria adopted in the light of the circumstances of the case will emerge the more convincingly -- one might almost say tangibly -- after the transition from the preliminary phase of choosing equitable criteria to the next phase, in which these criteria are to be reflected in the drawing of a particular delimitation line with the aid of appropriate practical methods.

199. ... Just as the criteria to which they must give effect are basically founded on geography, the practical methods in question can likewise only be methods appropriate for use against a background of geography. Moreover, like the underlying criteria, the methods employed to give them effect must, in this particular case, be just as suitable for the delimitation of the sea-bed and its subsoil as for the delimitation of the superjacent waters and their fishery resources. In the outcome, therefore, only geometrical methods will serve.

....

205. Regarding the choice and use of methods, one general observation must be made. The delimitation of the line to be drawn in a given area will depend upon the coastal configuration. But the configuration of the Gulf of Maine coastline, on which the delimitation of the maritime and submarine zones of the two countries depends throughout its length, is such as to exclude any possibility of the boundary's being formed by a basically unidirectional line, either over the whole distance between the point of departure and the terminal triangle or even over the sector between the point of departure and the closing line of the Gulf.

206. The Chamber has already considered this aspect...in commenting on the delimitation line proposed by Canada. It then expressed its disagreement precisely in relation to the fact that the Party in question had proposed a delimitation that failed to take into account of the fact that a change in the geographical perspective of the Gulf is to be noted at a certain point. Given the importance of this aspect, the Chamber considers that it will here be apposite, by way of reminder, to repeat its observation that it is only in the northeastern sector of the Gulf that the prevailing relationship of the coasts of the United States and Canada is that of lateral adjacency as between part of the coast of Maine and part of the Nova Scotian coast. In the sector close to the closing line, the prevailing relationship is, on the contrary, one of oppositeness as between the facing stretches of the Nova Scotian and Massachusetts coasts. Accordingly, in the first sector, geography itself demands that, whatever practical method is selected, the boundary should be a lateral delimitation line. In the second, it is once again geography which prescribes that the delimitation line should rather be a median line.for delimitation as between opposite coasts, and it is moreover geography again which requires that this

line, given the almost perfect parallelism of the two facing coasts involved, should also follow a direction practically parallel to theirs.

....

209. The first of the two segments is, then, the one belonging to the innermost sector of the Gulf, the sector closest to the international boundary terminus. As regards this sector, the Chamber is convinced that it constitutes the most appropriate location for effecting as far as possible -- since there is no special circumstance standing in the way -- an equal division of the area of overlapping created by the lateral superimposition of the maritime projections of the two States.

....

212. .... The essential premise of the operation, as the Chamber sees it, is to take note of the fact that the point of departure of the delimitation line to be drawn, and hence of its first segment, must be point A and no other point whatever its justification. That understood, the Chamber considers that the practical method to be applied must be a geometrical one based on respect for the geographical situation of the coasts between which the delimitation is to be effected, and at the same time suitable for producing a result satisfying the repeatedly mentioned criterion for the division of disputed areas.

213. Accordingly,...one may justifiably draw from point A two lines, respectively perpendicular to the two basic coastal lines here to be considered, namely the line from Cape Elizabeth to the international boundary terminus and from that latter point to Cape Sable. These perpendiculars form, at point A, on the one side an acute angle of about 82 degrees and on the other a reflex angle of about 278 degrees. It is the bisector of this second angle which the Chamber considers that it should adopt for the course of the first segment of the delimitation line. The Chamber believes that this practical method combines the advantages of simplicity and clarity with that of producing, in the instant case, a result which is probably as close as possible to equal division of the first area to be delimited....

214. ... [T]he Chamber will now turn its attention to the establishment of [the] second segment, which though it may be the shortest, will certainly be the central and most decisive segment for the whole of the delimitation line.

215. For the purpose of this operation, the Chamber considers, on account of the consideration already set forth, that it has first to make its choice of an appropriate practical method for use in provisionally establishing a base delimitation, and that it must then ascertain what corrections to it are rendered indispensable by the special circumstances of the case. A two-stage operation is therefore entailed.

216. The first stage involves the choice and concrete utilization of the practical method to be applied.... To use the terminology found in conventions and case law, there can be no doubt, in the Chamber's opinion, that, in the locations indicated, the coasts of the two States are opposite coasts. Here they do not possess the relationship of lateral adjacency which underlay the determination of the first segment of the delimitation line but face each other in confrontation. In such a geographical situation, the application of any method of geometrical origin, no matter which,...can in practice only result in the drawing of a median delimitation line. In this specific case, such a line can only be one approximately parallel to the approximately parallel lines of the two opposite coasts.

....

218. However,...it is...impossible to disregard the circumstance, which is of undeniable importance in the present case, that there is a difference in the length between the respective coastlines of the two neighbouring States which border on the delimitation area. Not to recognize this fact would be a denial of the obvious. The Chamber therefore reaffirms the necessity of applying to the median line...a correction which, though limited, will pay due heed to the actual situation.

....

221. ... [T]he Chamber notes that, according to the technical information at its disposal, the total length of the United States coastline in the Gulf...is approximately 284 nautical miles. The overall length of the Canadian coastline...is approximately 206 nautical miles....

222. The ratio between the coastal fronts of the United States and Canada on the Gulf of Maine as defined in the previous paragraphs, is thus 1.38 to 1. In the view of the Chamber, this ratio should be reflected in the location of the second segment of the delimitation line.... In the view of the Chamber it would then be proper to shift the line...in such a way as to reflect the ratio.... [The Chamber also corrected the line to account for the presence of islands off the Nova Scotia coast.]

223. The central segment of the delimitation will thus correspond, over its entire length, with the corrected median line so established. It will begin where this line intersects, within the Gulf, the bisector drawn from point A and constituting the first segment, and end on reaching the oft-mentioned closing line of the Gulf....

224. There now remains to be determined the course of the third segment of the delimitation line, e.e., the longest portion of its entire course. This is the segment concerning that part of the delimitation area which lies outside and over against the Gulf of Maine. Nevertheless, it appears beyond question that, in principle, the determination of the path of this segment must depend upon that of the previous two segments of the line, those segments within the Gulf which have just been described and whose path so obviously depended on the orientation of those coasts of the Parties that abut the waters of the Gulf.... From the geographical point of view, there is no point of reference, outside the actual shores of the Gulf, that can serve as a basis for carrying out the final operation required. That being so, it appears obvious that the only kind of practical method which can be considered for this purpose is, once again, a geometrical method. Within the range of such methods, the most appropriate is that recommended above all by its simplicity, namely in this instance the drawing of a perpendicular to the closing line of the Gulf.

....

226. Such being the Chamber's choice, the essential question remains to be resolved, namely that of determining the precise point on the closing line of the Gulf from which the perpendicular to that line should be drawn seawards. However, if it is considered necessary to remain guided by geography, all the considerations already set forth in regard to the determination of the final segment of the line militate in favour of having this new choice coincide with the very point where the corrected median line encounters the closing line of the Gulf....

230. ... [The Chamber's] last remaining task before formulating its final decision will be to ascertain whether the result thus arrived at may be considered as intrinsically equitable, in the light of all the circumstances which may be taken into account for purposes of this decision.

....

[In the remainder of the opinion, the Chamber reviewed what it had done and concluded that the line represented an equitable division of the fishing grounds and allocated to each country a broad expanse of submerged sea-bed.]

ED. NOTE: Examine, again, the maps at the end of the chapter, particularly comparing the lines originally proposed by the Parties to that drawn by the Chamber. You might speculate that the most important element of this case to the Parties was the question of allocating fishing grounds. If you did, you would be correct. Does the Chamber's line solve this problem? Think about whether one or both Parties could have presented this case in a way that would have achieved the result they both sought to achieve.

The most recent delimitation case involved a dipute between Canada and France over the martime boundaries in the Atlantic in an area surrounding the French islands of Saint Pierre and Miquelon off the Canadian coast of Newfoundland. The opinion of the arbitral tribunal follows.

CASE CONCERNING DELIMITATION OF MARITIME AREAS BETWEEN CANADA AND THE FRENCH REPUBLIC

....

Article 2

1. Ruling in accordance with the principles and rules of international law in the matter, the Court is requested to carry out the delimitation as between the Parties of the maritime areas appertaining to France and of those appertaining to Canada. This delimitation shall be effected from point 1 and from point 9 of the delimitation referred to in Article 8 of the Agreement of March 27, 1972 and described in the Annex thereto. The Court shall establish a single delimitation which shall govern all rights and jurisdiction which the Parties may exercise under international law in these maritime areas.

....

I. GEOGRAPHICAL DESCRIPTION OF THE AREA

18. The area within which the delimitation is to take place lies south of the Canadian island of Newfoundland, and east of the Canadian island of Cape Breton and the coast of mainland Nova Scotia. The coasts are indented by numerous bays and have many small islands and islets lying off them. To the east and south the area is open to the Atlantic Ocean.

19. The south coast of Newfoundland lies between Cape Race, at the eastern end, and Cape Ray about 260 nautical miles westward. From Cape Race the general direction of the coast is westerly for about 120 nautical miles to the southwestern end of the Burin Peninsula where the general direction turns abruptly north for nearly forty nautical miles, crossing the entrance to Fortune Bay, before turning west again towards Cape Ray. Placentia Bay, 48 nautical miles wide at its entrance and penetrating 60 nautical miles inland, has its eastern entrance 45 nautical miles west of Cape Race. Its western shore is the Burin Peninsula. Fortune Bay, north of the peninsula, is a further deep indentation about 30 nautical miles wide at its entrance and 60 nautical miles in length.

20. The north-eastern point of Cape Breton island lies approximately 60 nautical miles southwest of Cape Ray, from which it is separated by Cabot Strait which gives access to the Gulf of St. Lawrence. The east coast of the island stretches in a direction slightly east of south for 67 nautical

miles to Scatarie Island lying a mile offshore. There it turns to a southwesterly direction for a further 70 nautical miles, after which the east coast of mainland Nova Scotia continues in the same direction.

21. Sable Island is an isolated sandy island oriented in an east-west direction, 22 miles long and less than a mile wide, situated 120 nautical miles south of Scatarie Island, and about 88 nautical miles from mainland Nova Scotia. It has an area of 33 square kilometers.

22. The coasts of Newfoundland and Cape Breton Island from the Burin Peninsula to Scatarie Island, together with the opening to the Gulf of St. Lawrence, form a marked concavity. The French territory of Saint Pierre and Miquelon lies within this concavity, opposite the mouth of Fortune Bay and west and southwest of the Burin Peninsula. It has an area of 237 square kilometers and consists of two main islands, Miquelon and Saint Pierre, several smaller islands and islets and many drying rocks. Miquelon, which has a north-south axis and an area of 210 square kilometers, is about 27 nautical miles south of the mainland of Newfoundland. It consists of two parts: Grande Miquelon to the north and Langlade to the south, the two being joined by a narrow above-water sand bank or tombolo. The whole island is 21.6 nautical miles in length from north to south, and is about 7 nautical miles east to west at its widest point (Langlade). The island of Saint Pierre is situated 3 nautical miles south-west of Langlade and almost 10 nautical miles southwest of the Burin Peninsula. It is oriented northeast-southwest and has an area of 17 square kilometers and a length of 4.4 nautical miles.

23. The continental shelf in the area is agreed to be a geological continuum. The 200 metre isobath is generally about 120 nautical miles off the coasts described, except where it borders on the Laurentian Channel, a wide glacial valley about 50 nautical miles in width with an average depth of 400 metres, which runs in a southeast direction from Cabot Strait. This channel is a secondary feature which does not interrupt the continuity of the shelf. Further east and southeast of Newfoundland, the 200 metre isobath extends to a distance of nearly 250 miles from the coast. East of the Laurentian Channel the continental shelf is marked by further secondary features in the form of a series of plateaux or banks collectively known as the Grand Banks of Newfoundland. The easternmost and largest of these is the Grand Bank. West of it lie the smaller Whale, Green, St. Pierre and Burgeo Banks. The continental slope begins at about the 200 metre depth. The continental margin off Newfoundland generally extends beyond 200 nautical miles from the coasts.

II. THE RELEVANCE OF GEOGRAPHICAL FACTORS

24. Geographical features are at the heart of the delimitation process. The Chamber of the International Court of Justice in the Delimitation of the Maritime Boundary in the Gulf of Maine Area case said that the equitable criteria to be applied "are essentially to be determined in relation to what may be properly called the geographical features of the area".... In the Case concerning the delimitation of the continental shelf between the United Kingdom of Great Britain and Northern Ireland and the French Republic..., the Court declared that "it is the geographical circumstances which primarily determine the appropriateness of equidistance or any other method of delimitation in any given case".... However, geographical facts do not, in themselves, determine the line to be drawn. Rules of international law, as well as equitable principles, must be applied to determine the relevance and weight of the geographical features.

25. The delimitation process begins, as a rule, by identifying what the International Court of Justice has called "the geographical context of the dispute before the Court, that is to say the general area in which" the "delimitation which is the subject of the proceedings, has to be effected"....

26. In the present case both Parties have identified as the relevant area ("la region concernee") the geographical concavity formed by Newfoundland and Nova Scotia which Canada has termed the "Gulf Approaches" and France has described as "l'antichambre du Golfe". The French islands of Sant-

Pierre-et-Miquelon are within a concavity framed exclusively by Canadian coasts.

27. The Parties differ, however, in their identification of the coasts. Canada submits that the relevent Canadian coasts extend from Cape Race to Cape Canso, thus including (1) the entire southern coast of Newfoundland from Cape Race to Cape Ray; (2) a closing line across the Cabot Strait and (3) the eastern coasts of Cape Breton Island from Money Point (close east of Cape North) to Scatarie Island and from there to Cape Canso at the northeastern end of the mainland of Nova Scotia.

28. France would exclude significant segments of the southern coast of Newfoundland, such as the coast between Ramea Island and Cape Ray and the eastern and southern facade of the Burin Peninsula across Placentia Bay. Moreover, it would not consider the closing line across Cabot Strait as "coast". It would also exclude segments of the coast of Nova Scotia between Cape North and Low Point in Cape Breton Island and part of the line between Scatarie Island and Cape Canso. In support of these exclusions France has adduced that only those coasts that are in relation to one another and that generate projections which meet and overlap should be considered.

29. But the coastlines that France wants to exclude form the concavity of the Gulf approaches and all of them face the area where the delimitation is required, generating projections that meet and overlap, either laterally or in opposition. The closing line across the Cabot Strait represents coastlines inside the Gulf which are in direct opposition to Saint Pierre and Miquelon and are less than 400 nautical miles away. For similar reasons, the indentation of Placentia Bay cannot be ignored either.

30. On the other hand, the French argument justifiably excludes the Canadian line across Fortune Bay and opposite the north and east coast of Miquelon and Saint Pierre as far as the longitude of Point 9 of the 1972 agreement. The north and east coasts of Miquelon and Saint Pierre do not face on to the area in dispute, and thus were correctly left out of account in the estimate made in the Canadian Memorial of the total length of coasts of the French Islands. However, a similar treatment should apply to the opposite Canadian coast lying behind the French islands. Although this segment of coasts was taken into account in the 1972 agreement for an uninterrupted and continuous line of delimitation between the islands and the mainland, it should be omitted from the calculation of the length of coast fronting on the area of this dispute.

31. At the same time it is necessary to recognize that Saint Pierre and Miquelon face both westwards and southwards on to the area of dispute. This realistically cannot be represented by a single north-south oriented line as proposed by Canada. Instead it may be better represented by two segments; one from Cap du Nid a L'Aigle to Pointe du Ouest of 21.6 nautical miles, and the other from Pointe du Ouest to Cap Noir on Tete de Galantry of 8.25 nautical miles. The Court notes that although there is no difference between the distances, the method used to arrive at them differs from that described at footnote 28 of the Canadian Memorial.

32. France considered as a relevant Canadian coast a line from Scatarie Island to the tip of Cape Sable Island, lying 211 nautical miles to the southeast. A glance at the map shows "ictu-oculi" that this island lies outside the geographical configuration that forms the Gulf Approaches. The French Memorial has recognized that Sable Island is "situee en avance notable et isolee de toutes cotes au sud-ouest de la region ou doit se faire la delimitation"...

33. Both Parties admit that there is a marked disparity in the length of the relevant coasts. Measured by segments, according to their lines of general direction, the respective coastlines defined above have the

following lengths:

Canada 455.6 nautical miles

France 29.85 nautical miles

The ratio between the Canadian coastline and the French coastline is, then, 15.3 to 1 and not 21 to 1 as it is said in the Canadian Memorial....

34. Another important geographical feature concerning the coasts of the Parties is the relationship of these coasts to each other. The Canadian position is that the close contiguity of the coasts of the French islands to the south coast of Newfoundland signifies that the relationship between them is one of adjacency. The French position is that towards the west, the islands are opposite to the Canadian coasts that lie on the other side of the Laurentian Channel and that, in particular, they are in a relation of oppositeness to the Cape Breton Island. Towards the south and the southeast, France accepts that the relationship with the Burin and Avalon Peninsula is "plutot laterale".

35. It is the view of this Court that Saint Pierre and Miquelon are laterally aligned with the south coast of Newfoundland, so that the prevailing and overall relationship is one of adjacency. Historical evidence also confirms that the French islands have long been considered adjacent to Newfoundland. Article XIII of the 1713 Treaty of Utrecht implicitly included Saint Pierre and Miquelon in the clause assigning to Great Britain "the island called Newfoundland with the adjacent islands". The retrocession to France in the Treaty of Versailles of 1783 maintained Great Britain's rights with respect to the Island of Newfoundland and the adjacent islands, "excepting the islands of Saint Pierre and Miquelon". This explicit exception was required because otherwise the two French islands would have been included among the islands adjacent to Newfoundland.

III. THE APPLICABLE LAW

36. Article 2, para. 1 of the 1989 Agreement requires the Court to establish a single delimitation as between the Parties of the maritime areas appertaining to France and of those appertaining to Canada. The single delimitation is to govern all rights and jurisdiction which the parties may exercise under international law in these maritime areas.

37. The Parties have agreed to request an all purpose delimitation. As stated by the Chamber in the Case concerning the Delmitation of the Maritime Boundaries in the Gulf of Maine Area "there is certainly no rule of international law to the contrary, and, in the present case, there is no material impossibility in drawing a boundary of this kind".... Similarly, in the present case there is no material obstacle to the Court's drawing a single delimitation line as required by the Agreement.

38. The Parties are in agreement with respect to the fundamental norm to be applied in this case, which requires the delimitation to be affected in accordance with equitable principles, or equitable criteria, taking account of all the relevant circumstances, in order to achieve an equitable result. The underlying premise of this fundamental norm is the emphasis on equity and the rejection of any obligatory method. However, the Parties disagree with respect to the principles or criteria that should govern the equitable decision of this dispute, placing their emphasis on different principles or criteria.

39. In its Memorial Fance referred to the 1958 Convention on the Continental Shelf, ratified by both Parties, and contended that its Article 6 has a role to play in the present case and that the potential line resulting from the application of Article 6, which refers to equidistance, is an element that must be taken into account in determining the equitable character of the line to be drawn.

40. However this Court will adhere to the established judicial opinion to the effect that in a single or all purpose delimitation operation, Article 6 of the Convention on the Continental Shelf has not "mandatory force between States which are parties to the Convention".... The Chamber in the Gulf of Maine case ruled, rejecting a Canadian claim, that Article 6 was not applicable to a single

delimitation of both the sea-bed and the water column, because "such an interpretation would, in the final analysis, make the maritime water mass overlying the continental shelf a mere accessory of the shelf"....

41. Moreover, if the purpose of invoking Article 6 is to derive from it support for equidistance, it must be observed that Article 6 does not provide for equidistance "tout court" but equidistance when there are no special circumstances. The 1977 decision in the Anglo-French arbitration interpreted the reference in Article 6 to special circumstances as meaning "that the obligation to apply the equidistance principle is always one qualified by the condition `unless another boundary is justified by special circumstances'".... The Court added that a finding as to the existance of special circumstances "is very much a matter of appreciation in the light of the geographical and other circumstances".

42. In the course of these proceedings repeated reference was made by the Parties to the treatment given to the Channel Islands in the 1977 decisionin the Anglo-French Arbitration. This Court does not consider that decision to provide a precedent for the present case. The situation of the Channel Islands is substantially different from the present one, because of the proximity of the English coast. The Channel Islands were seen by the Court as an incidental feature of a delimitation between two mainland, and approximately commensurate, coasts.

IV. THE PRINCIPLES OF CRITERIA INVOKED BY FRANCE

43. In order to oppose the Canadian submission, which awards to Saint Pierre and Miquelon only a belt of 12 nautical miles from the baselines in those areas that have not yet been delimited, France relies on two basic principles: the principle of sovereign equality of States and the principle of the equal capacity of islands and mainland countries to generate maritime areas. On these grounds France asserts that the Canadian proposal is not only inequitable but also divorces the legal title to maritime areas from the delimitation operation. The French Government notes that the Canadian proposal would deny to the French islands any exclusive economic zone and continental shelf. It contends that the two islands are thus assimilated to "rocks which cannot sustain human habitation or economic life" of their own, while in accordance with Article 121(3) of the 1982 Convention on the Law of the Sea, it is only such rocks which "shall have no exclusive economic zone or continental shelf".

44. In answering the French contention that all coasts have an equal title, Canada introduced the notion of "relative reach", contending that all coasts do not necessarily have equal title and that their seaward projection is relative to their length. Canada asserted that coasts of limited length must have a correspondingly diminished prolongation as against longer coasts.

45. Undoubtedly, the difference in length of all the relevant coasts of the Parties is an important factor to take into account for an equitable delimitation, in order to avoid disproportionate results and, subsequently, to test the equitableness of the solution finally adopted. However, the Court cannot accept the contention that particular segments of coast may have an increased or diminished projection depending on their length. The extent of the seaward projections will depend, in every case, on the geographical circumstances; for example, a particular coast, however short, may have a seaward projection as far as 200 miles, if there are no competing coasts that could require a curtailed reach.

46. Another Canadian argument that France answers by invoking the principle of equality of States is the contention that Saint Pierre and Miquelon generate no continental shelf of their own because, from a physical point of view, the islands are superimposed upon the Canadian continental shelf itself. But the continental shelf in this area is a continuum characterized by the unity and uniformity of the whole sea-bed, "from the Arctic to Florida", as admitted by Canada and recognized by the Chamber of the International Court of Justice in the Gulf of Maine case. In that case the Chamber

concluded that "the continental shelf of the whole of this area is no more than an undifferentiated part of the continental shelf of the eastern seaboard of North America"... Since it is all one shelf it cannote be considered as exclusively Canadian. Each coastal segment has its share of shelf.

47. The Canadian invocation of the physical structure of the sea-bed does not adequately recognize that the continental shelf concept, as also the related concept of "natural prolongation", in spite of its physical origins has throughout its history become more and more a "complex and juridical concept".... It should not be forgotten, either, that the physical structure of the sea-bed ceases to be important when the object, as in this case, is to establish a single, all purpose delimitation both of the sea-bed and the superjacent waters.

48. By emphasizing the fact that the delimitation is to be carried out between two equally sovereign States, and that their sovereignty is indivisible, France seeks to refute a further argument invoked by Canada. The Canadian argument is to the effect that the status of political dependency of the French islands with respect to metropolitan France is a factor justifying less extensive maritime rights than if they constituted an independent island State.

49. In the view of this Court there are no grounds for contending that the extent of the maritime rights of an island depends on its political status. No distinction in this respect is made by Article 121 (para.2) of the 1982 Convention on the Law of the Sea or by the corresponding provisions of the 1958 Convention on the Territorial Sea and Contiguous Zone and on the Continental Shelf.

50. Canada has pointed out that in the Libya/Malta case the International Court of Justice recognized that Malta could hardly be given less weight as an independent State than as an offshore dependency, concluding that in indpendent island State could not be placed "in a worse position because of its independence".... However, this formulation suggests equality of treatment, rather than a diminished treatment for politically dependent islands.

51. Canada further observed that in the 1977 Anglo-French case the Court of arbitration underlined the importance of the distinction between dependent and independent islands, by attaching significance to the status of the Channel Islands as islands of the United Kingdom, and not as semi-independent States. This distinction is not relevant in the present case, since all the islands involved in the proceedings must be considered as islands of France or of Canada respectively, and none of them are independent or semi-independent States.

52. A relevant distinction was made by the Court of Arbitration in the 1977 Anglo-French case when it stated that "the case of the Channel Islands must, in the view of the Court, be differentiated from that of rocks or small islands" by reason of the presence of certain factors such as the "considerable population and a substantial agricultural and commerical economy".... Some of these factors are equally present in the case of Saint Pierre and Miquelon. Without comparing and even less equating the economic or political significance of the territories involved in this case, it must be concluded, from a strictly legal point of view, that Newfoundland, although much larger in size than Saint Pierre and Miquelon, is equally an island which does not enjoy the status of a politically independent or semi-independent State.

53. A further issue is raised by Canada's contention based on stipulations agreed upon in mutual declarations exchanged between the King of Great Britain and the King of France, when signing the 1783 Treaty of Versailles. Article IV of the 1783 Treaty of Versailles provided that the Islands of Saint Pierre and Miquelon "are ceded in full right, by the present Treaty to His Most Christian Majesty" i.e. the King of France. But the Declarations provided that the King of Great Britain

"in ceding the Islands of Saint Pierre and Miquelon to France, regards them as ceded for the purpose of serving as a real shelter to the French fishermen and in full confidence that those possessions will not become an object of jealousy between the two nations".

54. Differing views were taken by the Parties as to whether these provisions might be considered as being still in force and as restricting French rights to maritime areas beyond territorial waters, France strongly rejects this contention.

55. In the Court's view, even assuming that these stipulations are still in force, they cannot reasonably be construed as limiting the rights of France to maritime areas under the contemporary law of the sea. The reference to the islands as a "real shelter" for French fishermen has not be construed by Great Britain, or by Canada in later years, as limiting the right of Saint Pierre and Miquelon to be a base for fishing activities by its inhabitants. The stipulation that the islands will not become "an object of jealousy" between the Parties cannot plausibly be interpreted to mean that the legal rights of France under contemporary international law must be denied because of "jealousy".

V. THE PRINCIPLES OR CRITERIA INVOKED BY CANADA

56. In order to oppose the French claim for a delimitation based on equidistance, Canada invokes two principles or criteria developed by judicial opinion: the principle of non-encroachment and the equitable criterion defined as the need to take into account coastal lengths, so as to avoid disproportionate results.

57. The principle of non-encroachment was introduced by the judgment of the International Court of Justice in the North Sea Continental Shelf cases. In the operative part of that decision the Court stated that delimitation is to be effected "in such a way as to leave as much as possible to each Party all those parts of the continental shelf that constitutes a natural prolongation of its land territory into and under the sea, without encroachment on the natural prolongation of the land territory of the other"... An in the 1985 Libya/Malta case the Court referred to

> "the principle of non-encroachment by one party on the natural prolongation of the other, which is no more than the negative expression of the positive rule that the coastal State enjoys sovereign rights over the continental shelf off its coasts to the full extent authorized by international law in the relevant circumstances"....

58. As described by Canada, the principle of non-encroachment signifies that the delimitation must leave to a State the areas that constitute the natural prolongation or saward extension of its coasts, so that the delimitation must avoid any cut-off effect of those prolongations or seaward extensions. This means that, for an all-purpose delimitation, the concept of natural prolongation refers to the seaward projection of the coasts, both in respect of the sea-bed and of the water column. Canada adduces that in this case, of two adjacent coasts, one of them concave, with the French islands constituting a sort of pretuberance, the line of equidistance proposed by France would swing out laterally across the coastal front of the more concave coast, cutting Canada off from areas situated directly in front of its coasts. The use of equidistance in such situations, Canada contends, would, in the terms employed by the International Court of Justice in 1969, "cause areas which are the natural prolongation or extension of the territory of one State to be attributed to another".... In that case the Court added that this is to be avoided because the delimitation "must not encroach upon what is the natural prolongation of the territory of another State"....

59. Canada adds that a look at the map shows ictu-oculi that the line of equidistance captures too large a portion of the space seaward of the southern coast of Newfoundland, as the line balloons creating an inequitable cut-off of the natural projection of segments of that coast in maritime areas

lying directly in front of the southern coast of Newfoundland. This coast is, according to Canada, the most important one in this delimitation, for coasts project frontally, in the direction in which they face, as has been recognized by the judicial opinion. Canada pointed out that the judgment of 1969 in the North Sea Continental Shelf cases was clearly based on a directional concept of natural prolongation; the Court spoke of a coast, and, in a practical sense, this was the operative principle of the whole decision. Canada added that in the Gulf of Maine case it argued in favour of a radical projection based on the distance criterion but its arguments were not accepted by the Chamber of the International Court of Justice.

60. The second equitable criterion invoked by Canada in order to reject equidistance is described as the need to avoid a disproportionate relationship between the length of the relevant coasts of the Parties and the maritime areas which are found to correspond to each coast. Canada asserts that the premise underlying the relevance of the proportionality factor is that coasts constitute the legal basis of title and it is through their configuration and projection into the sea that the extent of a State's maritime jurisdiction is determined. Canada adduces that it is by way of the coast, the point of contact between the land and the sea, that territorial sovereignty over the land generates offshore rights and recalls that in the Libya/Malta case the Court declared that sovereignty over the landmass brings rights into effect "by means of the maritime front of this landmass, in other words, by its coastal opening"....

61. Canada pointed out that, according to established jurisprudence, there is a double role for the proportionality factor in a delimitation operation. On the one hand, it consists of a preliminary assessment of the relative extent of the abutting coasts in order to select the method of delimitation to be adopted; on the other hand, the ex-post comparison on the coastal length ration would be a test of the equity of the delimitation.

62. Canada invokes proportionality both as a criterion and as one of the relevant circumstances to take into account in the process of deciding on the choice of the method of delimitation. It contends that the marked disparity in the total length of the relevant coasts leads to the rejection of equidistance as the method to apply in this case in order to reach an equitable result. Canada adduces that there can be no basis for the use of this methodology when the adjacency relationship is coupled with such a marked disparity in the length of the coasts that equidisctance would inevitably lead to a disproportionate result. And Canada goes even further in opposing the use of a provisional equidistance line as a starting point, asserting that there is no point in beginning the process with a method that shows no prima facie likelihood of success in the geographical configuration to which it must be applied.

63. This Court considers that the proper use of proportionality as a test of equity was well described by the International Court of Justice in the Libya/Malta case. At para. 66 the Court defined its proper role:

> "It is however one thing to employ proportionality calculations to check a result; it is another thing to take note, in the course of the delimitation process, of the existance of a very marked difference in coastal lengths, and to attribute the appropriate significance to that coastal relationship, without seeking to define it in quantitative terms which are only suited to the ex-post assessment of relationships of coast to area".

> And in para. 58 the Court described the improper role of proportionality:

> "...to use the ratio of coastal lengths as of itself determinative of the seaward reach an area of continental shelf proper to each Party, is to go far beyond the use of proportionality as a test of equity, and as a corrective of the unjustifiable difference of treatment resulting from some method of drawing the boundary line. If such a use of proportionality were right, it is difficult

indeed to see what room would be left for any other consideration".

VI. EXAGGERATION IN THE CLAIMS OF BOTH PARTIES

64. Both Parties, in rebutting their opponent's claims, tend to contradict the very principles that have been invoked in support of non-encroachment and avoidance of cut off of its coastal projections towards the south and west, in order to oppose the French line of equidistance, while at the same time Canada denies, with its enclave proposal, any projection beyond the territorial sea to the coastal openings of Saint Pierre and Miquelon towards the South and the West. Similarly, France does not pay due regard to the principle of equality of States and equal title of islands when it denies, with its line of equidistance, any seaward projection to important segments of the southern coast of Newfoundland.

65. This Court does not have to consider that either of the proposed solutions provides even a starting point for the delimitation. The Court's conclusion is similar to that drawn by the Chamber of the International Court of Justice in the Gulf of Maine case, namely, "that it must undertake this final stage of the task entrusted to it and formulate its own solution independently of the proposals made by the Parties"....

VII. THE SOLUTION

66. In order to reach an equitable result, it is necessary to examine separately two different sectors of the maritime area where the delimitation is to be effected. This distinction between two separate seaward projections of the coasts of the French islands was suggested in the French Memorial, which says: "la zone dans laquelle doit intervenir la delimitation comporte des iles, l'autre au sud et au sud-est ce cese iles"....

67. With respect to the first sector, which may be called the western seaward projection, it is unavoidable that any seaward extension of the French coasts beyond their territorial sea would cause some degree of encroachment and cut off to the seaward projection towards the south from point located on the southern shore of Newfoundland. Both Parties, however, recognize that "some degree of cut off may be inherent in any delimitation", and such effect is "inherent in the mere presence of the islands close to the Newfoundland shore";... it has also been stated that any solution "amputera...ineluctablement une partie de leurs droits. Tel est l'esprit de toute operation de delimitation."...

68. This Court has already concluded that the specific Canadian proposal of the enclave is not equitable because it denies the islands any maritime area beyond that already recognized as territorial sea. A limited extension of the enclave beyond the territorial sea in this western sector would meet to some degree the reasonable expectations of France of title beyond the narrow belt of territorial sea, even if causing some encroachment to certain Canadian seaward projections.

69. A reasonable and equitable solution for the western sector would be to grant to Saint Pierre and Miquelon an additional twelve nautical miles from the limit of its territorial sea, for its exclusive economic zone. That area will have the extent of the contiguous zone referred to in Article 33 of the 1982 Convention on the Law of the Sea, which grants to the coastal State jurisdiction to prevent the infringement of its customs, fiscal, immigration or sanitary regulations. Beginning at point 9 of the delimitation referred to in Article 8 of the Agreement of 27 March, 1972, the line of delimitation shall be a straight line in a southwesterly direction to the furthest point of intersection of arcs of circles of 12 nautical miles radius centred on the nearest points of the baseline described below. Thence it shall be an equidistance line between Canada and the French islands to a position 24 nautical

miles from the nearest points on those baselines. In the case of Canada the baseline is to be that given in the Territorial Sea and Fishing Zones Geographical Co-ordinates Order..., and in the case of the French islands the baseline is to be the low-water line of the islands, islets, above-water rocks or low-tide elevations.

70. In the second sector, towards the south and the southeast the geographical situation is completely different. The French islands have a coastal opening towards the south which is unobstructed by any opposite or laterally aligned Canadian coast. Having such a coastal opening, France is fully entitled to a frontal seaward projection towards the south until it reaches the outer limit of 200 nautical miles, as far as any other segment of the adjacent southern coast of Newfoundland. There is no foundation for claiming that Saint Pierre and Miquelon frontal projection in this area should end at the 12 mile limit of the territorial sea. On the other hand, such a seaward projection must not be allowed to encroach upon or cut off a parallel frontal projection of the adjacent segments of the Newfoundland southern coast.

71. In order to achieve this result the projection towards the south must be measured by the breadth of the coastal opening of the French islands towards the south. Thus, a balanced application of the principles and criteria invoked by the Parties leads to the solution of a second maritime area for Saint Pierre and Miquelon, in the southern sector extending to a distance of 188 nautical miles from a 12 nautical miles limit measured from the baseline already described, with its axis extending due south along the meridian half way between the two meridian lines parallel to that axis and its width being determined by the distance between the meridians passing through the easternmost point of the island of St. Pierre and the westernmost point of Miquelon respectively and measured at the mean latitude of those two points, or approximately 10.5 nautical miles. From the northeastern point of the limit thus described, as far as point 1 referred to in the 1972 Agreement, the delimitation shall be a twelve nautical miles limit measured from the nearest points on the baselines of the French islands.

72. Canada has contended that in determining the seaward projection towards the South of Saint Pierre and Miquelon, account must be taken of the projection towards the east from the coasts of Cape Breton Island, 140 nautical miles away, or from other more distant points in Nova Scotia. Both Parties considered in this connection the hypothetical situation that would arise if Nova Scotia would have been an independent country. Canada contended that it could not derive less maritime rights for the sole reason that Nova Scotia is a Canadian province.

72. The objections of Canada against the southern projection of the coast of Saint Pierre and Miquelon, based on an eastern projection from Nova Scotia and Cape Breton Island are not compelling. Geographically, the coasts of Nova Scotia have open oceanic spaces for an unobstructed seaward projection towards the south in accordance with the tendencey, remarked by Canada, for coasts to project frontally, in the direction in which they face. In the hypothesis of a delimitation exclusively between Saint Pierre and Miquelon and Nova Scotia, as if the southern coast of Newfoundland did not exist, it is likely that corrected equidistance would be resorted to, the coasts being opposite. In that event it is questionable whether the area hypothetically corresponding to Nova Scotia, would reach the maritime areas towards the south appertaining to Saint Pierre and Miquelon.

74. In the light of the geographical situation, the Court finds no incompatibility or inconsistency in admitting a limited westward projection of the west coast of Saint Pierre and Miquelon, as well as a full seaward projection to 200 miles of the unobstructed south coast of the French islands.

VIII. THE QUESTION OF THE BROAD SHELF

75. The French Government, in its Memorial...indicates that from the available information

concerning profiles of the sea-bed, in the area South of Saint Pierre and Miquelon, it appears ("l'apparait") that the continental margin in that area extends beyond 200 nautical miles. Invoking Article 76, para. 4 a) ii) of the 1982 Convention on the Law of the Sea, France claims rights over the continental shelf beyond 200 miles, asserting that its shelf in the area extends as far as the outer edge of the continental margin. For these reasons the French Government requests the Court of Aribitration to decide that the lines of delimitation it establishes should be prolonged in order to delimit also the continental shelf of the parties beyond 200 miles. The French Memorial adds that if the Court does not prolong the delimitation line at least as far as the Canadian 200 nautical mile line, then its decision would result in denying France the right to a broad continental shelf extending as far as the outer edege of the continental margin...

76. On its part, Canada, in its Counter Memorial states that although the continental margin off Newfoundland generally extends beyond 200 nautical miles, the point at which France is making its claim may, in fact, lie beyond the edge of that margin determined in accordance with Article 76 of the 1982 Convention on the Law of the Sea, so that there is no reasonable basis for the French claim. Canada adds that it does not accept the French assertion concerning the location of the outer edge of the continental margin and observes that France itself does not know the location of the outer edge of the margin, which is fundamental to its claim, as shown by the fact that it did not complete the lines of that claim in Map 16 of the French Memorial....

77. There is a previous issue concerning the competence of this Court to pronounce on the discrepancy between the Parties as to whether the continental shelf at the relevant area extends beyond 200 miles. Under the Arbitration Agreement the Court has been requested "to carry out the delimitation as between the Parties of the maritime areas appertaining to France and of those appertaining to Canada".

78. Any decision by this Court recognizing or rejecting any rights of the Parties over the continental shelf beyond 200 nautical miles, would constitute a pronouncement involving a delimitation, not "between the Parties" but between each one of them and the international community, represented by organs entrusted with the administration and protection of the international sea-bed Area (the sea-bed beyond national jurisdiction) that has been declared to be the common heritage of mankind.

79. This Court is not competent to carry out a delimitation which affects the rights of a Party which is not before it. In this connection the Court notes that in accordance with Article 76, para. 8 and Annex II of the 1982 Convention on the Law of the Sea, a Commission is to be set up, under the title of "Commission on the Limits of the Continental Shelf", to consider the claims and data submitted by coastal States and issue recomendations to them. In conformity with this provision, only "the limits of the shelf established by a coastal State on the basis of these recommendations shall be final and binding".

80. Obviously, a denial of a pronouncement on the French claim, based on the absence of a competence of this Court cannot signify nor may be interpreted as prejudicing, accepting or refusing the rights that may be claimed by France, or by Canada, to a continental shelf beyond 200 nautical miles.

81. The disagreement between the Parties concerning the factual situation, namely, whether at the relevant location the geological and geomorphological data make Article 76 (4) applicable or not, was not elucidated during the oral proceedings. This deficiency strengthens the Court's decision to abstain from pronouncing on the substance of the matter. It is not possible for a tribunal to reach a decision by assuming hypothetically the eventuality that such rights will in fact exist. The French Memorial rightly states in a different context that "il est sur que le Tribunal ne peut tabler sir des actes futurs au contenu et a la date inconnus de lui"...

82. It follows from the above considerations that this Court is only competent to effect a delimitation reaching as far as the 200 nautical miles outer limit, which is the single delimitation applicable simultaneously both to the exclusive economic zone and to the normal continental shelf of the Parties, that is to say, the shelf which is not extended under Article 76 (4) of the 1982 Convention. In closing at the 200 nautical miles outer limit the two parallel lines conforming the seaward projection towards the south of the coastal opening of Saint Pierre and Miquelon, the Court is complying strictly with the 1989 Agreement, which enjoins it to "establish a single delimitation which shall govern all rights of jurisdiction which the Parties may exercise under international law in these maritime areas". This provision mandates a single boundary line that would apply both to the sea-bed and the superjacent waters in the area subject to the delimitation.

IX. THE RELEVANCE OF FISHERIES

83. It is evident from the pleadings that access to and control of fisheries in the disputed area are central to the dispute over delimitation. Both Parties have emphasized the economic dependence of their respective nationals on fishing in the area and both consider delimitation a critical factor in safeguarding the legitimate interests of their fishing communities. On the other hand, the Parties are in essential agreement that the criteria governing the delimitation are to be found primarily in the geographical facts. The Court, as already stated, shares this view. In particular, the Court recognizes that it has not been requested or authorized to apportion resources on the basis of need or other economic factors. Accordingly, economic dependence and needs were not taken into account in the process of delimitation, as described above.

84. However, the Court cannot close its eyes to the arguments and data presented by both parties concerning the impact of fishing rights and practices on the economic well-being of the people most affected by the delimitation. Having decided upon the delimitation in accordance with the geographical factors, the Court still has the obligation to assure itself that the solution reached is not "radically inequitable", the terms used by the Chamber of the International Court of Justice in the Gulf of Maine case. The Chamber defined "radically inequitable" as "likely to entail catastrophic repercussions for the livelihood and economic well-being of the population of the parties concerned"....

85. In the present case, the facts submitted to the Court indicate that the proposed demarcation will not have a radical impact on the existing pattern of fishing in the area. As both Parties have repeatedly stressed during the proceedings, the delimitation is without prejudice to their fishing rights, which will continue to be governed by the Agreement of 27 March, 1972. The main feature of that Agreement is that each Party is to give access to the nationals of the other in the fishing zones under its jurisdiction on the basis of full reciprocity. This principle is made subject to "possible measures for the conservation of resources, including the establishment of quotas".

86. The Arbitral Tribunal in the La Bretagne Case noted in its decision of 17 July, 1986 that the agreement of 27 March, 1972 "belongs to the category of reciprocity agreements, in that it involves the exchange of benefits of the same type between the two contracting States which grant each other fishing rights in the zones subject to their respective jurisdictions".... While it is not the function of this Court to apply or interpret the Agreement of 27 March, 1972, it is pertinent to note that the existing rights of the Parties under that Agreement will apply to the fishing zones subject to the delimitation.[1]

1. Articles 1 and 2 of the Agreement provide:

"Article 1. The Government of France renounces the privileges established to its advantage in fishery matters by the Convention signed at London, on April 8, 1904, between the United Kingdom and France. The present agreement supercedes all previous treaty provisions relating to fishing by French nationals off the Atlantic coast of Canada.

A restrictive interpretation of the Agreement in that respect would not be warranted. As noted by the Tribunal in the La Bretagne case:

> "In a treaty of this type, there appears to be no warrant for treating the rights of one of the parties as a statement of principle and the rights of the other as a statement of an exception which, as such, would justify a restrictive interpretation"....

87. Inasmuch as each of the Parties have valuable fishing resources in the areas under its jurisdiction, the Agreement for reciprocal rights has a true mutuality. The delimitation decided by the Court will not have the effect of depriving either Party of its existing fishing rights under that 1972 Agreement. The fact that the Parties have had differences in the past relating to quotas and claims of over-fishing does not deprive the Agreement of its essential utility. Both states have recognized the value of reciprocity in regard to the fishing resources that they have shared for centuries. They agree that quotas are to be fixed solely to conserve fishing resources. It is in the declared interest of both to maintain their cooperation and reciprocity. This Court is confident that by abiding in good faith with the 1972 Agreement, the Parties will be able to manage and exploit satisfactorily the fishing resources of the area. In these circumstances, the solution adopted by the Court on the basis of the geographical facts, equitable criteria and the principles of law will surely not have catastrophic repercussions for either Party.

88. By reason of the geography of the relevant area, the delimitation lines established by the Court result in economic zones that at certain points cross or intercept each other. This fact, as one examined in para. 87 above, will also have no adverse effects, concerning navigation and other rights and duties of the Parties. It is obvious, and is recognized by both Parties, that the navigational and other rights and duties within the 200 mile economic zone are governed by the relevant rules of international law. In the written and oral proceedings both Parties have underscored the importance they attach to the principles of freedom of navigation through the 200 mile zone guaranteed by Article 58 of the 1982 Convention, a provision that undoubtedly represents customary internationl law as much as the institution of the 200 mile zone itself. Even though this matter is not at issue in the present arbitration, the Court takes note of the concurrence of the Parties on this question.

XI. MINERAL RESOURCES

89. The Court was also informed by the Parties of their interest in potential hydrocarbon exploitation in areas of overlapping claims. Some permits had concurrently been issued for exploration by both governments but after reciprocal protests, no drilling was undertaken. In the present circumstances, the Court has no reason to consider the potential mineral resources as having a bearing on the delimitation.

90. The question of hydrocarbon resources was also brought to the Court's attention by reference to a document, called the Releve de Conclusions, by which France would accept a reduced shelf area off Saint Pierre and Miquelon in return for Canadian concessions to French companies to exploit oil and gas in the Canadian shelf area. This document was adopted in 1972 by the negotiators, ad referendum, to be submitted to the two governments for approval, but the approval was not given.

"Article 2. In return, the Canadian Government undertakes in the event of a modification to the juridical regime relating to the waters situated beyond the present limits of the territorial sea and fishing zones of Canada on the Atlantic coast, to recognize the right of French nationals to fish in these waters subject to possible measures for the conservation of resources, including the establishment of quotas. The French Government undertakes for its part to grant reciprocity to Canadian nationals off the coast of Saint Pierre and Miquelon "

France subsequently brought the Releve to the attention of the Court in the Anglo-French arbitration of 1977.

91. In the view of this Court, no conclusions may be derived from the Releve for purposes of the present delimitation. It refers only to the shelf and is therefore not relevant to the "all purpose" delimitation required here. Moreover, it did not receive the necessary approval of the two governments and therefore has no standing as an agreement between them.

XII. CHECKING THE RESULTS

92. The International Court of Justice has stated in the Libya/Malta case that:

"In the view of the Court, there is no reason of principle why the test of proportionality, more or less in the form in which it was used in the Tunisia-Libya case, namely the identification of `relevant coasts', the identification of `relevant areas' of continental shelf, the calculation of the mathematical ratios of the lengths of the coasts and the areas of shelf attributed, and finally the comparison of such ratios, should not be employed to verify the equity of a delimitation..."....

Yet the Court found that there were in that case practical difficulties which rendered it inappropriate to apply the proportionality test in that form. In particular there were practical difficulties in identifying the relevant coasts and the relevant areas. This is not the case here. The relevant coasts have been identified and their ratio established in para. 33 supra.

93. It is true that with respect to the size of the relevant areas the Parties have submitted different figures, some of them on a hypothetical basis. However, the geographical expert assisting this Court has calculated the size of the area relevant for the purpose of checking the resultes, as identified by the Court, to be close to 63,000 square nautical miles. The Court considers this calculation to be well founded because in comparing like with like it is necessary to take into account not only the projection to 200 miles awarded to France, but also the Canadian area resulting from an identical projection extending the relevant area eastwards along the Newfoundland 200 miles arc to a point due south of Cape Race, and so embracing the whole economic zone generated to the South by the south coast of Newfoundland. Thus, the southern limit of the relevant area consists of a line from Cape Canso to the intersection of the 200 mile limit from Cape Breton Island and the French islands, then the 200 mile limit from Newfoundland, and then the latter as far as a point due south from Cape Race. On those basis, the actual areas appertaining to each of the Parties are: for Canada, 59,434 n.m2; for the French islands, 3,617 n.m2, making a total area of 63,051 n.m2. This would produce a ratio of approximately 16.4 to 1, thus confirming that there is certainly no disproportion in the areas appertaining to each of the Parties. Consequently, the requirements of the test or proportionality, as an aspect of equity, have been satisfied.

For these reasons:

THE COURT OF ARBITRATION, by three votes to two, being in favour President Jimenez de Arechaga and Judges Schachter and Arangio-Ruiz, and against Judges Weil and Gotlieb, draws the following line of delimitation:

[Here follows points of latitude and longitude defining the line]

D. PROBLEMS OF ISLANDS.

Robert D. Hodgson, ISLANDS: NORMAL AND SPECIAL CIRCUMSTANCES (1973) 48-51, 71-72

Most of the provisions of the Convention on the Continental Shelf are very general and were drafted without a deep or acute examination of existing physical situations. The conference appeared to conceive of the world as relatively uncomplicated and regulated in its physical relationships. Unfortunately, even a brief description of conditions shows that simplifications do not prevail in the three-dimensional world of the shelf and the seabed. Islands and bathymetry combine to produce a myriad of potential combinations, each of which may defy solution based on the general principles of the Convention. These geographic relationships are far more complicated than those involved in the territorial sea, in scope as well as dimension. As a consequence, states may more quickly resort to the "special circumstances" clause to claim that inequities exist.

Two islands of differing sovereignty, for example, may be located on the same oceanic ridge. The "shelf" area of one of the islands may be more extensive than the other. The prolongation of the 200-meter isobath of Island A obviously extends closer in certain areas to the land territory of Island B than to its own baseline. Should the boundary be an equidistant line? Can one say that the shelf area about Island A should adhere to Island B, from which it is physically separated according to one criterion? How can one determine equity or, for that matter, really define it under the terms of the Convention? One may question whether equity relates to the resulting areal allocations, which are fairly equal, or to the justice of the geographic unity of the prolongation of the feature. How can the boundary expert balance parameters involving depth (200 meters), distance (adjacency), and technology (exploitability) in a rational and equitable manner? Boundary criteria must be altered -- simplified or clarified -- to clear the current jungle. If a depth criterion is used to determine seabed limit, boundary relationships between states should not relate, under all circumstances, to mileage, i.e., an equally distant line. Conversely, if the relationships are based on distance, bathymetry need not be deemed relevant.

However, the Convention remains valid and will prevail until replaced, revised, or expanded. Solutions to maritime boundary problems must relate to all aspects of the conventions on the territorial sea and the continental shelf as well as to developing customary practices of states and of the courts, e.g., the North Sea cases of the International Court of Justice. In the latter, however, many of the seemingly relevant points may prove geographically irrelevant. For example, under certain conditions, it may be possible to delimit "natural prolongations" in conditions of natural adjacency. How can one determine the limit between Dutch and German prolongations in the North Sea when nearly identical geographical conditions exist on land? In addition, the Court stated that the resulting division of the shelf, to be equitable, should relate to the respective coastal lengths of the adjacent states. The litigants -- Germany vs. Denmark and the Netherlands -- have virtually identical coastal morphology: low tidal flats fringed by islands aligned parallel to the coastline. A constant factor prevails. What would the relationships be if one state possessed many islands and the other few or none? Should the coastal lengths of the islands be added to that of the mainland? Should both the seaward and landward coasts of the islands be included in the measurements?

It would appear just that the bases for settlement should rest not only on seeming equity but also on equity based on relevant geographic facts. To include the total perimeter of an island or islands could lead to excesses and injustice. The comparison of coastal lengths should relate only to those portions of the coastline which directly affect the measurement of the territorial sea. These might be determined by the construction of special systems of straight baselines for the purpose, or by a direct comparison of the areas of the territorial sea involved (assuming, of course, identical breadth of claims). The latter probably would produce the greatest equity because it would remove from the influence areas of internal and tidal waters which do not directly relate to the territorial sea. Many irrelevancies would be eliminated as a result.

While the North Sea cases applied to adjacent states, the same conditions may prevail when state positions are opposite.... One may argue, on a depth criterion alone, that Island B, separated from the continental shelf of State A by water deeper than 200 meters, should receive only the circular shelf area immediately about it. Adjacency begs the issue and would assign to B a portion of the shelf which "prolongs" from A. Of greater complexity is the situation where B sits astride the same shelf areas but is separated from its parent state by deeper water. To a degree, the answers to these questions concern a) the relationships of islands to each other and to the mainlands, b) their size, as previously discussed, and c) their status.

These illustrations, however, focus on certain of the issues which have been raised and on which the language of the Convention and the North Sea cases do not assist. The Court cannot be expected to adjudicate the many maritime boundary problems which are evolving unless certain objective and specific criteria are created to assist in problems of delimitation for all jurisdictions: sovereignty, sovereign rights, economic resource zones, fisheries zones, etc.

It should be recognized that most current maritime boundary discussions have related to seabed resource allocations. If a fisheries convention is drafted, however, whether based on species or on a zonal approach, limits will be required between adjacent states and even, under certain conditions, between opposite states. The only alternative is a regional zone of common usage, but limits between zones will still be necessary. For example, how may one define the limits between the United States and Canada -- species or zonal -- for the allocation of fisheries rights or conservation? Will the same boundary for fisheries apply also to the shelf? Would two noncoextensive limits be acceptable? Do the same parameters prevail? Will additional "special circumstances" become issues?

....

There can be no question that islands, depending on location and relationships, cause gross deflections in equidistant boundaries. While equidistance is not the sole basis for the delimitation of territorial sea, continental shelf, and seabed boundaries, the principle has become established as "conventional wisdom" for maritime limits. It is the only method mentioned specifically in both conventions, and, because of this sanctification, states find the concept easy to accept.

The solution to the problems raised by the effects of islands on equidistant boundaries and seabed allocations may be determined rationally by varying the effects of islands on the limits under specific circumstances. Developing international practice and law point out several types of categorization of islands on their relationships to maritime boundaries....

....

Inequities multiply as distances from national baselines increase. Shelf boundaries, based on islands and equidistance, may prove to be unacceptable without considerable modification. Consequently, restrictions must be placed on the use of certain small islands in order to remove or reduce their distortions and to preserve a semblance of equity. An effort has been made here toward an objective analysis of islands as special circumstances within the limitations of the conventions on the territorial sea and the continental shelf.

ED. NOTE: A persistent problem concerning islands and the delimitation of maritime boundaries is caused by islands about which there are disputed claims to sovereignty. In the East China Sea, for example, the Senkaku Islands are claimed both by China and Japan. This complicates a solution to the claims of the two nations to the oil-rich continental shelf lying between them. In the

South China Sea, the Paracel Islands are likewise subject to multiple claims, in this case the Peoples Republic of China and Vientnam.

In the Aegean Sea, Greece and Turkey have been at loggerheads for years over the delimitation of the continental shelf. Greece claims that her archipelagic islands are entitled, in accordance with the provisions of the Convention on the Continental Shelf, to generate continental shelf jurisdiction the same as mainland areas. Turkey, in turn, denies that status for the Greek islands since to accept Greece's position would effectively eliminate Turkey from participation in any oil exploration in the area.

In 1975, Argentina began to dispute British title to the Falkland Islands, located in the South Atlantic off the Argentine coast. This dispute led to open warfare. In 1981, in a brief but intense battle, British forces occupied the island group. The sovereignty issued remains unsettled.

Other areas in which there are disputes include Spitzbergen, involving the Soviet Union and Norway, and Rockall Island, as between the British and the Irish.

1982 UNITED NATIONS CONVENTION ON THE LAW OF THE SEA

Article 121

Regime of islands

....

3. Rocks which cannot sustain human habitation or economic life of their own shall have no exclusive economic zone or continental shelf.

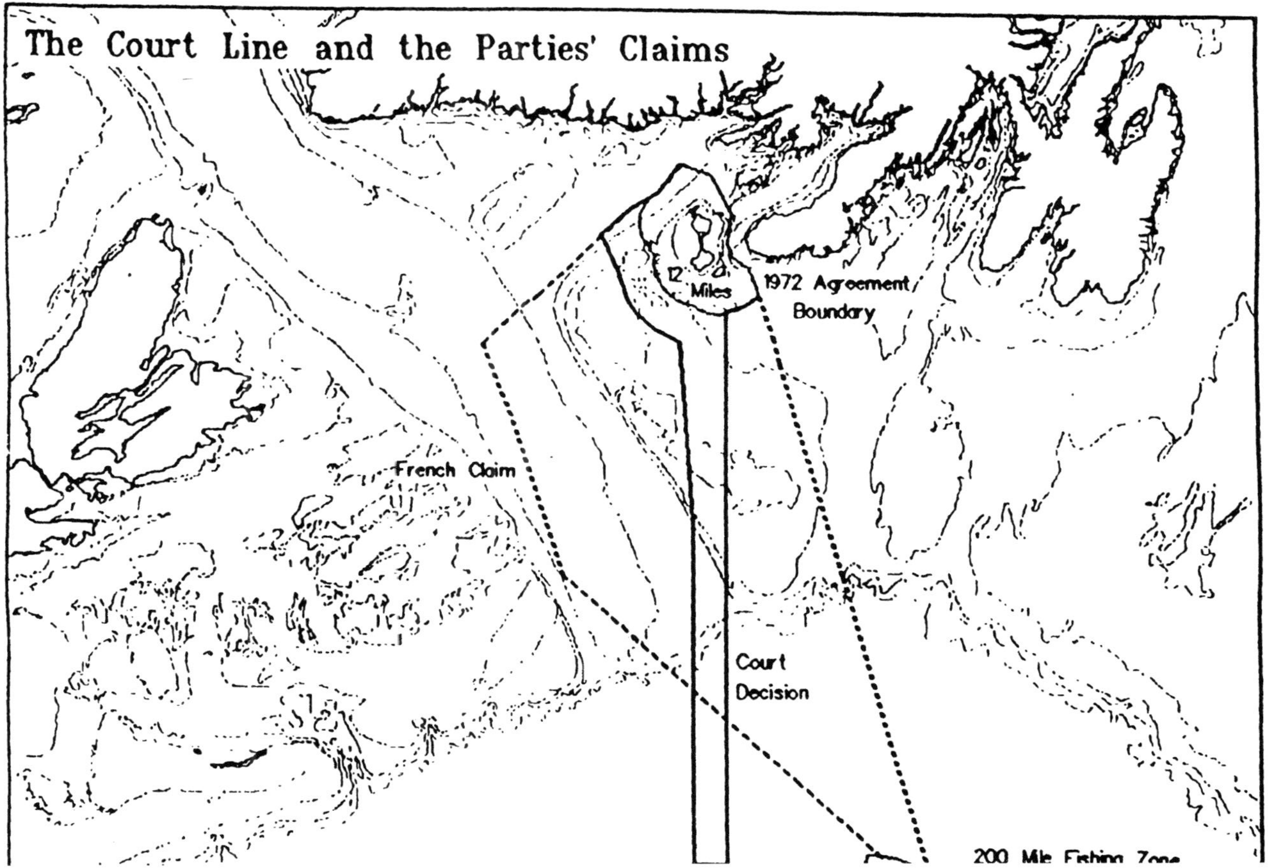

The Court Line and the Parties' Claims

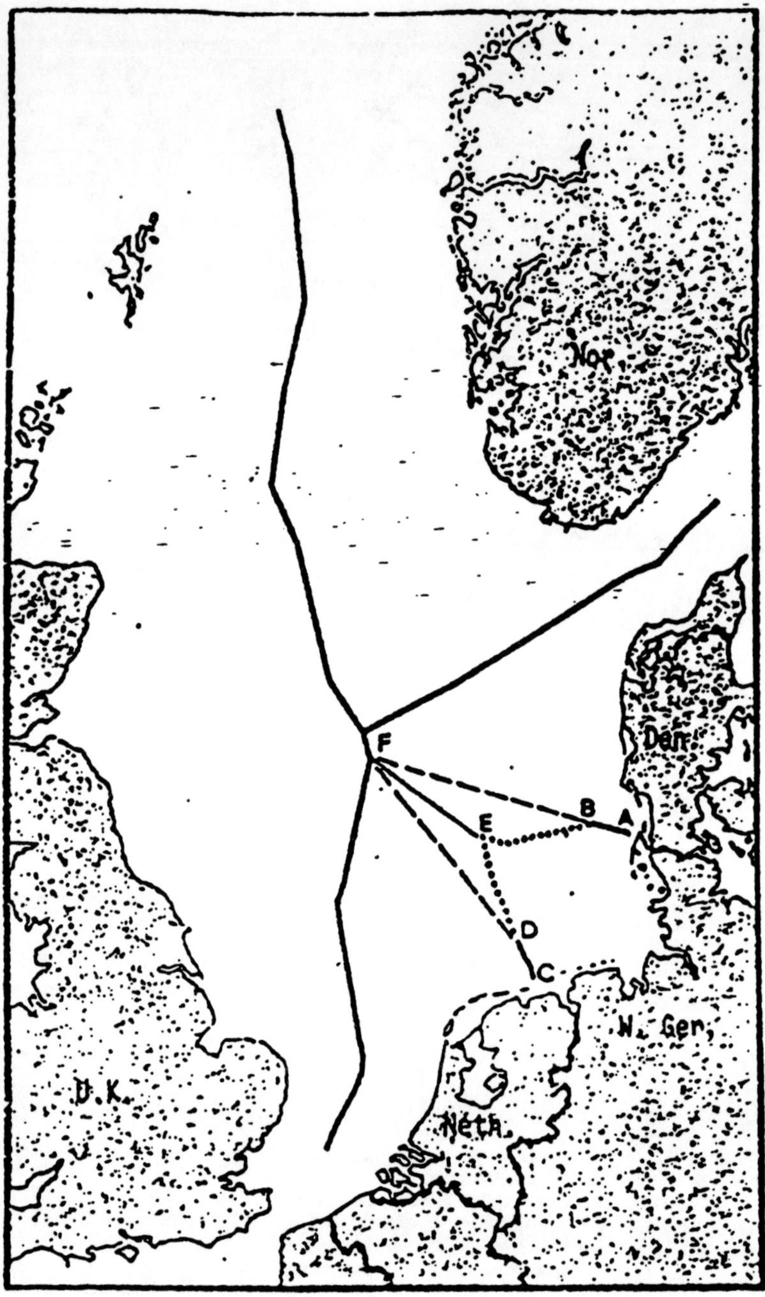

Nor.
Den.
F
B
A
E
D
C
N. Ger.
U.K.
Neth.

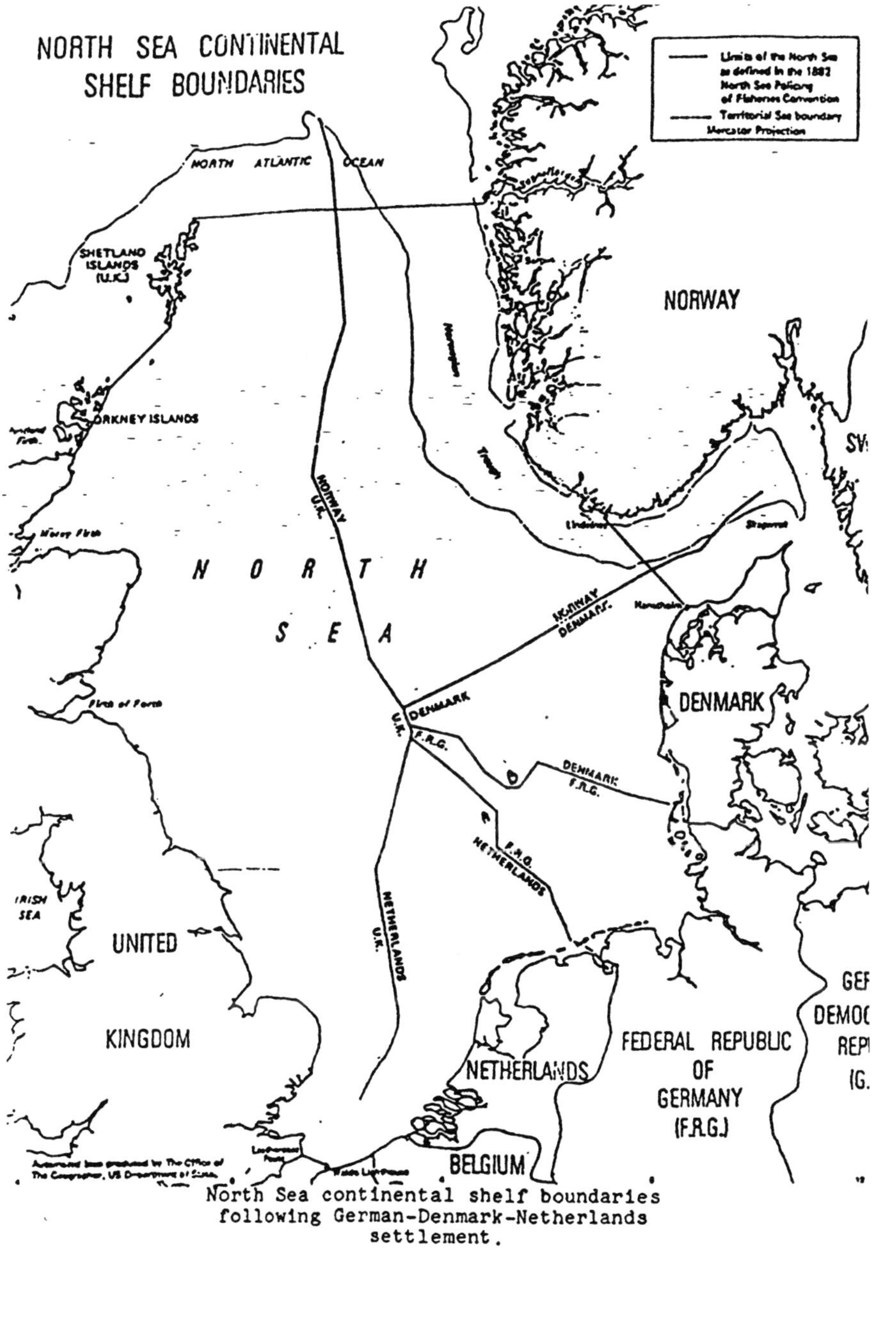

North Sea continental shelf boundaries following German-Denmark-Netherlands settlement.

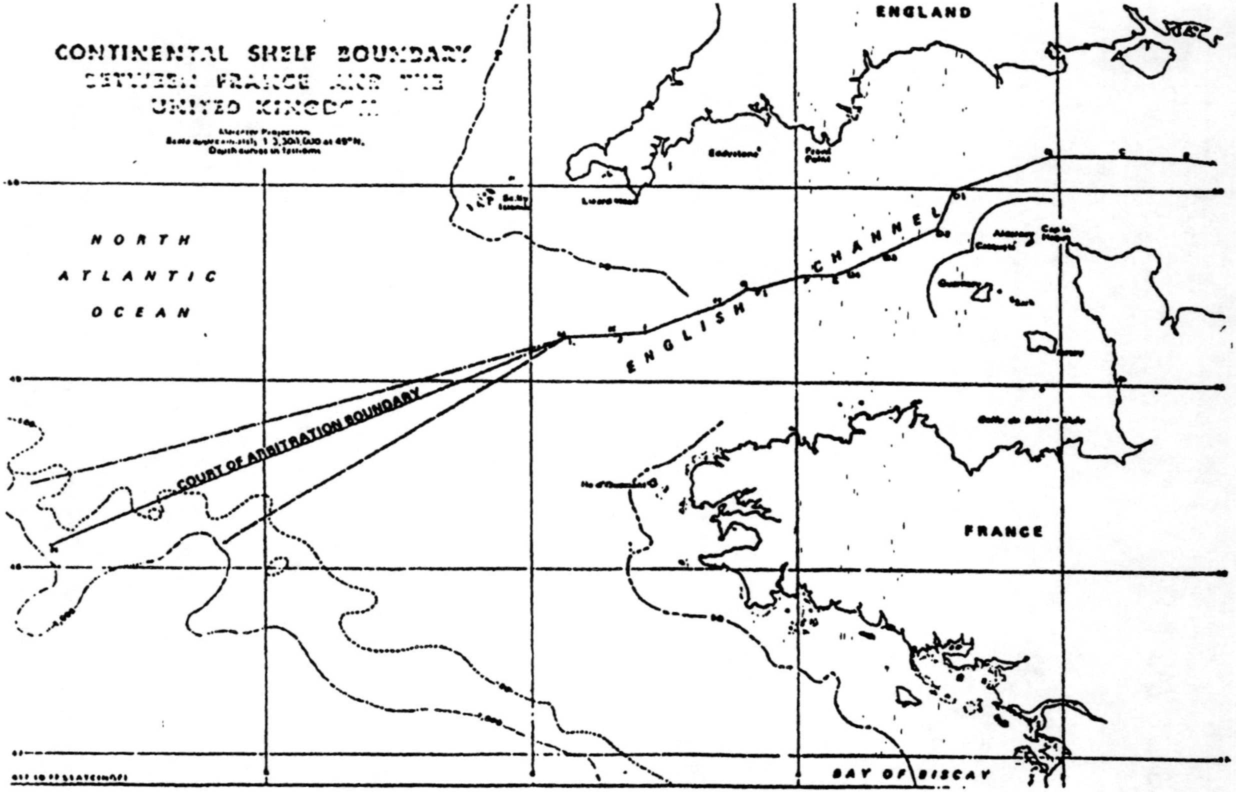

U.K.-France continental shelf boundary
as decided by Court of Arbitration in
Delimitation of the Continental Shelf case

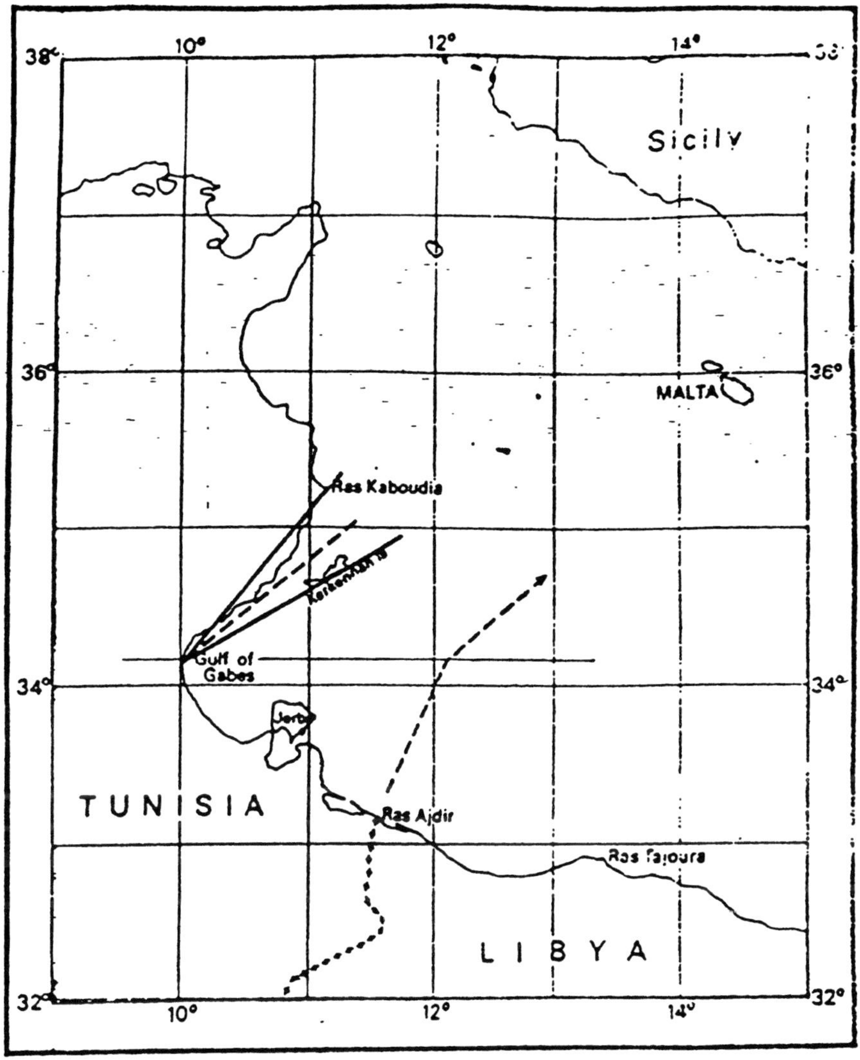

MAP No. 3

For illustrative purposes only, and without prejudice to the role of the experts in determining the delimitation line with exactness

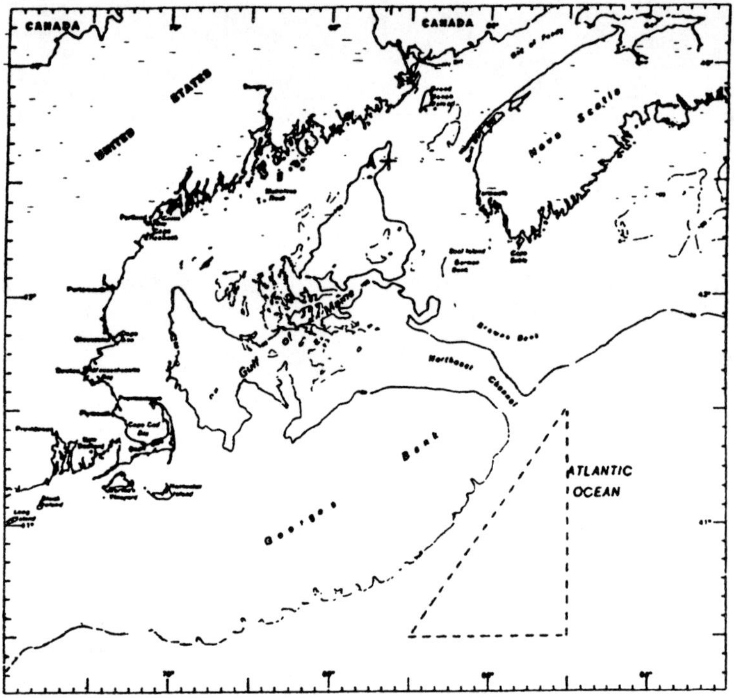

Map No. 1

General Map of the Region, Showing the Starting-Point for the Delimitation Line and the Area for its Termination

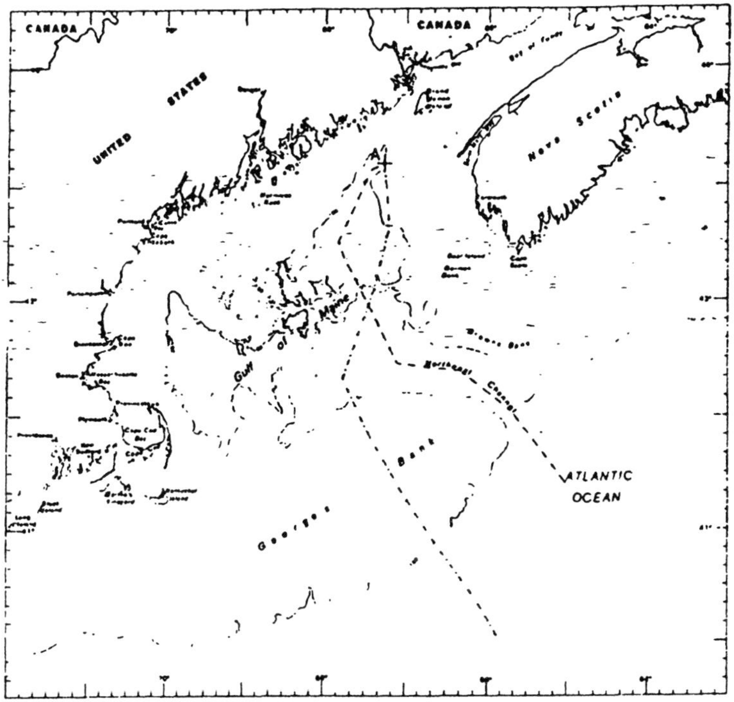

MAP NO 2

LIMITS OF FISHERY ZONES AND CONTINENTAL SHELF CLAIMED BY THE PARTIES, AT 1 MARCH 1977

(see paragraphs 68-70)

United States line - - - - - - -

Canadian line - · - · - -

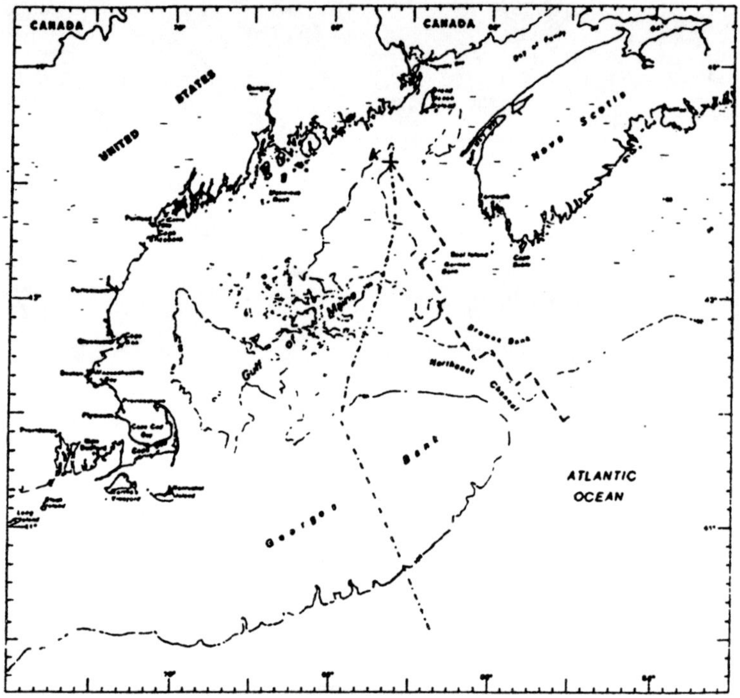

MAP NO. 3

DELIMITATION LINES PROPOSED BY THE PARTIES BEFORE THE CHAMBER

(see paragraphs 71, 77-78)

United States line - - - - - - -

Canadian line -·-·- -

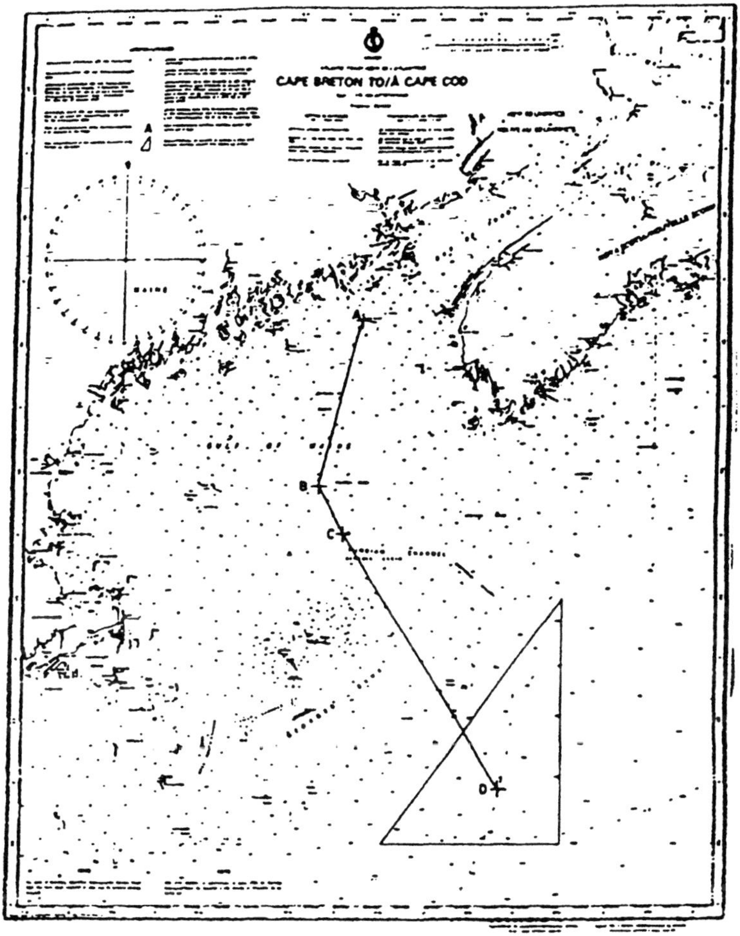

DELIMITATION LINE DRAWN BY THE CHAMBER

CHAPTER 8

THE DEEP OCEAN FLOOR; THE "SEABED QUESTION"

A. INTRODUCTION.

As most interpretations of the Convention on the Continental Shelf make clear, national (coastal state) jurisdiction over natural resources in the seabed and subsoil does not extend to mid-ocean but terminates at some point off the coast. This limit, should the 1982 treaty come into force, is defined by Article 76 of that convention. Once that formula is applied, there remains a large portion of the floor beyond the limits of national jurisdiction. Historically, the resources of that area have been considered *res nullius*, subject to appropriation by individuals or nations much in the same manner as free swimming fish beyond the limit of territorial waters.

In the early days of the Third U.N. Conference on the law of the sea, it became clear that some new legal regime and appropriate international organization would have to be developed to govern mining activities on the deep seabed. But major philosophical and ideological differences plagued the negotiations. The texts resulting from those negotiations remain to this day controversial, and are at the heart of what some describe as the failure of the conference to achieve its long-sought goals.

The materials in this chapter are organized, following an introductory section on seabed geology, into two main themes. The first is a brief examination of the history of the subject leading to the beginning of negotiations, from which the philosophical differences should become apparent. But the major emphasis in this chapter is placed on an examination of the texts that emerged from the negotiations, and a critical analysis of their adequacy to solve the seabed mining dilemma. Since the United States rejected the treaty primarily because of these provisions, the student should become familiar with the precise objections of the U.S. and be able to analyze their soundness. Because the provisions relating to seabed mining are complex, they will not be considered in order, but rather in clumps of provisions related to a particular functional issue, such as the organization, powers and functions of the International Seabed Authority, the access system, financial implications of the treaty, etc.

B. SOME MARINE GEOLOGY AND SEABED MINING TECHNOLOGY.

V. E. McKelvey and Frank F. H. Wang, "WORLD SEABED MINERAL RESOURCES," Department of the Interior, U.S. Geological Survey (1969)

The physiography of the large ocean basins beyond the continental margin and rise is also varied but is dominated by the following features...: (1) Oceanic ridges and rises, often called "midocean" although they do not everywhere occur in midocean. These form a nearly continuous but branching worldwide mountain chain with a total length of about 75,000 miles. A rift valley along the crest is a prominent feature of the ridges in many places, as are volcanoes and volcanic fields, many of which are islands. (2) Abyssal plains and hills, lying on both sides of the oceanic rises and underlain by a thin veneer of pelagic sediments. (3) Individual volcanoes and composite volcanic ridges formed by over-lapping volcanoes, and scattered over the ocean basins but often clustered to form groups of islands or seamounts and linear chains along oceanic margins. (4) Trenches, commonly present along volcanic island arcs or young mountain chains at the periphery of the large ocean basins.

In some places small ocean basins lie between two continents or between continents and offshore island arcs. Characteristically, they have an abyssal plain below a depth of 2000 meters, and a few also have trenches along the concave side of the bordering island arcs. Those that border land areas with large surface runoff have trapped erosional debris and hence contain thick accumulations of sediments analagous to those beneath the continental rises.

Many physiographic features of the ocean basins are related to volcanism, crustial subsidence, and possibly to a process of ocean-floor spreading that brings basaltic igneous rock to the surface along the oceanic ridges, and carries new crust away from the mid-oceanic ridge at the rate of a few to 10-15 cm a year. Much is still to be learned about this process, but many now believe that the continents have split apart, along what are now these oceanic ridges, and drifted away from each other, and that the continental mass is still in the process of separation in the Atlantic Ocean, Gulf of California, Red Sea, and African rift-valley system....

In contrast to continental crust, oceanic crust is thin and relatively uniform in composition. Basaltic bedrock lies at or near the surface over much of the oceanic rise and ridge; and, although sediments increase in thickness toward the edge of the ocean basin (reflecting the longer time available for their accumulation on the older parts of the ocean floor), they probably do not attain a thickness of more than a few hundred meters in most places. The basalt originates by partical melting of rocks in the underlying mantle; and while other rocks and minerals are produced in this process, they are not as varied in composition as those that result from the action and interaction of the processes operating on and within the continental crust. Nevertheless, the ocean basins contain large concentrations of manganese, nickel, copper, cobalt, and other metals in manganese-oxide nodules, crusts, and pavements on the surface of the sea bottom; and the ocean basins probably also contain these and other metals, such as zinc, mercury, chromite, and platinum, in other kinds of deposits formed from the differentiation of the mantle material from which the basalt itself was derived.

....

Surficial deposits of manganese-oxide nodules, crusts, and pavements, which are currently of more interest for their contents of nickel, copper, and cobalt than for manganese, are largely confined to the deep ocean floor, generally at depths of 3500 to 4500 meters, and to the seamounts within it. In several areas, however, they occur near land -- notably on the Blake Plateau off eastern United States, off the west coast of Baja California, in the Baltic Sea, and near some of the islands in large ocean basins.... In most of these nearshore areas, however, their metal content is much lower than that of the nodules far from land. Although bottom photographs and closely spaced samples show that nodules are extensive in many areas, the same kinds of data show that both their abundance and composition vary. Available information is not sufficient to infer their continuity between stations from which they have been reported or their absence in areas where they have not yet been found. Cores show that they are present in the sediments a few meters beneath the surface at some stations...where they are not present at the surface. Inspection of the results of available bottom photographs in the Pacific...however, suggests that nodules are absent from the surface of the bottom in some large areas and that they are particularly abundant in others.... Even if subsequent exploration shows that the nodules and related deposits are continuous over large areas, their minability may be adversely affected locally by irregularity of the bottom surface, presence of extensive crusts or pavements troublesome to break and lift, and deleterious impurities.

The composition of nodules also varies greatly. Again there appear to be regional variations, but published attempts to define the pattern of variation have not been satisfactory.... Manganese is nearly 50 percent in some samples, which are generally low in the other metals. Copper and nickel tend to vary roughly in proportion to each other and may be as much as 2 percent; cobalt may also be as much as 2 percent. Whether or not minable quantities contain such concentrations remains to be demonstrated.

The nodules constitute a huge resource. Mero estimates that they aggregate 1.7 trillion tons and contain 400 billion tons of manganese, 16.4 billion tons of nickel, 8.8 billion tons of copper, and 918 billion tons of cobalt....

"ECONOMIC IMPLICATIONS OF SEA-BED MINERAL DEVELOPMENT IN THE INTERNATIONAL AREA: REPORT OF THE SECRETARY-GENERAL," U.N. Doc. A/CONF.62/25 (22 May 1974), pp. 12-22

Deep sea-bed mining is a complex, multifaceted undertaking. Exploitation of nodules may be classified into three broad stages, namely: (1) the search for mineral deposits, (2) mining, and (3) metallurgical processing. A summary of the most important steps involved in each stage along with the most recent activities of companies and other institutions involved in research and development is presented below.

1. The search for nodule deposits

In the search for nodules, activities of a scientific character can generally be distinguished from the stages of exploration and evaluation because of their different objectives. Together they form a continuum of knowledge....

(a) Procedures used

Exploration is the broadly based survey using all available methods: the search generally begins over a large area and progressively narrows down to sites with mining potential. In industry circles this stage is generally referred to as "prospecting". It requires mapping, sampling of surficial and sub-bottom materials and making geophysical and geochemical measurements, and is best approached as a phased programme of increasingly more detailed surveys.

A large array of scientific instruments and devices are required to collect the necessary data.... Exploration vessels must carry sophisticated positioning equipment (satellite, celestial) and computers to correlate all sample data and other observations with precise co-ordinates. Acoustic and magnetic systems are used to obtain geophysical information about the nature of the sea bottom. The actual search for nodule deposits is made through optical systems such as closed-circuit T.V. and still and movie cameras.

The spacing at which samples are taken depends on results obtained, and generally range from 5 to 50 miles. The devices most commonly used for collecting samples are the free-fall sampler also called "boomerang", gravity-corer, piston-corer and dredge. The free-fall sampler is extensively used by institutions and industry groups such as Kennecott, Centre national pour l'exploration des oceans (CNEXO), Preussag, and Global Marine. These free-fall devices grab a small sample of nodules from an area of about 1 square foot. Corers are used to derive information on the sediments underlying the nodule deposit. Dredge sampling is used to collect a large volume of nodules for metallurigcal testing from areas known to contain attractive nodule deposits.

A detailed appraisal follows the discovery and outlining of a potential mine site. The objective is to provide information upon which to base feasibility studies. Recoverable nodule grade and concentration estimates are the key parameter sought in evaluation surveys. The equipment required for evaluation is similar to that needed for the exploration stage. However, greater attention must be given to the precise correlation of sample data and other observations with their geographic location.

....

2. Nodule mining technology

The mining systems under development comprise four major components: the mining/loading head; materials elevation/hoisting system; surface facility; and product transportation to shore plant....

(a) Nodule collection

Several forms of nodule gathering apparatus are under development. The dredge variety currently is thought to have the best potential for use in commercial production. Typically the dredge incorporates a sizing system to pick up nodules within a certain size range while excluding very large pieces as well as fine bottom silt. The mining equipment must be kept as mechanically simple as possible to minimize maintenance. One problem encountered, however, is the construction and operation of the very wide dredge head needed to collect the desired volume of nodules per hour (200 to 400 tons). The large dredge size is required because of the relatively low nodule concentration on the sea floor (1.5 to 5 lb/sq. ft.) and the maximum practical speed for operation of the system (1 to 3 knots).

....

(b) Materials elevation

Another critical factor in nodule mining is the materials elevation/hoisting system. Continuous systems can be based on: air lift, hydrolift (hydraulic hoisting), light-media lift and mechanical lift such as the CLB system. Batch systems include wireline dredging which, although useful for collecting tonnage samples, is not regarded as an economic large-scale production system due to its high cost when used at great depths. A bouyant hopper (submersible hopper) system has been proposed. Whether this system is being developed for materials elevation is not known, although the concept is somewhat akin to the Summa Corporation barge.

An air-lift is technically a three phase flow -- air, nodules and water. Compressed air is injected into the main pipe at various water depths to sustain the lifting action. Deepsea Ventures successfully tested an airlift device in 2,500 feet of water over the Blake Plateau in 1970....

A hydrolift is technically a two-phase flow -- nodules and water. The pump can be located close to the bottom or at an intermediate depth.... The technology for hydraulic and hydrolift pumping is well-developed and is used, for instance, in the coal industry. But working at such depths and lifting such volumes as required in nodule mining represent giant steps beyond current capability....

The Hughes system is thought to operate on the hydrolift principle. The major component of the system are the 36,000-ton Hughes Glomar Explorer and a sea floor mining vehicle which is connected to the ship by a string of 16-inch pipe and an umbilical cable that supplies electric power and control circuits. The mining vehicle is too large and heavy to be handled by the ship's gear in a conventional manner and must be installed onto a submersible barge which meets the ship in calm waters of a specified depth. There, the barge submerges and the docking legs of the ship engage the mining vehicle which is then connected to pipestring lowered from the ship's rugged derrick....

The CLB system uses a continuous polypropelene braided rope with dredge buckets attached. At the top, the loop is wound through traction motors while the bottom part of the loop drags along the ocean bottom. The CLB system was tested off Tahiti in August 1970. A later CLB test in August/September 1972 recovered seven tons of nodules off Hawaii. Several participants of the CLB consortium under the leadership of CNEXO of France, are continuing work on a modification of the CLB, which would use two ships working in tandem;...the main components of this modified system are expected to be ready for tests in 1974. Sumitomo is developing continuous ship handling equipment for the dredge baskets and is also doing additional research in the operation of the CLB system....

(c) Surface vessel

The so-called first generation mining systems are likely to use the ship itself as the surface platform. Tug assistance may be used for directional movement in some systems. A pipe system for nodule lifting will require a derrick aboard ship. Alternatives to a mine ship are a spar buoy or semi-submersible platform. A spar buoy is a long cigar-shaped semi-submersible which when tilted on one end creates a small but highly stable working platform on its other end. Semi-submersible floating platforms are extensively used in the off-shore oil industry for work in deeper waters.... Both the spar buoy and the semi-submersibles, however, have a poor capability for lateral movement.

The first generation of mining ships will do minimal processing at sea -- perhaps crushing and/or drying the nodules -- and the nodules will be tranported in bulk by the mining ship itself (particularly a CLB mining ship) or transferred at sea to a dry or bulk carrier.

3. Metallurgical processing

Nodules have a complex microscopic structure and are composed of fine-grained oxide material. They can vary widely in chemical and physical properties according to location, e.g. Blake Plateau nodules from the Atlantic are high in calcium, whereas those from the North Pacific are more siliceous. As a result, processing technology and costs for one type of nodule may not apply elsewhere.

....

The two basic approaches to nodule processing can be classified as pyrometallurgical and hydrometallurgical, the latter based on chloride, ammonia or sulfur oxide reaction. Some of these processes are considered technically possible, but not necessarily economically feasible. Heavy emphasis is being placed on the development of hydrometallurgical nodule processing systems.

ED. NOTE: The reference in the above study to the Hughes mining operation is of interest. At the time it was believed that Hughes was well advanced in the development of deep seabed mining. A few years later it was discovered that this was just a cover. The ship, barge and derrick was actually constructed by Hughes under contract with the CIA for use in recovering a sunken Russian submarine in the North Pacific Ocean and was never intended for mining.

C. THE "SEABED QUESTION" IN THE UNITED NATIONS.

1. EARLY PROCEEDINGS: THE SEABED COMMITTEE.

a. BACKGROUND

Hollick, U.S. FOREIGN POLICY AND THE LAW OF THE SEA (1981) 196-201[1]

The twenty-fifth General Assembly voted in December 1970 to convene the Third UN Conference on the Law of the Sea (UNCLOS III) in 1973. Three initiatives were instrumental in prompting the decision. The first was a proposal by Ambassador Arvid Pardo of Malta to create an international regime for the deep seabed. This proposal sparked the creation of the UN Seabed Committee to negotiate principles to govern an international seabed regime. The second action that laid the groundwork for UNCLOS III was the formulation by the U.S. government of a detailed draft treaty on a seabed mining regime for the area beyond the 200-meter isobath. The U.S. presented its draft to the UN Seabed Committee in August of 1970. The proposal signalled U.S. willingness to negotiate seriously on a deep seabed mining regime. The third major impetus to a conference evolved from bilateral discussions between the United States and the Soviet Union. Sharing similar navigational concerns, both powers proposed an international negotiation that would address the related issues of the territorial sea, transit through international straits, and fisheries. U.S. officially announced its position on these three issues in the spring of 1970 and called for an international negotiation. The sentiment prevailing among developing nations in the UN Seabed Committee augured ill for separating negotiations on seabed issues from those on territorial sea-related questions. Instead, developing countries pressed for a single conference to handle all law of the sea questions. They hoped in this manner to secure greater concessions from the developed world. Despite U.S. and Soviet concern over the feasibility of such a comprehensive undertaking, the UN General Assembly voted in favor of a comprehensive UN conference on the law of the sea.

The international politics of law of the sea influence, and were in turn affected by, domestic U.S. ocean policy. International pressure was channeled into the U.S. decision-making process through the UN negotiations. The U.S. government felt compelled to be responsive in the negotiations and sought in vain to formulate policies that would cast the U.S. in a leadership role. The development of a national policy acceptable to the various agencies of government and interest groups proved a formidible task. Prior to the establishment of the UN Seabed Committee, agencies such as Interior, Defense, and the National Science Foundation had pursued their individual ocean policies with little coordination and occasional conflict. As the use of the oceans intensified, defense considerations seemed to suggest a very different policy from that suited to seabed resource concerns. This emerging divergence in policy developed into a direct confrontation in 1969 and 1970. In spite of the need to formulate a national policy for the UN Seabed Committee, the Defense and Interior Departments could not agree on the optimal outer limit for the national continental shelf or the nature of the seabed regime beyond.

Under the new Nixon administration, the dispute was processed through the National Security Council system presided over by Henry Kissinger. The policy ultimately selected by President

---

[1]. Reprinted by permission of the Princeton University Press

Nixon in May 1970 was transposed into treaty language and presented to the UN Seabed Committee in August 1970 as a draft treaty on the seabed. It reflected a temporary victory for security concerns in that it limited national jurisdiction over the continental shelf to areas within the 200-meter isobath. Although this policy was subsequently eroded by the combined forces of domestic coastal resource interests and foreign coastal states, it set the direction for U.S. policy for two or three years. The process of arriving at the 1970 policy had an even more lasting impact. The policy dispute brought new actors into the debate. It also impelled the principal protagonists to consolidate the law of the sea offices within their respective agencies. And finally, it led to the establishment of an interagency coordinating mechanism which managed law of the sea questions for the duration of the UN negotiations.

THE U.S. AND THE UN SEABED COMMITTEE: 1967-1968

The Malta Initiative

On August 17, 1967, the Mission of Malta to the United Nations proposed including in the agenda of the General Assembly an item entitled "Declaration and Treaty Concerning the Reservation Exclusively for Peaceful Purposes of the Sea-Bed and of the Ocean Floor, Underlying the Seas Beyond the Limits of Present National Jurisdiction, and the Use of their Resources in the Interests of Mankind." The memorandum attached to the proposal expressed concern that the rapid development of marine technology by developed countries would promote national claims to the seabed, the appropriation of seabed resources for the benefit of the few, and the use of the ocean floor for military purposes. To prevent such a course of events, the memorandum went on, the seabed should be declared the "common heritage of mankind" and a treaty should be drafted which would provide that the seabed would not be subject to national appropriation, would be reserved exclusively for peaceful purposes, would be explored by means consistent with the principles and purposes of the UN charter, and would be used and exploited in the "interests of mankind." It further provided that the net financial benefits from such activities would be used primarily to assist the development of poor countries, and it suggested that an international agency be established to assure international jurisdiction over the seabed. No reference was made to aspects of the law of the sea unrelated to the seabed.

On September 21, 1967, when Ambassador Pardo presented his reasons for proposing this item to the General Assembly's General Committee, the response of the United States ambassador, Arthur J. Goldberg, was highly favorable. Ambassador Goldberg declared that the Maltese item was of great importance and wholeheartedly supported its inscription on the General Assembly's agenda. He agreed with Ambassador Pardo that efforts on ocean research must "be put on a more effective international footing." Goldberg then strongly endorsed "the expanding interest of the General Assembly in this field." He pointed out that "this organization is in a position to assume leadership in enlisting the peaceful cooperation of all nations in developing the world's oceans and ocean floor." He concluded that the item should be given "early consideration" in the first committee.

Ambassador Goldberg's enthusiasm for the Maltese proposal was not shared on Capitol Hill. Upon its appearance, resolutions pro and con were introduced in the Congress with the cons largely outnumbering the pros. Nearly two dozen resolutions were introduced in the House opposing any move to vest control over seabed resources in an international organization. A similar resolution was introduced in the United States Senate.

The House resolutions relating to the Malta proposal were referred to the Committee on Foreign Affairs and assigned to the Subcommittee on International Organizations and Actions. The House hearings began on September 22 and continued intermittently through October. In the course of the hearings, a number of congressmen expressed a deep hostility toward the United Nations. This hostility was combined with the conviction that the Maltese proposal for internationalizing seabed resources was highly detrimental to the national economic interest. In some cases the economic interest was perceived as requiring access for American industry to seabed resources extending as far as the middle of the oceans.

The State Department position on the Malta proposal was ambivalent, reflecting a division of opinion within the department as well as among the interested agencies. On the day after the enthusiastic Goldberg statement, David H. Popper, deputy assistant secretary of state for international organization affairs, displayed a notable lack of enthusiasm for the Malta proposal in testimony before the foreign affairs subcommittee. Mr. Popper assured the congressmen present that "we have no intention of taking substantive action on this proposal at this time," and that "we do not intend, in the course of consideration of the question in the General Assembly, to dispose of title to the deep-sea bottom, either to the United Nations or to any other recipient." The tenor of Mr. Popper's remarks may be partially explained by State's desire to prevent Congress from adopting restrictive measures. To this end, he assured the foreign affairs subcommittee that Congress would be fully consulted regarding any proposals that the United States might contemplate.

The attitude of the Congress was not uniform, however, and could not have been the sole cause of the State Department's vacillation on the Maltese item. Several resolutions were introduced in the House supporting the Maltese approach, and two of the three resolutions introduced in the Senate also favored it. The Senate resolutions were referred to the Committee on Foreign Relations and a hearing was scheduled for November 29. At the hearing, before a committee not unfavorably disposed to the Malta proposal, State Deparment officials clung to the view that a U.S. government position on the Malta proposal was premature at that time. Questioned about the merits of resolutions as far-reaching and detailed as those of Senator Pell, Joseph Sisco, assistant secretary of state for international organization affairs responded that the executive branch was "in favor of moving as rapidly as the accumulation of knowledge will permit...and we would hope that we can begin to move ahead with reasonable speed."

The inconsistency and hesitancy plaguing State Department efforts to develop a position on the Malta proposal were in large measure the result of simple unpreparedness. At the October 19 hearing before the House Foreign Affairs Committee, Herman Pollack, the director of the State Department's Bureau of International Scientific and Technological Affairs, confessed that the progress of the Ad Hoc Interagency Committee was "still developing preliminary governmental attitudes on the question." When the committee had been established, Pollack said, we had simply not "quite anticipated the speed at which the problem would be put before us." Over a month later, Mr. Pollack again testified on the progress of the ad hoc committee, this time before the Senate Foreign Relations Committee. Mr. Pollack indicated "that a number of working groups and task forces have been established to consider the variety of problems that are posed by the future of the ocean floor, and that the principal consequence at this point in time has been to scope the problem, to examine some of the possible alternatives." This was the extent of progress in the interagency committee during the three and one-half months following the Malta resolution.

The official position of the U.S. government as it emerged at the end of 1967 indicated a backing off from the approbation for the Malta proposal expressed in Goldberg's September 21 statement. Ambassador Goldberg's intervention in Committee One on November 8 accurately expressed this changed attitude and was notably reserved in its evaluation of the Malta proposal. Goldberg presented three suggestions that were intended as conservative alternatives to the Pardo proposal. He proposed that the General Assembly establish a committee on the oceans to plan a comprehensive program of international cooperation, and that the General Assembly, through the committee on the oceans begin to develop "general standards and principles to guide states and their nationals in the exploration and use of the deep ocean floor."

The manner in which the three proposals had been developed within the government indicates the extent of interagency disagreement on a U.S. position and illustrates the relatively free hand that the State Department had to formulate ocean policy in 1967. The Ad Hoc Interagency Committee had been unable to secure the concurrence of all its members to the proposals and, in the absence of agency-wide agreement, the committee could not formally recommend or endorse them. Herman Pollack nonetheless presented the proposals to the Congress and Ambassador Goldberg took them to the UN. Although obviously free to formulate ocean policy without the unanimous support of the Ad Hoc Interagency Committee, the State Department did not use this freedom to devise far-reaching proposals. Instead, the Department tacitly acknowledged the strength of the opposition to the Malta proposal in Congress and the executive branch by limiting itself to three very cautions offerings. The proposals for an ocean committee, a program of international cooperation, and the formulation of principles to guide ocean use merely skirted the Malta proposal while trying to lead UN deliberations in less dangerous directions.

The most important outcome of the Malta proposal in the Twenty-second General Assembly was the establishment of a committee to give sustained consideration to the seabed resources question. The General Assembly rejected both the Soviet position in favor of leaving ocean issues to the Intergovernmental Oceanographic Commission and the U.S. proposal for a committee dealing with all ocean issues. It voted instead to establish a thirty-five nation "Ad Hoc Committee to Study the Peaceful Uses of the Sea-Beds and Ocean Floor Beyond the Limits of National Jurisdiction." The Ad Hoc Seabed Committee was charged with preparing a study of "practical means to promote international cooperation in the exploration, conservation and use of the seabed and the ocean floor, and subsoil thereof...and of their resources."

Francis T. Christy, "ALTERNATIVE REGIMES FOR MARINE RESOURCES UNDERLYING THE HIGH SEAS", 1 Natural Resources Lawyer (No. 2) 63, 66 (1968)[2]

In considering the alternative regimes, the basic objective is to arrive at a regime that will be viable over the long-run and that will encourage the economically efficient, peaceful, and orderly exploitation of the minerals of the sea floor. Its success will be measured against three criteria. First it must permit economically efficient operations. Secondly, it must be acceptable to a sufficient number of nations both in the long and the short run. And third, it must be feasible.

2. Reprinted by permission of the American Bar Assocition

The prime requirement for an economically efficient operation is the assurance of exclusive rights for a sufficiently large area for a sufficient length of time. These rights should be adquate to permit both exploration and exploitation, as they do for oil leases on the U.S. continental shelf. Economic efficiency should be considered not only in terms of the entrepreneur, but also in terms of society. Social costs, such as those for protecting the entrepreneur's exclusive rights, of ensuring an efficient allocation of capital and labor, and, possibly, of preventing external effects (such as pollution) must also be considered in the measurement of benefits and costs by which efficiency is gauged. Efficient management programs for the minerals of the sea floor may require some payment to the public, whether the public be of the flag nation or the world community.

The second criterion is that of acceptability. The implementation and viability of any regime will depend upon how it is viewed by those nations that have an influence on the decisions. This is essentially the question of how the regime affects the distribution of the wealth of the seas' bottom -- or, more accurately, how each participant perceives his own net gains (economic and other) in relationship to the net gains of all other participants.

Assuming that the two criteria mentioned above can be met, the third test of a legal regime is that of feasibility. To meet this test, it may be necessary to devlop new institutions -- institutions for administration, enforcement, and adjudication. The necessity for new institutions should not be considered an impediment to the establishment of the regime. Indeed, it is in keeping that these totally new resources and totally new problems should require new institutions.

ED. NOTE: In the early days, there was disagreement among writers concerning the nature of any proposed mining regime. On the one hand, writers such as Browning, envisaged mining taking place under a regime that required the acquisition of property rights over portions of the deep sea bottom. Christy, on the other hand, in setting forth his three criteria, seems to envision a fixed time right to extract minerals under the supervision of some new international institution. Before reading on, which do you think is more preferrable or more feasible?

Lyndon B. Johnson, "REMARKS OF THE PRESIDENT OF THE UNITED STATES AT THE COMMISSIONING OF THE OCEANOGRAPHIC RESEARCH SHIP 'THE OCEANOGRAPHER'", July 13, 1966

> [U]nder no circumstances...must we ever allow the prospects of rich harvest and mineral wealth to create a new form of colonial competition among the maritime nations. We must be careful to avoid a race to grab and to hold the lands under the high seas. We must ensure that the deep seas and the ocean bottoms are, and remain, the legacy of all human beings.

b. AT THE UNITED NATIONS

There is a rich history of the steps taken by the United Nations General Assembly in the years leading up to the formal opening of the Third United Nations Conference on the Law of the Sea. Much of this history is reflected in a series of resolutions adopted by the General Assembly pertaining to this subject. The pertinent resolutions are summarized here, with the more important ones being set out in full.

The issue of the seabeds was first generated at the United Nations when, in 1967, the mission of Malta presented a note verbale to the Secretary General requesting that the following item be placed on the agenda of the twenty-second session of the Assembly: "Declaration and treaty concerning the reservation exclusively for peaceful purposes of the sea-bed and of the ocean floor, underlying the seas beyond the limits of present national jurisdiction, and the use of their resources in the interests of mankind." The note was accompanied by a memorandum setting forth the reasons, and concluding that:

"It is, therefore, considered that the time has come to declare the sea-bed and the ocean floor a common heritage of mankind and that immediate steps should be taken to draft a treaty embodying, *inter alia*, the following principles:

"(a) The sea-bed and ocean floor, underlying the seas beyond the limits of present national jurisdiction, are not subject to national appropriation in any manner whatsoever;

"(b) The exploration of the sea-bed and ocean floor beyond the limits of present national jurisdiction, shall be undertaken in a manner consistent with the Principles and Purposes of the Charter of the United Nations;

"(c) The use of the sea-bed and ocean floor, underlying the seas beyond the limits of present national jurisdiction, and their economic exploitation shall be undertaken with the aim of safeguarding the interests of mankind. The net financial benefits derived from the use and exploitation of the sea-bed and ocean floor shall be used primarily to promote the development of poor countries;

"(d) The sea-bed and ocean floor, underlying the seas beyond the limits of present national jurisdiction, shall be reserved exclusively for peaceful purposes in perpetuity."

The memorandum also called for the creation of an international agency to assume jurisdiction over the sea-bed, to regulate and supervise all activities thereon, and to ensure that these activities conform to the principals and provisions of the proposed treaty.

In response to discussion of this agenda item, the General Assembly, at its twenty-second session in 1967, established an Ad Hoc Committee to study the peaceful uses of the sea-bed in all aspects, and to report to the Secretary General (Resolution 2340 (XXII), December 18, 1967). The committee consisted of 35 designated countries. The report was to include a survey of activities taking place in the area or that had taken place, an account of scientific, technical, economic and legal aspects of the problem, and an indication of the means to promote cooperation in the exploration and use of the sea-bed.

The Ad Hoc Committee held three sessions (United Nations Headquarters, March 18-27 1968, and June 17-July 9, 1968; Rio de Janeiro, August 19-30, 1968). Two working groups were established, one concerned with economic and technical aspects of the item, and the other concerned with legal aspects. The chairman of the Ad Hoc Committee was Mr. Hamilton Shirley Amerasinghe of Ceylon (now Sri Lanka); the chairman of the Economic and Technical Working Group was Mr. Roger Denorme of Belgium; and the chairman of the Legal Working Group was Mr. Leopoldo Benites of Ecuador. The "Report of the Ad Hoc Committee to Study the Peaceful Uses of the Sea-Bed and the Ocean Floor Beyond the Limits of National Jurisdiction," U.N. Doc. A/7230, was adopted by the Committee on August 30, 2968, and was subsequently delivered to the twenty-third session of the General Assembly.

The Report of the Ad Hoc Committee was included on the agenda of the twenty-third session of the General Assembly and was allocated to the First Committee (Political and Security) for consideration and report. At the conclusion of its deliberations, the First Committee recommended to the General Assembly the adoption of four draft resolutions. The General Assembly considered these recommendations in December, 1968, and the resolutions were adopted by it without modification.

The Ad Hoc Committee fulfilled its mandate with the completion and approval of its report. But it was obvious that there was much more work to be accomplished. At its twenty-third session, therefore, the General Assembly adopted Resolution 2467 A (XXIII) establishing a Committee on the Peaceful Uses of the Sea-Bed and the Ocean Floor beyond the Limits of National Jurisdiction (the seabed committee, for short), composed of 42 states, and instructed the Committe to conduct further studies. Resolution 2467 C (XXIII) also adopted in 1968, requested the Secretary-General to undertake a study on the question of establishing in due time appropriate international machinery for the promotion of the exploration and exploitation of the seabed resources, and to report to the seabed committee.

The Seabed Committee began work in 1969 and continued until 1973. It met twice annually. Following each meeting, resolutions were proposed and adopted in the General Assembly. A narrative account of the work of the committee is far beyond the scope of this book, and would serve no particularly useful purpose at this stage. The Department of State Bulletins covering the period provides useful information of the substantive issues discussed, and are readily available to those having such an historical interest.

2. THE "MORATORIUM" AND "PRINCIPLES" RESOLUTIONS.

a. THE MORATORIUM.

In 1969, the General Assembly adopted four new resolutions. In Resolution 2574-A (XXIV), the Secretary General was asked to ascertain the views of member states on convening a conference on the law of the sea to review the regimes of the high seas, the continental shelf, the territorial sea and contiguous zone, fishing conservation of the living resources of the high seas, and the seabed. Resolution 2574-B (XXIV) urged the Seabed Committee to further and expedite its work. Resolution 2574-C (XXIV) requested the Secretary-General to prepare a futher study, in more detail, on the international machinery for the seabed. A much more important resolution adopted a moratorium on seabed activities, and the full text follows.

UNITED NATIONS GENERAL ASSEMBLY

RESOLUTION 2574-D (XXIV)

December 15, 1969

(Adopted by 62-28-28)

The General Assembly,

Recalling its resolution 2467 A (XXIII) of 21 December 1968 to the effect that the exploitation of the resources of the sea-bed and ocean floor, and the subsoil thereof, beyond the limits of national jurisdiction, should be carried out for the benefit of mankind as a whole, irrespective of the geographical location of States, taking into account the special interests and needs of the developing countries,

Convinced that it is essential, for the achievment of this purpose, that such activities be carried out under an international regime, including appropriate international machinery,

Noting that this matter is under consideration by the Committee on the Peaceful Uses of the Sea-Bed and the Ocean Floor beyond the Limits of National Jurisdiction,

Recalling its resolution 2340 (XXII) of 18 December 1967 on the importance of preserving the sea-bed and the ocean floor, and the subsoil thereof, beyond the limits of national jurisdiction, from actions and uses which might be detrimental to the common interests of mankind,

Declares that, pending the establishment of the aforementioned international regime:

(a) States and persons, physical or juridical, are bound to refrain from all activities of exploitation of the resources of the area of the sea-bed and ocean floor, and the subsoil thereof, beyond the limits of national jurisdiction;

(b) No claim to any part of that area or its resources shall be recognized.

"U.S. EXPLAINS ITS VOTES ON SEABED RESOLUTIONS," 62 DEP'T STATE BULL. 89 (1970)

....

We are unable...to support the amendments...which envisage a conference covering all law-of-the-sea issues arising under any of the various regimes of the high seas; we are, in fact, strongly opposed to these amendments and will vote against them. Briefly, our reasons are the following: First, Mr. Chairman, we feel that the previous experience of the international community in endeavoring to grapple with the enormously difficult issues of law of the sea teaches the very clear lesson that these issues must be divided into manageable packages if they are to be dealt with with any reasonable expeditiousness and chance of success. Such an omnibus conference...would take years to prepare, with preparation on all of the issues involved being slowed inevitably to the pace necessary for the most difficult.

Our second reason for opposition flows from the first: We have been most concerned, as we had assumed most members of the Assembly were, that the United Nations continue without interruption or delay to work toward the establishment of a legally effective international regime for the seabed in the foreseeable future. This, indeed, is the very raison d'etre of the Special Committee on the Seabed. It is of course clear that the question of the limits of area to which such a regime will apply is an integral part of the complex of issues which must be resolved before this objective can be achieved. The Seabed Committee could in theory, of course, draft any number of regimes on paper; there will, however, be no regime in fact until the area of its application is decided. Consequently, we would be most disturbed at any indication that the United Nations was willing to take an integral part of the seabed issue -- the question of limits -- and merge it inextricably with the whole range of law-of-the-sea issues generally, with the result that it could be acted on effectively only when all issues of the law of the sea were themselves capable of resolution. Such a signal from the United Nations that it was willing to postpone effective agreement on an international regime into the indefinite future would, we believe, have the most deleterious effects....

....

The United States delegation is opposed to [Resolution 2574-D] and will vote against it. I should like to explain again the reasons for our position.

First of all, it proceeds on a premise which is unsound and self-defeating: that the development of deep seabed exploitation, and accordingly the development of the technological capacity for such exploitation, should be retarded. What has struck us as doubly surprising about this proposition is that it is put forward in connection with an item whose very existence is due in substantial measure to the conviction that all mankind stands to benefit by the promotion of the exploitation of the deep seabed resources. The question is, therefore, whose interests -- if anybody's -- would such retardation serve? This is the question to which we have yet heard no adequate answer.

We are aware, of course, that a rather simplistic picture has sometimes been painted of developed maritime powers monopolizing seabed technology and rushing greedily to exhaust seabed resources before the international community can establish a regime to regulate their exploitation. To knowledgable people, however, this picture is defective in at least two respects. First, to the extent that the technology of deep seabed exploitation exists at all, it exists only in embryonic form. If its development does not move forward to the point where commercially viable exploitation of deep seabed resources is possible on a significant scale, there will be no exploitation of deep seabed resources and no benefit to anyone -- developed or developing, coastal or landlocked, east or west, north or south. Secondly, so far as my delegation is aware, there is simply no possibility of one country or group of countries having exclusive use of seabed exploitation technology, any more than one country or group of countries has exclusive use of the technology of exploiting resources on land.

If there are individual countries having special reasons for preferring a retardation of seabed exploitation, reasons not generally applicable and perhaps not generally understood, then it would be useful to have these considerations explained. Until convincing reasons are presented, however, we respectfully suggest that, in a time when the demands of economic development are being pressed insistently upon the entire international community, any proposal which posits the desirability of retarding development in a potentially important field requires looking at with a very skeptical eye indeed.

Secondly...the tendency of this resolution is to encourage national action which will make the issues now entrusted to the Seabed Committee for negotiation and solution progressively more difficult to solve. The resolution has been presented to us as a call for national self-restraint, intended to prevent unilateral action which would be prejudicial to the solution of issues currently pending before the committee. My delegation would not question the sincerity of these intentions; and in any case, motives are not the issue. What is the issue are practical consequences. In practical effect, this resolution is likely to encourage some states that may feel it useful or necessary to engage in exploration or exploitation of seabed resources to move toward unjustifiably expansive claims of national jurisdiction, just in order to remove these activities of exploitation from the scope of the prohibition contained in the resolution and thus render them in their view legitimate. It is not enough to say that the prohibition which the resolution contains is without binding legal effect; that is the case with almost any General Assembly resolution purporting to prescribe standards of conduct for states in the oceans. The point is that such a resolution by the Assembly may be taken by some to raise a question of the legitimacy of exploitation undertaken in certain areas of the seabed which, in view of the very substantial investment of capital which such exploitation or even exploration may require, might well be sufficient to generate an unjustifiably expansive claim of national jurisdiction as a precautionary measure.

b. THE PRINCIPLES.

As you know, a declaration of legal principles by the General Assembly of the United Nations carries much more weight than a resolution. In 1970, the Assembly adopted the following principles regarding the seabed.

UNITED NATIONS GENERAL ASSEMBLY

RESOLUTION 2749 (XXV)

December 17, 1970

(Adopted by 108-0-14)

The General Assembly,

Recalling its resolutions 2340 (XXII) of 18 December 1967, 2467 (XXIII) of 21 December 1968 and 2574 (XXIV) of 15 December 1969, concerning the area to which the title of the item refers,

Affirming that there is an area of the sea-bed and the ocean floor, and the subsoil thereof, beyond the limits of national jurisdiction, the precise limits of which are yet to be determined,

Recognizing that the existing legal regime of the high seas does not provide substantive rules for regulating the exploration of the aforesaid area and the exploitation of its resources,

Convinced that the area shall be reserved exclusively for peaceful purposes and that the exploration of the area and the exploitation of its resources shall be carried out for the benefit of mankind as a whole,

Believing it essential that an international regime applying to the area and its resources and including appropriate international machinery should be established as soon as possible,

Bearing in mind that the development and use of the area and its resources shall be undertaken in such a manner as to foster healthy development of the world economy and balanced growth of international trade, and to minimize any adverse economic effects caused by fluctuation of prices of raw materials resulting from such activities,

Solemnly declares that:

1. The sea-bed and ocean floor, and the subsoil thereof, beyond the limits of national jurisdiction (hereinafter referred to as the area), as well as the resources of the area, are the common heritage of mankind.

2. The area shall not be subject to appropriation by any means by States or persons, natural or juridical, and no State shall claim or exercise sovereignty or sovereign rights over any part thereof.

3. No State or person, natural or juridical, shall claim, exercise or acquire rights with respect to the area or its resources incompatible with the international regime to be established and the principles of this Declaration.

4. All activities regarding the exploration and exploitation of the resources of the area and other related activities shall be governed by the international regime to be established.

5. The area shall be open to use exclusively for peaceful purposes by all States whether coastal or land-locked, without discrimination, in accordance with the international regime to be established.

6. States shall act in the area in accordance with the applicable principles and rules of international law including the Charter of the United Nations and the Declaration of Principles of International Law concerning Friendly Relations and Co-operation among States in accordance with the Charter of the United Nations, adopted by the General Assembly on 24 October 1970, in the interests of maintaining international peace and security and promoting international co-operation and mutual understanding.

7. The exploration of the area and the exploitation of its resources shall be carried out for the benefit of mankind as a whole, irrespective of the geographical location of States, whether land-locked or coastal, and taking into particular consideration the interests and needs of the developing countries.

8. The area shall be reserved exclusively for peaceful purposes, without prejudice to any measures which have been or may be agreed upon in the context of international negotiations in the field of disarmament and which may be acceptable to a broader area. One or more international agreements shall be concluded as soon as possible in order to implement effectively this principle and to constitute a step towards the exclusion of the sea-bed, the ocean floor and the subsoil thereof from the arms race.

9. On the basis of the principles of this Declaration, an international regime applying to the area and its resources and including appropriate international machinery to give effect to its provisions shall be established by an international treaty of a universal character, generally agreed upon. The regime shall, inter alia, provide for the orderly and safe development and rational management of the area and its resources and for expanding opportunities in the use thereof and ensure the equitable sharing by States in the benefits derived therefrom, taking into particular consideration the interests and needs of the developing countries, whether land-locked or coastal.

10. States shall promote international co-operation in scientific research exclusively for peaceful purposes:

(a) By participation in international programmes and by encouraging co-operation in scientific research by personnel of different countries;

(b) Through effective publication of research programmes and dissemination of the results of research through international channels;

(c) By co-operation in measures to strengthen research capabilities of developing countries, including the participation of their nationals in research programmes.

No such activity shall form any legal basis for any claims with respect to any part of the area or its resources.

11. With respect to activities in the area and acting in conformity with the international regime to be established, States shall take appropriate measures for and shall co-operate in the adoption and implementation of international rules, standards and procedures for, *inter alia*:

(a) Prevention of pollution and contamination, and other hazards to the marine environment, including the coastline, and of interference with the ecological balance of the marine environment;

(b) Protection and conservation of the natural resources of the area and prevention of damage to the flora and fauna of the marine environment.

12. In their activities in the area, including those relating to its resources, States shall pay due regard to the rights and legitimate interests of coastal States in the region of such activities. Consultations shall be maintained with coastal States concerned with respect to activities relating to the exploration of the area and the exploitation of its resources with a view to avoiding infringement of such rights and interests.

13. Nothing herein shall effect:

(a) The legal status of the waters superjacent to the area or that of the air space above those waters;

(b) The rights of coastal States with respect to measures to prevent, mitigate or eliminate grave and imminent danger to their coastline or related interests from pollution or threat thereof resulting from, or from other hazardous occurences caused by, any activities in the area, subject to the international regime to be established.

14. Every State shall have the responsibility to ensure that activities in the area, including those relating to its resources, whether undertaken by governmental agencies, or non-governmental entities or persons under its jurisdiction, or acting on its behalf, shall be carried out in conformity with the international regime to be established. The same responsibility applies to international organizations and their members .

15. The parties to any dispute relating to activities in the area and its resources shall resolve such dispute by the measures mentioned in Article 33 of the Charter of the United Nations and such procedures for settling disputes as may be agreed upon in the international regime to be established.

D. THE THIRD U.N. CONFERENCE ON THE LAW OF THE SEA.

In 1970, the United Nations General Assembly, by resolution, decided to convene an international conference in 1973 to deal with the entire complex of ocean issues. At the same time, it expanded the Seabed Committee by 44 States and instructed it to, among other things, prepare a list of subjects and issues relating to the law of the sea for submission to the conference when it convened. The first session of the conference was scheduled for late 1973, to deal with organizational matters, including the rules of procedure. The second, substantive, session of the conference was scheduled to be held in Santiago, Chile, in the spring of 1974. Due to a coup in Chile, the situs was subsequently changed to Caracas, Venezuela.

Over the next years, until 1982, the conference held eleven sessions, and at the final session it adopted the text of the United Nations Convention on the Law of the Sea. The methodology of the conference is a subject which provides many lessons in international diplomacy on a large scale. Some of this methodology was discussed in an earlier chapter. A few of the important elements are reviewed here.

The conference proceeded under two basic tenets. The first was that the treaty was to be a "package deal", that is, that all parts of the convention would move forward at the same time, and that the final product would be adopted as a whole, and not piecemeal. The second principle was that the treaty was to be adopted by consensus. The object of this principle was to create a globally acceptable and accepted document.

At the outset, the conference had only two basic documents before it, though much discussion and drafting had taken place in the Seabed Committee. The first was the so-called "Gentleman's Agreement" which had been approved by the General Assembly in 1973. This read as follows:

> "Bearing in mind that the problems of ocean space are closely interrelated and need to be considered as a whole and the desirability of adopting a Convention on the Law of the Sea which will secure the widest possible acceptance.
>
> "The Conference should make every effort to reach agreement on substantive matters by way of consensus and there should be no voting on such matters until all efforts at consensus have been exhausted."

This agreement became the basis for discussions on voting procedure and mechanisms reflected in the rules of procedure adopted by the conference at its first session in New York. Rule 37 contains an elaborate procedure embodying the spirit of the Gentleman's Agreement.

The second document was the list of subjects and issues that the Seabed Committee had prepared for the conference. This was designed to be a road map for the negotiations. The list contained twenty-three subject areas that the conference would need to address, such as, inter alia, the territorial sea, straits used for international navigation, the seabed, etc. A glance at the table of contents of the 1982 convention reflects the breadth of subject matter contained in that list. Under each subject, there was a listing of issues that would need to be resolved. One example should suffice:

1. International Regime for the Sea-Bed and the Ocean Floor Beyond National Jurisdiction

1.1 Nature and Characteristics

1.2 International Machinery: Structure, Functions, Powers

1.3 Economic Implications

1.4 Equitable Sharing of Benefits Bearing in Mind the Special Interests and Needs of the Developing Countries, Whether Coastal or Landlocked

1.5 Definitions and Limits of the Area

1.6 Use Exclusively for Peaceful Purposes

Discussion of the issues provided the framework for delegates to commence and participate in the drafting of specific proposals for treaty articles.

The result of the negotiations were reduced to a text which then would be used as the basis for further negotiations with the goal of approaching a consensus. After many refinements, the time came, in 1982, to adopt the last version as a treaty. As noted above, while the procedures and machinations of the conference is a fascinating subject, it is not of great relevance to our study of the law. The scholar wishing to get a feel of how the texts proceeded through the process may wish to consult, for one view, the unclassified reports of the U.S. delegation to the conference, reproduced in Occasional Paper No. 33 of The Law of the Sea Institute, where those reports are set out in full. We turn now to a consideration of the final treaty provisions relating to the seabed, Part XI of the treaty, and related annexes.

E. THE NEW REGIME

The regime for seabed mining set forth in the treaty is complex and extensive. It would not seem particularly helpful to set the individual articles forth here in the order in which they appear in the treaty. Instead, the materials are presented in groups of articles relative to discreet subjects. This methodology is designed to make it easier to deal with this complicated subject.

1. Principles governing the area

Article 136

Common heritage of mankind

The Area and its resources are the common heritage of mankind.

Article 137

Legal status of the Area and its resources

1. No State shall claim or exercise sovereignty or sovereign rights over any part of the Area or its resources, nor shall any State or natural or juridical person appropriate any part thereof. No such claim or exercise of sovereignty or sovereign rights nor such appropriation shall be recognized.

2. All rights in the resources of the Area are vested in mankind as a whole, on whose behalf the Authority shall act. These resources are not subject to alienation. The minerals recovered from the Area, however, may only be alienated in accordance with this Part and the rules, regulations and procedures of the Authority.

3. No State or natural or juridical person shall claim, acquire or exercise rights with respect to the minerals recovered from the Area except in accordance with this Part. Otherwise, no such claim, acquisition or exercise of such rights shall be recognized.

2. Policies relating to mining

Article 150

Policies relating to activities in the Area

Activities in the Area shall, as specifically provided for in this Part, be carried out in such a manner as to foster healthy development of the world economy and balanced growth of international trade, and to promote international co-operation for the over-all development of all countries, expecially developing States, and with a view to ensuring:

(a) the development of the resources of the Area;

(b) orderly, safe and rational management of the resources of the Area, including the efficient conduct of activities in the Area and, in accordance with sound principles of conservation, the avoidance of unecessary waste;

(c) the expansion of opportunities for participation in such activities consistent in particular with articles 144 and 148;

(d) participation in revenues by the Authority and the transfer of technology to the Enterprise and developing States as provided for in this Convention;

(e) increased availability of the minerals derived from the Area as needed in conjunction with minerals derived from other sources, to ensure supplies to consumers of such minerals;

(f) the promotion of just and stable prices remunerative to producers and fair to consumers for minerals derived both from the Area and from other sources, and the promotion of long-term equilibrium between supply and demand;

(g) the enhancement of opportunities for all States Parties, irrespective of their social or economic systems or geographical location, to participate in the development of the resources of the Area and the prevention of monopolization of activities in the Area;

(h) the protection of developing countries from adverse effects on their economies or on their export earnings resulting from a reduction in the price of an affected mineral, or in the volume of exports of that mineral, to the extent that such reduction is caused by activities in the Area, as provided in article 151;

(i) the development of the common heritage for the benefit of mankind as a whole; and

(j) conditions of access to markets for the imports of minerals produced from the resources of the Area and for imports of commodities produced from such minerals shall not be more favourable than the most favourable applied to imports from other sources.

3. General structure and establishment of the International Seabed Authority

Article 156

Establishment of the Authority

1. There is hereby established the International Sea-Bed Authority.

2. All States Parties are *ipso facto* members of the Authority.

3. Observers at the Third United Nations Conference on the Law of the Sea who have signed the Final Act and who are not referred to in article 305, paragraph 1(c), (d), (e) or (f), shall have the right to participate in the Authority as observers, in accordance with its rules, regulations and procedures.

4. The seat of the Authority shall be in Jamaica.

5. The Authority may establish such regional centres or offices as it deems necessary for the exercise of its functions.

Article 157

Nature and fundamental principles of the Authority

1. The Authority is the organization through which States Parties shall, in accordance with this Part, organize and control activities in the Area, particularly with a view to administering the resources of the Area.

2. The powers and functions of the Authority shall be those expressly conferred upon it by this Convention. The Authority shall have such incidental powers, consistent with this Convention, as are implicit in and necessary for the exercise of those powers and functions with respect to activities in the Area.

3. The Authority is based on the principle of sovereign equality of all its members.

4. All members of the Authority shall fulfil in good faith the obligations assumed by them in accordance with this Part in order to ensure to all of them the rights and benefits resulting from membership.

Article 158

Organs of the Authority

1. There is hereby established, as the principal organs of the Authority, an Assembly, a Council and a Secretariate.

2. There is hereby established the Enterprise, the organ through which the Authority shall carry out the functions referred to in article 170, paragraph 1.

3. Such subsidiary organs as may be found necessary may be established in accordance with this Part.

4. Each principal organ of the Authority and the Enterprise shall be responsible for exercising those powers and functions which are conferred upon it. In exercising such powers and functions each organ shall avoid taking any action which may derogate from or impede the exercise of specific powers and functions conferred upon another organ.

Article 133

Use of terms

(a) "resources" means all solid, liquid or gaseous mineral resources in situ in the Area at or beneath the sea-bed, including polymetallic nodules;

(b) resources, when recovered from the Area, are referred to as "minerals".

Article 1

Use of terms and scope

(1) "Area" means the sea-bed and ocean floor and subsoil thereof, beyond the limits of national jurisdiction;

(2) "Authority" means the International Sea-Bed Authority;

(3) "activies in the Area" means all activities of exploration for, and exploitation of, the resources of the Area;

....

4. Composition, powers and decision-making in the Authority

(a) The Assembly

Article 159

Composition, procedure and voting

1. The Assembly shall consist of all the members of the Authority. Each member shall have one representative in the Assembly, who may be accompanied by alternates and advisers.

2. The Assembly shall meet in regular annual sessions and in such special sessions as may be declared by the Assembly, or convened by the Secretary-General at the request of the Council or of a majority of the members of the Authority.

3. Sessions shall take place at the seat of the Authority unless otherise decided by the Assembly.

4. The Assembly shall adopt its rules of procedure. At the beginning of each regular session, it shall elect its President and such other officers as may be required. They shall hold office until a new President and other officers are elected at the next regular session.

5. A majority of the members of the Assembly shall constitute a quorum.

6. Each member of the Assembly shall have one vote.

7. Decisions on questions of procedure, including decisions to convene special sessions of the Assembly, shall be taken by a majority of the members present and voting.

8. Decisions on questions of substance shall be taken by a two-thirds majority of the members present and voting, provided that such majority includes a majority of the members participating in the session. When the issue arises as to whether a question is one of substance or not, that question shall be treated as one of substance unless otherwise decided by the Assembly by the majority required for decisions on questions of substance.

9. When a question of substance comes up for voting for the first time, the President may, and shall, if requested by at least one fifth of he members of the Assembly, defer the issue of taking a vote on that question for a period not exceeding five calendar days. This rule may be applied only once to any question, and shall not be applied so as to defer the question beyond the end of the session.

10. Upon a written request addressed to the President and sponsored by at least one fourth of the members of the Authority for an advisory opinion on the conformity with this Convention of a proposal before the Assembly on any matter, the Assembly shall request the Sea-Bed Disputes Chamber of the International Tribunal for the Law of the Sea to give an advisory opinion thereon and shall defer voting on that proposal pending receipt of the advisory opinion by the Chamber. If the advisory opinion is not received before the final week of he session in which it is requested, the Assembly shall decide when it will meet to vote upon the deferred proposal.

Article 160

Powers and functions

1. The Assembly, as the sole organ of the Authority consisting of all the members, shall be considered the supreme organ of the Authority to which the other principal organs shall be accountable as specifically provided for in this Convention. The Assembly shall have the power to establish general policies in conformity with the relevant provisions of this Convention on any question or matter within the competence of the Authority.

2. In addition, the powers and functions of the Assembly shall be:

(a) to elect the members of the Council in accordance with article 161;

(b) to elect the Secretary-General from among the candidates proposed by the Council;

(c) to elect, upon the recommendation of the Council, the members of the Governing Board of the Enterprise and the Director-General of the Enterprise;

(d) to establish such subsidiary organs as it finds necessary for the exercise of its functions in accordance with this Part. In the composition of these subsidiary organs due account shall be taken of the principle of equitable geographical distribution and of the special interests and the need for members qualified and competent in the relevant technical questions dealt with by such organs;

(e) to assess the contributions of members to the administrative budget of the Authority in accordance with an agreed scale of assessment based upon the scale used for the regular budget of the United Nations until the Authority shall have sufficient income from other sources to meet its administrative expenses;

(f) (i) to consider and approve, upon the recommendation of the Council, the rules, regulations and procedures on the equitable sharing of financial and other economic benefits derived from activities in the Area and the payments and contributions made pursuant to article 82, taking into particular consideration the interests and needs of developing States and peoples who have not attained full independence or other self-governing status. If the Assembly does not approve the recommendations of the Council, the Assembly shall return them to the Council for reconsideration in the light of the views expressed by the Assembly;

(ii) to consider and approve the rules, regulations and procedures of the Authority, and any amendments thereto, provisionally adopted by the Council pursuant to article 162, paragraph 2(o)(ii). These rules, regulations and procedures shall relate to prospecting exploration and exploitation in the Area, the financial management and internal administration of the Authority, and, upon the recommendation of the Governing Board of the Enterprise, to the transfer of funds from the Enterprise to the Authority;

(g) to decide upon the equitable sharing of financial and other economic benefits derived from activities in the Area, consistent with this Convention and the rules, regulations and procedures of the Authority;

(h) to consider and approve the proposed annual budget of the Authority submitted by the Council;

(i) to examine periodic reports from the Council and from the Enterprise and special reports requested from the Council or any other organ of the Authority;

(j) to initiate studies and make recommendations for the purpose of promoting international co-operation concerning activities in the Area and encouraging and progressive development of international law relating thereto and its codification;

(k) to consider problems of a general nature in connection with activities in the Area arising in particular for developing States, as well as those problems for States in connection with activities in the Area that are due to geographical location, particularly for land-locked and geographically disadvantated States;

(l) to establish, upon the recommendation of the Council, on the basis of advice from the Economic Planning Commission, a system of compensation or other measures of economic adjustment assistance as provided in article 151, paragraph 10;

(m) to suspend the exercise of rights and privileges of membership pursuant to article 185;

(n) to discuss any question or matter within the competence of the Authority and to decide as to which organ of the Authority shall deal with any such question or matter not specifically entrusted to a particular organ, consistent with the distribution of powers and functions among the organs of the Authoity.

(b) The Council

Article 161

Composition, procedure and voting

1. The Council shall consist of 36 members of the Authority elected by the Assembly in the following order:

(a) four members from among those States Parties which, during the last five years for which statistics are available, have either consumed more than 2 per cent of the total world consumption or have had net imports of more than 2 per cent of total world imports of the commodities produced from the categories of minerals to be derived from the Area, and in any case one State from the Eastern European (Socialist) region, as well as the largest consumer;

(b) four members from among the eight States Parties which have the largest investments in preparation for and in the conduct of activities in the Area, either directly or through their nationals, including at least one State from the Eastern European (Socialist) region;

(c) four members from among States Parties which on the basis of production in areas under their jurisdiction are major net exporters of the categories of minerals to be derived from the Area, including at least two developing States whose exports of such minerals have a substantial bearing upon their economies;

(d) six members from among developing States Parties, representing special interests. The special interests to be represented shall include those of States with large populations, States which are land-locked or geographically disadvantaged, States which are major importers of the categories of minerals to be derived from the Area, States which are potential producers of such minerals, and least developed States;

(e) eighteen members elected according to the principles of ensuring an equitable distribution of seats in the Council as a whole, provided that each geographical region shall have at least one member elected under this subparagraph. For this purpose, the geographical regions shall be Africa, Asia, Eastern European (Socialist), Latin America and Western European and Others;

2. In electing the members of the Council in accordance with paragraph 1, the Assembly shall ensure that:

(a) land-locked and geographically disadvantated States are represented to a degree which is reasonably proportionate to their representation in the Assembly;

(b) coastal States, especially developing States, which do not qualify under paragraph (1)(a), (b), (c) or (d) are represented to a degree which is reasonably proportionate to their representation in the Assembly;

(c) each group of States Parties to be represented on the Council is represented by those members, if any, which are nominated by that group.

3. Elections shall take place at regular sessions of the Assembly. Each member of the Council shall be elected for four years. At the first election, however, the term of one half of the members of each group referred to in paragaph 1 shall be two years.

4. Members of the Council shall be eligible for re-election, but due regard should be paid to the desirability of rotation of membership.

5. The Council shall function at the seat of the Authority, and shall meet as often as the business of the Authority may require, but not less than three times a year.

6. A majority of the members of the Council shall constitute a quorum.

7. Each member of the Council shall have one vote.

8. (a) Decisions on questions of procedure shall be taken by a majority of the members present and voting.

(b) Decisions on questions of substance arising under the following provisions shall be taken by a two-thirds majority of the members present and voting, provided that such majority includes a majority of the members of the Council: article 162, paragraph 2, subparagraphs (f); (g); (h); (i); (n); (p); (v); article 191.

(c) Decisions on questions of substance arising under the following provisions shall be taken by a three-fourths majority of the members present and voting, provided that such majority includes a majority of the members of the Council: article 162, paragraph 1; article 162, paragraph 2, subparagraphs (a); (b); (c); (d); (e); (l); (q); (r); (s); (t); (u) in cases of non-compliance by a contractor or a sponsor; (w) provided that orders issued thereunder may be binding for not more than 30 days unless confirmed by a decision taken in accordance with subparagraph (d); article 162, paragraph 2, subparagraphs (x); (y); (z); article 163, paragraph 2; article 174, paragraph 3; Annex IV, article 11.

(d) Decisions on questions of substance arising under the following provisions shall be taken by consensus: article 162, paragraph 2(m) and (o); adoption of amendments to Part XI.

(e) For the purposes of subparagrahs (d), (f), and (g), "consensus" means the absence of any formal objection. Within 14 days of the submission of a proposal to the Council, the President of the Council shall determine whether there would be a formal objection to the adoption of the proposal. If the President determines that there would be such an objection, the President shall establish and convene, within three days following such determination, a conciliation committee consisting of not more than nine members of the Council, with the President as chairman, for the purpose of reconciling the differences and producing a proposal which can be adopted by consensus. The committee shall work expeditiously and report to the Council within 14 days following its establishment. If the committee is unable to recommend a proposal which can be adopted by consensus, it shall set out in its report the grounds on which the proposal is being opposed.

(f) Decisions on questions not listed above which the Council is authorized to take by the rules, regulations and procedures of the Authority or otherwise shall be taken pursuant to the subparagraphs of this paragraph specified in the rules, regulations and procedures or, if not specified therein, then pursuant to the subparagraph determined by the Council if possible in advance, by consensus.

(g) When the issue arises as to whether the question is within subparagraph (a), (b), (c), or (d), the question shall be treated as being within the subparagraph requiring the higher or highest majority or consensus as the case may be, unless otherwise decided by the Council by the said majority or consensus.

9. The Council shall establish a procedure whereby a member of the Authority not represented on the Council may send a representative to attend a meeting of the Council when a request is made by such member, or a matter particularly affecting it is under consideration. Such a representative shall be entitled to participate in the deliberations but not to vote.

Article 162

Powers and functions

1. The Council is the executive organ of the Authority. The Council shall have the power to establish, in conformity with this Convention and the general policies established by the Assembly, the specific policies to be pursued by the Authority on any question or matter within the competence of the Authority.

2. In addition, the Council shall:

(a) supervise and co-ordinate the implementation of the provisions of this Part on all questions and matters within the competence of the Authority and invite the attention of the Assembly to cases of non-compliance;

(b) propose to the Assembly a list of candidates for the election of the Secretary-General;

(c) recommend to the Assembly candidates for the election of the members of the Governing Board of the Enterprise and the Director-General of the Enterprise;

(d) establish, as appropriate, and with due regard to economy and efficiency, such subsidiary organs as it finds necessary for the exercise of its functions in accordance with this Part. In the composition of subsidiary organs, emphasis shall be placed on the need for members qualified and competent in relevant technical matters dealt with by those organs provided that due account shall be taken of the principle of equitable geographical distribution and of special interests;

(e) adopt its rules of procedure including the method of selecting its president;

(f) enter into agreements with the United Nations or other international organizations on behalf of the Authority and within its competence, subject to approval by the Assembly;

(g) consider the reports of the Enterprise and transmit them to the Assembly with its recommendations;

(h) present to the Assembly annual reports and such special reports as the Assembly may request;

(i) issue directives to the Enterprise in accordance with article 170;

(j) approve plans of work in accordance with Annex III, article 6. The Council shall act upon each plan of work within 60 days of its submission by the Legal and Technical Commission at a session of the Council in accordance with the following procedures:

(i) if the Commission recommends the approval of a plan of work, it shall be deemed to have been approved by the Council if no member of the Council submits in writing to the President within 14 days a specific objection alleging non-compliance with the requirments of Annex III, article 6. If there is an objection, the conciliation procedure set forth in article 161, paragraph 8(e), shall apply. If, at the end of the conciliation procedure, the objection is still maintained, the plan of work shall be deemed to have been approved by the Council unless the Council disapproves it by consensus among its members excluding any State or States making the application or sponsoring the applicant;

(ii) if the Commission recommends the disapproval of a plan of work or does not make a recommendation, the Council may approve the plan of work by a three-fourths majority of the members present and voting, providing that such majority includes a majority of the members participating in the session;

(k) approve plans of work submitted by the Enterprise in accordance with Annex IV, article 12, applying, *mutatis mutandis*, the procedures set forth in subparagraph (j);

(l) exercise control over activities in the Area in accordance with article 153, paragraph 4, and the rules, regulations and procedures of the Authority;

(m) take, upon the recommendation of the Economic Planning Commission, necessary and appropriate measures in accordance with article 150, subparagraph (h), to provide protection from the adverse economic effects specified therein;

(n) make recommendations to the Assembly, on the basis of advice from the Economic Planning Commission, for a system of compensation or other measures of economic adjustment assistance as provided in article 151, paragraph 10;

(o) (i) recommend to the Assembly rules, regulations and procedures on the equitable sharing of financial and other economic benefits derived from activities in the Area and the payments and contributions made pursuant to article 82, taking into particular consideration the interests and needs of the developing States and peoples who have not attained full indendence or other self-governing status;

(ii) adopt and apply provisionally, pending approval by the Assembly, the rules, regulations and procedures of the Authority, and any amendments thereto, taking into account the recommendations of the Legal and Technical Commission or other subordinate organ concerned. These rules, regulations and procedures shall relate to prospecting, exploration and exploitation in the Area and the financial management and internal administration of the Authority. Priority shall be given to the adoption of rules, regulations and procedures for the exploration for and exploitation of polymetallic nodules. Rules, regulations and procedures for the exploration for and exploitation of any resource other than polymetallic nodules shall be adopted within three years from the date of a request to the Authority by any of its members to adopt such rules, regulations and procedures in respect of such resource. All rules, regulations and procedures shall remain in effect on a provisional basis until approved by the Assembly or until amended by the Council in the light of any views expressed by the Assembly;

(p) review the collection of all payments to be made by or to the Authority in connection with operations pursuant to this Part;

(q) make the selection from among applicants for production authorizations pursuant to Annex III, article 7, where such selection is required by that provision;

(r) submit the proposed annual budget of the Authority to the Assembly for its approval;

(s) make recommendations to the Assembly concerning policies on any question or matter within the competence of the Authority;

(t) make recommendations to the Assembly concerning suspension of the exercise of the rights and privileges of membership pursuant to article 185;

(u) institute proceedings on behalf of the Authority before the Sea-Bed Disputes Chamber in cases of non-compliance;

(v) notify the Assembly upon a decision by the Sea-Bed Disputes Chamber in proceedings instituted under subparagraph (u), and make any recommendations which it may find appropriate with respect to measures to be taken;

(w) issue emergency orders, which may include orders for the suspension or adjustment of operations, to prevent serious harm to the marine environment arising out of activities in the Area;

(x) disapprove areas for exploitation by contractors or the Enterprise in cases where substantial evidence indicates the risk of serious harm to the marine environment;

(y) establish a subsidiary organ for the elaboration of draft financial rules, regulations and procedures relating to:

(i) financial management in accordance with articles 171 to 175; and

(ii) financial arrangements in accordance with Annex III, article 13 and article 17, paragraph 1(c);

(z) establish appropriate mechanisms for directing and supervising a staff of inspectors who shall inspect activities in the Area to determine whether this Part, the rules, regulations and procedures of the Authority, and the terms and conditions of any contract with the Authority are being complied with.

* * * *

QUESTIONS: Before moving on to the next section dealing with subsidiary organs, having read carefully the provisions on the powers, functions and voting of the two primary organs, consider the following questions.

1. Which of the two primary organs, the Council or the Assembly, is the most powerful?

2. Why such an elaborate voting system for the Council?

3. One of the objections the U.S. has voiced concerning the treaty is that while the socialist bloc is guaranteed three seats on the Council, the U.S. is not guaranteed a seat. Read the articles again. Do you think this is true?

* * * *

(c) Subsidiary organs

Article 163

Organs of the Council

1. There are hereby established the following organs of the Council:

(a) an Economic Planning Commision;

(b) a Legal and Technical Commission.

2. Each Commission shall be composed of 15 members, elected by the Council from among the candidates nominated by the States Parties. However, if necessary, the Council may decide to increase the size of either Commission having due regard to economy and efficiency.

3. Members of a Commission shall have appropriate qualifications in the area of competence of that Commission. States Parties shall nominate candidates of the highest standards of competence and integrity with qualifications in relevant fields so as to ensure the effective exercise of the functions of the Commissions.

4. In the election of members of the Commissions, due account shall be taken of the need for equitable geographical distribution and the representation of special interests.

5. No State Party may nominate more than one candidate for the same Commission. No person shall be elected to serve on more than one Commission.

6. Members of the Commissions shall hold office for a term of five years. They shall be eligible for re-election for a further term.

7. In the event of the death, incapacity or resignation of a member of a Commission prior to the expiration of the term of office, the Council shall elect for the remainder of the term, a member from the same geographical region or area of interest.

8. Members of Commissions shall have no financial interest in any activity relating to exploration and exploitation in the Area. Subject to their responsibilities to the Commissions upon which they serve, they shall not disclose, even after the termination of their functions, any industrial secret, proprietary data which are transferred to the Authority in accordance with Annex III, article 14, or any other confidential information coming to their knowledge by reason of their duties for the Authority.

9. Each Commission shall exercise its functions in accordance with such guidelines and directives as the Council may adopt.

10. Each Commission shall formulate and submit to the Council for approval such rules and regulations as may be necessery for the efficient conduct of the Commission's functions.

11. The decision-making procedures of the Commissions shall be established by the rules, regulations and procedures of the Authority. Recommendations to the Council shall, where necessary, be accompanied by a summary on the divergencies of opinion in the Commission.

12. Each Commission shall normally function at the seat of the Authority and shall meet as often as is required for the efficient exercise of its functions.

13. In the exercise of its functions, each Commission may, where appropriate, consult another commission, any competent organ of the United Nations or of its specialized agencies or any international organizations with competence in the subject-matter of such consultation.

Article 164

The Economic and Planning Commission

1. Members of the Economic and Planning Commission shall have appropriate qualifications such as those relevant to mining, management of mineral resource activities, international trade or international economics. The Council shall endeavour to ensure that the membership of the Commission reflects all appropriate qualifications. The Commission shall include at least two members from developing States whose exports of the categories of minerals to be derived from the Area have a substantial bearing upon their economies.

2. The Commission shall:

(a) propose, upon the request of the Council, measures to implement decisions relating to activities in the Area taken in accordance with this Convention;

(b) review the trends of and the factors affecting supply, demand and prices of minerals which may be derived from the Area, bearing in mind the interests of both importing and exporting countries, and in particular of the developing States among them;

(c) examine any situation likely to lead to the adverse effects referred to in article 150, subparagraph (h), brought to its attention by the State Party or States Parties concerned, and make appropriate recommendations to the Council;

(d) propose to the Council for submission to the Assembly, as provided in article 151, paragraph 10, a system of compensation or other measures of economic adjustment assistance for developing States which suffer adverse effects caused by activities in the Area. The Commission shall make the recommendations to the Council that are necessary for the application of the system or other measures adopted by the Assembly in specific cases.

Article 165

The Legal and Technical Commission

1. Members of the Legal and Technical Commission shall have appropriate qualifications such as those relevant to exploration for and exploitation and processing of mineral resources, oceanology, protection of the marine environment, or economic or legal matters relating to ocean mining and related fields of expertise. The Council shall endeavour to ensure that the membership of the Commission relects all appropriate qualifications.

2. The Commission shall:

(a) make recommendations with regard to the exercise of the Authority's functions upon the request of the Council;

(b) review formal written plans of work for activities in the Area in accordance with article 153, paragraph 3, and submit appropriate recommendations to the Council. The Commission shall base its recommendations solely on the grounds stated in Annex III and shall report fully thereon to the Council;

(c) supervise, upon the request of the Council, activities in the Area where appropriate, in consultation and collaboration with any entity carrying out such activities or State or States concerned and report to the Council;

(d) prepare assessments of the environmental implications of activities in the Area;

(e) make recommendations to the Council on the protection of the marine environment, taking into account the views of recognized experts in that field;

(f) formulate and submit to the Council the rules, regulations and procedures referred to in article 162, paragraph 2(o), taking into account all relevant factors including assessments of the environmental implications of activities in the Area;

(g) keep such rules, regulations and procedures under review and recommend to the Council from time to time such amendments thereto as it may deem necessary or desirable;

(h) make recommendations to the Council regarding the establishment of a monitoring programme to observe, measure, evaluate and analyse, by recognized scientific methods, on a regular basis, the risk or effects of pollution of the marine environment resulting from activities in the Area, ensure that existing regulations are adequate and are complied with and co-ordinate the implementation of the monitoring programme approved by the Council;

(i) recommend to the Council that proceedings be instituted on behalf of the Authority before the Sea-Bed Disputes Chamber, in accordance with this Part and the relevant Annexes taking into account particularly article 187;

(j) make recommendations to the Council with respect to measures to be taken, upon a decision by the Sea-Bed Disputes Chamber in proceedings instituted in accordance with subparagraph (i);

(k) make recommendations to the Council to issue emergency orders, which may include orders for the suspension or adjustment of operations, to prevent serious harm to the marine environment arising out of activities in the Area. Such recommendations shall be taken up by the Council on a priority basis;

(l) make recommendations to the Council to disapprove areas for exploitation by contractors or the Enterprise in cases where substantial evidence indicates the risk of serious harm to the marine environment;

(m) make recommendations to the Council regarding the direction and supervision of a staff of inspectors who shall inspect activities in the Area to determine whether the provisions of this Part, the rules, regulations and procedures of the Authority, and the terms and conditions of any contract with the Authority are being complied with;

(n) calculate the production ceiling and issue production authorizations on behalf of the Authority pursuant to article 151, paragraphs 2 to 7, following any necessary selection among applicants for production authorizations by the Council in accordance with Annex III, article 7.

3. The members of the Commission shall, upon request by any State Party or other party concerned, be accompanied by a representative of such State or other party concerned when carrying out their function of supervision and inspection.

(d) The Secretariate.

Subsection D of Part XI of the treaty (articles 166 to 170) deal with the establishment and functions of a secretariate to service the Authority, including the establishment of the post of Secretary-General of the Authority. Since these provisions are similar to those for other international organizations, they will not be considered in detail here. You are referred to the particular provisions cited above for details.

5. The System of Access

(a) The Parallel System

Article 153(2)

....

2. Activities in the Area shall be carried out as prescribed in paragraph 3:

(a) by the Enterprise, and

(b) in association with the Authority by States Parties, or state enterprises or natural or juridical persons which possess the nationality of States Parties or are effectively controlled by them or their nationals, when sponsored by such States, or any group of the foregoing which meets the requirements provided in this Part and in Annex III.

....

(b) The Banking System

ANNEX III

Article 8

Reservation of areas

Each application, other than those submitted by the Enterprise or by any other entities for reserved areas, shall cover a total area, which need not be a single continuous area, sufficiently large and of sufficient estimated commercial value to allow two mining operations. The applicant shall indicate the co-ordinates dividing the area into two parts of equal estimated commercial value and submit all the data obtained by him with respect to both parts. Without prejudice to the powers of the Authority persuant to article 17 of this Annex, the data to be submitted concerning polymetallic nodules shall relate to mapping, sampling, the abundance of nodules, and their metal content. Within 45 days of receiving such data, the Authority shall designate which part is to be reserved solely for the conduct of activities by the Authority through the Enterprise or in association with developing States. This designation may be deferred for a further period of 45 days if the Authority requests an independent expert to assess whether all the data required by this article has been submitted. The area designated shall become a reserved area as soon as the plan of work for the non-reserved area is approved and the contract is signed.

Article 9

Activities in reserved areas

1. The Enterprise shall be given an opportunity to decide whether it intends to carry out activities in each reserved area. This decision may be taken at any time, unless a notification pursuant to paragraph 4 is received by the Authority, in which event the Enterprise shall take its decision within a reasonable time. The Enterprise may decide to exploit such areas in joint ventures with the interested State or entity.

2. The Enterprise may conclude contracts for the execution of part of its activities in accordance with Annex IV, article 12. It may enter into joint ventures for the conduct of such activities with any entities which are eligible to carry out activities in the Area pursuant to article 153, paragraph 2(b). When considering such joint ventures, the Enterprise shall offer to States Parties which are developing States and their nationals the opportunity of effective participation.

3. The Authority may prescribe, in its rules, regulations and procedures substantive and procedural requirements and conditions with respect to such contracts and joint ventures.

4. Any State Party which is a developing State or any natural or juridical person sponsored by it and effectively controlled by it or by other developing State which is a qualified applicant, or any group of the foregoing, may notify the Authority that it wishes to submit a plan of work pursuant to article 6 of this Annex with respect to a reserved area. The plan of work shall be considered if the Enterprise decides, pursuant to paragraph 1, that it does not intend to carry out activities in the Area.

6. Plans of work

(a) Requirements for plans of work

Article 153(3)

....

3. Activities in the Area shall be carried out in accordance with a formal written plan of work drawn up in accordance with Annex III and approved by the Council after review by the Legal and Technical Commission. In the case of activities in the Area carried out as authorized by the Authority by the entities specified in paragraph 2(b), the plans of work shall, in accordance with Annex III, article 3, be in the form of a contract. Such contracts may provide for joint arrangements in accordance with Annex III, article 11.

....

Annex III

Article 3

Exploration and exploitation

1. The Enterprise, States Parties, and the other entities referred to in article 153, paragraph 2(b), may apply to the Authority for approval of plans of work for activities in the Area.

2. The Enterprise may apply with respect to any part of the Area, but applications by others with respect to reserved areas are subject to the additional requirements of article 9 of this Annex.

3. Exploration and exploitation shall be carried out in areas specified in plans of work referred to in article 153, paragraph 3, and approved by the Authority in accordance with this Convention and the relevant rules, regulations and procedures of the Authority.

4. Every plan of work shall:

(a) be in conformity with this Convention and the rules, regulations and procedures of the Authority;

(b) provide for control by the Authority of activities in the Area in accordance with article 153, paragraph 4;

(c) confer on the operator, in accordance with the rules, regulations and procedures of the Authority, the exclusive right to explore for and exploit the specified categories of resources in the area covered by the plan of work. If, however, the applicant presents for approval a plan of work covering only the stage of exploration or the stage of exploitation, the approved plan of work shall confer such exclusive right with respect to that stage only.

5. Upon its approval by the Authority, every plan of work, except those presented by the Enterprise, shall be in the form of a contract concluded between the Authority and the applicant or applicants.

(b) Qualifications of applicants

Annex III

Article 4

Qualifications of applicants

1. Applicants, other than the Enterprise, shall be qualified if they have the nationality or control and sponsorship required by article 153, paragraph 2(b), and if they follow the procedures and meet the qualification standards set forth in the rules, regulations and procedures of the Authority.

2. Except as provided in paragraph 6, such qualification standards shall relate to the financial and technical capabilities of the applicant and his performance under any previous contracts with the Authority.

3. Each applicant shall be sponsored by the State Party of which it is a national unless the applicant has more than one nationality, as in the case of a partnership or consortium of entities from several States, in which event all States Parties involved shall sponsor the application,or unless the applicant is effectively controlled by another State Party or its nationals, in which event both States Parties shall sponsor the application. The criteria and procedures for implementation of the sponsorship shall be set forth in the rules, regulations and procedures of the Authority.

4. The sponsoring State or States shall, pursuant to article 139, have the responsibility to ensure, within their legal systems, that a contractor so sponsored shall carry out activities in the Area in conformity with the terms of its contract and its obligations under this Convention. A sponsoring State shall not, however, be liable for damage caused by any failure of a contractor sponsored by it to comply with its obligations if that State Party has adopted laws and regulations and taken administrative measures which are, within the framework of its legal system, reasonably appropriate for securing compliance by persons under its jurisdiction.

5. The procedures for assessing the qualifications of States Parties which are applicants shall take into account their character as States.

6. The qualification standards shall require that every applicant, without exception, shall as part of his application undertake:

(a) to accept as enforceable and comply with the applicable obligations created by the provisions of Part XI, the rules, regulations and procedures of the Authority, the decisions of the organs of the Authority and terms of his contracts with the Authority;

(b) to accept control by the Authority of activities in the Area, as authorized by this Convention;

(c) to provide the Authority with a written assurance that his obligations under the contract will be fulfilled in good faith;

(d) to comply with the provisions on the transfer of technology set forth in article 5 of this Annex.

(c) Size of areas.

Annex III

Article 17(2)

....

2. Rules, regulations and procedures on the following items shall fully reflect the objective criteria set out below:

(a) Size of areas:

The Authority shall determine the appropriate size of areas for exploration which may be up to twice as large as those for exploitation in order to permit intensive exploration operations. The size of areas shall be calculated to satisfy the requirements of article 8 of this Annex on reservation of areas as well as stated production requirements consistent with article 151 in accordance with the terms of the contract taking into account the state of the art of technology then available for sea-bed mining and the relevant physical characteristics of the areas. Areas shall be neither smaller nor larger than necessary to satisfy this objective.

....

(d) Flow of contract approval

Under this category we examine how a plan of work is processed through the system to the point of approval. The plan, in the form of a contract, is first submitted to the Legal and Technical Commission for review under article 165(2)(b). According to that provision, the Commission will make recommendations on the approval of the plan to the Council. In considering its recommendation, the Commission "shall base its recommendations solely on the ground stated in Annex III". As we have seen, the only grounds that the Commission can consider are the applicant's financial and technical capabilities and any performance the applicant may have demonstrated under any prior contract.

Next, the plan is forwarded to the Council with the Commission's recommendations. The Council has the power to approve or disapprove the plan regardless of the recommendations of the Commission. Article 162(2)(j) establishes a special procedure for this process. Notice that the plan will be deemed approved if there is no written objection. Even if there is an objection, after conciliation, the plan will still be deemed to be approved unless the Council disapproves it by consensus. If the Commission's recommendation is negative, the Council may still approve the plan by a three-fourths vote.

Further details concerning approval of plans of work are found in Annex III:

Article 6

Approval of plans of work

1. Six months after the entry into force of this Convention, and thereafter each fourth month, the Authority shall take up for consideration proposed plans of work.

2. When considering an application for approval of a plan of work in the form of a contract, the Authority shall first ascertain whether:

(a) the applicant has complied with the procedures established for applications in accordance with article 4 of this Annex and has given the Authority the undertakings and assurances required by that article. In cases of non-compliance with these procedures or in the absence of any of these undertakings and assurances, the applicant shall be given 45 days to remedy these defects;

(b) the applicant possesses the requisite qualifications provided for in article 4 of this Annex.

3. All proposed plans of work shall be taken up in the order in which they are received. The proposed plans of work shall comply with and be governed by the relevant provisions of this Convention and the rules, regulations and procedures of the Authority, including those on operational requirements, financial contributions and the undertakings concerning the transfer of technology. If the proposed plans of work conform to these requirements, the Authority shall approve them provided that they are in accordance with the uniform and non-discriminatory requirements set forth in the rules, regulations and procedures of the Authority, unless:

(a) part or all of the area covered by the proposed plan of work is included in an approved plan of work or a previously submitted proposed plan of work which has not yet been finally acted on by the Authority;

(b) part or all of the area covered by the proposed plan of work is disapproved by the Authority pursuant to article 162, paragraph 2(x); or

(c) the proposed plan of work has been submitted or sponsored by a State Party which already holds:

(i) plans of work for the exploration and exploitation of polymetallic nodules in non-reserved areas that, together with either part of the area covered by the application for a plan of work, exceed in size 30 per cent of a circular area of 400,000 square kilometers surrounding the center of either part of the area covered by the proposed plan of work;

(ii) plans of work for the exploration and exploitation of polymetallic nodules in non-reserved areas which, taken together, constitute 2 per cent of the total sea-bed area which is not reserved or disapproved for exploitation pursuant to article 162, paragraph 2(x).

....

7. Production authorizations

Approval of a plan of work does not entitle the contractor to begin work. It must first obtain a production authorization. This is also covered by Annex III:

Article 7

Selection among applicants for production authorizations

1. Six months after the entry into force of this Convention, and therafter each fourth month, the Authority shall take up for consideration applications for production authorizations submitted during the immediately preceding period. The Authority shall issue the authorizations applied for if all such applications can be approved without exceeding the production limitation or contravening the obligations of the Authority under a commodity agreement or arrangement to which it has become a party, as provided in article 151.

2. When a selection must be made among applicants for production authorizations because of the production limitation set forth in article 151, paragraphs 2 to 7, or because of the obligations of the Authority under a commodity agreement or arrangement to which it has become a party, as provided for in article 151, paragraph 1, the Authority shall make the selection on the basis of objective and non-discriminatory standards set forth in its rules, regulations and procedures.

3. In the application of paragraph 2, the Authority shall give priority to those applicants which:

(a) give better assurance of performance, taking into account their financial and technical qualifications and their performance, if any, under previously approved plans of work;

(b) provide earlier prospective financial benefits to the Authority, taking into account when commercial production is scheduled to begin;

(c) have already invested the most resources and effort in prospecting or exploration.

4. Applicants which are not selected in any period shall have priority in subsequent periods until they receive a production authorization.

5. Selection shall be made taking into account the need to enhance opportunities for all States Parties, irrespective of their social and economic systems or geographical locations so as to avoid discrimination against any State or system, to participate in activities in the Area and to prevent monopolization of those activities.

6. Whenever fewer reserved areas than non-reserved areas are under exploitation, applications for production authorizations with respect to reserved areas shall have priority.

7. The decisions referred to in this article shall be taken as soon as possible after the close of each period.

8. Production limitations

This subject is linked to that of production authorizations in the sense that it is the trigger that causes prioritization of such authorizations. The underlying theory of production limitations is that they may be necessary to protect land-based producers of metals derived from the Area.

Article 151

Production policies

1. (a) Without prejudice to the objectives set forth in article 150 and for the purpose of implementing subparagraph (h) of that article, the Authority, acting through existing forums or such new arrangements or agreements as may be appropriate, in which all interested parties, including both producers and consumers, participate, shall take measures necessary to promote the growth, efficiency and stability of markets for those commodities produced from the minerals derived from the Area, at prices remunerative to producers and fair to consumers. All States Parties shall cooperate to this end.

(b) The Authority shall have the right to participate in any commodity conference dealing with those commodities and in which all interested parties including both producers and consumers participate. The Authority shall have the right to become a party to any arrangement or agreement resulting from such conferences. Participation of the Authority in any organs established under those arrangements or agreements and shall be in respect of production in the Area and in accordance with the relevant rules of those organs.

(c) The Authority shall carry out its obligations under the arrangements or agreements referred to in this paragraph in a manner which assures a uniform and non-discriminatory implementation in respect of all production in the Area of the minerals concerned. In doing so, the Authority shall act in a manner consistent with the terms of existing contracts and approved plans of work of the Enterprise.

2. (a) During the interim period specified in paragraph 3, commercial production shall not be undertaken pursuant to an approved plan of work until the operator has applied for and has been issued a production authorization by the Authority. Such production authorizations may not be applied for or issued more than five years prior to the planned commencement of commercial production under the plan of work unless, having regard to the nature and timing of project development, the rules, regulations and procedures of the Authority prescribe another period.

(b) In the application for the production authorization, the operator shall specify the annual quantity of nickel expected to be recovered under the approved plan of work. The application shall include a schedule of expenditures to be made by the operator after he has received the authorization which are reasonably calculated to allow him to begin commercial production on the date planned.

(c) For the purposes of subparagraphs (a) and (b), the Authority shall establish appropriate performance requirements in accordance with Annex III, article 17.

(d) The Authority shall issue a production authorization for the level of production applied for unless the sum of that level and the levels already authorized exceeds the nickel production ceiling, as calculated pursuant to paragraph 4 in the year of issuance of the authorization, during any year of planned production falling within the interim period.

(e) When issued, the production authorization and approved aplication shall become a part of the approved plan of work.

(f) If the operator's application for a production authorization is denied pursuant to subparagraph (d), the operator may apply again to the Authority at any time.

3. The interim period shall begin five years prior to 1 January of the year in which the earliest commercial production is planned to commence under an approved plan of work. If the earliest commercial production is delayed beyond the year originally planned, the beginning of the interim period and the production ceiling originally calculated shall be adjusted accordingly. The interim period shall last 25 years or until the end of the Review Conference referred to in article 155 or until the day when such new arrangements or agreements as are referred to in paragraph 1 enter into force, whichever is earliest. The Authority shall resume the power provided for in this article for the remainder of the interim period if the said arrangements or agreements should lapse or become ineffective for any reason whatsoever.

4. (a) The production ceiling for any year of the interim period shall be the sum of:

(i) the difference betwen the trend line values for nickel consumption, as calculated pursuant to subparagraph (b), for the year immediately prior to the year of the earliest commercial production and the year immediately prior to the commencement of the interim period; and

(ii) sixty per cent of the difference between the trend line values for nickel consumption, as calculated pursuant to subparagraph (b), for the year for which the production authorization is being applied for and the year immediately prior to the year of the earliest commecial production.

(b) For the purposes of subparagraph (a):

(i) trend line values used for computing the nickel production ceiling shall be those annual nickel consumption values on a trend line computed during the year in which a production authorization is issued. The trend line shall be derived from a linear regression of the logarithms of actual nickel consumption for the most recent 15-year period for which such data are available, time being the independent variable. This trend line shall be referred to as the original trend line;

(ii) if the annual rate of increase of the original trend line is less than 3 per cent, then the trend line used to determine the quantities referred to in subparagraph (a) shall be one passing through the original trend line at the value for the first year of the relevant 15-year period, and increasing at 3 per cent annually; provided however that the production ceiling established for any year of the interim period may not in any case exceed the difference between the original trend line value for the year immediately prior to the commencement of the interim period.

5. The Authority may reserve to the Enterprise for its initial production a quantity of 38,000 metric tonnes of nickel from the available production ceiling calculated pursuant to paragraph 4.

6. (a) An operator may in any year produce less than or up to 8 per cent more than the level of annual production of minerals from polymetallic nodules specified in his production authorization, provided that the over-all amount of production shall not exceed that specified in the authorization. Any excess over 8 per cent and up to 20 per cent in any year, or in excess in the first and subsequent years following two consecutive years in which excesses occur, shall be negotiated with the Authority, which may require the operator to obtain a supplementary production authorization to cover additional production.

(b) Applications for such supplementary production authorizations shall be considered by the Authority only after all pending applications by operators who have not yet received production authorizations have been acted upon and due account has been taken of other likely applicants. The Authority shall be guided by the principle of not exceeding the total production allowed under the production ceiling in any year of the interim period. It shall not authorize the production under any plan of work of a quantity in excess of 46,500 metric tonnes of nickel per year.

7. The levels of production of other metals such as copper, cobalt and manganese extracted from the polymetallic nodules that are recovered pursuant to a production authorization should not be higher than those which would have been produced had the operator produced the maximum level of nickel from those nodules pursuant to this article. The Authority shall establish rules, regulations and procedures pursuant to Annex III, article 17, to implement this paragraph.

8. Rights and obligations relating to unfair economic practices under relevant multilateral trade agreements shall apply to the exploration for and exploitation of minerals from the Area. In the settlement of disputes arising under this provision, States Parties which are Parties to such multilateral trade agreements shall have recourse to the dispute settlement procedures of such agreements.

9. The Authority shall have the power to limit the level of production of minerals from the Area, other than minerals from polymetallic nodules, under such conditions and applying such methods as may be appropriate by adopting regulations in accordance with article 161, paragraph 8.

10. Upon the recommendation of the Council on the basis of advice from the Economic Planning Commission, the Assembly shall establish a system of compensation or take other measures of economic adjustment assistance including co-operation with specialized agencies and other international organizations to assist developing countries which suffer serious adverse effects on their export earnings or economies resulting from a reduction in the price of an affected mineral or in the volume of exports of that mineral, to the extent that such reduction is caused by activities in the Area. The Authority on request shall initiate studies on the problems of those States which are likely to be most seriously affected with a view to minimizing their difficulties and assisting them in their economic adjustment.

9. Financial implications

(a) Financing the International Sea-Bed Authority

Article 171

Funds of the Authority

The funds of the Authority shall include:

(a) assessed contributions made by members of the Authority in accordance with article 160, paragraph 2(e);

(b) funds received by the Authority pursuant to Annex III, article 13, in connection with activities in the Area;

(c) funds transferred from the Enterprise in accordance with Annex IV, article 10;

(d) funds borrowed pursuant to article 174;

(e) voluntary contributions made by members or other entities; and

(f) payments to a compensation fund, in accordance with article 151, paragraph 10, whose sources are to be recommended by the Economic Planning Commission.

[You will wish to refer to article 160 (2)(e) which ties contributions to the administrative budget to the the scale of assessments used for contributions to the U.N. budget. For the U.S., the contribution for the last years has been 25 per cent of the budget.]+

(b) Financing the enterprise

Annex IV

Article 11

Finances

1. The funds of the Enterprise shall include:

(a) amount received from the Authority in accordance with article 173, paragraph 2(b);

(b) voluntary contributions made by States Parties for the purpose of financing actities of the Enterprise;

(c) amounts borrowed by the Enterprise in accordance with paragraphs 2 and 3;

(d) income of the Enterprise from its operations;

(e) other funds made available to the Enterprise to enable it to commence operations as soon as possible and to carry out its functions.

2. (a) The Enterprise shall have the power to borrow funds and to furnish such collateral or other security as it may determine. Before making a public sale of its obligations in the financial markets or currency of a State Party, the Enterprise shall obtain the approval of that State Party. The total amount of borrowings shall be approved by the Council upon the recommendation of the Governing Board.

(b) States Parties shall make every reasonable effort to support applications by the Enterprise for loans on capital markets and from international financial institutions.

3. (a) The Enterprise shall be provided with the funds necessary to explore and exploit one mine site, and to transport, process and market the minerals recovered therefrom and the nickel, copper, cobalt and manganese obtained, and to meet its initial administrative expenses. The amount of the said funds, and the criteria and factors for its adjustment, shall be included by the Preparatory Commission in the draft rules, regulations and procedures of the Authority.

(b) All States Parties shall make available to the Enterprise an amount equivalent to one half of the funds referred to in subparagraph (a) by way of long-term interest-free loans in accordance with the scale of assessments for the United Nations regular budget in force at the time when the assessments are made, adjusted to take into account the States which are not members of the United Nations. Debts incurred by the Enterprise in raising the other half of the funds shall be guaranteed by all States Parties in accordance with the same scale.

(c) If the sum of the financial contributions of States Parties is less than the funds provided to the Enterprise under subparagraph (a), the Assembly shall, at its first session, consider the extent of the shortfall and adopt by consensus measures for dealing with this shortfall, taking into account the obligations of States Parties under subparagraphs (a) and (b) and any recommendatons of the Preparatory Commission.

(d) (i) Each State Party shall, within 60 days after the entry into force of this Convention, or within 30 days after the deposit of its instrument of ratification or accession, whichever is later, deposit with the Enterprise irrevocable, non-negotiable, non-interest-bearing promissory notes in the amount of the share of such State Party of interest-free loans pursuant to subparagraph (b).

(ii) The Board shall prepare, at the earliest practicable date after this Convention enters into force, and thereafter at annual or other appropriate intervals, a schedule of the magnitude and timing of its requirements for the funding of its administrative expenses and for activities carried out by the Enterprise in accordance with article 170 and article 12 of this Annex.

(iii) The States Parties shall, thereupon, be notified by the Enterprise, through the Authority, of their respective shares of the funds in accordance with paragraph 3(b), required for such expenses. The Enterprise shall encash such amounts of the promissory notes as may be required to meet the expenditure referred to in the schedule with respect to interest-free loans.

(iv) States Parties shall, upon receipt of the notification, make available their respective shares of debt guarantees for the Enterprise in accordance with subparagraph (b).

(e) (i) If the Enterprise so requests, States Parties may provide debt guarantees in addition to those provided in accordance with the scale referred to in subparagraph (b).

(ii) In lieu of debt guarantees, a State Party may make a voluntary contribution to the Enterprise in an amount equivalent to that portion of the debts which it would otherwise be liable to guarantee.

(f) Repayment of the interest-bearing loans shall have priority over the repayment of interest-free loans. Repayment of interest-free loans shall be in accordance with a schedule adopted by the Assembly, upon the recommendation of the Council and the advice of the Board. In the exercise of this function the Board shall be guided by the relevant provisions of the rules, regulations and procedures of the Authority, which shall take into account the paramount importance of ensuring the effective functioning of the Enterprise and, in particular, ensuring its financial independence.

(g) Funds made available to the Enterprise shall be freely usuable currencies or currencies which are freely available and effectively usable in he major foreign exchange markets. These currencies shall be defined by the rules, regulations and procedures of the Authority in accordance with prevailing international monetary practice. Except as provided in paragraph 2, no State Party shall maintain or impose restrictions on the holding, use or exchange by the Enterprise of these funds.

(h) "Debt guarantees" means a promise of a State Party to creditors of the Enterprise to pay, pro rata in accordance with the appropriate scale, the financial obligations of the Enterprise covered by the guarantee following notice by the creditors to the State Party of a default by the Enterprise. Procedures for the payment of those obligations shall be in conformity with the rules, regulations and procedures of the Authority.

4. The funds, assets and expenses of the Enterprise shall be kept separate from those of the Authority. This article shall not prevent the Enterprise from making arrangements with the Authority regarding facilities, personnel and services and arrangements for reimbursement of administrative expenses paid by either on behalf of the other.

5. The records, books and accounts of the Enterprise, including its annual financial statements, shall be audited annually by an independent auditor appointed by the Council.

(c) Financial terms of mining contracts

Annex III

Article 13

Financial terms of contracts

1. In adopting rules, regulations and procedures concerning the financial terms of a contract between the Authority and the entities referred to in article 153, paragraph 2(b), and in negotiating those financial terms in accordance with Part XI and those rules, regulations and procedures, the Authority shall be guided by the following objectives:

(a) to ensure optimum revenues for the Authority from the proceeds of commercial production;

(b) to attract investments and technology to the exploration and exploitation of the Area;

(c) to ensure equality of financial treatement and comparable financial obligations for contractors;

(d) to provide incentives on a uniform and non-discriminatory basis for contractors to undertake joint arrangments with the Enterprise and developing States or their nationals, to stimulate the transfer of technology thereto, and to train the personnel of the Authority and of devleloping States;

(e) to enable the Enterprise to engage in sea-bed mining effectively at the same time as the entities referred to in article 153, paragraph 2(b); and

(f) to ensure that, as a result of the financial incentives provided to contracters under paragraph 14, under the terms of contracts reviewed in accordance with article 19 of this Annex or under the provisions of article 11 of this Annex with respect to joint ventures, contractors are not subsidized so as to be given an artificial advantage with respect to land-based miners.

2. A fee shall be leveled for the administrative cost of processing an application for approval of a plan of work in the form of a contract and shall be fixed at an amount of $US 500,000 per application. The amount of the fee shall be reviewed from time to time by the Council in order to ensure that it covers the administrative cost incurred. If such administrative cost incurred by the Authority in processing an application is less than the fixed amount the Authority shall refund the difference to the applicant.

3. A contractor shall pay an annual fixed fee of $US 1 million from the date of entry into force of the contract. If the approved date of commencement of commercial productions is postponed because of a delay in issuing the production authorization, in accordance with article 151, the annual fixed fee shall be waived for the period of postponment. From the date of commencement of commercial production, the contractor shall pay either the production charge or annual fixed fee, whichever is greater.

4. Within a year of the date of commencement of commercial production in conformity with paragraph 3, a contractor shall choose to make his financial contribution by either:

(a) paying a production charge only; or

(b) paying a combination of a production charge and a share of net proceeds.

5. (a) If a contractor chooses to make his financial contribution to the Authority by paying a production charge only, it shall be fixed at a percentage of the market value of the processed metals produced from the polymetallic nodules recovered from the area covered by the contract. This percentage shall be fixed as follows:

(i) years 1-10 of commercial production 5 per cent

(ii) Years 11 to end of commercial production 12 per cent

(b) The said market value shall be the product of the quantity of the processed metals produced from the polymetallic nodules extracted from the area covered by the contract and the average price for those metals during the relevant accounting year, as defined in paragraphs 7 and 8.

6. If a contractor chooses to make his financial contribution to the Authority by paying a combination of a production charge and a share of net proceeds, such payments shall be determined as follows:

(i) first period of commercial production 2 per cent
(ii) second period of commercial production 4 per cent

If, in the second period of commercial production, as defined in subparagraph (d), the return on investment in any accounting year as defined in subparagraph (m) falls below 15 per cent as a result of the payment of the production charge at 4 per cent, the production charge shall be 2 per cent instead of 4 per cent in that accounting year.

(b) The said market value shall be the product of the quantity of the processed metals produced from the polymetallic nodules recovered from the area covered by the contract and the average price for those metals during the relevant accounting year as defined in paragraphs 7 and 8.

(c) (i) The Authority's share of net proceeds shall be taken out of that portion of the contractor's net proceeds which is attributable to the mining of the resources of the area covered by the contract, referred to hereinafter as attributable net proceeds.

(ii) The Authority's share of attributable net proceeds shall be determined in accordance with the following incremental schedule:

Portion of attributable net proceeds

Share of the Authority

First period of commercial production

Second period of commercial production

That portion representing a return on investment which is greater than 0 per cent, but less than 10 per cent

35 per cent

40 per cent

That portion representing a return on investment which is greater than 10 per cent, but less than 20 per cent

42.5 per cent

50 per cent

That portion representing a return on investment which is 20 per cent or greater

50 per cent

70 per cent

....

[The remaining parts of this article, which is extensive, consists of definitions of terms. You are referred to the treaty itself for those definitions.]

[For provisions concerning the distribution of revenues from seabed mining, see articles 165(2)(f), 162(2)(o), and 160(2)(f)(i).]

Why have alternative methods of making payments? Why not just a straight royalty system as used in the U.S. for oil and gas?

10. Transfer of technology

Annex III

Article 5

Transfer of technology

1. When submitting a plan of work, every applicant shall make available to the Authority a general description of the equipment and methods to be used in carrying out activities in the Area, and other relevant non-proprietary information about the characteristics of such technology and information as to where such technology is available.

2. Every operator shall inform the Authority of revisions in the description and information made available pursuant to paragraph 1 whenever a substantial technological change or innovation is introduced.

3. Every contract for carrying out activities in the Area shall contain the following undertakings by the contractor:

(a) to make available to the Enterprise on fair and reasonable commercial terms and conditions, whenever the Authority so requests, the technology which he uses in carrying out activities in the Area under the contract, which the contractor is legally entitled to transfer. This shall be done by means of licenses or other appropriate arrangements which the contractor shall negotiate with the Enterprise and which shall be set forth in a specific agreement supplementary to the contract. This undertaking may be invoked only if the Enterprise finds that it is unable to obtain the same or equally efficient and useful technology on the open market on fair and reasonable commercial terms and conditions;

(b) to obtain a written assurance from the owner of any technology used in carrying out activities in the Area under the contract, which is not generally available on the open market and which is not covered by subparagraph (a), that the owner will, whenever the Authority so requests, make that technology available to the Enterprise under license or other appropriate arrangements and on fair and reasonable commercial terms and conditions, to the same extent as made available to the contractor. If this assurance is not obtained, the technology in question shall not be used by the contractor in carrying out activities in the Area;

(c) to acquire from the owner by means of an enforceable contract, upon the request of the Enterprise and if it is possible to do so without substantial cost to the contractor, the legal right to transfer to the Enterprise any technology used by the contractor, in carrying out activities in the Area under the contract, which is not generally available on the open market. In cases where there is a substantial corporate relationship between the contractor and the owner of the technology, the closeness of this relationship and the degree of control or influence shall be relevant to the determination whether all feasible measures have been taken to acquire such a right. In cases where the contractor exercises effective control over the owner, failure to acquire form the owner the legal right shall be considered relevant to the contractor's qualification for any subsequent application for approval of a plan of work.

(d) to facilitate, upon the request of the Enterprise, the acquisition by the Enterprise of any technology covered by subparagraph (b), under license or other appropriate arrangements and on fair and reasonable terms and conditions, if the Enterprise decides to negotiate directly with the owner of the technology;

(e) to take the same measures as are prescribed in subparagraphs (a), (b), (c) and (d) for the benefit of developing States or group of developing States which has applied for a contract under article 9 of this Annex, provided that these measures shall be limited to the exploitation of the part of the area proposed by the contractor which has been reserved pursuant to article 8 of this Annex and provided that activities under the contract sought by the developing State or group of developing States would not involve transfer of technology to a third State or nationals of a third State. The obligation under this provision shall only apply with respect to any given contractor where technology has not been requested by the Enterprise or transferred by that contractor to the Enterprise.

4. Disputes concerning undertakings required by paragraph 3, like other provisions of the contracts, shall be subject to compulsory dispute settlement in accordance with Part XI and, in cases of violations of these undertakings, suspension or termination of the contract or monetary penalties may be ordered in accordance with article 18 of this Annex. Disputes as to whether offers made by the contractor are within the range of fair and reasonable commercial terms and conditions may be submitted by either party to binding commercial arbitration in accordance with the UNCITRAL Aribitration Rules or such other arbitration rules as may be prescribed in the rules, regulations and procedures of the Authority. If the finding is that the offer made by the contractor is not within the range of fair and reasonable commercial terms and conditions, the contractor shall be given 45 days to revise his offer to bring it within that range before the Authority takes any action in accordance with article 18 of this Annex.

5. If the Enterprise is unable to obtain on fair and reasonable commercial terms and conditions appropriate technology to enable it to commence in a timely manner the recovery and processing of minerals from the Area, either the Council or the Assembly may convene a group of States Parties composed of those which are engaged in activities in the Area, those which have sponsored entities which are engaged in activities in the Area and other States Parties having access to such technology. This group shall consult together and shall take effective measures to ensure that such technology is made available to the Enterprise on fair and reasonable commercial terms and conditions. Each such State Party shall take all feasible measures to this end within its own legal system.

6. In the case of joint ventures with the Enterprise, transfer of technology will be in accordance with the terms of the joint venture agreement.

7. The undertakings required by paragraph 3 shall be included in each contract for the carrying out of activities in the Area until 10 years after the commencement of commercial production by the Enterprise, and may be invoked during that period.

8. For the purposes of this article, "technology" means the specialized equipment and technical know-how, including manuals, designs, operating instructions, training and technical advice and assistance, necessary to assemble, maintain and operate a viable system and the legal right to use these items for that purpose on a non-exclusive basis.

Article 302

Disclosure of information

Without prejudice to the right of a State Party to resort to the procedures for the settlement of disputes provided for in this Convention, nothing in this Convention shall be deemed to require a State Party, in the fulfilment of its obligations under this Convention, to supply informaton the disclosure of which is contrary to the essential interests of its security.

11. Review Conference

Article 155

The Review Conference

1. Fifteen years from 1 January of the year in which the earliest commercial production commences under an approved plan of work, the Assembly shall convene a conference for the review of those provisions of this Part and the relevant Annexes which govern the system of exploration and exploitation of the resources of the Area. The Review Conference shall consider in detail in the light of the experience acquired during that period:

(a) whether the provisions of this Part which govern the system of exploration and exploitation of the resources of the Area have achieved their aims in all respects, including whether they have benefited mankind as a whole;

(b) whether, during the 15-year period, reserved areas have been exploited in an effective and balanced manner in comparison with non-reserved areas;

(c) whether the development and use of the Area and its resources have been undertaken in such a manner as to foster healthy development of the world economy and balanced growth of international trade;

(d) whether monopolization of activities in the Area has been prevented;

(e) whether the policies set forth in articles 150 and 151 have been fulfilled; and

(f) whether the system has resulted in the equitable sharing of benefits derived from activities in the Area, taking into particular consideration the interests and needs of the developing States.

2. The Review Conference shall ensure the maintenance of the principle of the common heritage of mankind, the international regime designed to ensure equitable exploitation of the resources of the Area for the benefit of all countries, especially the developing States, and an Authority to organize, conduct and control activities in the Area. It shall also ensure the maintenance of the principles laid down in this Part with regard to the exclusion of claims or exercise of sovereignty over any part of the Area, the rights of States and their general conduct in relation to the Area, and their participation in activities in the Area in conformity with this Convention, the prevention and monopolization of activities in the Area, the use of the Area exclusively for peaceful purposes, economic aspects of activities in the Area, marine scientific research, transfer of technology, protection of the marine environment, protection of human life, rights of coastal States, the legal status of the waters superjacent to the Area and that of the air space above those waters and accomodation between activities in the Area and other activities in the marine environment.

3. The decision-making procedure applicable at the Review Conference shall be the same as that applicable at the Third United Nations Conference on the Law of the Sea. The Conference shall make every effort to reach agreement on any amendments by way of consensus and there should be no voting on such matters until all efforts at achieving consensus have been exhausted.

4. If, five years after its commencement, the Review Conference has not reached agreement on the system of exploration and exploitation of the resources of the Area, it may decide during the ensuing 12 months, by a three-fourths majority of the States Parties, to adopt and submit to the States Parties for ratification or accession such amendments changing or modifying the system as it determines necessary and appropriate. Such amendments shall enter into force for all States Parties 12 months after the deposit of instruments of ratification or accession by three fourths of the States Parties.

5. Amendments adopted by the Review Conference pursuant to this article shall not affect rights acquired under existing contracts.

12. Amendments to the treaty other than by review conference

Article 312

Amendment

1. After the expiry of a period of 10 years from the date of entry into force of this Convention, a State Party may, by written communication addressed to the Secretary-General of the United Nations, propose specific amendments to this Convention, other than those relating to activities in the Area, and request the convening of a conference to consider such proposed amendments. The Secretary-General shall circulate such communication to all States Parties. If, within 12 months from the date of the circulation of the communication, not less than one half of the States Parties reply favourably to the request, the Secretary-General shall convene the conference.

2. The decision-making procedure applicable at the amendment conference shall be the same as that applicable at the Third United Nations Conference on the Law of the Sea unless otherwise decided by the conference. The conference should make every effort to reach agreement on any amendments by way of consensus and there should be no voting on them until all efforts at consensus have been exhausted.

Article 313

Amendment by simplified procedure

1. A State Party may, by written communication addressed to the Secretary-General of the United Nations, propose an amendment to this Convention, other than an amendment relating to activities in the Area, to be adopted by the simplified procedure set forth in this article without convening a conference. The Secretary-General shall circulate the communication to all States Parties.

2. If, within a period of 12 months from the date of the circulation of the communication, a State Party objects to the proposed amendment or to the proposal for its adoption by the simplified procedure, the amendment shall be considered rejected. The Secretary-General shall immediately notify all States Parties accordingly.

3. If, 12 months from the date of the circulation of the communication, no State Party has objected to the proposed amendment or to the proposal for its adoption by the simplified procedure, the proposed amendment shall be considered adopted. The Secretary-General shall notify all States Parties that the proposed amendment has been adopted.

Article 314

Amendments to the provisions of this Convention relating exclusively to activities in the Area

1. A State Party may, by written communication addressed to the Secretary-General of the United Nations, propose an amendment to the provisions of this Convention relating exclusively to activities in the Area, including Annex VI, section 4. The Secretary-General shall circulate such communication to all States Parties. The proposed amendment shall be subject to the approval by the Assembly following its approval by the Council. Representatives of States Parties in those organs shall have full powers to consider and approve the proposed amendment. The proposed amendment as approved by the Council and the Assembly shall be considered adopted.

2. Before approving any amendment under paragraph 1, the Council and the Assembly shall ensure that it does not prejudice the system of exploration and exploitation of the resources of the Area, pending the Review Conference in accordance with article 155.

13. Entry into force of amendments

Article 316

Entry into force of amendments

1. Amendments to this Convention, other than those referred to in paragraph 5, shall enter into force for all States Parties ratifying or acceding to them on the thirtieth day following the deposit of instruments of ratification or accession by two thirds of the States Parties or by 60 States Parties, whichever is greater. Such amendments shall not affect the enjoyment by other States of their rights or the performance of their obligations under this Convention.

2. An amendment may provide that a large number of ratifications or accessions shall be required for entry into force than are required by this article.

3. For each State Party ratifying or acceding to an amendment referred to in paragraph 1 after the deposit of the required number of instruments of ratification or accession, the amendment shall enter into force on the thirtieth day following the deposit of its instrument of ratification or accession.

4. A State which becomes a Party to this Convention after the entry into force of an amendment in accordance with paragraph 1 shall, failing an expression of a different intention by that State:

(a) be considered as a Party to the Convention as so amended; and

(b) be considered as a Party to the unamended Convention in relation to any State Party not bound by the amendment.

5. Any amendment relating exclusively to activities in the Area and any amendment to Annex XI shall enter into force for all States Parties one year following the deposit of instruments of ratification or accession by three fourths of the States Parties.

6. A State which becomes a Party to this Convention after the entry into force of amendments in accordance with paragraph 5 shall be considered as a Party to the Convention as so amended.

14. Investment protection

When negotiations were completed on the treaty in 1981, it was realized that the Convention would in all likelihood not enter into force for several years. At this writing, it is still not in force. This raised a problem with respect to those mining consortia that were already making substantial investments in mining research and development, and which anticipated, at that time, moving into exploration before the expiration of much time. The question was how to protect these mining investments during this exploratory period between the time the treaty was concluded and adopted, and the time at which it entered into force. The treaty, for example, places the power to approve applications for plans of work in the Authority, but until the treaty enters into force, there will be no Authority. This problem was addressed in two resolutions adopted by the Conference. Resolution I created a Preparatory Commission to begin drafting provisional rules, regulations and procedures to submit to the Authority at its first session for consideration and adoption. Resolution II turns to the Preparatory Commission as a temporaty substitution for the Authority during the exploratory period before the Convention enters into force. Its provisions are somewhat unique.

RESOLUTION II

GOVERNING PREPARATORY INVESTMENT IN PIONEER ACTIVITIES RELATING TO POLYMETALLIC NODULES

The Third United Nations Conference on the Law of the Sea,

Having adopted the Convention on the Law of the Sea (the "Convention"),

Having established by resolution I the Preparatory Commission for the International Sea-Bed Authority and for the International Tribunal for the Law of the Sea (the "Commission") and directed it to prepare draft rules, regulations and procedures, as necessary to enable the Authority to commence its functions, as well as to make recommendations for the early entry into effective operation of the Enterprise,

Desirous of making provision for investments by States and other entities in a manner compatable with the international regime set forth in Part XI of the Convention and the Annexes relating thereto before the entry into force of the Convention,

Recognizing the need to ensure that the Enterprise will be provided with the funds, technology and expertise necessary to enable it to keep pace with the States and other entities referred to in the preceding paragraph with respect to activities in the Area,

Decides as follows:

1. For the purposes of this resolution:

(a) "pioneer investor" refers to:

(i) France, India, Japan and the Union of Soviet Socialist Republics, or a state enterprise of each of those States or one natural or juridical person which possesses the nationality of or is effectively controlled by each of those States, or their nationals, provided that the State concerned signs the Convention and the State or state enterprise or natural or juridical person has expended, before 1 January 1983, an amount equivalent to at least $US 30 million (United States dollars calculated in constant dollars relative to 1982) in pioneer activities and has expended no less than 10 per cent of that amount in the location, survey and evaluation of the area referred to in paragraph 3(a);

(ii) four entities, whose components being natural or juridical persons[3] possess the nationality of one or more of the following States, or are effectively controlled by one or more of them or their nationals: Belgium, Canada, the Federal Republic of Germany, Italy, Japan, the Netherlands, the United Kingdom of Great Britain and Northern Ireland, and the United States of America, provided that the certifying State or States sign the Convention and the entity concerned has expended, before 1 January 1983, the levels of expenditures for the purpose stated in subparagraph (i);

(iii) any developing State which signs the Convention or any state enterprise or natural or juridical person which possesses the nationality of such State or is effectively controlled by it or its nationals, or any group of the foregoing, which, before 1 January 1985, has expended the levels of expenditures for the purpose stated in subparagraph (i);

The rights of the pioneer investor may devolve upon its successor in interest.

(b) "pioneer activities" means undertakings, commitments of financial and other assets, investigations, findings, research, engineering development and other activities relevant to the determination of the technical and economic feasibility of exploitation. Pioneer activities include:

(i) any at-sea observation and evaluation activity which has as its objective the establishment and documentation of the nature, shape, concentration, location and grade of polymetallic nodules and of the environmental, technical and other appropriate factors which must be taken into account before exploitation;

(ii) the recovery from the Area of polymetallic nodules with a view to the designing, fabricating and testing of equipment which is intended to be used in the exploitation of polymetallic nodules;

(c) "certifying State" means a State which signs the Convention, standing in the same relation to a pioneer investor as would a sponsoring State pursuant to Annex III, article 4, of the Convention and which certifies the levels of expenditures specified in subparagraph (a);

(d) "polymetallic nodules" means one of the resources of the Area consisting of any deposit or accretion of nodules, on or just below the surface of the deep sea-bed, which contain manganese, nickle, cobalt and copper;

(e) "pioneer area" means an area allocated by the Commission to a pioneer investor for pioneer activities pursuant to this resolution. A pioneer area shall not exceed 150,000 square kilometers. The pioneer investor shall relinquish portions of the pioneer area to revert to the Area, in accordance with the following schedule:

---

3. For their identity and composition see "Sea-bed mineral resource development: recent activities of the international Consortia" and addendum, published by the Department of International Economic and Social Affairs of the United Nations (ST/ESA/107 and Add.1).

(i) 20 per cent of the area allocated by the end of the third year from the date of the allocation;

(ii) an additional 10 per cent of the area allocated by the end of the fifth year from the date of the allocation;

(iii) an additional 20 per cent of the area allocated or such larger amount as would exceed the exploitation area decided upon by the Authority in its rules, regulations and procedures, after eight years from the date of the allocation of the area or the date of the award of a production authorization, whichever is earlier;

(f) "Area", "Authority", "activities in the Area" and "resources" have the meanings assigned to them in the Convention.

2. As soon as the Commission begins to function, any State which has signed the Convention may apply to the Commission on its behalf or on behalf of any state enterprise or entity or natural or juridical person specified in paragraph 1(a) for registration as a pioneer investor. The Commission shall register the applicant as a pioneer investor if the application:

(a) is accompanied, in the case of a State which has signed the Convention, by a statement certifying the level of expenditure made in accordance with paragraph 1(a), and, in all other cases, a certificate concerning such level of expenditure issued by a certifying State or States; and

(b) is in conformity with the other provisions of this resolution, including paragraph 5.

3. (a) Every application shall cover a total area which need not be a single continuous area, sufficiently large and of sufficient estimated commercial value to allow two mining operations. The application shall indicate the co-ordinates of the area defining the total area and dividing it into two parts of equal estimated commercial value and shall contain all the data available to the applicant with respect to both parts of the area. Such data shall include, *inter alia*, information relating to mapping, testing, the density of polymetallic nodules and their metal content. In dealing with such data, the Commission and its staff shall act in accordance with the relevant provisions of the Convention and its Annexes concerning the confidentiality of data.

(b) Within 45 days of receiving the data required by subparagraph (a), the Commission shall designate the part of the area which is to be reserved in accordance with the Convention for the conduct of activities in the Area by the Authority through the Enterprise or in association with developing States. The other part of the area shall be allocated to the pioneer investor as a pioneer area.

4. No pioneer investor may be registered in respect of more than one pioneer area. In the case of a pioneer investor which is made up of two or more components, none of such components may apply to be registered as a pioneer investor in its own right under paragraph 1(a)(iii).

5. (a) Any State which has signed the Convention and which is a prospective certifying State shall ensure, before making applications to the Commission under paragraph 2, that areas in respect of which applications are made do not overlap one another or areas previously allocated as pioneer areas. The States concerned shall keep the Commission currently and fully informed of any efforts to resolve conflicts with respect to overlapping claims and of the results thereof.

(b) Certifying States shall ensure, before the entry into force of the Convention, that pioneer activities are conducted in a manner compatible with it.

(c) The prospective certifying States, including all potential claimants, shall resolve their conflicts as required under subparagraph (a) by negotiations within a reasonable period. If such conflicts have not been resolved by 1 March 1983, the prospective certifying States shall arrange for the submission of all such claims to binding arbitration in accordance with UNCITRAL Arbitration Rules to commence not later than 1 May 1983 and to be completed by 1 December 1984. If one of the States concerned does not wish to participate in the arbitration, it shall arrange for a juridical person of its nationality to represent it in the arbitration. The arbitral tribunal may, for good cause, extend the deadline for the making of the award for one or more 30-day periods.

(d) In determining the issue as to which applicant involved in a conflict shall be awarded all or part of each area in conflict, the arbitral tribunal shall find a solution which is fair and equitable, having regard, with respect to each applicant involved in the conflict, to the following factors:

(i) the deposit of a list of relevant co-ordinates with the prospective certifying State or States not later than the date of adoption of the Final Act or 1 January 1983, whichever is earlier;

(ii) the continuity and extent of past activities relative to each area in conflict and to the application area of which it is a part;

(iii) the date on which each pioneer investor concerned or predecessor in interest or component organization thereof commenced activities at sea in the application area;

(iv) the financial cost of activities measured in constant United States dollars relevant to each area in conflict and to the application area of which it is a part; and

(v) the time when those activities were carried out and the quality of activities.

6. A pioneer investor registered pursuant to this resolution, shall from the date of registration, have the exclusive right to carry out pioneer activities in the pioneer area allocated to it.

7. (a) Every applicant for registration as a pioneer investor shall pay to the Commission a fee of $US 250,000. When the pioneer investor applies to the Authority for a plan of work for exploration and exploitation the fee referred to in Annex III, article 13, paragraph 2, of the Convention, shall be $US 250,000.

(b) Every registered pioneer investor shall pay an annual fixed fee of $US 1 million commencing from the date of the allocation of the pioneer area. The payments shall be made by the pioneer investor to the Authority upon approval of its plan of work for exploration and exploitation . The financial arrangements undertaken pursuant to such plan of work shall be adjusted to take account of the payments made pursuant to this paragraph.

(c) Every registered pioneer investor shall agree to incur periodic expenditures, with respect to the pioneer area allocated to it, until approval of its plan of work pursuant to paragraph 8, of an amount to be determined by the Commission. The amount should be reasonably related to the size of the pioneer area and the expenditures which would be expected of a *bona fide* operator who intends to bring that area into commercial production within a reasonable time.

8. (a) Within six months of the entry into force of the Convention and certification by the Commission in accordance with paragraph 11, of compliance with this resolution, the pioneer investor so registered shall apply to the Authority for approval of a plan of work for exploration and exploitation, in accordance with the Convention. The plan of work in respect of such application shall comply with and be governed by the relevant provisions of the Convention and the rules, regulations and procedures of the Authority, including those on the operational requirements, the financial requirements and the undertakings concerning the transfer of technology. Accordingly, the Authority shall approve such application.

(b) When an application for approval of a plan of work is submitted by an entity other than a State, pursuant to subparagraph (a), the certifying State or States shall be deemed to be the sponsoring State for the purposes of Annex III, article 4, of the Convention, and shall thereupon assume such obligations.

(c) No plan of work for exploration and exploitation shall be approved unless the certifying State is a Party to the Convention. In the case of the entities referred to in paragraph 1(a)(ii), the plan of work for exploration and exploitation shall not be approved unless all the States whose natural or juridical persons comprise those entities are Parties to the Convention. If any such State fails to ratify the Convention within six months after it has received a notification from the Authority that an application by it, or sponsored by it, is pending, its status as a pioneer investor or certifying State, as the case may be, shall terminate, unless the Council, by a majority of three fourths of its members present and voting, decides to postpone the terminal date for a period not exceeding six months.

9. (a) In the allocation of production authorizations, in accordance with article 151 and Annex III, article 7, of the Convention, the pioneer investors who have obtained approval of plans of work for exploration and exploitation shall have priority over all applicants other than the Enterprise which shall be entitled to production authorization for two mine sites including that referred to in article 151, paragraph 5, of the Convention. After each of the pioneer investors has obtained production authorization for its first mine site, the priority for the Enterprise contained in Annex III, article 7, paragraph 6, of the Convention shall apply.

(b) Production authorizations shall be issued to each pioneer investor within 30 days of the date on which that pioneer investor notifies the Authority that it will commence commercial production within five years. If a pioneer investor is unable to begin production within the period of five years for reasons beyond its control, it shall apply to the Legal and Technical Commission for an extension of time. That Commission shall grant the extension of time, for a period not exceeding five years and not subject to further extension, if it is satisfied that the pioneer investor cannot begin on an economically viable basis at the time originally planned. Nothing in this subparagraph shall prevent the Enterprise or any other pioneer applicant, who has notified the Authority that it will commence commercial production within five years, from being given a priority over any applicant who has obtained an extension of time under this subparagraph.

(c) If the Authority, upon being given notice, pursuant to subparagraph (b), determines that the commencement of commercial production within five years would exceed the production ceiling in article 151, paragraphs 2 to 7, of the Convention, the applicant shall hold a priority over any other applicant for the award of the next production authorization allowed by the production ceiling.

(d) If two or more pioneer investors apply for production authorizations to begin commercial production at the same time and article 151, paragraphs 2 to 7, of the Convention, would not permit all such production to commence simultaneously, the Authority shall notify the pioneer investors concerned. Within three months of such notification, they shall decide whether and, if so, to what extent they wish to apportion the allocable tonnage among themselves.

(e) If, pursuant to subparagaph (d), the pioneer investors concerned decide not to apportion production among themselves they shall agree on an order of priority of production authorizations and all subsequent applications for production authorizations will be granted after those referred to in this subparagraph have been approved.

(f) If, pursuant to subparagraph (d), the pioneer investors concerned decide to apportion the available production among themselves, the Authority shall award each of them a production authorization for such lesser quantity as they have agreed. In each case the stated production requirements of the applicant will be approved and their full production will be allowed as soon as the production ceiling admits of additional capacity sufficient for the applicants involved in the competition. All subsequent applications for production authorizations will only be granted after the requirements of this subparagraph have been met and the applicant is no longer subject to the reduction of production provided for in this subparagraph.

(g) If the parties fail to reach agreement within the stated time period, the matter shall be decided immediately by the means provided for in paragraph 5(c) in accordance with the criteria set forth in Annex III, article 7, paragraphs 3 and 5, of the Convention.

10. (a) Any rights acquired by entities or natural or juridical persons which possess the nationality of or are effectively controlled by a State or States whose status as certifying State has been terminated, shall lapse unless the pioneer investor changes its nationality and sponsorship within six months of the date of such termination, as provided for in subparagraph (c).

(b) A pioneer investor may change its nationality and sponsorship from that existing at the time of its registration as a pioneer investor to that of any State Party to the Convention which has effective control over the pioneer investor in terms of paragraph 1(a).

(c) Changes of nationality and sponsorship pursuant to this paragraph shall not affect any right or priority conferred on a pioneer investor pursuant to paragraphs 6 and 8.

11. The Commission shall:

(a) provide each pioneer investor with the certificate of compliance with the provisions of this resolution referred to in paragraph 8; and

(b) include in its final report required by paragraph 11 of resolution I of the Conference details of all registration of pioneer investors and allocation of pioneer areas pursuant to this resolution.

12. In order to ensure that the Enterprise is able to carry out activities in the Area in such a manner as to keep pace with States and other entities:

(a) every registered pioneer investor shall:

(i) carry out exploration, at the request of the Commission, in the area reserved, pursuant to paragraph 3 in connection with its application, for activities in the Area by the Authority through the Enterprise or in association with developing States, on the basis that the costs so incurred plus interest thereon at the rate of 10 per cent per annum shall be reimbursed;

(ii) provide training at all levels for personnel designated by the Commission;

(iii) undertake before the entry into force of the Convention, to perform the obligations prescribed in the Convention relating to transfer of technology;

(b) every certifying State shall:

(i) ensure that the necessary funds are made available to the Enterprise in a timely manner in accordance with the Convention, upon its entry into force; and

(ii) report periodically to the Commission on the activities carried out by it, by its entities or natural or juridical persons.

13. The Authority and its organs shall recognize and honour the rights and obligations arising from this resolution and the decisions of the Commission taken pursuant to it.

14. Without prejudice to paragraph 13, this resolution shall have effect until the entry into force of the Convention.

15. Nothing in this resolution shall derogate from Annex III, article 6, paragraph 3(c), of the Convention.

F. RELATED DOCUMENTS

To deal with disputes arising concerning deep seabed mining, a mechanism is established by the treaty. We will deal with this subject in a separate chapter on dispute resolution. The following materials contain the U.S. legislation on mining, and the so-called "mini" treaty as alternatives to the law of the sea Convention.

DEEP SEABED HARD MINERAL RESOURCES ACT, 30 U.S.C. 1401 et seq. (1980)

1401. Congressional findings and declaration of purpose

(a) Findings

The Congress finds that--

(1) the United States' requirements for hard minerals to satisfy national industrial needs will continue to expand and the demand for such minerals will increasingly exceed the available domestic sources of supply;

(2) in the case of certain hard minerals, the United States is dependent upon foreign sources of supply and the acquisition of such minerals from foreign sources is a significant factor in the national balance-of-payments position;

(3) the present and future national interest of the United States requires the availability of hard mineral resources which is independent of the export policies of foreign nations;

(4) there is an alternate source of supply, which is significant in relation to national needs, of certain hard minerals, including nickel, copper, cobalt and manganese, contained in the nodules existing in great abundance on the deep seabed;

(5) the nations of the world, including the United States, will benefit if the hard mineral resources of the deep seabed beyond limits of national jurisdiction can be developed and made available for their use;

(6) in particular, future access to the nickel, copper, cobalt and manganese resources of the deep seabed will be important to the industrial needs of the nations of the world, both developed and developing;

(7) on December 17, 1970, the United States supported (by affirmative vote) the United Nations General Assembly Resolution 2749(XXV) declaring inter alia the principle that marine resources of the deep seabed are the common heritage of mankind, with the expectation that this principle would be legally defined under the terms of a comprehensive international Law of the Sea Treaty yet to be agreed upon;

(8) it is in the national interest of the United States and other nations to encourage a widely acceptable Law of the Sea Treaty, which will provide a new legal order for the oceans covering a broad range of ocean interests, including exploration for and commercial recovery of hard mineral resources of the deep seabed;

(9) the negotiations to conclude such a Treaty and establish the international regime governing the exercise of rights over, and exploration of, the resources of the deep seabed, referred to in General Assembly Resolution 2749(XXV) are in progress but may not be concluded in the near future;

(10) even if such negotiations are concluded promptly, much time will elapse before such an international regime is established and in operation;

(11) development of technology required for the exploration and recovery of hard mineral resources from the deep seabed will require substantial investment for many years before commercial production can occur, and must proceed at this time if deep seabed minerals are to be available when needed;

(12) it is the legal opinion of the United States that exploration and commercial recovery of hard mineral resources of the deep seabed are freedoms of the high seas subject to a duty of reasonable regard to the interests of other states in their exercise of those and other freedoms recognized by general principles of international law;

(13) pending a Law of the Sea Treaty, and in the absence of agreement among states on applicable principles of international law, the uncertainty among potential investors as to the future legal regime is likely to discourage or prevent the investments necessary to develop deep seabed mining technology;

(14) pending a Law of the Sea Treaty, the protection of the marine environment from damage caused by exploration or recovery of hard mineral resources of the deep seabed depends upon the enactment of suitable interim national legislation;

(15) a Law of the Sea Treaty is likely to establish financial arrangements which obligate the United States or United States citizens to make payments to an international organization with respect to exploration or recovery of hard mineral resources of the deep seabed; and

(16) legislation is required to establish an interim legal regime under which technology can be developed and exploration and recovery of the hard mineral resources of the deep seabed can take place until such time as the Law of the Sea Treaty enters into force with respect to the United States.

(b) Purposes

The Congress declares that the purposes of this chapter are--

(1) to encourage the successful conclusion of a comprehensive Law of the Sea Treaty, which would give legal definition to the principle that the hard mineral resources of the deep seabed are the common heritage of mankind and which will assure, among other things, nondiscriminatory access to such resources for all nations;

(2) pending the ratification by, and entering into force with respect to, the United States of such a Treaty, to provide for the establishment of an international revenue-sharing fund the proceeds of which shall be used for sharing with the international community pursuant to such a Treaty;

(3) to establish, pending the ratification by, and entering into force with respect to, the United States of such a Treaty, an interim program to regulate the exploration for and commercial recovery of hard mineral resources of the deep seabed by United States citizens;

(4) to accelerate the program of environmental assessment of exploration for and commercial recovery of hard mineral resources of the deep seabed and assure that such exploration and recovery activities are conducted in a manner which will encourage the conservation of such resources, protect the quality of the environment, and promote the safety of life and property at sea; and

(5) to encourage the continued development of technology necessary to recover the hard mineral resources of the deep seabed.

1402 International objectives

(a) Disclaimer of extraterritorial sovereignty

By the enactment of this chapter, the United States--

(1) exercises its jurisdiction over United States citizens and vessels and foreign persons and vessels otherwise subject to its jurisdiction, in the exercise of the high seas freedom to engage in exploration for, and commercial recovery of, hard mineral resources of the deep seabed in accordance with generally accepted principles of international law recognized by the United States; but

(2) does not thereby assert sovereignty or sovereign or exclusive rights or jurisdiction over, or the ownership of, any areas or resources in the deep seabed.

(b) Secretary of State

(1) The Secretary of State is encouraged to negotiate successfully a comprehensive Law of the Sea Treaty which, among other things, provides assured and nondiscriminatory access to the hard mineral resources of the deep seabed for all nations, gives legal definition to the principle that the resources of the deep seabed are the common heritage of mankind, and provides for the establishment of requirements for the protection of the quality of the environment as stringent as those promulgated pursuant to this chapter.

(2) Until such a Treaty is concluded, the Secretary of State is encouraged to promote any international actions necessary to adequately protect the environment from adverse impacts which may result from an exploration for and commercial recovery of hard mineral resources of the deep seabed carried out by persons not subject to this chapter.

....

1411. Prohibited activities by United States citizens

(a) Prohibited activities and exceptions

(1) No United States citizen may engage in any exploration or commercial recovery unless authorized to do so under--

(A) a license or permit issued under this subchapter;

(B) a license, permit, or equivalent authorization issued by a reciprocating state; or

(C) an international agreement which is in force with respect to the United States.

(2) The prohibitions of this subsection shall not apply to any of the following activities:

(A) Scientific research, including that concerning hard mineral resources.

(B) Mapping, or the taking of any geophysical, geochemical, oceanographic, or atmospheric measurements or random bottom samplings of the deep seabed, if such taking does not significantly alter the surface or subsurface of the deep seabed or significantly effect the environment.

(C) The design, construction, or testing of equipment and facilities which will or may be used for exploration or commercial recovery, if such design, construction, or testing is conducted on shore, or does not involve the recovery of any but incidental hard mineral resources.

(D) The furnishing of any machinery, products, supplies, services, or materials for any exploration or commercial recovery conducted under a license or permit issued under this subchapter, a license or permit or equivalent authorization issued by a reciprocating state, or under an international agreement.

(E) Activities, other than exploration or commercial recovery activities, of the Federal Government.

....

(c) interference

No United States citizen may interfere or participate in interference with any activity conducted by any licensee or permittee which is authorized to be undertaken under a license or permit issued by the United States to the licensee or permittee under this chapter or with any activity conducted by the holder of, and authorized to be undertaken under, a license or permit or equivalent authorization issued by a reciprocating state for the exploration or commercial recovery of hard mineral resources. United States citizens shall exercise their rights on the high seas with reasonable regard for the interests of other states in their exercise of the freedoms of the high seas.

1412. Licenses for exploration and permits for commercial recovery

(a) Authority to issue

Subject to the provisions of this chapter, the Administrator shall issue to applicants who are elegible therefor licenses for exploration and permits for commercial recovery.

(b) Nature of licenses and permits

(1) A license or permit issued under this subchapter shall authorize the holder thereof to engage in exploration or commercial recovery, as the case may be, consistent with the provisions of this chapter, the regulations issued by the Administrator to implement the provisions of this chapter, and the specific terms, conditions and restrictions applied to the license or permit by the Administrator.

(2) Any license or permit issued under this subchapter shall be exclusive with respect to the holder thereof as against any other United States citizen or any citizen, national or governmental agency of, or any legal entity organized or existing under the laws of any reciprocating state.

(3) A valid existing license shall entitle the holder, if otherwise eligible under the provisions of this chapter and regulations issued under this chapter, to a permit for commercial recovery. Such a permit recognizes the right of the holder to recover hard mineral resources, and to own, transport, use and sell hard mineral resources recovered, under the permit and in accordance with the requirements of this chapter.

(4) In the event of interference with the exploration or commercial recovery activities of a licensee or permittee by nationals of other states, the Secretary of State shall use all peaceful means to resolve the controversy by negotiation, conciliation, aribtration, or resort to agreed tribunals.

....

1413. License and permit applications, review, and certification

....

(b) Priority of right for issuance

Subject to section 1411(b) of this title, priority of right for the issuance of licenses to applicants shall be established on the basis of the chronological order in which license applications which are in substantial compliance with the requirements established under subsection (a)(2) of this section are filed with the Administrator. Priority of right shall not be lost in the case of any application filed which is in substantial but not full compliance with such requirements if the applicant thereafter brings the application into conformity with such requirements within a reasonable period of time as the Administrator shall prescribe in regulations.

....

1415. License and permit terms, conditions, and restrictions; issuance and transfer of licenses and permits

(a) Eligibility for issuance or transfer of license or permit

Before issuing or transferring a license for exploration or permit for commercial recovery, the Administrator must find in writing, after consultation with interested departments and agencies pursuant to section 1413(e) of this title, and upon considering public comments received with respect to the license or permit, that the exploration or commercial recovery proposed in the application--

(1) will not unreasonably interefere with the exercise of the freedoms of the high seas by other states, as recognized under general principles of international law;

(2) will not conflict with any international obligation of the United States established by any treaty or international convention in force with respect to the United States;

(3) will not create a situation which may reasonably be expected to lead to a breach of international peace and security involving armed conflict;

(4) cannot reasonably be expected to result in a significant adverse effect on the quality of the environment, taking into account the analyses and information in any applicable environmental impact statement prepared pursuant to section 1419(c) or 1419(d) of this title; and

(5) will not pose an indordinate threat to the safety of life and property at sea.

....

1419. Protection of the environment

(a) Environmental assessment

(1) Deep ocean mining environmental study (DOMES)

The Administrator shall expand and accelerate the program assessing the effects on the environment from exploration and commercial recovery activities, including seabased processing and the disposal at sea of processing wastes, so as to provide an assessment, as accurate as practicable, of environmental impacts of such activities for the implemenation of subsections (b), (c), and (d) of this section.

....

(c) Programmatic environmental impact statement

(1) If the Administrator, in consultation with the Administrator of the Environmental Protection Agency and with the assistance of other appropriate Federal agencies, determines that a programmatic environmental impact statement is required, the Adminstrator shall, as soon as practicable after June 28, 1980, with respect to the areas of the oceans in which any United States citizen is expected to undertake exploration and commercial recovery under the authority of this chapter--

(A) prepare and publish draft programmatical environmental impact statements which assess the environmental impacts of exploration and commercial recovery in such areas;

(B) afford all interested parties a reasonable time after such dates of publication to submit comments to the Administrator on such draft statements; and

(C) thereafter prepare (giving full consideration to all comments submitted under subparagraph (B)) and publish final programmatice environmental impact statements regarding such areas.....

(d) Environmental impact statements on issuance of licenses and permits

The issuance of, but not the certification of an application for, any license or permit under this subchapter shall be deemed to be a major Federal action significantly affecting the quality of the human environment for purposes of section 4332 of Title 42....

1421. Prevention of interference with other uses of the high seas

Each license and permit issued under this subchapter shall include such restrictions as may be necessary and appropriate to ensure that exploration or commercial recovery activities conducted by the licensee or permittee do not unreasonably interfere with the interests of other states in their exercise of the freedom of the high seas, as recognized under general principles of international law.

1428. Reciprocating states

(a) Designation

The Administrator, in consultation with the Secretary of State and the heads of other appropriate departments and agencies, may designate any foreign nation as a reciprocating state if the Secretary of State finds that such foreign nation--

(1) regulates the conduct of its citizens and other persons subject to its jurisdiction engaged in exploration for, and commercial recovery of, hard mineral resources of the deep seabed in a manner compatible with that provided in this chapter and the regulations issued under this chapter, which includes adequate measure for the protection of the environment, the conservation of natural resources, and the safety of life and property at sea, and includes effective enforcement provisions;

(2) recognizes licenses and permits issued under this subchapter to the extent that such nations, under its laws, (A) prohibits any person from engaging in exploration or commercial recovery which conflicts with that authorized under any license or permit and (B) complies with the date for issuance of licenses and the effective date for permits provided in section 1412(c)(1)(D) of this title;

(3) recognizes, under its procedures, priorities of right, consistent with those provided in this chapter and the regulations issued under this chapter, for application for licenses for exploration or permits for commercial recovery, which applications are made either under its procedures or under this chapter; and

(4) provides an interim legal framework for exploration and commercial recovery which does not unreasonably interefere with the interests of other states in the exercise of the freedoms of the high seas, as recognized under general principles of international law.

(b) Effect of designation

No license or permit shall be issued under this subchapter permitting any exploration or commercial recovery which will conflict with any license, permit, or equivalent authorization issued by any foreign nation which is designated as a reciprocating state under subsection (a) of this section.

(c) Notification

Upon receipt of any application for a license or permit under this subchapter, the Administrator shall immediately notify all reciprocating states of such application. The notification shall include those portions of the exploration plan or recovery plan submitted with respect to the application, or a summary thereof, and any other appropriate information not required to be withheld from public disclosure by section 1423(c) of this title.

(d) Revocation of reciprocating state status

The Administrator, in consultation with the Secretary of State and the heads of other appropriate departments and agencies, shall revoke the designation of a foreign nation as a reciprocating state if the Secretary of State finds that such foreign nation no longer complies with the requirements of subsection (a) of this section. At the request of any holder of a license, permit, or equivalent authorization of such foreign nation, who obtained the license, permit, or equivalent authorization while such foreign nation was a reciprocating state, the Administrator, in consultation with the Secretary of State, may decide to recognize the license, permit, or equivalent authorization for purposes of subsection (b) of this section.

(e) Authorization

The President is authorized to negotiate agreements with foreign nations necessary to implement this section.

(f) International consultations

The Administrator, in consultation with the Secretary of State and the heads of other appropriate departments and agencies, shall consult with foreign nations which enact, or are preparing to enact, domestic legislation establishing an interim legal framework for exploration and commercial recovery of hard mineral resources. Such consultations shall be carried out with a view to facilitating the designation of such nations as reciprocating states and, as necessary, the negotiation of agreements with foreign nations authorized by subsection (e) of this section. In addition, the Administrator shall provide such foreign nations with information on environmental impacts of exploration and commercial recovery activities, and shall provide any technical assistance requested in designing regulatory measures to protect the environment.

SUBCHAPTER II--TRANSITION TO INTERNATIONAL AGREEMENT

1441. Declaration of Congressional intent

It is the intent of Congress--

(1) that any international agreement to which the United States becomes a party should, in addition to promoting other national oceans objectives--

(A) provide assured and nondiscriminatory access, under reasonable terms and conditions, to the hard mineral resources of the deep seabed for United States citizens, and

(B) provide security of tenure by recognizing the rights of United States citizens who have undertaken exploration or commercial recovery under subchapter I of this chapter before such agreement enters into force with respect to the United States to continue their operations under terms, conditions, and restrictions which do not impose significant new economic burdens upon such citizens with respect to such operations with the effect of preventing the continuation of such operations on a viable economic basis;

(2) that the extent to which any such international agreement conforms to the provisions of paragraph (1) should be determined by the totality of the provisions of such agreement, including, but not limited to, the practical implications for the security of investments of any discretionary powers granted to an international regulatory body, the structures and decisionmaking procedures of such body, the availability of impartial and effective procedures for the settlement of disputes, and any features that tend to discriminate against exploration and commercial recovery activities undertaken by United States citizens; and

(3) that this chapter should be transitional pending--

(A) the adoption of an international agreement at the Third United Nations Conference on the Law of the Sea, and the entering into force of such agreement, or portions thereof, with respect to the United States, or

(B) if such adoption is not forthcoming, the negotiation of a multilateral or other treaty concerning the deep seabed, and the entering into force of such treaty with respect to the United States.

1442. Effect of international agreement

If an international agreement enters into force with respect to the United States, any provision of subchapter I of this chapter, this subchapter, or subchapter III of this chapter, and any regulation issued under any such provision, which is not inconsistent with such international agreement shall continue in effect with respect to United States citizens. In the implementation of such international agreement the Administrator, in consultation with the Secretary of State, shall make every effort, to the maximum extent practicable consistent with the provisions of that agreement, to provide for the continued operation of exploration and commercial recovery activities undertaken by United States citizens prior to entry into force of the agreement. The Administrator shall submit to the Congress, within one year after the date of such entry into force, a report on the actions taken by the Administrator under this section, which report shall include, but not be limited to--

(1) a description of the status of deep seabed mining operations of United States citizens under the international agreement; and

(2) an assessment of whether United States citizens who were engaged in exploration or commercial recovery on the date such agreement entered into force have been permitted to continue their operations.

....

SUBCHAPTER III--ENFORCEMENT AND MISCELLANEOUS PROVISIONS

1461. Prohibited acts

It is unlawful for any person who is a United States citizen, or a foreign national on board a vessel documented or numbered under the laws of the United States, or subject to the jurisdiction of the United States under a reciprocating state agreement negotiated under section 1428(e) of this title--

(1) to violate any provision of this chapter, any regulation issued under this chapter, or any term, condition, or restriction of any license or permit issued to such person under this chapter;

(2) to engage in exploration or commercial recovery after the revocation, or during the period of suspension, of an applicable license or permit issued under this chapter, to engage in a particular exploration or commercial recovery activity during the period such activity has been suspended under this chapter, or to fail to modify a particular exploration or commercial recovery activity for which modification was required under this chapter.

(3) to refuse to permit any Federal officer or employee authorized to monitor or enforce the provisions of this chapter, as provided in sections 1424 and 1464 of this title, to board a vessel documented or numbered under the laws of the United States, or any vessel for which such boarding is authorized by a treaty or executive agreement, for purposes of conducting any search or inspection in connection with the monitoring or enforcement of this chapter, or any regulation, term, condition, or restriction referred to in paragraph (1);

(4) to forcibly assault, resist, oppose, impede, intimidate, or interfere with any such authorized officer or employee in the conduct of any search or inspection described in paragraph (1);

(5) to resist a lawful arrest for any act prohibited by this section;

(6) to ship, transport, offer for sale, sell, purchase, import, export, or have custody, control, or possession of any hard mineral resource recovered, processed, or retained in violation of this chapter or any regulation, term, condition, or restriction referred to in paragraph (1); or

(7) to interfere with, delay, or prevent, by any means, the apprehension or arrest of any other person subject to this section knowing that such other person has committed any act prohibited by this section.

....

FRANCE-FEDERAL REPUBLIC OF GERMANY-UNITED KINGDOM-UNITED STATES: AGREEMENT CONCERNING INTERIM ARRANGEMENTS RELATING TO POLYMETALLIC NODULES OF THE DEEP SEA BED [Done at Washington and entered into force, September 2, 1982]

THE PARTIES TO THIS AGREEMENT:

--HAVING regard to investments made in exploration, research and other pioneer activities relating to the polymetallic nodules of the deep sea bed;

--NOTING the adoption by the Third United Nations Conference on the Law of the Sea of a Convention on the Law of the Sea and of a Resolution Governing Preparatory Investment in Pioneer Activities Relating to Polymetallic Nodules prior to the entry into force of the Convention on the Law of the Sea, and the provision of that Resolution concerning resolution of conflicts among pioneer operators;

--RECALLING the interim character of legislation with respect to deep sea bed operations enacted by certain Parties;

--DESIRING to make appropriate provisions for avoiding overlaps in the areas claimed for future pioneer activities in the deep sea bed and to ensure that, during the interim period, such activities are carried out in an orderly and peaceful manner;

--EMPHASIZING that this Agreement is without prejudice to the decisions of the Parties with respect to the Convention on Law of the Sea adopted by the Third United Nations Conference on the Law of the Sea;

--DESIRING also to avoid any discrimination among Parties in the implementation of this Agreement;

--DESIRING further to insure that adquate areas containing polymetallic nodules remain available for operations by other states and entities in conformity with international law;

HAVE AGREED AS FOLLOWS:

1. The object of the present Agreement is to facilitate the identification and resolution of conflicts which may arise from the filing and processing of applications for authorizations made by Pre-Enactment Explorers (PEEs) on or before March 12, 1982 under legislation in respect of deep sea bed operations enacted by any of the Parties.

2. In the case of a conflict between the areas claimed in such applications, the Parties shall afford the applicants adequate opportunity, and shall encourage them, to resolve such conflict in a timely manner by voluntary procedures.

3. The Parties with whom applications for authorizations have been made by PEEs on or before March 12, 1982 shall follow the procedures set out in Part I of the Schedule hereto in respect of such applications.

4. The Parties shall consult together:

(a) with a view to coordinating and reviewing implementation of this Agreement;

(b) before issuing any authorization under their respective laws relating to deep sea bed operations;

(c) in regard to consideration of any arrangement to facilitate mutual recognitions of such authorizations, it being understood that any such arrangement shall not enter into force before January 1, 1983;

(d) before entering into any other bilateral or any multilateral arrangement between themselves or any arrangement with other States, with respect to deep sea bed operation.

5. In the event that any of the Parties with whom applications for authorizations have been made by PEEs on or before March 12, 1982 enter into an agreement for the mutual recognition of authorizations granted under their respective laws in respect of deep sea bed operations, the Parties concerned shall apply the procedures and impose the requirements set out in Part II of the Schedule hereto.

6. To the extent permissible under national law, a Party shall maintain the confidentiality of the coordinates of application areas and other proprietary or confidential commercial information received in confidence from any other Party in pursuance of cooperation under this Agreement in accordance with the principles set out in Part III of the schedule hereto.

7. The Parties shall settle any dispute arising from the interpretation or application of this Agreement by appropriate means. The Parties to the dispute shall consider the possibility of recourse to binding arbitration and, if they agree, shall have recourse to it.

8. The Schedule hereto is an integral part of this Agreement and Part IV thereof shall apply for the interpretation of this Agreement.

9. The Parties shall not enter into any supplementary international agreement inconsistent with this Agreement.

10. This Agreement may be amended by written agreement of all the Parties.

11. This Agreement shall enter into force upon signature.

12. After entry into force of this Agreement, additional States may be invited to accede to this Agreement at any time with the consent of all Parties.

13. Any Party may denounce this Agreement on 30 days notice to the Government of the United States of America, and in no case shall the denunciation have effect before January 3, 1983.

DONE at Washington this second day of September, 1982, in the English, German and French languages, all texts being equally authentic, in a single copy of which shall be deposited in the archives of the Government of the United States of America, which will transmit a duly certified copy to each of the other signatory Governments.

THE SCHEDULE

PART I

APPLICATION PROCEDURES FOR PRE-ENACTMENT EXPLORERS

1. Each Party as provided in paragraph 3 of the Agreement shall forthwith inform the other Parties of entities which have filed applications with it.

2. Any application filed before March 12, 1982 shall be deemed to be filed on that date.

3. Each Party shall with all dispatch determine whether:

(a) each application filed with it fulfills its domestic requirements;

(b) the applicant is a PEE with respect to the area applied for (an applicant filing on behalf of a PEE shall itself be deemed a PEE for that application);

(c) the area is bounded by a continuous boundary;

(d) the area is reasonably compact.

4. Each Party shall:

(a) notify the other Parties of the results of the initial processing under paragraph 3 above;

(b) with the other Parties establish the final list of applications to which this Agreement applies;

(c) inform the other Parties whether the applicant has applied for the same area, or substantially the same area, to one or more Parties;

(d) if the applicant agrees, inform the other Parties of the coordinates of the area specified in any application filed with it;

(e) endeavor to determine the exact locations of any conflicts.

5. No Party shall issue any authorization before January 3, 1983.

6. Where it is informed of the relevant coordinates, each Party shall notify each of its applicants who is involved in a conflict that a conflict exists. Such notification shall include coordinates identifying the areas in conflict and the identity of each applicant with whom conflict has arisen.

7. Each Party shall ensure that domestic conflicts are resolved pursuant to its respective domestic requirements. Upon agreement of the applicants, domestic conflicts may be resolved in accordance with the international conflict resolution procedures specified in the Schedule. The Parties shall enter into consultations if it appears that the resolution of a domestic conflict might affect the international conflict resolution procedures, or vice versa.

8. (1) Each Party shall accept amendments to applications to which this Agreement applies only if they:

(a) pertain to areas with respect to which the applicant is a PEE (the area applied for in an amendment need not be adjacent to the area applied for in the original application); and

(b) are made in order to resolve an existing conflict with respect to that application.

(2) Each Party shall process any amendment filed pursuant to this paragraph in accordance with the procedures described in the foregoing provisions of this Part except that paragraphs 2, 3(c), 3(d), and 4(c) shall not apply to amendments.

(3) Amendments filed under paragraph 8 of the Schedule shall be eligible for mutual recognition in accordance with the terms of an agreement entered into by any of the Parties pursuant to paragraph 5 of the Agreement.

PART II

CONFLICT RESOLUTION FOR PRE-ENACTMENT EXPLORERS

9. (1) Where there is an international conflict, the Parties shall use their good offices to assist the applicants to resolve the conflict by voluntary procedures.

(2) If, within six months from the entry into force of an agreement between the Parties referred to in paragraph 5 of the Agreement, notwithstanding the good offices of the Parties, all applicants involved in an international conflict have not resolved that conflict, or are not parties to a written agreement submitting the conflict to a specified binding conflict resolution procedure, the conflict shall be resolved by binding arbitration in accordance with Appendices 1 and 2 if a Party so elects.

(3) The procedures provided in the Appendices shall commence ten days after a Party notifies the other Party or Parties of the decision to elect arbitration.

PART III

PRINCIPLES OF CONFIDENTIALITY

10. In implementing the provisions of paragraph 6 of the Agreement, Parties shall apply the following principles:

(a) The confidentiality of the coordinates of application areas shall be maintained until any conflict involving such area is resolved and the relevant authorization is issued, except on the basis of a demonstrated need to know and adequate assurances that the confidentiality of the information shall be maintained by the recipient;

(b) The confidentiality of other proprietary or confidential commercial information shall be maintained in accordance with domestic lasw as long as such information retains its character as such.

PART IV

DEFINITIONS

11. In this Agreement:

(a) "activities" means the undertakings, commitments of resources, investigations, findings, research, engineering devlopment, and other activities relevant to the identification, discovery, and systematic analysis and evaluation of polymetallic nodules and to the determination of the technical and economic feasibility of exploitation;

(b) "authorization" means any license, permit, or other authorization issued under the national law of a Party which authorizes the holder to engage in deep sea be operations in a specified area or areas;

(c) "conflict" means the existence of one or more than one application or amendment covered by this Agreement submitted by different applicants:

(1) whether filed with the same Party or with more than one Party; and

(2) in which the deep sea bed areas applied for overlap in whole or in part, to the extent of the overlap;

"international conflict" means a conflict arising from applications or amendments filed with more than one Party;

"domestic conflict" means any other conflict;

(d) a "pre-enactment explorer" ("PEE") is an entity which was engaged, prior to the earliest date of enactment of domestic legislation by any Party, in deep sea bed polymetallic nodule exploration by substantial surveying activity with respect to the area applied for; and

(e) "polymetallic nodules" means any deposit or accretion on or just below the surface of the deep sea bed consisting of nodules which contain manganese, nickel, cobalt, or copper.

APPENDIX 1

Arbitration Procedure

1. In this Appendix, "Party" means a Party to this Agreement which is also concerned in the arbitration, and "other Party" includes any such Party or Parties.

2. The parties presenting the case shall seek to agree in writing within sixty days after the expiry of the ten-day period provided by paragraph 9(3) of the Schedule on three arbitrators, or, if they agree to have only one arbitrator, on that one arbitrator.

3. Any Party may ojbect to the choice of any arbitrator or arbitrators under paragraph 2, by written notice received by the other Party within thirty days after the expiry of the period provided by paragraph 2 above. Upon objection to any arbitrator by a Party, the other Party may, when three arbitrators have been chosen under paragraph 2, object to either or both of the other arbitrators by written notice received by the other Party within fifteen days after the expiry of the period provided by the immediately preceding sentence.

4. If a Party objects to the choice of any arbitrator in accordance with paragraph 3 or if an arbitrator becomes unable to act, the parties presenting the case shall seek to agree on a replacement in writing within sixty days after receipt of the notice of objection or after the date when the arbitrator becomes unable to act.

If agreement is reached, a Party may object to the choice of a replacement by written notice received by the other Party within thirty days. If the parties presenting the case have not reached agreement, of or a Party objects to the choice of a replacement in accordance with this paragraph, the Secretary-General of the Permanent Court of Arbitration shall appoint a replacement without delay.

5. If the parties presenting the case fail to agree on three arbitrators (or an arbitrator) within the period provided by paragraph 2, three arbitrators shall, on request of a Party, be appointed without delay by the Secretary-General of the Permanent Court of Arbitration.

6. Any arbitrator appointed by the Secretary-General of the Permanent Court of Arbitration shall not be a citizen of a Party, shall have international standing and expertise, and shall have personal characteristics which place him in a neutral position with respect to the subject of the dispute. The Secretary-General shall not be confined to any particular list of arbitrators in making this selection. Appointments by the Secretary-General shall not be open to challenge.

7. Insofar as any matter is not dealt with by Appendix 2 and other relevant provisions of the Agreement, the arbitrator or arbitrators shall, consistent with Appendix 2, be guided by the general principles of law recognized by the Parties, which, where the case is presented by a Party or Parties means the general principles of public international law (lex lata) as recognized by the Parties.

8. The arbitrator or arbitrators shall decide where he or they shall sit and shall, in consultation with the parties presenting the case, adopt rules of procedure consistent with this Appendix.

9. The case will be presented by a Party or by its applicants involved in the conflict, at the option of the Party and each side of the case shall be represented as it sees fit.

10. A Party may intervene as a matter of right.

11. An arbitrator may not abstain from voting on the award. If there are three arbitrators, their award shall be made by majority vote.

12. The award of the arbitrator or arbitrators shall be rendered within one year from the date of the final appointment of the arbitrator or arbitrators unless all Parties or parties presenting the case otherwise agree or unless the arbitrator or arbitrators for good cause extend the deadline for the making of the award for one or more 30 day periods, in any case not to exceed 120 days.

The award shall be final and binding on the applicants involved in the conflict and on the Parties and shall be enforced by the Parties. The applicants involved in the conflict shall without delay file amendments to their applications consistent with the arbitral award. Within two months of the date of the award, a Party or any applicant represented in the arbitration may request an interpretation of the award. Such interpretation shall be provided within four months of the request.

13. The expense of the arbitration, including the remuneration of the arbitrators, shall be borne by the parties presenting the case. Unless the arbitrator or arbitrators determine otherwise because of the particular circumstances of the case, the parties presenting the case shall bear the expenses in equal shares.

14. If an applicant of a Party is involved in conflicts with two or more applicants of two or more States Parties to this Agreement, every effort shall be made to consolidate the arbitration proceedings.

APPENDIX 2

Principles for Resolution of Conflicts

1. In determing the issue as to which applicant involved in a conflict shall be awarded all or part of each area in conflict, the arbitral tribunal shall find a solution which is fair and equitable, having regard, with respect to each applicant involved in the conflict, to the following factors:

(a) the continuity and extent of activities relevant to each area in conflict and the application of area of which it is a part;

(b) the date on which each applicant involved in the conflict or predecessor in interest or component organization thereof commenced activities at sea in the application area;

(c) the financial cost of activities relevant to each area in conflict and to the application area of which it is a part, measured in constant terms;

(d) the time when activites were carried out, and the quality of activities; and

(e) such additional factors as the tribunal determines to be relevant, but excluding a consideration of the future plans of work of the applicants involved in the conflict.

2. When considering the factors specified in paragraph 1, the arbitral tribunal shall hear, and shall, except for purposes of apportionment pursuant to paragraph 3, limit its consideration to all evidence based on the activities specified in paragraph 1, which were conducted on or before January 1, 1982, provided, however, that an applicant must prove at-sea prospecting in the conflict area prior to June 28, 1980 as a pre-condition to presentation of further evidence to the arbitral tribunal regarding activities in the conflict area.

3. In making its determination, the arbitral tribunal may award the entire area in conflict to one applicant involved in the conflict, or the arbitral tribunal may apportion the area among any or all of the applicants involved in the conflict. If, after applying the provisions of paragraph 1 of this Appendix, the arbitral tribunal determines the area in conflict should be apportioned, then the arbitral tribunal shall, to the maximum extent practicable consistent with its application of those provisions, apportion the area in a manner designed to satisfy the plan of work set forth in the application of each applicant which is awarded part of the area.

ED.NOTE: Representatives of the Parties announced, on August 3, 1984, that they had resolved all conflicts between areas in which they had an interest.

G. RECENT DEVELOPMENTS

There has been considerable activity in furtherance of an acceptable regime for deep seabed mining since the conclusion of the Convention. This activity has taken place in two separate forums, in addition to the General Assembly itself. The primary forum has been the Preparatory Commission which was established by conference resolution at the conclusion of its work. The Preparatory Commission has as its task the development of rules and regulations concerning seabed mining, the Secretariate, and the Law of the Sea Tribunal, as called for in the Convention. The Commission has been meeting regularly since the conclusion of the treaty to accomplish this task. In addition, the Commission has taken it upon itself to coordinate the filing of applications for pioneer status as set forth in Conference Resolution II, considered earlier.

A second, later, but equally important initiative has been the holding, in New York, a series of consultations by the Secretary-General of the United Nations with a view toward making the seabed mining provisions of the treaty more acceptable to a number of States which have either rejected those provisions or severely criticized them.

The work of the Preparatory Commission has produced a raft of documents containing proposed rules and regulations too numerous to be produced here. However, the following paper summarizes both of the above-mentioned initiatives sufficiently for the purposes of this chapter. Ambassador Nandan is the former Under-Secretary General of the United Nations and Special Representative of the Secretary-General for the Law of the Sea.

Nandan, THE UNITED NATIONS CONVENTION ON THE LAW OF THE SEA: TEN YEARS AFTER SIGNATURE [4]

When the Conference ended in 1982 the international community which had laboured for long years to achieve a consensus found itself divided over the Convention. There was disappointment and acrimony in the air at the closing session of the Conference at Montego Bay, and in the discussions in the General Assembly. There was also confusion and division on what should be the role of the U.N. Secretariate now that the Conference was over. At the same time, the Secretary-General was asked by the General Assembly...to assume all the responsibilities imposed upon him by the United Nations Convention on the Law of the Sea and the relevant resolutions of the Third United Nations Conference on the Law of the Sea.

4. Paper delivered at the annual meeting of the Law of the Sea Institute, Genoa, Italy, June 1992 Reprinted by permission of the Law of the Sea Institute.

In the absence of a clear policy directive from the General Assembly on how the responsibilities of the Secretary-General were to be discharged, the Secretary-General, through the Office of the Special Representative for the Law of the Sea, adopted two basic approaches for ensuring the universality of the Convention. First, to ensure the widest possible acceptance of the Convention and, secondly, to ensure the widest possible application of its provisions in State practice. Both these principles were translated into the programme for the Office of the Special Representative for the Law of the Sea (later the Office for Ocean Affairs and the Law of the Sea) adopted by the General Assembly in December 1983....

In practical terms the strategy that the United Nations has followed for the past ten years through the Secretary-General's Special Representative for the Law of the Sea may be summarised as follows:

1) To encourage all States to sign the Convention by 9th December 1984, the closing date for signature of the Convention, and to encourage the ratification of it or accession to it, thereafter.

2) To promote the acceptance and application of the Convention in national legislation of States and in their relations on maritime issues with other States.

3) To assist States, especially developing States, in the implementation of the Convention and in their development of national marine policies within the framework of the Convention.

4) To effectively service the Preparatory Commission for the International Seabed Authority and the International Tribunal for the Law of the Sea. In doing so to ensure that the differences over the deep seabed mining part of the Convention would not be aggravated or widened.

5) To maintain dialogue on ocean matters with all States whether signatories of the Convention or not, and to await the opportunity to promote dialogue on the difficultes that some industrialized States have with Part XI of the Convention and to assist in resolving them.

With respect to the signature of the Convention the efforts of the United Nations were highly successful. Through direct approaches to States it was possible to increase the number of signatures to 159 by the closing date in 1984. This was a record number for a complex and comprehensive instrument. Its significance in substantive terms was even greater in that 159 States and entities from all regions of the world and from all interest groups had agreed at least provisionally to accept the Convention even though some had reservations with respect to Part XI. This level of support certainly enhanced the status and authority of the Convention and made it easier for States to proceed to incorporate its provisions in their national legislation. It was an important step in building confidence in the Convention.

Promoting the acceptance and application of the Convention at national, sub-regional, regional and global levels was perhaps one of the most important tasks. It does not serve the goal of universality of the Convention if States only subscribed to it in formal terms but fail to apply its provisions in practice. It was equally important to ensure that State practice did not deviate from the provisions of the Convention to a point that would unravel the very delicate balance that was achieved on many key issues. The United Nations Office for Ocean Affairs and the Law of the Sea provided advice and assistance to States in an effort to encourage uniform and consistent application of the provisions of the Convention. This task took may forms. Direct assistance to States in formulating certain legislation, reviewing and assisting with prospective legislation, clarifying certain provisions of the Convention, providing studies and publications on the antecedents of some of the key provisions, providing compendiums on national legislation or some key concepts and providing information through the annual reports of the Secretary-General to the General Assembly and through the Law of the Sea Bulletin on current developments relating to the oceans.

The success that has been achieved in developing a uniform and consistent application of the Convention is remarkable and beyond all expectations....

The Law of the Sea Convention is multi-faceted. It addresses all uses of the oceans and their resources. It creates a multitude of rights and imposes a multitude of responsibilities on States. Effective implementation of this complex and comprehensive Convention requires the development of national ocean management policy. The inter-related nature of the rights and duties and the inter-dependency of the different uses of the oceans presents a major challenge to many States, expecially developing States. It was therefore imperative that if the Convention was to be meaningful to States, the United Nations and the United Nations system provided States with assistance in implementing it. Addressing the needs of States in this context has been an important part of the strategy for promoting universality of the Convention....

Servicing the Preparatory Commission has been a very delicate and difficult matter in the light of there being no consensus over the deep seabed mining provisions of the Convention. The United Nations Secretariate took the view that every effort should be made to avoid further polarization of the developed and developing States or to further aggravate the situation between signatories and non-signatories of the Convention. This was made more difficult by the fact that one important State, the United States, had decided to boycott the Preparatory Commission. One of the measures taken by the Secretariate in this regard was to assume the responsibility for presenting the basic negotiating texts for the rules and regulations that were to be prepared by the Commission for the Mining Code and for the setting-up of the various institutions under the Convention. This strategy had the effect on positions which would have re-ignited acrimonious debates and on the other hand of providing delegations a common text for their negotiations from a neutral source. The maintenance of a smooth and harmonious atmosphere in the Preparatory Commission was essential to the confidence-building in the Convention as a whole notwithstanding the differences that persisted on substance between the industrialised and the developing States in respect of Part XI. The Preparatory Commission, thanks to the leadership provided by its first Chairman, Mr. Joseph Warioba, during the Commission's formative years has established from the beginning a record of constructive and workman-like approach to its work. It systematically worked on those areas where broad agreement existed and set aside for discussion later those issues where major differences were well-established.

A major challenge to the universal acceptance of the Convention lay in the implementation of the pioneer investors regime contained in resolution II of the Conference. In today's heady days of East-West cooperation it is easy to forget the competition and tension that existed between the East and the West until only recently. In the specific case of the deep seabed regime, it manifested itself in the claims to mine sites most of which were concentrated in a narrow belt of the North-East Pacific between the Clarion and Clipperton fractures. Given the limited area and the number of known claimants in that region the potential for overlaps in the areas to be claimed was recognised in resolution II. It, in fact, prescribed the procedure for resolving such overlaps through negotiations and if necessary by arbitration before an application for registration as a pioneer investor was made.

In 1984 when the Soviet Union and then France and Japan deposited their respective applications as pioneer investors with the Special Representative of the Secretary-General for the Law of the Sea, it became known that the overlap that existed between France and Japan had been resolved as had been the overlaps amongst a number of potential applicants based in the United States. There was, however, no dialogue on this matter between the Soviet Union on the one hand and France and Japan on the other, nor with other potential Western applicants. The Soviet Union in fact insisted that its claim should be registered as a matter of priority since it was lodged before that of France and Japan. It also insisted that the Commission could not take into account any unilateral claims made outside the Commission especially by non-signatories to the Convention.

The Preparatory Commission and the United Nations were put in an extremely difficult position. Any precipitous action by the Commission would have not only aggravated the relations among States but also had the potential to destroy Part XI of the Convention itself. It would have possibly lost the cooperation of many industrialized States and threatened the viability of the Convention as a whole.

The Commission wisely insisted on the four applicants which included India whose claim was in the Indian Ocean, that they should exchange coordinates to ascertain any overlaps in their claims and resolve them.

When in 1985 the Special Representative of the Secretary-General for the Law of the Sea in exercise of his good offices convened a meeting of the four applicants in Geneva so that the coordinates of each applicant could be exchanged with the others, it was discovered that there were major overlaps in the claims of France and the Soviet Union and a substantial overlap between Japan and the Soviet Union. It was also apparent that there were further overlaps between the claims of the Soviet Union and three of the four U.S. based consortia.

The extent and nature of the overlaps were such that the parties especially France and the Soviet Union did not find it possible to resolve them without help. Eventually in August 1985 at a technical meeting convened by the Special Representative with the three States, an agreement was reached on three priniciples on the basis of which the parties would try to resolve the conflicts in their claims. They were as follows:

1) The three applicants will reduce their respective claims for pioneer areas to be allocated to them through an advanced relinquishment by one half, that is, from 150,000 sq. kms. to 75,000 sq. kms., thereby making it easier for them to divide the prime areas which were the subject of the overlaps.

2) In resolving their own overlaps the three applicants must jointly ensure that the Authority has a viable mine site in the central zone where most of the first generation prime sites existed and where the overlaps had occurred.

3) That the interest of potential applicants for pioneer investor status should be taken into account before registration could take place.

Early in 1986, on the basis of the first two principles, France, Japan and the Soviet Union were able to resolve their overlaps through what is known as the "Arusha Understanding". The third principle could not be implemented without the participation of the potential pioneer investors, in particular the United States. Since the United States was not participating in the Preparatory Commission its other partners in the four multinational consortia namely Belgium, Canada, Federal Republic of Germany, Italy, Japan, the Netherlands and United Kingdom opened a dialogue with the Soviet Union. This eventually culminated in what is known as the "mid-night agreement" of 14th August 1987 on all overlaps following two-tier negotiations. One between the Soviet Union and the other signatories to the Convention, and the other, a less formal meeting between the Soviet Union and the other signatories plus the three non-signatories -- the Federal Republic of Germany, the United Kingdom and the United States.

The Arusha Understanding and the "mid-night agreement" with some further negotiations in the Preparatory Commission paved the way for the unanimous decision to register the applicants sponsored by France, Japan and the Soviet Union as pioneer investors on 17th December 1987. India having been registered already on 17th August 1987. This was a historic achievement in international law. For the first time States had acquired international areas in the deep ocean by the common consent of the international community. We now have six registered pioneer investors.

The importance of recapitulating the process of resolving the conflicts that had arisen in the mining areas claimed by different States is to underscore that the States concerned (signatories and non-signatories), the Preparatory Commission and the United Nations played critical and constructive roles in ensuring that the broad support that the Convention enjoyed was not put into question. The responsible manner in which the Preparatory Commission acted in the matter augers well for the future International Seabed Authority and argues in favour of universal participation in the Convention.

An essential strategy that was followed by the Secretary-General and by his Special Representative over the past ten years has been to maintain dialogue on law of the sea matters with Member States of the United Nations whether signatories of the Convention or not. There was a deliberate effort on the part of the Secretary-General to involve some of the non-signatories together with signatories in the activities of the Office for Ocean Affairs and the Law of the Sea such as the experts groups on a number of technical matters arising out of the implementation of the provisions of the Convention. The purpose was to keep all States engaged in the implementation of the Convention provisions on which there was already a broad consensus while waiting for an opportunity to open up a dialogue on the outstanding issues relating to Part XI.

By 1989 the number of ratifications or accessions to the Convention steadily increased towards the required sixty. At the same time there was improvement in international relations, from tension and confrontation, towards cooperation in resolving outstanding global issues. The Secretary-General, following an extensive sounding by his Special Representative with States and his own bilateral exchanges with some of the key non-signatory States decided to convene informal consultations on the outstanding issues. The first of these consulations took place on 19th July 1990 and by the end of 1991 six such consultations had taken place. The result of these consultations were summarised by me on 31st January 1992 and circulated to all States. Since there is not enough time for me to deal fully with this important matter, I have attached a copy of this summary as annex II to this statement.

The participants in these consultations included a representative group of some 30 States from all regions and all interest groups including Germany, the United Kingdom and the United States. After ascertaining the willingness of the participants to examine the outstanding issues relating to Part XI of the Convention, the Secretary-General identified nine areas that needed to be addressed. These are: 1) cost to States Parties; 2) the Enterprise; 3) decision-making; 4) Review Conference; 5) transfer of technology; 6) production limitation; 7) compensation fund; 8) financial terms of contract; and 9) environmental considerations.

Participants agreed to examine these issues one-by-one. To facilitate discussion, Information Notes on the issues were provided by the Special Representative. These contained background information, identified questions that needed to be addressed and suggested possible approaches towards their resolution.

On 11th December 1991, Secretary-General Javier Perez de Cuellar summarised the results of the consultations as follows:

"In the process of examining the areas of difficulties, a solid foundation has been laid for resolving them which should be built upon. It is apparent that some of the issues need to be dealt with in detail at this stage. Other, however, can be resolved by way of agreement on certain fundamental principles, on the basis of which detailed rules and regulations may be established when commercial production of metals from the deep seabed becomes feasible."

The Secretary-General also stated that the next step in the process was to give more precision to the emerging approaches towards resolving the issues. This suggests that the emerging understanding on each issue should be reflected in a series of concise statements as a step towards eventually converting them into draft articles of an agreement.

While the United States remains very hesitant and tentative about the process, the fact, nevertheless, is that the process of reconciliation on Part XI has begun and it is the responsibility of all States to take advantage of this window of opportunity. I believe the most difficult task, that of engaging everyone in the process has been accomplished. The Group of 77 (the group of developing States) must be given full credit for agreeing to participate in the dialogue without any precondition. They have already shown ample disposition towards resolving the outstanding issues in a manner satisfactory to all.

By identifying the key issues and by discussing possible approaches towards resolving them, the participants have already gone a long way down the road towards an agreement. I believe that the process which has been carefully prepared over the past ten years and delicately and firmly launched over the past 3 years will eventually succeed. If it does we would have indeed succeeded in making the Convention a truly universal instrument.

****

The parallel effort of the Secretary-General has been directed and exploring problems that some States are having with the existing seabed mining provisions, and exploring possible ways to correct or modify them without disrupting the entire system. The status of those consultations, at the present stage, are reflected in the following document dated November 1993. A preambulatory paragraph emphasises that the document does not necessarily reflect the positions of any country, but that all participants thought it provided a basis for negotiation.

DRAFT RESOLUTION FOR ADOPTION BY THE GENERAL ASSEMBLY

The United Nations Convention on the Law of the Sea

The General Assembly

Recalling resolution (48/...of...December 1993) on the Law of the Sea;

Recalling that Part XI and related provisions of the 1982 United Nations Convention on the Law of the Sea (the Convention) established a regime for the international seabed area ("the Area") and its resources;

Reaffirming that the Area and its resources are the common heritate of mankind;

Recognizing that political and economic changes, including in particular a growing reliance on market principles, show the need to re-evaluate some aspects of the regime;

Noting the initiative of the Secretary-General since 1990 to promote dialogue aimed at achieving universal participation in the Convention;

Welcoming the report of the Secretary-General pursuant to General Assembly resolution (48/....) and, in particular, the results of the Secretary-General's informal consultations set out in paragraphs [....] of the report;

Taking note of the report of the Preparatory Commission for the International Seabed Authority and for the International Tribunal for the Law of the Sea;

Considering that the objective of universal participation in the Convention may best be achieved by the adoption of an agreement relating to the implementation of Part XI and related provisions of the Convention and to give effect to the results of the Secretary-General's informal consultations;

1. *Endorses* the results of the Secretary-General's consultations set out in paragraphs [....] of the report of the Secretary-Gemeral;

2. *Adopts* the Agreement relating to the implementation of Part XI and related provisions of the Convention ("the Agreement"), the text of which is attached to this resolution;

3. *Considers* that future ratifications of formal confirmations of or accessions to the Convention should be taken to relate to the Convention together with the Agreement;

4. *Calls on* States and other entities referred to in Article 3 of the Agreement to act in accordance with the object and purpose of the Agreement pending its entry into force;

5. *Requests* the Secretary-General to transmit certified copies of the Agreement to the States and other entities referred to in Article 3 thereof, with a view to facilitating uniiversal participation in the Convention together with the Agreement.

AGREEMENT RELATTING TO THE IMPLEMENTATION OF PART XI OF THE 1982 UNITED NATIONS CONVENTION ON THE LAW OF THE SEA

The States Parties to this Agreement,

Recognizing the sifnificant contribution of the 1982 United Nations Convention on the Law of the Sea ("the Convention") to the maintenance of peace, justice and progress for all peoples of the world;

Having considered the report of the Secretary-General of the United Nations on the results of the informal consulations held from 1990 to 1994 on outstanding issues relating to Part XI and related provisions of the Convention ("Part XI");

Wishing to take account of important political and economic developments affecting the implementation of those provisions, in order to facilitatte universal participation in the Convention;

Considering that an Agreement relating to the implementation of Part XI would best meet that objective;

Have agreed as follows:

Article I

Implementation of Part XI

1. The States Parties to this Agreement undertake to implement Part XI in accordance with this Agreement.

2. The Annex forms an integral part of this Agreement.

Article 2

Relationship between this Agreement and Part XI

1. The Provisions of Part XI and this Agreement shall be interpreted and applied together as one single instrument. In the event of any inconsistency, the provisions of this Agreement shall prevail.

2. Articles 309 to 319 of the Convention shall apply to this Agreement as they apply to the Convention.

3. After the adoption of this Agreement, any instrument of ratification or formal confirmation of or accession to the Convention shall represent also an accession to this Agreement.

Article 3

Accession

This Agreement shall be open for accession by those States and other entities referred to in Article 305 of the Convention which have ratified, formally confirmed or acceded to the Convention or which are simultaneously ratifying, formally confirming or acceding to the Convention and this Agreement.

Accession by the entities referred to in Article 305 of the Convention shall be in accordance with Annex IX of the Convnetion. Instruments of accession shall be deposited with the Secretary-General of the United Nations.

Article 4

Simplified Procedure

A State or entity which has deposited before the date of the adoption of this Agreement an instrument of ratification, formal confirmation or accession in respect of the Convention shall be considered a party to this Agreement if that States has not notified the Depositary within [....] months of the adoption of this Agreement that it is not having recorse to the simplified procedure set out in this Article. In the event of such notification being made, accession to the Agreement shall take place in accordance with Article 3.

Article 5

Entry into Force

1. This Agreement shall enter into force on the day of deposit of the [....] instrument of accession to this Agreement, provided that at least [....] of those instruments have been deposited by States to which paragraph 1(a)(i),(ii) or (iii) of Resolution II of the Third United Nations Conference on the Law of the Sea ("Resolution II") applies.

2. For each State acceding to the Agreement after its entry into force, the Agreement shall come into force on the date of deposit by such State of its instrument of accession.

3. States which have recourse to the simplified procedure in Article 4 shall be regared as having acceded upon expiry of the period of [....] months specified in that Article, or upon entry into force on the date of deposit by such State of its instrument of accession.

Article 6

States Parties

For the purposes of this Agreement, "States Parties" means States and entities which have consented to be bound by this Agreement and for which it has entered into force.

Article 7

Depositary

The Secretary-General of the United Nations shall be the depostary of this Agreement.

Article 8

Authentic Texts and Depositary

The original of this Agreement, of which the Arabic, Chinese, English, French, Russian and Spanish texts are equally authentic, shall be deposited in the archives of the Secretariat of the United Nations.

ANNEX

SECTION 1. COSTS TO STATES PARTIES AND INSTITUTIONAL ARRANGEMENTS

1. The Authority is the organization through which States Parties to the Convention shall, in accordance with the regime for the international seabed area ("Area") established in Part XI and this Agreement, organize and control activities in the Area, particularly with a view to administering the resources of the Area. The powers and functions of the Authority shall be those expressly conferred upon it by the Convention. The Authority shall have such incidental powers consistent with the Convention, as are implicit in, and necessary for, the exercise of those powers and functions with respect to the activities of the Area.

2. In order to minimize costs to State Parties, all organs and subsidiary bodies to be established under the Convention and this Agreement shall be cost-effective. This principle shall also apply to the frequency, length and scheduling of meetings.

3. The setting up and the operation of the various organs and subsidiary bodies shall be based on an evolutionary approach, taking into account the functional needs of the organs and subsidiary bodies concerned in order that they may discharge effectively their respective responsibilities at various stages of the development of activities in the Area.

4. The functions of the Authority upon entry into force of the Convention shall be carried out by the Assembly, the Council, the Legal and Technical Commission and the Finance Committee, which shall work in accordance with Section 9 of this Annex. The functions of the Economic Planning Commission shall be performed by the Legal and Technical Commission until such time as the Council decides otherwise or until the approval of the first plan of work for exploitation.

5. The Assembly and the Council, as well as their respective subsidiary bodies, shall meet only as frequently as required for the adequate and timely performance of their function.

6. Between the entry into force of the Convention and the approval of the first plan of work for exploitation, the Authority shall concentrate on:

(a) processing of applications for approval of plans of work for exploration in accordance with Part XI and this Agreement;

(b) monitoring of compliance with plans of work for exploration approved in the form of contracts;

(c) implementation of decisions of the Preparatory Commission for the International Seabed Authority and for the International Tribunal for the Law of the Sea (Preparatory Commission) relating to the registered pioneer investors and their certifying States, including their rights and obligations, in accordance with the provisions of Article 308, paragraph 5 of the Convention and Resolution II, paragraph 13;

(d) study of the potential impact of mineral production from the Area on the economies of developing land-based producers of those minerals which are likely to be most seriously affected, with a view to minimizing the difficulties and assisting them in their economic adjustment, taking into account the work done in this regard by the Preparatory Commission;

(e) promotion and encouragement of the conduct of marine scientific research with respect to activities in the Area and the collection and dissemination of the results of such research and analysis, when available, with particular emphasis on research related to the environmental impact of activities in the Area;

(f) acquisition of scientific knowledge and the monitoring of the development of marine technology relevant to activities in the Area;

(g) adoption of rules, regulations and procedures, including those relating to the protection and preservation of the marine environment, necessary for the conduct of activities in the Area as they progress. Notwithstanding the provisions of Annex III, Article 17(2)(b) and (c) of the Convention, such rules, regulations and procedures shall take into account the terms of this Agreement, the changed economic circumstances since the Convention was adopted, the prolonged delay in commercial deep seabed mining and the likely pace of activities in the Area;

(h) monitoring and review of trends and developments relating to deep seabed mining activities, including regular analysis of world metal market conditions and metal prices, trends and prospects;

(i) assessment of available data relating to prospecting and exploration; and

(j) timely elaboration of rules, regulations and procedures for explotiation.

7(a) The application for the approval of a plan of work for exploration shall be considered by the Council following the receipt of a recommendation on the application from the Legal and Technical Commission. The processing of an application for the approval of a plan of work for exploration shall be in accordance with the provisions of the Convention, including its Annex III, and this Agreement, provided that:

(i) a plan of work for exploration submitted on behalf of a State or entity, or any component of such entity, referred to in Resolution II, paragraph 1(a)(ii) and (iii), other than a registered pioneer investor, which had already undertaken substantial activities in the Area prior to entry into force of the Convention or their successors in interest, shall be considered to have met the financial and technical qualificationns necessary for approval of a plan of work, if the sponsoring State certifies that the applicant has expended an amount equivalent to at least $US30 million in research and exploration activities and has expended no less than ten (10) per cent of that amount in thee location, survey and evaluation of the area referred to in the plan of work. If the plan of work otherwise satisfies the requirements of the Convention and any rules, regulations and procedures adopted pursuant thereto, it shall be approved by the Council in the form of a conract, notwithstanding the provisions of Section 3, paragraph 10 of this Annex.

(ii) upon the request of a registered pioneer investor, its plan of work for exploration consisting of documents, reports and other data submitted to the Preparatory Commission before and after registration together with an indication of plans for future activities, if any, shall be approved in the form of a contract by the Council in accordance with *Part XI and this agreement, notwithstanding the provisions of Section 3, paragraph 10 of this Annex. Resolution II, paragraph 8(c) shall not apply and a request for approval of a plan of work for exploration of a pioneer investor may be made by a sponsoring State as a State Party or as a provisional member of the Authority pursuant to paragraph 14. The fee to be paid by a pioneer investor upon application for a plan of work, in accordance with the provisions of Resolution II, paragraph 7(a), and Annex III, Article 13, paragraph 2 of the Convention, shall be deferred until the pioneer investor submits a plan of work for exploitation, taking into account the $250,000 fee paid pursuant to Resolution II, paragraph 7(a), which shall be deemed to be the fee relating to the exploration phase pursuant to Section 8, paragraph 3 of this Annex. The period following entry into force of the Convention within which a registered pioneer investor may request approval of a plan f work pursuant to Resolution II, paragraph 8(a) shall be extended from six months to twenty four months; and

(iii) in accordance with the principle of non-discrimination a contract with a State or entity or anhy component of such entitie referred to in (i) above, shall include arrangments which shall be similar to and no less favourable than those agreed with any State or entity or any component of such entity referred to in (ii) above. In the case of contracts with the States or entities or any components of such entities referred too in (ii) above, the Council shall make such adjustments, as are equitable, to the rights and obligations assumed by them under Resolution II and the decisions of the reparatory Commission.

(b) The approval of a plan of work for exploration shall be in accordance with Article 153, paragraph 3 of the Convention.

8. Appications for plans of work shall be accompanied by an assessment of the potential environmental impacts of the proposed activities in accordance with the rules, regulations and proceddures adopted by the Authority.

9. Applications for approval of plans of work for exploration other than those referred to in paragraph 7 shall be processed in accordance with the procedures set out in Section 3, paragraph 10 of this Annex.

10. A plan of work for exploration shall be approved for a period of ten years. Upon the expiration of a plan of work for exploration the contractor shall apply for a plan of work for exploitation unless the contractor has received an extension for the plan of work for exploration. Contractors may apply for such extensions for periods of not more than five years each. Such extension shall be approved if the contractor has made good faith efforts to comply with the requirements of the plan of work but for reasons beyond the contractor's control has been unable to complete the necessary preparatory wwork for proceeding to the exploitation stage or the prevailing economic circumstances have not justified proceeding to the exploitation stage.

11. The reference in the last sentence of Annex III, Article 10 of the Convention to performance which has not been satisfactory shall be interpreted to mean that the contractor has failed to comply with the requirements of an approved plan of work despite written warning or warnings from the Authority to the contractor to comply therewith.

12. The Authority shall elaborate and adopt, in accordance with Article 162, paragraph 2(o)(ii) of the Convention, rules, regulations and procedures based on the principles contained in Sections 2, 5, 6, 7, and 8 of this Annex, as well as any additional rules, regulations and procedures necessary to facilitate the approval of plans of work for exploration or exploitation, as follows:

(a) The Council may undertake such elaboration at any time it deems all or any of such rules, regulations or procedures are required for the conduct of activities in the Area, or when it determines that commercial exploitation is imminent, or at the request of a State whose national is in a position to apply for approval of a plan of work for exploitation.

(b) If a request is made by a State referred to in subparagraph (a) the Council shall, in accordance with Article 162, paragraph 2(o) of the Convention, complete the adoption of such rules, regulations and procedures within two years of such a request.

(c) If the Council has not completed rules, regulations and procedures relating to exploitation within the prescribed time, and an application for the approval of a plan of work for exploitation is pending, it shall nonetheless consider and provisionally approve such plan of work based on the provisions of the Convention and any rules, regulations and procedures that the Council may have adopted provisionally, or on the basis of the norms contained in the Convention and the terms and principles contained in this Annex as well as the principle of non-discrimination among contractors.

13. The Authority shall have its own budget. The administrative expenses of the Authority shall be met [by assessed contributions of its members, including its provisional members, in accordance with Article 173 of the Convention and this Agreement] [through the budget of the United Nations] until such time as the Authority becomes self-financing. The Authority shall not exercise its power referred in Article 174, paragraph 1 of the Convention to borrow funds to finance its administrative budget.

14. States and entities referred to in Article 305 of the Convention which have not established their consent to be bound by it shall be eligible to become provisional members of the Authority on the following basis:

(a) Such membership shall take effect upon notification to the depositary of the Convention by a State or entity of its intention to participate as a provisional member of the Authority and shall terminate two years after the date of entry into force of the Convention or upon ratification or formal confirmation of, or accession to, the Convention and this Agreement by such a State. The Council may, upon request of the State or entity concerned, extend provisional membership by up to two years if the Council is satisfied that the State or entity has been making efforts in good faith to become a party, provided that provisional membership shall not extend beyond four years after the date of entry into force of the Convention.

(b) Provisional members shall apply the terms of Part XI and this Agreement provisionally and shall have the same rights and obligations as other members, inclduding:

(i) the obligation to contribute to the budget of the Authority based on assessed contributions, in accordance with their national laws, regulations and annualy budgetaary appropriations; and

(ii) the right to sponsor an application for a plan of work for exploration. In the case of entities whose components are natural or juridical persons possessing the nationality of more than one State, a plan of work shall not be approved unless all the States whose natural or juridical persons comprise those entities are provisional members or States Parties.

15. The draft rules, regulations and procedures and any recommendations relating to the provisions of Part XI, as contained in the reports and recommendations of the Preparatory Commission, shall be taken into account by the Authority in the adoption of rules, regulations and procedures in accordance with Part XI and this Agreement.

16. The relevant provisions of Part XI, Section 4 shall be interpreted and applied in accordance with this Agreement.

SECTION 2. THE ENTERPRISE

1. The Enterprise shall conduct its initial operation through joint ventures. It shall commence its functioning on the issuance of a directive by the Council pursuant to Article 170, paragraph 2 of the Convention.

2. The obliations to fund one mine site of the Enterprise as provided for in Annex IV, Article 11, paragraph 3 of the Convention, shall not apply and States parties to the Convention shall be under no obligation to finance any of the operations in any mine site of the Enterprise or under its joint venture arrangements.

3. The Secretariat of the Authority shall perform the preparatory functions necessary for the commencement of the functioning of the Enterprise. These shall include the monitoring of developments in the deep seabed mining sector, in particular the prevailing conditions in the world metal market, developments in deep seabed mining technology, and data and information on the environmental impact of activities in the Area.

4. The obligations applicable to contractors shall apply to the Enterprise. Notwithstanding the provisions of Article 153, paragraph 3 of the Convention, and Annex III, Article 3, paragraph 5 of the Convention, a plan of work for the Enterprise upon its approval shall be in the form of a contract concluded between the Authority and the Enterprise.

5. A contractor which has contributed a particular area to the Authority as a reserved area shall have priority to enter into a joint venture arrangement with the Enterprise for exploration and exploitation of that area, subject to agreement on the terms and conditions of the joint venture arrangement. If the Enterprise does not commence activities on such a reserved site within ten years of the commencement of its functioning or within ten years of the date on which that area is reserved for the Authority, whichever is the later, the contractor which contributed shall be entitled to apply for a plan of work for that area provided it offers to include the Enterprise as a joint venture partner.

6. Article 170, paragraph 4, Annex IV and other provisions of the Convention relating to the Enterprise shall be interpreted and applied in accordance with this Part.

SECTION 3. DECISION-MAKING

1. The general policies of the Authority shall be established by the Assembly in collaboration with the Council.

2. Decision-making in the organs of the Authority, as a general rule, should be by consensus and there should be no voting until all efforts to reach a decision by consensus have been exhausted.

3. If consensus cannot be reached, decisions by voting in the Assembly on matters of procedure shall be taken by a majority of States present and voting, and decisions on matters of substance shall be taken by a two-thirds majority of States present and voting, as provided for in Article 159, paragraph 8 of the Convention.

4. Decisions of the Assembly on any matter for which the Council also has competence on any administrative, budgetary or financial matters shall be based on the recommendations of the Council. If the Assembly does not accept the recommendation of the Council on any matter, it shall return the matter to the Council for further consideration. The Council shall reconsider the matter in the light of the views expressed by the Assembly.

5. Decisions by the Council or the Assembly having financial or budgetary implications shall be based on the recommendations of the Finance Committee.

6. The major categories of interests in paragraph 14(a) to (c) shall be treated as chambers for the purposes of decision-making in the Council. Before electing the members of the Council, the Assembly shall establish lists of countries fulfilling the criteria for the membership in the interests groups identified in subparagraphs 14(a) to (d). If a country fulfills the criteria for membership in more than one interest group, it may only be proposed by one interest group for election to the Council and it shall represent only that interest group in voting in the Council.

7. Each interes group identified in paragraph 14(a) to (d) shall be represented in the Council by those members nominated by that interest group. Each interest groups shall only nominate as many candidates as the number of seats that are required to be filled by that group. When the number of potential candidates in each of the categories referred to in paragraph 14(a) to (e) exceeds the number of seats available in each of those respective categories, as a general rule, the principle of rotation shall apply. States members of those categories shall determine how this principle shall apply in those categories. This principle, however, shall not apply to the two States specifically referred to in paragraph 14(a).

8. Decisions by voting in the Council on questions of procedure shall be taken by a majority of the members present and voting, and decisions on questions of substance, exept where the Covention provides for decisions by consensus in the Council, shall be taken by a two-thirds majority of members present and voting, provided that such decisions are not opposed by a majority in any one of the chambers referred to above.

9. The Council may postpone the taking of a decision in order to facilitate further negotiation whenever it appears that all efforts at achieving a consensus on a question have not been exhausted.10(a) The Council shall approve a recommendation by the Legal and Technical Commission for approval of a plan of work unless by a two-thirds majority of its members present and voting, including a majority of members present and voting in each of the chambers of the Council, the Council decides to disapprove a plan of work. If the Council does not take a decision on a recommendation for approval of a plan of work whithin a prescribed period, the recommendation shall be deemed to have been approved by the

Council at the end of that period. The prescribed period shall normally be 60 days unless the Council decides to provide for a longer period. If the Commission recommends disapproval of a plan of work or does not make a recommendation, the Council may neverthe less approve the plan of work in accordance with its normal rules ofprocedure on matters of substance.

(b) The provisions of Article 162, paragraph 2(j) of the Convention shall not apply.

11. Where a dispute arises relating to the disapproval of a plan of work, such dispute shall be submitted to the dispute settlement mechanism contained in the Convention.

12. Decisions by voting in the Legal and Technical Commission shall be by a majority of members present and voting.

13. Part XI, Section 4, sub-sections B and C shall be interpreted and applied in accordance with this Part.

14. The Council shall consist of 36 members of the Authority elected by the Assembly in the following order:

(a) four members from among States Parties, each of which, during the last five years for which statistics are available, have either consumed more than 2 per cent in value terms of the total world consumption, or have had net imports of more than 2 percent in value terms of total world imports of the commodities produced from the categories of minerals to be derived from the Area, provided that the four members shall include one State from the Eastern European region having the largest economy in terms of gross domestic product and the State, at the time of entry into force of the Convention, having the largest economy in terms of gross domestic product, if such States wish to be represented in this category;

(b) four members from among the eight States Parties which have made the largest investments in preparation for, and in the conduct of, activities in the Area, either directly or through their nationals;

(c) four members from among States Parties which, on the basis of production in areas under their jurisdiction, are major net importers of the categories of minerals to be derived from the Area, including at least two developing States whose exports of such minerals have a substantial bearing on their economies;

(d) six members from among developing States, representing special interests. The special interests to be represented shall consist of States with large populations, States which are land-locked or geographically disadvantaged, island States, States which are major importers of the categories of minerals to be derived from the Area, States which are potential producers of such minerals and least developed States; and

(e) eighteen members elected according to the principle of ensuring an equitable geographic distribution of seats in the Council as a whole, provided that each geographical region shall have at least one member elected under this subparagraph. For this purpose, the geographical regions shall be Africa, Asia, Eastern European, Latin America and Western European and Others.

15. The Provisions of Article 161, paragraph 1 of the Convention shall not apply.

16(a) Decisions on questions of substance in the Council, except decisions governed by Article

161, paragraph 8(d) of the Convention, shall be taken by a two-thirds majority of members present and voting, provided that such decisions are not opposed by a majority in any one of the categories mentioned in paragaph 14(a), (b) or (c).

(b) The provisions of Article 161, paragraph 8(b) and (c) of the Convention shall not apply.

SECTION 4. REVIEW CONFERENCE

In the light of the present Agreement and the changed circumstances in respect of seabed mining since the Convention was adopted, and the changes in approaches to economic issues, the provisions relating to the Review Conference in Article 155, paragraphs 1, 3, and 4 of the Convention shall not apply. Nothwithstanding the provisions of Article 314, paragraph 2 of the Convention, the Authority may undertake at any time a review of the matters referred to in Article 155, paragraph 1 of the Convention. Amendments relating to Part XI shall be subject to the procedures contained in Articles 314, 315 and 316 of the Convention, provided that:

(a) the principles, regime and other terms of Article 155, paragraph 2 of the Convention shall be maintained, and the rights referred to in paragraph 5 of that Article shall not be affected; and

(b) amendments shall enter into force on a date determined by the Council by a three-fourths majority of the members present and voting, including a majority of members of each chamber of the Council at that time.

SECTION 5. TRANSFER OF TECHNOLOGY

1. Transfer of technology, for the purposes of Part XI, shall be governed by the provisions of Article 144 of the Convention and the following principles:

(a) The Enterprise shall take measures to obtain the technology required for its operations on the open market or through its joint venture arrangements.

(b) If the technology in question is not available on the open market, the Authority may invite any or all of the contractors and their respective sponsoring State or States to cooperate with it in facilitating acquisition of technology by the Enterprise or its joint venture, or a developing State or States seeking to acquire such technology on fair and reasonable commercial terms and conditions, including effective protection of intellectual property rights. States Parties undertake to cooperate fully and effectively with the Authority for this purpose and to ensure that contractors sponsored by them also fully cooperate with the Authority.

(c) States Parties shall promote international technical and scientific cooperation with regard to activities in the Area either between the parties concerned or by developing training, technical assistance and scientific cooperation programmes.

2.The provisions of Annex III, Article 5 of the Convention shall not apply.

SECTION 6. PRODUCTION POLICY

1. The production policy of the Authority shall be based on the following principles:

(a) The rights and obligations relating to unfair economic practices under the General

Agreement on Tariffs and Trade, its relevant codes and successor agreements, shall apply to activities in the Area.

(b) In particular, there shall be no subsidisation of acctivities in the Area except as permitted under the agreements referred to in subparagraph (a). Subsidisation for the purpose of these articles shall be defined in terms of the agreements referred to in subparagraph (a).

(c) There shall be no discrimination between minerals derived from the Area and from other sources. There shall be no preferential access to markets for such minerals or for imports of commodities produced from such minerals, in particular:

(i) b;y use of tariff or non-tariff barriers; and

(ii) given by States Parties to such minerals or commodities produced by their state enterprises or by natural or juridical persons which possess their nationality or are controlled by them or their nationals.

(d) The plan of work for exploitation approved by the Authority in respect of each mining area shall indicate an anticipated production schedule which shall include the estimated maximum amounts of minerals that would be produced per year under the plan of work.

(e) In the settlement of disputes concerning the provisions of the agreements referred to in subparagraph (a), States Parties which are parties to such agreements shall have recourse to the dispute settlement procedures of such agreements; and

(f) In circumstances where a determination is made under the agreements referred to in subparagraph (a) that a State Party has engaged in subsidisation which is prohibited or has resulted in adverse effects to the interests of another State Party and appropriate steps have not been taken by the relevant State Party or States Parties, a State Party may request the Council to take appropriate measures.

2. The principles contained in paragraph 1 shall nnot affect rights and obligations under any provision of the agreements referred to in paragraph 1(a), as well as relevant free trade and customs union agreements, in relations between States Parties which are parties to such agreements.

3. The acceptance, by a contractor, of subsidies other than those which may be permitted under the agreements referred to in paragraph 1(a) shall constitute a violation of the fundamental terms of the contract forming a plan of work for the carrying out of activities in the Area.

4. Any State Party which has reason to believe that there has bee;n a breach of the requirements of pargraph 1(a) to (d) may initiate dispute settlement procedures in conformity with paragraph 1(e) or (f).

5. The Authority shall develop rules, regulations and procedures which ensure the implementation of the provisions of this Part. This shall include relevant rules, regulations and procedures governing the approval of plans of work.

6. The provisions of Article 162, paragraph 2(q), Article 165, paragraph 2(n), Article 151, paragraphs 1 to 7 and paragraph 9 and Annex III, Article 7 of the Convention shall nnot apply.

SECTION 7. ECONOMIC ASSISTANCE

1. The policy of the Authority to assist developing countries which suffer serious effects on their export earnings or economies resulting from a reduction in the price of an affected mineral, or in the volume of exports of that mineral, to the extent that such reduction is caused by activities in the Area, shall be based on the following principles:

(a) Developing land-based producer States whose economies have been determined to be seriously affected by production of minerals from the deep seabed shall be assisted from the economic assistance fund of the Authority.

(b) The Authority shall establish an economic assistance fund from a portion of funds of the Authority which exceeds those necessary to cover the administrative expenses of the Authority, provided that the amount set aside for this purpose shall be determined by the Council from time to time, upon the recommendation of the Finance Committee. Only funds from payments received from contractors, including the Enterprise, and voluntary contributions, shall be used for the establishment of the economic assistance fund.

(c) The Authority shall provide assistance from the fund to affected developoing land-based producer states, where appropriate, in cooperation with existing global or regional development institutions which have the infrastructure to carry out such assistance programmes.

(d) The extent and period of such assistance shall be determined on a case-by-case basis. In doing so, due consideration shall be given to the nature and magnitude of the problems encountered by affected developing land-based producer states.

2. Article 151, paragraph 10 of the Convention shall be implemented by means of measures of economic assistance referred to in paragraph 1. Article 160, paragraph 2(l), Article 162, paragraph 2(n), Article 164, paragraph 2(d), Articlce 171, paragraph (f) and Article 173, paragraph 2(c) of the Convention shall be interpreted accordingly.

SECTION 8. FINANCIAL TERMS OF CONTRACT

1. The following procedures shall provide the basis for establishing rules, regulations and procedures for financial terms of contract:

(a) The system of financial payments to the Authority shall be fair both to the contractor and the Authority.

(b) The rates of financial payments under the system shall be within the range of those prevailing in respect of land-based mining of the same or similar minerals in order to avoid giving deep seabed miners an artificial competitive advantage or imposing on them a competitive disadvantage.

(c) The system of financial payments may be revised periodically in view of changing circumstances, however, they shall be applied in a non-discriminatory manner and they may apply retroactively to existing contracts only at the election of the contractor. Any subsequent change in the choice of they systems shall, however, be by agreement of the Council.

(d) While the system should not be complicated and should not impose major administrative costs on the Authority or on a contractor, consideration should be given to the adoption of a royalty system or a combination of a royalty and profit sharing system. If alternative systems are decided upon the choice of the system applicable to an individual contract shall be at the election of the contractor. However, any subsequent change of system shall be by agreement of the Council.

(e) An annual fixed fee shall be payable from the date of commencement of commercial production. However, such fee may be credited against other payments due under the system adopted in accordance with subparagrap (d). The amount of such fee shall be established by the Council.

(f) Any disputes concerning the interpretation or application of the rules and regulations based on these principles shall be subject to the dispute settlement procedures under the Convention.

2. The provisions of Annex III, Article 13, paragraphs 3 to 10 of the Convention shall not apply.

3. With regard to the implementation of Annex III, Article 13, paragraph 2 of the Convention, the fee for processing applications for approval of a plan of work limited to one phase, either the exploration phase or the exploitation phase, shall be $250,000.

SECTION 9. THE FINANCE COMITTEE

1. There is hereby established a Finance Committee. The Finance Committee shall be composed of 15 membeers with appropriate qualifications relevant to financial matters. States Parties shall nominate candidates of the highest standards of competence and integrity. In the election of members of the Finance Committee, due account shall be taken of the need for equitable geographical distribution and representation of special interests. Until the Authority is self-financing, the membership of the Committee shall include the five largest financial contributors to the administrative budget of the Authority.

2. No two members of the Finance Committee shall be nationals of the same State Party.

3. Members of the Finance Committee shall be elected by the Assembly. Each category referred to in Section 3, paragraph 14(a), (b), (c) and (d) of this Annex shall be represented on the Finance Committee by at least one member. After the Authority becomes self-financing, the election of one member from each category shall be on the basis of nomination by the members of the respective categoroy, without prejudice to the possibility of further members being elected from each such category.

4. Members of the Committee shall hold office for a term of five y ears. They shall be eligible for re-election for a further term.

5. In the event of death, incapacity or resignation of a member of the Committee prior to the expiration of the term of office, the Assembly shall elect for the remainder of the term a member from the same geographical region or interest group.

6. Members of the Committee shall have no financial interest in any activity relating to matters upon which the Committee has the responsibility to make recommendations. They shall not disclose, even after the termination of their functions, any confidential information coming to their knowledge by reason of their duties for the Authority.

7. Decisions by the Council and the Assembly on the following issues shall take into account recommendations by the Finance Committee:

(a) Draft financial rules, regulations and procedures of the various organs of the Authority and the financial management and internal financial administration of the Authority.

(b) Assessment of contributions of members to the adminisstrative budget of the Authority in accordance with Article 160, paragraph 2(e) of the Convention.

(c) All relevant financial matters inclding the proposed annual budget prepared by the Secretary-General (Article 172 of the Convention), the financial aspects of the implementation of the programmes of work of the Secretariat.

(d) The administrative budget.

(e) Financial obligations of States Parties arising from the operation of Part XI and its related annexes as well as on the administrative and budgetary implications of proposals and recommendations involving expenditure from the funds of the Authority.

(f) Rules, regulations and procedures on the equitable sharing of financial and other economic benefits and the decisions to be made on that basis.

8. Recommendations of the Committee shall, where necessary, be accompanid by a summary of the range of opinions in the Committee.

9. Decisions in the Finance Committee on questions of procedure shall be taken by a majority of members present and voting. Decisions on questions of substance shall be taken by consensus.

10. The requirement of Article 162, paragraph 2(y) of the Convention to establish a subsidiary organ to deal with financial matters shall be deemed to have been fulfilled by the establishment of the Finance Committee in accordance with this Section.

ED. NOTE: The categories of issues set forth in the foregoing "Boat Paper" are those which many, mostly industrialized, countries objected to in Part XI and its related provisions. At this point, you should review the relevant provisions of the treaty and ask yourself whether the Boat Paper sufficiently corrects the perceived deficiencies. Do you think that U.S. interests, if this paper is put into effect, are sufficiently protected to enable it to accept the Convention along with the Agreement?

Until recently, the United States played a role of reluctant observer in the consultations conducted by the Secretary-General. It is now fully engaged. Perhaps that fact, plus the following exchange before the U.S. Senate can be seen as a signal of a renewed U.S. interest in a generally acceptable Convention.

EXCERPT FROM SENATE CONFIRMATION HEARING FOR THE SECRETARY OF STATE DESIGNATE MR. WARREN CHRISTOPHER, 13 January 1993

<u>Senator Pell</u>: The law of the sea is a subject that has been of some interest, I think, to you in your previous government service, and I know it has been for me for many years. It has languished under

previous Administrations. As you know, we have the PREPCOM meetings in Jamaica, and we don't have an observer there. I was hoping that that might be in your thoughts as being dusted off and revised. What are your views about it?

Mr. Christopher: I do have a long standing interest, Mr. Chairman, in the law of the sea, and I hope we can do something to revive that. As I am sure you know better than I, I'm just getting re-acquainted in that area. There's only one aspect of the law of the sea treaty to which we have not been able to give approval, and that is the deep seabed regime.

Senator Pell: Article 40...Article 11, I think.

Mr. Christopher: Your memory of those numbers is better than mine. But I do understand that there may be some movement in that deep seabed regime, and there is some hope that there may be a restatement or perhaps some revision of that Article that would make it more acceptable to the United States and the interests here. It's unfortunate, with all the positive things there are in the law of the sea treaty, that we have been unable to adhere to that. Without knowing about it in detail, Mr. Chairman, or wanting to pose as an expert of the character of Elliot Richardson on the subject, I will assure you that we will see if we can't reactivate interest in the law of the sea in a way that protects US interests. Of course, the reason that we have not adhered is because we feel that are interests are not adequately protected under the law, under the deep seabed articles.

Senator Pell: I would agree with you. Except for the deep seabed, the rest of the provisions are accepted as established in international law. The deep seabed does, upon reflection, contain elements in it adverse to the United States, and I would hope that that Part could be handled by a Protocol or a separate side arrangement.

* * * * * *

ED. NOTE: On November 16, 1993, Guyana became the sixtieth State to ratify the 1982 United Nations Law of the Sea Convention. Accordingly, under the terms of Article 308 of the Convention, the Convention will enter into force on November 16, 1994 for all States that have ratified.

CHAPTER 9

EXPLOITATION OF LIVING RESOURCES

A. INTRODUCTION

In this chapter we shall examine the basic principles involved in the management of the living resources of the sea. This is a complex problem, and resource managers have been struggling with it for decades. There has been almost constant debate among experts as to the appropriate criteria to be applied to fishery management. There are many relevant considerations. The objective of good management may be seen as biological in nature: to provide the maximum amount of protein for food consistent with proper conservation measures.

There is also an economic aspect: the need for efficiency in the fishing industry, as well as preserving the economic well-being of coastal fishing communities. Finally, there may be ecological considerations to be taken into account, such as the effect that fishing a targeted species may have on other species that are biologically linked to it or may depend upon the targeted species for its own food. To take all of these factors into account calls for management techniques of almost gargantuan proportions.

In addition to the above considerations, assuming that we can identify the goals and techniques of proper fisheries management, there remains the question of what is the best way to achieve good management programs, and who should be making the decisions in what way. There is also a difficult issue with regard to how the manager should allocate the available fish stocks among the various participants in the fishery.

We must begin this investigation with an examination of some of the objectives that one might wish to attain. During your consideration of the preliminary materials, you may wish to consult the graph, figure 1, at the end of the chapter.

B. OBJECTIVES OF FISHERY MANAGEMENT

Johnston, THE INTERNATIONAL LAW OF FISHERIES (1965), 47-5[1]

OBJECTIVES

Exploiters

The general objective of all direct exploiters of fishery resources is to reap a profitable harvest from the sea, so as to secure the maximum return for the labor and capital expended. The fisherman is not concerned, as an exploiter, with the permanent stature and needs of the fishery, except in so far as it affects his means of livelihood. He places a high value on his personal intitiative and independence; the sea and the storm are his natural enemies; and no reward can be too high in good times to offset the dangers and disappointments of the bad. A "lucky catch," when it happens, is just something that happens, unrelated to previous effort. If the exploitation is intense and undisciplined, he will, however,

---

1. Reprinted by permission of the Free Press.

be made witness to "the great law of fishing," the general tendency of free fishing to become unprofitable. Whether he cooperates with conservers to restrict fishing will depend on many factors, both personal and nonpersonal, but it cannot affect his basic objective as an exploiter.

The larger units of exploitation, viewed as companies, industries, and governments, are obliged by the scale of their operation to adopt more flexible standards and longer perspectives. Less than maximum immediate benefits will be an acceptable objective if this runs in their long-term interest, and the viewpoint is institutional rather than personal. The national government is, of course, at the top of the tree of responsibility and has the advantage of the broadest range of vision. Normally it is more likely to take a long-term view of its objectives, since it also represents the consumers, but if the fishing industry makes an important contribution to the export trade, a national government may be tempted to adopt a short-term objective in order to contend with an unexpected shift in the world market. Iceland, for example, in constant fear of losing foreign markets, may have difficulty in adhering consistently to the conservation measures recommended in the interest of the resource. In Norway, too, the immediate necessity of promoting exports is paramount for the fishing industry, and the establishment of efficient, hygienic freezing and processing plants to maintain high standards of quality for the export trade could have the unplanned effect of increasing demand to a point at which production would be in excess of the optimum output, as measured by long-term and conservation criteria.

It is often assumed that underdeveloped countries embarking on a fisheries expansion program are motivated chiefly by the desire to improve the food supply for their own consumption, but it should be remembered that India actually exports more fish than she imports, and that the spectacular development of the Peruvian *anchoveta* fishery has been acccomplished to establish a huge fishmeal industry. Yet in most poor countries where food production lags behind population growth, it can be expected that two objectives will be predominant in fishery policy: to bring about a rapid increase in production so as to improve the intake of animal protein; and to make parallel improvements in marketing and distribution facilities. Fishery objectives for underdeveloped and developing countries must be framed in broader terms than for developed countries, since they are more immediately related to general social and political objectives, such as the social welfare of the fisherman, the economic conditions of the fishing community, and the nutritional level of the national population.

Often such financial aid as is allocated to fishery development in an emerging country is directed at small independent fishermen who are the least capable of investing it with durable effects, so that the necessity for aid tends to become permanent rather than temporary. The problem of fishery development is of course only part of the larger question of economic growth and a whole range of nonfinancial factors play their part. The rate of advance will depend upon the character and ability of the people, especially their capacity and willingness to learn, experiment, and apply improved methods; the acumen of the entrepreneurs; the creation of adequate incentives to encourage effort and capital investment; general economic and social policy and customs; and the ability and integrity of government administrators.

Conservers

To state the general objective of conservers is to beg one of the most difficult and controversial questions in the whole study of fishery problems. Conservation is associated, *prima facie*, with the restriction or postponement of exploitation, but these are perhaps more properly regarded as methods of attaining a more positive ulterior objective. The ulterior objective might be cast in strictly biological terms -- such as the combination of the highest sustainable yield with the best biological condition of the resource -- or in socioeconomic terms, such as the perpetuation and rationalization of the whole fishery complex (resource, men, capital and enterprise) at the highest level of efficiency.

Most fishery scientists throughout the world are prepared to agree on three possible objectives of conservation:

1. biggest total yield (i.e. maximum gross physical yield)

2. biggest average size and best average quality of fish (i.e. genetic optimum)

3. biggest catch per unit of effort (i.e. maximum net economic yield)

The first of these is likely to appeal most to national governments, since they represent both the domestic consumers and the export trade. The second is primarily a scientific challenge, but is commercially significant in certain established fisheries where the young fish are not being protected enough to maintain the abundance of stocks, and it is economic in the sense that the best marketable size of fish represents the best price and profit per unit. The third of these objectives, that of maximum net economic yield, treats as axiomatic the premise that "a prime motive in any commercial fishery is to obtain as much income in the form of yield as is possible with a given expenditure in fishing....

At the International Technical Conference on the Conservation of the Living Resources of the Sea, held at Rome in 1955, it was agreed that "the principal objective of conservation of the living resources of the sea is to obtain the optimum sustainable yield so as to secure a maximum supply of food and other marine products." This biological objective of the optimum sustainable yield [OSY] was accepted more or less uncritically by the International Law Commission, called upon by the General Assembly to prepare draft articles for the codification of the law of the sea; and at the codifying conference itself, held at Geneva in 1958, the same objective found its way into Article 2 of the Convention on Fishing and Conservation of the Living Resources of the High Seas. But although accepted by diplomats and lawyers, the concept of optimum sustainable yield has been subjected to criticism from several quarters.

C. ALTERNATIVES FOR MANAGEMENT

Over the years, there has been an ongoing debate regarding the most appropriate objective for fisheries management. Historically, most international fisheries agreements, bilateral or multilateral, were based upon the objective of maximizing the total amount of protein to be obtained in a fishery, while at the same time assuring that stays at a sustainable level over an indefinite period of time. This goal is usually referred to as "Maximum Sustainable Yield" (MSY), although sometimes known as "Optimum Sustainable Yield" (OSY). The latter phrase, as we will see, takes on a slightly different meaning in the 1982 United Nations Convention on the Law of the Sea. This objective is purely biologial in nature, and it does not take into account the desirability of promoting economic efficiency, or that of protecting social values, such as the cultural history of the fishing industry.

Christy has argued that a better objective for fisheries management would be one that maximizes the economic rent from the fishery, rather than putting stress on maximum biological yield: "Maximum Economic Yield" (MEY). As will be seen, to achieve MEY, it would be necessary to reduce the waste, i.e., to reduce the amount of fishing effort expended in a given fishery. This means reducing the number of fishermen. The desirability of increasing efficiency in the fishery, therefore, conflicts with that of increasing employment opportunities, and thus this goal has been difficult to explain to, much less achieve the support of, those fishermen who would be affected by the adoption of MEY as the primary fishery management objective.

These concepts are best understood by examining figure 1 at the end of this chapter. MSY and OSY are both biological goals. As noted above, if this objective is used, the idea is to obtain the maximum amount of protein from the resource wihthout, at the same time, depleting the resource below a biological optimal level. In figure 1, the relationship between fishing effort and fishing yield is represented by a parabollic curve. As indicated, yield can be represented by thousands of tons or millions of dollars. Effort, on that graph, is represented in terms of thousand vessel-days. But this would be accurate only if it is presumed that all vessels in the fishery were of the same design and power, and utilized the same fishing techniques and gear.

The point of maximum sustainable yield is marked point A. Any fishing effort less than that required to reach point A will produce a lower yield, but also, any fishing effort in excess of that amount will produce the same result.

Another way to describe MSY is to say that it is the amount of fishing effort that produces a catch that exactly equals the amount of protein that enters the fishery each year. Fishery stocks are measured in terms of year classes. It is not desirable to fish a year class of a stock until it reaches maturity. Younger fish should be allowed to remain. MSY is achieved if the yield for that year, resulting from fishing, plus the depletion of the stock from natural mortality, exactly equals the number of mature fish entering the fishery for that year. Because a fishery manager utilizing MSY will not wish to fish at efforts to the right of point A on the graph, it follows that some limitations must be placed on the fishermen.

This could be done by limiting the number of vessel-days. On the illustration, that would be a limit of five thousand vessel-days. This, in turn, would require a limitation on either the number of vessels or the number of fishing days, or a combination of each. Since it is always politically difficult, if not impossible, to put a limit on the number of boats that might fish, the alternative of reducing the length of the fishing season is by far the more popular device. Another alternative is to make fishing less efficient by putting a limit on the type of gear that can be used. Christy made reference to this alternative in his example concerning oystering in the Maryland waters of Chesapeake Bay.

But Christy's major point is that by regulating fishing in a way that permits as many boats as may wish to fish into the fishery while still protecting the stock from a conservation point of view means that the boats must be less efficient. In the graph, the amount of "economic rent", that is, the amount of profits in the fishery as a whole, is represented by the vertical distance between the curve (total revenues) and the cost line. In the example, this would be the difference between 13 million dollars in revenue and 5 million dollars in costs, or 8 million dollars.

Christy obviously opts for economic efficiency. His argument is that there is a point along the effort curve where the length of the vertical line, and hence economic rents, is at a maximum. In the illustration, this occurs at point C. You can easily see that the vertical line is longer there than at point A. Thus the rents available are maximized. In this case, the difference between revenues of 12 million dollars and costs of 3 million dollars, or 9 million dollars.

But the problem with using MEY as an objective, again using the illustration, is that to reach that optimum rent, it would be necessary to reduce the fishing effort from 5 thousand vessel-days to 3 thousand vessel-days. This is a forty percent reduction in effort. Since the objective is to eliminate wasted capital from the industry, the only way to do that would be to reduce the number of vessels allowed to fish. Perhaps now you can understand why the industry has so strenuously resisted adoption of any fishery goal based upon this concept. Fishermen will, however, accept MSY, even though it requires some limitation on their effort, because most know that if they do not, it will just be a matter of time before the stock is depleted below levels from which it cannot recover, and the fishery will be gone along with their jobs and boats.

It must be emphasized, at this stage, that setting MSY is not as simple as it sounds. It is very complicated. It should be based on scientific evidence, but such evidence is scant and research is underfunded. It can be estimated, however, by estimating how much food is in the food chain on which the stock is dependent, or by sampling the stock for the number of mature fish in a given area. But the result is usually only at best an estimate, and it will need to be tested by its application and subsequent sampling to see if the catch per unit of effort starts to fall off. If it does, the MSY has been set too high and will have to be reduced. The problem is further complicated by the fact that the illustration is for a single stock of fish only, and it does not take into account the interrelationship between stocks, such as the predator-prey relationship, nor does it (or can it) predict environmental variations that might affect recruitment into the stock.

1. LIMITED ENTRY

The above note mentions the problem of reaching a management goal of MEY, which requires limiting entry to the fishery to a finite number of boats. In U.S. law, this might create legal challenges. The following article discusses some of them.

Lansford, LEGAL IMPEDIMENTS TO LIMITED ENTRY SCHEMES IN MISSISSIPPI AND ALABAMA, 12 Water Log (1992), 3 - 6[2]

INTRODUCTION

Open access to the seas for commercial and sport fishing, which has long been a right in the United States, has over time caused serious depletion of the stocks of the country's fisheries, and measures such as area closings and seasonal limits on catches have proven inadequate to protect fisheries from further exhaustion. "Limited entry" is a general term used to describe any program that restricts a fisherman's access to open fisheries or limits the catch he is allowed to retain. This article will examine two forms of limited entry in use in the United States and will then discuss legal impediments to limited entry legislation....

OVERVIEW OF LIMITED ENTRY

Most fishery regulations in American waters are controlled by the federal government under the Magnuson Fishery Conservation and Management Act (FCMA), 16 U.S.C. 1801 *et seq*. These regulations, however, only govern waters more than three miles off the coast. Waters within three miles of the coast are regulated by the individual states. Most traditional methods used for fishery conservation have been implemented for the purpose of maintaining the "maximum sustainable yield" (MSY). The MSY is a theoretical level of the amount of stock that can be taken from a fishery in a season and still allow a full harvest to be available in perpetuity. It would be easy to assume the more plentiful the stock, the more bountiful the harvest. But the last few decades have seen a rapidly escalating demand on fishery resources and a corresponding decrease in the ocean's bounty. Limited entry programs are designed to promote the greatest economic efficiency of fisheries while at the same time ensuring that stocks will be able to replenish themselves.

A limited entry scheme may be effected either by limited licensing or by individual tradeable quotas. Limited licensing consists of issuing licenses to the greatest number of people who can fish the waters without hurting the fishery. A system of individual tradeable quotas (ITQs) allocates shares of

---

2. Reprinted by permission of the University of Mississippi Law Center.

the available stock of the fishery to fishermen, who are then allowed to catch whatever portion they have rights in.

Since limited entry entails restricting the amount of fishing that may be done in an area in which all people have a common propterty status, inevitable constitutional claims will be made. It is likely that these claims will assert either a denial of equal protection (the limited entry program must bear a rational relationship to its intended purpose), due process of law (the state must provide sufficient procedural safeguards to protect the fishermen's rights), or just compensation (the state must pay for any property it deprives the fishermen of).

METHODS OF EFFECTING LIMITED ENTRY

Limited Licensing

License limitation restricts the number of vessels, fishermen, gear, areas, or any combination thereof that are allowed to participate in fishing operations. Licence limitation has emerged as the favored method of limited entry. The manner of selecting which fishermen, vessels, or gear qualify for these licenses ranges from a simple lottery or a moratorium (capping the total amount allowed in a fishery at the existing level) to selection based on an individual's fishing history, his dependence on the fishery, and his past performance in the fishery.

The first and most difficult problem with limited licensing is determining who will be allowed entry. The system by which a state decides to issue licenses will greatly determine its success in defending a constitutional challenge. If a court finds that a definable group was excluded from a fair opportunity at receiving a license, it may feel free to strike down the program as violative of equal protection.

Provided licenses are issued in a valid manner, the next problem is with transferability. If the state makes licenses freely transferable, the risk arises that most of the licenses will eventually come into the hands of a few, possibly creating monopoly and anti-trust problems. On the other hand, free transferability would allow the value of the license to fluctuate so as to reflect its market price, thus allowing the fisherman to make an economically profitable decision to leave the fishery. Along with the ability to use the license as a security interest for loans and the possible creation of a property right, the development of a satisfactory transferability scheme for licenses is one of the most difficult aspects of devising a valid limited entry program.

Individual Tradeable Quotas

Individual tradeable quotas (ITCs) come in two forms. They can either be shares or percentages of an annually determined "total allowable catch," or they can be expressed as a fixed yearly catch. As with license limitation, the primary challenge will likely be directed against the method by which the shares are distributed. Since a fisherman's shares are transferable, the market price of his shares will rise and fall depending on the value of the stock. Fleets can therefore make a reasonably prudent decision about how much stock they can afford to catch in a given season. Another benefit of ITQs is with enforcement: a state regulatory agency may have to spend immense sums of money to ensure that fishermen are not taking more than their share. Further, because shares are tradeable, the quota system might tend to create a fishery dominated by large fishing concerns. While a state may limit the number of shares owned by one entity, such a solution would curb a major factor of ITQs which makes the system appealing.

Most troubling is the prospect that this system could encourage wanton discard of caught fish. Since vessels would be limited to the number of fish they could land, they might embark on a course of "high grading" their catch; this means retaining only the largest fish of the catch and discarding the rest. Whether the total allowable catch can be expressed in a weight limit rather than a limit on the number of fish caught is unclear.

FEDERAL CONSTITUTIONAL ISSUES

Equal Protection

State governments wield power to enact legislation to protect the public's natural resources. A state can enforce a total prohibition on using certain resources in order to protect those resources from depletion or destruction. But the power to ban the use of a natural resource does not include power merely to limit or restrict the use of a resource. While a total prohibition has an equal effect on all who wish to use the resource, limitation carries with it the potential for unequal treatment. This disparity in treatment is likely to be the argument of those who oppose limited entry.

Under the equal protection clause of the fourteenth amendment to the United States Constitition, a licensing classification will be upheld as long as the legislative classification bears a rational relationship to a legitimate state purpose or interest. This standard is relatively low. To survive equal protection scrutiny, the state would only have to show that its method of allocating entry into the fisheries was legitimately designed to effect its purpose. The Supreme Court, when deciding cases involving economic regulation or resource management, has shown a desire to affirm the state's legislative evaluations of the public's economic and social welfare. Since limited entry is a legitimate way of achieving economic efficiency in fisheries and preserving the natural resources of a state, as long as the access classifications are rationally related to this stated purpose, and equal protection claim would almost certainly fail.

Traditional licensing was a way for states to finance the administration of fishing regulations. Licenses are required in every state to fish, but unlike this traditional purpose, license limitation is intended to exclude people from fisheries. For a license limitation scheme to pass muster on an equal protection claim, the state must distribute licenses in a rational manner to achieve its purpose and not exclude any definable class of persons. While a limited entry program could be challenged on equal protection grounds by claiming that the plan violates its stated purpose (typically "the economic well-being of fishermen"), a state can easily avoid this problem by announcing in the statute that its goal is "economic efficiency" or "conservation of fisheries."

Of course all equal protection problems are avoided by distributing licenses through a lottery, but the political backlash from such a system would make certain that this method would not be used. Another method of distribution that could be used is sale or auction. This method has its own drawbacks in that it may create a class of wealthy fishermen. However, the Supreme Court has never held a legislative classification based on wealth subject to the heightened scrutiny of equal protection.

Due Process

A second constitutional claim that could be brought against a limited entry scheme in general is one of due process. There are two facets to due process, one substantive and the other procedural. Courts review substantive due process claims challenging industry regulations in much the same manner as they do equal protection. There need only be the same rational relationship between the regulation and its purpose. A substantive due process claim would likely assert that the right to fish (liberty) or the fish or fishing gear (property) had been taken without due process of law. It is therefore unlikely that a substantive due process claim would succeed in invalidating a limited entry scheme. Procedural due process requires a state to administer sufficient procedures to ensure that any entry rights are distributed and rescinded fairly. The procedures that are required are those of notice of the state's revocation, the right to a hearing upon revocation, and the right to judicial review of that hearing. It is assumed that any implementation of a limited entry program would fulfill the requirements of procedural due process (notice, right to hearing, and right to review), so a successful due process claim would be unlikely.

Takings and Just Compensation

The final potential constitutional claim against limited entry in general is one of a takings under the fifth amendment. The fifth amendment of the United States Constitution requires the federal and state governments to pay just compensation for any property or property right taken from a private citizen. For any takings claim to be successful, the claimant must have a cognizable property interest in the subject of the taking. No fisherman has an individual property right to fish. Generally, licenses and permits, required for fishing in every state, are deemed to confer a privilege, revocable at the discretion of the issuing agency. Even in cases where fishermen have challenged legislation that had the effect of rendering their equipment useless, the Supreme Court has held there was no taking. Since a fisherman presumably has no cognizable property right in uncaught fish, and since the courts have held that statutes having the effect of rendering fishing gear useless do not work a taking, an argument grounded in the fifth amendment is not likely to be successful.

Transferability

Any successful licensing program must describe the scope of the property rights vested in the license. This goes to the heart of the transferability problem. At one end of the scale there is no transferability: the license immediately reverts to the state whenever its holder is no longer entitled to it. At the other extreme is free transferability. In the former instance, the state would be granting a use privilege in issuing a license, thus avoiding the creation of any property rights. But the use of this system would discourage efficient fishing entities from expanding their operations and less efficient fishing entities from exiting the fishery. In the latter situation, the state would almost assuredly be inviting the creation of a property right. Therefore, whenever a state tried to defeat a license holder's right to fish, it would have to provide proper due process and possible just compensation. A free transferability scheme could also create monopoly and anti-trust problems and the previously mentioned classifications based on wealth that are subject to stricter scrutiny from the courts.

To achieve the goals of limited entry and to avoid the potential legal entanglements of vested property rights, any transferability scheme would have to take the positive aspects of both approaches. Some suggestions for this approach have been to make any transfer subject to the approval of the state's management agency. Limiting the number of licenses one entity could own, or allowing only natural persons, not corporations or organizations, to own licenses, has also been suggested.

Closely related to transferability are the legal problems associated with the disposition of fishery-related interests upon death and their use as security interests. A state could devise a program that required any receiving heir to qualify for a license. Others have suggested that a better system would be to have the state automatically buy back all licenses upon death. Besides the unattractive expense of such a scheme, it would probably result in multiple just compensation claims.

As a general rule, licenses should not be available as security interest on loans. Though some argue that using the license as a security interest may increase capital investments in the fisheries, legal entanglements that would result upon default would be horrendous. In addition, allowing a license to be used as security would give fishermen another argument that the license created some sort of property interest.

Property Rights in Uncaught Fish?

Property law has traditionally held that individuals have no right in fish while free. But if a state were to award a fisherman a fixed percentage of the total allowable catch in a given area, this would appear to give the fisherman a property interest in the fish before they were caught. In theory this might seem attractive to the state. It would encourage the economic efficiency that a limited entry program seeks to achieve and would also promote private enforcement of fishing regulations.

Creating a private property interest in the fish may also help deter water polluters. Typically states and the federal government have the only causes of action against polluters, with their remedies having little deterrent value. If a property interest was created, all fishermen holding an ITQ would have an independent cause of action against the polluter, with a generous amount of damages almost certain. The threat of numerous expensive lawsuits would have a far greater deterrent value than any cause of action held by the state or the federal government. However, the negative aspects of creating a property interest weigh much heavier than the positive. Though recognizing a property interest in the fish might encourage private enforcement of fishing regulations, the state would then be required to respect this property interest. This means that should the law ever be changed so as to deprive a fisherman of his proportion of the total allowable catch, he would have a valid due process and "takings" claim. Since ITQs only allow a percentage of the total allowable catch, a state could determine that no catch was allowable and effectively deprive all fishermen of their right to fish.

....

D. MANAGEMENT OF INTERNATIONAL FISHERIES

Assuming that the makers of policy have selected the goal that best suits their needs, there still must some mechanism for putting into effect the appropriate conservation measures designed to attain that goal. This brings into consideration a number of factors.

Let us consider briefly the situation before the adoption of the 1982 Convention, and then we can compare that with the existing regime.

Prior to the adoption of the new Convention, States claimed varying distances for the purposes of the management and regulation of fisheries. Prior to 1976, for example, the United States claimed jurisdiction for this purpose to 12 nautical miles from the baseline. Beyond that limit, fishing was considered to be a freedom of the high seas, and thus foreign vessels could remain outside that limit and apply as much fishing effort as they desired. The impact on the stock inside the limit must be obvious. It was impossible to conserve stocks of fish in this manner, but, lacking jurisdiction outside that limit the U.S. could not enforce fishing regulations on foreign vessels without their consent.

Since consent was required, a complicated set of international agreements needed to be negotiated. These could be of a bilateral nature, or they could, where there were a number of foreign participants in the fishery, be managed by an international fishing commission which the participants and relevant coastal States might set up.

The character and functions of these commissions varied according to the characteristics of the particular fisheries. For example, one system of regulation might be appropriate for coastal pelagic fisheries, but totally unsuited for anadromous fish (primarily salmon) or highly migratory fisheries (primarily tuna) because of the widely disparate migratory and spawning patterns of a particular specie.

In 1976, the Congress of the United States enacted the Fishery Conservation and Management Act. We will examine that act in some detail later, but for the present purposes, the major advance included in that legislation was the creation of a fishery management zone of 200 miles adjacent to the U.S. coast. It was similar, but with less jurisdictional content, to the Exclusive Economic Zone created by the new treaty. This solved several previous management problems. However, it is not totally comprehensive and there is still a need for various bilateral arrangements and international regulatory bodies. For that reason, we shall take a look at some of the prior agreements.

1. BILATERAL ARRANGEMENTS

Prior to 1976, the U.S. chose to deal with conservation and allocation of fisheries near its coast, in some cases, by negotiating bilateral arrangements. This was especially true in the Northwest Pacific -- the Gulf of Alaska, the Bering Sea, and to a lesser extent, the coasts of California, Oregon and Washington. The biggest control and management problems were presented by the fishing fleets of Japan and the then Soviet Union. Faced with the choice of dealing with them separately or forming a commission to regulate the fishery, the U.S. chose the bilateral route. There was a feeling on the part of at least some U.S. fishery managers that a commission having these countries as members would give them too much opportunity to sabotage sound conservation measures and too much power to negotiate a larger share of the resource.

Accordingly, each nation was negotiated with separately, taking into account individual problems that were unique to the situation. Obviously, no two bilateral fishery agreements are alike. Some are relatively simple, but others, dealing with multiple stocks of fish, can be amazingly complex. But, typically, these arrangements tend to address the same kinds of questions. They address such matters as permitted levels of catch, seasons, permissible gear, areas to be fished, exchange of statistics, port calls, and the like. The following is an example of a rather simple bilateral agreement between the United States and the Soviet Union.

July 18, 1975

AGREEMENT BETWEEN THE UNITED STATES OF AMERICA AND THE GOVERNMENT OF THE UNION OF SOVIET SOCIALIST REPUBLICS RELATING TO FISHING FOR KING AND TANNER CRAB

The Government of the United States of America and the Government of the Union of Soviet Socialist Republics,

Having considered in a spirit of understanding their problems relating to the king and tanner crab fisheries on the continental shelf in light of their ratifications of the Convention on the Continental Shelf adopted at Geneva, 1958,

Taking into account the existing fishery of the Soviet Union for king and tanner crab in the eastern Bering Sea, and

Desiring to adopt the necessary measures for conserving the stocks of king crab and tanner crab in the fisheries areas provided for by the agreement,

Have agreed as follows:

1. The king crab and tanner crab are natural resources of the continental shelf over which the coastal state exercises sovereign rights for the purposes of exploration and exploitation in accordance with the provisions of Article 2 of the Convention on the Continental shelf.

2. Nationals and vessels of the Soviet Union may continue to carry out fishing for king and

tanner crab on the continental shelf of the United States during 1975 and 1976 in that area of the eastern Bering Sea described in the Appendix to this Agreement, provided that the annual commercial catch of king crab and tanner crab by Soviet nationals and vessels in such area shall not exceed 112,000 king crabs and 4.05 million tanner crabs each in 1975 and 1976.

3. Each Government will apply the measures specified in paragraphs 3 and 4 of the Appendix to this Agreement to its nationals and vessels engaged in the king and tanner crab fisheries in the eastern Bering Sea. Either Government shall, if requested by the other Government, provide opportunity for observation of the conduct of enforcement of the provisions of this Agreement and for that purpose shall permit duly authorized officers of the other Government to board its vessels engaged in the king and tanner crab fisheries in the eastern Bering Sea. These officers will make a report on the results of their observations; the report will be forwarded to the Government of the flag state for appropriate action, if such action should be necessary.

4. The two Governments will continue and intensify their study of the king and tanner crab resources in the eastern Bering Sea and will exchange annually by November 30 the data resulting from such study including also, to the extent possible, an estimate of the maximum sustainable yield of the resources. The data to be furnished by each Government may be prepared in accordance with its own methodology and shall include, but not be limited to, the categories of data described in the Appendix to this Agreement. The two Governments will also provide for the exchange of scientific personnel engaged in the study of the king crab and tanner crab resources.

5. This Agreement shall replace the Agreement of February 21, 1973 between the two Governments relating to fishing for king and tanner crab, as extended by an exchange of notes. It shall enter into force on August 1, 1975 and shall remain in force through December 31, 1976. At the request of either Government, representatives of the two Governments will meet at a mutually convenient time within sixty days of such request with a view to modifying the present Agreement. In any event, representatives of the two Governments will meet at a mutually convenient time prior to the expiration of the period of validity of this Agreement to review the operation of the Agreement and to decide on future arrangements. Nothwithstanding the above, at any time during the period of force of the Agreement, either Government may communicate to the other Government its intention to denounce this Agreement, in which case the Agreement shall terminate one month from the date of receipt of the communication. As soon as possible after receipt of such communication, representatives of the two Governments will meet to discuss possible future arrangements.

IN WITNESS WHEREOF, the undersigned, being duly authorized for this purpose, have signed this Agreement.

DONE at Washington, July 18, 1975, in duplicate, in the English and Russian languages, both texts being equally authentic.

FOR THE GOVERNMENT OF THE UNITED STATES OF AMERICA

Thomas A. Clingan, Jr.

FOR THE GOVERNMENT OF THE UNION OF SOVIET SOCIALIST REPUBLICS

Vladimir M. Kamentsev

APPENDIX

1. The area referred to in paragraph 2 of the Agreement is that portion of the southeastern Bering Sea lying seaward of twelve nautical miles from the baseline from which the United States territorial sea is measured west of 164° West Longitude and north of 55° 30' North Latitude.

The annual commercial catch of king crab and tanner crab by Soviet nationals and vessels referred to in paragraph 2 of the Agreement shall not exceed:

a. 750,000 tanner crabs (750 metric tons) in the area bounded by straight lines connecting the following coordinates in the order listed: [there follows a listing of boundary points by latitude and longitude]

b. 112,000 king crabs (356 metric tons) and 3.3 million tanner crabs (2,310 metric tons) in the waters north and west of and adjacent to the area designated in subparagraph a above.

3. a. Female king and tanner crabs, king crabs less than 15.8 cm. in maximum carapice width, and soft-shelled king and tanner crabs shall not be retained and used. Any such crabs taken incidentally, any king crabs taken in excess of the agreed quotas, and any tanner crabs taken in excess of the agreed quotas in each of the areas shall be returned immediately to the sea with a minimum of injury.

b. King crabs and tanner crabs shall not be taken by means of fishing gear other than pots.

4. Unless otherwise agreed by the two Governments, only pots may be used to capture king crabs and tanner crabs for commercial purposes and no trawling by Soviet fishing vessels may be conducted for other species in that area lying seaward of twelve nautical miles from the baseline from which the United States territorial sea is measured within the following boundaries: a line running from a point on the Bering Sea coast of the Alaska Peninsula due west along 55° 54' North Latitude to its intersection with a line connecting two points 56° 20' North Latitude, 163° 00' West Longitude, and 55° 16' North Latitude, 166° 10' West Longitude, thence southwesterly along the said line to its intersection with a line passing between Cape Navarin and Cape Sarachef at 55° 16' North Latitude, 166° 10' West Longitude, thence southeasterly along the Cape Navarin-Sarichef line to Cape Sarichef.

5. The data referred to in paragraph 4 of the Agreement are:

a. Biological Data.

(1) Tag returns: tag number and/or tag; date and location of capture (latitude and longitude); sex, length, width, and weight of crab; condition of shell.

(2) Life history data: length, width, weight, and age of crab by sex; moult data;

breeding habits, feeding habits, migration habits.

(3) Publications dealing with king crabs and tanner crabs in the Bering Sea and North Pacific.

b. Catch Statistics.

Total amount and monthly catches by 1° of longitude.

c. Effort Statistics.

(1) Description of pots; number of pot lifts per month by 1° of longitude.

(2) Number of fleets operated by dates of operations; number of pot boats.

d. Production Statistics.

(1) Canned crab: number of cases, number of crabs per case, quantity of meat per case.

(2) Frozen crab: description of units and number of units; number of crabs.

* * * *

Such bilateral arrangements were not particularly successful, but given the lack of fishery jurisdiction beyond 12 miles at the time, they represented the best effort of the Government to conserve the resources. There were many problems. First, since it was necessary to make gains in the negotiations, it was equally necessary to make concessions. Thus, while a particular agreement might represent an overall gain for the United States, that gain could not usually be more than marginal. The size of the gain depended directly on the amount of bargaining leverage the negotiator had at his disposal, and this was normally quite small. The possible trade-offs were greater if a number of stocks of fish, not just one or two, were the subject of negotiation. In such a case, a U.S. negotiator might be able to agree to allowing the other side to take an increased share of one stock of fish that was relatively in healthy condition, and for which U.S. fishermen had little or no interest, in exchange for agreement that the other side would cut back on stocks of special interest to the United States. This negotiating technique was used, for example, in the U.S./Japanese bilateral where the U.S. would agree to allow the Japanese to take increased catches of Pollock, a fish in which at that time the U.S. had little interest, in exchange for Japanese agreement to cut back on their take of King Crab.

Other issues could be used to advantage, as well. For example, the Soviet Union attached significance to their need to be authorized to use selected U.S. ports for exchange of crews, re-supply, and rest and recreation. That need could be taken into account. Also, the Soviets had an interest in having access to sheltered areas within 12 miles for the transfer of cargo to transport ships. These things were of some value in extracting concessions from them, but it was a painful process.

A second defect in the process was the lack of sufficient independent scientific information upon which to make reasoned decisions regarding the safe upper limits of total catch. Both sides had their scientists, and, as can be imagined, there was no agreement among them, leaving the chief negotiators no goals to attain except on a purely political basis.

Third, the negotiators were hampered by other foreign policy considerations. Although the negotiations were only concerned with the regulation of fishing, it was impossible to ignore the impact of a particular set of regulations which, if successfully attained, would have on the overall bilateral relations of the two countries. A regulation, for example, that would have the effect of closing down an entire segment of the Japanese industry would have a real impact on our relations.

All of these factors, and others like them, made significant conservation progress difficult, and the improvement of benefits to the American fishing industry at the expense of foreign fishermen almost impossible. And the evidence was mounting to indicate that these agreements not only were not improving the situation but that certain stocks were actually in decline, as reflected in the following excerpt:

REPORT OF THE HOUSE MERCHANT MARINE AND FISHERIES COMMITTEE TO THE COMMITTEE OF THE WHOLE HOUSE No. 94-445, April 20, 1975

....

The decline in many of the fisheries off our coast has been coincidental with increased foreign fishing in major areas along our continental shelf and beyond our existing 12-mile fishery jurisdictional limit. Current international, national and state conservation efforts are not successfully preventing the depletion of fisheries resources of the greatest economic importance. The normal process of negotiating fishery agreements is time consuming and complex. Nations wishing to continue a high level of fishing effort while negotiating can easily slow down or impede the progress of such negotiations, and without mutual agreement, there are no binding treaties. Moreover, a number of existing agreements admittedly have resulted in over-fishing, and the signatory nations have been reluctant to reduce their efforts accordingly. Presently, the United States is a party to well over a score of international fishing agreements and periodically engages in bilateral and multilateral negotiations with foreign nations to restructure these treaties and to frame new ones which seek to conserve fish resources. Nearly all of the stocks of fish considered to be depleted or threatened with depletion are subject to these international agreements.

In those instances where agreements are reached, the problem of enforcement has been chronic. Traditionally, international fishery agreements provide for the enforcement by each signatory nation as to their own citizens. For example, if a Soviet fleet is operating off U.S. shores pursuant to an international agreement, it is the duty of Soviet officials to enforce that agreement on their own citizens. It is easy to see, however, why a nation, which on the one hand has directed its fishing fleet to return a high quota of fish, may not be as diligent as is necessary to enforce full compliance with international fishery agreements. In many cases, it would appear that effective sanctions are completely lacking and violations often go unpunished. Meanwhile, U.S. fishermen see themselves as being tightly regulated by Government officials to comply with U.S. responsibilities under any such agreement. They claim that while they must toe the line, foreign fishermen are not forced to toe the same line. Furthermore, it is difficult to imagine that a nation with a long distance fishing fleet which can pick up and move to any part of the world would ever be strongly concerned about conserving fisheries in any one particular area. In contrast, fishermen who live a relatively short distance from a fishing ground have a much greater interest in conserving the fish that inhabit the waters near their home.

....

* * * *

It was rarely possible during negotiations to get foreign fishing States to agree to really good enforcement measures, and never to get them to allow enforcement by U.S. officials. It was not even possible to get agreement to permit the U.S. to place observers on their vessels to verify the size and type of catch.

2. MULTILATERAL ARRANGEMENTS

As noted previously, where a particular area was being subjected, outside of U.S. jurisdiction, to fishing by a substantial number of fishing States, it would be much too complex to seek to deal with the problems by a series of bilateral agreements. It is hard enough to do so where there are only one or two major participants. As an example, if the U.S., based on the best available scientific evidence, could establish the total catch allowable for the year within conservation limits, the manager still had to decide how to allocate this catch as between the participants. On such decisions, the success or failure of bilateral arrangements might rest.

For that reason, the United States participated in the work of a number of multilateral fishery commissions, whose task was the conservation of several resources in the area for which the commission took responsibility. Like bilateral arrangments, the agreements establishing such commissions took a number of different forms. But these commissions were not any more successful than bilateral arrangements, and perhaps less so in some regards. Most of the agreements creating fishery commissions restricted themselves to matters of conservation. With multiple participants, both distant water fishermen and coastal States, it was rarely possible to create a commission having the power to allocate the fish among themselves, for obvious reasons. Second, some of the agreements did not make the recommendations of the commission binding on the participating States. Third, the enforcement problems were just as severe as those under bilateral arrangements.

Assuming that one wished to negotiate an agreement to create a new fishery commission, there were difficult questions to be addressed. What States should be invited to join? How are decisions to be taken by the commission? Will these decisions be binding on States Parties? Will the commission be given power to allocate the available stocks of fish among the participants, and, if so, how will the commission deal with new entrants -- that is, States not presently fishing in the area, but subsequently ask to join the arrangment? How will scientific data be obtained upon which to base decisions? How will the conservation measures be enforced?

Different commissions dealt with these issues in different ways. The following is an example of how these issues were dealt with in one international commission of which the United States was a member.

NORTHWEST ATLANTIC FISHERIES

....

International Convention for the Northwest Atlantic Fisheries

The Governments whose duly authorized representatives have subscribed hereto, sharing a substantial interest in the conservation of the fishery resources of the Northwest Atlantic Ocean, have resolved to conclude a convention for the investigation, protection and conservation of the fisheries of the Northwest Atlantic Ocean, in order to make possible the maintenance of a maximum sustained catch from those fisheries and to that end have, through their duly authorized representatives, agreed as follows:

Article I

1. The area to which this Convention applies, hereinafter referred to as "the Convention area", shall be all waters, except territorial waters, bounded by a line....[Article I goes on to describe the precise area by latitude and longitude points].

2. Nothing in this Convention shall be deemed to affect adversely (prejudice) the claims of any Contracting Government in regard to the limits of territorial waters or to the jurisdiction of a coastal state over fisheries.

3. The Convention area shall be divided into five sub-areas, the boundaries of which shall be those defined in the Annex to this Convention....

Article II

1. The Contracting Governments shall establish and maintain a Commission for the purposes of this Convention. The Commission shall be known as the International Commission for the Northwest Atlantic Fisheries, hereinafter referred to as "the Commission".

2. Each of the Contracting Governments may appoint not more than three Commissioners and one or more experts or advisers to assist its Commissioner or Commissioners.

3. The Commission shall elect from its members a Chairman and a Vice Chairman, each of whom shall serve for a term of two years and shall be eligible for re-election but not to a succeeding term. The Chairman and Vice Chairman must be Commissioners from different Contracting Governments.

4. The seat of the Commission shall be in North America at a place to be chosen by the Commission.

5. The Commission shall hold a regular annual meeting at its seat or at such place in North America as may be agreed upon by the Commission.

6. Any other meeting of the Commission may be called by the Chairman at such time and place as he may determine, upon the request of the Commissioner of a Contracting Government and subject to the concurrence of the Commissioners of two other Contracting Governments, including the Commissioner of a Government in North America.

7. Each Contracting Government shall have one vote which may be cast by any Commissioner from that Government. Decisions of the Commission shall be taken by a two-thirds majority of the votes of all the Contracting Governments.

8. The Commission shall adopt, and amend as occasion may require, financial regulations and rules and by-laws for the conduct of its meetings and for the exercise of its functions and duties.

Article III

1. The Commission shall appoint an Executive Secretary according to such procedure and on such terms as it may determine.

2. The staff of the Commission shall be appointed by the Executive Secretary in accordance with such rules and procedures as may be determined and authorized by the Commission.

3. The Executive Secretary shall, subject to the general supervision of the Commission, have full power and authority over the staff and shall perform such other functions as the Commission shall prescribe.

Article IV

1. The Contracting Governments shall establish and maintain a Panel for each of the sub-areas provided for in Article I, in order to carry out the objectives of this Convention. Each Contracting Government participating in any Panel shall be represented on such Panel by its Commissioner or Commissioners, who may be assisted by experts or advisers. Each Panel shall elect from its members a Chairman who shall serve for a period of two years and shall be eligible for reelection but not to a succeeding term.

2. After this Convention has been in force for two years, but not before that time, Panel representation shall be reviewed annually by the Commission, which shall have the power, subject to consultation with the Panel concerned, to determine representation on each Panel on the basis of current substantial exploitation in the sub-area concerned of fishes in the cod group (*Gadiformes*), of flat-fishes (*Pleuronectiformes*), and of rosefish (*genus Sebastes*), except that each Contracting Government with coastline adjacent to a sub-area shall have the right of representation on the Panel for the sub-area.

3. Each Panel may adopt, and amend as occasion may require, rules of procedure and by-laws for the conduct of its meetings and for the exercise of its functions and duties.

4. Each Government participating in a Panel shall have one vote, which shall be cast by a Commissioner representing that Government. Decisions of the Panel shall be taken by a two-thirds majority of the votes of all the Governments participating in that Panel.

5. Commissioners of Contracting Governments not participating in a particular Panel shall have the right to attend the meetings of such Panel as observers, and may be accompanied by experts and advisers.

6. The Panels shall, in the exercise of their functions and duties, use the services of the Executive Secretary and the staff of the Commission.

Article V

1. Each Contracting Government may set up an Advisory Committee composed of persons, including fishermen, vessel owners and others, well informed concerning the problems of the fisheries of the Northwest Atlantic....

Article VI

1. The Commission shall be responsible in the field of scientific investigation for obtaining and collating the information necessary for maintaining those stocks of fish which support international fisheries in the Convention area and the Commission may, through or in collaboration with agencies of the Contracting Governments or other public or private agencies and organizations or, when necessary, independently:

(a) make such investigations as it finds necessary into the abundance, life history and ecology of any species of aquatic life in any part of the Northwest Atlantic Ocean;

(b) collect and analyze statistical information relating to the current conditions and trends of the fishery resources in the Northwest Atlantic Ocean;

(c) study and appraise information concerning the methods for maintaining and increasing stocks of fish in the Northwest Atlantic Ocean;

(d) hold or arrange such hearings as may be useful or essential in connection with the development of factual information necessary to carry out the provisions of this Convention;

(e) conduct fishing operations in the Convention area at any time for purposes of scientific investigation;

(f) publish and otherwise disseminate reports of its findings and statistical, scientific and other information relating to the fisheries of the Northwest Atlantic Ocean as well a such other reports as fall within the scope of this Convention.

2. Upon the unanimous recommendation of each Panel affected, the Commission may alter the boundaries of the sub-areas set out in the Annex. Any such alteration shall forthwith be reported to the Depositary Government which shall inform the Contracting Governments, and the sub-areas defined in the Annex shall be altered accordingly.

3. The Contracting Governments shall furnish to the Commission at such time and in such form as may be required by the Commission, the statistical information referred to in paragraph 1(b) of this Article.

Article VII

1. Each Panel established under Article IV shall be responsible for keeping under review the fisheries of its sub-area and the scientific and other information relating thereto.

2. Each Panel, upon the basis of scientific investigations, may make recommendations to the Commission for joint action by the Contracting Governments on matters specified in paragraph 1 of article VIII.

3. Each Panel may recommend to the Commission studies and investigations within the scope of this Convention which are deemed necessary in the development of factual information relating to a particular sub-area.

4. Any Panel may make recommendations to the Commission for the alteration of the boundaries of the sub-areas defined in the Annex.

5. Each Panel shall investigate and report to the Commission upon any matter referred to it by the Commission.

6. A Panel shall not incur any expenditure except in accordance with directions given by the Commission.

Article VIII

1. The Commission may, on the recommendations of one or more Panels, and on the basis of scientific investigations, transmit to the Depositary Government proposals, for joint action by the Contracting Governments, designed to keep the stocks of those species of fish which support international fisheries in the Convention area at a level permitting the maximum sustained catch by the

application, with respect to such species of fish, of one or more of the following measures:

(a) establishing open and closed seasons;

(b) closing to fishing such portions of a sub-area as the Panel concerned finds to be a spawning area or to be populated by small or immature fish;

(c) establishing size limits for any species;

(d) prescribing the fishing gear and appliances the uses of which is prohibited;

(e) prescribing an over-all catch limit for any species of fish.

2. Each recommendation shall be studied by the Commission and thereafter the Commission shall either:

(a) transmit the recommendation as a proposal to the Depositary Government with such modifications or suggestions as the Commission may consider desirable, or

(b) refer the recommendation back to the Panel with comments for its reconsideration.

3. The Panel may, after reconsidering the recommendation returned to it by the Commission, reaffirm that recommendation, with or without modification.

4. If, after a recommendation is reaffirmed, the Commission is unable to adopt the recommendation as a proposal, it shall send a copy of the recommendation to the Depositary Government with a report of the Commission's decision. The Depositary Government shall transmit copies of the recommendation and of the Commission's report to the Contracting Governments.

5. The Commission may, after consultation with all the Panels, transmit proposals to the Depositary Government within the scope of paragraph 1 of this Article affecting the Convention area as a whole.

6. The Depositary Government shall transmit any proposal received by it to the Contracting Governments for their consideration and may make such suggestions as will facilitate acceptance of the proposal.

7. The Contracting Governments shall notify the Depositary Government of their acceptance of the proposal, and the Depositary Government shall notify the Contracting Governments of each acceptance communicated to it, including the date of receipt thereof.

8. The proposal shall become effective for all Contracting Governments four months after the date on which notifications of acceptance shall have been received by the Depositary Government from all the Contracting Governments participating in the Panel or Panels for the sub-area or sub-areas to which the proposal applies.

9. At any time after the expiration of one year from the date on which a proposal becomes effective, any Panel Government for the sub-area to which the proposal applies may give to the Depositary Government notice of the termination of its acceptance of the proposal and, if that notice is not withdrawn, the proposal shall cease to be effective for that Panel Government at the end of one year from the date of receipt of the notice by the Depositary Government. At any time after a proposal ceased to be effective for a Panel Government under this paragraph, the proposal shall cease to be

effective for any other Contracting Giovernment upon the date a notice of withdrawal by such Government is received by the Depositary Government. The Depositary Government shall notify all Contracting Governments of every notice under this paragraph immediately upon the receipt thereof.

....

ED. NOTE: At this point, read and consider the provisions of the Convention on Fishing and Conservation of the Living Resources of the High Seas, contained in the annexes to this book. What are the policies being advanced? Through what mechanisms? How effective do you think the regime established by that Convention would be?

The agreement shown above was a regional commission. Most of them are, but some commissions have a global concern. The most important, perhaps, is the International Whaling Commission which has the task of regulating commercial whaling anywhere in the world. But, again, in this instance the problem is the binding nature of the IWC's regulations. Under that agreement, recommendations of the commission are submited to member Governments. If any member objects within 90 days, the regulation will not apply to it. If that occurs, all other member States will have a period in which to decide whether they wish to object as well. For a case in U.S. law involving the matter of objection, see Adams v. Vance, 570 F.2d 950 (D.C. Cir. 1978).

On first glance, it would seem that the creation of the Exclusive Economic Zone, giving coastal States jurisdiction over their fisheries to 200 miles would eliminate the need for fisheries commissions. Not so, however. As noted before, some stocks of fish range beyond that limit, and some mechanism still needs to be created to deal with conservation issues regarding such stocks.

E. EXCLUSIVE FISHING ZONES

As a result of the shortcomings of the above arrangements, States began to make unilateral claims to broad fishing zones adjacent to their coasts. These zones had the advantage of giving coastal States greater control over the conservation of their living resources. In most instances, other States could still gain access to these zones by paying fees and buying licenses. However, there was no rule of international law that required granting access or setting the terms and conditions of access. Accordingly, these unilateral moves created the potential for conflict.

In addition, some States, like the U.S., had for a long time difficulty in deciding its policy on this issue. This is because the U.S. fishing industry is not entirely coastal. There is a substantial distant-water fishery as well. Thus there was no industry consensus on whether to ask for an expanded fishery zone.

For some time, the fishing zone of the U.S. was quite modest. It extended to only 12 miles under the Twelve Mile Exclusive Fishery Zone Act of 1966. But the statute proved simply inadequate to protect U.S. fisheries. When the Third United Nations Conference on the Law of the Sea began its work, it soon became clear that a substantially expanded resource zone must be a part of an overall comprehensive agreement. As the Exclusive Economic Zone concept began to attract widespread support, States began to broaden their claims. As of May, 1990, 2 nations claimed zones of 12 miles, 1 claimed 25 miles, 1 nation claimed 50 miles, but 95 nations claimed 200 miles.

At first, the United States sought to deal with the problem of fisheries beyond 12 miles, as we have seen, by negotiation. This system was established by the following proclamation.

PRESIDENTIAL PROCLAMATION NO. 2668 (SEPTEMBER 28, 1945), 3 C.F.R., 1943-1948 Comp., p. 68, 13 Dep't State Bull. 486 (1945)

"Policy of the United States with Respect to Coastal Fisheries in Certain Areas of the High Seas"

Whereas for some years the Government of the United States of America has viewed with concern the inadequacy of present arrangements for the protection and perpetuation of the fishery resources contiguous to its coasts, and in view of the potentially disturbing effect of this situation, has carefully studied the possibility of improving the jurisdictional basis for conservation measures and international cooperation in this field; and

Whereas such fishery resources have a special importance to coastal communities as a source of livelihood and to the nation as a food and industrial resource; and

Whereas the progressive development of new methods and techniques contributes to intensified fishing over wide sea areas and in certain cases seriously threatens fisheries with depletion; and

Whereas there is an urgent need to protect coastal fishery resources from destructive exploitation, having due regard to conditions peculiar to each region and situation and to the special rights and equities of the coastal State and of any other State which may have established a legitimate interest therein;

Now, therefore, I, Harry S. Truman, President of the United States of America, do hereby proclaim the following policy of the United States of America with respect to coastal fisheries in certain areas of the high seas:

In view of the pressing need for conservation and protection of fishery resources, the Government of the United States regards it as proper to establish conservation zones in those areas of the high seas contiguous to the coasts of the United States wherein fishing activities have been or in the future may be developed and maintained on a substantial scale. Where such activities have been or shall hereafter be developed by its nationals alone, the United States regards it as proper to establish explicitly bounded conservation zones in which fishing activities shall be subject to the regulation and control of the United States. Where such activities have been or shall hereafter be legitimately developed and maintained jointly by nationals of the United States and nationals of other States, explicitly bounded conservation zones may be established under agreements between the United States and such other States; and all fishing activities in such zones shall be subject to regulation and control as provided in such agreements. The right of any State to establish conservation zones off its shores in accordance with the above principle is conceded, provided that corresponding recognition is given to any fishing interests of nationals of the United States which may exist in such areas. The character as high seas of the areas in which such conservation zones are established and the right to their free and unimpeded navigation are in no way thus affected.

NOTE: Not long after the U.S. took this step, certain latin American countries took steps far beyond the policies reflected in the Truman Proclamation. The following is an example.

AGREEMENTS BETWEEN CHILE, ECUADOR, AND PERU, SIGNED AT THE FIRST CONFERENCE ON THE EXPLOITATION AND CONSERVATION OF THE MARITIME RESOURCES OF THE SOUTH PACIFIC, SANTIAGO, CHILE, AUGUST 18, 1952.

(a) Declaration on the Maritime Zone

1. Governments are bound to ensure for their peoples access to necessary food supplies and to furnish them with the means of developing their economy.

2. It is therefore the duty of each Government to ensure the conservation and protection of its natural resources and to regulate the use thereof to the greatest possible advantage of its country.

3. Hence it is likewise the duty of each Government to prevent the said resources from being used outside the area of its jurisdiction so as to endanger their existence, integrity and conservation to the prejudice of peoples so situated geographically that their seas are irreplaceable sources of essential food and economic materials.

For the foregoing reasons the Governments of Chile, Ecudador and Peru, being resolved to preserve for and make available to their respective peoples the natural resources of the areas of sea adjacent to their coasts, hereby declare as follows:

(I) Owing to the geological and biological factors affecting the existence, conservation and development of the marine fauna and flora of the waters adjacent to their coasts of the declarant countries, the former extent of the territorial sea and contiguous zone is insufficient to permit of the conservation, development and use of those resources, to which the coastal countries are entitled.

(II) The Governments of Chile, Ecuador and Peru therefore proclaim as a principle of their international maritime policy that each of them possesses sole sovereignty and jurisdiction over the area of sea adjacent to the coast of its own country and extending not less than 200 nautical miles from the said coast.

(III) Their sole jurisdiction and sovereignty over the zone thus described includes sole sovereignty and jurisdiction over the sea floor and subsoil thereof.

(IV) The zone of 200 nautical miles shall extend in every direction from any island or group of islands forming part of the territory of a declarant country. The maritime zone of an island or group of islands belonging to one declarant country and situated less than 200 nautical miles from the general maritime zone of another declarant country shall be bounded by the parallel of latitude drawn from the point at which the land frontier between the two countries reaches the sea.

(V) This Declaration shall not be construed as disregarding the necessary restrictions on the exercise of sovereignty and jurisdiction imposed by international law to permit the innocent and inoffensive passage of vessels of all nations through the zone aforesaid.

(VI) The Governments of Chile, Ecuador and Peru state that they intend to sign agreements or conventions to put into effect the principles set forth in this Declaration and to establish general regulations for the control and protection of hunting and fishing in their respective maritime zones and the control and co-ordination of the use and working of all other natural products or resources of common interest present in the said waters.

ED. NOTE: The Santiago Declaration was issued in response to the desires of the coastal States involved to manage their tuna resources. This declaration was not accepted by the United

States, which has an extensive distant-water tuna fishing fleet, and many conflicts arose, including the seizure of American tuna clippers. But unilateral extensions were not limited to the tuna problem. In 1958, Iceland extended its fishing zone from 4 to 12 miles, causing a dispute with the United Kingdom whose boats had traditionally fished in the area. This dispute was finally settled through negotiation in 1961. By an exchange of notes, the UK tacitly accepted the 12 mile limit in exchange for a promise on the part of Iceland to refer any further extensions to the International Court of Justice for adjudication. In 1972, Iceland made such a further extension to 50 miles, and the United Kingdom filed suit. Iceland refused to recognize the jurisdiction of the Court over this dispute, but Iceland's non-appearance did not deprive the Court of its jurisdiction. It granted temporary relief to the UK and then proceeded to hear the case on the merits. In July 1974, the Court handed down its opinion, which sets forth the state of international law as the Court perceived it at that time.

INTERNATIONAL COURT OF JUSTICE, FISHERIES JURISDICTION CASES (UNITED KINGDOM v. ICELAND) I.C.J. [1974], 3, 22-34

....

52.... Two concepts have crystallized as customary law in recent years arising out of the general consensus revealed at [the 1960] Conference.... The second is the concept of preferential rights of fishing in adjacent waters in favour of the coastal State in a situation of special dependence on its coastal fisheries, this preference operating in regard to other States concerned in the exploitation of the same fisheries, and to be implemented in the way indicated in paragraph 57 below.

....

55. The concept of preferential rights for the coastal State in a situation of special dependence on coastal fisheries originated in proposals submitted by Iceland at the Geneva Conference of 1958. Its delegation drew attention to the problem which would arise when, in spite of adequate fisheries conservation measures, the yield ceased to be sufficient to satisfy the requirements of all those who were interested in fishing in a given area. Iceland contended that in such a case, when a catch-limitation becomes necessary, special consideration should be given to the coastal State whose population is overwhelmingly dependent on the fishing resources in its adjacent waters.

56. An Icelandic proposal embodying these ideas failed to obtain the majority required, but a resolution was adopted at the 1958 Conference concerning the situation of countries or territories whose people are overwhelmingly dependent upon coastal fisheries for their livelihood or economic development. This resolution, after "recognizing that such situations call for exceptional measures befitting particular needs" recommended that:

> "...where, for the purpose of conservation, it becomes necessary to limit the total catch of a stock or stocks of fish in an area of the high seas adjacent to the territorial sea of a coastal State, any other States fishing in that area should collaborate with the coastal State to secure just treatment of such situation, by establishing agreed measures which shall recognize any preferential requirements of the coastal State resulting from its dependence upon the fishery concerned while having regard to the interests of the other States".

The resolution futher recommended that "appropriate conciliation and arbitral procedures shall be established for the settlement of any disagreement".

57. At the Plenary Meetings of the 1960 Conference the concept of preferential rights was embodied in a joint amendment presented by Brazil, Cuba and Uruguay which was subsequently

incorporated by a substantial vote into a joint United States-Canadian proposal concerning a 6-mile territorial sea and an additional 6-mile fishing zone, thus totalling a 12-mile exclusive fishing zone, subject to a phasing-out period. This amendment provided, independently of the exclusive fishing zone, that the coastal State had:

> "...the faculty of claiming preferential fishing rights in any area of the high seas adjacent to its exclusive fishing zone when it is scientifically established that a special situation or condition makes the exploitation of the living resources of the high seas in that area of fundamental importance to the economic development of the coastal State or the feeding of its population."
>
> It also provided that:
>
> "A special situation or condition may be deemed to exist when:
>
> (a) The fisheries and the economic development of the coastal State or the feeding of its population are so manifestly interrelated that, in consequence, that State is greatly dependent on the living resources of the high seas in the area in respect of which preferential fishing is being claimed;
>
> (b) It becomes necessary to limit the total catch of a stock or stocks of fish in such areas..."

The contemporary practice of States leads to the conclusion that the preferential rights of the coastal State in a special situation are to be implemented by agreement between the States concerned, either bilateral or multilateral, and, in case of disagreement, through the means for the peaceful settlement of disputes provided for in Article 33 of the Charter of the United Nations....

58. State practice on the subject of fisheries reveals an increasing and widespread acceptance of the concept of preferential rights for coastal States, particularly in favour of countries or territories in a situation of special dependence on coastal fisheries.....

....

60. The preferential rights of the coastal State come into play only at the moment when an intensification in the exploitation of fishery resources makes it imperative to introduce some system of catch-limitation and sharing of those resources, to preserve the fish stocks in the interests of their rational and economic exploitation....

....

62. The concept of preferential rights is not compatible with the exclusion of all fishing activities of other States. A coastal State entitled to preferential rights is not free, unilaterally and according to its own uncontrolled discretion, to determine the extent of those rights. The characterization of the coastal State's rights as preferential implies a certain priority, but cannot imply the extinction of the concurrent rights of other States, and particularly a State which, like the applicant, has for many years been engaged in fishing in the waters in question, such fishing activity being important to the economy of the country concerned. The coastal State has to take into account and pay regard to the position of such other States, particularly when they have established an economic dependence on the same fishing grounds. Accordingly, the fact that Iceland is entitled to claim preferential rights does not suffice to justify its claim unilaterally to exclude the Applicant's fishing vessels from all fishing activity in the waters beyond the limits agreed to in the 1961 Exchange of Notes.

63. In this case, the Applicant has pointed out that its vessels have been fishing in Icelandic

waters for centuries and that they have done so in a manner comparable with their present activites for upwards of 50 years. Published statistics indicate that from 1920 onwards, fishing of demersal species by United Kingdom vessels in the disputed area has taken place on a continuous basis from year to year, and that, except for the period of the Second World War, the total catch of those vessels has been remarkably steady. Similar statistics indicate that the waters in question constitute the most important of the Applicant's distant-water fishing grounds for demersal species.

64. The Applicant further states that in view of the present situation of fisheries in the North Atlantic, which has demanded the establishment of agreed catch-limitations of cod and haddock in various areas, it would not be possible for the fishing effort of the United Kingdom vessels displaced from the Icelandic area to be diverted at economic levels to other fishing grounds in the North Atlantic. Given the lack of alternative fishing opportunity, it is further contended, the exclusion of British fishing vessels from the Icelandic area would have very serious adverse consequences, with immediate results for the affected vessels and with damage extending over a wide range of supporting and related industries. It is pointed out in particular that wide-spread unemployment would be caused among all sections of the British fishing industry and in ancillary industries and that certain ports -- Hull, Grimsby and Fleetwood -- specially reliant on fishing in the Icelandic area, would be seriously affected.

65. Iceland has for its part admitted the existence of the Applicant's historic and special interests in the fishing in the disputed waters. The Exchange of Notes as a whole and in particular its final provision requiring Iceland to give advance notice to the United Kingdom of any extension of its fishery limits impliedly acknowledged the existence of United Kingdom fishery interests in the waters adjacent to the 12-mile limit. The discussions which have taken place between the two countries also imply an acknowledgment by Iceland of the existence of such interests. Furthermore, the Prime Minister of Iceland stated on 9 November 1971:

> "...the British have some interests to protect in this connection. For a long time they have been fishing in Icelandic waters... The well-being of specific British fishing towns may nevertheless to some extent be connected with the fisheries in Icelandic waters..."

66. Considerations similar to those which have prompted the recognition of the preferential rights of the coastal State in a special situation apply when coastal populations in other fishing States are also dependent on certain fishing grounds. In both instances the economic dependence and the livelihood of whole communities are affected. Not only do the same considerations apply, but the same interest in conservation exists. In this respect the Applicant has recognized that the conservation and efficient exploitation of the fish stocks in the Iceland area are of importance not only to Iceland but also to the United Kingdom.

67. The provisions of the Icelandic Regulations of 14 July 1972 and the manner of their implementation disregard the fishing rights of the Applicant. Iceland's unilateral action thus constitutes an infringement of the principle enshrined in Article 2 of the 1958 Geneva Convention on the High Seas which requires that all States, including coastal States, in exercising their freedom of fishing, pay reasonable regard to the interests of other States. It also disregards the rights of the Applicant as they result from the Exchange of Notes of 1961. The Applicant is therefore justified in asking the Court to give all necessary protection to its own rights, while at the same time agreeing to recognize Iceland's preferential position. Accordingly, the Court is bound to conclude that the Icelandic Regulations of 14 July 1972 establishing a zone of exclusive fisheries jurisdiction extending to 50 nautical miles from the baseline around the coast of Iceland, are not opposable to the United Kingdom, and the latter is under no obligation to accept the unilateral termination by Iceland of United Kingdom fishery rights in the area.

68. The findings stated by the Court in the preceding paragraphs suffice to provide a basis for the decision of the present case, namely: that Iceland's extension of its exclusive fisheries jurisdiction beyond 12 miles is not opposable to the United Kingdom; that Iceland may on the other hand claim preferential rights in the distribution of fishery resources in the adjacent waters; that the United Kingdom also has established rights in the distribution of fishery resources in question; and that the principle of reasonable regard for the interests of other States enshrined in Article 2 of the Geneva Convention on the High Seas of 1958 requires Iceland and the United Kingdom to have due regard to each other's interests, and to the interests of other States, in those resources.

69. It follows from the reasoning of the Court in this case that in order to reach an equitable solution of the present dispute it is necessary that the preferential fishing rights of Iceland, as a State specially dependent on coastal fisheries, be reconciled with the traditional fishing rights of the Applicant. Such a reconciliation cannot be based, however, on a phasing-out of the Applicant's fishing, as was the case in the 1961 Exchange Notes in respect of the 12-mile fishery zone. In that zone, Icleand was to exercise exclusive fishery rights while not objecting to continued fishing by the Applicant's vessels during a phasing-out period. In adjacent waters outside that zone, however, a similar extinction of rights of other fishing States, particularly when such rights result from a situation of economic dependence and long-term reliance on certain fishing grounds, would not be compatible with the notion of preferential rights as it was recognized at the Geneva Conferences of 1958 and 1960, nor would it be equitable. At the 1960 Conference, the concept of preferential rights of a coastal State in a special situation was recognized in the joint amendment referred to in paragraph 57 above, under such limitations and to such extent as is found "necessary by reason of the dependence of the coastal State on the stock or stocks of fish, while having regard to the interests of other States in the exploitation of the same stock or stocks of fish". The reference to the interests of other States in the exploitation of the same stocks clearly indicates that the preferential rights of the coastal State and the established rights of other States were considered as, in principle, continuing to co-exist.

70. This is not to say that preferential rights of a coastal State in a special situation are a static concept, in the sense that the degree of the coastal State's preference is to be considered as fixed for ever at some given moment. On the contrary, the preferential rights are a function of the exceptional dependence of such a coastal State on the fisheries in the adjacent waters and may, therefore, vary as the extent of that dependence changes. Furthermore, as was expressly recognized in the 1961 Exchange of Notes, a coastal State's exceptional dependence on fisheries may relate not only to the livelihood of its people but to its economic development. In each case, it is essentially a matter of appraising the dependence of the coastal State on the fisheries in question in relation to that of the other State concerned and of reconciling them in as equitable a manner as is possible.

71. In view of the Court's finding (paragraph 67 above) that the Icelandic Regulations of 14 July 1972 are not opposable to the United Kingdom for the reasons which have been stated, it follows that the Government of Iceland is not in law entitled unilaterally to exclude United Kingdom fishing vessels from sea areas to seaward of the limits agreed to in the 1961 Exchange of Notes or unilaterally to impose restrictions on their activities in such areas. But the matter does not end there; as the Court has indicated, Iceland is, in view of its special situation, entitled to preferential rights in respect of the fish stocks of the waters adjacent to its coasts. Due recognition must be given to the rights of both Parties, namely the rights of the United Kingdom to fish in the waters in dispute, and the preferential rights of Iceland. Neither right is an abolute one: the preferential rights of the coastal State are limited according to the extent of its special dependency on the fisheries and by its obligation to take account of the rights of other States and the needs of conservation; the established rights of other fishing States are in turn limited by reason of the coastal State's dependence on the fisheries and its own obligation to take acount of the rights of other States, including the coastal State, and of the needs of conservation.

72. It follows that even if the Court holds that Iceland's extension of its fishery limits is not opposable to the Applicant, this does not mean that the Applicant is under no obligation to Iceland with respect to fishing in the disputed waters in the 12-mile to 50-mile zone. On the contrary, both States have an obligation to take full account of each other's rights and of any fishery conservation measures the necessity of which is shown to exist in those waters. It is one of the advances in maritime international law, resulting from the intensification of fishing, that the former *laissez-faire* treatment of the living resources of the sea in the high seas has been replaced by the recognition of a duty to have due regard to the rights of other States and the needs of conservation for the benefit of all. Consequently, both Parties have the obligation to keep under review the fishery resources in the disputed waters and to examine together, in the light of scientific and other available information, the measures required for the conservation and development, and the equitable exploitation, of those resources, taking into account any international agreement in force between them, such as the North-East Atlantic Fisheries Convention of 24 January 1959, as well as such other agreements as may be reached in the matter in the course of further negotiation.

73. The most appropriate method for the solution of the dispute is clearly that of negotiation. Its objective should be the delimitation of the rights and interests of the Parties, the preferential rights of the coastal State on the one hand and the rights of the Applicant on the other, to balance and regulate equitably questions such as those of catch-limitation, share allocations and "related restrictions concerning areas closed to fishing, number and type of vessels allowed and forms of control of the agreed provisions"....

....

78. In the fresh negotiations which are to take place on the basis of the present Judgment, the Parties will have the benefit of the above appraisal of their respective rights, and of certain guidelines defining their scope. The task before them will be to conduct their negotiations on the basis that each must in good faith pay reasonable regard to the legal rights of the other in the waters around Iceland outside the 12-mile limit, thus bringing about an equitable apportionment of the fishing resources based on the facts of the particular situation, and having regard to the interests of other States which have established fishing rights in the area. It is not a matter of finding simply an equitable solution, but an equitable solution derived from the applicable law....

79. For these reasons,

The Court,

by ten votes to four,

(1) finds that the Regulations concerning the Fishery Limits off Iceland...promulgated by the Government of Iceland on 14 July 1972 and constituting a unilateral extension of the exclusive fishing rights of Iceland to 50 nautical miles from the baselines specified therein are not opposable to the Government of the United Kingdom;

(2) finds that, in consequence, the Government of Iceland is not entitled unilaterally to exclude United Kingdom fishing vessels from areas between the fishery limits agreed to in the Exchange of Notes of 11 March 1961 and the limits specified in the Icelandic Regulations of 14 July 1972, or unilaterally to impose restrictions on the activities of those vessels in such areas;

(3) holds that the Government of Iceland and the Government of the United Kingdom are under mutual obligations to undertake negotiations in good faith for the equitable solution of their

differences concerning their respective fishery rights in the areas specified in subparagraph 2;

by ten votes to four,

(4) holds that in these negotiations the Parties are to take into account, *inter alia*:

(a) that in the distribution of the fishing resources in the areas specified in subparagraph 2 Iceland is entitled to a preferential share to the extent of special dependence of its people upon the fisheries in the seas around its coasts for their livelihood and economic development;

(b) that by reason of its fishing activities in the areas specified in subparagraph 2, the United Kingdom also has established rights in the fishery resources of the said areas on which elements of its people depend for their livelihood and economic well-being;

(c) the obligation to pay due regard to the interests of other States in the conservation and equitable exploitation of these resources;

(d) that the above-mentioned rights of Iceland and of the United Kingdom should each be given effect to the extent compatible with the conservation and development of the fishery resources in the areas specified in subparagraph 2 and with the interests of other States in their conservation and equitable exploitation;

(e) their obligation to keep under review those resources and examine together, in the light of scientific and other available information, such measures as may be required for the conservation and development, and equitable exploitation, of those resources, making use of the machinery established by the North-East Atlantic Fisheries Convention or such other means as may be agreed upon as a result of international negotiations.

ED. NOTE: The Court's judgment did not end the matter. In fact, it may have made a solution more difficult. In October, 1975, Iceland extended her fishing limits from 50 to 200 miles, setting off another round in the cod war, this time involving naval units of both Britain and Iceland. Even the NATO alliance was threatened by Iceland's threat to withdraw from the organization. In November, 1975, Belgium and the Federal Republic of Germany signed agreements with Iceland concerning the conduct of their fishing activities within Iceland's 200-mile fishing zone. In June, 1976, Iceland and the United Kingdom finally reached an agrement on British fishing within the 200-mile limit, providing for a substantial reduction in British fishing effort.

By the early 1970's political pressure began to build in the Congress of the United States to do something about fisheries conservation. The fishing industry mounted a tremendous effort toward new legislation. As a result, the Congress enacted the Fishery Conservation and Management Act of 1976, declaring for the U.S. a 200-mile fishery zone, and creating a complex mechanism for making management decisions. In 1983, upon completion of the Law of the Sea Conference, the President of the United States declared for the United States an Exclusive Economic Zone, and the Act, set forth below, was amended accordingly. Before considering this material, however, we should examine the provisions of the 1982 Convention dealing with fisheries. Earlier we considered the juridical nature of the EEZ. Recall that Article 56 of the Convention bestows jurisdiction upon the coastal State over the natural resources of that zone. As we now see, however, that coastal State jurisdiction is not unrestricted.

1. FISHING IN THE EXCLUSIVE ECONOMIC ZONE: THE CONVENTION

1982 UNITED NATIONS CONVENTION ON THE LAW OF THE SEA

Article 61

Conservation of the living resources

1. The coastal State shall determine the allowable catch of the living resources in its exclusive economic zone.

2. The coastal State, taking into account the best scientific evidence available to it, shall ensure through proper conservation and management measures that the maintenance of the living resources in the exclusive economic zone is not endangered by over-exploitation. As appropriate, the coastal State and competent international organizations, whether subregional, regional or global, shall co-operate to this end.

3. Such measures shall also be designed to maintain or restore populations of harvested species at levels which can produce the maximum sustainable yield, as qualified by relevant environmental and economic factors, including the economic needs of coastal fishing communities and the special requirements of developing States, and taking into account fishing patterns, the interdependence of stocks and any generally recommended international minimum standards, whether subregional, regional or global.

4. In taking such measures the coastal State shall take into consideration the effects on species associated with or dependent upon harvested species with a view to maintaining or restoring populations of such associated or dependent species above levels at which their reproduction may become seriously threatened.

5. Available scientific information, catch and fishing effort statistics, and other data relevant to the conservation of fish stocks shall be contributed and exchanged on a regular basis through competent international organizations, whether subregional, regional or global, where appropriate and with participation by all States concerned, including States whose nationals are allowed to fish in the exclusive economic zone.

Article 62

Untilization of the living resources

1. The coastal State shall promote the objective of optimum utilization of the living resources in the exclusive economic zone without prejudice to article 61.

2. The coastal State shall determine its capacity to harvest the living resources of the exclusive economic zone. Where the coastal State does not have the capacity to harvest the entire allowable catch, it shall, through agreements or other arrangements pursuant to the terms, conditions, laws and regulations referred to in paragraph 4, give other States access to the surplus of the allowable catch, having particular regard to the provisions of articles 69 and 70, especially in relation to the developing States mentioned therein.

3. In giving access to other States to its exclusive economic zone, the coastal State shall take into account all relevant factors, including, *inter alia*, the significance of the living resouces of the area

to the economy of the coastal State concerned and its other national interests, the provisions of articles 69 and 70, the requirements of developing States in the subregion or region in harvesting part of the surplus and the need to minimize economic dislocation in States whose nationals have habitually fished in the zone or which have made substantial efforts in research and identification of stocks.

4. Nationals of other States fishing in the exclusive economic zone shall comply with the terms and conditions established in the laws and regulations of the coastal State. These laws and regulations shall be consistent with this Convention and may relate, *inter alia*, to the following:

(a) licensing of fishermen, fishing vessels and equipment, including payment of fees and other forms of remuneration, which, in the case of developing coastal States, may consist of adequate compensation in the field of financing, equipment and technology related to the fishing industry;

(b) determining the species which may be caught, and fixing quotas of catch, whether in relation to particular stocks or groups of stocks or catch per vessel over a period of time or to the catch by nationals of any State during a specified period;

(c) regulating seasons and areas of fishing, the types, sizes and amount of gear, and the types, sizes and number of fishing vessels that may be used;

(d) fixing the age and size of fish and other species that may be caught;

(e) specifying information required of fishing vessels, including catch and effort statistics and vessel position reports;

(f) requiring, under the authorization and control of the coastal State, the conduct of specified fisheries research programmes and regulating the conduct of such research, including the sampling of catches, disposition of samples and reporting of associated scientific data;

(g) the placing of observers or trainees on board such vessels by the coastal State;

(h) the landing of all or any part of the catch by such vessels in the ports of the coastal State;

(i) terms and conditions relating to joint ventures or other co-operative arrangements;

(j) requirements for the training of personnel and the transfer of fisheries technology, including enhancement of the coastal State's ability of undertaking fisheries research;

(k) enforcement procedures.

5. Coastal States shall give due notice of conservation and management laws and regulations.

Article 63

Stocks occurring within the exclusive economic zones of two or more coastal States or both within the exclusive economic zone and in an area beyond and adjacent to it.

1. Where the same stock or stocks of associated species occur within the exclusive economic zones of two or more coastal States, these States shall seek, either directly or through appropriate subregional or regional organizations, to agree upon the measures necessary to co-ordinate and ensure

the conservation and development of such stocks without prejudice to the other provisions of this Part.

2. Where the same stock or stocks of associated species occur both within the exclusive economic zone and in an area beyond and adjacent to the zone, the coastal State and the States fishing for such stocks in the adjacent area shall seek, either directly or through appropriate subregional and regional organizations, to agree upon the measures necessary for the conservation of these stocks in the adjacent area.

Article 64

Highly migratory species

1. The coastal State and other States whose nationals fish in the region for the highly migratory species listed in Annex I shall co-operate directly or through appropriate international organizations with a view to ensuring conservation and promoting the objective of optimum utilization of such species throughout the region, both within and beyond the exclusive economic zone. In regions for which no appropriate international organization exists, the coastal State and other States whose nationals harvest these species in the region shall co-operate to establish such an organization and participate in its work.

2. The provisions of paragraph 1 apply in addition to the other provisions of this Part.

Article 65

Marine mammals

Nothing in this Part restricts the right of a coastal State or the competence of an international organization, as appropriate, to prohibit, limit or regulate the exploitation of marine mammals more strictly than provided for in this Part. States shall co-operate with a view to the conservation of marine mammals and in the case of cetaceans shall in particular work through the appropriate international organizations for their conservation, management and study.

Article 66

Anadromous species

1. States in whose rivers anadromous stocks originate shall have the primary interest in and responsibility for such stocks.

2. The State of origin of anadromous stocks shall ensure their conservation by the establishment of appropriate regulatory measures for fishing in all waters landward of the outer limits of its exclusive economic zone and for fishing provided for in paragraph 3(b). The State of origin may, after consultation with the other States referred to in paragraphs 3 and 4 fishing these stocks, establish total allowable catches for stocks originating in its rivers.

3. (a) Fisheries for anadromous stocks shall be conducted only in waters landward of the outer limits of exclusive economic zones, except in cases where this provision would result in economic dislocation for a State other than the State of origin. With respect to such fishing beyond the outer limits of the exclusive economic zone, States concerned shall maintain consultations with a view to achieving agreement on terms and conditions of such fishing giving due regard to the conservation requirements and the needs of the State of origin in respect of these stocks.

(b) The State of origin shall co-operate in minimizing economic dislocation in such other

States fishing these stocks, taking into account the normal catch and the mode of operations of such States, and all the areas in which such fishing has occurred.

(c) States referred to in subparagraph (b), participating by agreement with the State of origin in measures to renew anadromous stocks, particularly by expenditures for that purpose, shall be given special consideration by the State of origin in the harvesting of stocks originating in its rivers.

(d) Enforcement of regulations regarding anadromous stocks beyond the exclusive economic zone shall be by agreement between the State of origin and the other States concerned.

4. In cases where anadromous stocks migrate into or through the waters landward of the outer limits of the exclusive economic zone of a State other than the State of origin, such State shall co-operate with the State of origin with regard to the conservation and management of such stocks.

5. The State of origin of anadromous stocks and other States fishing these stocks shall make arrangements for the implementation of the provisions of this article, where appropriate, through regional organizations.

Article 67

Catadromous species

1. A coastal State in whose waters catadromous species spend the greater part of their life cycle shall have responsibility for the managment of these species and shall ensure the ingress and egress of migrating fish.

2. Harvesting of catadromous species shall be conducted only in waters landward of the outer limits of exclusive economic zones. When conducted in exclusive economic zones, harvesting shall be subject to this article and the other provisions of this Convention concerning fishing in those zones.

3. In cases where catadromous fish migrate through the economic zone of another State, whether as juvenile or maturing fish, the management, including harvesting, of such fish shall be regulated by agreement between the State mentioned in paragraph 1 and the other State concerned. Such agreement shall ensure the rational management of the species and take into account the responsibilities of the State mentioned in paragraph 1 for the maintenance of these species.

Article 68

Sedentary species

This Part does not apply to sedentary species as defined in article 77, paragraph 4.

Article 69

Right of land-locked States

1. Land-locked States shall have the right to participate, on an equitable basis, in the exploitation of an appropriate part of the surplus of the living resources of the exclusive economic zones of coastal States of the same subregion or region, taking into account the relevant economic and geographic circumstances of all the States concerned and in conformity with the provisions of this article and of articles 61 and 62.

2. The terms and modalities of such participation shall be established by the States concerned through bilateral, subregional or regional agreements taking into account, *inter alia*:

(a) the need to avoid effects detrimental to fishing communities or fishing industries of the coastal State;

(b) the extent to which the land-locked State, in accordance with the provisions of this article, is participating or is entitled to participate under existing bilateral, subregional or regional agreements in the exploitation of the living resources of the exclusive economic zones of other coastal States;

(c) the extent to which other land-locked States and geographically disadvantaged States are participating in the exploitation of the living resources of the exclusive economic zone of the coastal State and the consequent need to avoid a particular burden for any single coastal State or a part of it;

(d) the nutritional needs of the populations of the respective States.

3. When the harvesting capacity of a coastal State approaches a point which would enable it to harvest the entire allowable catch of the living resources in its exclusive economic zone, the coastal State and other States concerned shall co-operate in the establishment of equitable arrangements on a bilateral, subregional or regional basis to allow for participation of developing land-locked States of the same subregion or region in the exploitation of the living resources of the exclusive economic zones of coastal States of the subregion or region, as may be appropriate in the circumstances and on terms satisfactory to all parties. In the implementation of this provision the factors mentioned in paragraph 2 shall also be taken into account.

4. Developed land-locked States shall, under the provisions of this article, be entitled to participate in the exploitation of the living resources only in the exclusive economic zones of developed coastal States in the same subregion or region having regard to the extent to which the coastal State, in giving access to other States to the living resources of its exclusive economic zone, has taken into account the need to minimize detrimental effects on fishing communities and economic dislocation in States whose nationals have habitually fished in the zone.

5. The above provisions are without prejudice to arrangements agreed upon in subregions or regions where the coastal States may grant to land-locked States of the same subregion or region equal or preferential rights for the expoitation of the living resources in the exclusive economic zone.

Article 70

Rights of geographically disadvantaged States

1. Geographically disadvantaged States shall have the right to participate, on an equitable basis, in the exploitation of an appropriate part of the surplus of the living resources of the exclusive economic zones of the same subregion or region, taking into account the relevant economic and geographical circumstances of all the States concerned and in conformity with the provisions of this article and of articles 61 and 62.

2. For the purposes of this Part, "geographically disadvantaged States" means coastal States, including States bordering enclosed or semi-enclosed seas, whose geographical situation makes them dependent upon the exploitation of the living resources of the exclusive economic zones of other States in the subregion or region for adequate supplies of fish for the nutritional purposes of their populations or parts thereof, and coastal States which can claim no exclusive economic zones of their own.

3. The terms and modalities of such participation shall be established by the States concerned through bilateral, subregional or regional agreements taking into account, inter alia:

(a) the need to avoid effects detrimental to fishing communities or fishing industries of the coastal State;

(b) the extent to which the geographically disadvantaged State, in accordance with the provisions of this article, is participating or is entitled to participate under existing bilateral, subregional or regional agreements in the exploitation of living resources of the exclusive economic zones of other coastal States;

(c) the extent to which other geographically disadvantaged States and land-locked States are participating in the exploitation of the living resources of the exclusive economic zone of the coastal State and the consequent need to avoid a particular burden for any single coastal State or a part of it;

(d) the nutritional needs of the populations of the respective States.

4. When the harvesting capacity of a coastal State approaches a point which would enable it to harvest the entire allowable catch of the living resources in its exclusive economic zone, the coastal State and other States concerned shall co-operate in the establishment of equitable arrangements on a bilateral, subregional or regional basis to allow for the participation of developing geographically disadvantaged States of the same subregion or region in the exploitation of the living resources of the exclusive economic zones of coastal States of the subregion or region, as may be appropriate in the circumstances and on terms satisfactory to all parties. In the implementation of this provision the factors mentioned in paragraph 3 shall also be taken into account.

5. Developed geographically disadvantaged States shall, under the provisions of this article, be entitled to participate in the exploitation of the living resources only in the exclusive economic zones of developed coastal States of the same subregion or region having regard to the extent to which the coastal State, in giving access to other States to the living resources of its exclusive economic zone, has taken into account the need to minimize detrimental effects on fishing communities and economic dislocation in States whose nationals have habitually fished in the zone.

6. The above provisions are without prejudice to arrangments agreed upon in subregions or regions where the coastal States of the same subregion or region may grant to geographically disadvantaged States of the same subregion or region equal or preferential rights for the exploitation of the living resources in the exclusive economic zones.

Article 71

Non-applicability of articles 69 and 70

The provisions of articles 69 and 79 do not apply in the case of a coastal State whose economy is overwhelmingly dependent on the exploitation of the living resources of its exclusive economic zone.

Article 72

Restrictions on transfer of rights

1. Rights provided under articles 69 and 70 to exploit living resources shall not be directly or indirectly transferred to third States or their nationals by lease or license, by establishing joint ventures or in any other manner which has the effect of such transfer unless otherwise agreed by the States concerned.

2. The foregoing provision does not preclude the States concerned from obtaining technical or financial assistance from third States or international organizations in order to facilitate the exercise of the rights pursuant to articles 69 and 70, provided that it does not have the effect referred to in paragraph 1.

Article 73

Enforcement of laws and regulations of the coastal State

1. The coastal State may, in the exercise of its sovereign rights to explore, exploit, conserve and manage the living resources in the exclusive economic zone, take such measures, including boarding, inspection, arrest and judicial proceedings, as may be necessary to ensure compliance with the laws and regulations adopted by it in conformity with this Convention.

2. Arrested vessels and their crews shall be promptly released upon the posting of reasonable bond or other security.

3. Coastal State penalties for violations of fisheries laws and regulations in the exclusive economic zone may not include imprisonment, in the absence of agreements to the contrary by the States concerned, or any other form of corporal punishment.

4. In cases of arrest or detention of foreign vessels the coastal State shall promptly notify the flag State, through appropriate channels, of the action taken and of any penalties subsequently imposed.

ANNEX I. HIGHLY MIGRATORY SPECIES

1. Albacore tuna: *Thunnus alalunga*.
2. Bluefin tuna: *Thunnus thynnus*.
3. Bigeye tuna: *Thunnus obesus*.
4. Skipjack tuna: *Katsuwonus pelamis*.
5. Yellowfin tuna: *Thunnus albacares*.
6. Blackfin tuna: *Thunnus atlanticus*.
7. Little tuna: *Euthynnus alletteratus; Euthynnus affinis*.
8. Southern bluefin tuna: *Thunnus maccoyii*.
9. Frigate mackerel: *Auxis thazard; Auxis rochei*.
10. Pomfrets: Family *Bramidae*.
11. Marlins: *Tetrapturus angustirostris; Tetrapturus belone; Tetrapus pfluegeri; Tetrapturus albidus; Tetrapturus audax; Tetrapturus georgei; Makaira mazara; Makaira indica; Makaira nigricans*.
12. Sail-fishes: *Istiophorus platypterus; Istiophorus albicans*.
13. Swordfish: *Xiphias gladius*.
14. Sauries: *Scomberesox saurus; Cololabis saira; Cololabis adocetus; Scomberesox saurus scomboides*.
15. Dolphin: *Coryphaena hippurus; Coryphaena equiselis*.
16. Oceanic sharks: *Hexanchus griseus; Cetorhinus maximus*; Family *Alopiidae; Rhincodon typus*; Family *Carcharhinidae; Family Sphyrnidae; Family Isurida*.
17. Cetaceans: Family *Physeteridae*; Family *Balaenopteridae*; Family *Balaenidae*; Family *Eschrichtiidae*; Family *Monodontidae*; Family *Ziphiidae*; Family *Delphinidae*.

NOTE: The following provisions are applicable beyond the limits of the exclusive economic zone.

SECTION 2. CONSERVATION AND MANAGEMENT OF THE LIVING RESOURCES OF THE HIGH SEAS

Article 116

Right to fish on the high seas

All States have the right for their nationals to engage in fishing on the high seas subject to:

(a) their treaty obligations;

(b) the rights and duties as well as the interests of coastal States provided for, inter alia, in article 63, paragraph 2, and articles 64 to 67; and

(c) the provisions of this section.

Article 117

Duty of States to adopt with respect to their nationals measures for the conservation of the living resources of the high seas

All States have the duty to take, or to co-operate with other States in taking, such measures for their respective nationals as may be necessary for the conservation of the living resources of the high seas.

Article 118

Co-operation of States in the conservation and management of living resources

States shall co-operate with each other in the conservation and management of living resources in the areas of the high seas. States whose nationals exploit identical living resources, or different living resources in the same area, shall enter into negotiations with a view to taking the measures necessary for the conservation of the living resources concerned. They shall, as appropriate, co-operate to establish subregional or regional fisheries organizations to this end.

Article 119

Conservation of the living resources of the high seas

1. In determining the allowable catch and establishing other conservation measures for the living resources in the high seas, States shall:

(a) take measures which are designed, on the best scientific evidence available to the States concerned, to maintain or restore populations of the harvested species at levels which can produce the maximum sustainable yield, as qualified by relevant environmental and economic factors, including the special requirements of the developing States, and taking into account fishing patterns, the interdependence of stocks and any generally recommended international minimum standards, whether subregional, regional or global;

(b) take into consideration the effects on species associated with or dependent upon harvested species with a view to maintaining or restoring populations of such associated or dependent species above levels at which their reproduction may become seriously threatened.

2. Available scientific information, catch and fishing effort statistics, and other data relevant to the conservation of fish stocks shall be contributed and exchanged on a regular basis through competent international organizations, whether subregional, regional or global, where appropriate and with participation by all States concerned.

3. States concerned shall ensure that conservation measures and their implementation do not discriminate in form or in fact against the fishermen of any State.

Article 120

Marine mammals

Article 65 also applies to the conservation and management of marine mammals in the high seas.

2. DOMESTIC FISHERIES MANAGEMENT

The major legislation on this subject is the Fishery Management and Conservation Act of 1976. Its original enactment was designed to establish a 200-mile fishery zone for the United States. It was subsequently modified to take into account the following proclamation.

PROCLAMATION ON AN EXCLUSIVE ECONOMIC ZONE

By the President of the United States of America

A Proclamation

THE WHITE HOUSE, Proclamation 5030, March 10, 1983

Whereas the Government of the United States of America desires to facilitate the wise development and use of the ocean consistent with international law;

Whereas international law recognizes that, in a zone beyond its territory and adjacent to its territorial sea, known as the Exclusive Economic Zone, a coastal State may assert certain sovereign rights over natural resources and related jurisdiction; and

Whereas the establishment of an Exclusive Economic Zone by the United States will advance the development of ocean resources and promote the protection of the marine environment, while not affecting other lawful uses of the zone, including the freedoms of navigation and overflight, by other States;

Now, Therefore, I, Ronald Reagan, by the authority vested in me as President by the Constitution and laws of the United States of America, do hereby proclaim the sovereign rights and jurisdiction of the United States of America and confirm also the rights and freedoms of all States within an Exclusive Economic Zone, as described herein.

The Exclusive Economic Zone of the United States is a zone contiguous to the territorial sea, including zones contiguous to the territorial sea of the United States, the Commonwealth of Puerto Rico, the Commonwealth of the Northern Mariana Islands (to the extent consistent with the Covenant and the United Nations Trusteeship Agreement), and United States overseas territories and possessions. The Exclusive Economic Zone extends to a distance 200 nautical miles from the baseline from which the breadth of the territorial sea is measured. In cases where the maritime boundary with a neighboring State remains to be determined, the boundary of the Exclusive Economic Zone shall be determined by the United States and the other State concerned in accordance with equitable principles.

Within the Exclusive Economic Zone, the United States has, to the extent permitted by international law, (a) sovereign rights for the purpose of exploring, exploiting, conserving and managing natural resources, both living and non-living, of the seabed and subsoil and the superjacent waters and with regard to other activities for the economic exploitation and exploration of the zone, such as the production of energy from the water, currents and winds; and (b) jurisdiction with regard to the establishment and use of artificial islands, and installations and structures having economic purposes, and the protection and preservation of the marine environment.

This Proclamation does not change existing United States policies concerning the continental shelf, marine mammals and fisheries, including highly migratory species of tuna which are not subject to United States jurisdiction and require international agreements for effective management.

The United States will exercise these sovereign rights and jurisdiction in accordance with the rules of international law.

Without prejudice to the sovereign rights and jurisdiction of the United States, the Exclusive Economic Zone remains an area beyond the territory and territorial sea of the United States in which all States enjoy the high seas freedoms of navigation, overflight, the laying of submarine cables and pipelines, and other internationally lawful uses of the sea.

In Witness Whereof, I have hereunto set my hand this tenth day of March, in the year of our Lord nineteen hundred and eighty-three, and of the Independence of the United States of America the two hundred and seventh.

Ronald Reagan

ED. NOTE: The Fishery Conservation and Management Act, as amended, does basically two things. First, it provides for a conservation management system to apply within the U.S. EEZ, and, second, it creates fishery management councils to carry out the provisions of the Act. The Act is set forth in some detail here as a reference.

THE FISHERY CONSERVATION AND MANAGEMENT ACT OF 1976, P.L. 94-265, April 13, 1976, 16 U.S.C. 1801 et seq.

Sec. 1802. Definitions.

As used in this Act, unless the context otherwise requires--

....

(6) The term "exclusive economic zone" means the zone established by Proclamation

Numbered 5030, dated March 10, 1983. For purposes of applying this chapter, the inner boundary of that zone is a line coterminous with the seaward boundary of each of the coastal States.

....

(10) The term "fishing" means--

(A) the catching, taking, or harvesting of fish;

(B) the attempted catching, taking, or harvesting of fish;

(C) any other activity which can reasonably be expected to result in the catching, taking, or harvesting of fish; or

(D) any operations at sea in support of, or in preparation for, any activity described in subparagraphs (A) through (C).

Such term does not include any scientific research activity which is conducted by a scientific research vessel.

....

(14) The term "highly migratory species" means species of tuna which, in the course of their life cycle, spawn and migrate over great distances in waters of the ocean.

....

(18) The term "optimum", with respect to the yield from a fishery, means the amount of fish--

(A) which will provide the greatest overall benefit to the Nation, with particular reference to food production and recreational opportunities; and

(B) which is prescribed as such on the basis of the maximum sustainable yield from such fishery, as modified by any relevant economic, social, or ecological factor.

....

(20) The term "Secretary" means the Secretary of Commerce or his designee.d

....

(23) The term "treaty" means any international fishery agreement which is a treaty within the meaning of section 2 of article II of the Constitution.

SUBCHAPTER II--FISHERY MANAGEMENT AUTHORITY OF THE UNITED STATES

Sec. 1811. United States sovereign rights to fish and fishery management authority

(a) In the exclusive economic zone

Except as provided in section 1812 of this title, the United States claims, and will exercise in the manner provided for in this chapter, sovereign rights and exclusive fishery management authority over all fish, and all Continental Shelf fishery resources, within the exclusive economic zone.

(b) Beyond the exclusive economic zone

The United States claims, and will exercise in the manner provided for in this chapter, exclusive fishery management authority over the following:

(1) All anadromous species throughout the migratory range of each such species beyond the exclusive economic zone; except that management authority does not extend to any such species during the time they are found within any foreign nation's territorial sea or exclusive economic zone (or equivalent), to the extent that that sea or zone is recognized by the United States.

(2) All Continental Shelf fishery resources beyond the exclusive economic zone.

Sec. 1812. Exclusion for highly migratory species

The sovereign rights and exclusive fishery management authority asserted by the United States under section 1811 of this title over fish do not include, and may not be construed to extend to, highly migratory species of fish.

SUBCHAPTER II--FOREIGN FISHING AND INTERNATIONAL FISHERY AGREEMENTS

Sec. 1821. Foreign fishing

(a) In general

After February 28, 1977, no foreign fishing is authorized within the exclusive economic zone, or for anadromous species or Continental Shelf fishery resources beyond the exclusive economic zone, unless such foreign fishing--

(1) is authorized under subsection (b) or (c) of this section;

(2) is not prohibited by subsection (g) of this section; and

(3) is conducted under, and in acordance with, a valid and applicable permit issued pursuant to section 1824 of this title.

(b) Existing international fishery agreements

Foreign fishing described in subsection (a) of this section may be conducted pursuant to an international fishery agreement (subject to the provisions of section 1822(b) or (c) of this title), if such agreement--

(1) was in effect on April 13, 1976; and

(2) has not expired, been renegotiated, or otherwise ceased to be of force and effect with respect to the United States.

(c) Governing international fishery agreements

Foreign fishing described in subsection (a) of this section may be conducted pursuant to an international fishing agreement (other than a treaty) which meets the requirements of this subsection if such agreement becomes effective after application of section 1823 of this title. Any such international fishery agreement shall hereafter in this chapter be referred to as a "governing international fishery agreement". Each governing international fishery agreement shall acknowledge the exclusive fishery management authority of the United States as set forth in this chapter....

(d) Total allowable level of foreign fishing

(1) As used in this subsection--

(A) The term "base harvest" means, with respect to any United States fishery, the total allowable level of foreign fishing during the 1979 harvesting season.

(B) The term "harvesting season" means the period established under this chapter by the Secretary during which foreign fishing is permitted within a United States fishery. For purposes of this subsection, a harvesting season is designated by the calendar year in which the last day of the harvesting season occurs, regardless of whether fishing is not permitted on that day due to emergency or other closure of the fishery.

(C) The term "calculation factor" means, with respect to each United States fishery, 15 percent of the base harvest.

(D) The term "reduction factor amount" means, with respect to each United States fishery, for any harvesting season after the 1980 harvesting season--

(i) an amount equal to 15 percent of the base harvest for that fishery, if, in addition to the level of harvest by vessels of the United States in the designated preceding harvesting season for the fishery, such vessels harvest, in one or more harvesting seasons, not less than 75 percent of the calculation factor;

(ii) an amount equal to 10 percent of the base harvest for the fishery, if, in addition to the level of harvest by vessels of the United States in the designated preceding harvesting season for the fishery, such vessels harvest, in one or more harvesting seasons, not less than 50 percent, but less than 75 percent, of the calculation factor; or

(iii) an amount equal to 5 percent of the base harvest for the fishery, if, in addition to the level of harvest by vessels of the United States in the designated preceding harvesting season for the fishery, such vessels harvest, in one or more harvesting seasons, not less than 25 percent, but less than 50 percent, of the calculation factor.

For purposes of this paragraph, the term "designated preceding harvesting season" means--

(I) until a reduction factor amount is first achieved under this paragraph with respect to the fishery concerned, the 1979 harvesting season, and

(II) after such amount is first achieved, the most recent harvesting season in which a reduction factor was achieved.

(E) The term "annual fishing level" for any United States fishery during any harvesting season after the 1980 harvesting season is the base harvest for the fishery reduced by--

(i) an amount equal to the reduction factor amount for that harvesting season; and

(ii) an amount equal to the increased level of harvest by vessels of the United States over the level achieved by such vessels in the 1979 harvesting season for the fishery.

(F) The term "United States fishery" means any fishery subject to the exclusive management authority of the United States.

(2) The total allowable level of foreign fishing, if any, with respect to any United States fishery for each harvesting season after the 1980 harvesting season shall be--

(A) the level representing that portion of the optimum yield of such fishery that will not be harvested by vessels of the United States as determined in accordance with the provisions of this chapter (other than those relating to the determination of annual fishing levels), or

(B) the annual fishing level determined purusant to paragraph (3) for the harvesting season.

(3) For each United States fishery, the appropriate fishery management council, on a timely basis, may determine and certify to the Secretary of State and the Secretary the annual fishing level for that fishery for each harvesting season after the 1980 harvesting season.

(4) If with respect to any harvesting season for any United States fishery for which the total allowable level of foreign fishing is determined under paragraph (2)(B), the Secretary, in consultation with the Secretary of State, approves the determination by any appropriate fishery management council that any portion of the optimum yield for that harvesting season will not be harvested by vessels of the United States, the Secretary of State, in accordance with subsection (e) of this section, may allocate such portion for use during that harvesting season by foreign fishing vessels, except that if--

(A) the making available of such portion (or any part thereof) during that harvesting season is determined to be detrimental to the development of the United States fishing industry; and

(B) such portion or part will be available for harvest in the immediately succeeding harvesting season, as determined on the basis of the best available scientific information;

then such portion or part may be allocated for use by foreign fishing vessels in such succeeding harvesting season. The determinations required to be made under subparagraphs (A) and (B) of the preceding sentence shall be made by the Secretary in consultation with the Secretary of State and on the basis of any recommendation of any appropriate fishery management council.

(e) Allocation of allowable level

(1)(A) The Secretary of State, in cooperation with the Secretary, may make allocations to foreign nations from the total allowable level of foreign fishing which is permitted with respect to each fishery subject to the exclusive fishery management authority of the United States.

(B) From the determinations made under subparagraph (A), the Secretary of State shall compute the aggregate of all of the fishery allocations made to each foreign nation.

(C) The Secretary of State shall initially release to each foreign nation for harvesting up to 50 percent of the allocations aggregate computed for such nation under subparagraph (B), and such release of allocation shall be apportioned by the Secretary of State, in cooperation with the Secretary, among the individual fishery allocations determined for that nation under subparagraph (A). The basis on which each aportionment is made under this subparagraph shall be stated in writing by the Secretary of State.

(D) After the initial release of fishery allocations under subparagraph (C) to a foreign nation, any subsequent release of an allocation for any fishery to such nation shall only be made--

(i) after the lapse of such period of time as may be sufficient for purposes of making the determination required under clause (ii); and

(ii) if the Secretary of State and the Secretary, after taking into account the size of the allocation for such fishery and the length and timing of the fishing season, determine in writing that such nation is complying with the purposes and intent of this paragraph with respect to such fishery.

If the foreign nation is not determined under clause (ii) to be in such compliance, the Secretary of State shall reduce, in a manner and quantity he considers appropriate (I) the remainder of such allocation, or (II) if all of such allocation has been released, the next allocation of such fishery, if any, made to such nation.

(E) The determination required to be made under subparagraphs (A) and (D)(ii), and the apportionments required to be made under subparagraph (C), with respect to a foreign nation shall be based on--

(i) whether, and to what extent, such nation imposes tariff barriers or nontariff barriers on the importation, or otherewise restricts the market access, of both United States fish and fishery products, particularly fish and fishery products for which the foreign nation has requested an allocation;

(ii) whether, and to what extent, such nation is cooperating with the United States in both the advancement of existing and new opportunities for fisheries exports from the United States through the purchase of fishery products from United States processors, and the advancement of fisheries trade through the purchase of fish and fishery products from the United States, particularly fish and fishery products for which the foreign nation has requested an allocation;

(iii) whether, and to what extent, such nation and the fishing fleets of such nation have cooperated with the United States in the enforcement of United States fishing regulations;

(iv) whether, and to what extent, such nation requires the fish harvested from the exclusive economic zone for its domestic consumption;

(v) whether, and to what extent, such nation otherwise contributes to, or fosters the growth of, a sound and economic United States fishing industry, including minimizing gear conflicts with fishing operations of United States fishermen, and transferring harvesting or processing technology which will benefit the United States fishing industry;

(vi) whether, and to what extent, the fishing vessels of such nation have traditionally fished in such fishery;

(vii) whether, and to what extent, such nation is cooperating with the United States in, and making substantial contributions to, fishery research and the identification of fishery resources; and

(viii) such other matters as the Secretary of State, in cooperation with the Secretary, deems appropriate.

....

Sec. 1822. International fishery agreements

(a) Negotiations

The Secretary of State--

(1) shall renegotiate treaties as provided for in subsection (b) of this section;

(2) shall negotiate governing international fishery agrements as described in section 1821(c) of this title;

(3) may negotiate boundary agreements as provided for in subsection (d) of this section;

(4) shall, upon the request of and in cooperation with the Secretary, initiate and conduct negotiations for the purpose of entering into international fishery agreements--

(A) which allow fishing vessels of the United States equitable access to fish over which foreign nations assert exclusive fishery management authority, and

(B) which provide for the conservation and management of anadromous species and highly migratory species; and

(5) may enter into such other negotiations, not prohibited by subsection (c) of this section, as may be necessary and appropriate to further the purposes, policy and provisions of this chapter.

(b) Treaty renegotiation

The Secretary of State, in cooperation with the Secretary, shall initiate, promptly after April 13, 1976, the renegotiation of any treaty which pertains to fishing within the exclusive economic zone (or within the area that will constitute such zone after February 28, 1977), or for anadromous species or Continental Shelf fishery resources beyond such zone or area, and which is in any manner inconsistent with the purposes, policy or provisions of this chapter, in order to conform such treaty to such purposes, policy or provisions. It is the sense of Congress that the United States shall withdraw from any such treaty, in accordance with its provisions, if such treaty is not so renegotiated within a reasonable period of time after April 13, 1976.

(c) International fishery agreements

No international fishery agreement (other than a treaty) which pertains to foreign fishing within the exclusive economic zone (or within the area that will constitute such zone after February 28,

1977), or for anadromous species or Continental Sheld fishery resources beyond such zone or area--

(1) which is in effect on June 1, 1976, may thereafter be renewed, extended, or amended; or

(2) may be entered into after May 31, 1976;

by the United States unless it is in accordance with the provisions of section 1821(c) of this title.

(d) Boundary negotiations

The Secretary of State, in cooperation with the Secretary, may initiate and conduct negotiations with any adjacent or opposite foreign nation to establish the boundary of the exclusive economic zone of the United States in relation to any such nation.

(e) Nonrecognition

It is the sense of Congress that the United States Government shall not recognize the claim of any foreign nation to a [sic] exclusive economic zone (or the equivalent) beyond such nation's territorial sea, to the extent that such sea is recognized by the United States, if such nation--

(1) fails to consider and take into account traditional fishing activity of fishing vessels of the United States;

(2) fails to recognize and accept that highly migratory species are to be managed by applicable international fishery agreements, whether or not such nation is a party to any such agreement; or

(3) imposes on fishing vessels of the United States any conditions or restrictions which are unrelated to fishery conservation and management.

Sec. 1823. Congressional oversight of governing international fishing agreements

(a) In general

No governing international fishery agreement shall become effective with respect to the United States before the close of the first 60 calendar days of continuous session of the Congress after the date on which the President transmits to the House of Representatives and the Senate a document setting forth the text of such governing international fishery agreement. A copy of the documents shall be delivered to each House of Congress on the same day and shall be delivered to the Clerk of the House of Representatives, if the House is not in session, and to the Secretary of the Senate, if the Senate is not in session.

....

(d) Congressional procedures

....

(2) "Fishery agreement resolution" defined

For purposes of this subsection, the term "fishery agreement resolution" refers to a joint resolution of either House of Congress--

(A) the effect of which is to prohibit the entering into force and effect of any governing international fishery agreement the text of which is transmitted to the Congress pursuant to subsection (a) of this section; and

(B) which is reported from the Committee on Merchant Marine and Fisheries of the House or Representatives or the Committee on Commerce or the Committee on Foreign Relations of the Senate, not later than 45 days after the date on which the document described in subsection (a) of this section relating to that agreement is transmitted to Congress.

(3) Placement on calendar

Any fishery agreement resolution upon being reported shall immediately be placed on the appropriate calendar.

(4) Floor consideration in House

....

(5) Floor consideration in Senate

....

Unconstitutionality of Legislative Veto Provisions

The provisions of section 1254(c)(2) of Title 8, Aliens and Nationality, which authorize a House of Congress, by resolution, to invalidate an action of the Executive Branch, were declared unconsitutional in Immigration and Naturalization Service v. Chadha, 1983, 103 S.Ct. 2764, 457 U.S. 830, 73 L.Ed.2d 418. See similar provisions in this section.

....

Sec. 1824. Permits for foreign fishing

(a) In general

After February 28, 1977, no foreign fishing vessel shall engage in fishing within the exlusive economic zone, or for anadromous species or Continental Shelf fishery resources beyond such zone, unless such vessel has on board a valid permit issued under this section for such vessel.

(b) Applications and permits governing international fishery agreements

(1) Eligibility; duration

Each foreign nation with which the United States has entered into a governing international fishery agreement shall submit an application to the Secretary of State each year for a permit for each of its fishing vessels that wishes to engage in fishing described in subsection (a) of this section. No permit issued under this section may be valid for longer than a year; and section 558(c) of Title 5, does not apply to the renewal of any such permit.

(2) Forms

The Secretary, in consultation with the Secretary of State and the Secretary of the department in which the Coast Guard is operating, shall prescribe the forms for permit applications submitted under this subsection and for permits issued pursuant to any such application.

(3) Contents

Any application made under this subsection shall specify--

(A) the name and official number or other identification of each fishing vessel for which a permit is sought, together with the name and address of the owner thereof;

(B) the tonnage, hold capacity, speed, processing equipment, type and quantity of fishing gear, and such other pertinent information with respect to the characteristics of each such vessel as the Secretary may require;

(C) each fishery in which each such vessel wishes to fish;

(D) the estimated amount of tonnage of fish which will be caught, taken, or harvested in each such fishery by each such vessel during the time the permit is in force;

(E) the amount or tonnage of United States harvested fish, if any, which each vessel proposes to receive at sea from vessels of the United States; and

(F) the ocean area in which, and the season or period during which such fishing will be conducted;

and shall include any other pertinent information and material which the Secretary may require.

....

(10) Fees

(A) Fees shall be paid to the Secretary by the owner or operator of a foreign fishing vessel for which a permit is issued pursuant to this subsection. The Secretary, in consultation with the Secretary of State, shall establish a schedule of such fees which shall apply nondiscriminatorily to each foreign nation.

(B) Unless subparagraph (C) applies, the fees imposed under subparagraph (A) shall be at least in an amount sufficient to return to the United States an amount which bears to the total coast of carrying out provisions of this chapter during each fiscal year the same ratio as the aggregate quantity of the harvest within the exclusive economic zone during the preceding year bears to the aggregate quantity of fish harvested by both foreign and domestic fishing vessels within such zone and the territorial waters of the United States during such preceding year.

....

Sec. 1825. Import prohibitions

(a) Determinations by Secretary of State

If the Secretary of State determines that--

(1) he has been unable, within a reasonable period of time, to conclude with any foreign nation an international fishery agreement allowing fishing vessels of the United States equitable access to fisheries over which that nation asserts exclusive fishery management authority, as recognized by the United States, in accordance with traditional fishing activities of such vessels, if any, and under terms not more restrictive than those established under sections 1821(c) and (d) and 1824(b)(7) and (10) of this title, because such nation (A) has refused to commence negotiatons, or (B) failed to negotiate in good faith;

(2) any foreign nation is not allowing fishing vessels of the United States to engage in fishing for highly migratory species in accordance with an applicable international fishery agreement, whether or not such nation is a party thereto;

(3) any foreign nation is not complying with its obligations under any existing international fishery agreement concerning fishing by fishing vessels of the United States in any fishery over which that nation asserts exclusive fishery management authority; or

(4) any fishing vessel of the United States, while fishing in waters beyond any foreign nation's territorial sea, to the extent such sea is recognized by the United States, is seized by any foreign nation-

(A) in violation of an applicable international fishery agreement;

(B) without authorization under an agreement between the United States and such nation; or

(C) as a consequence of a claim of jurisdiction which is not recognized by the United States;

he shall certify such determination to the Secretary of the Treasury.

(b) Prohibitions

Upon receipt of any certification from the Secretary of State under subsection (a) of this section, the Secretary of the Treasury shall immediately take such action as may be necessary and appropriate to prohibit the importation into the United States--

(1) of all fish and fish products from the fishery involved, if any; and

(2) upon recommendation of the Secretary of State, such other fish or fish products, from any fishery of the foreign nation concerned, which the Secretary of State finds to be appropriate to carry out the purposes of this section.

(c) Removal of prohibitions

If the Secretary of State finds that the reasons for the imposition of any import prohibition under this section no longer prevail, the Secretary of State shall notify the Secretary of the Treasury, who shall promptly remove such import prohibition.

(d) Definitions

As used in this section--

(1) The term "fish" includes any highly migratory species.

....

SUBCHAPTER IV--NATIONAL FISHERY MANAGEMENT PROGRAM

Sec. 1851. National standards for fishery conservation and management

(a) In general

Any fishery management plan prepared, and any regulation promulgated to implement any such plan, pursuant to this subchapter shall be consistent with the following national standards for fishery conservation and management:

(1) Conservation and managment measures shall prevent overfishing while achieving, on a continuing basis, the optimum yield from each fishery for the United States fishing industry.

(2) Conservation and management measures shall be based upon the best scientific information available.

(3) To the extent practicable, an individual stock of fish shall be managed as a unit throughout its range, and interrelated stocks of fish shall be managed as a unit or in close coordination.

(4) Conservation and management measures shall not discriminate between residents of different States. If it becomes necessary to allocate or assign fishing privileges among various United States fishermen, such allocation shall be (A) fair and equitable to all such fishermen; (B) reasonably calculated to promote conservation; and (C) carried out in such manner that no particular individual, corporation, or other entity acquires an excessive share of such privileges.

(5) Conservation and management measures shall, where practicable, promote efficiency in the utilization of fishery resources; except that no such measure shall have economic allocation as its sole purpose.

(6) Conservation and management measures shall take into account and allow for variations among, and contingencies in, fisheries, fishery resources, and catches.

(7) Conservation and management measures shall, where practicable, minimize costs and avoid unecessary duplication.

(b) Guidelines

The Secretary shall establish guidelines (which shall not have the force and effect of law), based on national standards, to assist in the development of fishery management plans.

Sec. 1852. Regional fishery management councils

(a) Establishment

There shall be established, within 120 days after April 13, 1976, eight Regional Fishery Management Councils, as follows:

(1) New England Council

The New England Fishery Management Council shall consist of the States of Maine, New Hampshire, Massachusetts, Rhode Island, and Connecticut and shall have authority over the fisheries in the Atlantic Ocean seaward of such States. The New England Council shall have 17 voting members, including 11 appointed by the Secretary in accordance with subsection (b)(2) of this section (at least one of whom shall be appointed from each such State).

(2) Mid-Atlantic Council

The Mid-Atlantic Fishery Management Council shall consist of the States of New York, New Jersey, Delaware, Pennsylvania, Maryland, and Virginia and shall have authority over the fisheries in the Atlantic Ocean seaward of such States. The Mid-Atlantic Council shall have 19 members, including 12 appointed by the Secretary in accordance with subsection (b)(2) of this section (at least one of whom shall be appointed from each such State).

(3) South Atlantic Council

The South Atlantic Fishery Management Council shall consist of the States of North Carolina, South Carolina, Georgia, and Florida and shall have authority over the fisheries of the Atlantic Ocean seaward of such States. The South Atlantic Council shall have 13 voting members, including 8 appointed by the Secretary in accordance with subsection (b)(2) of this section (at least one of whom shall be appointed from each such State).

(4) Caribbean Council

The Caribbean Fishery Management Council shall consist of the Virgin Islands and the Commonwealth of Puerto Rico and shall have authority over the fisheries in the Caribbean Sea and Atlantic Ocean seaward of such States. The Caribbean Council shall have 7 voting members, including 4 appointed by the Secretary in accordance with subsection (b)(2) of this section (at least one of whom shall be appointed from each such State).

(5) Gulf Council

The Gulf of Mexico Fishery Management Council shall consist of the States of Texas, Louisiana, Mississippi, Alabama, and Florida and shall have authority over the fisheries in the Gulf of Mexico seaward of such States. The Gulf Council shall have 17 voting members, including 11 appointed by the Secretary in accordance with subsection (b)(2) of this section (at least one of whom shall be appointed from each such State).

(6) Pacific Council

The Pacific Fishery Management Council shall consist of the States of California, Oregon, Washington, and Idaho and shall have authority over the fisheries in the Pacific Ocean seaward of such States. The Pacific Council shall have 13 voting members, including 8 appointed by the Secretary in accordance with subsection (b)(2) of this section (at least one of whom shall be appointed from each such State).

(7) North Pacific Council

The North Pacific Fishery Management Council shall consist of the States of Alaska, Washington, and Oregon and shall have authority over the fisheries in the Arctic Ocean, Bering Sea, and Pacific Ocean seaward of Alaska. The North Pacific Council shall have 11 voting members, including 7 appointed by the Secretary in accordance with subsection (b)(2) of this section (5 of whom shall be appointed from the State of Alaska and 2 of whom shall be appointed from the State of Washington).

(8) Western Pacific Council

The Western Pacific Fishery Management Council shall consist of the States of Hawaii, American Samoa, Guam, and the Northern Mariana Islands and shall have authority over the fisheries in the Pacific Ocean seaward of such States and of the Commonwealths, territories, and possessions of the United States in the Pacific Ocean area. The Western Pacific Council shall have 13 voting members, including 8 appointed by the Secretary in accordance with subsection (b)(2) of this section (at least one of whom shall be appointed from each of the following States: Hawaii, American Samoa, Guam, and the Northern Mariana Islands).

Each Council shall reflect the expertise and interest of the several constituent States in the ocean area over which such Council is granted authority.

(b) Voting members

(1) The voting members of each Council shall be:

(A) The principle State official with marine fishery management responsibility and expertise in each constituent State, who is designated as such by the Governor of the State, so long as the official continues to hold such position, or the designee of such official.

(B) The regional director of the National Marine Fisheries Service for the geographic area concerned, or his designee, except that if two such directors are within such geographical area, the Secretary shall designate which of such directors shall be the voting member.

(C) The members required to be appointed by the Secretary in accordance with subsection (b)(2) of this section.

(2)(A) The members of each Council required to be appointed by the Secretary must be individuals who are knowledgeable and experienced with regard to the conservation and management, or the recreational or commercial harvest, of the fishery resources of the geographical area concerned. The Secretary, in making appointments under this section, shall, to the extent practicable, ensure a fair apportionment, on a rotating basis, of the active participants (or their representatives) involved in the fisheries under Council jurisdiction.

(B) The Secretary shall appoint the members of each Council from a list of individuals submitted by the Governor of each applicable constituent State. A Governor may not submit the names of individuals to the Secretary for appointment unless the Governor has, to the extent practicable, first consulted with representatives of the commercial and recreational fishing interests of the state regarding those individuals. Each such list shall contain the names and pertinent biographical data of not less than three individuals for each applicable vacancy. The Secretary shall review each list submitted by a Governor to ascertain if the individuals on the list are qualified for the vacancy on the basis of the required knowledge and experience required by subparagraph (A), If the Secretary determines that any individual is not qualified, he shall notify the appropriate Governor of that determination. The Governor shall then submit a revised list or resubmit the original list with an additional explanation of the qualifications of the individual in question. An individual is not eligible for appointment by the Secretary until that individual complies with the applicable financial disclosure requirements under subsection (k) of this section.

(C) Whenever the Secretary makes an appointment to a Council, he shall make a public announcement of such appointment not less than 45 days before the first day on which the individual is to take office as a member of the Council.

(3) Each voting member appointed to a Council by the Secretary in accordance with subsection (b)(2) of this section shall serve for a term of 3 years; except that the Secretary may designate a shorter term if necessary to provide for balanced expiration to terms of office.

(c) Nonvoting members

(1) The nonvoting members of each Council shall be:

(A) The regional or area director of the United States Fish and Wildlife Service for the geographical area concerned, or his designee.

(B) the commander of the Coast Guard district for the geographical area concerned, or his designee; except that, if two Coast Guard districts are within such geographical area, the commander designated for such purpose by the commandant of the Coast Guard.

(C) The executive director of the Marine Fisheries Commission for the geographical area concerned, if any, or his designee.

(D) One representative of the Department of State designated for such purpose by the Secretary of State, or his designee.

(2) The Pacific Council shall have one additional nonvoting member who shall be appointed by, and serve at the pleasure of, the Governor of Alaska.

(d) Compensation and expenses

The voting members of each Council, who are not employed by the Federal Government or any State or local government, shall receive compensation at the daily rate for GS-18 of the General Schedule when engaged in the actual performance of duties for such Council. The voting members of each Council, any nonvoting member described in subsection (c)(1)(C) of this section, and the nonvoting member appointed pursuant to subsection (c)(2) of this section shall be reimbursed for actual expenses incurred in the performance of such duties, and the other nonvoting members may be reimbursed for actual expenses.

(e) Transaction of business

(1) A majority of the voting members of any Council shall constitute a quorum, but one or more members designated by the Council may hold hearings. All decisions of any Council shall be by

majority vote of the voting members present and voting.

(2) The voting members of each Council shall select a Chairman for such Council from among the voting members.

(3) Each Council shall meet in the geographical area concerned at the call of the Chairman or upon the request of a majority of its members.

(4) If any voting member of a Council disagrees with respect to any matter which is transmitted to the Secretary by such Council, such member may submit a statement to the Secretary setting forth the reasons for such disagreement.

(f) Staff and administration

(1) Each Council may appoint, and assign duties to, an executive director and such other full- and part-time administrative employees as the Secretary determines are necessary to the performance of its functions.

(2) Upon the request of any Council, and after consultation with the Secretary, the head of any Federal agency is authorized to detail such Council, on a reimbursable basis, any of the personnel of such agency, to assist such Council in the performance of its functions under this chapter.

(3) The Secretary shall provide to each Council such administrative and technical support services as are necessary for the effective functioning of such Council.

(4) The Administrator of General Services shall furnish each Council with such offices, equipment, supplies, and services as he is authorized to furnish any other agency or instrumentality of the United States.

(5) The Secretary and the Secretary of State shall furnish each Council with relevant information concerning foreign fishing and international fishery agreements.

(6) Each Council shall determine its organization, and prescribe it practices and procedures for carrying out its functions under this chapter, in accordance with such uniform standards as are prescribed by the Secretary. The procedures of a Council, and of its scientific and statistical committee and advisory panels established under subsection (g) of this section, must be consistent with the procedural guidelines set forth in subsection (i)(2) of this section. Each Council shall publish and make available to the public a statement of its organization, practices, and procedures.

(7) The Secretary shall pay--

(A) the compensation and expenses provided for in subsection (d) of this section;

(B) appropriate compensation to employees appointed under paragraph (1);

(C) the amounts required for reimbursement of other Federal agencies under paragraphs (2) and (4);

(D) the actual expenses of the members of the committees and panels established under subsection (g) of this section; and

(E) such other costs as the Secretary determines are necessary to the performance of the functions of the Councils.

(g) Committees and panels

(1) Each Council shall establish and maintain, and appoint the members of a scientific and statistical committee to assist it in the development, collection, and evaluation of such statistical, biological, economic, social, and other scientific information as is relevant to such Council's development and amendment of any fishery management plan.

(2) Each Council shall establish such other advisory panels as are necessary or appropriate to assist it in carrying out its functions under this chapter.

(h) Functions

Each Council shall, in accordance with the provisions of this chapter--

(1) prepare and submit to the Secretary a fishery management plan with respect to each fishery within its geographical area of authority that requires conservation and management and, from time to time, such amendments to each such plan as are necessary;

(2) prepare comments on any application for foreign fishing transmitted to it under section 1824(b)(4)(C) of this title, and any fishery management plan or amendment transmitted to it under section 1854(c)(2) of this title;

(3) conduct public hearings, at appropriate times and in appropriate locations in the geographical area concerned, so as to allow all interested persons an opportunity to be heard in the development of fishery management plans and amendments to such plans, and with respect to the administration and implementation of the provisions of this chapter (and for purposes of this paragraph, the term "geographical area concerned" may include an area under the authority of another Council if the fish in the fishery concerned migrate into, or occur in, that area or if the matters being heard affect the fishermen of that area; but not unless such other Council is first consulted regarding the conduct of such hearings within its area);

(4) submit to the Secretary such periodic reports as the Council deems appropriate, and any other relevant report which may be requested by the Secretary;

(5) review on a continuing basis, and revise as appropriate, the assessments and specifications made pursuant to section 1853(a)(3) and (4) of this title with respect to the optimum yield from, the capacity and extent to which United States fish processors will process United States harvested fish from, and the total allowable level of foreign fishing in, each fishery within the geographical area of authority; and

(6) conduct any other activities which are required by, or provided for in, this chapter or which are necessary and appropriate to the foregoing functions.

(i) Fishery habitat concerns

Each Council may comment on, or make recommendations concerning, any activity undertaken, or proposed to be undertaken, by any State or Federal agency that, in the view of the Council, may affect the habitat of a fishery resource under its jurisdiction. Within 45 days after receiving such a comment or recommendation from a Council, a Federal agency must provide a detailed response, in writing, to the Council regarding the matter.

(j) Procedural matters

(1) The Federal Advisory Committee Act (5 U.S.C.App.) shall not apply to the Councils or to the scientific and statistical committee and advisory panels of a Council:

(A) Unless closed in accordance with paragraph (3), each regular meeting and each emergency meeting shall be open to the public.

(B) Emergency meetings shall be held at the call of the chairman or equivalent presiding officer.

(C) Timely public notice of each regular meeting and emergency meeting, including the time, place, and agenda of the meeting, shall be published in local newspapers in the major fishing ports of the Council's region (and in other major fishing ports having a direct interest in the affected fishery) and such notice may be given by such other means as will result in wide publicity. Timely notice of each regular meeting shall also be published in the Federal Register.

(D) Interested persons shall be permitted to present oral or written statements regarding the matters on the agenda at meetings.

(E) Minutes of each meeting shall be kept and shall contain a record of the persons present, an accurate description of matters discussed and conclusions reached, and copies of all statements filed.

(F) Subject to the procedures established by the Council under paragraph (4), and the guidelines prepared by the Secretary under section 1853(d) of this title, relating to confidentiality, the administrative record, including minutes required under subparagraph (E), of each meeting, and records or other documents which were made available to or prepared for the Council, committee, or panel incident to the meeting, shall be available for public inspection and copying at a single location in the offices of the Council.

(3)(a) Each Council, scientific and statistical committee, and advisory panel--

(i) shall close any meeting, or portion thereof, that concerns matters or information that bears a national security classification; and

(ii) may close any meeting, or portion thereof, that concerns matters or information that pertains to national security, employment matters, or briefings on litigation in which the Council is interested;

and if any meeting or portion is closed, the Council, committee, or panel concerned shall publish notice of the closure in local newspapers in the major fishing ports within its region (and other major, affected fishing ports), including the time and place of the meeting. Subparagraphs (D) and (F) shall not apply to any meeting or portion thereof that is so closed.

(4) Each Council shall establish appropriate procedures applicable to it and to its committee and advisory panels for ensuring the confidentiality of the statistics that may be submitted to it by Federal or State authorities, and may be voluntarily submitted to it by private persons; including, but not limited to, procedures for the restriction of council employee access and the prevention of conflicts of interest; except that such procedures, in the case of statistics submitted to the Council by a State or

by the Secretary under section 1853(d) of this title, must be consistent with the laws and regulations of that State, or with the procedures of the Secretary, as the case may be, concerning the confidentiality of the statistics.

(5) Each Council shall specify those procedures that are necessary or appropriate to ensure that the committee and advisory panels established under subsection (g) of this section are involved, on a continuing basis, in the development and amendment of fishery management plans.

(k) Disclosure of financial interest

(1) For the purposes of this subsection, the term "affected individual" means an individual who--

(A) is nominated by the Governor of a State for appointment as a voting member of a Council in accordance with subsection (b)(2) of this section;

(B) is a voting member of the Council appointed under subsection (b)(2) of this section; or

(C) is the executive director of a Council.

(2) Each affected individual must disclose any financial interest held by--

(A) that individual;

(B) the spouse, minor child, or partner of that individual; and

(C) any organization (other than the Council) in which that individual is serving as an officer, director, trustee, partner, or employee;

in any harvesting, processing, or marketing activity that is being, or will be, undertaken within any fishery over which the Council has jurisdiction.

(3) The discosure required under paragraph (2) shall be made--

(A) in the case of an affected individual referred to in paragraph (1)(A), before appointment by the Secretary; and

(B) in the case of an affected individual referred to in paragraph (1)(B) or (C), within 45 days of taking office.

(4) An affected individual referred to in paragraph (1)(B) or (C) must update his or her disclosure form at any time such financial interest is acquired, or substantially changed, by any person referred to in paragraph (2)(A), (B), or (C).

(5) The financial interest disclosures required by this subsection shall--

(A) be made on such forms, in accordance with such procedures, and at such times, as the Secretary shall by regulation prescribe; and

(B) be kept on file, and made available for public inspection at reasonable hours, at the Council office.

(6) The participation by an affected individual referred to in paragraph (1)(B) or (C) in an action by a Council during any time in which that individual is not in compliance with the regulations prescribed under paragraph (5) may not be treated as cause for the invalidation of that action.

(7) Section 208 of Title 18, does not apply to an affected individual referred to in paragraph (1)(B) or (C) during any time in which that individual is in compliance with the regulations prescribed under paragraph (5).

Sec. 1853. Contents of fishery management plans

(a) Required provisions

Any fishery management plan which is prepared by any Council, or by the Secretary, with respect to any fishery, shall--

(1) contain the conservation and management measures, applicable to foreign fishing and fishing by vessels of the United States, which are--

(A) necessary and appropriate for the conservation and management of the fishery;

(B) described in this subsection or subsection (b) of this section, or both; and

(C) consistent with the national standards, the other provisions of this chapter, and any other applicable law.

(2) contain a description of the fishery, including, but not limited to, the number of vessels involved, the type and quantity of fishing gear used, the species of fish involved and their location, the cost likely to be incurred in management, actual and potential revenues from the fishery, any recreational interests in the fishery, and nature and extent of foreign fishing and Indian treaty fishing rights, if any;

(3) assess and specify the present and probable future condition of, and the maximum sustainable yield and optimum yield from, the fishery, and include a summary of information utilized in making such specification;

(4) assess and specify--

(A) the capacity and extent to which fishing vessels of the United States, on an annual basis, will harvest the optimum yield specified under paragraph (3),

(B) the portion of such optimum catch which, on an annual basis, will not be harvested by fishing vessels of the United States and can be made available for foreign fishing, and,

(C) the capacity and extent to which United States fish processors, on an annual basis, will process that portion of such optimum yield that will be harvested by fishing vessels of the United States;

(5) specify the pertinent data which shall be submitted to the Secretary with respect to the fishery, including, but not limited to, information regarding the type and quantity of fishing gear used, catch by species in numbers of fish or weight thereof, areas in which fishing was engaged in, time of

fishing, number of hauls, and the estimated processing capacity of, and the actual processing capacity utilized by, United States fish processors,

(6) consider, and may provide for, temporary adjustments after consultation with the Coast Guard and persons utilizing the fishery, regarding access to the fishery for vessels otherwise prevented from harvesting because of weather or other ocean conditions affecting the safety of the vessels; and

(7) include readily available information regarding the significance of habitat to the fishery and assessment as to the effects which changes to that habitat may have upon the fishery.

(b) Discretionary provisions

Any fishery management plan which is prepared by any Council, or by the Secretary, with respect to any fishery, may--

(1) require a permit to be obtained from, and fees to be paid to, the Secretary with respect to any fishing vessel of the United States fishing, or wishing to fish, in the exclusive economic zone, or for anadromous species or Continental Shelf fishery resources beyond such zone;

(2) designate zones where, and periods when, fishing shall be limited, or shall not be permitted, or shall be permitted only by specified types of fishing vessels or with specified types and quantities of fishing gear;

(3) establish specified limitations on the catch of fish (based on area, species, size, number, weight, sex, incidental catch, total biomass, or other factors), which are necessary and appropriate for the conservation and management of the fishery;

(4) prohibit, limit, condition, or require the use of specified types and quantities of fishing gear, fishing vessels, or equipment for such vessels, including devices which may be required to facilitate enforcement of the provisions of this chapter;

(5) incorporate (consistent with the national standards, the other provisions of this chapter, and any other applicable law) the relevant fishery conservation and management measures of the coastal State nearest to the fishery;

(6) establish a system for limiting access to the fishery in order to achieve optimum yield if, in developing such system, the Council and the Secretary take into account--

(A) present participation in the fishery,

(B) historical fishing practices in, and dependence on, the fishery,

(C) the economics of the fishery,

(D) the capability of fishing vessels used in the fishery to engage in other fisheries,

(E) the cultural and social framework relevant to the fishery, and

(F) any other relevant considerations;

(7) assess and specify the effect which the conservation and management measures of the plan will have on the stocks of naturally spawning anadromous fish in the region; and

(8) prescribe such other measures, requirements, or conditions and restrictions as are determined to be necessary and appropriate for the conservation and management of the fishery.

(c) Proposed regulations

The proposed regulations which the Council deems necessary or appropriate for purposes of carrying out the plan or amendment of a plan shall be submitted to the Secretary simultaneously with the plan or amendment for action by the Secretary under sections 1854 and 1855 of this title.

(d) Confidentiality of statistics

Any statistic submitted to the Secretary by any person in compliance with any requirement under subsection (a)(5) of this section shall be confidential and shall not be disclosed; except--

(1) to Federal employees and Council employees who are responsible for management plan development and monitoring; or

(2) when required by court order.

The Secretary shall, by regulation, prescribe such procedures as may be necessary to preserve such confidentiality, except that the Secretary may release or make public any such statistics in any aggregate or summary form which does not directly or indirectly disclose the identity or business of any person who submits such statistics.

(e) Data collecting programs

If a Council determines that additional information and data (other than information and data that would disclose proprietary or confidential commercial or financial information regarding fishing operations or fish processing operations) would be beneficial for the purposes of--

(1) determining whether a fishery management plan is needed for a fishery; or

(2) preparing a fishery management plan;

the Council may request that the Secretary implement a data collection program for the fishery which would provide the types of information and data (other than information and data that would disclose proprietary or confidential commercial or financial information regarding fishing operations or fish processing operations) specified by the Council.

The Secreaty shall approve such a data collection program if he determines that the need is justified, and shall promulgate regulations for such determination in writing.

The determinations of the Secretary under this subsection regarding a Council request shall be made within a reasonable period of time after he receives that request.

Sec. 1854. Action by Secretary

(a) Action by Secretary upon receipt of plan

(1) After the Secretary receives a fishery management plan, or amendment to a plan, which was prepared by the Council, the Secretary shall--

(A) immediately make a preliminary evaluation of the management plan or amendment for purposes of deciding if it is consistent with the national standards and sufficient in scope and substance to warrant review under this subsection and--

(i) if that decision is affirmative, implement subparagraphs (B),(C), and (D) with respect to the plan or amendment, or

(ii) if that decision is negative--

(I) disapprove the plan or amendment, or

(II) notify the Council, in writing, of the disapproval and of those matters specified in subsection (b)(2)(A), (B) and (C) of this section as they relate to the plan or amendment;

(B) immediately commence a review of the management plan or amendment to determine whether it is consistent with the national standards, the other provisions of this chapter, and any other applicable law;

(C) immediately publish in the Federal Register a notice stating that the plan or amendment is available and that written data, views, or comments of interested persons on the plan or amendment may be submitted to the Secretary during the 60-day period beginning on the receipt date; and

(D) by the 15th day after the receipt date--

(i) make such changes in the proposed regulations submitted for the plan or amendment under section 1853(c) of this title as may be necessary for the implementation of the plan, and

(ii) publish such proposed regulations, including any changes made under clause (i), in the Federal Register together with an explanation of those changes which are substantive.

(2) In undertaking the reveiw required under paragraph (1)(B), the Secretary shall--

(A) take into account the data, views, and comments received from interested persons;

(B) consult with the Secretary of State with respect to foreign fishing; and

(C) consult with the Secretary of the department in which the Coast Guard is operating with respect to enforcement at sea and to fishery access adjustments referred to in section 1853(a)(6) of this title.

(3)(A) the Secretary shall take action under this section on any fishery management plan or amendment to a plan which the Council characterizes as being a final plan or amendment.

(B) For purposes of this section, the term "receipt date" means the 5th day after the day on which a Council transmits to the Secretary a fishery management plan, or an amendment to a plan, that it characterizes as a final plan or amendment.

(1) A plan or amendment shall take effect and be implemented in accordance with section 1855(c) of this title if--

(b) Review by the Secretary

(A) the Secretary does not notify the Council in writing of--

(i) his disapproval under section (a)(1)(A)(ii) of this section, or

(ii) his disapproval, or partial disapproval, under paragraph (2), of the plan or amendment before the close of the 95th day after the receipt date; or

(B) at any time subsequent to the 60th day after the receipt date and before such 95th day, the Secretary notifies the Council in writing that he does not intend to disapprove, or partially disapprove, the plan or amendment.

2) If after review under subsection (a) of this section the Secretary determines that the plan or amendment is not consistent with the criteria set forth in paragraph (1)(B) of that subsection, the Secretary shall notify the Council in writing of his disapproval or partial disapproval of the plan or amendment. Such notice shall specify--

((A) the applicable law with which the plan or amendment is inconsistent;

(B) the nature of such inconsistency; and

(C) recommendations concerning the actions that could be taken by the Council to conform such plan or amendment to the requirements of applicable law.

(3)(A) If the Secretary disapproves a proposed plan or amendment under subsection (a)(1)(A)(ii) of this section, or disapproves, or partially disapproves, a proposed plan or amendment under paragraph (2), the Council may submit a revised plan or amendment, accompanied by appropriately revised proposed regulations, to the Secretary.

(B) After the Secretary receives a revised plan or amendment under subparagraph (A) or (C)(ii), the Secretary shall immediately--

(i) commence review of the plan or amendment to determine whether it complies with the criteria set forth in subsection (a)(1)(B) of this section;

(ii) publish in the Federal Register a notice stating that the revised plan or amendment is available and that written data, views, or comments of interested persons on the plan or amendment may be submitted during the 30-day period beginning on the date (hereinafter in this paragraph referred to as the "revised receipt date") the plan or amendment was submitted to the Secretary under subparagraph (A) or (C)(ii); and

(iii) review the revised proposed regulations, if any, submitted by the Council and make such changes to them as may be necessary for the implementation of the plan, and thereafter publish such revised proposed regulations in the Federal Register together with an explanation of each of such changes that is substantive.

(C)(i) Before the close of the 60th day after the revised receipt date, the Secretary, after taking account of any data, views, or comments received under subparagraph (B)(ii), shall complete the review required under subparagraph (B)(i) and determine whether the plan or amendment complies with the criteria set forth in subsection (a)(1)(B) of this section. If the Secretary determines that a plan or amendment is not in compliance with such criteria, he shall immediately notify the Council of his disapproval of the plan or amendment.

(ii) After notifying the Council of a disapproval under clause (i), the Secretary shall promptly provide to the Council a written statement of the reasons on which the disapproval was based and advise the Council that it may submit a further revised plan or amendment, together with appropriately revised regulations, for review and determination under this paragraph.

(D) A revised plan or amendment shall take effect and be implemented in accordance with section 1855(c) of this title if the Secretary does not notify the Council, in writing, by the close of the 60th day after the revised receipt date of his disapproval of the plan or amendment.

(c) Preparation by the Secretary

(1) The Secretary may prepare a fishery management plan, with respect to any fishery, or any amendment to any such plan, in accordance with the national standards, the other provisions of this chapter, and any other applicable law, if--

(A) the appropriate Council fails to develop and submit to the Secretary, after a reasonable time, a fishery management plan for such fishery, or any necessary amendment to such a plan, if such fishery requires conservation and management; or

(B) the Secretary disapproves or partially disapproves any such plan or amendment, or disapproves a revised plan or amendment, and the Council involved fails to submit a revised or further revised plan or amendment, as the case may be.

In preparing any such plan or amendment, the Secretary shall consult with the Secretary of State with respect to foreign fishing and with the Secretary of the department in which the Coast Guard is operating with respect to enforcement at sea. The Secretary shall also prepare such proposed regulations as he deems necessary or appropriate to carry out each plan or amendment prepared by him under this paragraph.

(2)(A) Whenever, under paragraph (1), the Secretary prepares a fishery management plan or amendment, the Secretary shall immediately--

(i) submit such plan or amendment, and proposed regulations to implement such plan or amendment, to the appropriate Council for consideration and comment;

(ii) publish in the Federal Register a notice stating that the plan or amendment is available and that written data, views, or comments of interested persons on the plan or amendment may be submitted to the Secretary during the 60-day period beginning on the date the plan or amendment was submitted under clause (i); and

(iii) by the 15th day after the date of submission under clause (i), submit for publication in the Federal Register the proposed regulations to implement the plan or amendment.

(B) The appropriate council must submit its comments and recommendations, if any, regarding the plan or amendment to the Secretary before the close of the 60-day period referred to in subparagraph (A)(ii). After the close of such 60-day period, the Secretary, after taking into account any such comments and recommendations, as well as any views, data, or comments submitted under subparagraph (A)(ii), may implement such plan or amendment under section 1855(c) of this title.

(3) Notwithstanding paragraph (1), the Secretary may not include in any fishery management plan, or any amendment to any such plan, prepared by him, a provision establishing a limited access system described in section 1853(b)(6) of this title, unless such system is first approved by a majority of the voting members, present and voting, of each appropriate Council.

(d) Establishment of fees

The Secretary shall by regulation establish the level of any fees which are authorized to be charged pursuant to section 1853(b) of this title. The Secretary may enter into a cooperative agreement with the States concerned under which the States administer the permit system and the agreement may provide that all or part of the fees collected under the system shall accrue to the States. The level of fees charged under this subsection shall not exceed the administrative costs incurred in issuing the permits.

(e) Fisheries research

The Secretary shall initiate and maintain, in cooperation with the Councils, a comprehensive program of fishery research to carry out and further the purposes, policy, and provisions of this chapter. Such program shall be designed to acquire knowledge and information, including statistics, on fishery conservation and management and on the economics of fisheries, including, but not limited to, biological research concerning the interdependence of fisheries or stocks of fish, the impact of pollution on fish, the impact of wetland and estuarine degradation, and other matters bearing upon the abundance and availability of fish. The Secretary shall annually review and update the comprehensive program and make the results of review and update available to the Councils.

(f) Misellaneous duties

(1) If any fishery extends beyond the geographical area of authority of any one Council, the Secretary may--

(A) designate which Council shall prepare the fishery management plan for such fishery and any amendment to such plan; or

(B) may require that the plan and amendment be prepared jointly by the Councils concerned.

(2) The Secretary shall establish the boundaries between the geographical areas of authority of adjacent Councils.

Sec. 1855. Implementation of fishery management plans

(a), (b) Repealed

(c) implementation

The Secretary shall promulgate each regulation that is necessary to carry out a plan or amendment--

(1) within 110 days after the plan or amendment was received by him for action under section 1854(a) of this title, if such plan or amendment takes effect under section 1854(b) of this title;

(2) within 75 days after a revised plan or amendment was received by him under section 1854(b) of this title, if such plan or amendment takes effect under paragraph (3)(D) of such section; or

(3) within such time as he deems appropriate in the case of a plan or amendment prepared by him under section 1854(c) of this title.

(d) Judicial review

Regulations promulgated by the Secretary under this chapter shall be subject to judicial review to the extent authorized by, and in accordance with, chapter 7 of Title 5, if a petition for review is filed within 30 days after the date on which the regulations are promulgated; except that (1) section 705 of such title is not applicable, and (2) the appropriate court shall only set aside any such regulation on a ground specified in section 706(2)(A),(B),(C), or (D) of such title.

(e) Emergency actions

(1) If the Secretary finds that an emergency exists involving any fishery, he may promulgate emergency regulations necessary to address the emergency, without regard to whether a fishery managment plan exists for such fishery.

(2) If a Council finds that an emergency exists involving any fishery within its jursidiction, whether or not a fishery management plan exists for such fishery--

(A) the Secretary shall promulgate emergency regulations under paragraph (1) to address the emergency if the Council, by unanimous vote of the members who are voting members, requests the taking of such action; and

(B) the Secretary may promulgate emergency regulations under paragraph (1) to address the emergency if the Council, by less than a unanimous vote, requests the taking of such action.

(3) Any emergency regulation which changes any existing fishery management plan or amendment shall be treated as an amendment to such plan for the period in which the regulation is in effect. Any emergency regulation promulgated under this subsection--

(A) shall be published in the Federal Register together with the reasons therefor;

(B) shall remain in effect for not more than 90 days after the date of such publication, except that any such regulation may, by agreement of the Secretary and the Council, be promulgated for one additional period of not more than 90 days; and

(C) may be terminated by the Secretary at an earlier date by publication in the Federal Register of a notice of termination, except for emergency regulations promulgated under paragraph (2) in which case such early termination may be made only upon agreement of the Secretary and the Council concerned.

(f) Repealed

(g) Responsibility of Secretary

The Secretary shall have general responsibility to carry out any fishery management plan or amendment approved or prepared by him, in accordance with the provisions of this chapter. The Secretary may promulgate such regulations, in accordance with section 553 of Title 5, as may be necessary to discharge such responsibility or to carry out any other provision of this chapter.

(h) Effect of certain laws on certain time requirements

The Paperwork Reduction Act of 1980 (44 U.S.C. 3501 et seq.), the Regulatory Flexibility Act (5 U.S.C. 601 et seq.), and Executive Order Numbered 12291, dated February 17, 1981, shall be complied with within the time limitations specified in subsection (c) of this section or section 1854(a) and (b) of this title as they apply to the functions of the Secretary under such provisions.

Sec. 1856. State jurisdiction

(a) in general

(1) Except as provided for in subsection (b) of this section, nothing in this chapter shall be construed as extending or diminishing the jurisdiction or authority of any State within its boundaries.

(2) For the purposes of this chapter, except as provided in subsection (b) of this section, the jurisdiction and authority of a State shall extend--

(A) to any pocket of waters that is adjacent to the State and totally enclosed by lines delimiting the territorial sea of the United States pursuant to the Geneva Convention on the Territorial Sea and Contiguous Zone or any successor convention to which the United States is a party.

(B) with respect to the body of water commonly known as Nantucket Sound, to the pocket of water west of the seventieth meridian west of Greenwich; and

(C) to the waters of southeastern Alaska (for the purpose of regulating fishing for other than any species of crab) that are--

(i) north of the line representing the international boundary at Dixon Entrance and the westward extension of that line; east of 138 degrees west longitude; and not more than three nautical miles seaward from the coast, from the lines extending from headland to headland across all bays, inlets, straits, passes, sounds, and entrances, and from any island or group of islands, including the islands of the Alexander Archipelago (except Forrester Island); or

(ii) between the islands referred to in clause (i) (except Forrester Island) and the mainland.

(3) Except as otherwise provided by paragraph (2), a State may not directly or indirectly regulate any fishing vessel outside its boundaries, unless the vessel is registered under the law of that State.

(b) Exception

(1) If the Secretary finds, after notice and an opportunity for a hearing in accordance with section 554 of Title 5, that--

(A) the fishing in a fishery, which is covered by a fishery management plan implemented under this chapter, is engaged in predominantly within the exclusive economic zone; and

(B) any State has taken any action, or omitted to take any action, the results of which will substantially and adversely affect the carrying out of such fishery management plan;

the Secretary shall promptly notify such State and the appropriate Council of such finding and of his intention to regulate the applicable fishery within the boundaries of such State (other than internal waters), pursuant to such fishery management plan and the regulations promulgated to implement such plan.

(c) Exception regarding foreign fish processing in internal waters

(1) A foreign fishing vessel may engage in fish processing within the internal waters of a State if, and only if--

(A) the vessel is qualified for purposes of this paragraph pursuant to paragraph (4)(C); and

(B) the owner or operator of the vessel applies to the Governor of the State for, and (subject to paragraph (2)) is granted, permission for the vessel to engage in such processing.

(2) The Governor of a State may not grant permission for a foreign fishing vessel to engage in fish processing under paragraph (1)(B) if he determines that the fish processors within the State have adequate capacity, and will utilize such capacity, to process all of the United States harvested fish from the fishery concerned that are landed in the State.

(3) Nothing in this subsection may be construed as relieving a foreign fishing vessel from the duty to comply with all applicable Federal and State laws while operating within the internal waters of a State incident to permission obtained under paragraph (1)(B).

(4) For purposes of this subsection--

(A) The term "fish processing" includes, in addition to processing, the performance of any other activity relating to fishing, including, but not limited to, preparation, supply, storage, refrigeration, or transportation.

(B) The phrase "internal waters of a State" means all waters within the boundaries of a State except those seaward of the baseline from which the breadth of the territorial sea is measured.

(C) A foreign fishing vessel shall be treated as qualified for purposes of paragraph (1) if the foreign nation under which it is flagged will be a party to (i) a governing international fishery agreement or (ii) a treaty described in section 1821(b) of this title during the time the vesel will engage in the fish processing for which permission is sought under paragraph (1)(B).

....

Sec. 1861. Enforcement

(a) Responsibility

The provisions of this chapter shall be enforced by the Secretary and the Secretary of the department in which the Coast Guard is operating. Such Secretaries may, by agreement, on a reimbursable basis or otherwise, utilize the personnel, services, equipment (including aircraft and vessels), and facilities of any other Federal agency, including all elements of the Department of Defense, and of any State agency, in the performance of such duties....

ED. NOTE: Among the purposes stated in the Act's preambulary language are the following:

(1) to take immediate action to conserve and manage the fishery resources found off the coasts of the United States, and the anadromous species and Continental Shelf fishery resources of the United States, by exercising (A) sovereign rights for the purposes of exploring, exploiting, conserving, and managing all fish except highly migratory species, within the exclusive economic zone established by Presidential Proclamation 5030, dated March 10, 1983, and (B) exclusive fishery management authority beyond the exclusive economic zone over such anadromous species and Continental Shelf fishery resources;

(2) to support and encourage the implementation and enforcement of international fishery agreements for the conservation and management of highly migratory species, and to encourage the negotiation and implementation of such agreements as necessary;

(3) to promote domestic commercial and recreational fishing under sound conservation and management principles;

(4) to provide for the preparation and implementation in accordance with national standards, of fishery management plans which will achieve and maintain, on a continuing basis, the optimum yield from each fishery;

In the policy statement section, Congress indicated its intentions in adopting the Act as being:

(1) to maintain without change the existing territorial or other ocean jurisdiction of the United States for all purposes other than the conservation and management of fishery resources, as provided for in this chapter;

(2) to authorize no impedement to, or interference with, recognized legitimate uses of the high seas, except as necessary for the conservation and management of fishery reesources, as provided for in this chapter;

(3) to assure that the national fishery conservation and management program utilizes, and is

based upon, the best scientific information available; involves, and is responsive to the needs of, interested and affected States and citizens; promotes efficiency, draws upon Federal, State, and academic capabilities in carrying out research, administration, management, and enforcement; and is workable and effective;

(4) to permit foreign fishing consistent with the provisions of this chapter; and

(5) to support and encourage active United States efforts to obtain internationally acceptable agreements which provide for effective conservation and management of fishery resources.

* * * *

In your judgment, how well does the statute carry out these objectives? Are there any provisions in the statute that run directly contrary to the 1982 Convention?

In 1990, Congress deleted the exclusion of highly migratory species from the statute, and substituted the following:

> The United States shall cooperate directly or through appropriate international organizations with those nations involved in fisheries for highly migratory species with a view to ensuring their conservation and promoting the objective of optimum utilization of such species throughout their range, both within and beyond the exclusive economic zone.

This brought the statute into line with the Convention, reversed a long-standing U.S. position that tuna were not under the jurisdiction of the coastal State, and removed a serious irritant to our Latin American neighbors.

The statute, as you have already noted, deals with the special problems of anadromous and sedentary species. Those species considered to be sedentary by the United States are listed in the Act. They are:

Sec. 1802. Definitions

....

(4) The term "Continental Shelf fishery resources" means the following:
COLENTERATA
Baboo Coral -- Acanella spp.;
Black Coral -- Antipathes spp.;
Gold Coral -- Callogorgia spp.;
Precious Red Coral -- Corallium spp.;
Bamboo Coral -- Keratoisis spp.; and
Gold Coral -- Parazoanthus spp.
CRUSTACEA
Tanner Crab -- Chionoecetes tanneri;
Tanner Crab -- Chionoecetes opilio;
Tanner Crab -- Chionoecetes angulatus;
Tanner Crab -- Chionoecetes bairdi;
King Crab -- Paralithodes camtschatica;
King Crab -- Paralithodes platypus;

King Crab -- Paralithodes brevipes;
Lobster -- Homarus americanus;
Dungeness Crab -- Cancer magister;
California King Crab -- Paralithodes californiensis;
California King Crab -- Paralithodes rathbuni;
Northern Stone Crab -- Lithodes maja;
Stone Crab -- Menippe mercenaria; and
Deep-sea Red Crab -- Geryon quinquedens
MOLLUSKS
Red Abalone -- Haliotis rufescens;
Pink Abalone -- Haliotis corrugata;
Japanese Abalone -- Haliotis Kamtschatkana;
Queen Conch -- Strombus gigas;
Surf Clam -- Spisula solidissima; and
Ocean Quahog -- Artica islandica.
SPONGES
Glove Sponge -- Hippiospongia canaliculata;
Sheepswool sponge -- Hippiospongia lachne;
Grass Sponge -- Spongia graminea; and
Yellow Sponge -- Spongia barbera.

If the Secretary determines, after consultation with the Secretary of State, that living organisms of any other sedentary species are, at the harvestable stage, either--

(A) immobile on or under the seabed, or

(B) unable to move except in constant physical contact with the seabed or subsoil,

of the Continental Shelf which appertains to the United States, and publishes notice of such determination in the Federal Register, such sedentary species shall be considered to be added to the foregoing list and included in such term for purposes of this chapter.

* * * *

Note that the list includes crab and the American lobster. Do you think that these fulfill the requirements for sedentary species in the 1982 Convention? Note also that the list includes the American lobster (the two-claw variety) that is found off the coast of New England, but excludes the spiny lobster found in Florida waters. Can you imagine why?

For a criticism of the structural make-up and bias of the fisheries councils in the United States, see Pontecorvo, Fishery Management and the General Welfare: Implications of the New Structure, 52 Wash.L.Rev. 641 (1977).

F. INTERNATIONAL ENFORCEMENT PROBLEMS

Enforcement of fisheries regulations in the EEZ is relatively straight forward. The Convention provides sweeping enforcement powers for the coastal State. On the high seas, however, it is a different matter. Because fishing is a freedom of the high seas beyond the limits of the EEZ, enforcement is essentially a matter for the application by flag States of their own laws to their own vessels.

If there was a clear demarcation between stocks of fish within the EEZ and those beyond, there would be no difficulty. A severe problem arises, however, where the same stocks of fish inhabit both the EEZ and the waters beyond. This raises the possibility that what vessels do with regard to conservation, or more importantly, what they do not do on the high seas may have a significant impact on the efforts of coastal States to establish a meaningful conservation regime in their own economic zones. The following article deals with this problem of "straddling stocks".

Miles and Burke, PRESSURES ON THE UNITED NATIONS CONVENTION ON THE LAW OF THE SEA OF 1982 ARISING FROM NEW FISHERIES CONFLICTS: THE PROBLEM OF STRADDLING STOCKS 20 O.D.I.L. 343-356 (1989)[3]

Even before entry into force, a variety of pressures place strains on the balance of interests underlying the 1982 Convention on the Law of the Sea. The most urgent demands relate to navigational and fisheries activities. A most important recent issue concerns *straddling stocks*, i.e., stocks that occur both within the EEZ and adjacent to it.

From the perspective of a growing number of important coastal states, the 1982 Convention on the Law of the Sea did not adequately settle the issue of straddling stocks, those stocks within and adjacent to the EEZ. Article 63 of the Convention stipulates that the coastal states and states fishing for straddling stocks beyond the EEZ shall seek to agree on conservation measures applicable beyond the EEZ, either directly or through appropriate regional or subregional organizations. In addition, Article 116 establishes that the coastal state has the superior right, duty, and interest in straddling stocks beyond the EEZ. However, the precise distribution of competences to make these effective is not prescribed in the treaty. The failure to specify consequences for failure to agree on conservation measures for high seas fishing, the uncertain extent of the coastal state's superior right, and the absence of express enforcement measures beyond the EEZ -- all these contribute to a situation of high uncertainty and growing dissatisfaction.

At the final session of UNCLOS III in April 1982, a coalition of states led by Canada and including Australia, Cape Verde, Iceland, Philippines, Sao Tome and Principe, Senegal and Sierra Leone introduced a compromise proposal...on the issue of straddling stocks, which sought to link failure to agree on conservation measures to the compulsory dispute settlement procedures included in the Convention. Failure to agree, in this case, would mean that the Law of the Sea Tribunal would determine the necessary conservation measures. Not surprisingly, distant-water fishing states strongly resisted this proposal and, given the fact that the Convention was nearing final approval, it was withdrawn by its sponsors. Since that time, as disagreements arise about excessive fishing outside the EEZ on common stocks, conflict on this issue has been heating up at sea and pressures have been building within coastal states to extend their jurisdiction beyond 200 miles to protect the stocks in question.

The most important conflicts are currently occurring in the Northwest Atlantic, the Southwest Atlantic, the East Central and Southeast Pacific, and in the Northeast Pacific (Bering Sea). Since some states are parties, either directly or indirectly, to several or all of these conflicts, there are definite connections between them in a policy sense.

---

[3] Reprinted by permission of the Journal of Ocean Development and International Law.

[The authors consider each of these problem areas. However, we shall deal here only with the Bering Sea problem.]

The facts are that since 1984 Japanese-directed fishing for pollock...in the U.S. zone in the Eastern Bering Sea has been phased out. In response, the Japanese rapidly increased their fishing effort on pollock in the international area of the Central Bering Sea, popularly known as the "Doughnut Hole." The Japanese reported catch in the "Doughnut Hole" jumped from 135,000 mt. in 1985 to 695,000 mt. in 1986 and 802,646 mt. in 1987, with more than 90 Japanese vessels operating. This catch, combined with those of other fleets operating in the area, led to an agreed estimate of total catch in 1986 of 1 million mt. and in 1987 of a total catch of close to 1.3 mt.

The U.S. industry concerned, and the North Pacific Fishery Management Council, assert that these stocks of pollock are straddling stocks and that such a high level of effort and catch adversely affects the recruitment and catch levels on pollock in the U.S. EEZ. In contrast, the Japanese industry contend that these pollock stocks are completely independent of other stocks in the U.S. EEZ, since pollock stock structure in the Bering Sea as a whole consists of essentially six independent subpopulations. Neither side in fact yet has the data to support either position conclusively, and the issue is complicated by dramatic confirmation of significant Japanese illegal fishing in the U.S. zone. Clamor by U.S. interest groups for punitive action has escalated rapidly, but here serious complications are encountered by both the United States and the USSR.

This disagreement, though the most recent of all, is the most ominous since it casts both the USA and the USSR in the role of coastal states versus Japan, China, ROK, Poland, Taiwan, and potentially others. Consequently, this situation is a potential trigger that can release repercussions severely destabilizing to the United Nations Convention of 1982 depending on the policy choices made by the coastal states.

Important fishing interests in both coastal states, and especially in the United States, seem to be pushing hard for unilateral or bilateral extensions of jurisdiction on legal grounds that are questionable or nonexistent. But, were either or both coastal states to extend jurisdiction, this would put intolerable pressure on the Canadian government to do the same. It would be difficult for Canada to resist these pressures indefinitely, and Canadian action, combined with super power action, would most probably stimulate similar moves elsewhere.

Within the United States, the relevant industry group, the North Pacific Council, and their congressional allies, claiming that the issue is one of straddling stock management and that emergency action is needed, called for unilateral U.S. extension of jurisdiction beyond 200 miles. When this was rejected by the United States, reportedly based on objections by the Defense Department and the Legal Advisor's Office of the Department of State, the U.S. industry coalition fell back to a demand for joint US/USSR extensions of jurisdiction and for declaring the "Doughnut Hole" a sanctuary in which no fishing would be permitted. This recommendation was never officially adopted by the U.S. government (although a nonbinding resolution calling for a moratorium was passed by the Senate), but the United States did invite the Soviets to consider jointly what response could be taken.

Recognizing the need for better data on the stocks, the USA and the Soviet Union agreed to seek more information on pollock stock structure in the Central Bering Sea and an international meeting was quickly convened on the status of pollock stocks. Beyond this, the complications are considerable for both parties because each is constrained by conflicts of interest. For instance, if the United States declares that these are straddling stocks and that the United States has superior or dominant rights concerning their use and conservation, the same principle may be invoked against U.S. vessels fishing in the NAFO Convention area beyond 200 miles. Similarly, the USSR cannot espouse this straddling stock hypothesis withour facing the prospect of its application to the Soviet Bloc fleets off Chile and Argentina. As a result, fisheries elements in both governments seek alternative approaches to managing fisheries beyond 200 miles.

The approach that was reportedly explicitly considered, and that has so far been rejected, calls for the invocation of Article 123 on enclosed and semi-enclosed seas of the UN Convention. Proponents in both the USSR and the USA apparently seek to use Article 123 as a basis for joint control of foreign fishing in the "Doughnut Hole" by the coastal States. Unfortunately for this hypothesis, Article 123 does not provide any rights to coastal states beyond those already available in the EEZ or territorial sea. If Article 123 were used to mask impermissible extensions of coastal state jurisdiction beyond 200 miles to protect fisheries by a superpower, it would also call into question all the other protections of superpower navigational interests in the UN Convention. One would expect, therefore, that member states of CPPS, plus Mexico, Argentina, Canada, and indeed all other coastal states, share a keen interest in the ways in which the USA and USSR seek to resolve this problem.

....

A Proposed Approach

How might such an arrangement be crafted? Let us first consider the applicable international law.

The key initial question is what authority exists for the USA and the USSR, as states bordering the Bering Sea, to take conservation action within the central Bering Sea affecting high seas fishing by foreign vessels fishing for groundfish. Could these states, separately or together, lawfully declare that the foreign fishing in the "Doughnut Hole" must terminate or that it must be limited to a particular quantity of fish, or number of days, or to the use of certain gear? Or, for example, that special provisions must be observed to protect marine mammals or other incidental catch and that these measures will be enforced by the bordering states?

An initial alternative is to consider what obligations high seas fishing states have regarding conservation of the resources they exploit in the high seas. Exploration of this alternative is in two parts. The first part assumes that such resources are found and occur only beyond any area of national jurisdiction. It is further assumed that international law on this question is found in the 1982 Convention. The obligations derived from the Convention, Part VII, Section 2 are:

(1) To take necessary conservation measures (Art. 117);

(2) To cooperate with other states in taking such measures (Art. 117);

(3) To enter into negotiations with other states fishing the same or different resources in the same area "with a view to taking the measures necessary for the conservation of the living resources concerned" (Art. 118);

(4) Where appropriate, to cooperate in establishing fisheries organizations to facilitate taking the necessary conservation measures (Art. 118);

(5) To take measures "designed, on the best scientific evidence available to the states concerned, to maintain or restore populations of harvested species at levels which can produce the maximum sustainable yield, as qualified by relevant environment and economic factors..." (Art. 119);

(6) To contribute and exchange "available scientific information, catch and fishing effort statistics, and other data relevant to the conservation of the fish stocks" (Art. 119);

(7) To make such exchange through "competent international organizations, whether subregional, regional or global" (Art. 119);

(8) To ensure that the measures adopted are nondiscriminatory against the fishermen of any state (Art. 119).

States fishing on the high seas thus have substantial obligations to take measures to conserve fish stocks there and to cooperate with other states to that end. The most basic obligation is that of contributing and exchanging "basic scientific information, catch and fishing effort statistics, and other data relevant to conservation." The range of further cooperative action is as wide as the measure that might contribute to conservation including "negotiations with a view to taking" the necessary measures. Even if negotiations do not lead to agreed measures, an obligation would still apply to each fishing state to take unilaterally conceived measures affecting its own flag vessels.

If these obligations are owed, to whom are they owed? At least three recipients are possible: another state or states fishing on the high seas, the general community of states (as where no other states fish the stocks involved), and coastal states adjoining on the high seas area. It is conceivable that states of a region or subregion might be the beneficiaries of the obligation as well. If the fishery in question is subject to an international agreement, the fishing state may also have obligations arising from that agreement.

Although it is evident that high seas fishing states have conservation obligations and duties irrespective of the involvement of other states in the same area, certainly such obligations and duties may be invoked when the interests of other states are directly affected. According to Article 118, the several states fishing in an area have an obligation to each other regarding conservation. Any of these states might take measures to seek to secure the discharge of an obligation of another state. Nothing in the 1982 treaty or other customary law, however, authorizes one high seas fishing state to take action on the high seas to enforce a conservation obligation owed to it by another state. This does not mean that there is no recourse.

Diplomatic action (protests), domestic remedies (embargoes on fishery or other trade, refusal of access to ports for logistic support, denials of economic assistance, suspension of particular benefits), international sanctions (remedies available under international agreements, including trade agreements) are all possible instrumentalities. Whether any of these is available and, if so, feasible to employ is another question -- the point is that a state (including a high seas fishing state) whose interests are harmed by refusal of a high seas fishing state to take necessary conservation measures is not necessarily helpless. If the 1982 Convention on the Law of the Sea were in force and in effect between the states concerned, disputes about the applications of foreign high seas fishing woud be subject to compulsory dispute settlement proceedings in Part XV.

[The authors sum up that the provisions of the Convention calling for agreement on conservation measures. States must negotiate in good faith. If efforts at agreement are successful, the problem is solved, and if they are not successful, the superior position of the coastal state would permit it to prescribe its own conservation measures, demand that the fishing state comply, and go to compulsory dispute settlement in the event of noncompliance. The authors further suggest that states adopt a provision similar to one in the 1958 Convention requiring fishing states to enforce conservation measures against their own nationals.]

....

Were such an approach adopted, it would effectively settle the "Doughnut Hole" problem without prejudice to the strategic interests of the USA and USSR in global stability in the law of the sea.

[Finally, the authors address the problem of new entries. New entries are states who had not previously fished for the stock or stocks in question. The authors take the position that if a new entry refuses to take part in a conservation scheme or ignores conservation regulations, as a last resort the coastal state may take unspecified "unilateral action". The authors concede that this "may appear to go somewhat beyond existing international law".]

* * * *

At this point, you may wish to recall the materials on the Presential Sea.

G. MARINE MAMMALS AND GATT

Upon occasion, law of the sea issues become entangled with and in conflict with other seemingly unrelated areas of international and domestic law. A very recent example involves the imposition of an embargo on imports of tuna from certain countries, in accordance with U.S. law, for failure to adhere to international fisheries agreements. A panel convened at the request of Mexico by GATT held that such an embargo was an illegal barrier to trade under the GATT rules. The following article discusses the most recent attempt to resolve the problem.

PRESIDENT SIGNS TUNA-DOLPHIN MORATORIUM LEGISLATION, Oceans Policy News, Vol. IX, No. 11, November 1992

On 26 October 1992, President Bush signed into law H.R. 5419, the International Dolphin Conservation Act of 1992 (the "Act") (P.L.102-523). With the support of the Administration and interested environmental organizations, the Act had previously passed both Houses of Congress with broad bi-partisan support.

H.R. 5419 provides for a global moratorium on the catching of tuna by encircling dolphins and other marine mammals. This fishing technique, which uses large purse-seine nets, was developed originally by the San Diego-based U.S. tuna industry to take advantage of the little-understood relationship between tuna (other than albacore tuna) and dolphins in the Eastern Tropical Pacific Ocean, as a result of which tuna often school beneath dolphins. It has since been adopted by the international tuna industry.

The Marine Mammal Protection Act (MMPA), 16 USC 1361 et seq, was passed in 1972 to address the significant dolphin mortality that results from the fishing technique of "setting on" dolphins, but did not anticipate that, even as mortality from U.S. operations declined, the problem would become international in scope as other nations' fleets adopted the technique. NOAA's National Marine Fisheries Service has estimated that in excess of 6 million dolphins have been killed as a result of U.S. and foreign tuna-fishing operations since 1959. See, 57 FR 27010 (17 June 1992). As a result of concerns over rising international dolphin mortality, the MMPA's embargo provisions were amended in 1984 (P.L. 98-364) to require that each nation exporting yellowfin tuna to the U.S. provide proof that it had reduced dolphin mortality to levels "comparable" to those achieved by the intensively regulated

U.S. fleet, and again in 1988 (P.L. 100-711) to clarify the standards that would apply to determine if an embargo was warranted.

Efforts to enforce the amended embargo provisions initiated a long and somewhat arduous path through the judicial system. A federal court ordered in August 1990 an embargo on the importation of tuna from Mexico, Venezuela, Vanuatu, Panama and Ecuador. In September 1990, the embargo was lifted for Mexico, Venezuela and Vanuatu, but then reimposed for Mexico and Venezuela in October 1990. A stay of the embargo, issued by a federal appeals court in November 1990, was lifted but the embargo again went into effect with respect to Mexico on 22 February 1991 and with respect to Venezuela on 26 March 1991. Panama and Ecuador have now prohibited their fleets from setting on dolphin and are no longer affected by the embargo; the embargo against Vanuatu was lifted in January 1992. Also in 1992, imports from Colombia became subject to an embargo and "secondary embargoes" were ordered against twenty "intermediary nations" which ship tuna products to the U.S. All but five of these "secondary embargoes" have now been lifted. See Earth Island Institute v. Mosbacher, 785 F.Supp. 826 (N.D. Cal. 1992), and related cases.

Mexico requested, in January 1991, that a GATT Panel rule on the GATT-consistency of the U.S. embargo. The Panel ruled in September 1991 that the U.S. embargo was inconsistent with GATT because, among other things, the GATT does not permit its contracting parties to maintain GATT-inconsistent measures for the purpose of protecting the life or health of animals beyond its jurisdiction. The dolphin in question are killed principally in the Eastern Tropical Pacific Ocean, an area of the Pacific Ocean designated by international agreement and lying in international waters.

The Panel's ruling is, under GATT practice, preliminary in nature, and Mexico has not yet sought to force its adoption by the GATT Council. However, certain EC countries are also subject to a secondary embargo and the EC has also sought a GATT Panel on the embargo question, which will likely reach a similar conclusion. Adoption of either Panel decision would place the U.S. marine mammal protection framework -- and the enforcement of a number of other environmental statutes and agreements -- at variance with GATT.

Principal Features of the Act

The Act was proposed by the Administration, and approved by Congress, in an effort to avoid the necessity of confronting head-on the implications of the GATT Panel decision for the U.S. marine mammal program, while addressing the immediate problems created for those nations, such as Mexico, denied access to U.S. markets by the embargo. The Administration's proposal followed consultations with Mexico regarding the steps necessary to lift the embargo without altering the basic provisions of the MMPA. Mexico needed some assurance that the embargo issue could be resolved while agreeing not to press its case in the GATT, and the U.S. needed assurance that the adoption of the unpopular GATT decision would be deferred while a solution acceptable to the Congress and the U.S. environmental community was worked out.

At first glance the Act appears to offer a solution acceptable to all the parties. Its principal features are as follows:

1. *Global Moratorium*. The Act authorizes the Secretary of State to negotiate and enter into international agreements providing for a five-year moratorium on the practice of encircling dolphin with purse-seine nets in order to catch tuna. Thne moratorium would go into effect on 1 March 1994. Signatory countries would be required to participate in an international research program and take all necessary and appropriate steps to ensure compliance with the moratorium, while encouraging other countries to do so as well. U.S. compliance with the moratorium could be terminated only upon recommendation of the Secretary of State and a joint resolution of Congress.

2. *Lifting of the Current Embargo*. The Act prohibits the Secretary of Treasury from imposing a tuna embargo on any country that commits to enter into the 5-year moratorium in 1994 and agrees, in the meantime, to achieve significant reductions in tuna (sic) mortality in both 1992 and 1993. Any country making this commitment will be free of any MMPA embargo unless the Secretary of Treasury determines that it has failed to implement its commitments. The Act provides for a two-tiered response in the event of such a determination. First, the embargo is reinstated with respect to imports of that country's yellowfin tuna products. Then, if the country does not certify within 60 days its full compliance with its commitments, the statute authorizes a sanction banning 40% of the previous year's imports with respect to any fish or fish product categories.

3. *U.S. Domestic Ban*. The Act further amends the MMPA to prohibit the sale in the U.S. of "dolphin-unsafe tuna" after 1 June 1994, and commits the U.S. tuna fleet to progressive reductions in dolphin mortality, to approach zero by the end of 1999 even if no other country joins the U.S. in the moratorium.

4. *Redefinition of "Intermdiary Nation*." The Act creates a statutory definition of the term "intermediary nation" which permits the U.S. to ameliorate, but not entirely remove, the problems associated with the "secondary embargo" on nations that transship, but do not engage in fishing for, yellowfin tuna. The new defition includes only those countries that transship yellowfin tuna that is directly subject to a primary embargo (i.e., tuna from Mexico, Venezuela and Colombia). It also excludes any country that certifies that it has not shipped such tuna for 6 months.

As a result of this change, the National Marine Fisheries Service announced on 30 October 1992 that it had instructed the Customs Service to lift the embargo with respect to 6 nations: Canada, Colombia (as to the secondary embargo only, the primary embargo remains), Malaysia, Netherlands Antilles, Singapore and the United Kingdom. The "secondary" embargo remains in effect for only 5 nations: Costa Rica, France, Italy, Japan and Spain.

Prospects for the Future

One of the purposes of the Act was to remove a substantial irritant in trade between the U.S. and Mexico at a time when the Bush Administration was seeking to solidify and expand these relations through the North American Free Trade Agreement ("NAFTA"). However, whether the Act will ultimately be successful in this regard remains to be seen. During its consideration by the Congress, the Inter-American Tropical Tuna Commission ("IATTC") concluded a multilateral agreement calling for substantial reductions in dolphin mortality in the Eastern Tropical Pacific through 1999.

Although Mexico is not a member of the IATTC, it formally ratified the IATTC agreement, which includes provision for substantial research on dolphin-safe fishing techniques and for 100 percent IATTC observer coverage (but does not prohibit setting on dolphins as a fishing technique). These measures will impact heavily on Mexico's tuna fleet, and Mexico may resist the 1994 moratorium required by the Act as a precondition to lifting the current embargo. Mexico has criticized the Act's embargo provisions as going beyond what it had agreed to in principle at the outset of the legislative process. These criticisms may reflect a substantial stiffening of Mexico's position. Further negotiations are likely over these issues, and will possibly occur even as Congress considers the NAFTA during 1993.

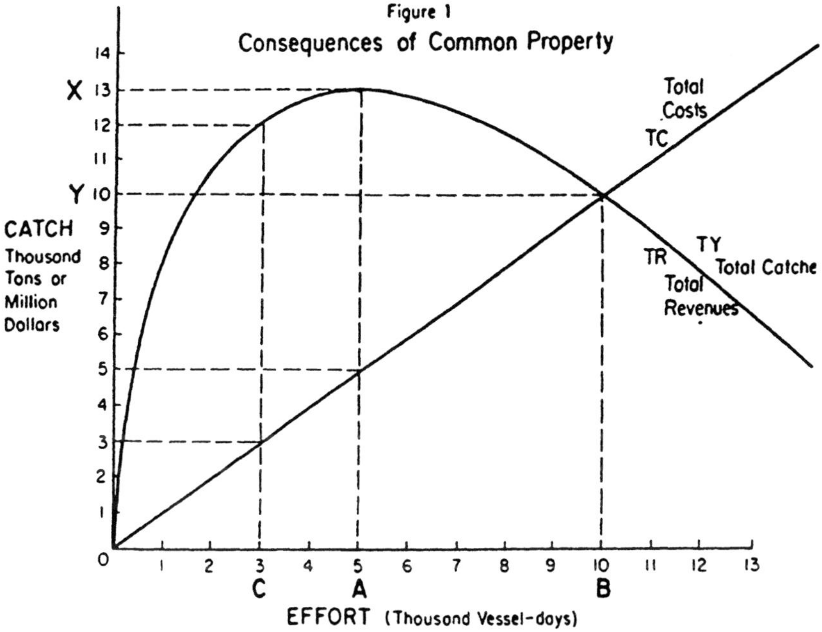

Figure 1
Consequences of Common Property

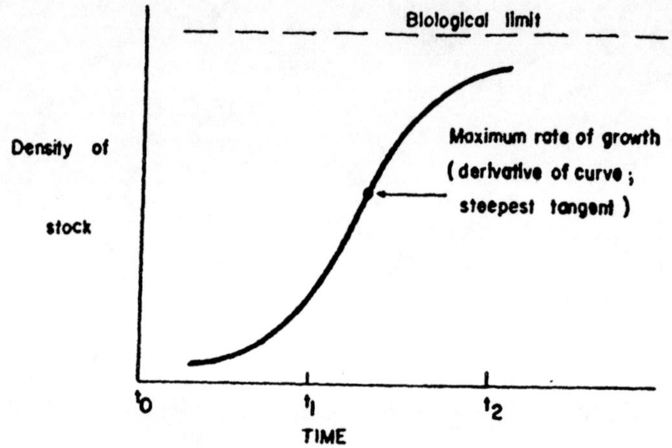
Biological limit
Density of
stock
Maximum rate of growth
(derivative of curve;
steepest tangent)
t_0
t_1
t_2
TIME

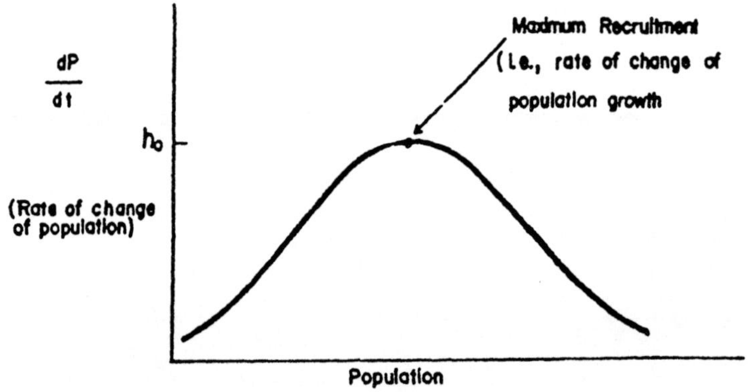
Maximum Recruitment
(i.e., rate of change of
population growth
$\frac{dP}{dt}$
h_0
(Rate of change
of population)
Population

CHAPTER 10

MARINE SCIENTIFIC RESEARCH

A. INTRODUCTION

Before examining the international law regarding the conduct of marine scientific research, it is a good idea to have a perspective on the information and uses that such research generates. In reading the materials in this chapter, keep in mind that the products of scientific research in the oceans can be utilized in many different ways. The academic researcher is interested only in obtaining data to be able to better understand the marine environment and to predict its behavior. The data developed by such research, however, has implications for resource extraction and military uses as well. Thus it is possible to understand the suspicion among developing countries about what all this information is being used for. This translates, as we shall see, into the difficulty in defining marine scientific research in a way that could remove that suspicion. But first, a look at what marine researchers, in the academic sense, do. While this material is a little lengthy it is helpful. It tells us what the marine scientists are interested in and why they think its important. It also highlights how little, despite many years of sophisticated research, scientists really know about the oceans.

B. GOALS OF MARINE SCIENTIFIC RESEARCH

OPPORTUNITIES IN OCEANOGRAPHIC RESEARCH, Report on the Panel on Oceanography, President's Science Advisory Committee (1966) 41-54

OBSERVATION

Until recently oceanographic observations could be characterized as being exploratory in nature. Expeditions were undertaken, usually with a single ship, to survey unknown regions or observe special phenomena discovered on an earlier expedition. Exploratory surveys have frequently provided new information which has been useful in asking questions of critical scientific importance but not so often in answering them. Another consequence of the emphasis given to exploratory observation is that oceanographers have been physically and intellectually isolated from their colleagues in basic disciplines and in other geophysical sciences.

In recent years exploratory observations, although they still dominate oceanography, have begun to yield more systematic observations designed for specific purposes. There are a number of reasons for this change.

First, there is a growing awareness that the most challenging scientific problems encompass two or more of the environmental sciences. For example, oceanic circulation cannot be understood apart from atmospheric circulation, nor can atmospheric circulation be predicted for periods of more than a few days without considering the ocean. Development of a theory of climate will require treating the oceans and atmosphere as a thoroughly interacting system. The complexities of the interactions are illustrated by the process of sedimentation on the bottom of the sea. These processes are governed by physical and biological conditions within the volume of the oceans, which depend on the interaction of the oceans and the atmosphere.

Second, new platforms and sensors are becoming available which permit new observations.

Acoustic and electromagnetic probes make possible remote sensing, "swallow" floats give unequivocal records of subsurface currents, thermistor chains can furnish continuous records of temperature distribution and "hot wires" provide information about the turbulent spectrum. Many other examples could be cited.

Third, developments in data processing and methods of data analysis represent major advances. Telemetering techniques provide vast quantities of data far beyond that available a decade ago, and the newer computers permit systematic analysis of these data and facilitate study of mathematical models by integration of governing differential equations. A consequence of these new capabilities in data processing and analysis is that quantitative determinations are begining to replace qualitative and intuitive accounts which characterized geophysical sciences a few years ago. For example, direct measurement of vertical flux and wind stress can now be made by spectral analysis of fluctuations. New insights into the mechanism of nonlinear coupling, made possible by computer technology, have contributed significantly to theories of wave generation and motions of a variety of scales.

These developments in observational techniques, data processing, and interpretation have proved equally valuable in studies of the oceans, atmosphere, and solid earth. A strong coupling of research among various fields of geophysics exists. There is a basic commonality in obsevational platforms, techniques of analysis and underlying theory. A fruitful idea in one field is likely to be equally profitable in other geophysical fields. Thus, broadly trained, creative scientists may provide crucial leadership in several fields simultaneously.

A close connection also exists between geophysical and biological problems, despite the fact that these connections have often been overlooked. Certain regions owe their great biological productivity to subtle combinations of chemical and physical processes which vitally need to be understood. Oceanographers are well aware of the importance of these relationships, and in the future we see a closer relationship between biological and physical studies of the sea. This will be especially important as modification of the environment becomes more widespread.

Our new abilities to observe and interpret the environment have brought within the range of possibility a number of major scientific and technological enterprises. These require increased understanding of systems far more complex than those which can be studied in the laboratory. Consequently, they are of the highest intrinsic scientific interest, as well as great practical importance.

PREDICTION

We are in the very early stages of developing the capability for ocean prediction. Until World War II ocean predictions were limited to truly periodic phenomena whose mechanism was clearly understood -- tides and seasons. Tidal predictions are still imperfect, and improvements based on more complete treatment of nonlinear effects and transients associated with surface winds and pressures are within reach.

In the past two decades methods have been devised for:

(a) Prediction of surface waves based on observations and predictions of surface wind distribution.

(b) Warnings of tsunamis produced by earthquakes which are readily detected at great distances.

These methods have proved vital for safety and economy in coastal areas, in commercial shipping and for many military operations. Further improvement in wave prediction is tied clsely to atmospheric prediction, for which atmospheric observations over the oceans are required. In a similar way prediction of the depth of the surface mixed layer, still in its early stages, is closely tied to the meteorological problem. Understanding the process occurring in the surface mixed layer is important for acoustic transmission applications within the sea and for marine biological problems.

We have reason to think that these phenomena, for which rather simple prediction methods are available, fail to encompass other characteristic, important features of the ocean. From the fragmentary evidence we have at present, it appears that a wide range of time-dependent phenomena do indeed occur in the ocean, as our experience with stratified fluids in the laboratory or in the atmosphere would lead us to expect. Ocean weather may be as varied and complex as the weather in the atmosphere. For example, we see indications of internal gravity waves, inertial motions associated with the earth's rotation, turbulence, meanders in the Gulf Stream and other currents and fluctuations in surface temperatures over large areas; but we have not yet adequately described any of these phenomena. Whether current systems occur which are comparable in size to atmospheric planetary waves remains to be discovered. The extent to which prediction of these phenomena is inherently feasible and for what scales of time and space remains unknown; these problems appear destined to become some of the most exciting objectives of ocean research in the next decade. The answers are not obvious, for although the governing differential equations are well known, we do not know the strength of coupling between observable and unobservable scales.

We do know, however, that lack of ocean surface-layer observations restricts effective atmospheric prediction to a few days.

Until the prediction problem is better understood, the potentialities of deliberate ocean modification cannot be determined. Without such understanding, large-scale experiments addressed to diverting ocean currents, to melting the Arctic ice or to overturning large regions of ocean water would be extravagant and highly irresponsible. However, inadvertant modification of coastal areas, already of local concern, is likely to become more serious. In order to plan wisely for use and development of coastal areas we must learn to predict such effects as increased pollution, changes in coastlines, and deepening of harbors.

Finally, a remark should be made concerning the space and scale of ocean observations envisioned by this Panel. For the present and for the foreseeable future ocean observations should be undertaken as research and development programs, specifications closely linked to objectives and with results linked to subsequent planning. The first stages should be distinctly limited in scope and areal extent; but one should anticipate observational systems covering very large areas. It will be necessary to establish and maintain numbers of observing platforms in, on and above the sea. Reliable communication systems of considerable complexity will be needed. Furthermore, the inherently global nature of many scientific problems will require support of research on a larger and more stable basis than has been the case heretofore.

PHYSICAL PROCESSES

A catalog on research problems in physical oceanograpy captures neither the flavor nor the intellectual quality of scientific challenges posed by the oceans. For example in the ocean bottom a well-documented history of our planet is recorded, perhaps containing far more information about the early stages of evolution of our planet and the solar system than on the moon's scarred surface. The oceans are a giant laboratory for fluid dynamics, which illustrates the full complexity of hydrodynamics. The oceans, in turn, interact with both the solid earth and atmosphere in direct and subtle ways, and one can never hope to gain a comprehensive understanding from study limited to the oceans themselves.

We will not compose a detailed framework of oceanographic research nor catalog the variety of work in progress at existing institutions. Instead, we will concentrate on defining specific, new types of large-scale projects not yet underway which seem to offer great potential for increased knowledge. The emphasis on large-scale projects in this section does not imply that progress in oceanography can be achieved only in this way. The large-scale projects originate through the efforts of individual researchers seeking answers to problems posed by theoretical, laboratory or small-scale observational studies.

Benthic Boundary. At the bottom of the deep ocean there is a transition from fluid, to fluid with suspended particles, to solid insterstitial fluid, to solid. The detailed nature of this boundary is unknown, as well as whether its characteristics result primarily from physical or biological processes. An understanding of this boundary is essential in order to solve such problems as long-range transmission of powerful sonars, occupation at the bottom in permanent or semi-permanent structures and search for objects at or near the bottom. The study of the benthic boundary is now possible because of the development of recording devices and probes which measure temperature, velocity, and pressure fluctuations at great depths.

This benthic boundary is a base for studying the earth below. Beneath the oceans the earth's crust is thin, and environmental conditions for measurement are quiet. A recent surprising discovery is that standard geophyisical methods of exploration (seismic, gravimetric, magnetic, and geothermal) yield better results than on land. The greater technical difficulties of working on the sea bottom are more than compensated by advantages of a uniform environment. There remains, of course, great ambiguity about the deeper material. This can only be resolved by coring the sediments and the layer beneath.

An opportunity exists for adapting other geophysical techniques developed on land for marine use. For example, measurements on the sea bottom of the fluctuating electric and magnetic fields at various frequencies could provide information about the variation of conductivity with depth; from this, one can, in principle infer temperature and ultimately horizontal stresses between oceans and continents. Our understanding of mountain making and of the very existence of oceans and continents depends on assessment of stresses at the margins of basins.

It is now possible to make deep-ocean tide measurements from instruments lowered to the seabed. Theories of the origin of the moon depend critically on the efficacy of tides in disposing of the mechanical energy of the earth-moon system. Do tides in the solid earth slow down the earth's rotation and move the moon outward or are the ocean tides responsible? Additional tidal measurements on a global scale are required in order to settle the problem.

Further understanding of the benthic boundary depends on continued development of instruments operable at great depths. Many observational programs require data-collection over long periods of time, and substantial technological problems exist in collecting these data. Furthermore, the ocean bottom is not uniform, and isolated observations are unlikely to yield a proper view. We can thus expect continuing expansion of measurements on a global scale. The opportunity exists for perhaps solving an important cosmological problem, and we recommend that tidal measurements be made for many parts of the oceans to determine once and for all the nature and magnitude of oceanic tidal friction.

The Abyssal Ocean. The deep distribution of oceanic variables (temperature, salinity, current, etc.), and planktonic and sedimentary particles appears to be determined by upwelling and turbulent fluxes. The most urgent need is for observational studies of the turbulent mixing processes. A thorough, well-planned effort to study the turbulent microstructure of the main thermocline would provide insight on the general circulation of the oceans, global weather and climatic fluctuations as well. It is intolerable that direct measurements of turbulent fluxes at depth are not being attempted. In our judgment this is within present-day technological capability but might require substantial engineering. A few pioneering studies made with sensors mounted on submarines and lowered by wire from surface vessels have shown fascinating microstructures. Submarines are essential to the study of water under ice sheets. This cold water, of high salinity and density, eventually becomes the water at the greatest depths. The development of the bottom water remains largely unkown.

....

Buoy Programs. During the past few years several draft plans have been submitted to international bodies for oceanwide observational programs employing dozens of ships extending over several years -- purportedly to study variability of ocean circulation. To us they have seemed ill-designed from the standpoint of sampling, because we believe it would be better to study smaller scales and higher frequencies first, even though these do not provide busywork for fleets of oceanographic vessels. In fact instrumented buoys seem better adapted to variability studies, although ships will, of course, be necessary to service them.

To date, use of moored buoys has been largely limited to efforts of individuals who, lacking the resources, logistic support, and necessary organization, have been unable to maintain dense enough arrays for a long enough time to gather statistically significant data.... Oceanographers need to evolve some fairly elaborate measuring arrays, with limited regions heavily instrumented. They are in the position of radio astronomers who need a radio telescope of a novel design, a facility quite beyond the capability of a single individual to design, build and operate. The oceanographic community has been too concerned with conventional research and fund-raising and has devoted insufficient attention to exciting new scientific projects such as a viable buoy program.

....

BIOLOGICAL PROCESSES

....

The Panel believes that marine biology must be regarded in broad terms. Specifically, marine biology embraces four major areas of research:

1. Animal and plant populations and their interaction with each other and the ocean.

2. The unique characteristics of diverse marine organisms that enable them to survive in the ocean.

3. Utilization of marine organisms as unique experimental material for investigation of biomedical problems.

4. The processes and factors involved in food production from the sea.

....

Populations in the Sea. The conversion of photosynthetic plants to animal protein on land is relatively well understood. In the sea, however, photosynthetic plants are restricted largely to microscopic planktonic algae (phytoplankton); conversion to animals large enough to serve as food for man usually involves many intermediate steps. Our knowledge of the complex and diverse food chains and food webs of the sea is very sparse. The natural foods of even the best-known marine animal species are unknown except in general terms. Central and prerequisite to scientific control and ultimate management of marine food resources is further knowledge of essential nutritional requirements, of feeding habits and food preferences, and of efficiency in converting planktonic algae to animal protein.

Plants and Photosynthesis. Photosynthetic plants in the sea and on land use solar energy to synthesize organic matter from inorganic materials. In agriculture, solar energy is channeled into production of plants that are useful to mankind, either directly as plant products or indirectly as animal food. Growth of plants in the sea, on the other hand, is a process over which we have no control and little knowledge. Some species of planktonic algae are recognized as food organisms for marine animals; others are "weed" species of little or no nutritional value; still others, such as "red tide" organisms, are noxious or lethal to marine life. To increase significantly the amount of food obtained from the sea, we must learn to control the kinds of phytoplankton produced as the primary food source. Expanded and intensified programs in marine microbiology in its broadest sense, including both laboratory and field studies, are needed to provide fundamental background and practical experience.

Environmental Studies. Although human intervention is increasingly affecting natural populations of organisms, very little is known about environmental conditions that govern these populations in nature. Without adequate knowledge it is difficult to predict the effects of human intervention or to define proper procedures for management and exploitation. The complexity of the marine environment has limited the rate of progress in understanding.

....

[For example,] [i]f a sea level canal is opened across Central America, many biological problems of great potential consequence will emerge. A number of species have close relatives on opposite sides of the present land mass which has existed for 80 million years. These closely related species show different amounts of divergence. What will happen if the barrier is breached so that organisms can move between oceans through such a canal? Will changing selection pressures and competition eliminate species? Will closely related species interbreed and form a hybrid population or remain separate with, perhaps, accompanying changes in their genetic, physiological, behavioral, and populations characteristics? Will present populations resist invasions unchanged, or will serious disruptions occur, accompanied by violent oscillations in the composition and abundance of species?

....

Biomedical Applications. Our present understanding of many biomedical problems is based largely upon research initially conducted on lower organisms. The insights so afforded are valid because many biological processes of most kinds of organisms are fundamentally alike. Understanding of mammalian genetics stems in part from research on insects amd micro-organisms; our understanding of human biochemistry derives from studies of lower animals and plants; and many of our present insights into the phenomena of fertilization and embryonic development are derived primarily from investigations of marine organisms.

....

The list of pharmacologically active substances extracted from marine organisms is expanding as more investigators enter this virtually untapped field of research in natural products. With development of biochemical analyses and refined techniques for cultivating many marine organisms that produce chemicals which may prove to be of medical importance, the time is now ripe for intensified research in marine biochemistry and pharmacology.

....

ED. NOTE: The above excerpts tell us much about how academic marine scientists view the importance of their work. They are looking at the use of marine scientific research to attack sometimes global problems, such as weather prediction and modification, or earthquake warning systems, or the production of food and medicines. Were that the only perception of marine scientists, the negotiation of treaty provisions providing for broad freedom of access for such scientists into the various zones of coastal State jurisdiction would have been no problem. Unfortunately for them, the nations involved were quite aware that data from marine scientific research could be put to commercial and/or military uses.

It seems obvious, therefore, that an initial task for the negotiators was to draft a definition of marine scientific research that would distinguish, and treat differently, so-called "pure" scientific research from "applied" scientific research. That task, however, was not so simple. Most proposed definitions were overly broad. Consider the following suggestions.

NETHERLANDS

Marine scientific research is any study of and related experimental work in the marine environment excluding industrial exploration and other activities aimed at the direct exploitation of marine resources, designed to increase man's knowledge and conducted for peaceful purposes.

SUDAN

Marine scientific research is any study and related experimental work conducted in the interest of peace and human welfare and aimed at increasing mankind's knowledge.

SPAIN

Marine scientific research means any study and related experimental work designed to increase mankind's knowledge of the marine environment.

EGYPT

Scientific research lends itself to all investigations dealing with natural phenomena in the marine environment and the atmosphere thereabove, as well as to promotion of methodology for abatement of marine pollution and other abnormalities. Scientific research is contradictory to all non-peaceful aspects, and does not cover activities aimed at the direct exploitation of the marine resources.

* * * *

In considering the provisions of the treaty that actually emerged from the negotiations, you will note that the regime is quite restrictive. Given that fact, can you think of any reason why a major researching State that is also a major maritime power, such as the United States, would be uncomfortable with any of those proposed definitions? Also take note of the fact that the chapter on marine scientific research contains no definition at all.

In the 1958 Conventions there was very little mention of marine scientific research.

CONVENTION ON THE CONTINENTAL SHELF

Article 5

1. The exploration of the continental shelf and the exploitation of its natural resources must not...result in any interference with fundamental oceanographic or other scientific research carried out with the intention of open publication.

.....

8. The consent of the coastal State shall be obtained in respect of any research concerning the continental shelf and undertaken there. Nevertheless, the coastal State shall not normally withhold its consent if the request is submitted by a qualified institution with a view to purely scientific research into the physical or biological characteristics of the continental shelf, subject to the proviso that the coastal State shall have the right, if it so desires, to particpate or be represented in the research, and that in any event the results shall be published.

C. THE CONDUCT OF MARINE SCIENTIFIC RESEARCH UNDER THE 1982 CONVENTION

As previously noted, developing coastal States were deeply suspicious of the motives of marine scientists, in part due to the fact that many of the smaller States lacked any significant scientific infrastructure, and their negotiators, lacking scientific input, had little if any ability to understand the problems faced by marine scientists in carrying out their investigations. Furthermore, some States' suspicions were only fueled by the knowledge that in the United States and the then Soviet Union, much of the cost of conducting research activities was borne by the military (in the case of the U.S., the National Science Foundation and the Office of Naval Research). While marine scientists valiantly struggled for complete freedom to conduct marine scientific research in the oceans, it was not possible to negotiate such a regime. This was despite the distribution of many excellent papers prepared by them explaining the need to have maximum access to the entire fluid system of the oceans. Now, let us examine the regime that emerged.

1982 UNITED NATIONS CONVENTION ON THE LAW OF THE SEA

PART XIII

SECTION 1. GENERAL PROVISIONS

Article 238

Right to conduct marine scientific research

All States, irrespective of their geographical location, and competent international organizations have the right to conduct marine scientific research subject to the rights and duties of other States as provided for in this Convention.

Article 239

Promotion of marine scientific research

States and competent international organizations shall promote and facilitate the development of marine scientific research in accordance with this Convention.

Article 240

General principles for the conduct of marine scientific research

In the conduct of marine scientific research the following principles shall apply:

(a) marine scientific research shall be conducted exclusively for peaceful purposes;

(b) marine scientific research shall be conducted with appropriate scientific methods and means compatible with this Convention;

(c) marine scientific research shall not unjustifiably interfere with other legitimate uses of the sea compatible with this Convention and shall be duly respected in the course of such uses;

(d) marine scientific research shall be conducted in compliance with all relevant regulations adopted in conformity with this Convention including those for the protection and preservation of the marine environment.

Article 241

Non-recognition of marine scientific research activities as the legal basis for claims

Marine scientific research activities shall not constitute the legal basis for any claim to any part of the marine environment or its resources.

SECTION 2. INTERNATIONAL CO-OPERATION

Article 242

Promotion of international co-operation

1. States and competent international organizations shall, in accordance with the principle of respect for sovereignty and jurisdiction and on the basis of mutual benefit, promote international co-operation in marine scientific research for peaceful purposes.

2. In this context, without prejudice to the rights and duties of States under this Convention, a State, in the application of this Part, shall provide, as appropriate, other States with a reasonable opportunity to obtain from it, or with its co-operation, information necessary to prevent and control damage to the health and safety of persons and to the marine environment.

Article 243

Creation of favourable conditions

States and competent international organizations shall co-operate, through the conclusion of bilateral and multilateral agreements, to create favourable conditions for the conduct of marine scientific research in the marine environment and to integrate the efforts of scientists in studying the essence of phenomena and processes occurring in the marine environment and the interrelationships between them.

Article 244

Publication and dissemination of information and knowledge

1. States and competent international organizations shall, in accordance with this Convention, make available by publication and dissemination through appropriate channels information on proposed major programmes and their objectives as well as knowledge resulting from marine scientific research.

2. For this purpose, States, both individually and in co-operation with other States and with competent international organizations, shall actively promote the flow of scientific data and information and the transfer of knowledge resulting from marine scientific research, especially to the developing States, as well as the strengthening of the autonomous marine scientific research capabilities of developing States through, *inter alia*, programmes to provide adequate education and training of their technical and scientific personnel.

SECTION 3. CONDUCT AND PROMOTION OF MARINE SCIENTIFIC RESEARCH

Article 245

Marine scientific research in the territorial sea

Coastal States, in the exercise of their sovereignty, have the exclusive right to regulate, authorize and conduct marine scientific research in their territorial sea. Marine scientific research therein shall be conducted only with the express consent of and under the conditions set forth by the coastal State.

Article 246

Marine scientific research in the exclusive economic zone and on the continental shelf

1. Coastal States, in the exercise of their jurisdiction, have the right to regulate, authorize and conduct marine scientific research in their exclusive economic zone and on their continental shelf in accordance with the relevant provisions of this Convention.

2. Marine scientific research in the exclusive economic zone and on the continental shelf shall be conducted with the consent of the coastal State.

3. Coastal States shall, in normal circumstances, grant their consent for marine scientific research projects by other States or competent international organizations in their exclusive economic zone or on their continental shelf to be carried out in accordance with this Convention exclusively for peaceful purposes and in order to increase scientific knowledge of the marine environment for the

benefit of all mankind. To this end, coastal States shall establish rules and procedures ensuring that such consent will not be delayed or denied unreasonably.

4. For the purposes of applying paragraph 3, normal circumstances may exist in spite of the absence of diplomatic relations between the coastal State and the researching State.

5. Coastal States may however in their discretion withhold their consent to the conduct of a marine scientific research project of another State or competent international organization in the exclusive economic zone or on the continental shelf of the coastal State if that project:

(a) is of direct significance for the exploration and exploitaton of natural resources, whether living or non-living;

(b) involves drilling into the continental shelf, the use of explosives or the introduction of harmful substances into the marine environment;

(c) involves the construction, operation or use of artificial islands, installations and structures referred to in articles 60 and 80;

(d) contains information communicated pursuant to article 248 regarding the nature and objectives of the project which is inaccurate or if the researching State or competent international organization has outstanding obligations to the coastal State from a prior research project.

6. Notwithstanding the provisions of paragraph 5, coastal States may not exercise their discretion to withhold consent under subparagraph (a) of that paragraph in respect of marine scientific research projects to be undertaken in accordance with the provisions of this Part on the continental shelf, beyond 200 nautical miles from the baselines from which the breadth of the territorial sea is measured, outside those specific areas which coastal States may at any time publicly designate as areas in which exploitation or detailed exploratory operations focussed on those areas are occurring or will occur within a reasonable period of time. Coastal States shall give reasonable notice of the designation of such areas, as well as any modifications thereto, but shall not be obliged to give details of the operations therein.

7. The provisions of paragraph 6 are without prejudice to the rights of coastal States over the continental shelf as established in article 77.

8. Marine scientific research activities referred to in this article shall not unjustifiably interfere with activities undertaken by the coastal State in the exercise of their sovereign rights and jurisdiction provided for in this Convention.

Article 247

Marine scientific research projects undertaken by or under the auspices of international organizations

A coastal State which is a member of or has a bilateral agreement with an international organization, and in whose exclusive economic zone or on whose continental shelf that organization wishes to carry out a marine scientific research project, directly or under its auspices, shall be deemed to have authorized the project to be carried out in conformity with the agreed specifications if that State approved the detailed project when the decision was made by the organization for the undertaking of the project or is willing to participate in it, and has not expressed any objection within four months of notification of the project by the organization to the coastal State.

Article 248

Duty to provide information to the coastal State

States and competent international organizations which intend to undertake marine scientific research in the exclusive economic zone or on the continental shelf of a coastal State shall, not less than six months in advance of the expected starting date of the marine scientific research project, provide that State with a full description of:

(a) the nature and objectives of the project;

(b) the method and means to be used, including name, tonnage, type and class of vessels and a description of scientific equipment;

(c) the precise geographical areas in which the project is to be conducted;

(d) the expected date of first appearance and final departure of the research vessels, or deployment of the equipment and its removal, as appropriate;

(e) the name of the sponsoring institution, its director, and the person in charge of the project; and

(f) the extent to which it is considered that the coastal State should be able to participate or to be represented in the project.

Article 249

Duty to comply with certain conditions

1. States and competent international organizations when undertaking marine scientific research in the exclusive economic zone or on the continental shelf of a coastal State shall comply with the following conditions:

(a) ensure the right of the coastal State, if it so desires, to participate or be represented in the marine scientific research project, especially on board research vessels and other craft or scientific research installations, when practicable, without payment of any remuneration to the scientists of the coastal State and without obligation to contribute towards the costs of the project;

(b) provide the coastal State, at its request, with preliminary reports, as soon as practicable, and with the final results and conclusions after the completion of the research;

(c) undertake to provide access for the coastal State, at its request, to all data and samples derived from the marine scientific research project and likewise to furnish it with data which may be copied and samples which may be divided without detriment to their scientific value;

(d) if requested, provide the coastal State with an assessment of such data, samples and research results or provide assistance in their assessment or interpretation;

(e) ensure, subject to paragraph 2, that the research results are made internationally available through appropriate national or international channels, as soon as practicable;

(f) inform the coastal State immediately of any major change in the research programme;

(g) unless otherwise agreed, remove the scientific research installations or equipment once the research is completed.

2. This article is without prejudice to the conditions established by the laws and regulations of the coastal State for the exercise of its discretion to grant or withhold consent pursuant to article 246, paragraph 5, including requiring prior agreement for making internationally available the research results of a project of direct significance for the exploration and exploitation of natural resources.

Article 250

Communications concerning marine scientific research projects

Communications concerning the marine scientific research projects shall be made through appropriate official channels, unless otherwise agreed.

Article 251

General criteria and guidelines

States shall seek to promote through competent international organizations the establishment of general criteria and guidelines to assist States in ascertaining the nature and implications of marine scientific research.

Article 252

Implied consent

States or competent international organizations may proceed with a marine scientific research project six months after the date upon which the information required pursuant to article 248 was provided to the coastal State unless within four months of receipt of the communication containing such information the coastal State has informed the State or organization conducting the research that:

(a) it has withheld its consent under the provisions of article 246; or

(b) the information given by that State or competent international organization regarding the nature or objectives of the project does not conform to the manifestly evident facts; or

(c) it requires supplementary information relevant to conditions and the information provided for under articles 248 and 249; or

(d) outstanding obligations exist with respect to a previous marine scientific research project carried out by that State or organization, with regard to conditions established in article 249.

Article 253

Suspension or cessation of marine scientific research activities

1. A coastal State shall have the right to require the suspension of any marine scientific research activities in progress within its exclusive economic zone or on its continental shelf if:

(a) the research activities are not being conducted in accordance with the information communicated as provided under article 248 upon which the consent of the coastal State was based; or

(b) the State or competent international organization conducting the research activities fails to comply with the provisions of article 249 concerning the rights of the coastal State with respect to the marine scientific research project.

2. A coastal State shall have the right to require the cessation of any marine scientific research activities in case of any non-compliance with the provisions of 248 which amounts to a major change in the research project or the research activities.

3. a coastal State may also require the cessation of marine scientific research activities in any of the situations contemplated in paragraph 1 are not rectified within a reasonable period of time.

4. Following notification by the coastal State of its decision to order suspension or cessation, States or competent international organizations authorized to conduct marine scientific research activities shall terminate the research activities that are the subject of such a notification.

5. An order of suspension under paragraph 1 shall be lifted by the coastal State and the marine scientific research activities allowed to continue once the researching State or competent international organization has complied with the conditions required under articles 248 and 249.

Article 254

Rights of neighbouring land-locked and geographically disadvantaged States

1. States and competent international organizations which have submitted to a coastal State a project to undertake marine scientific research referred to in article 246, paragraph 3, shall give notice to the neighbouring land-locked and geographically disadvantaged States of the proposed research project, and shall notify the coastal State thereof.

2. After the consent has been given for the proposed marine scientific research project by the coastal State concerned, in accordance with article 246 and other relevant provisions of this Convention, States and competent international organizations undertaking such a project shall provide to the neighbouring land-locked and geographically disadvantaged States, at their request and when appropriate, relevant information as specified in article 248 and article 249, paragraph 1(f).

3. The neighbouring land-locked and geographically disadvantaged States referred to above shall, at their request, be given the opportunity to participate, whenever feasible, in the proposed marine scientific research project through qualified experts appointed by them and not objected to by the coastal State, in accordance with the conditions agreed for the project, in conformity with the provisions of this Convention, between the coastal State concerned and the State or competent international organizations conducting the marine scientific research.

4. States and competent international organizations referred to in paragraph 1 shall provide to the above-mentioned land-locked and geographically disadvantaged States, at their request, the information and assistance specified in article 249, paragraph 1(d), subject to the provisions of article 249, paragraph 2.

Article 255

Measures to facilitate marine scientific research and assist research vessels

States shall endeavour to adopt reasonable rules, regulations and procedures to promote and facilitate marine scientific research conducted in accordance with this Convention beyond their territorial sea and, as appropriate, to facilitate, subject to the provisions of their laws and regulations, access to their harbours and promote assistance for marine scientific research vessels which comply with the relevant provisions of this Part.

Article 256

Marine scientific research in the Area

All States, irrespective of their geographical location, and competent international organizations have the right, in conformity with the provisions of Part XI, to conduct marine scientific research in the Area.

Article 257

Marine scientific research in the water column beyond the exclusive economic zone

All States, irrespective of their geographic location, and competent international organizations have the right, in conformity with this Convention, to conduct marine scientific research in the water column beyond the limits of the exclusive economic zone.

SECTION 4. SCIENTIFIC RESEARCH INSTALLATIONS OR EQUIPMENT IN THE MARINE ENVIRONMENT

Article 258

Deployment and use

The deployment and use of any type of scientific research installations or equipment in any area of the marine environment shall be subject to the same conditions as are prescribed in this Convention for the conduct of marine scientific research in such area.

Article 259

Legal status

The installations or equipment referred to in this section do not possess the status of islands. They have no territorial sea of their own, and their presence does not affect the delimitation of the territorial sea, the exclusive economic zone or the continental shelf.

Article 260

Safety zones

Safety zones of a reasonable breadth not exceeding a distance of 500 metres may be created around scientific research installations in accordance with the relevant provisions of this Convention. All States shall ensure that such safety zones are respected by their vessels.

Article 261

Non-interference with shipping routes

The deployment and use of any type of scientific research installations or equipment shall not constitute an obstacle to established international shipping routes.

Article 262

Identification markings and warning signals

Installations or equipment referred to in this section shall bear indentification markings indicating the State or registry or the international organization to which they belong and shall have adequate internationally agreed warning signals to ensure safety and sea and safety of air navigation, taking into account rules and standards established by competent international organizations.

SECTION 5. RESPONSIBILITY AND LIABILITY

Article 263

Responsibility and liability

1. States and competent international organizations shall be responsible for ensuring that marine scientific research, whether undertaken by them or on their behalf, is conducted in accordance with this Convention.

2. States and competent international organizations shall be responsible and liable for the measures they take in contravention of this Convention in respect of marine scientific research conducted by other States, their natural or juridical persons or by competent international organizations, and shall provide compensation for damage resulting from such measures.

3. States and competent international organizations shall be responsible and liable pursuant to article 235 for damage caused by pollution of the marine environment arising out of marine scientific research undertaken by them or on their behalf.

SECTION 6. SETTLEMENT OF DISPUTES AND INTERIM MEASURES

Article 264

Settlement of disputes

Disputes concerning the interpretation or application of the provisions of this Convention with regard to marine scientific research shall be settled in accordance with Part XV, sections 2 and 3.

Article 265

Interim measures

Pending settlement of a dispute in accordance with Part XV, sections 2 and 3, the State or competent international organization authorized to conduct a marine scientific research project shall not allow research activities to commence or continue without the express consent of the coastal State concerned.

ED. NOTE: While U.S. marine scientists viewed the evolution of the above provisions with considerable alarm during the negotiations, now that the conference has concluded, these provisions are receiving mixed reviews in the U.S. scientific community. Consider the following comments by one of the most distinguished U.S. oceanographers.

Wooster, SEA LAW AND OCEAN RESEARCH: VIEW FROM THE NORTHWEST, 63 Ore. L. Rev. 121, 128-130 (1984)[1]

The Convention provisions regulating marine scientific research differ only in degree from the recent practice of many coastal States. The principal change introduced by the Convention has been the extension of jurisdiction over research to two hundred miles offshore. It could be argued that this disadvantageous step (from a marine research perspective) is balanced by several improvements over recent practice. For example, standardization of the coastal State requirements, the granting of consent expeditiously under normal circumstances, and implied consent in the absence of a timely response should facilitate distant water research.

In fact, the impact of the new regime on marine scientific research depends entirely on the spirit in which it is implemented. If the provisions are interpreted liberally so as to promote marine research and are administered fairly and efficiently, the conditions for international marine research could be significantly better than they have been during the last decade, which was marked by uncertainty and the harsh positions that accompanied the negotiations. On the other hand, the Convention strengthens the ability of the coastal State to block all research by foreign scientists if it so desires. The United States rejection of the Convention could exacerbate such worst-case scenarios if coastal States annoyed with the U.S. position choose to interpret the Convention provisions harshly, or to impose even more stringent conditions. If this happens, then some coastal regions where difficulties are too great will be abandoned as research sites.

The consequences of the Convention provisions on U.S. scientists, assuming they will be required to follow them, can be divided into three categories: (1) those affecting the process of seeking clearance, (2) those concerning the predictability of action and likelihood of approval, and (3) those affecting the research operation and the post-cruise period. On a more general level, it should be noted that the geographical area within which marine research will be controlled by the coastal State has greatly expanded so that a significant number of U.S. operations are likely to be affected by the Convention.

The entire process of seeking clearance will become more formal under article 250, with casual arrangements between scientific institutions becoming a thing of the past. Because all applications will presumably be handled by the State Department, there is a danger that research will be held hostage to political considerations here and in the coastal State. The paperwork for the

1. Reprinted by permission. Copyright c by University of Oregon.

applying institution is likely to increase, and the time required for the total process will be extended to at least half a year under article 248.

Under article 246 of the Convention, the predictability of coastal State action in response to clearance requests is increased because consent is to be granted under normal circumstances for most research not related to natural resources. Action by the coastal State within four months is encouraged under article 252. It is difficult to judge whether approval of research projects is more or less likely under these provisions. The chance of approval is probably increased for research clearly not related to resources and decreased for resource-related work.

The Convention allows a coastal State to regulate research and post-cruise operations. Even after the coastal State has consented to a research project, the project may be suspended or terminated under article 253 if, for example, unavoidable modifications are not approved. After the end of the cruise, final results must be made available to the coastal State and the research entity's interpretation of those findings may be required. This obligation may continue indefinitely, so that careful recording of all reporting actions will be necessary. Under article 249, the coastal State can restrict what the research entity publishes about its project.

The costs of conducting international marine research are likely to increase in order to meet fully the obligations incurred in gaining access to the site. The additional costs will include: participation by coastal State scientists, in some cases from cruise planning to post-cruise analysis of data and samples; reporting fully on findings; and providing an assessment or interpretation of data, samples, and results. There are also costs connected with rescheduling or reprogramming of ship operations when clearance is delayed or denied. While the expense of sharing information should be modest and a good investment in scientific cooperation, assessments, rescheduling, and reprogramming are likely to be costly, and it is not clear how they will be funded.

D. INTERNATIONAL COOPERATION IN MARINE SCIENTIFIC RESEARCH

Introduction: The many references to "competent international organizations" in the texts of the 1982 Convention is a recognition that there already exists a strong network of international organizations related to scientific inquiry in the oceans. These organizations are both governmental and non-governmental in nature. They all have the common goal of cooperation for the advancement of marine scientific research and related enterprises. These international arrangments are of a multilateral and bilateral character. In the following materials, you are introduced to some of them.

Soons, MARINE SCIENTIFIC RESEARCH AND THE LAW OF THE SEA, (Kluwer, 1982), 20-23[2]

There can be several reasons for international cooperation in scientific research in general. First, the very nature of the research topic can be such that the field work required cannot be restricted to the territory of one nation. Secondly, international cooperation may also be necessary to make possible the cross-fertilization of ideas, particularly in newer and highly specialized fields where only close collaberation by scientists from a number of countries is likely to provide the necessary critical mass of activity. And thirdly, the provision of the very expensive equipment and operations required by large-scale scientific research may only be possible by cost sharing between countries.

---

2. Reprnted by permission of the T.M.C. Asser Institute.

These general reasons are all applicable to marine scientific research. In particular, international cooperation is required in the compilation and exchange of information, the standardization and inter-calibration of instruments and methods, and in the organisation of field investigations. The importance of international data exchange has already been dealt with above. Standardization and inter-calibration of instruments and methods is essential in order to improve the comparability of data. Since many investigations require the pooling of data from a number of sources, synthesis can be particularly difficult when different methods and standards have been used. The need for international cooperation in the organisation of field investigations is a result of the fact that some oceanic research projects can only be carried out by means of simultaneous observations on short time scales, requiring many ships or other platforms. Few nations are capable of providing these on their own. Other research projects may require only a few platforms, but for long periods. Such projects can often only be carried out if the costs are shared by several nations. An additional advantage of joining forces in international operations is that the cost-effectiveness of the research for each participating nation will be substantially increased.

Cooperative research programmes can be either "problem oriented", i.e., concerned with specific problems, or "area oriented", i.e., concerned with a particular geographical regions. A number of large-scale international cooperative investigations of both kinds have already been carried out during the past two decades. The first one was the International Indian Ocean Expedition (1959-1965) in which 23 countries participated with 40 research vessels which undertook 180 research cruises of varying duration and complexity. During 1963 and 1964, Internation Cooperative Investigations of the Tropical Atlantic were carried out in three stages by 13 ships from eight countries. The next expedition was the Cooperative Study of the Kuroshio and Adjacent Regions of the Pacific (1965-1966), involving 36 research vessels from eight countries. Similar cooperative investigations have been carried out in such areas as the eastern tropical Atlantic (EASTROPAC), the northeast central Atlantic (CINECA) and the Caribean and adjacent regions (CICAR). An example of a project exclusively concerned with atmospheric research is GATE, the GARP (Global Atmospheric Research Programme) Atlantic Tropical Experiment, carried out in 1974. About 40 research vessels participated in this project; in addition a great number of buoys, moorings and aircraft were deployed.

The basis, however, for all international cooperation in marine science is provided by a number of organizations. A distinction must be made between governmental international organizations and non-governmental international organizations. The latter will be dealt with first.

The functions performed by non-governmental international organizations in the marine science field are threefold. In the first place they facilitate communication, in order to help scientists exchange their ideas and experience. Secondly, they bring together scientists from different countries to work out agreements on methodology or on other technical problems where an exchange of views and accepted opinion is now required. Their third function is monitoring, evaluation and comment on intergovernmental programs.

The most important non-governmental international organization in the area of marine science is the Scientific Committee on Oceanic Research (SCOR), established in 1957 by the International Council of Scientific Unions (ICSU), an organization having consultative status with UNESCO ("A" status). Other scientific organizations in this field, operating within the framework of ICSU, include:

- the Commission on Marine Geology (CMG), of the International Union of Geodesy and Geophysics (IUGG);

- the International Association of Biological Oceanography (IABO), of the International Union of Biological Science (IUBS);

- the International Association for the Physical Sciences of the Ocean (IAPSO), of the International Union of Geological Scienses (IUGS); and

- the Scientific Committee for Antarctic Research (SCAR).

Intergovernmental organizations concerned with marine scientific research can be either regional or global. Apart from a number of regional fisheries commissions having competence in the field of scientific reesarch, two regional intergovernmental organizations established specifically to promote and coordinate marine research exist. In 1906 the International Council for the Exploration of the Sea (ICES) was founded. ICES, which now has 17 members, is primarily concerned with the North Atlantic Ocean and deals particularly with research related to living resources. A similar organization was established in 1919 for the Mediterranean Sea area: the International Commission for the Scientific Exploration of the Mediterranean Sea (ICSEM), also now having 17 members.

The only global intergovernmental organization exclusively concerned with marine scientific research is the Intergovernmental Oceanographic Commission (IOC). The IOC was established as an autonomous body within UNESCO in 1960. Its purpose is "to promote scientific investigation with a view to learning more about the nature and resources of the ocean through the concerted action of its members". It further functions as the coordinating body within the UN system for marine science and related activities. Cooperative scientific investigations of the ocean as well as world-wide ocean services, combined with a programme of training, education and mutual assistance form the chief components of IOC's work. Membership is open to any member State of any one of the organizations of the UN system; on March 1979 103 States were members of the IOC. The Secretariate of the IOC is located in UNESCO Headquarters in Paris.

A number of other global intergovernmental organizations is concerned with marine research. Of these, the most important ones are:

- the Food and Agricultural Organization of the United Nations (FAO), active in the fields of fisheries research, marine biological research and marine pollution research;

- the World Health Organization (WHO), mainly interested in marine pollution research;

- the World Meteorological Organization (WMO), which is involved in meteorological and physical oceanographic research;

- the Intergovernmental Maritime Consultative Organization (IMCO), interested in marine pollution research;

- the International Atomic Energy Agency (IAEA), active in the field of marine pollution research; and

- the United Nations Environment Programme (UNEP), also interested in marine pollution research.

Coordination between these organizations is ensured through the Inter-secretariate Committee on Scientific Programs Relating to Oceanography (ICSPRO).

ED. NOTE: A counterpart to ICES has recently been created for the North Pacific, known as PICES. IMCO, also referred to in the above materials recently changed its name to the International

Maritime Organization (IMO). Further elaboration on the organization and functions of some of these organizations is found in the following excerpt.

Alexander, ORGANIZATIONAL RESPONSES TO NEW OCEAN SCIENCE AND TECHNOLOGY DEVELOPMENTS, 9 J.Ocean Development and International Law, 241, 250-256[3]

....

(1) *Intergovernmental Oceanographic Commission* (IOC) The IOC's stated purpose is "to promote scientific investigation with a view to learning more about the nature and resources of the oceans through the concerted action of its members." It further functions as the coordinating body within the marine system for marine science and related activities. Functionally, IOC works through three sections, Ocean Science, Ocean Services, and Training, Education and Mutual Assistance in the marine sciences (TEMA).

Within the framework of Ocean Science are the regional cooperative investigations, such as those of the Kuroshio and Adjacent Regions, and of the Eastern Central Atlantic, which are multination, multiship projects. Interest in these investigations has tended to lag as operational costs have mounted, and as the results of the efforts have failed to produce tangible economic or other benefits for developing member states. One investigation in the Caribbean, IOCARIBE, (IOC Association for the Caribbean and Adjacent Regions), was eventually transformed into a regional association with a permanent director and staff. Other regional associations are expected to follow. Another ocean science activity of IOC is the Global Investigation of Pollution in the Marine Environment (GIPME).

There are three major forms of the Ocean Services section: Integrated Global Ocean Station System (IGOSS), International Oceanographic Data Exchange (IODE), and Tsunami Warning System in the Pacific (ITSU)> IGOSS has recently established a Marine Pollution Monitoring Pilot Project, under which petroleum pollutants will be monitored by a network of countries in such areas as the Persian (Arabian) Gulf, and along tanker routes from the Gulf to Japan and Europe.

TEMA, the third section of IOC, seeks to act as a catalyst to bring together countries interested in the marine sciences so they can develop their own programs and intitiate plans for joint ventures.

Although this brief list does not cover all of IOC's activities, it gives an indication of the scope of cooperative marine science activities which the Commission endeavors (with a very small staff and budget) to carry out. One of its stated functions is "to promote freedom of scientific investigation of the oceans for the benefit of mankind"; given the new ocean regime, this function, if successfully carried out, may prove to be one of IOC's most important activities.

(2) *Intergovernmental Maritime Consultative Organization* (IMCO) This organization is designed to promote maritime safety, efficiency of navigation, and the prevention and control of marine pollution from ships. it is also concerned with intergovernmental cooperation concerning regulations and practices related to technical matters affecting commercial shipping. In addition, it provides technical assistance to developing states, and performs depository and other functions with respect to conventions and agreements related to shipping.

IMCO is responsible for a number of global treaties, among them the 1954 Convention on the

[3]. Reprinted by permission of the Journal for Ocean Development and International Law.

Prevention of Pollution of the Sea by Oil, the 1973 International Convention on the Prevention of Pollution from Ships (MARPOL), and the 1974 Convention on the Safety of Life at Sea (SOLAS). IMCO is a consultative body, and can only act as a catalyst for the adoption by its 113 members of new conventions; once adopted, a convention must then proceed through the lengthy process of ratification by the required number of states in order to enter into force.

(3) *Food and Agriculture Organization* (FAO) Within FAO, the Department of Fisheries, headed by an Assistant Director General, is the organization responsible for living resources of the oceans and of fresh waters. The four main functions of the Department are: (1) to collect, analyze, and disseminate information on all aspects of fisheries; (2) to assess fishery resources of the world and the state of exploitation of the major living aquatic resources; (3) to assist developing countries in utilizing their fishery resources to the best advantage; and (4) to provide assistance in the establishment, maintenance, and expansion of national and regional training institutions, and in accelerating the transfer of technology through field operations.

Under FAO auspices nine multinational regional fisheries commissions and councils have been established. The membership in these bodies is composed largely of developing countries, and the organizations' functions are restricted to data collection and assessment, to advisory roles, and to assistance in developing management functions; only a few are entitled to recommend conservation measures to the member states. The nine regional bodies are:

Regional Fisheries Advisory Commission for the Southwest Atlantic (CARPAS)

Fishery Committee for the Eastern Central Atlantic (CECAF)

General Fisheries Council for the Mediterranean (GFCM)
Indian Ocean Fishery Commission (IOFC)
Indo-Pacific Fishery Commission (IPFC)
Western Central Atlantic Fisheries Advisory Commission (WECAFC)

Committee for Inland Fisheries Advisory Commission (CIFA)

European Inland Fisheries Advisory Commission (EIFAC)
Commission for Inland Fisheries of Latin America (COPESCAL)

Two areas where the potentially severe ecological impacts of technological advances in fish harvesting might be felt lie outside the framework of the FAO fisheries bodies. These are in whaling and the harvesting of fish in the Southern Ocean. Both issues have been addressed by organizations outside the UN system. FAO regional fisheries organizations have the opportunity to play important roles (1) in improving knowledge of fisheries stocks and alternative conservation measures within the organizations' areas of competence; (2) in providing education and training for fisheries personnel in developing member states; and (3) in assisting states in developing national fisheries infrastructures, including vessels, ports, processing facilities, etc.

....

(10) *World Meteorological Organization* (WMO) Many aspects of the marine scientific research activities of IOC are closely related to the work of WMO. The World Meteorological Organization facilitates worldwide cooperation in the establishment of meteorological observation stations, and promotes systems for the rapid exchange of meteorological data. Through its World Weather Watch, WMO provides continuous information on the state of the oceans at any given place. It conducts studies in the physical processes of the atmosphere, including forms of air/sea interaction,

and cooperates with UNEP in carrying out baseline studies of pollution patterns in semienclosed seas.

(11) *World Health Organization* (WHO) The programs of WHO impact most directly on the marine environment are those concerning coastal areas. WHO has published a set of International Sanitary Regulations which include restrictions on the discharge of sewage, garbage, or other wastes from ships into harbors or estuaries. In cooperation with FAO, the Organization has worked on problems of the hygiene of fish and shellfish, as well as drafting an international monitoring program on seafood contamination. It also works closely with UNEP in its action plans.

....

ED. NOTE: Occasionally, for scientic or political reasons, or both, it is advantageous for two countries to enter into a long-term cooperative arrangement apart from the kind discussed above. This is usually done through a bilateral agreement. A typical such agreement follows.

AGREEMENT BETWEEN THE GOVERNMENT OF THE UNITED STATES OF AMERICA AND THE GOVERNMENT OF THE UNION OF SOVIET SOCIALIST REPUBLICS ON CO-OPERATION IN OCEAN STUDIES OF 1 JUNE 1990

The Government of the United States of America and the Government of the Union of Soviet Socialist Republics (hereinafter referred to as "the Parties");

Recognizing the importance of comprehensive studies of the oceans of the world for peaceful purposes and for the well-being of mankind;

Striving for more complete knowledge and rational utilization of the oceans of the world by all nations through broad international co-operation in oceanographic investigations and research;

Aware of the capabilities and resources of both countries for studies of the oceans of the world and the extensive history and successful results of previous co-operation between them;

Desiring to combine their efforts in the further investigation of the oceans of the world and to use the results for the benefit of the peoples of both countries and of all mankind;

Noting the General Agreement between the Government of the United States of America and the Government of the Union of Soviet Socialists Republics on Contacts, Exchanges and Co-operation in Scientific, Technical, Educational, Cultural and Other Fields, signed 21 November 1985; the Agreement on Co-operation in the Field of Environmental Protection, signed 23 May 1972; and the Agreement on Co-operation in the Field of Basic Scientific Research, signed 8 January 1989; and

Desiring to continue the co-operation carried out under the Agreement on Co-operation in Studies of the World Ocean, signed 19 June 1973;

Have agreed as follows:

Article 1

1. The Parties will develop and carry out co-operation in ocean studies on the basis of equality, overall reciprocity and mutual benefit.

2. All co-operation under this Agreement will be subject to approval of the Parties and to the

national laws, regulations and international obligations of each country, as well as the availability of appropriated funds and personnel.

Article 2

1. In their ocean studies, the Parties will direct co-operative efforts to the investigation of important and mutually agreed scientific topics.

2. Co-operative efforts may be considered in the areas of: (a) physical oceanography; (b) chemical and biological oceanography; (c) geological, geophysical and geochemical investigations of oceans; (d) biological productivity and the functioning of oceanic biological communities; and (e) marine meteorology.

3. Projects of initial co-operation are set forth in Annex I, which constitutes an integral part of the Agreement. Other projects may be added by mutual agreement of the Parties.

Article 3

1. Co-operation provided for in the preceding articles may take the following forms:

a. Co-operative scientific research projects, including field studies; the exchange of participating scientists, specialists and researchers; and the exchange and joint publication of their results;

b. Joint scientific conferences, symposia and workshops;

c. Exchange of scientific information and documentation;

d. Appropriate participation by both countries in multilateral co-operative activities sponsored by international scientific organizations;

e. Facilitation by both Parties of use of appropriate port facilities of the two countries for ships' services and supplies, including provision for rest and changes of ships' personnel, in connection with carrying out co-operative activities.

2. Other forms of co-operation may be added by mutual agreement of the Parties.

Article 4

1. Co-operation in ocean studies under this Agreement will be within the framework of jointly approved projects and programmes and in accordance with written arrangements for their implementation.

2. The Parties will ensure, in accordance with agreed co-operative activity, that access to institutes, scientists and other specialists participating in joint co-operative activity under this Agreement, and to scientific data, will be made available on an equal, reciprocal and mutually beneficial basis.

Article 5

1. The implementation of this Agreement will be carried out by a US-USSR Joint Committee on Co-operation in Ocean Studies. This Joint Committee shall meet, as a rule, once a year,

alternatively in the United States and the Soviet Union, unless otherwise mutually agreed.

2. The Joint Committee shall take such action as is necessary for effective implementation of this Agreement, including, but not limited to, approval of specific projects and programmes of co-operation; designation of agencies and organizations to be responsible for carrying out co-operative activities; and making recommendations, as appropriate, to the Parties.

3. Each Party shall have an Executive Agent to assist the Joint Committee. The Executive Agent of the United States of America will be the National Oceanic and Atmospheric Administration (NOAA), a constituent agency of the U.S. Department of Commerce. The Executive Agent for the Union of Soviet Socialist Republics will be the USSR State Committee for Science and Technology (GKNT).

4. The Executive Agents of the Parties will be responsible for carrying out this Agreement during the period between meetings of the Joint Committee. The Executive Agents will maintain contact with each other; keep each other informed of activities and the progress in implementing this Agreement; and co-ordinate and supervise the development and implementation of co-operative activities conducted under this Agreement.

Article 6

Nothing in this Agreement will be interpreted to prejudice other agreements between the Parties or commitments of either Party to other international oceanographic programmes.

Article 7

Each Party, with the consent of the other Party, may invite third countries to participate in co-operative activities engaged in under this Agreement. Such participation will be consistent with the provisions of this Agreement.

Article 8

Protection of intellectual property and rights thereto shall be as set forth in Annex II, which constitutes an integral part of this Agreement.

Article 9

1. This Agreement will enter into force upon signature by both Parties and will remain in force for five years. It may be modified or extended by written agreement of the Parties.

2. Co-operative activities being conducted when the effective period of this Agreement ends will, unless terminated by either Party, be continued to their conclusion in accordance with the terms of this Agreement.

3. Either Party has the right to terminate this Agreement on six months notice to the other Party.

4. Upon entry into force, this Agreement shall supercede the 1973 US-USSR Agreement on Co-operation in Studies of the World Ocean, as amended and extended.

IN WITNESS WHEREOF, the undersigned, being duly authorized by their respective governments, have signed this Agreement.

ANNEX I

To the Agreement between the Government of the United States of America and the Government of the Union of Soviet Socialist Republics on Co-operation in Ocean Studies

Co-operation under this Agremeent will initially be implemented in the following projects:

a. Southern Ocean Dynamics
b. Mid-Atlantic Ridge Crest Processes
c. Geochemistry of Marine Sediments
d. Arctic Erosional Processes with Special Attention to Gas Hydrates

ANNEX II

[This annex covers such intellectual property matters as copyrights, inventions, business-confidential information, and the like]

E. TRANSFER OF MARINE TECHNOLOGY

Introduction: In this section, consideration will be given to the provisions of the treaty dealing with the transfer of marine technology. Before examining them, consider for yourself the more fundamental question. Is a program requiring the transfer of marine technology from developed to developing countries a good idea at all? Given some countries' economic conditions, is it wise to give any kind of priority to marine science? Would not such countries have much more pressing social and economic problems toward which scarce financial and intellectual resources should first be directed? For example, if country A has extremely limited scientific capability, would it not be more appropriate for it to direct its resources to, say, medical science than marine science? If so, is it moral or ethical to tempt that country to move in the direction of marine science?

Assuming that the above question is adequately resolved, then one must face the question of what is meant by transfer of technology and the modes and mechanisms for accomplishing it. Obviously, we are concerned here with much more than the physical transfer of equipment. Local scientists are going to require rather sophisticated training in using the equipment and interpreting and assessing scientific results. How is this best accomplished? Should, for example, those scientists be brought to a developed country for advanced training? Or would it be better for scientists from the developed countries to establish training programs within the developing States? And what are the implications of making that decision? As you can see, the subject, apparently simple on its face, is not at all.

1982 UNITED NATIONS CONVENTION ON THE LAW OF THE SEA

PART XIV

DEVELOPMENT AND TRANSFER OF MARINE TECHNOLOGY

SECTION 1. GENERAL PROVISIONS

Article 266

Promotion of the development and transfer of marine technology

1. States, directly or through competent international organizations, shall co-operate in accordance with their capabilities to promote actively the development and transfer of marine science and marine technology on fair and reasonable terms and conditions.

2. States shall promote the development of the marine scientific and technological capacity of States which may need and request technical assistance in this field, particularly developing States, with regard to the exploration, exploitation, conservation and management of marine resources, the protection and preservation of the marine environment, marine scientific research and other activities in the marine environment compatible with this Convention, with a view to accelerating the social and economic development of the developing States.

3. States shall endeavour to foster favourable economic and legal conditions for the transfer of marine technology for the benefit of all parties concerned on an equitable basis.

Article 267

Protection of legitimate interests

States, in promoting co-operation pursuant to article 266, shall have due regard for all legitimate interests including, *inter alia*, the rights and duties of holders, suppliers and recipients of marine technology.

Article 268

Basic objectives

States, directly or through competent international organizations, shall promote:

(a) the acquisition, evaluation and dissemination of marine technological knowledge and facilitate access to such information and data;

(b) the development of appropriate marine technology;

(c) the development of the necessary technological infrastructure to facilitate the transfer of marine technology;

(d) the development of human resources through training and education of nationals of developing States and countries and especially the nationals of the least developed among them;

(e) international co-operation at all levels, particularly at the regional, subregional and bilateral levels.

Article 269

Measures to achieve the basic objectives

In order to achieve the objectives referred to in article 268, States, directly or through competent international organizations, shall endeavour, *inter alia*, to:

(a) establish programmes of technical co-operation for the effective transfer of all kinds of marine technolgy to States which may need and request technological assistance in this field, particularly the developing land-locked and geographically disadvantaged States, as well as other developing States which have not been able either to establish or develop their own technological capacity in marine science and in the exploration and exploitation of marine resources or to develop the infrastructure of such technology;

(b) promote favourable conditions for the conclusion of agreements, contracts and other similar arrangements, under equitable and reasonable conditions;

(c) hold conferences, seminars and symposia on scientific and technological subjects, in particular on policies and methods for the transfer of marine technology;

(d) promote the exchange of scientists and technological and other experts;

(e) undertake projects and promote joint ventures and other forms of bilateral and multilateral co-operation.

Article 270

Ways and means of international co-operation

International co-operation for the development and transfer of marine technology shall be carried out, where feasible and appropriate, through existing bilateral, regional or multilateral programmes, and also through expanded and new programmes in order to facilitate marine scientific research, the transfer of marine technology, particularly in new fields, and appropriate international funding for ocean research and development.

Article 271

Guidelines, criteria and standards

States, directly or through competent international organizations, shall promote the estabishment of generally accepted guidelines, criteria and standards for the transfer of marine technology on a bilateral basis or within the framework of international organizations and other fora, taking into account, in particular, the interests and needs of developing States.

Article 272

Co-ordination of international programmes

In the field of transfer of marine technology, States shall endeavour to ensure that competent international organizations co-ordinate their activities, including any regional or global programmes, taking into account the interests and needs of developing States, particularly land-locked and geographically disadvantaged States.

Article 273

Co-operation with international organizations and the Authority

States shall co-operate actively with competent international organizations and the Authority to encourage and facilitate the transfer to developing States and their nationals and the Enterprise of skills and marine technology with regard to activities in the Area.

Article 274

Objectives of the Authority

Subject to all legitimate interests including, *inter alia*, the rights and duties of holders, suppliers and recipients of technology, the Authority, with regard to activities in the Area, shall ensure that:

(a) on the basis of the principle of equitable geographical distribution, nationals of developing States, whether coastal, land-locked or geographically disadvantaged, shall be taken on for the purposes of training as members of the managerial, research and technical staff constituted for its undertakings;

(b) the technical documentation on the relevant equipment, machinery, devices and processes is made available to all States, in particularl developing States which may need and request technical assistance in this field;

(c) adequate provision is made by the Authority to facilitate the acquistion of technical assistance in the field of marine technology by States which may need and request it, in particular developing States, and the acquisition by their nationals of the necessary skills and know-how, including professional training;

(d) States which may need and request technical assistance in this field, in particular developing States, are assisted in the acquisition of necessary equipment, process, plant and other technical know-how through any financial arrangements provided for in this Convention.

SECTION 3. NATIONAL AND REGIONAL MARINE SCIENTIFIC AND TECHNOLOGICAL CENTRES

Article 275

Establishment of national centres

1. States, directly or through competent international organizations and the Authority, shall promote the establishment, particularly in developing States, of national marine scientific and technological research centres, in order to stimulate and advance the conduct of marine scientific research by developing coastal States and to enhance their national capabilities to utilize and preserve their marine resources for their economic benefit.

2. States, through competent international organizations and the Authority, shall give adequate support to facilitate the establishment and strengthening of such national centres so as to provide for advanced training facilities and necessary equipment, skills and know-how as well as technical experts to such States as may need and request such assistance.

Article 276

Establishment of regional centres

1. States, in co-ordination with the competent international organizations and the Authority and national marine and technological research institutions, shall promote the estabishment of regional marine scientific and technological research centres, particularly in developing States, in order to stimulate and advance the conduct of marine scientific research by developing States and foster the transfer of marine technology.

2. All States of a region shall co-operate with the regional centres therein to ensure the more effective achievment of their objectives.

Article 277

Functions of regional centres

The functions of such regional centres shall include, *inter alia*:

(a) training and educational programmes at all levels on various aspects of marine scientific and technological research, particularly marine biology, including conservation and management of living resources, oceanograpy, hydrography, engineering, geological exploration of the sea-bed, mining and desalination technologies;

(b) management studies;

(c) study programmes related to the protection and preservation of the marine environment and the prevention, reduction and control of pollution;

(d) organization of regional conferences, seminars and symposia;

(e) acquisition and processing of marine scientific and technological data and information;

(f) prompt dissemination of results of marine scientifc and technological research in readily available publications;

(g) publicizing national policies with regard to the transfer of marine technology and systematic comparative study of those policies;

(h) compilation and systematization of information on the marketing of technology and on contracts and other arrangements concerning patents;

(i) technical co-operation with States of the region.

SECTION 4. CO-OPERATION AMONG INTERNATIONAL ORGANIZATIONS

Article 278

Co-operation among international organizations

The competent international organizations referred to in this Part and in Part XIII shall take appropriate measures to ensure, either directly or in close co-operation among themselves, the effective discharge of their functions and responsibilities under this Part.

ED. NOTE: After examining these provisions, do you think they are well-balanced? How much of the cooperation called for, in your judgment, is likely to take place in the forseeable future? Would a much more modest undertaking be more likely to receive the enthusiastic support of developed countries having the technologies referred to? Finally, you are reminded that there are provisions related to this subject in Part XI of the Convention and related Annexes dealing with deep seabed mining, particularly those related to mandatory transfer of technology. You may wish to review them at this time.

CHAPTER 11

PROTECTION AND PRESERVATION OF THE MARINE ENVIRONMENT

In this chapter, we shall examine some of the international and national rules relating to the preservation and protection of the marine environment. The major focus will be on the subject of pollution from ships, although it is quite clear that this source of pollution is a relatively minor contributor to the degradation of the oceans. Our attention will be directed both to treaties negotiated under the auspices of the International Maritime Organization (IMO) and the provisions of the United Nations Convention on the Law of the Sea, which represent an important addition to the international law on this subject.

A. THE NATURE OF THE PROBLEM: SOURCES OF POLLUTION

Clingan, LAW AFFECTING THE QUALITY OF THE MARINE ENVIRONMENT, 26 Miami L. Rev. 223, 224-231 (1971-72)[1]

Pollutants are resources where they do not belong. These unwanted resources can be introduced into the oceans deliberately or inadvertently. The wastes most commonly dumped into the oceans include dredge spoils, industrial wastes, sewage sludge, construction and demolition debris, solid waste, explosive and chemical munitions, and radioactive wastes. Those inadvertently finding their way to the sea include oil (although this should also be included among deliberate introductions) and various other organic and inorganic toxic substances such as lead, cadmium, mercury, vanadium, nitrilotracetic acid, orthonitrochorobenzine, and polychlorinated biphenyls.

Also among the forms of pollutants affecting the marine environment are excessive nutrients, heat from power and industrial plants, and sediments from land erosion, all of which exert their own peculiar influence on the totality of water quality. Complicating the pollution problem is the fact that some chemicals tend to react synergistically causing problems that would not exist had each chemical been introduced into the water by itself. No attempt will be made to go into detail concerning each of the previously mentioned substances, but a brief survey of some of the more threatening pollutants will be provided.

A. Oil

Oil spills attract a great deal of attention and have, to be sure, influenced the quality of the marine environment. However, the massive spills such as the widely publicized *Torrey Canyon* incident, while generating substantial economic impact, are normally localized and of debatable long-term ecological impact. Perhaps the greater threat is the pervasive oil pollution from underwater activities and operational spills in connection with the routine transport of oil by sea. Routine spills originating from the operations of oil-carrying tankers, other ships, refineries, petro-chemical plants, and submarine oil wells represent, according to one source, 90 percent of the estimated 2.1 million metric tons of oil introduced annually into the oceans. The remaining ten percent represents the spectacular spills caused by major marine accidents.

---

1. "Reprinted from the University of Miami Law Review 26 U.MIAMI L. REV. 223 (1971)," which holds copyright on this article.

Effects of oil pollution on marine life are subject to debate. In general, there are five principal ways in which oil may affect marine animals : (1) tainting of the flesh; (2) poisoning by ingestion; (3) disturbance of food chains; (4) physical fouling with coats of oil; and (5) repellant effects. It has been stated that while there has been no final conclusion concerning the effects of oil on marine life, the generally accepted opinion is that pollution by crude oil is not significantly harmful to living organisms. However, there is highly respected authority to the contrary. The best that can be said is that the subject requires a great deal more study before a definite conclusion can be substantiated. Limited information is available with respect to the effect of oil on filter-feeding mollusks, such as clams, oysters, scallops, and mussels, and there are indications that concentrations of 25 parts of oil per million parts of water may be toxic to these animals. At any rate, there definitely is an impact on the shellfish market in economic terms due to tainting. The effect of oil on seabirds is probably the most dramatic. The coating of feathers with oil can cause death by drowning, loss of body heat, or inability to feed. Oil pollution also damages aquatic plants and other forms of life that constitute a part of the marine food chain.

The other special effects of oil spills should be mentioned. First, a possibly serious result could accrue from the fact that chlorinated hydrocarbons such as DDT and dieldrin are highly soluble in oil. Measurements of the effects of an oil slick on Biscayne Bay, Florida, indicated that the concentration of dieldrin in the top one millimeter of water containing the slick was more than 10,000 times higher than the rest of the water. Because many animals within the food chain feed near or on the surface, this effect can be of significant magnitude. Second, deleterious consequences for marine life have been noted to result from the use of detergents and similar compounds used for dispersing oil which are sometimes improperly attributed to the oil itself.

B. Toxic Substances

This category covers a wide range of organic and inorganic materials having varying effects on portions of the environment. Man produces more than a million kinds of products, many of which eventually wind up as waste in one form or another. Toxic substances among these products can be classified as metallic or organic. Among the metals, lead is perhaps the oldest known pollutant, and its presence in the oceans is steadily increasing. One of the major factors contributing lead to the environment is the automobile. According to one estimate in 1968, 180,000 tons of lead were emitted from internal combustion engines, representing 14 percent of all the lead consumed in the U.S. during that year. Much of this lead ultimately reaches the sea. However, the more spectacular cases of heavy metal poisoning in recent years involve mercury. It was long thought that mercury was environmentally inert and simply settled to the bottom of a river or estuary when discharged there. Mercury-caused deaths at Minimata, Japan, between 1953 and 1960 served to dispell this misconception and indicated that mercury can be changed by sea-borne bacteria into methylmercury. Methylmercury is an extremely toxic compount that enters the food chain and may reach hazardous concentrations. Newspapers have recently carried a number of stories concerning the concentrations of mercury discovered in tuna and swordfish. Although the dangers inherent in consumption of tuna have recently been discounted, the swordfishing industry in the United States has virtually come to a standstill. Other metals now being investigated as possible hazards to marine ecology are cadmium, vanadium, berryllium, and barium.

Among the common organic compounds, the most notorious threat to the marine envivonment is DDT. It has been shown that DDT in sea-water affects growth, reproduction, and mortality in marine animals in concentrations currently found in some coastal aquatic environments. While all pesticides present a threat, the so-called "hard" pesticides, the chlorinated hydrocarbons such as DDT, aldrin, dieldrin, endrin, heptaclor, and toxaphene, are especially dangerous because they are extremely persistent and easily concentrated in the food chain. Plankton, at the base of the food chain, are primary concentrators, hence marine fish are almost universally contaminated to one degree or another. Shrimps, crabs, and zooplankton are killed by exposure to DDT, and the growth of oysters is inhibited by such exposure.

Other synthetic organic compounds which are being deposited in the oceans include dyes and pigments (which may also include heavy metals), plastics and associated resins, rubber products, and surface active agents such as solvents, detergents, dispersing agents, and emulsifiers. Much of these are deposited as a result of household and industrial detergents. Other deposits come from the processing of leather and textiles, or the manufacture of a variety of other products.

The effects of toxic substances on man are not fully understood. While standard texts list the toxicity of more than 1,000 commerical chemical compounds at high levels of exposure, little is known of the longer range effects of exposure at lower levels. Further, the toxicity of a compound can be a function of the form it takes, as well as the metabolism and other physical characteristics of the individual exposed to it. The recent report on toxic substances of the Council on Environmental Quality refers to the effects of a few of the better known compounds. It points out that compounds of nickel and beryllium may cause respiratory disease, or heart, intestinal, or nervous disorders. Lead has been thought to produce sterility, child mortality, and permanent mental impairment. Mercury compounds destroy brain cells, cause tremors, and produce birth defects. The inescapable conclusion seems to be that the effects of toxic substances are probably sufficiently severe to call for the careful monitoring of the oceans and their products to detect the presence of these substances.

C. Heat

The increasing population in the United States creates a constant demand for more electrical power. Standard power plants generate electricity through the utilization of steam produced by the combustion of various fuels. Each plant condenses its steam for re-use through the utilization of large quantities of cooling water. The amount of water which is necessary depends on the efficiency of the plant and the designed temperature differential betwen intake and outfall. The temperature rise due to steam condensation is normally 10 to 20 degrees Fahrenheit, with an average increase of about 13 degrees. The demand on fresh water for cooling is so great that it is estimated that by 1980, the power industry will require about one-fifth of the total fresh water runoff of the United States for cooling. Today, approximately 68 percent of the heat produced by nuclear-fueled plants and 50 percent of the heat produced by fossil-fueled plants is removed by cooling water. It takes approimately 129 billion gallons of water a day to accomplish this task.

The discharge of heated effluents into the streams and bays of the nation has been the subject of considerable recent controversy, and a great amount of research has been conducted seeking to ascertain the seriousness of the effects of such discharges. One writer has speculated that heated effluents affect not only the growth and reproduction of fish and wildlife, but also recreation, public water supplies, and agricultural and industrial uses. As previously noted, effects of thermal increases are not yet thoroughly understood despite intensive research on the subject. It has been fairly well established, however, that a ten degree increase in water temperature can be expected to produce certain ecological imbalances. Some of the possible effects on fish are: (1) internal injury or inability to escape predators due to decreased mobility; (2) starvation due to inability to catch food; (3) starvation because of a decrease in food supply; (4) thermal shock due to the rapid rise in surrounding water temperature; (5) inability to digest food; (6) insufficient oxygen supply to sustain life; and, (7) disruption or cessation of the reproductive process.

Not all thermal discharges need to be considered detrimental. Research is being undertaken to determine whether heated effluents can be utilized beneficially. It has been proposed, for example, that waste heat be utilized to keep rivers free from ice and thereby improve navigation, to attract fish in certain areas, to warm recreational swimming beaches, or even to heat villages. Despite such promises, however, the heat problem remains serious, particularly in tropical and subtropical areas where marine life is often found in waters which are already near the upper levels of thermal tolerance.

D. Nutrients

An apt example of pollutants resulting from excess resources is the presence of excess nutrients in the marine environment. Nitrates, phosphates, and potassium compounds, introduced into the water from sewage and agricultural wastes, nourish algal growth. An exess of algal growth constitutes a threat to marine life, particularly in the vital estuarine regions where almost 90 percent of the commercially important species of fish spend at least a part of their life cycle. The problem is summarized in the following passage:

> Eutrophication of waters through overfertilization (principally with phosphorus and nitrogen) produces an excess of organic matter that decomposes, removing oxygen and killing the fish. Estuaries are increasingly being eutrophied. Pollution of coastal regions eliminates the nursery grounds of fish, including many commercial species that inhabit the oceans.
>
> Approximately 60 percent of the phosphorous causing over-enrichment of water bodies comes from municipal wastes. Urban and rural runoff contribute the remainder. A major contributor to the latter is runoff from feedlots, manured lands, and eroding soil.
>
> Trends in both nutrient use and loss are rising. Fertilizer consumption is expected to increase greatly in both developed and developing countries in the next decade, increasing the nutrient runoff from agricultural lands. Concentration of animal production will continue, with the result that losses of nutrients from feedlot runoff will rise sharply. Urban waste production is also expected to increase rapidly, resulting in greater potential loss of nutrients directly into coastal waters.

Injection of sewage into the environment also creates problems of oxygen depletion. Organic wastes demand oxygen to decompose. If the waste loads from sewage are heavy, the oxygen is nearly, or completely, depleted from the water and this depletion causes anaerobic bacteria to produce malodorous amounts of hydrogen sulfide and methane. An example of overnutrition can be found in the reports of the Moriches Bay, New York, experience. Moriches Bay, prior to 1950, was fed in part by a continual flow of salt water through Moriches Inlet. About 1951, the inlet became closed due to tidal action resulting in reduced salinity of the Bay. At the same time, the area was heavily fertilized with nitrates and phosphates caused by the runoff of duck wastes from the large number of poultry farms nearby. The resulting bloom of a unicellular plankton called *Nannachloris* destroyed the once prosperous oyster industry, and affected the supply of clams and other fish. In 1953, the inlet was reopened, salinity increased, and the counts of algae declined to near zero. The filling of Moriches Inlet poses a continuing problem to the area, however, an effort is being made to control the amount of nitrates and phosphates allowed to run off from the duck farms in order to reduce the threat of a repeat performance.

E. Sediments

Sediments, the product of erosion, constitute the greatest volume of waste materials entering surface waters. In the United States this volume has been estimated at 700 times the total sewage discharge into these waters. Normal erosion carry-away plus sediments resulting from dredge and fill operations sometimes cause severe local problems in estuaries. Light for photosynthesis is reduced, increased turbidity interferes with with visibility of marine species, and most important, sediments often interfere with oyster larval attachment and egg survival in other species. A serious example of this type of effect has been observed in the New York Bight area as the result of sewage sludge and dredge spoil dumping. The "Crown of Thorns" starfish plague in the Pacific has also been attributed to sediments from blasting, dredging, and dumping which protect the larval starfish from their natural predators. The potential damage from this type of pollution is quite high, and legislation is pending to control ocean dumping through a permit system. This legislation, of course, will solve only a part of the problem.

ED. NOTE: It goes without saying that much has occurred in the twenty years since this article was written. Legislation is in place eliminating or reducing the release of many of the substances mentioned, and ocean dumping. More is known about the effects of the various substances, including the effects of oil on the oceans and their resources. The article, if written today, would have to take account of these changes. However, it does serve to illustrate the complexity and variety of agents impacting, actually or potentially, upon coastal and oceanic waters and upon the living resources therein.

COMPETENCE TO ESTABLISH STANDARDS FOR THE CONTROL OF VESSEL SOURCE POLLUTION: WORKING PAPER PRESENTED BY THE UNITED STATES OF AMERICA, U.N. Doc. A/AC.138/SC.III/L.36 (April 2, 1973)

There are many sources of pollution of the marine environment including outflow from rivers and outfall structures, atmospheric transport of pollutants from land, natural seepage, offshore mineral development activities, vessel oil discharge and other cargoes into the oceans from vessels due to collisions and other marine casualties.

Land-based sources provide the largest quantities of pollutants to the marine environment. Land-based pollutants include riverborne substances from domestic sewage, industrial wastes and agricultural run-off, air-borne pollutants such as vaporized hydrocarbons, and direct discharges of sewage and other wastes from coastal communities. With regard to petroleum, land-based sources account for an estimated 50 to 90 per cent of the estimated total of 2 to 5 million metric tons of oil which enter the oceans annually. There are significant quantities of oil entering the marine environment from air-borne hydrocarbons which are very difficult to detect and measure (and which may be considerably larger than the entire total shown above). Although international co-operative efforts such as the Stockholm Conference on the Human Environment and the London Conference on Ocean Dumping have begun to deal with these problems, further work is urgently needed to insure effective protection of the oceans. The United States shares the view, however, that the Sea-Bed Committee does not have the expertise to deal adequately of the technical aspects of these sources of complex problems. While the general undertaking relating to all sources of marine pollution can be fruitfully discussed here, the specific problems involved in controls on land-based sources raise may issues of a very different order from those that will be discussed at the Law of the Sea Conference.

A second source of pollutants to the marine environment is the natural seepage from the sea-bed. The amount of pollution from natural seepage is not known although there is some evidence that it may be signifient. There is, of course, no known method of controlling this source and it is thus not dealt with in this paper.

A third source is pollution from sea-bed mineral development. Such activities provide a small percentage of total marine pollution. For example, it is estimated that the predominant sea-bed resource activity of oil development produces less than 2 per cent of the oil pollution of the oceans. If only maritime sources are considered, sea-bed activities make up about 5 per cent of ocean oil pollution with vessels accounting for the other 95 per cent. Of course, sea-bed exploitation will intensify, and the United States has presented specific draft treaty articles for a regime and machinery to deal with pollution from the deep sea-bed as well as on the continental margin.

A fourth principal source of pollution to the marine environment is pollution from vessels....

B. RESPONSIBILITY AND LIABILITY

1. RESPONSIBILITY

a. GENERAL PRINCIPLES OF INTERNATIONAL LIABILITY

Barros and Johnson, THE INTERNATIONAL LAW OF POLLUTION (1974) 73-75[2]

It is commonly asserted that the international law of pollution is still at the embryonic stage of development. What is normally meant by this statement is that legal development in this area has not yet been evidenced by any growing acceptance of general principles of state responsibility for environmental injury beyond territorial limits. One may quarrel with this emphasis on general principles on the ground that it represents an unduly narrow view of how international law evolves, expecially in an area that is likely to be characterized by a growing proliferation of environmental agreements. On the other hand, it is unlikely that an international law of pollution will emerge holistically from universal lawmaking conventions in the near future. International legal principles of environmental responsibility are likely to emerge chiefly from two sources: from international declarations and resolutions that lack the form and, arguably, the effect of lawmaking treaties and from the express commitments and implied assumptions common to a growing variety of international environmental agreements of limited scope. But it will be easier to derive generally binding principles from either of these sources if they can be shown to be a development or modification of existing principles of international responsibility.

The textbooks show that the doctrine of international responsibility is not highly developed. Primarily it deals with the responsibility of a state for injuries to aliens in its territory and only marginally with state responsibility for direct injury to the rights of other states. Even in the latter category, there are few references to general principles that pertain specifically to situations of environmental injury. It is generally assumed that liability for such an injury would arise upon proof of an "international delinquency," an unlawful act or omission by one state resulting in loss or damage to another. But the injury need not be accompanied by fault or negligence on the part of the individual or agency whose delinquent conduct is ascribed to the state. The doctrine of strict or absolute liability in international law is, however, limited to a few areas designated by treaty under arrangements for the allocation of risks associated with extremely dangerous activities. Recent examples are found in the 1960 and 1963 treaties on third-party liability for nuclear damage and the 1962 Brussels Convention on the Liability of Operators of Nuclear Ships. In these instances the provisions deal with civil liability under the applicable domestic law, and state responsibility under international law is not a primary concern. The activities themselves are dangerous but not unlawful. Although those agreements on risk distribution are certainly part of the evolving international law of pollution, they are marginal to the basic question of state responsibility for environmental damage extending beyond territorial limits.

Earlier approaches to that basic question are found rather in applications of the principle of noninterference established by customary international law and described in the vague maxim sic utere

2. Reprinted by permission of the Free Press.

ut alienum non laedas (use your property in such a manner as not to injure that of another). Obviously, this maxim is of minimal utility in the assessment of international environmental responsibility without the provision of specific criteria. It belongs to an even more nebulous order of vagueness than the civil law doctrine of abuse of rights (*abus de droit*). The observations in the *Trail Smelter* Arbitration and the .*Corfu Channel* case, reproduced below, belong essentially to this category. In the latter case, although the "environmental" danger lay hidden *within* territorial limits, the state's responsibility would have been recognized if the danger had "escaped" beyond these limits.

Another source of general principles of state responsibility for extraterritorial injury might be traced by analogy with the doctrine of equitable utilization applied to international rivers and lakes. This doctrine, enunciated in the unofficial Helsinki Rules adopted by the nongovernmental International Law Association in 1966, has evolved in state practice in most areas of the world, but it really does little more than introduce the "reasonable man" test for determining what is a lawful share in the beneficial use of the waters of an international drainage basin. Thus, according to the Helsinki Rules, a state causing pollution of such waters is not under a duty to take prevention or control measures that would deprive it of equitable utilization; and liability arises only where the water use is inconsistent with that principle and causes substantial injury in the territory of another state.

The famous *Trail Smelter* decision has been interpreted in many ways. Some, for example, have argued that it introduced the concept of strict (or absolute) liability into international law. some maintain that it merely invokes the rudimentary principle of sic utere tuo. Other have suggested that it hints at an acceptance of the doctrine of eqitable utilization. As this decision was an arbital award and not a judicial decision, the controversy will never be authoritatively resolved. More important, the *Trail Smelter* heritage has now been appropriated by the international community in the Stockholm Declaration on the Human Environment. Whether the language of the Declaration is wholly faithful to the *Trail Smelter* doctrine is now academic: it has transcended it.

THE TRAIL SMELTER ARBITRATION: UNITED STATES AND CANADA

The tribunal, therefore, finds...under the principles of international law, as well as of the law of the United States, no State has the right to use or permit the use of its territory in such a manner as to cause injury by fumes in or to the territory of another or the properties or persons therein, when the case is of serious consequence and the injury is established by clear and convincing evidence.

THE CORFU CHANNEL CASE: UNITED KINGDOM AND ALBANIA

From all the facts and observations mentioned above, the Court draws the conclusion that the laying of the minefield which caused the explosions on October 22nd, 1946, could not have been accomplished without the knowledge of the Albanian Government.

The obligations resulting for Albania from this knowledge are not disputed between the Parties. Counsel for the Albanian Government expressly recongized that "if Albania had been informed of the operation before the incidents of October 22nd, and in time to warn the British vessels and shipping in general of the existence of mines in the Corfu Channel, her responsibility would be involved...."

The obligations incumbent upon the Albanian authorities consisted in notifying, for the benefit of shipping in general, the existence of a minefield in Albanian territorial waters and in warning the approaching British warships of the imminent danger to which the minefield exposed them. Such obligations are based, not on the Hague Convention of 1907, No. VIII, which is applicable in time of war, but on certain general and well-recognized principles, namely; elementary considerations of humanity, even more exacting in peace than in war; the principle of the freedom of maritime communication, *and every State's obligation not to allow knowingly its territory to be used for acts contrary to the rights of other States*. [Emphasis added.]

In fact, Albania neither notified the existence of the minefield, nor warned the British warships of the danger they were approaching.

But Albania's obligation to notify shipping of the existence of mines in her waters depends on her having obtained knowledge of that fact in sufficient time before October 22nd, and the duty of the Albanian coastal authorities to warn the British ships depends on the time that elapsed between the moment that these ships were reported and the moment of the first explosion.

DECLARATION, STOCKHOLM CONFERENCE ON THE HUMAN ENVIRONMENT (1972)

Principle No. 7

States shall take all possible steps to prevent pollution of the Seas by substances that are liable to create hazards to human health, to harm living resources and marine life, to damage amenities or to interfere with other legitimate uses of the sea.

b. RESPONSIBILITY UNDER TREATY LAW

CONVENTION ON THE HIGH SEAS

Article 24

Every State shall draw up regulations to prevent pollution of the seas by the discharge of oil from ships or pipelines or resulting from the exploitation and exploration of the seabed and its subsoil, taking account of existing treaty provisions on the subject.

Article 25

1. Every State shall take measures to prevent pollution of the seas from the dumping of radio-active waste, taking into account any standards and regulations which may be formulated by the competent international organizations.

2. All States shall co-operate with the competent international organizations in taking measures for the prevention of pollution of the seas or air space above, resulting from any activities with radio-active materials or other harmful agents.

1982 UNITED NATIONS CONVENTION ON THE LAW OF THE SEA

PART XII

PROTECTION AND PRESERVATION OF THE MARINE ENVIRONMENT

SECTION 1. GENERAL PROVISIONS

Article 192

General obligation

States have the obligation to protect and preserve the marine environment.

Article 193

Sovereign right of States to exploit their natural resources

States have the sovereign right to exploit their natural resources pursuant to their environmental policies and in accordance with their duty to protect and preserve the marine environment.

Article 194

Measures to prevent, reduce and control pollution of the marine environment

1. States shall take, individually or jointly as appropriate, all measures consistent with this Convention that are necessary to prevent, reduce and control pollution of the marine environment from any sources, using for this purpose the best practicable means at their disposal and in accordance with their capabilities, and they shall endeavour to harmonize their policies in this connection.

2. States shall take all measures necessary to ensure that activities under their jurisdiction or control are so conducted as not to cause damage by pollution to other States and their environment, and that pollution arising from accidents or activities under their jurisdiction or control does not spread beyond the area where they exercise sovereign rights in accordance with this Convention.

3. The measures taken pursuant to this Part shall deal with all sources of pollution of the marine environment. These measures shall include, *inter alia*, those designed to minimize to the fullest possible extent:

(a) the release of toxic, harmful or noxious substances, especially those which are persistent, from land-based sources, from or through the atmosphere or by dumping;

(b) pollution from vessels, in particular measures for preventing accidents and dealing with emergencies, ensuring the safety of operations at sea, preventing intentional and unintentional discharges, and regulating the design, construction, equipment, operation and manning of vessels;

(c) pollution from installations and devices used in exploration or exploitation of the natural resources of the sea-bed or subsoil, in particular measures for preventing accidents and dealing with emergencies, ensuring the safety of operations at sea, and regulating the design, construction, equipment, operation and manning of such installations or devices;

(d) pollution from other installations and devices operating in the marine environment, in particular measures for preventing accidents and dealing with emergencies, ensuring safety of operations at sea, and regulating the design, construction, equipment, operation and manning of such installations or devices.

4. In taking such measures to prevent, reduce or control pollution of the marine environment, States shall refrain from unjustifiable interference with activities carried out by other States in the exercise of their rights and in pursuance of their duties in conformity with this Convention.

5. The measures taken in accordance with this Part shall include those necessary to protect and preserve rare or fragile ecosystems as well as the habitat of depleted, threatened or endangered species and other forms of marine life.

Article 195

Duty not to transfer damage or hazards or transform one type of pollution into another

In taking measures to prevent, reduce or control pollution of the marine environment, States shall act so as not to transfer, directly or indirectly, damage or hazards from one area to another or transform one type of pollution into another.

Article 196

Use of technologies or introduction of alien or new species

1. States shall take all measures necessary to prevent, reduce and control pollution of the marine environment resulting from the use of technologies under their jurisdiction or control, or the intentional or accidental introduction of species, alien or new, to a particular part of the marine environment, which may cause significant and harmful changes thereto.

2. This article does not affect the application of this Convention regarding the prevention, reduction and control of pollution of the marine environment.

2. LIABILITY

a. LIABILITY UNDER TREATIES OTHER THAN LOS

In this and following sections, we will examine some existing Conventions that were negotiated under the auspices of the International Maritime Organization (IMO -- its earlier name was the Intergovernmental Maritime Consultative Organization -- IMCO). In this note, information on the structure and responsibilities of IMO are set forth.

The IMO is a specialized agency of the United Nations created by international agreement in 1948. It was not until 1958 that the treaty was actually implemented, and IMO (then IMCO) came into being. The purpose of IMO was seen to be the promotion of international cooperation with respect to all technical matters affecting shipping, to discourage discriminatory shipping practices, and to promote availability of shipping.

In practice, IMO has been extremely active in promotion of safety at sea, and in the control of oil pollution from ships. It has sponsored conferences resulting in major agreements, a few of which are to be found in this chapter. It is composed of an assembly in which each member has one vote, a council, and several working committees. The principle ones of these are the Maritime Safety Committee, and the Legal Committee.

The Maritime Safety Committee (MSC) is central to the work of the organization. MSC deals with the technical aspects of maritime problems, the most important of which, for our purposes, is marine pollution. It is this committee that gathers and disseminates technical information and lays the groundwork for the negotiation of international agreements. All recommendations from the committees go to the Council and then to the Assembly for adoption.

For a complete description of the work of IMO, see Mensah, The IMCO Experience, in Law, Institutions, and the Global Environment (1972) at 227 et seq.

INTERNATIONAL CONVENTION ON CIVIL LIABILITY FOR OIL POLLUTION DAMAGE, 1969

....

Article II

This Convention shall apply exclusively to pollution damage caused on the territory including the territorial sea of a Contracting State and to preventive measures taken to prevent or minimize such damage.

Article III

1. Except as provided in paragraphs 2 and 3 of this article, the owner of a ship at the time of an incident, or where the incident consists of a series of occurrences at the time of the first occurrence, shall be liable for any pollution damage caused by oil which has escaped or been discharged from the ship as a result of the incident.

2. No liability for pollution damage shall attach to the owner if he proves that the damage:

(a) resulted from an act of war, hostilities, civil war, insurrection or a natural phenomenon of an exceptional, inevitable and irresistible character, or

(b) was wholly caused by an act or omission done with intent to cause damage by a third party, or

(c) was wholly caused by the negligence or other wrongful act of any government or other authority responsible for the maintenance of lights or other navigational aids in the exercise of that function.

3. If the owner proves that the pollution damage resulted wholly or partly either from an act or omission done with intent to cause damage by the person who suffered the damage or from the negligence of that person, the owner may be exonerated wholly or partially from his liability to such person.

4. No claim for compensation for pollution damage shall be made against the owner otherwise than in accordance with this Convention. No claim for pollution damage under this Convention or

otherwise may be made against the servants or agents of the owner.

5. Nothing in this Convention shall prejudice any right of recourse of the owner against third parties.

Article IV

When oil has escaped or has been discharged from two or more ships, and pollution damage results therefrom the owners of all the ships concerned, unless exonerated under Article III, shall be jointly and severally liable for all such damage which is not reasonably separable.

Article V

1. The owner of a ship shall be entitled to limit his liability under this Convention in respect of any one accident to an aggregate amount of 2,000 francs for each ton of the ship's tonnage. However, this aggregate amount shall not in any event exceed 210 million francs.

....

INTERNATIONAL CONVENTION ON THE ESTABLISHMENT OF AN INTERNATIONAL FUND FOR COMPENSATION FOR OIL POLLUTION DAMAGE, 1971

....

Article 2

1. An International Fund for compensation for pollution damage, to be named "The International Oil Pollution Compensation Fund" and hereinafter referred to as "The Fund," is hereby established with the following aims:

(a) to provide compensation for pollution damage to the extent that the protection offered by the Liability Convention is inadequate;

(b) to give relief to shipowners in respect of the additional financial burden imposed on them by the Liability Convention, such relief being subject to conditions designed to insure compliance with safety at sea and other conventions;

(c) to give effect to the related purposes set out in this Convention.

2. The Fund shall in each Contracting State be recognized as a legal person capable under the laws of that state of assuming rights and obligations and of being a party in legal proceedings before the courts of that state. Each Contracting State shall recognize the Director of the Fund (hereinafter referred to as "The Director") as the legal representative of the Fund.

Article 3

This Convention shall apply:

1. with regard to compensation according to Article 4, exclusively to pollution damage caused on the territory including the territorial sea of a Contracting State and to preventive measures taken to

prevent or minimize such damage.

2. with regard to indemnification of shipowners and their guarantors according to Article 5, exclusively in respect of pollution damage caused on the territory including the territorial sea of a state party to the Liability Convention, by a ship registered in or flying the flag of a Contracting State and in respect of preventive measures taken to prevent or minimize such danger.

ED. NOTE: For the provision covering responsibility and liability under the 1982 Convention, see Article 235, *infra*.

C. VESSEL SOURCE POLLUTION

COMPETENCE TO ESTABLISH STANDARDS FOR THE CONTROL OF VESSEL SOURCE POLLUTION: WORKING PAPER PRESENTED BY THE UNITED STATES OF AMERICA, U.N. Doc. A/AC.138/SC.III/L.36 (April 2, 1973)

Vessels introduce pollutants into the marine environment in three principal ways -- through oil and other cargoes entering the water due to collisions or other maritime casualties, through loading, unloading and bunkering operations, and through the intentional operational discharge of oil. There are, of course, other pollutants released from vessels such as sewage and garbage but these do not present problems of the same magnitude (there are international efforts underway to develop technical means of control for such pollutants).

A. Collisions and Other Maritime Casualties

Most casualties occur in congested areas in internal waters, at port entrances or in heavily traveled shipping lanes close to the coast. Thus, individual States can and should act effectively to reduce pollution from such incidents by the provision of adequate navigational aids, warnings of dangers to navigation and other assistance to the mariner to ensure that collisions, groundings and other casualties are minimized. Also, such international actions as provision of compulsory traffic separation schemes in congested areas, and requiring double-bottom construction for large tankers, as proposed by the United States in these and IMCO negotiations, can assist in solving these problems. In addition, authority to take remedial action is given to coastal States in the Convention Relating to Intervention on the High Seas in Cases of Oil Pollution Casualties (which is presently being revised to expand it to cover other substances in addition to oil). Oil spills resulting from casualties contribute about 10 per cent of vessel source oil pollution and methods for preventing such spills must continue to be developed.

B. Loading and bunkering operations

It is estimated that approximately 5 to 10 per cent of vessel source oil pollution is caused by spills occurring during bunkering and loading operations. This source of pollution is being reduced through provision of automatic loading controls on large tankers and improved personnel training. Also, significant advances are being made in the development of new techniques to clean up spills. Many ports are now providing the equipment and personnel to deal rapidly and effectively with such spills but continuing efforts are needed by maritime and port States.

C. Operational discharges

The major source of vessel pollution is the intentional operational discharge of oily wastes from commercial vessels. Operational discharge is due to the pumping of oily bilge wastes, tanker ballasting operations, and the cleaning of tanker cargo tanks prior to a change in the type of cargo or prior to overhaul. Such discharges are estimated to account for approximately three fourths of all oil pollution from vessels, with tank washing and ballasting providing about twice as much oil pollution as bilge pumping.

After discharging a cargo of oil, a tanker must take aboard seawater in her cargo tanks for use as ballast to facilitate handling in port and to provide proper seakeeping characteristics. For example, safe navigation requires ballast of approximately 40 per cent of dead weight tonnage under normal conditions and as much as 80 per cent in extreme weather conditions. Since some oil remains in the tanks by adhering to the tank surface, the ballast water will mix with that residue and become "oily". As the tanks must be empty before a new cargo of oil can be taken aboard, the oily ballast water must be disposed of in one of two ways -- direct discharge at sea or separation of the oil and its retention on board under the "load-on-top" system. In tankers structurally equipped for "load-on-top", the tanks are washed with sea water which is then collected in a slop tank (the other tanks are then clean and can take on water for ballast). During the ballast voyage the oily water in the slop tank slowly separates into a layer of oil and a layer of water, after which the water can be discharged. A new cargo can then be loaded on top of the retained oil or the retained oil can be discharged into a shore reception facility. This procedure is not fully effective since settling is affected by turbulent sea conditions and other factors and since some voyages are simply not lengthy enough for the process to be completed, but it is estimated that the system is 80 per cent effective. Although "load-on-top" tankers carry three fourths of the oil transported by sea, they produce only about one fourth of the operational oil discharge due to ballasting and tank cleaning.

INTERNATIONAL CONVENTION FOR THE PREVENTION OF POLLUTION OF THE SEA BY OIL, 1954, As amended, 1962, 1969, 1971

Article I

(1) For the purposes of the present Convention, the following expressions shall (unless the context otherwise requires) have the meanings hereby respectively assigned to them that is to say:

....

`Discharge' in relation to oil or oily mixture means any discharge or escape howsoever caused;

....

`Nearest land'. The term `from the nearest land' means `from the base-line from which the territorial sea of the territory in question is estabished in accordance with the Geneva Convention on the Territorial Sea and the Contiguous Zone, 1958':

`Oil' means crude oil, fuel oil, heavy diesel oil and lubricating oil, and `oily' shall be construed accordingly;

`Oily mixture' means a mixture with any oil content;

`Organization' means the Inter-Governmental Maritime Consultative Organization;

`Ship' means any sea-going vessel of any type whatsoever, including floating craft, whether self-propelled or towed by another vessel, making a sea voyage; and `tanker' means a ship in which the greater part of the cargo space is constructed or adapted for the carriage of liquid cargoes in bulk and which is not, for the time being, carrying a cargo other than oil in that part of its cargo space.

....

Article II

(1) The present Convention shall apply to ships registered in any of the territories of a Contracting Government and to unregistered ships having the nationality of a Contracting Party, except:

(a) tankers of under 150 tons gross tonnage and other ships of under 500 tons gross tonnage, provided that each Contracting Government will take the necessary steps, so far as is reasonable and practicable, to apply the requirements of the Convention to such ships also, having regard to their size, service and the type of fuel used for their propulsion;

(b) ships for the time being engaged in the whaling industry when actually employed on whaling operations;

(c) ships for the time being navigating the Great Lakes of North America and their connecting and tributary waters as far east as the lower exit of St. Lambert Lock at Montreal in the Province of Quebec, Canada;

(d) naval ships and ships for the time being used as naval auxiliaries.

(2) Each Contracting Government undertakes to adopt appropriate measures ensuring that requirements equivalent to those of the present Convention, so far as is reasonable and practicable, are applied to the ships referred to in subparagraph (d) of paragraph (1) of this Article.

Article III

Subject to the provisions of Articles IV and V:

(a) the discharge from a ship to which the present Convention applies, other than a tanker, of oil or oily mixture shall be prohibited except when the following conditions are satisfied:

(i) the ship is proceeding en route;

(ii) the instantaneous rate of discharge of oil content does not exceed 60 litres per mile;

(iii) the oil content of the discharge is less than 200 parts per 1,000,000 parts of the mixture;

(iv) the discharge is made as far as practicable from land;

(b) the discharge from a tanker to which the present Convention applies of oil or oily mixture shall be prohibited except when the following conditions are satsified:

(i) the tanker is proceeding en route;

(ii) the instantaneous rate of discharge of oil content does not exceed 60 litres per mile;

(iii) the total quantity of oil discharged on a ballast voyage does not exceed 1/15,000 of the total cargo-carrying capacity;

(iv) the tanker is more than 50 miles from the nearest land;

(c) the provisions of sub-paragraph (b) of this Article shall not apply to:

(i) the discharge of ballast from a cargo tank which, since the cargo was last carried therein, has been so cleaned that any effluent therefrom, if it were discharged from a stationary tanker into clean calm water on a clear day, would produce no visible traces of oil on the surface of the water; or

(ii) the discharge of oil or oily mixture from machinery bilge spaces, which shall be governed by the provisions of sub-paragraph (a) of this Article.

Article IV

Article III shall not apply to:

(a) the discharge of oil or oily mixture from a ship for purpose of securing the safety of a ship, preventing damage to a ship or cargo, or saving life at sea;

(b) the escape of oil or oily mixture resulting from damage to a ship or unavoidable leakage, if all reasonable precautions have been taken after the occurrence of the damage or discovery of the leakage for the purpose of preventing or minimizing the escape;

Article V

Article III shall not apply to the discharge of oily mixture from the bilges of a ship during the period of twelve months following the date on which the present Convention comes into force for the relevant territory in accordance with paragraph (1) of Article II.

Article VI

(1) Any contravention of Articles III and IX shall be an offense punishable under the law of the relevant territory in respect of the ship in accordance with paragraph (1) of Article II.

(2) The penalties which may be imposed under the law of any of the territories of a Contracting Government in respect of the unlawful discharge from a ship of oil or oily mixture outside the territorial sea of that territory shall be adequate in severity to discourage any such unlawful discharge and shall not be less than the penalties which may be imposed under the law of that territory in respect of the same infringements within the territorial sea.

(3) Each Contracting Government shall report to the Organization the penalties actually imposed for each infringement.

Article VI bis

(1) Every tanker to which the present Convention applies and for which the building contract

is placed on or after the date of coming into force of this Article shall be constructed in accordance with the provisions of Annex C. In addition, every tanker to which the present Convention applies and for which the building contract is placed, or in the absence of a building contract the keel of which is laid or which is at a similar state of construction, before the date of coming into force of this Article shall be required, within two years after that date, to comply with the provisions of Annex C, where such a tanker falls into either of the following categories:

(a) a tanker, the delivery of which is after 1 January 1977; or

(b) a tanker to which both the following conditions apply:

(i) delivery is not later than 1 January 1977; and

(ii) the building contract is placed after 1 January 1972, or in cases where no building contract has previously been placed, the keel is laid or the tanker is at a similar stage of construction, after 30 June 1972.

(2) A tanker required under paragraph (1) of this Article to be constructed in accordance with Annex C and so constructed shall carry on board a certificate issued or authorized by the responsible Contracting Government attesting to such compliance. A tanker which under paragraph (1) of this Article is not required to be constructed in accordance with Annex C shall carry on board a certificate to that effect issued or authorized by the responsible Contracting Government, or if the tanker does comply with Annex C although not required to do so, it may carry on board a certificate issued or authorized by the responsible Contracting Government attesting such compliance. A Contracting Government shall not permit such tankers under its flag to trade unless the appropriate certificate has been issued.

(3) Certificates issued under the authority of a Contracting Government shall be accepted by the other Contracting Governments for all purposes covered by the present Convention. They shall be regarded by the other Contracting Governments as having the same force as certificates issued by them.

(4) If a Contracting Government has clear grounds for believing that a tanker required under paragraph (1) of this Article to be constructed in accordance with Annex C entering ports in its territory or using the off-shore terminals under its control does not in fact comply with Annex C, such Contracting Government may for this reason deny such a tanker access to ports or to off-shore terminals under its control until such time as the Contracting Government is satisfied that the tanker does comply.

Article VII

(1) As from a date twelve months after the present Convention comes into force for the relevant territory in respect of a ship in accordance with paragraph (1) of Article II, such a ship shall be required to be so fitted as to prevent, as far as reasonable and practicable, the escape of oil into bilges, unless effective means are provided to ensure that the oil in the bilges is not discharged in contravention of this Convention.

(2) Carrying water ballast in oil fuel tanks shall be avoided if possible.

Article VIII

(1) Each Contracting Government shall take all appropriate steps to promote the provision of

facilities as follows:

(a) according to the needs of the ships using them, ports shall be provided with facilities adequate for the reception, without causing undue delay to ships, of such residues and oily mixtures as would remain for disposal from ships other than tankers if the bulk of the water had been separated from the mixture;

(b) oil loading terminals shall be provided with facilities adequate for the reception of such residues and oily mixtures as would similarly remain for disposal by tankers;

(c) ship repair ports shall be provided with facilities adquate for the reception of such residues and oily mixtures as would similarly remain for disposal by all ships entering for repairs.

(2) Each Contracting Government shall determine which are the ports and oil loading terminals in its territories suitable for the purposes of sub-paragraphs (a), (b) and (c) of paragraph (1) of this Article.

(3) As regards paragraph (1) of this Article, each Contracting Government shall report to the Organization, for transmission to the Contracting Government concerned, all cases where the facilities are alleged to be inadequate.

Article IX

(1) Of the ships to which the present Convention applies, every ship which uses oil fuel and every tanker shall be provided with an oil record book, whether as part of the ship's official log book or otherwise, in the form specified in the Annex to the Convention.

(2) The oil record book shall be completed on each occasion, on a tank-to-tank basis, whenever any of the following operations take place in the ship:

(a) for tankers:

(i) loading of oil cargo;

(ii) transfer of oil cargo during voyage;

(iii) discharge of oil cargo;

(iv) ballasting of cargo tanks;

(v) cleaning of cargo tanks;

(vi) discharge of dirty ballast;

(vii) discharge of water from slop-tanks;

(viii) disposal of residues;

(ix) discharge overboard of bilge water containing oil which has accumulated in machinery spaces whilst in port, and the routine discharge at sea of bilge water containing oil unless the latter has been entered in the appropriate log book.

In the event of such discharge or escape of oil or oily mixture as is referred to in Article IV, a statement shall be made in the oil record book of the circumstances of, and the reason for, the discharge or escape.

(3) Each operation described in paragraph (2) of this Article shall be fully recorded without delay in the oil record book so that the entries in the book appropriate to that operation are completed. Each page of the book shall be signed by the officer or officers in charge of the operations concerned and, when the ship is manned, by the master of the ship. The written entries in the oil record book shall be in an official language of the relevant territory in respect of the ship in accordance with paragraph (1) of Article II, or in English or French.

(4) Oil record books shall be kept in such a place as to be readily available for inspection at all reasonable times, and, except in the case of unmanned ships under tow, shall be kept on board the ship. They shall be preserved for a period of two years after the last entry has been made.

(5) The competent authorities of any of the territories of a Contracting Government may inspect on board any ship to which the present Convention applies, while within a port in that territory, the oil record book required to be carried in the ship in compliance with the provisions of this Article, and may make a true copy of any entry in that book and may require the master of the ship to certify that the copy is a true copy of such entry. Any copy so made which purports to have been certified by the master of the ship as a true copy of an entry in the ship's oil record book shall be made admissible in any judicial proceedings as evidence of the facts stated in the entry. Any action by the competent authorities under this paragraph shall be taken as expeditiously as possible and the ship shall not be delayed.

Article X

(1) Any Contracting Government may furnish to the Government of the relevant territory in respect of the ship in accordance with paragraph (1) of Article II particulars in writing of evidence that any provision of the present Convention has been contravened in respect of that ship, wheresoever the alleged contravention may have taken place. If it is practicable to do so, the competent authorities of the former Government shall notify the master of the ship of the alleged contravention.

(2) Upon receiving such particulars, the Government so informed shall investigate the matter, and may request the other Government to furnish further or better particulars of the alleged contravention. If the Government so informed is satisfied that sufficient evidence is available in the form required by its law to enable proceedings against the owner or master of the ship to be taken in respect of the alleged contravention, it shall cause such proceedings to be taken as soon as possible. That Government shall promptly inform the Government whose official has reported the alleged contravention, as well as the Organization, of the action taken as a consequence of the information communicated.

Artice XI

Nothing in the present Convention shall be construed as derogating from the powers of any Contracting Government to take measures within its jurisdiction in respect of any matter to which the Convention relates or as extending the jurisdiction of any Contracting Government.

Article XII

Each Contracting Government shall send to the Bureau and to the appropriate organ of the United Nations:

(a) the text of laws, decrees, orders and regulations in force in its territories which give effect to the present Convention;

(b) all official reports or summaries of official reports in so far as they show the results of the application of the provisions of the Convention, provided always that such reports or summaries are not, in the opinion of that Government, of a confidential nature.

Article XIII

Any dispute between Contracting Governments relating to the interpretation or appplication of the present Convention which cannot be settled by negotiation shall be referred at the request of either party to the International Court of Justice for decision unless the parties to the dispute agree to submit it to arbitration.

....

INTERNATIONAL CONVENTION RELATING TO INTERVENTION ON THE HIGH SEAS IN CASES OF OIL POLLUTION CASUALTIES, 1969

The States Parties to the present Convention,

CONSCIOUS of the need to protect the interests of their peoples against the grave consequences of a maritime casualty resulting in danger of oil pollution of sea and coastlines,

CONVINCED that under these circumstances measures of an exceptional character to protect such interests might be necessary on the high seas and that these measures do not affect the principle of freedom of the high seas,

HAVE AGREED as follows:

Article I

1. Parties to the present Convention may take such measures on the high seas as may be necessary to prevent, mitigate or eliminate grave and imminent danger to their coastline or related interests from pollution or threat of pollution of the sea by oil, following upon a maritime casualty or acts related to such a casualty, which may reasonably be expected to result in major harmful consequences.

2. However, no measures shall be taken under the present Convention against any warship or other ship being owned or operated by a State and used, for the time being, only on government non-commercial service.

Article II

For the purposes of this Convention:

1. "maritime casualty" means a collision of ships, stranding or other incident of navigation, or other occurrence on board a ship or external to it resulting in material damage or imminent threat of material damage to a ship or cargo;

....

4. "related interests" means the interests of a coastal State directly affected or threatened by the maritime casualty. such as:

(a) maritime coastal, port or estuarine activities, including fisheries activities, constituting an essential means of livelihood for the persons concerned;

(b) tourist attractions of the area concerned;

(c) the health of the coastal population and the well-being of the area concerned, including the conservation of living marine resources and of wildlife;

....

Article III

When a coastal State is exercising the right to take measures in accordance with Article I, the following provisions shall apply:

(a) before taking any measure, a coastal State shall proceed to consultations with the other States affected by the maritime casualty, particularly with the flag State or States;

(b) the coastal State shall notify without delay the proposed measures to any persons physical or corporate known to the coastal State, or made known to it during the consultations, to have interests which can reasonably be expected to be affected by those measures. The coastal State shall take into account any views they may submit;

(c) before any measure is taken, the coastal State may proceed to a consultation with independent experts, whose names shall be chosen from a list maintained by the Organization.

(d) in cases of extreme urgency requiring measures to be taken immediately, the coastal State may take measures rendered necessary by the urgency of the situation, without prior notification or consultation or without continuing consultations already begun;

(e) a coastal State shall, before taking such measures and during their course, use its best endeavours to avoid any risk to human life, and to afford persons in distress any assistance of which they may stand in need, and in appropriate cases to facilitate the repatriation of ships' crews, and to raise no obstacle thereto;

(f) measures which have been taken in application of Article I shall be notified without delay to the States and to the known physical or corporate persons concerned, as well as to the Secretary-General of the Organization.

....

Article V

1. Measures taken by the coastal State in accordance with Article I shall be proportionate to the damage actual or threatened to it.

2. Such measures shall not go beyond what is reasonably necessary to achieve the end

mentioned in Article I and shall cease as soon as that end has been achieved; they shall not unnecessarily interfere with the rights and interests of the flag State, third States and of any persons, physical or corporate, concerned.

3. In considering whether the measures are proportionate to the damage, account shall be taken of:

(a) the extent and probability of imminent damage if those measures are not taken; and

(b) the likelihood of those measures being effective; and

(c) the extent of the damage which may be caused by such measures.

Article VI

Any Party which has taken measures in contravention of the provisions of the present Convention causing damage to others, shall be obliged to pay compensation to the extent of the damage caused by measures which exceed those reasonably necessary to achieve the end mentioned in Article I.

....

INTERNATIONAL CONVENTION FOR THE PREVENTION OF POLLUTION FROM SHIPS, 1973

The parties to the Convention, being conscious of the need to preserve the human environment in general and the marine environment in particular,

Recognizing that deliberate, negligent or accidental release of oil and other harmful substances from ships constitutes a serious source of pollution, Recognizing also the importance of the International Convention for the Prevention of Pollution of the Sea by Oil, 1954, as being the first multilateral instrument to be concluded with the prime objective of protecting the environment, and appreciating the significant contribution which that Convention has made in preserving the seas and coastal environment from pollution,

Desiring to achieve the complete elimination of intentional pollution of the marine environment by oil and other harmful substances and the minimization of accidental discharge of such substances,

Considering that this object may best be achieved by establishing rules not limited to oil pollution having a universal purport,

Have agreed as follows:

Article 1

(1) The Parties to the Convention undertake to give effect to the provisions of the present Convention and those Annexes by which they are bound, in order to prevent the pollution of the marine environment by the discharge of harmful substances or effluents containing such substances in contravention of the Convention.

(2) Unless expressly provided for otherwise, a reference to the present Convention constitutes at the same time a reference to its Protocols and to the Annexes.

Article 2

For the purposes of this Convention, unless expressly provided for otherewise:

....

(2) "Harmful substance" means any substance which, if introduced into the sea, is liable to create hazards to human health, to harm living resources and marine life, to damage amenities or to interfere with other legitimate uses of the sea, and includes any substance subject to control by the present Convention.

(3) (a) "Discharge", in relation to harmful substances or effluents containing such substances, means any release howsoever caused from a ship and includes any escape, disposal, spilling, leaking, pumping, emitting or emptying.

(b) "Discharge" does not include:

(i) dumping within the meaning of the Convention on the Prevention of Marine Pollution by Dumping of Wastes and other Matter done at London on 13 November 1972;

(ii) release of harmful substances directly arising from the exploration, exploitation and associated off-shore processing of sea-bed mineral resources; or

(iii) release of harmful substances for purposes of legitimate scientific research into pollution abatement or control.

....

Article 3

....

(3) The present Convention shall not apply to any warship, naval auxiliary or other ship owned or operated by a State and used, for the time being, only on government non-commercial service. However, each Party shall ensure by the adoption of appropriate measures not impairing the operations or operational capabilities of such ships owner or operated by it, that such ships act in a manner consistent, so far as is reasonable and practicable, with the present Convention.

Article 4

(1) Any violation of the requirements of the present Convention shall be prohibited and sanctions shall be established therefor under the law of the Administration of the ship concerned wherever the violation occurs. If the Administration is informed of such a violation and is satisfied that sufficient evidence is available to enable proceedings to be brought in respect of the alleged violation, it shall cause such proceedings to be taken as soon as possible, in accordance with its law.

(2) Any violation of the requirements of the present Convention within the jurisdiction of any Party to the Convention shall be prohibited and sanctions shall be established therefor under the law of that Party. Whenever such a violation occurs, that Party shall either:

(a) cause proceedings to be taken in accordance with its law; or

(b) furnish to the Administration of the ship such information and evidence as may be in its possession that a violation has occurred.

(3) Where information or evidence with respect to any violation of the present Convention by a ship is furnished to the Administration of that ship, the Administration shall promptly inform the Party which has furnished the information or evidence, and the Organization, of the action taken.

(4) The penalties specified under the law of a Party pursuant to the present Article shall be adequate in severity to discourage violations of the present Convention and shall be equally severe irrespective of where the violations occur.

....

Article 6

(1) Parties to the Convention shall co-operate in the detection of violations and the enforcement of the provisions of the present Convention, using all appropriate and practicable measures of detection and environmental monitoring, adequate procedures for reporting and accumulation of evidence.

(2) A ship to which the present Convention applies may, in any port or off-shore terminal of a Party, be subject to inspection by officers appointed or authorized by that Party for the purpose of verifying whether the ship has discharged any harmful substances in violation of the provisions of the Regulations. If an inspection indicates a violation of the Convention, a report shall be forwarded to the Administration for any appropriate action.

(3) Any Party shall furnish to the Administration evidence, if any, that the ship has discharged harmful substances or effluents containing such substances in violation of the provisions of the Regulations. If it is practicable to do so, the competent authority of the former Party shall notify the master of the ship of the alleged violation.

(4) Upon receiving such evidence, the Administration so informed shall investigate the matter, and may request the other Party to furnish further or better evidence of the alleged contravention. If the Administration is satisfied that sufficient evidence is available to enable proceedings to be brought in respect of the alleged violation, it shall cause such proceedings to be taken in accordance with its law as soon as possible. The Administration shall promptly inform the Party which has reported the alleged violation, as well as the Organization, of the action taken.

(5) A Party may also inspect a ship to which the present Convention applies when it enters the ports or off-shore terminals under its jurisdiction, if a request for an investigation is received from any Party together with sufficient evidence that the ship has discharged harmful substances or effluents containing such substances in any place. The report of such investigation shall be sent to the Party requesting it and the the Administration so that the appropriate action may be taken under the present Convention.

Article 7

(1) All possible efforts shall be made to avoid a ship being unduly contained or delayed under Articles 4, 5 and 6 of the present Convention.

(2) When a ship is unduly detained or delayed under Articles 4, 5 and 6 of the present Convention, it shall be entitled to compensation for any loss or damage suffered.

H. Gary Knight, "ISSUES BEFORE THE THIRD UNITED NATIONS CONFERENCE ON THE LAW OF THE SEA," 34 Louisiana Law review 155, 187-188 (1974)[3]

The Inter-Governmental Maritime Consultative Organization ("IMCO") has been engaged in attempts to reduce or restrict the discharge of pollutants from vessels for many years. However, many developing nations have charged -- and perhaps not incorrectly -- that IMCO has by and large been the tool of the major maritime powers and its efforts at pollution prevention have been token at best. It was such a reaction to the unwillingness or inability of IMCO to move rapidly in the Artic pollution situation that led Canada to take unilateral action by way of a 100 miles pollution prevention zone in which the construction and operation of ships is strictly regulated, ostensibly for the purpose of protecting the fragile Arctic environment. Nonetheless, developments have proceeded at IMCO, most recently resulting in the adoption of the text of the International Conventionfor the Prevention of Pollution from Ships, 1973.

The Seabed Committee has also placed the question of vessel source pollution on its agenda and there have been a number of proposals in this area. As with other issues involved in the negotiations, the issue no longer appears to be whether to retain absolute freedom of the high seas as opposed to establishment of jurisdictional bases for management, but rather the nature of the jurisdictional base. Major maritime powers are generally opposed to zonal approaches to jursidiction -- whether in regard to fisheries jurisdiction, vessel pollution control, or regulation of scientific research -- while most developing nations perceive that their national interests can best be protected through establishment of broad offshore zones of national jurisdiction. The situation is particularly acute with respect to the pollution issue, where the potential for imposition of excessive cost burdens on maritime transport is great if each coastal state should be free to estabish its own pollution standards within a 200 mile zone. This situation would not be unlike that which would exist if trucks traveling from Maine to California were required to have a different type of pollution control device operative in each state through which they passed -- the costs of acquiring thirteen or fourteen different devices, plus the time expended in changing them at each state boundary, would greatly raise the cost to the consumer of the goods being transported.

....

The United States' fear -- indeed that of most major maritime powers -- is that extensive pollution zones might be abused to adversely affect maritime commerce. Of course, developing nations probably import proportionately more goods by ocean borne transport than do developed countries, yet the potential for disruption of maritime commerce as an outgrowth of ocean related controversy remains. The United States, in August, 1973, delivered a statement to the Seabeds Committee pointing out that the majority of coastal nations of the world are "zone locked," i.e., vessels bound from their ports to areas beyond any 200 mile economic resource zone would of necessity pass through the economic resource zone (and, if the zonal approach were taken, the pollultion control zone) of at least one other nation. If pollution control zones were used to inhibit maritime transport, the effect would obviously be felt not only by the United States and other maritime powers, but by the majority of the world's coastal nations. Thus the form which pollution control agreements take concerning the

[3]. Originally published in 34 Louisiana Law Review at 187-188.

appropriate jurisdiction to promulgate and enforce rules may well be of greater importance than the substantive rules themselves.

COMPETENCE TO ESTABLISH STANDARDS FOR THE CONTROL OF VESSEL SOURCE POLLUTION: WORKING PAPER PRESENTED BY THE UNITED STATES OF AMERICA, U.N. Doc. A/AC.138/SC.III/L.36 (April 2, 1973)

A fundamental objective of the Law of the Sea Conference is to reach agreement on effective measures which will protect the marine environment. This objective is shared by all nations. Another fundamental objective, shared by all nations, is protection of the freedom of navigation -- an objective which is vital for international trade, communication and peaceful relations among nations.

A principal issue in the consideration of standards to control vessel source pollution is the authority to establish standards which will eliminate or minimize environmental damage caused by vessels. Only a system of exclusively international standards will provide an effective means to control vessel source pollution while protecting the community interest in both of these fundamental objectives. There are at least five principal reasons which support exclusively international standards.

First, the international community has basic interests which should be represented in the formulation of such standards. One basic concern, of particular interest to coastal States, is to protect the marine environment from pollution. A second basic concern, of particular interest to exporting States, importing States, and maritime States, is the avoidance of unnecessary increases in transportation costs. Participation by these concerned States in the establishment of standards will ensure that a proper balance is maintained.

On the other hand, if coastal States were to be given the authority to establish standards by themselves, such standards might not adequately reflect either the interests of existing maritime States or the developing States as they become maritime nations or the interests of the international community in effective protection of the marine environment.

Second, because of the difficulty or impossibility of a vessel complying with several sets of different, and possibly inconsistent standards, there should be a single set of uniform standards observed by all States. Although vessels utilizing major ocean routes pass close to shore for only a fraction of a normal voyage, they could be subject to many separate sets of standards in an area adjacent to the territorial sea. For example, on a voyage from the Persian Gulf to Europe, a heavily traveled oil transport route, a vessel might be subject to as many as 15 different sets of standards. Since compliance with differing standards might be difficult and costly, vessels may try to avoid these areas, if possible, thus increasing voyage length and time. Avoidance of these areas might even force a vessel into a different load line area, thus requiring a lighter cargo load. The result would be higher shipping costs, which in the end would be passed on to producers and consumers. A legal regime which accords coastal States the authority to supplement international standards does not avoid those problems. Moreover, it should be kept in mind that the higher costs associated with divergent standards will not necessarily result in improved protection for the marine environment.

Third, exclusively international standards are required for effective protection of the full marine environment. Since ocean currents carry some amounts of pollution from one ocean area to another and from far offshore to inshore areas, individual coastal State standards could not as effectively reduce such pollution. All of the principal oceans have major currents flowing generally from one continent to another and across broad expanses of open ocean. To demonstrate the magnitude of these currents, the major North American current system washes the shores of 23 coastal States of Africa, South America, North America and Europe. In crossing any major oceans, ships will encounter one or more of these major currents and may discharge oil into them many miles from shore. Inshore currents may carry quantities of oil onto beaches and inshore areas hundreds of miles away from the point of discharge. Because of the size of the areas and the distances involved, individual coastal State pollution control standards cannot possibly cope with the entire problem. Moreover, individual coastal State standards may simply tranfer the effects of pollution from one State to another. Such a transfer could add to friction between nations and would not meaningfully contribute to the protection of the marine environment. Certain areas, of course, may require special measures for effective protection. Such measures, however, could and should be internationally established.

Fourth, an exclusively international approach is better able to respond to changes in the technology for the control of pollution and to new knowledge about threats to the marine environment. Our concern, of course, must be protection of the entire marine environment. In meeting that concern, it is far more efficient to continually update one set of international standards than to alter over 100 national standards. Moreover, an international approach provides a focus for utilizing the expertise of all nations in establishing international standards.

Fifth, concerns regarding economic advantage and disadvantage among States are increasingly evident in attempts to deal effectively with environmental problems. Individual States may fear the economic effects on themselves of imposing environmental controls that others may not impose. A system of exclusively international standards would largely eliminate these competitive economic concerns and would encourage a willingness to impose higher standards on an agreed basis.

ED. NOTE: Against this background, we must now compare the results of the negotiations to see how well these concerns were met. As you examine the treaty texts, you may be struck by the complexity of the problems that emerged, in large part due to the fact that the Conference did in fact adopt basically a zonal approach to the law of the sea. In addition to dealing with the problem of standard setting, and the relationship of international rules with national legislation, the problem of enforcement was a difficult one, and it was necessary to simultaneously consider the problem of the resolution of disputes. While dispute resolution is dealt with in a separate chapter, you will certainly recognize that setting up a system of regulation of this type, it is absolutely essential that it must be accompanied by international mechanisms such as tribunals to curb excesses. In addition, the Conference, while focussing primarily on vessel source pollution, felt it necessary to provide, at least in part, for the protection of the marine environment from pollution from other sources.

1982 UNITED NATIONS CONVENTION ON THE LAW OF THE SEA

PART XII

PROTECTION AND PRESERVATION OF THE MARINE ENVIRONMENT

SECTION 5. INTERNATIONAL RULES AND NATIONAL LEGISLATION TO PREVENT, REDUCE AND CONTROL POLLUTION OF THE MARINE ENVIRONMENT

Article 207

Pollution from land-based sources

1. States shall adopt laws and regulations to prevent, reduce and control pollution of the marine environment from land-based sources, including rivers, estuaries, pipelines and outfall

structures, taking into account internationally agreed rules, standards and recommended practices and procedures.

2. States shall take other measures as may be necessary to prevent, reduce and control such pollution.

3. States shall endeavour to harmonize their policies in this connection at the appropriate regional level.

4. States, acting especially through competent international organizations or diplomatic conference, shall endeavour to establish global and regional rules, standards and recommended practices and procedures to prevent, reduce and control pollution of the marine environment from land-based sources, taking into account characteristic regional features, the economic capacity of developing States and their need for economic development. Such rules, standards and recommended practices and procedures shall be re-examined from time to time as necessary.

5. Laws, regulations, measures, rules, standards and recommended practices and procedures referred to in paragraphs 1, 2 and 4 shall include those designed to minimize, to the fullest extent possible, the release of toxic, harmful or noxious substances, especially those which are persistent, into the marine environment.

Article 108

Pollution from sea-bed activities subject to national jurisdiction

1. Coastal States shall adopt laws and regulations to prevent, reduce and control pollution of the marine environment arising from or in connection with sea-bed activities subject to their jurisdiction and from artificial islands, installations and structures under their jurisdiction, pursuant to articles 60 and 80.

2. States shall take other measures as may be necessary to prevent, reduce and control such pollution.

3. Such laws, regulations and measures shall be no less effective than international rules, standards and recommended practices and procedures.

4. States shall endeavour to harmonize their policies in this connection at the appropriate regional level.

5. States, acting through competent international organizations or diplomatic conference, shall establish global and regional rules, standards and recommended practices and procedures to prevent, reduce and control pollution of the marine environment referred to in paragraph 1. Such rules, standards and recommended practices and procedures shall be re-examined from time to time as necessary.

Article 209

Pollution from activities in the Area

1. International rules, regulations and procedures shall be established in accordance with Part XI to prevent, reduce and control pollution of the marine environment from activities in the Area. Such rules, regulations and procedures shall be re-examined from time to time as necessary.

2. Subject to the relevant provisions of this section, States shall adopt laws and regulations to prevent, reduce and control pollution of the marine environment from activities in the Area undertaken by vessels, installations, structures and other devices flying their flag or of their registry or operating under their authority, as the case may be. The requirements of such laws and regulations shall be no less effective than the international rules, regulations and procedures referred to in paragraph 1.

Article 210

Pollution by dumping

1. States shall adopt laws and regulations to prevent, reduce and control pollution of the marine environment by dumping.

2. States shall take other measures as may be necessary to prevent, reduce and control such pollution.

3. Such laws, regulations and measures shall ensure that dumping is not carried out without the permission of the competent authorities of States.

4. States, acting especially through competent international organizations or diplomatic conference, shall endeavour to establish global and regional rules, standards and recommended practices and procedures to prevent, reduce and control such pollution. Such rules, standards and recommended practices and procedures shall be re-examined from time to time as necessary.

5. Dumping within the territorial sea and the exclusive economic zone or onto the continental shelf shall not be carried out without the express approval of the coastal State, which has the right to permit, regulate and control such dumping after due consideration of the matter with other States which by reason of their geographical situation may be adversely affected thereby.

6. National laws, regulations and measures shall be no less effective in preventing, reducing and controlling such pollution than the global rules and standards.

Article 211

Pollution from vessels

1. States, acting through the competent international organization or diplomatic conference, shall establish international rules and standards to prevent, reduce and control pollution of the marine environment from vessels and promote the adoption, in the same manner, wherever appropriate, of routeing systems designed to minimize the threat of accidents which might cause pollution of the marine environment, including the coastline, and pollution damage to the related interests of coastal States. Such rules and standards shall, in the same manner, be re-examined from time to time as necessary.

2. States shall adopt laws and regulations for the prevention, reduction and control of pollution of the marine environment from vessels flying their flag or of their registry. Such laws and regulations shall at least have the same effect as that of generally accepted international rules and standards established through the competent international organization or general diplomatic conference.

3. States which establish particular requirements for the prevention, reduction and control of pollution of the marine environment as a condition for the entry of foreign vessels into their ports or

internal waters or for a call at their off-shore terminals shall give due publicity to such requirements and shall communicate them to the competent international organization. Whenever such requirements are established in identical form by two or more coastal States in an endeavour to harmonize policy, the communication shall indicate which States are participating in such co-operative arrangments. Every State shall require the master of a vessel flying its flag or of its registry, when navigating within the territorial sea of a State participating in such co-operative arrangements, to furnish, upon the request of that State, information as to whether it is proceeding to a State of the same region participating in such co-operative arrangements and, if so, to indicate whether it complies with the port entry requirements of that State. This article is without prejudice to the continued exercise by a vessel of its right of innocent passage or to the application of article 25, paragraph 2.

4. Coastal States may, in the exercise of their sovereignty within their territorial sea, adopt laws and regulations for the prevention, reduction and control of marine pollution from foreign vessels, including vessels exercising the right of innocent passage. Such laws and regulations shall, in accordance with Part II, section 3, not hamper innocent passage of foreign vessels.

5. Coastal States, for the purpose of enforcement as provided for in section 6, may in respect of their exclusive economic zones adopt laws and regulations for the prevention, reduction and control of pollution from vessels conforming to and giving effect to generally accepted international rules and standards established through the competent international organization or diplomatic conference.

6. (a) Where the international rules and standards referred to in paragraph 1 are inadequate to meet special circumstances and coastal States have reasonable grounds for believing that a particular, clearly defined area of their respective exclusive economic zones is an area where the adoption of special mandatory measures for the prevention of pollution from vessels is required for recognized technical reasons in relation to its oceanographical and ecological conditions, as well as its utilization or the protection of its resources and the particular character of its traffic, the coastal States, after appropriate consultations through the competent international organization with any other States concerned, may, for that area, direct a communication to that organization, submitting scientific and technical evidence in support and information on necessary reception facilities. Within 12 months after receiving such a communication the organization shall determine whether the conditions in that area correspond to the requirements set out above. If the organization so determines, the coastal State may, for that area, adopt laws and regulations for the prevention, reduction and control of pollution from vessels implementing such international rules and standards or navigational practices as are made applicable, through the organization, for special areas. These laws and regulations shall not become applicable to foreign vessels until 15 months after the submission of the communication to the organization.

(b) The coastal States shall publish the limits of any such particular, clearly defined area.

(c) If the coastal States intend to adopt additional laws and regulations for the same area for the prevention, reduction and control of pollution from vessels, they shall, when submitting the aforesaid communication, at the same time notify the organization thereof. Such additional laws and regulations may relate to discharges or navigational practices but shall not require foreign vessels to observe design, construction, manning or equipment standards other than generally accepted international rules and standards; they shall become applicable to foreign vessels 15 months after the submission of the communication to the organization, provided that the organization agrees within 12 months after the submission of the communication.

7. The international rules and standards referred to in this article should include *inter alia* those related to prompt notification to coastal States, whose coastline or related interests may be

affected by incidents, including maritime casualties, which involve discharges or probability of discharges.

Article 212

Pollution from or through the atmosphere

1. States shall adopt laws and regulations to prevent, reduce and control pollution of the marine environment from or through the atmosphere, applicable to the air space under their sovereignty and to vessels flying their flag or vessels or aircraft of their registry, taking into account internationally agreed rules, standards and recommended practices and procedures and the safety of air navigation.

2. States shall take other measures as may be necessary to prevent, reduce and control such pollution.

3. States, acting especially through competent international organizations or diplomatic conference, shall endeavour to establish global and regional rules, standards and recommended practices and procedures to prevent, reduce and control such pollution.

SECTION 6. ENFORCEMENT

Article 213

Enforcement with respect to pollution from land-based sources

States shall enforce their laws and regulations adopted in accordance with article 207 and shall adopt laws and regulations and take other measures necessary to implement applicable international rules and standards established through competent international organizations or diplomatic conference to prevent, reduce and control pollution of the marine environment from land-based sources.

Article 214

Enforcement with respect to pollution from sea-bed activities

States shall enforce their laws and regulations adopted in accordance with article 208 and shall adopt laws and regulations and take other measures necessary to implement applicable international rules and standards established through competent international organizations or diplomatic conference to prevent, reduce and control pollution of the marine environment arising from or in connection with sea-bed activities subject to their jurisdiction and from artificial islands, installations and structures under their jurisdiction, pursuant to articles 60 and 80.

Article 215

Enforcement with respect to pollution from activities in the Area

Enforcement of international rules, regulations and procedures established in accordance with Part XI to prevent, reduce and control pollution of the marine environment from activities in the Area shall be governed by that Part.

Article 216

Enforcement with respect to pollution from dumping

1. Laws and regulations adopted in accordance with this Convention and applicable international rules and standards established through competent international organizations or diplomatic conference for the prevention, reduction and control of pollution of the marine environment by dumping shall be enforced:

(a) by the coastal State with regard to dumping within its territorial sea or its exclusive economic zone or onto its continental shelf;

(b) by the flag State with regard to vessels flying its flag or vessels or aircraft of its registry;

(c) by any State with regard to acts of loading of wastes or other matter occurring within its territory or at its off-shore terminals.

2. No State shall be obliged by virtue of this article to institute proceedings when another State has already instituted proceedings in accordance with this article.

Article 217

Enforcement by flag States

1. States shall ensure compliance by vessels flying their flag or of their registry with applicable international rules and standards, established through the competent international organization or general diplomatic conference, and with their laws and regulations adopted in accordance with this Convention for the prevention, reduction and control of pollution of the marine environment from vessels and shall accordingly adopt laws and regulations and take other measures necessary for their implementation. Flag States shall provide for the effective enforcement of such rules, standards, laws and regulations, irrespective of where a violation occurs.

2. States shall, in particular, take appropriate measures in order to ensure that vessels flying their flag or of their registry are prohibited from sailing, until they can proceed to sea in compliance with the requirements of the international rules and standards referred to in paragraph 1, including requirements in respect of design, construction, equipment and manning of vessels.

3. States shall ensure that vessels flying their flag or of their registry carry on board certificates required by and issued pursuant to international rules and standards referred to in paragraph 1. States shall ensure that vessels flying their flag are periodically inspected in order to verify that such certificates are in conformity with the actual condition of the vessels. These certificates shall be accepted by other States as evidence of the condition of the vessels and shall be regarded as having the same force as certificates issued by them, unless there are clear grounds for believing that the condition of the vessel does not correspond substantially with the particulars of the certificates.

4. If a vessel commits a violation of rules and standards established through the competent international organization or general diplomatic conference, the flag State, without prejudice to articles 218, 220 and 228, shall provide forimmediate investigation and where appropriate institute proceedings in respect of the alleged violation irrespective of where the violation occurred or where the pollution caused by such violation has occurred or has been spotted.

5. Flag States conducting an investigation of the violation may request the assistance of any

other State whose co-operation could be useful in clarifying the circumstances of the case. States shall endeavour to meet appropriate requests of flag States.

6. States shall, at the written request of any State, investigate any violation alleged to have been committed by vessels flying their flag. If satisfied that sufficient evidence is available to enable proceedings to be brought in respect of the alleged violation, flag States shall without delay institute proceedings in accordance with their laws.

7. Flag States shall promptly notify the requesting State and the competent international organization of the action taken and its outcome. Such information shall be available to all States.

8. Penalties provided for by the laws and regulations of States for vessels flying their flag shall be adequate in severity to discourage violations wherever they occur.

Article 218

Enforcement by port States

1. When a vessel is voluntarily within a port or at an off-shore terminal of a State, that State may undertake investigations and, where the evidence so warrants, institute proceedings in respect of any discharge from that vessel outside the internal waters, territorial sea or exclusive economic zone of that State in violation of applicable international rules and standards esablished through the competent international organization or general diplomatic conference.

2. No proceedings pursuant to paragraph 1 shall be instituted in respect of a discharge violation in the internal waters, territorial sea or exclusive economic zone of another State unless requested by that State, the flag State, or a State damaged or threatened by the discharge violation, or unless the violation has caused or is likely to cause pollution in the internal waters, territorial sea or exclusive economic zone of the State instituting the proceedings.

3. When a vessel is voluntarily within a port or at an off-shore terminal of a State, that State shall, as far as practicable, comply with requests from any State for investigation of a discharge violation referred to in paragraph 1, believed to have occured in, caused, or threatened damage to the internal waters, territorial sea or exclusive economic zone of the requesting State. It shall likewise, as far as practicable, comply with requests from the flag State for investigation of such a violation, irrespective of where the violation occurred.

4. The records of the investigation carried out by a port State pursuant to this article shall be transmitted upon request to the flag State or to the coastal State. Any proceedings instituted by the port State on the basis of such an investigation may, subject to section 7, be suspended at the request of the coastal State when the violation has occurred within its internal waters, territorial sea or exclusive economic zone. The evidence and records of the case, together with any bond or other financial security posted with the authorities of the port State, shall in that event be transmitted to the coastal State. Such transmittal shall preclude the continuation of proceedings in the port State.

Article 219

Measures relating to seaworthiness of vessels to avoid pollution

Subject to section 7, States which, upon request or on their own initiative, have ascertained that a vessel within one of their ports or at one of their off-shore terminals is in violation of applicable international rules and standards relating to seaworthiness of vessels and thereby threatens damage to the marine environment shall, as far as practicable, take admimnistrative measures to prevent the vessel from sailing. Such States may permit the vessel to proceed only to the nearest appropriate repair yard and, upon removal of the causes of the violation, shall permit the vessel to continue immediately.

Article 220

Enforcement by coastal States

1. When a vessel is voluntarily within a port or at an off-shore terminal of a State, that State may, subject to section 7, institute proceedings in respect of any violation of its laws and regulations adopted in accordance with this Convention or applicable international rules and standards for the prevention, reduction and control of pollution from vessels when the violation has occurred within the territorial sea or exclusive economic zone of that State.

2. Where there are clear grounds for believing that a vessel navigating in the territorial sea of a State has, during its passage therein, violated laws and regulations of that State adopted in accordance with this Convention or applicable international rules and standards for the prevention, reduction and control of pollution from vessels, that State, without prejudice to the application of the relevant provisions of Part II, section 3, may undertake physical inspection of the vessel relating to the violation and may, where the evidence so warrants, institute proceedings, including detention of the vessel, subject to the provisions of section 7.

3. Where there are clear grounds for believing that a vessel navigating in the exclusive economic zone or the territorial sea of a State has, in the exclusive economic zone, committed a violation of applicable international rules and standards for the prevention, reduction and control of pollution from vessels or laws and regulations of that State conforming and giving effect to such rules and standards, that State may require the vessel to give information regarding its identity and port of registry, its last and next port of call and other relevant information required to establish whether a violation has occurred.

4.States shall adopt laws and regulations and take other measures so that vessels flying their flag comply with requests for information pursuant to paragraph 3.

5. Where there are clear grounds for believing that a vessel navigating in the exclusive economic zone or the territorial sea of a State has, in the exclusive economic zone, committed a violation referred to in paragraph 3 resulting in a substantial discharge causing or threatening significant pollution of the marine environment, that State may undertake physical inspection of the vessel for matters relating to the violation if the vessel has refused to give information or if the information supplied by the vessel is manifestly at variance with the evident factual situation and if the circumstances of the case justify such an inspection.

6. Where there is clear objective evidence that a vessel navigating in the exclusive economic zone or the territorial sea of a State has, in the exclusive economic zone, committed a violation referred to in paragraph 3 resulting in a discharge causing major damage or threat of major damage to the coastline or related interests of the coastal State, or to any resources of its territorial sea or exclusive economic zone, that State may, subject to section 7, provided that the evidence so warrants, institute proceedings, including detention of the vessel, in accordance with its laws.

7. Notwithstanding the provisions of paragraph 6, whenever appropriate procedures have been established, either through the competent international organization or as otherwise agreed, whereby

compliance with requirements for bonding or other appropriate financial security has been assured, the coastal State if bound by such procedures shall allow the vessel to proceed.

8. The provisions of paragraphs 3, 4, 5, 6 and 7 also apply in respect of national laws and regulations adopted pursuant to article 211, paragraph 6.

Article 221

Measures to avoid pollution arising from maritime casualties

1. Nothing in this Part shall prejudice the right of States, pursuant to international law, both customary and conventional, to take and enforce measures beyond the territorial sea proportionate to the actual or threatened damage to protect their coastline or related interests, including fishing, from pollution or threat of pollution following upon a maritime casualty or acts relating to such a casualty, which may reasonably be expected to result in major harmful consequences.

2. For purposes of this article, "maritime casualty" means a collision of vessels, stranding or other incident of navigation, or other occurrence on board a vessel or external to it resulting in material damage or imminent threat of material damage to a vessel or cargo.

Article 222

Enforcement with respect to pollution from or through the atmosphere

States shall enforce, within the air space under their sovereignty or with regard to vessels flying their flag or vessels or aircraft of their registry, their laws and regulations adopted in accordance with article 212, paragraph 1, and with other provisions of this Convention and shall adopt laws and regulations and take other measures necessary to implement applicable international rules and standards established through competent international organizations or diplomatic conference to prevent, reduce and control pollution of the marine environment from or through the atmosphere, in conformity with all relevant international rules and standards concerning the safety of air navigation.

SECTION 7. SAFEGUARDS

Article 223

Measures to facilitate proceedings

In proceedings instituted pursuant to this Part, States shall take measures to facilitate the hearing of witnesses and the admission of evidence submitted by authorities of another State, or by the competent international organization, and shall facilitate the attendance at such proceedings of official representatives of the competent international organization, the flag State and any State affected by pollution arising out of any violation. The official representatives attending such proceedings shall have such rights and duties as may be provided under national laws and regulations or international law.

Article 224

Exercise of powers of enforcement

The powers of enforcement against foreign vessels under this Part may only be exercised by officials or by warships, military aircraft, or other ships or aircraft clearly marked and identifiable as being on government service and authorized to that effect.

Article 225

Duty to avoid adverse consequences in the exercise of the powers of enforcement

In the excercise under this Convention of their powers of enforcement against foreign vessels, States shall not endanger the safety of navigation or otherwise create a hazard to a vessel, or bring it in to an unsafe port or anchorage, or expose the marine environment to an unreasonable risk.

Article 226

Investigation of foreign vessels

1. (a) States shall not delay a foreign vessel longer than is essential for purposes of the investigations provided for in articles 216, 218 and 220. Any physical inspection of a foreign vessel shall be limited to an examination of such certificates, records or other documents as the vessel is required to carry by generally acceptable international rules and standards or of any similar documents which it is carrying, further inspection of the vessel may be undertaken only after such an examination and only when:

(i) there are clear grounds for believing that the condition of the vessel or its equipment does not correspond substantially with the particulars of those documents;

(ii) the contents of such documents are not sufficient to confirm or verify a suspected violation; or

(iii) the vessel is not carrying valid certificates and records.

(b) If the investigation indicates a violation of applicable laws and regulations or international rules and standards for the protection and preservation of the marine environment, release shall be made promptly subject to reasonable procedures such as bonding or other appropriate financial security.

(c) Without prejudice to the applicable international rules and standards relating to the seaworthiness of vessels, the release of a vessel may, whenever it would present an unreasonable threat of damage to the marine environment, be refused or made conditional upon proceeding to the nearest appropriate repair yard. Where the release has been refused or made conditional, the flag State of the vessel must be promptly notified, and may seek release of the vessel in accordance with Part XV.

Article 227

Non-discrimination with respect to foreign vessels

In exercising their rights and performing their duties under this Part, States shall not discriminate in form or in fact against vessels of another State.

Article 228

Suspension and restrictions on institution of proceedings

1. Proceedings to impose penalties in respect of any violation of applicable laws and regulations or international rules and standards relating to the prevention, reduction and control of

pollution from vessels committed by a foreign vessel beyond the territorial sea of the State instituting proceedings shall be suspended upon the taking of proceedings to impose penalties in respect of corresponding charges by the flag State within six months of the date on which proceedings were first instituted, unless those proceedings relate to a case of major damage to the coastal State or the flag State in question has repeatedly disregarded its obligation to enforce effectively the applicable international rules and standards in respect of violations committed by its vessels. The flag Sate shall in due course make available to the State previously instituting proceedings a full dossier of the case and the records of proceedings, whenever the flag State has requested the suspension of proceedings in accordance with this article. When proceedings instituted by the flag State have been brought to a conclusion, the suspended proceedings shall be terminated. Upon payment of costs incurred in respect of such proceedings, any bond posted or other financial security provided in connection with the suspended proceedings shall be released by the coastal State.

2. Proceedings to impose penalties on foreign vessels shall not be instituted after the expiry of three years from the date on which the violation was committed, and shall not be taken by any State in the event of proceedings having been instituted by another State subject to the provisions set out in paragraph 1.

3. The provisions of this article are without prejudice to the right of the flag State to take any measures, including proceedings to impose penalties, according to its laws irrespective of prior proceedings by another State.

Article 229

Institution of civil proceedings

Nothing in this Convention affects the institution of civil proceedings in respect of any claim for loss or damage resulting from pollution of the marine environment.

Article 230

Monetary penalties and the observance of recognized rights of the accused

1. Monetary penalties only may be imposed with respect of violations of national laws and regulations or applicable international rules and standards for the prevention, reduction and control of pollution of the marine environment, committed by foreign vessels beyond the territorial sea.

2. Monetary penalties only may be imposed with respect of national laws and regulations or applicable international rules and standards for the prevention, reduction and control of pollution of the marine environment, committed by foreign vessels in the territorial sea, except in a case of a wilful and serious actg of pollution in the territorial sea.

3. In the conduct of proceedings in respect of such violations committed by a foreign vessel which may result in the imposition of penalties, recognized rights of the accused shall be observed.

Article 231

Notification to the flag State and other States concerned

States shall promptly notify the flag State and any other State concerned of any measures taken pursuant to section 6 against foreign vessels, and shall submit to the flag State all official reports concerning such measures. However, with respect to violations committed in the territorial sea, the foregoing obligations of the coastal State apply only to such measures as are taken in proceedings. The diplomatic agents or consular officers and where possible the maritime authority of the flag State, shall be immediately informed of any such measures taken pursuant to section 6 against foreign vessels.

Article 232

Safeguards with respect to straits used for international navigation

Nothing in sections 5, 6 and 7 affects the legal regime of straits used for international navigation. However, if a foreign ship other than those referred to in section 10 has committed a violation of the laws and regulations referred to in article 42, paragraph 1(a) and (b), causing or threatening major damage to the marine environment of the straits, the States bordering the straits may take appropriate enforcement measures and if so shall respect *mutatis mutandis* the provisions of this section.

SECTION 8. ICE-COVERED AREAS

Article 234

Ice-covered areas

Coastal States have the right to adopt and enforce non-discriminatory laws and regulations for the prevention, reduction and control of marine pollution from vessels in ice-covered areas within the limits of the exclusive economic zone, where particularly severe climatic conditions and the presence of ice covering such areas for most of the year create obstructions or exceptional hazards to navigation, and pollution of the marine environment could cause major harm to or irreversible disturbance of the ecological balance. Such laws and regulations shall have due regard to navigation and the protection and preservation of the marine environment based on the best available scientific evidence.

SECTION 9. RESPONSIBILITY AND LIABILITY

Article 235

Responsibility and Liability

1. States are responsible for the fulfilment of their international obligations concerning the protection and preservation of the marine environment. They shall be liable in accordance with international law.

2. States shall ensure that recourse is available in accordance with their legal systems for prompt and adequate compensation or other relief in respect of damage caused by pollution of the marine environment by natural or juridical persons under their jurisdiction.

3. With the objective of assuring prompt and adequate compensation in respect of all damage caused by pollution of the marine environment, States shall co-operate in the implementation of existing international law and the further development of international law relating to responsibility and liability for the assessment of and compensation for damage and the settlement of related disputes, as well as, where appropriate, development of criteria and procedures for payment of adequate compensation, such as compulsory insurance or compensation funds.

SECTION 10. SOVEREIGN IMMUNITY

Article 236

Sovereign immunity

The provisions of this Convention regarding the protection and preservation of the marine environment do not apply to any warship, naval auxiliary, other vessels or aircraft owned or operated by a State and used, for the time being, only on government non-commercial service. However, each State shall ensure, by the adoption of appropriate measures not impairing operations or operational capabilities of such vessels or aircraft owned or operated by it, that such vessels or aircraft act in a manner consistent, so far as is reasonable and practicable, with this Convention.

SECTION 11. OBLIGATIONS UNDER OTHER CONVENTIONS ON THE PROTECTION AND PRESERVATION OF THE MARINE ENVIRONMENT

Article 237

Obligations under other conventions on the protection and preservation of the marine environment

1. The provisions of this Part are without prejudice to the specific obligations assumed by States under special conventions and agreements concluded previously which relate to the protection and preservation of the marine environment and to agreements which may be concluded in furtherance of the general principles set forth in this Convention.

2. Specific obligations assumed by States under special conventions, with respect to the protection and preservation of the marine environment, should be carried out in a manner consistent with the general principles and objectives of this Convention.

D. OCEAN DUMPING

Kindt, Ocean Dumping, 13 Den. J. Int'l. L. & Pol'y (1984), 335-338[4]

The oceans are the earth's greatest single natural resource. Covering 71 percent of the earth's surface, they are crucial to maintaining the balance of the global ecosystem. "The importance of the oceans needs little emphasis as this planet's last great economic frontier, the potential source for enormous food supplies, the final buffer against ecological catastrophe, and a recreational outlet for restoration of body and spirit of man."

As important as the oceans are to mankind, it seems irrational that human enterprise would abuse them. Man's dumping of wastes into the ocean has always occurred. However, due to accelerating industrial development and population growth, the quantities and concentrations of wastes dumped have begun to tax the assimilative capacity of the oceans.

The reasons for the growing use of the ocean as a dump site are readily observable because mankind tends to "regard the oceans as a convenient, limitless receptacle for wastes." "But as problems of waste disposal on land multiply, pressures to use the oceans as a dumping ground become stronger." Ocean dumping often provides the least expensive method of disposal. Since the sites are far removed

[4]. Reprinted by permission of the Denver Journal of International Law and Policy.

from land, the adverse effects are less noticable and therefore less objectionable. However, experience and research have revealed that despite its vastness, the ocean's natural ability to accept, decompose, and recycle wastes is limited. Once saturation levels of waste assimilation develop, irreversible consequences may result, for the "deep sea has a turnover rate measured in thousands of years."

Of the pollution entering the world's oceans, approximately 10 percent are due to direct ocean dumping. In 1970 the U.S. Council on Environmental Quality (CEQ) identified seven sources of ocean dumping. The seven categories and their definitions are as follows:

a."*Dredge spoils* -- the solid materials removed from the bottom of water bodies generally for the purpose of improving navigation: sand, silt, clay, rock, and pollutants that have been deposited from municipal and industrial discharges."

b. "*Industrial wastes* -- acids; refinery, pesticides, and paper mill wastes; and assorted liquid wastes."

c. "*Sewage sludge* -- the solid material remaining after municipal waste treatment; residual human wastes and other organic and inorganic wastes."

d. "*Construction and demolition debris* -- masonry, tile, stone, plastic, wiring, piping, shingles, glass, cinderblock, tar, tarpaper, plaster, vegetation, and excavation dirt."

e. "*Solid wastes* -- more commonly called refuse, garbage, or trash -- the material generated by residences; commercial, agricultural, and industrial establishments; hospitals and other institutions; and municipal operations: chiefly paper, food wastes, garden wastes, steel and glass containers, and other miscellaneous materials."

f. *Explosives and chemical munitions* -- no official definition but includes "[u]nserviceable or obslolete shells, mines, solid rocket fuels, and chemical warfare agents."

g. "*Radioactive wastes* -- the liquid and solid wastes that result from processing of irradiated fuel elements, nuclear reactor operations, medical use of radioactive isotopes, and research activities and from equipment and containment vessels which become radioactive by induction."

These sources are listed in decreasing order of their deleterious impact on the marine environment. Of the 10 percent of ocean dumped materials, dredged spoils constitute 80 percent of the total. Approximately 1 to 10 percent of the dredged sediment taken from waterways and harbors has been contaminated to potentially unacceptable levels because of industrial, urban, and agricultural activities. Even non-toxic dredged spoils can physically damage marine organisms in ways ranging from inhibiting the penetration of light (due to suspended sediments) to somthering organisms on the ocean floor where large quantities are dumped.

The dumping of dredged material, sewage sludge, and other wastes has a measurable impact on ecosystems, such as the New York Bight, and has led to cadmium and PCB concentrations that have approached intolerable levels. Toxic pollutants dumped into the ocean, either industrial wastes or municipal sewage sludge, enter into the tissue of marine organisms. As large forms feed on contaminated organisms, toxic substances accumulate and reach concentrations where immediate physical harm can occur to marine mammals, birds, and man. For example, biomagnification of PCB's in marine food chains has been reported, and levels involving birds and mammals have been magnified "by a factor on the order of 10 to 100 at each step."

Pollutants may be highly biodegradable and have only a local adverse effect, whereas less or non-biodegradable pollutants may have long-term effects on both local and global marine environments. Pollutants can be classified into several categories: (1) hydrocarbons (basically oil and gas); (2) hydrocarbon compounds utilized as organic contaminants, inhibitors, and poisons; (3) heavy metals; (4) radioactive wastes; and (5) solid wastes (including particulate pollution). Of these, heavy metals, poisons, and radioactive wastes are especially hazardous because they tend to bioaccumulate in marine organisms.

The adverse effects of these hazardous wastes are numerous. High levels of pollutants which bioaccumulate have lead to "bioconcentration" that kills marine organisms or anything which feeds on them. This phenomenon has killed marine stocks and made surviving stocks inedible, thus causing severe economic loss to the fishing industry.

More serious is the long-range impact of pollutants on the marine environment. First, pollutants affect some species more than others. The resulting diminution of species variety is known to upset the ecobalance. Secondly, organic wastes, particularly sewage sludge, require oxygen for decomposition. When organic wastes are dumped, they deplete the oxygen in adjacent waters to the extent that some organisms cannot survive. This cycle is accelerated when deceased organisms decompose and further deplete oxygen concentrations in that process. A vicious cycle of death, decay and depletion ensues which threatens the hardiest marine organisms. The oxygen deficiency may continue for years -- long after the dumping has ceased.

Due to the volume and types of wastes dumped annually, particularly toxic materials and radioactive wastes, the need to understand the impact of these wastes and to expand international environmental cooperation must receive priority.

....

CONVENTION ON THE PREVENTION OF MARINE POLLUTION BY DUMPING OF WASTES AND OTHER MATTER, 1972

Preamble

The Contracting Parties to this Convention

Recognizing that the marine environment and the living organisms which it supports are of vital importance to humanity, and all people have an interest in assuring that it is so managed that its quality and resources are not impaired;

Recognizing that the capacity of the sea to assimilate wastes and render them harmless, and its ability to regenerate natural resources, is not unlimited;

Recognizing that States have, in accordance with the Charter of the United Nations and the principles of international law, the sovereign right to exploit their own resources pursuant to their own environmental policies, and the responsibility to ensure that activities within their jurisdiction or control do not cause damage to the environment of other States or of areas beyond the limits of national jurisdiction;

Recalling Resolution 2749 (XXV) of the General Assembly of the United Nations on principles governing the seabed and the ocean floor and the subsoil thereof, beyond the limits of national jurisdiction;

Noting that marine pollution originates in many sources, such as dumping and discharges through the atmosphere, rivers, estuaries, outfalls and pipelines, and that it is important that States use the best practicable means to prevent such pollution and develop products and processes which will reduce the amount of harmful wastes to be disposed of;

Being convinced that international action to control the pollution of the sea by dumping can and must be taken without delay but that this action should not preclude discussion of measures to control other sources of marine pollution as soon as possible and;

Wishing to improve protection of the marine environment by encouraging States with a common interest in particular geographical areas to enter into appropriate agreements supplementary to this Convention:

Have agreed as follows:

Article I

Contracting Parties shall individually and collectively promote the effective control of all sources of pollution of the marine environment, and pledge themselves especially to take all practicable steps to prevent the pollution of the sea by the dumping of waste and other matter that is liable to create hazards to human health, to harm living resources or marine life, to damage amenities or to interfere with other legitimate uses of the sea.

Article II

Contracting Parties shall, as provided for in the following Articles, take effective measures individually, according to their scientific, technical and economic capabilities, and collectively, to prevent marine pollution caused by dumping and shall harmonize their policies in this regard.

Article III

For the purposes of this Convention:

1. a. "Dumping" means:

(i) any deliberate disposal at sea of wastes or other matter from vessels, aircraft, platforms or other man-made structures at sea.

(ii) any deliberate disposal at sea of vessels, aircraft, platforms or other man-made structures at sea;

b. "Dumping" does not include:

(i) the disposal at sea of wastes or other matter incidental to, or derived from the normal operations of vessels, aircraft, platforms or other man-made structures at sea and their equipment, other than wastes or other matter transported by or to vessels, aircraft, platforms or other man-made structures at sea, operating for the purpose of disposal of such matter or derived from the treatment of such wastes or other matter from such vessels, aircraft, platforms or structures;

(ii) placement of matter for a purpose other than the mere disposal thereof, provided that such placement is not contrary to the aims of this Convention;

c. The disposal of wastes or other matter directly arising from, or related to the exploration, exploitation and associated off-shore processing of seabed mineral resources will not be covered by the provisions of this Convention.

....

Article IV

1. In accordance with the provisions of this Convention, Contracting Parties shall prohibit the dumping of any wastes or other matter in whatever form or condition except as otherwise specified below:

a. The dumping of wastes or other matter listed in Annex I is prohibited;

b. The dumping of wastes or other matter listed in Annex II requires a prior special permit;

c. The dumping of all other wastes or matter requires a prior general permit.

2. Any permit shall be issued only after careful consideration of all the factors set forth in Annex III, including prior studies of the characteristics of the dumping site, as set forth in Sections B and C of that Annex.

3. No provision of this Convention is to be interpreted as preventing a Contracting Party from prohibiting, insofar as that Party is concerned, the dumping of wastes or other matter not mentioned in Annex I. That Party shall notify such measures to the Organization.

Article V

1. The provisions of Article IV shall not apply when it is necessary to secure the safety of human life or of vessels, aircraft, platforms or other man-made structures at sea or in cases of force majeure caused by stress of weather, or in any case which constitutes a danger to human life or a real threat to vessels, aircraft, platforms or other man-made structures at sea, if dumping appears to be the only way of averting the threat and there is every probability that the damage consequent upon such dumping will be less than would otherwise occur. Such dumping shall be conducted as to minimize the likelihood of damage to human or marine life and shall be reported forthwith to the Organization.

2. A Contracting Party may issue a special permit as an exception to Article IV 1 a, in emegencies, posing unacceptable risk relating to human health and admitting no other feasible solution. Before doing so the Party shall consult any other country or countries that are likely to be affected and the Organization which, after consulting other Parties, and international organizations as appropriate, shall, in accordance with Article XIV 4 e promptly recommend to the Party the most appropriate procedures to adopt. The Party shall follow these recommendations to the maximum extent feasible consistent with the time within which action must be taken and with the general obligation to avoid damage to the marine environment and shall inform the Organization of the action it takes. The Parties pledge themselves to assist one another in such situations.

3. Any Contracting Party may waive its rights under paragraph 2 at the time of, or subsequent to ratification of, or accession to this Convention.

Article VI

1. Each Contracting Party shall designate an appropriate authority or authorities to:

a. issue special permits which shall be required prior to, and for, the dumping of matter listed in Annex II and in the circumstances provided for in Article V 2;

b. issue general permits which shall be required prior to, and for, the dumping of all other matter;

c. keep records of the nature and quantities of all matter permitted to be dumped and the location, time and method of dumping;

d. monitor individually, or in collaboration with other Parties and competent international organizations, the condition of the seas for the purposes of this Convention;

2. The appropriate authority or authorities of a Contracting Party shall issue prior special or general permits in accordance with paragraph 1 in respect of matter intended for dumping:

a. loaded in its territory;

b. loaded by a vessel or aircraft registered in its territory or flying its flag, when the loading occurs in the territory of a State not party to this Convention.

3. In issuing permits under subparagraphs 1 a and b above, the appropriate authority or authorities shall comply with Annex III, together with such additional criteria, measures and requirements as they may consider relevant.

4. Each Contracting Party, directly or through a Secretariate established under a regional agreement, shall report to the Organization, and where appropriate to other Parties, the information specified in subparagraphs c, a and d of paragraph 1 above, and the criteria, measures and requirements it adopts in accordance with paragraph 3 above. The procedure to be followed and the nature of such reports shall be agreed by the Parties in consultation.

Article VII

1. Each Contracting Party shall apply the measures required to implement the present Convention to all:

a. vessels and aircraft registered in its territory or flying its flag;

b. vessels and aircraft loading in its territory or territorial seas matter which is to be dumped;

c. vessels and aircraft and fixed or floating platforms under its jurisdiction believed to be engaged in dumping.

2. Each Party shall take in its territory appropriate measures to prevent and punish conduct in contravention of the provisions of this Convention.

3. The Parties agree to cooperate in the development of procedures for the effective application of this Convention particularly on the high seas, including procedures for the reporting of vessels and aircraft observed dumping in contravention of the Convention.

4. This Convention shall not apply to those vessels and aircraft entitled to sovereign immunity under international law. However each Party shall ensure by the adoption of appropriate measures that such vessels and aircraft owned or operated by it act in a manner consistent with the object and

purpose of this Convention, and shall inform the Organization accordingly.

5. Nothing in this Convention shall affect the right of each Party to adopt other measures, in accordance with the principles of international law, to prevent dumping at sea.

....

ANNEX I

1. Organohalogen compounds.

2. Mercury and mercury compounds.

3. Cadmium and cadmium compounds.

4. Persistent plastics and other persistent synthetic materials, for example, netting and ropes, which may float or remain in suspension in the sea in such a manner as to interfere materially with fishing, navigation or other legitimate uses of the sea.

5. Crude oil, fuel oil, heavy diesel oil, and lubricating oils, hydraulic fluids, and any mixtures containing any of these, taken on board for the purpose of dumping.

6. High-level radioactive wastes or other high-level radioactive matter, defined on public health, biological or other grounds, by the competent international body in this field, at present the International Atomic Energy Agency, as unsuitable for dumping at sea.

7. Materials in whatever form (e.g., solids, liquids, semi-liquids, gases or in a living state) produced for biological and chemical warfare.

8. The preceding paragraphs of this Annex do not apply to substances which are rapidly rendered harmless by physical, chemical or biological processes in the sea provided they do not:

(i) make edible marine organisms unpalatable,

or

(ii) endanger human health or that of domestic animals. The consultative procedure provided for under Article XIV should be followed by a Party if there is doubt about the harmlessness of the substance.

9. This Annex does not apply to wastes or other materials (e.g., sewage sludges and dredged spoils) containing the matters referred to in paragraphs 1-5 above as trace contaminants. Such wastes shall be subject to the provisions of Annexes II and III as appropriate.

ANNEX II

The following substances and materials requiring special care are listed for the purposes of Article VI 1 a.

A. Wastes containing significant amounts of the matters listed below:

arsenic

lead

copper

zinc

organosilicon compounds

cyanides

flourides

pesticides and their by-products not covered in Annex I.

B. In the issue of permits for dumping of large quantities of acids and alkalis, consideration shall be given to the possible presence in such wastes of the substances listed in paragraph A and to the following additional substances:

berryllium

chromium

nickel

vanadium

C. Container, scrap metal and other bulky wastes liable to sink to the sea bottom which may present a serious obstacle to fishing or navigation.

D. Radioactive wastes or other radioactive matter not included in Annex I. In the issue of permits for the dumping of this matter, the Contracting Parties should take full account of the recommendations of the competetent international body in this field, at present the International Atomic Energy Agency.

ANNEX III

Provisions to be considered in establishing criteria governing the issue of permits for the dumping of matter at sea, taking into account Article IV 2 include:

A. Characteristics and Composition of the Matter.

1. Total amount and average composition of matter dumped (e.g., per year).

2. Form (e.g., solid, sludge, liquid, or gaseous).

3. Properties: physical (e.g., solubility and density), chemical and biochemical (e.g., oxygen demand, nutrients) and biological (e.g., presence of viruses, bacteria, yeasts, parasites).

4. Toxicity.

5. Persistence: physical, chemical and biological.

7. Susceptibility to physical, chemical and biochemical changes and interaction in the aquatic environment with other dissolved organic and inorganic materials.

8. Probability of production of taints or other changes reducing market-ability of resources (fish, shellfish, etc.).

B. Characteristics of Dumping Site and Method of Deposit

1. Location (e.g., co-ordinates of the dumping area, depth and distance from the coast), location in relation to other areas (e.g., amenity areas, spawning, nursery and fishing areas and exploitable resources).

2. Rate of disposal per specific period (e.g., quantity per day, per week, per month).

3. Methods of packaging and containment, if any.
4. Initial dilution achieved by proposed method of release.

5. Dispersal characteristics (e.g., effects of currents, tides and wind on horizontal transport and vertical mixing).

6. Water characteristics (e.g., temperature, pH, salinity, stratification, oxygen indicies of pollution -- dissolved oxygen (DO), chemical oxygen demand (COD), biochemical oxygen demand (BOD) -- nitrogen present in organic and mineral form including ammonia, suspended matter, other nutrients and productivity).

7. Bottom characteristics (e.g., topography, geochemical and geological characteristics and biological productivity).

8. Existence and effects of other dumpings which have been made in the dumping area (e.g., heavy metal background reading and organic carbon content).

9. In issuing a permit for dumping, Contracting Parties should consider whether an adequate scientific basis exists for assessing the consequences of such dumping, as outlined in this Annex, taking into account seasonal variations.
C. General Considerations and Conditions

1. Possible effects on amenities (e.g., presence of floating or stranded material, turbidity, objectionable odour, discolouration and foaming).

2. Possible effects on marine life, fish and shellfish culture, fish stocks and fisheries, seaweed harvesting and culture.

3. Possible effects on other uses of the sea (e.g., impairment of water quality for industrial use, underwater corrosion of structures, interference with ship operations from floating materials, interference with fishing or navigation through deposit of wastes or solid objects on the sea floor and protection of areas of special importance for scientific or conservation purposes).

4. The practical availability of alternative land-based methods of treatment, disposal or elimination, or of treatment to render the matter less harmful for dumping at sea.

* * * *

In U.S. domestic law, the primary statute dealing with ocean dumping is the Marine Protection, Research and Sanctuaries Act (33 U.S.C. 1401 et seq.). Under the first two titles of that Act, referred to as the Ocean Dumping Act, four agencies have responsibilities: the Environmental Protection Agency (EPA), the Corps of Engineers (CE), the National Oceanic and Atomspheric Administration (NOAA), and the Coast Guard (USCG). Title I of the statute authorizes the EPA to designate specific ocean disposal sites, establishes a permit system for the use of such sites, and directs EPA to establish ocean dumping criteria based on specific factors. The EPA administers the permit program for all dumping except for dredged spoil which is under the jurisdition of the Corps of Engineers.

Title II requires EPA and NOAA to conduct research and monitoring on ocean dumping. Title III deals with the establishment of marine sanctuaries. The most relevant sections are set out below.

MARINE PROTECTION, RESEARCH AND SANCTUARIES ACT

Sec. 1411. Prohibited acts

(a) Except as may be authorized by a permit issued pursuant to section 1412 or section 1413 of this title, and subject to regulations issued pursuant to section 1418 of this title,

(1) no person shall transport from the United States, and

(2) in the case of a vessel or aircraft registered in the United States or flying the United States flag or in the case of a United States department, agency, or instrumentality, no person shall transport from any location

any material for the purpose of dumping it into ocean waters.

(b) Except as may be authorized by a permit issued pursuant to section 1412 of this title, and subject to regulations issued pursuant to section 1418 of this title, no person shall dump any material transported from a location outside the United States (1) into the territorial sea of the United States, or (2) into a zone contiguous to the territorial sea of the United States, extending to a line twelve nautical miles seaward from the base line from which the breadth of the territorial sea is measured, to the extent that it may affect the territorial sea or the territory of the United States.

Sec. 1412. Dumpinmg permit program

(a) Environmental Protection Agency permits

Except in relation to dredged material, as provided for in section 1413 of this title, and in relation to radiological, chemical, and biological warfare agents and high-level radioactive wastes, for which no permit may be issued, the Administrator may issue permits, after notice and opportunity for public hearings, for the transportation from the United States or, in the case of an agency or instrumentality of the United States, or in the case of a vessel or aircraft registered in the United States or flying the United States flag, for the transportation from a location outside the United States, of material for the purpose of dumping it into ocean waters, or for the dumping of material into waters described in section 1411(b) of this title, where the Administrator determines that such dumping will not unreasonably degrade or endanger human health, welfare, or amenities, or the marine environment, ecological systems, or economic potentialities. The Administrator shall establish and apply criteria for reviewing and evaluating such permit applications, and, in establishing or revising such criteria, shall consider, but not be limited in his consideration to, the following:

(A) The need for the proposed dumping.

(B) The effect of such dumping on human health and welfare, including economic, esthetic, and recreational values.

(C) The effect of such dumping on fisheries resources, plankton, fish, shellfish, wildlife, shore lines and beaches.

(D) The effect of such dumping on marine ecosystems, particularly with respect to --

(i) the transfer, concentration, and dispersion of such material and its byproducts through biological, physical, and chemical processes,

(ii) potential changes in marine ecosystem diversity, productivity, and stability, and

(iii) species and community population dynamics.

(E) The persistence and permanence of the effects of the dumping.

(F) The effect of dumping particular volumes and concentrations of such materials.

(G) Appropriate locations and methods of disposal or recycling, including land-based alternatives and the probable impact of requiring use of such alternate locations or methods upon considerations affecting the public interest.

(H) The effect on alternate uses of oceans, such as scientific study, fishing, and other living resource exploitation, and nonliving resource exploitation.

(I) In designating recommended sites, the Administrator shall utilize wherever feasible locations beyond the edge of the Continental Shelf.

....

****

There are quite a few other statutes that bear upon the question of ocean dumping, either directly or indirectly. The include the Clean Water Act (33 U.S.C. 1251 et seq.), the Clean Air Act (42 U.S.C. 7401 et seq.), the Coastal Zone Management Act (16 U.S.C 1451 et seq.), The Comprehensive Environmental Response, Compensation, and Liability Act (41 U.S.C. 9601 et seq.), The Endangered Species Act (16 U.S.C. 1531 et seq.), the National Environmental Policy Act (42 U.S.C. 4321 et seq.), the National Ocean Pollution Planning Act (33 U.S.C. 1701 et seq.), the Port and Tanker Safety Act (33 U.S.C. 1221 et seq.), the Safe Water Drinking Act (42 U.S.C. 300(f) et seq.), the Toxic Substances Control Act (15 U.S.C. 2601 et seq.), and the Low-Level Radioactive Waste Policy Amendments Act (42 U.S.C. 2021(b) et seq.). In addition, the Resource Conservation and Recovery Act (42 U.S.C. 690 et seq.) is relevant because it makes dumping of hazardous wastes on land more difficult and expensive, thus making the oceans more attractive as a disposal site.

In 1992, UNCED was held in Rio. As a part of its work it was inevitable that the conference would address oceans issues. As a result of that meeting, a report was issued that contained a chapter on the oceans. The following excerpts will give you an idea concerning the direction management issues may take in the future.

E. UNITED NATIONS CONFERENCE ON THE ENVIRONMENT AND DEVELOPMENT (UNCED)

CHAPTER 17

Protection of oceans, all kinds of seas, including enclosed and semi-enclosed seas, and coastal areas and the protection, rational use and development of their living resources

INTRODUCTION

17.1 The marine environment -- including the oceans and all seas and adjacent coastal areas -- form an integrated whole that is an essential component of the global life-support system and a positive asset that presents opportunities for sustainable development. International law, as reflected in the provisions of the United Nations Convention on the Law of the Sea, referred to in this chapter of Agenda 21, sets forth rights and obligations of States and provides the international basis upon which to pursue the protection and sustainable development of the marine and coastal environment and its resources. This requires new approaches to marine and coastal area management and development, at the national, subregional, regional and global levels, approaches that are integrated in content, and are precautionary and anticipatory in ambit, as reflected in the following program areas:

(a) Integrated management and sustainable development of coastal areas, including exclusive economic zones;

(b) Marine environmental protection;

(c) Sustainable use and conservation of marine living resources of the high seas;

(d) Sustainable use and conservation of marine living resources under national jurisdiction;

(e) Addressing critical uncertainties for the management of the marine environment and climate change;

(f) Strengthening international, including regional, cooperation and coordination;

(g) Sustainable development of islands.

17.2 The implementation by developing countries of the activities set forth below shall be commensurate with their individual technological and financial capacities and priorities in allocating resources for development needs and ultimately depends on the technology transfer and financial resources required and made available to them.

....

C. Sustainable use and conservation of marine living resources of the high seas

Basis for action

17.44 Over the last decade, fisheries on the high seas have considerably expanded and currently represent approximately five per cent of total world landings. The provisions of the United

Nations Convention on the Law of the Sea on the marine living resources of the high seas sets forth rights and obligations of States with respect to conservation and utilization of those resources.

17.45 However, management of high seas fisheries, including the adoption, monitoring and enforcement of effective conservation measures, is inadequate in many areas and some resources are overutilized. There are problems of unregulated fishing, overcapitalization, excessive fleet size, vessel reflagging to escape controls, insufficiently selective gear, unreliable data bases and lack of sufficient cooperation among States. Action by States whose nationals and vessels fish on the high seas as well as cooperation at the bilateral, subregional, regional and global levels, is essential, particularly for highly migratory species and straddling stocks. Such action and cooperation should address inadequacies in fishing practices as well as in biological knowledge, fisheries statistics and improvement in systems for handling data. Emphasis should also be on multi-species management and other approaches which take into account the relationships among species, especially in addressing depleted species, but also in identifying the potential of underutilized or unutilized populations.

CHAPTER 12

DISPUTE SETTLEMENT

A. INTRODUCTION.

From the time the law of the sea negotiations began in earnest in Caracas in 1974, most participants understood that the adoption of a comprehensive and widely accepted law of the sea treaty would not indefinitely resolve all ocean space use problems. Just as customary international law rules are subject to interpretations based upon one's view of state practice, so a treaty must be interpreted in the light of its object and purpose so as to give effect to the intent of the drafters. If the treaty interpretation process simply falls back on traditional negotiation of disputes among affected nations, then not a great deal will have been gained by an LOS treaty over customary international law practice, save for those areas in which agreement is clear-cut and explicit. Likewise, many areas involved in the negotiations resulted in texts which are deliberately ambiguous in order to accommodate the views of States with differing perspectives on and interests in the issue, or to at least have some text regarding issues for which no agreement could be reached on a clearer rule. These "deliberate ambiguities" only result in transference of the problem from a conflict of practice to a conflict of treaty interpretation unless some method were devised for their orderly resolution.

Thus, it was important to include within the new treaty a dispute settlement mechanism along with the substantive articles. Part B of this chapter contains the provisions regarding dispute settlement contained in the 1982 United Nations Convention on the Law of the Sea.

Before examining those provisions, the following indicates some of the traditional kinds of methods for resolving international disagreements.

Clingan, COMPULSORY SETTLEMENT OF FISHERIES DISPUTES[1]

INTRODUCTION

The settlement of international disputes is a subject of distinct complexity. The application of procedures for dispute settlement is frequently at odds with its supportive theory. Compulsory dispute settlement is, by its nature, contrary to one of the most basic and honored traditions of international law. This is well characterized in the writing of Lauterpacht:

> The function of law is to regulate the conduct of men by reference to rules whose formal -- as distinguished from their historical -- source of validity lies, in the last resort, in a precept imposed from outside. Within the community of nations, this essential feature of the rule of law is constantly put in jeopardy by the conception of the sovereignty of States which deduces the binding force of international law from the will of each individual member of the international community. This is the reason why any inquiry of a general character in the field of international law finds itself at the very start confronted with the doctrine of sovereignty.

This doctrine, the equality of sovereigns, operates as a permanent restraint on the concept of compulsory settlement of disputes, for if sovereigns cannot in theory be subject to the will of another, they can no less be subject to the will of a group of sovereigns or to an international tribunal. This is an

[1]. From Fisheries Conflicts in the North Atlantic, Pontecorvo Ed., Law of the Sea Institute, 1974. Reproduced by permission of the Law of the Sea Institute.

historical element which must be kept in mind while evaluating the acceptability of options open to nations within the international community. It is a political reality which nations must adopt or change.

Even so, nations have frequently worked out individual or multilateral arrangements to settle quarrels in advance of the actual disputes. In structuring these agreements for pacific dispute settlement, nations often attempt to characterize the kinds of problems which party nations agree to submit to binding settlement. One cannot say that these attempts have been particularly successful. Occasionally, states have reserved those disputes which are "justiciable" for binding arbitration or other judicial settlement. The problem here is, of course, determining which such disputes are justiciable, and which are not. While this problem is analogous to the question of justiciability in domestic law, the nature of international law makes the definition of the term more difficult where more than one nation is involved. Occasionally, the problem is described in terms of questions of law as opposed to political questions, but this characterization is of only limited help.

A look at history may provide better perspective. Article 38 of the Hague Convention for the Pacific Settlement of Disputes of 1907 dealt with the identification of justiciable disputes as follows:

> In questions of a legal nature, and especially in the interpretation and application of international conventions, arbitration is recognized by the signatory Powers as the most effective, and at the same time the most equitable, means of settling disputes which diplomacy has failed to settle.

The phrase "questions of a legal nature" adds nothing by way of precision, but the modifying clause concerning the interpretation and application of conventions is of some limited value.

The first two paragraphs of Article 13 of the Covenant of the League of Nations handled the difficulty this way:

> 1. The Members of the League agree that whenever any dispute shall arise between them which they recognize to be suitable for submission to arbitration, and which cannot be satisfactorily settled by diplomacy, they will submit the whole subject-matter to arbitration.
>
> 2. Disputes as to the interpretation of a treaty, as to any question of international law, as to the existence of any international obligation, or as to the extent and nature of the reparation to be made for any such breach, are declared to be among those which are generally suitable for submission to arbitration.

These guidelines are more precise: yet, note that the language is structured to suggest that the parties must themselves recognize the subject matter as being suitable for arbitration before such submission can be effected. From these examples we can see that as the obligation to arbitrate becomes more precise, the responsibility to do so without reservation becomes less clear.

Article 36 of the Statute of the International Court of Justice gives jurisdiction to the court for all cases referred to it by the parties, and, in addition, for matters provided for in the U.N. Charter and treaties in force. But it further declares:

> 2. The states parties to the present Statute may at any time declare that they recognize as compulsory ipso facto and without special agreement, in relation to any other state accepting the same obligation, the jurisdiction of the court in all legal disputes concerning:
>
> a. the interpretation of a treaty;
>
> b. any question of international law;

c. the existence of any fact which, if established, would constitute a breach of an international obligation;

d. the nature or extent of the reparation to be made for the breach of an international obligation.

3. The declarations referred to above may be made unconditionally or on condition of reciprocity on the part of several or certain states, or for a certain time.

The international community at large seems to treat disputes of a legal nature differently from those which are purely political. The problem, of course, is to differentiate between them. Lauterpacht points out the attempt to do so by concluding that if parties to a dispute ask only for the application or interpretation of existing international law, the dispute is legal in nature, or "justiciable." However, if, instead of setting forth rights under existing international law, the parties profess to disregard an existing rule, and seek to change the law, the dispute is more than likely political -- a conflict of national interests not of a justiciable character.

The more one thinks about these matters, the more the interplay between justiciability and sovereignty becomes evident. Matters of high national interest creating new obligations between sovereigns have been left to negotiation between those sovereigns on a plane of equality. Justiciable disputes interpreting the results of those negotiations, determinations of fact bearing upon those interpretations, and matters of reparation arising out of the interpretations have been considered fit subjects for binding adjudication, but only, in many instances, where the parties to the dispute agree to that kind of procedure. For this reason, dispute settlement for fisheries cannot be discussed limiting oneself to binding or compulsory procedures alone. Fisheries disputes are fraught with mixed questions calling into play all of the skill and all of the legal tools available to the respective parties. Thus it will be necessary to depart from the assigned topic, reviewing and analyzing all the traditional legal tools, both compulsory and voluntary in nature, to establish a comparative base from which to depart. The material on international dispute settlement is voluminous. The purpose of this paper is not to exhaust the topic, but simply to provide a sufficient background in general theory so that discussions can focus on the advisability of one or another method for any particular aspect of the problems of this workshop. We must, as J. P. Cot advised, be prepared to choose between the Wise Man and the Prince.

TYPES OF INTERNATIONAL DISPUTE SETTLEMENT PROCEDURES

At this point, thought should be given to identifying points of commonality as well as differences between the various traditional methods of international dispute settlement.

Diplomatic Negotiations

Direct negotiation is, of course, still a primary method of first level dispute settlement. Because most such negotiations are conducted in privacy, one can never be sure of the degree to which problems are solved by this method. However, the number of bilateral and multilateral agreements which are openly published gives an indication that the total number of difficulties handled by direct diplomatic negotiations between states is substantial. Furthermore, present-day importance of negotiation in the international community is reflected in the number of documents which preface any requirement for submission of disputes to a binding mechanism with a requirement that there first be an attempt to settle the issue by diplomacy. Language typical of this form of approach is found in the following excerpt from the treaty between Belgium and Czechoslovakia dated April 23, 1929, Article 1:

> Disputes of every kind which may arise between the High Contracting Parties and which it has not been possible to settle by diplomacy shall be submitted, under the conditions laid down in the present Convention, to settlement by judicial means or arbitration, preceded, according to circumstances, as a compulsory or optional measure, by recourse to the procedure of conciliation.

This device, obviously, raises a question with regard to how long negotiation must continue before recourse can be had to other processes. Accordingly it is quite common to add a statement that a solution must be reached by negotiation within a reasonable period of time. Another facet of the problem was noted by Sohn. He pointed out that where a group of nations have in common a dispute with one other nation, it would be irresponsible to require each nation to negotiate individually with that nation before it could be found that the requirement of prerequisite negotiation had been satisfied. In such situations, other procedures could be adopted without completely exhausting all administrative remedies through negotiations. Diplomatic negotiations, by their very nature, are non-compulsory, yet they may take on an aura or gloss of binding quality when written in as part of a package which provides for binding procedures where negotiations fail.

Good Offices

When negotiations fail, it is sometimes appropriate for a third state, or a prominent international official, to make an offer of *good offices*. The offer, of course, must be acceptable to the parties to a dispute in order to set the procedure in motion. Upon acceptance by the parties, the third state is authorized to attempt to bring the parties together and to assist them in reaching an adequate solution between or among themselves. This can be done in a number of ways. The third state can act as a go-between, a line of communication between the parties, and usually has as its role the re-establishment of direct negotiations between the disputing parties. Once negotiations are resumed, good offices automatically cease unless the parties invite the third state to be present at further diplomatic negotiations. The primary factor that differentiates good offices from other forms of dispute settlement is that the state proffering good offices plays no other role than acting as an intermediary. If that state (or other party) assumes an active role in bringing about a settlement, then the process is converted into mediation.

Mediation

The function of a mediator has been defined as assisting the parties "in the simplest and most direct manner, avoiding formalities and seeking an acceptable solution." Mediation proceedings are normally informal in the sense that they are without a report and are confidential in nature. Mediation normally continues until an agreement is reached, or until the mediator or the parties declare that the solutions proposed by him are not acceptable. In that sense, the advice given by the mediator is not binding upon the parties, and it must live or die based upon its inherent logic and persuasive force. Sohn points out that in practice the functions of good offices and mediation are often confused, and are often exercised simultaneously without a clear distinction between the two functions. He notes:

> For instance, when the Committee of Good Offices was discussed in the Indonesian Question, the United States representative on the Security Council stated that should "the parties accept the Council's good offices, they could request it to act as a mediator or conciliator and to suggest a method of settlement, or ask it to perform any other service they desired. So long as both parties join in making such a request, there is obviously no limit to the services which the Council can perform in facilitating a just and lasting settlement of this dispute."

Sohn concludes:

> While the powers of the Security Council and its subsidiary organs can thus be extended by an agreement between the parties to a dispute, it does not seem proper to put all these functions under the much narrower label of "good offices."

While it may not be technically proper to combine the functions of the two devices, Sohn's observation that it is often done is correct, and the combination must have certain attractions that would lead parties to consider the formula as an alternative. Flexibility would appear to be the major of these attractions. Thus it appears that in the Inter-American Treaty on Good Offices and Mediation of 1936, the parties provided first for negotiation, then:

> The High Contracting Parties may have recourse to the good offices or mediation of an eminent citizen of any of the other American countries, preferably chosen from a general list made up in accordance with the following Article.

The second article calls for the nomination of persons "most eminent by reason of their high character and juridical learning," which suggests that the parties had mediation more than good offices in mind. Yet the third article again makes reference to both forms of settlement; thus one could conclude that fexibility was the goal to be achieved.

According to H. G.. Darwin, the functions of a mediator are broad and flexible, falling into two categories. First, it is his responsibility to conduct interstate negotiations. In other words, in an atmosphere of reticence and perhaps even resentment, he must be prepared to introduce new elements into the discussion and relax tensions where possible. In doing this, he may discuss ideas with parties individually, and may actually advance the thought of one of the parties to the other without disclosing its origin. Any and all devices of persuasion are open to him. Secondly, he may within the course of discussions offer one or more substantive solutions to the dispute. This is a matter of judgment on his part, and, if he has particularly high credentials, he may wish to ponder carefully the question of diluting his potential influence by offering too many proposed solutions. On the other hand, a person of stature may not wish to risk failure on the success of a single proposal. Thus the personal factor is important to the selection of an appropriate mediator. Often the mediator will be a government, rather than an individual, providing the advantage of a large staff and greater input to the process. The advantage of an unallied mediating individual is, of course, his flexibility, which may not be evident if the same person operates as an agent of a government. The problem of selection of ad hoc vs. permanent mechanisms is a perpetual one involved in most dispute settlement procedures, and will be discussed later. However, it might be useful to note the following of Darwin's guidelines:

> 1. Though mediation can only be of assistance where the parties in dispute are fundamentally willing to settle their dispute, it can help towards a settlement.
>
> 2. Since flexibility is an essential element of the procedure, only to a limited extent could it be useful to attempt to establish institutions or standard procedures for mediation.
>
> 3. Though States will continue to be able to offer mediation, the appointment of individuals as mediators is a useful alternative possibility.
>
> 4. Since the choice of a mediator depends on the nature of the dispute and a large number of other factors, including nationality, it is important that there should be a wide field from which mediators may be chosen.

5. In the view of the personal qualities and experience desirable in an individual mediator, he might best be found from among persons with experience in the United Nations or other international organizations, either as a national representative or in the Secretariate.

Commission of Inquiry

Such commissions normally address themselves to ascertainment of facts; assisting parties to disputes by providing a fair and impartial determination of the bases from which a dispute might have arisen. In doing so, commissions may be regarded as playing an important part in the process which, upon occasion, has resulted in elimination of further proceedings. Fact finding is also recognized as an independent procedure under Article 33 of the Charter of the United Nations, which requires parties to a dispute which is likely to endanger peace and security to seek a solution by "negotiation, *inquiry*, mediation, conciliation, arbitration, resort to regional agencies or arrangements, or other peaceful means of their own choice" [emphais added].

Inquiry was also specifically provided for by the Hague Convention on Pacific Settlement of Disputes of 1907 for questions of fact. Article 9 provides:

> In disputes of an international nature involving neither honor nor vital interests, and arising from a difference of opinion on points of fact, the contracting powers deem it expedient and desirable that means of diplomacy should, as far as circumstances allow, to facilitate a solution of these disputes by elucidating the facts by means of an impartial and conscientious investigation.

The only case submitted to a commission of inquiry under the 1899 Hague Convention, the precursor of the above, was the *North Sea* or *Dogger Bank* case. In October, 1904, during the Russo-Japanese War, a squadron of the Russian fleet passing through the North Sea fired on British fishing vessels from Hull, thinking them to be Japanese torpedo boats. One of the trawlers was sunk, and several fishermen were killed or wounded. A commission of inquiry was set up consisting of admirals from France, Austria-Hungary, the United States, Great Britain, and Russia, and it was authorized to inquire into the circumstances surrounding the incident and to decide questions of responsibility and blame. While some lawyers might dispute whether the question of fault is a question of fact, the commission avoided that issue by finding that there were no torpedo boats among the fishing vessels, rendering the ultimate question somewhat moot. Eventually the Russians paid compensation.

In another "naval" case, a dispute arose out of the sinking of the Netherlands steamer *Tubantia* in 1916, possibly by a German submarine. A commission of inquiry was eastablished by the parties in 1921 consisting of a former member of the Swiss Federal Council as chairman, and naval officers from Denmark, Sweden, Germany and the Netherlands, and it was charged with determining the cause of the sinking. In this case, the commission concluded that the sinking was the result of "the explosion of a torpedo launched by a German submarine," but it assiduously avoided deciding the issue of fault, suggesting that the *Tubantia* may have struck a floating, inert torpedo previously expended against some other target. Nonetheless, the Germans responded in damages once the facts were ascertained.

Several other cases of the same nature indicate that they tend to involve isolated instances, so that fact-finding is relatively simple. A comparison between the *Dogger Bank* case and the *Tubantia* indicates another important characteristic of commissions of inquiry. They do not normally derive conclusions from presumptions. That is, in the *Dogger Bank* case, the commission concluded that there were no Japanese torpedo boats in the fleet fired upon, and in *Tubantia* there was no conclusion of fault; thus, unlike a court, no presumptions of guilt, innocence, or fault are used to fill a gap created by the failure to carry a given burden of proof. The facts are recounted and established for the use of he parties, and nothing more is attempted.

It is of note that many cases handled by commissions of inquiry involved naval matters, and were for the large part resolved by experts experienced in such matters. It is also notable that in all such cases deemed appropriate for submission to commissions of inquiry, findings of fact invariably led to settlement. The authority of the report of the commission of inquiry bears a direct relationship to the original scope of the charge. When the charge is limited solely to fact finding, it is almost impossible for one of the parties to reject the findings without appearing in bad faith. Thus, for example, in the case of the *Tubantia*, Germany could hardly deny the distinguished panel's findings that the *Tubantia* had been sunk by a German torpedo. Where, however, the charge to the commission includes broader goals, the appropriateness of a commission of inquiry to make such findings may be challenged, and the question is inevitably raised whether the question should have been referred to a better-suited mechanism.

Conciliation

In his work on international conciliation, Cot makes reference to Sir John Fischer Williams' observation that with respect to conciliation "No nice definition is called for." Yet Cot observes:

> Conciliation is a concept, rather than an institution. The intervention of third parties in the settlement of an international dispute can assume many forms, and must adapt itself to the nature of each individual case. All that matters is success; the procedure is of little importance. The factor that is essential to ensure success is still the wisdom and experience of those who are called upon to give their opinion; the institutional set-up that enables them to intervene is secondary.

Conciliation is to be distinguished from mediation in that the process involves an independent body rather than a third state or other prominant negotiator. It is different from a commission of inquiry in that in addition to elucidating facts, a conciliation commission makes positive proposals for the settlement of disputes. But unlike arbitration, the parties have no obligation to accept the commission's conclusions as binding. According to M. Rolin, when rapporteur to the Institut de Droit International on international conciliation, conciliation has four advantages:

> 1. It offers the parties to the dispute information and a knowledge of the oponent's case which is invaluable.
>
> 2. It affords an opportunity to the lawyers and politicians involved in the dispute at a national level to refer the matter to a small body of independent and qualified persons for their objective appraisal of the issues and for proposals for their settlement.
>
> 3. It takes full account of the sensitivity, susceptibilities and prestige of governments in that it is easier to accept a third party's solution than that offered by the opponent.
>
> 4. It leaves unchallenged the liberty and sovereignty of the parties. There is complete secrecy, no obligation to accept the Commission's proposals, no loss of rights or abandonment of postion. A state retains its sovereign control to the last stage of the proceedings.

Oppenheim, on the other hand, finds the procedure suspect. He points out that the lack of obligation of the parties to accept the commission's proposals makes matter uncertain, subject to the whims of neutral members who have no objective criteria at their disposal while developing a solution.

The procedure of conciliation has only rarely been adopted. The most noted of these was the Conciliation Commission for Palestine established by the General Assembly in 1948 "to assist the

Governments and authorities concerned to achieve a final settlement of all questions outstanding between them." The commission has not yet completed its task but is viewed as having some useful purpose.

Sir Hersch Lauterpacht has been one of conciliation's most searching critics. He rejects the concept of conciliation as a valid device on two grounds. First, conciliation is not mandatory, hence states adopting the procedure have by that act undermined judicial procedure while at the same time giving the illusion that they are agreeing to peaceful settlemnt. Secondly, he contends, conciliation erodes the foundations of the Rule of Law, for if a state can choose between a settlement having the force of law, and one which is nonjuridical, it will normally opt for the procedure which meets its political interests. Hence, by clothing conciliation with the appearances of a juridical procedure, the states involved "saction[s] the degradation of the Rule of Law by reducing it to the level of simple political argument."

Cot, however, disagrees, pointing out that:

> Conciliation is indeed a method of either modifying or setting aside the Rule of Law. Recourse is not had to a conciliator for strict enforcement of the law. Nevertheless the solution proposed by the Commission does take into account the Rule of Law and makes the relationship to it clear.

Thus one can view conciliation as the intervention in the settlement of an international dispute by a body having no political authority of its own, but enjoying the confidence of the parties to the dispute and entrusted with the task of investigating every aspect of the dispute and proposing a nonbinding solution. Because a conciliation commission rests its effectiveness, if any, solely on the trust and confidence of the parties, it is better suited to resolving specific conflicts than it is to relaxing long-standing tensions involving a number of incidents, or traditional mistrust. Problems of the constitution of commissions will be deferred to later.

Arbitration

Arbitration and juridial tribunals have been left for treatment until last because these are the two methods which truly raise the question of sovereign rights. Modern arbitration has changed little from the form in which it emerged at the end of the nineteenth century. Article 15 of the Hague Convention of 1899 offers the following definition:

> International arbitration has for its object the settlement of differences between States by judges of their own choice, and on the basis of a respect for law.

The 1907 version adds the following: "Recourse to arbitration implies an engagement to submit in good faith to the award." Arbitration, as envisaged by the Hague Convention, is seen as the most effective and equitable way of dealing with questions of a legal nature, particularly the interpretation or application of treaties.

Arbitration is preserved for use within the United Nations structure by Article 33, insofar as disputes the continuance of which is likely to endanger the maintenance of international peace and security are concerned. It is listed as one of the devices that should be used before resort to the Security Council under the terms of Article 37. If the order in which devices are listed is indicative of their nature, it would be of interest that arbitration is listed between conciliation and referral to judicial settlement. The distinction between conciliation and arbitration is clearer than the distinction between arbitration and judicial settlement. In fact, arbitration is a judicial process, and as indicated by the

Hague Convention, should be conducted by "judges." However, one distinction between them has been noted by Sohn:

> It is generally agreed that there is at least one difference, formal or structural rather than substantive, between arbitral tribunals and international courts. Traditionally, that difference lies not in their respective functions but in the method of selection of the arbitrators and judges. While the parties usually have free choice with respect to membership of an arbitral tribunal, they have to adopt a court as it is and can vary its membership only to a slight degree.

Of course, this distinction becomes even less in importance in the case where arbitration is conducted under a permanent framework such as the Permanent Court of Arbitration rather than on an ad hoc basis.

Furthermore, there does in fact seem to be some difference between cases handled by the International Court of Justice and arbitral tribunals. This division tends to fall along functional lies. While any case might be referred to arbitration without reference to whether it is abitrable, so long as the parties agree, the converse is not usually true for judicial tribunals to which only "legal questions" are normally referred. Thus the only time one may expect a general dispute over the jurisdiction of an arbitral tribunal is in those cases where a governing treaty specifies certain categories of disputes that are agreed to be the subject of arbitration. Time and space do not permit an examination here of the many cases that would shed light on the distinction between arbitration and judicial tribunals. Let it suffice for the present discussion to say that while judicial tribunals are limited to questions of legal interpretation and the application of legal norms, panels of arbitrators have been known to consider not only such disputes but disputes of a nonlegal character, provided that the nonlegal disputes do not encroach on the vital interest or national honor, or affect the territorial integrity of one or both of the parties. In looking over the cases referred to arbitration outside of the commercial area, however, there seems to be a growing tendency to reserve to courts all questions of legal interpretation (but not claims to change existing law), and to retain nonlegal disputes to arbitration after an attempt has first been made to utilize conciliation. As noted by Hazel Fox, "[many] factors have contributed to the decline in the use of ad hoc arbitration as a method of settling disputes today. Its proper function today -- and it is well to recognize this frankly without further analysis of defects -- must be as a useful residual process where no special tribunal or separate procedure exists." Thus arbitration seems a natural as a compulsory device demanding more flexibility than can normally be afforded by courts, both in the selection of judges and in the type of mechanisms and subjects of disputes.

Juridical Courts

From what has been said thus far, one can clearly see that courts occupy the upper end of the justicial scale in terms of both formality and juridicality. The tribunal is today typified by the International Court of Justice. Its function under Article 38(1) of the Statute of the Court is to decide disputes in accordance with international law. In this sense, the court is the living symbol of the rule of law as opposed to the rule of force. It adds stability to the international legal process by providing a forum of permanence by whose jurisprudence the law is allowed to mature. Against this background of expectations, one must view the reality that the tribunal of which we speak now is clearly the greatest threat to nations jealous of sovereignty, thus is least likely to be either the chosen or the most effective forum for the resolution of disputes involving international relations which, while resolvable by principles of law, have strong political overtones. This is best typified by Litvinov's axiom "only an angel could be unbiased in Russian affairs."

The facts belie the expectations. The expectations for the Internationl Court were as follows:

> ...the First Committee ventures to foresee a significant role for the new Court in the

> international relations of the future. The judicial process will have a central place in the plans of the United Nations for the settlement of international disputes by peaceful means.... In establishing the International Court of Justice, the United Nations hold before a war-stricken world the beacons of Justice and Law and offer the possibility of substituting orderly judicial processes for the vicissitudes of war and the reign of brutal force.

Between 1945 and 1970, 175 treaties conferred jurisdiction on the International Court of Justice. During that same period, proceedings were instituted in fifty cases, of which fourteen were requests for advisory opinions and only fifteen proceeded to judgments on the merits. Furthermore, analysis of the cases reveal that all but nine were between nations having no major ideological differences. Thus while the court has many advantages, the statistics indicate a need for further investigation and improvement. The record is not impressive.

A number of proposals have been made to change the court. These proposals cover a wide range of ideas relating to procedure, the membership and competence of the court, the basis of jurisdiction, and other such areas. More will be said about these problems susbsequently, but suffice it to say at this point that while some changes could be salutory, the basic problem with the International Court remains one of widespread lack of confidence. In adjudications before the court one party wins and one loses. In the world of international politics, particularly in the sphere of negotiations, it is not necessary for there to be a complete "winner" and a total "loser". Political compromise is possible so that face-saving becomes an alternative. Added to this fact is the fear that members of the court are suspected not to fairly reflect the interests of the nations parties to the dispute, or that they might indeed apply provisions of law which one or both the parties might view as out of date or reflecting the interests of a special power group. The attitude of Canada with respect to its 100-mile pollution zone legislation is typical of this feeling. The enormous increase in the number of independent states in the last two decades has added much fuel to this fire, particularly with respect to law of the sea matters. The political shift from an essentially West European-American orientation to a greatly varied international community approach; thus nations would seem at this point in history to be uncertain as to the path of international jurisprudence, and, hence, the future of compulsory adjudication by a permanent court.

Another question often discussed relates to the respective role of the International Court of Justice and the possible roles of subsidiary international courts basing their jurisdiction upon geography or expertise. It has been variously suggested that regional courts be established, or that courts such as the proposed Law of the Sea Tribunal be created to deal with problems of special expertise. One must ask whether the creation of such tribunals would add to the cause of adjudication of international disputes or detract from it. On the one hand, creation of subsidiary instruments would detract from the prestige of the World Court. On the other, it may ultimately enhance its usefulnes by creating an atmosphere where nations become more accustomed to the fact of international adjudication.

Clearly, with all of its faults, a permanent adjudicatory institution will continue to exist. Perhaps more than one will be required. It may be that adjudication by judges on questions of legal interpretation of treaties alone will not be sufficient, and that other types of machinery will be needed such as the World Equity Tribunal proposed by Clark and Sohn to deal with disputes not primarily of a legal nature.

Relevant to the subject of specialized courts, the U.S. proposal for the settlement of disputes with relation to the law of the sea would create a unique tribunal. Article 1 of that draft first provides for other means of settlement.

> In any dispute between the Contracting Parties relating to the interpretation or application of the present Convention, any party to the dispute may invite the other party or parties to the dispute to settle the dispute by direct negotiation, good offices, mediation, conciliation,

arbitration, or through special procedures provided for by an international or regional organization.

While such optional procedures are made available, any party to a dispute which is required by the terms of the Law of the Sea Convention to be submitted to compulsory settlement may at any time refer the dispute to the Law of the Sea Tribunal created by the articles. Thus the ultimate decision rests in the hands of the tribunal if all other methods fail. While the tribunal would be established by the procedure provided for the International Court of Justice, it would also be assisted in the consideration of technical cases by four technical assessors sitting without right to vote. The specialized nature of the court is indicated by that provision, and by the provision in the draft which would provide the owner or operator of a vessel detained by any state the right to bring the question of detention before the tribunal to secure its prompt release, even though the dispute relating to the initial seizure of that vessel was being handled by some other procedure, such as arbitration.

....

ED. NOTE: The paper goes on to discuss some of the practical problems related to dispute settlement. There are questions relating to the number and qualifications of adjudicators. For example, in arbitration, should there be three or five arbitral judges? Who should pick them? Should they be selected from a permanent list, or selected by the parties to the dispute? And so forth.

With this background in mind, let us go on to the next section dealing specifically with the procedures finally adopted as part of the Law of the Sea Convention.

B. DISPUTE SETTLEMENT PROCEDURES

1982 UNITED NATIONS CONVENTION ON THE LAW OF THE SEA

PART XI.

THE AREA

SECTION 5. SETTLEMENT OF DISPUTES AND ADVISORY OPINIONS

Article 186

Sea-Bed Disputes Chamber of the International Tribunal for the Law of the Sea

The establishment of the Sea-Bed Disputes Chamber and the manner in which it shall exercise its jurisdiction shall be governed by the provisions of this section, of Part XV and of Annex VI.

Article 187

Jurisdiction of the Sea-Bed Disputes Chamber

The Sea-Bed Disputes Chamber shall have jurisdiction under this Part and the Annexes relating thereto in disputes with respect to activities in the Area falling within the following categories:

(a) disputes between States Parties concerning the interpretation and application of this Part and the Annexes relating thereto;

(b) disputes between a State Party and the Authority concerning:

(i) acts or omissions of the Authority or of a State Party alleged to be in violation of this Part or the Annexes relating thereto or of rules, regulations and procedures of the Authority adopted in accordance therewith; or

(ii) acts of the Authority alleged to be in excess of jurisdiction or a misuse of power;

(c) disputes between parties to a contract, being States Paraties, the Authority or the Enterprise, state enterprises and natural or juridical persons referred to in article 153, paragraph 2(b), concerning:

(i) the interpretation or application of a relevant contract or a plan of work; or

(ii) acts or omissions of a party to the contract relating to activities in the Area and directed to the other party or directly affecting its legitimate interests;

(d) disputes between the Authority and a prospective contractor who has been sponsored by a State as provided in article 153, paragraph 2(b), and has duly fulfilled the conditions referred to in Annex III, article 4, paragraph 6, and article 13, paragraph 2, concerning the refusal of a contract or a legal issue arising in the negotiation of the contract;

(e) disputes between the Authority and a State Party, a state enterprise or a natural or juridical person sponsored by a State Party as provided for in article 153, paragraph 2(b), where it is alleged that the Authority has incurred liability as provided in Annex III, article 22;

(f) any other disputes for which the jurisdiction of the Chamber is specifically provided in this Convention.

Article 188

Submission of disputes to a special chamber of the International Tribunal for the Law of the Sea or an ad hoc chamber of the Sea-Bed Disputes Chamber or to binding commercial arbitration

1. Disputes between States Parties referred to in article 187, subparagraph (a), may be submitted:

(a) at the request of the parties to the dispute, to a special chamber of the International Tribunal for the Law of the Sea to be formed in accordance with Annex VI, articles 25 and 17; or

(b) at the request of any party to the dispute, to an *ad hoc* chamber of the Sea-Bed Disputes Chamber to be formed in accordance with Annex VI, article 36.

2. (a) Disputes concerning the interpretation and application of a contract referred to in article 187, subparagraph (c)(i), shall be submitted, at the request of any party to the dispute, to binding commerical arbitration, unless the parties otherwise agree. A commercial arbitral tribunal to which the dispute is submitted shall have no jurisdiction to decide any question of interpretation of this Convention. When the dispute also involves a question of the interpretation of Part XI and the Annexes relating thereto, with respect to activities in the Area, that question shall be referred to the Sea-Bed Disputes Chamber for a ruling.

(b) If, at the commencement of or in the course of such arbitration, the arbitral tribunal determines, either at the request of any party to the dispute or *proprio motu*, that its decision depends upon a ruling of the Sea-Bed Disputes Chamber, the arbitral tribunal shall refer such question to the Sea-Bed Disputes Chamber for such ruling. The arbitral tribunal shall then proceed to render its award in conformity with the ruling of the Sea-Bed Disputes Chamber.

(c) In the absence of a provision in the contract or the arbitration procedure to be applied in the dispute, the arbitration shall be conducted in accordance with the UNCITRAL Arbitration Rules or such other arbitration rules as may be prescribed in the rules, regulations and procedures of the Authority, unless the parties to the dispute otherwise agree.

Article 189

Limitations on jurisdiction with regard to decisions of the Authority

The Sea-Bed Disputes Chamber shall have no jurisdiction with regard to the exercise by the Authority of its discretionary powers in accordance with this Part; in no case shall it substitute its discretion for that of the Authority. Without prejudice to article 191, in exercising its jurisdiction purusant to article 187, the Sea-Bed Disputes Chamber shall not pronounce itself on the question of whether any rules, regulations and procedures of the Authority are in conformity with this Convention, nor declare invalid any such rules, regulations and procedures. Its jurisdiction in this regard shall be confined to deciding claims that the application of any rules, regulations and procedures of the Authority in individual cases would be in conflict with the contractual obligations of the parties to the dispute or their obligations under this Convention, claims concerning excess of jurisdiction or misuse of power, and to claims for damages to be paid or other remedy to be given to the party concerned for the failure of the other party to comply with its contractual obligations or its obligations under this Convention.

Article 190

Participation and appearance of sponsoring States Parties in proceedings

1. If a natural or juridical person is a party to a dispute referred to in article 187, the sponsoring State shall be given notice thereof and shall have the right to participate in the proceedings by submitting written or oral statements.

2. If an action is brought against a State Party by a natural or juridical person sponsored by another State Party in a dispute referred to in article 187, subparagraph (c), the respondent State may request the State sponsoring that person to appear in the proceedings on behalf of that person. Failing such appearance, the respondent State may arrange to be represented by a juridical person of its nationality.

Article 191

Advisory opinions

The Sea-Bed Disputes Chamber shall give advisory opinions at the request of the Assembly or the Council on legal questions arising within the scope of their activities. Such opinions shall be given as a matter of urgency.

PART XV. SETTLEMENT OF DISPUTES

SECTION 1. GENERAL PROVISIONS

Article 279

Obligation to settle disputes by peaceful means

States Parties shall settle any dispute between them concerning the interpretation or application of this Convention by peaceful means in accordance with Article 2, paragraph 3, of the Charter of the United Nations and, to this end, shall seek a solution by the means indicated in Article 33, paragraph 1, of the Charter.

Article 280

Settlement of disputes by any peaceful means chosen by the parties

Nothing in this Part impairs the right of any States Parties to agree at any time to settle a dispute between them concerning the interpretation or application of this Convention by any peaceful means of their own choice.

Article 281

Procedure where no settlement has been reached by the parties

1. If the States Parties which are parties to a dispute concerning the interpretation or application of this Convention have agreed to seek settlement of the dispute by peaceful means of their own choice, the procedures provided for in this Part apply only where no settlement has been reached by recourse to such means and the agreement between the parties does not exclude any further procedure.

2. If the parties have also agreed on a time-limit, paragraph 1 applies only upon the expiration of that time-limit.

Article 282

Obligations under general, regional or bilateral agreements

If the States Parties which are parties to a dispute concerning the interpretation or application of this Convention have agreed, through a general, regional or bilateral agreement or otherwise, that such dispute shall, at the request of any party to the dispute, be submitted to a procedure that entails a binding decision, that procedure shall apply in lieu of the procedures provided for in this Part, unless the parties to the dispute otherwise agree.

Article 283

Obligation to exchange views

1. When a dispute arises between States Parties concerning the interpretation or application of this Convention, the parties to the dispute shall proceed expeditiously to an exchange of views regarding its settlement by negotiation or other peaceful means.

2. The parties shall also proceed expeditiously to an exchange of views where a procedure for the settlement of such a dispute has been terminated without a settlement or where a settlement has been reached and the circumstances require consultation regarding the manner of implementing the settlement.

Article 284

Conciliation

1. A State Party which is a party to a dispute concerning the interpretation or application of this Convention may invite the other party or parties to submit the dispute to conciliation in accordance with the procedure under Annex V, section 1, or another conciliation procedure.

2. If the invitation is accepted and if the parties agree upon the conciliation procedure to be applied, any party may submit the dispute to that procedure.

3. If the invitation is not accepted or the parties do not agree upon the procedure, the conciliation proceedings shall be deemed to be terminated.

4. Unless the parties otherwise agree, when a dispute has been submitted to conciliation, the proceedings may be terminated only in accordance with the agreed conciliation procedure.

Article 285

Application of this section to disputes submitted pursuant to Part XI

This section applies to any dispute which pursuant to Part XI, section 5, is to be settled in accordance with procedures provided for in this Part. If an entity other than a State Party is a party to such a dispute, this section applies *mutatis mutandis*.

SECTION 2. COMPULSORY PROCEDURES ENTAILING BINDING DECISIONS

Article 286

Application of procedures under this section

Subject to section 3, any dispute concerning the interpretation or application of this Convention shall, where no settlement has been reached by recourse to section 1, be submitted at the request of any party to the dispute to the court or tribunal having jurisdiction under this section.

Article 287

Choice of procedure

1. When signing, ratifying or acceding to this Convention or at any time thereafter, a State shall be free to choose, by means of a written declaration, one or more of the following means of the settlement of disputes concerning the interpretation or application of this Convention:

(a) the International Tribunal for the Law of the Sea established in accordance with Annex VI;

(b) the International Court of Justice;

(c) an arbitral tribunal constituted in accordance with Annex VII;

(d) a special arbitral tribunal constituted in accordance with Annex VIII for one or more of the categories of disputes specified therein.

2. A declaration made under paragraph 1 shall not affect or be affected by the obligation of a State Party to accept the jurisdiction of the Sea-Bed Disputes Chamber of the International Tribunal for the Law of the Sea to the extent and in the manner provided for in Part XI, section 5.

3. A State Party, which is a party to a dispute not covered by a declaration in force, shall be deemed to have accepted arbitration in accordance with Annex VII.

4. If the parties to a dispute have accepted the same procedure for the settlement of the dispute, it may be submitted only to the that procedure, unless the parties otherwise agree.

5. If the parties to a dispute have not accepted the same procedure for the settlement of the dispute, it may be submitted only to arbitration in accordance with Annex VII, unless the parties otherwise agree.

6. A declaration made under paragraph 1 shall remain in force until three months after notice of revocation has been deposited with the Secretary-General of the United Nations.

7. A new declaration, a notice of revocation or the expiry of a declaration does not in any way affect proceedings pending before a court or tribunal having jurisdiction under this article, unless the parties otherwise agree.

8. Declarations and notices referred to in this article shall be deposited with the Secretary-General of the United Nations, who shall transmit copies thereof to the States Parties.

Article 288

Jurisdiction

1. A court or tribunal referred to in article 287 shall have jurisdiction over any dispute concerning the interpretation or application of this Convention which is submitted to it in accordance with this Part.

2. A court or tribunal referred to in article 287 shall also have jurisdiction over any dispute concerning the interpretation or application of an international agreement related to the purposes of this Convention, which is submitted to it in accordance with the agreement.

3. The Sea-Bed Disputes Chamber of the International Tribunal for the Law of the Sea established in accordance with Annex VI, and any other chamber or arbitral tribunal referred to in Part XI, section 5, shall have jurisdiction in any matter which is submitted to it in accordance therewith.

4. In the event of a dispute as to whether a court or tribunal has jurisdiction, the matter shall be settled by decision of that court or tribunal.

Article 289

Experts

In any dispute involving scientific or technical matters, a court or tribunal exercising jurisdiction under this section may, at the request of a party or *proprio motu*, select in consulation with the parties no fewer than two scientific or technical experts chosen preferably from the relevant list prepared in accordance with Annex VIII, article 2, to sit with the court or tribunal but without the right to vote.

Article 290

Provisional measures

1. If a dispute has been duly submitted to a court or tribunal which considers that *prima facie* it has jurisdiction under the Part or Part XI, section 5, the court or tribunal may prescribe any provisional measures which it considers appropriate under the circumstances to preserve the respective rights of the parties to the dispute or to prevent serious harm to the marine environment, pending the final decision.

2. Provisional measures may be modified or revoked as soon as the circumstances justifying them have changed or ceased to exist.

3. Provisional measures may be prescribed , modified or revoked under this article only at the request of a party to the dispute and after the parties have been given the opportunity to be heard.

4. The court or tribunal shall forthwith give notice to the parties to the dispute, and to such other States Parties as it considers appropriate, of the prescription, modification or revocation of provisional measures.

5. Pending the constitution of an arbitral tribunal to which a dispute is being submitted under this section, any court or tribunal agreed upon by the parties or, filing such agreement within two weeks from the date of the request for provisional measures, the International Tribunal for the Law of the Sea or, with respect to activities in the Area, the Sea-Bed Disputes Chamber, may prescribe, modify or revoke provisional measures in accordance with this article if it considers that *prima facie* the tribunal which is to be constituted would have jurisdiction and that the urgency of the situation so requires. Once constituted, the tribunal to which the dispute has been submitted may modify, revoke or affirm those provisional measures, acting in conformity with paragraphs 1 to 4.

6. The parties to the dispute shall comply promptly with any provisional measures prescribed under this article.

Article 291

Access

1. All the dispute settlement procedures specified in this Part shall be open to States Parties.

2. The dispute settlement procedures specified in this Part shall be open to entities other than States Parties only as specifically provided for in this Convention.

Article 292

Prompt release of vessels and crews

1. Where the authorities of a State Party have detained a vessel flying the flag of another State Party and it is alleged that the detaining State has not complied with the provisions of this Convention for the prompt rlease of the vessel or its crew upon the posting of a reasonable bond or other financial security, the question of release from detention may be submitted to any court or tribunal agreed upon by the parties, or, failing such agreement within 10 days from the time of detention, to a court or tribunal accepted by the detaining State under article 287 or to the International Tribunal for the Law of the Sea, unless the parties otherwise agree.

2. The application for release may be made only by or on behalf of the flag State of the vessel.

3. The court or tribunal shall deal without delay with the application for release and shall deal only with the question of release, without prejudice to the merits of any case before the appropriate domestic forum against the vessel, its owner or its crew. The authorities of the detaining State remain competent to release the vessel or its crew at any time.

4. Upon the posting of the bond or other financial security determined by the court or tribunal, the authorities of the detaining State shall comply promptly with the decision of the court or tribunal concerning the release of the vessel or its crew.

Article 293

Applicable law

1. A court or tribunal having jurisdiction under this section shall apply this Convention and other rules of international law not incompatible with this Convention.

2. Paragraph 1 does not prejudice the power of the court or tribunal under this section to decide a case *ex aequo et bono*, if the parties so agree.

Article 294

Preliminary proceedings

1. A court or tribunal provided for in article 287 to which an application is made in respect to a dispute referred to in article 297 shall determine at the request of a party, or may determine *proprio motu*, whether the claim constitutes an abuse of legal process or whether *prima facie* it is well founded. If the court or tribunal determines that the claim constitutes an abuse of legal process or is *prima facie* unfounded, it shall take no further action in the case.

2. Upon receipt of the application, the court or tribunal shall immediately notify the other party or parties of the application, and shall fix a reasonable time-limit within which they may request it to make a determination in accordance with paragraph 1.

3. Nothing in this article affects the right of any party to a dispute to make preliminary objections in accordance with the applicable rules of procedure.

Article 295

Exhaustion of local remedies

Any dispute between States Parties concerning the interpretation or application of this Convention may be submitted to the procedures provided for in this section only after local remedies have been exhausted where this is required by international law.

Article 296

Finality and binding force of decisions

1. Any decision rendered by a court or tribunal having jurisdiction under this section shall be final and shall be complied with by all the parties to the dispute.

2. Any such decision shall have no binding force except between the parties and in respect of that particular dispute.

SECTION 3. LIMITATIONS AND EXCEPTIONS TO APPLICABILITY OF SECTION 2

Article 297

Limitations on applicabilitly of section 2

1. Disputes concerning the interpretation or application of this Convention with regard to the exercise by a coastal State of its sovereign rights or jurisdiction provided for in this Convention shall be subject to the procedures provided for in section 2 in the following cases:

(a) when it is alleged that a coastal State has acted in contravention of the provisions of this Convention in regard to the freedoms and rights of navigation, overflight or the laying of submarine cables and pipelines or in regard to other internationally lawful uses of the sea specified in article 58;

(b) when it is alleged that a State in exercising the aformentioned freedoms, rights or uses has acted in contravention of this Convention or of laws or regulations adopted by the coastal State in conformity with this Convention and other rules of international law not incompatible with this Convention; or

(c) when it is alleged that a coastal State has acted in contravention of specified international rules and standards for the protection and preservation of the marine environment which are applicable to the coastal State and which have been established by this Convention or through a competent international organization or diplomatic conference in accordance with this Convention.

2. (a) Disputes concerning the interpretation or application of the provisions of this Convention with regard to marine scientific research shall be settled in accordance with section 2, except that the coastal State shall not be obliged to accept the submission to such settlement of any dispute arising out of:

(i) the exercise by the coastal State of a right or discretion in accordance with article 246; or

(ii) a decision by the coastal State to order suspension or cessation of a research project in accordance with article 253

(b) a dispute arising from an allegation by the researching State that with respect to a specific project the coastal State is not exercising its rights under articles 246 and 253 in a manner compatible with this Convention shall be submitted, at the request of either party, to conciliation under Annex V, section 2, provided that the conciliation commission shall not call in question the exercise by the coastal State of its discretion to designate specific areas as referred to in article 246, pargraph 6, or of its discretion to withhold consent in accordance with article 246, paragraph 5.

3(a) Disputes concerning the interpretation or application of the provisions of this Convention with regard to fisheries shall be settled in accordance with section 2, except that the coastal State may not be obliged to accept the submission of any dipute relating to its sovereign rights with respect to the living resources in the exclusive economic zone or their exercise, including its discretionary powers for determining the allowable catch, its harvesting capacity, the allocation of surpluses to other States and the terms and conditions established in its conservation and management laws and regulations.

(b) Where no settlement has been reached by recourse to section 1 of this Part, a dispute shall be submitted to conciliation under Annex V, section 2, at the request of any party to the dispute, when it is alleged that:

(i) a coastal State has manifestly failed to comply with its obligations to ensure through proper conservation and management measures that the maintenance of the living resources in the exclusive economic zone is not seriously endangered;

(ii) a coastal State has arbitrarily refused to determine, at the request of another State, the allowable catch and its capacity to harvest living resources with respect to stocks which that other State is interested in fishing; or

(iii) a coastal State has arbitrarily refused to allocate to any State, under articles 62, 69 and 70 and under the terms and conditions established by the coastal State consistent with this Convention, the whole or any part of the surplus it has declared to exist.

(c) In no case shall the conciliation commission susbstitute its discretion for that of the coastal State.

(d) The report of the conciliation commission shall be communicated to the appropriate international organizations.

(e) In negotiating agreements pursuant to article 69 and 70, States Parties, unless they otherwise agree, shall include a clause on measures which they shall take in order to minimize the possibility of a disagreement concerning the interpretation or application of the agreement, and on how they should proceed if a disagreement nevertheless arises.

Article 298

Optional exceptions to the applicability of section 2

1. When signing, ratifying or acceding to this Convention or at any time thereafter, a State may, without prejudice to the obligations arising under section 1, declare in writing that it does not accept any one or more of the procedures provided for in section 2 with respect to one or more of the following categories of disputes:

(a)(i) disputes concerning the interpretation or application of articles 15, 74 and 83 relating to sea boundary delimitations, or those involving historic bays or titles, providing that a State having made such a declaration shall, when such a dispute arises subsequent to the entry into force of this Convention and where no agreement within a reasonable period of time is reached in negotiations between the parties, at the request of any party to the dispute, accept submission of the matter to conciliation under Annex V, section 2; and provided further that any dispute that necessarily involves the concurrent consideration of any unsettled dispute concerning sovereignty or other rights over continental or insular land territory shall be excluded from such submission;

(ii) after the conciliation commission has made its report, which shall state the reasons on which it is based, the parties shall negotiate an agreement on the basis of that report; if these negotiations do not result in an agreement, the parties shall, by mutual consent, submit the question to one of the procedures provided for in section 2, unless the parties otherwise agree;

(iii) this subparagraph does not apply to any sea boundary dispute finally settled by an agreement between the parties, or to any such dispute which is to be settled in accordance with bilateral or multilateral agreement binding upon those parties;

(b) disputes concerning military activities, including military activities by government vessels and aircraft engaged in non-commerical service, and disputes concerning law enforcement activities in regard to the exercise of sovereign rights or jurisdiction excluded from the jurisdiction of a court or tribunal under article 297, paragraph 2 or 3;

(c) disputes in respect of which the Security Council of the United Nations is exercising the functions assigned to it by the Charter of the United Nations, unless the Security Council decides to remove the matter from its agenda or calls upon the parties to settle it by the means provided for in this Convention.

2. A State Party which has made a declaration under paragraph 1 may at any time withdraw it, or agree to submit a dispute excluded by such declaration to any procedure specified in this Convention.

3. A State Party which has made a declaration under paragraph 1 shall not be entitled to submit any dispute falling within the excepted category of disputes to any procedure in this Convention as against another State Party, without the consent of that party.

4. If one of the States Parties has made a declaration under paragraph 1(a), any other State Party may submit any dispute falling within an excepted category against the declarant party to the procedure specified in such declaration.

5. A new declaration, or the withdrawal of a declaration, does not in any way affect proceedings pending before a court or tribunal in accordance with this article, unless the parties otherwise agree.

6. Declarations and notices of withdrawal of declarations under this article shall be deposited with the Secretary-General of the United Nations, who shall transmit copies thereof to the States Parties.

Article 299

Right of the parties to agree upon a procedure

1. A dispute excluded under article 297 or excepted by a declaration made under article 298 from the dispute settlement procedures provided for in section 2 may be submitted to such procedures

only by agreement of the parties to the dispute.

2. Nothing in this section impairs the right of the parties to the dispute to agree to some other procedure for the settlement of such dispute or to reach an amicable settlement.

ANNEX V. CONCILIATION

SECTION 1. CONCILIATION PROCEDURE PURSUANT TO SECTION 1 OF PART XV

Article 1

Institution of proceedings

If the parties to a dispute have agreed, in accordance with article 284, to submit it to conciliation under this section, any such party may institute the proceedings by written notification addressed to the other party or parties to the dispute.

Article 2

List of conciliators

A list of conciliators shall be drawn up and maintained by the Secretary-General of the United Nations. Every State Party shall be entitled to nominate four conciliators, each of whom shall be a person enjoying the highest reputation for fairness, competence and integrity. The names of the persons so nominated shall constitute the list. If at any time the conciliators nominated by a State Party in the list so constituted shall be fewer than four, that State Party shall be entitled to make further nominations as necessary. The name of a conciliator shall remain on the list until withdrawn by the State Party which made the nomination, provided that such conciliator shall continue to serve on any conciliation commission to which that conciliator has been appointed until the completion of the proceedings before that commission.

Article 3

Constitution of conciliation commission

The conciliation commission shall, unless the parties otherwise agree, be constituted as follows:

(a) Subject to subparagraph (g), the conciliation commission shall consist of five members.

(b) The party instituting the proceedings shall appoint two conciliators to be chosen preferably from the list referred to in article 2 of this Annex, one of whom may be its national, unless the parties otherwise agree. Such appointments shall be included in the notification referred to in article 1 of this Annex.

(c) The other party to the dispute shall appoint two conciliators in the manner set forth in subparagraph (b) within 21 days of receipt of the notification referred to in article 1 of this Annex. If the appointments are not made within that period, the party instituting the proceedings may, within one week of the expiration of that period, either terminate the proceedings by notification addressed to the other party or request the Secretary-General of the United Nations to make the appointments in accordance with subparagraph (e).

(d) Within 30 days after all four conciliators have been appointed, they shall appoint a fifth conciliator chosen from the list referred to in article 2 of this Annex, who shall be chairman. If the appointment is not made within that period, either party may, within one week of the expiration of that period, request the Secretary-General of the United Nations to make the appointment in accordance with subparagraph (e).

(e) Within 30 days of the receipt of a request under subparagraph (c) or (d), the Secretary-General of the United Nations shall make the necessary appointments from the list referred to in article 2 of this Annex in consultation with the parties to the dispute.

(f) Any vacancy shall be filled in the manner prescribed for the initial appointment.

(g) Two or more parties which determine by agreement that they are in the same interest shall appoint two conciliators jointly. Where two or more parties have separate interests or there is a disagreement as to whether they are of the same interest, they shall appoint conciliators separately.

(h) In disputes involving more than two parties having separate interests, or where there is a disagreement as to whether they are of the same interest, the parties shall apply subparagraphs (a) to (f) in so far as possible.

Article 4

Procedure

The conciliation commission shall, unless the parties otherwise agree, determine its own procedure. The commission may, with the consent of the parties to the dispute, invite any State Party to submit its views orally or in writing. Decisions of the commission regarding procedural matters, the report and recommendations shall be made by a majority vote of its members.

Article 5

Amicable settlement

The commission may draw the attention of the parties to any measures which might facilitate an amicable settlement of the dispute.

Article 6

Functions of the commission

The commission shall hear the parties, examine their claims and objections, and make proposals to the parties with a view to reaching an amicable settlement.

Article 7

Report

1. The commission shall report within 12 months of its constitution. Its report shall record any agreements reached and, failing agreement, its conclusions on all questions of fact or law relevant to the matter in dispute and such recommendations as the commission may deem appropriate for an amicable settlement. The report shall be deposited with the Secretary-General of the United Nations and shall immediately be transmitted by him to the parties to the dispute.

2. The report of the commission, including its conclusions or recommendations, shall not be binding upon the parties.

Article 8

Termination

The conciliation proceedings are terminated when a settlement has been reached, when the parties have accepted or one party has rejected the recommendations of the report by written notification addressed to the Secretary-General of the United Nations, or when a period of three months has expired from the date of transmission of the report to the parties.

Article 9

Fees and expenses

The fees and expenses of the commission shall be borne by the parties to the dispute.

Article 10

Right of parties to modify procedure

The parties to the dispute may by agreement applicable solely to that dispute modify any provision of this Annex.

SECTION 2. COMPULSORY SUBMISSION TO CONCILIATION PROCEDURE PURSUANT TO SECTION 3 OF PART XV

Article 11

Institution of proceedings

1. Any party to a dispute which, in accordance with Part XV;, section 3, may be submitted to conciliation under this section, may institute the proceedings by written notification addressed to the other party or parties to the dispute.

2. Any party to the dispute, notified under paragraph 1, shall be obliged to submit to such proceedings.

Article 12

Failure to reply or to submit to conciliation

The failure of a party or parties to the dispute to reply to notification of institution of proceedings or to submit to such proceedings shall not constitute a bar to the proceedings.

Article 13

Competence

A disagreement as to whether a conciliation commission acting under this section has competence shall be decided by the commission.

Article 14

Application of section 1

Articles 2 to 10 of section 1 of this Annex apply subject to this section.

ANNEX VI. STATUTE OF THE INTERNATIONAL TRIBUNAL FOR THE LAW OF THE SEA

Article 1

General provisions

1. The International Tribunal for the Law of the Sea is constituted and shall function in accordance with the provisions of this Convention and this Statute.

2. The seat of the Tribunal shall be in the Free and Hanseatic City of Hamburg in the Federal Republic of Germany.

3. The Tribunal may sit and exercise its functions elsewhere whenever it considers this desirable.

4. A reference of a dispute to the Tribunal shall be governed by the provisions of Parts XI and XV.

SECTION 1. ORGANIZATION OF THE TRIBUNAL

Article 2

Composition

1. The Tribunal shall be composed of a body of 21 independent members, elected from among persons enjoying the highest reputation for fairness and integrity and of recognized competence in the field of the law of the sea.

2. In the Tribunal as a whole the representation of the principle legal systems of the world and equitable geographical distribution shall be assured.

Article 3

Membership

1. No two members of the Tribunal may be nationals of the same State. A person who for the purposes of membership in the Tribunal could be regarded as a national of more than one State shall be deemed to be a national of the one in which he ordinarily exercises civil and political rights.

2. There shall be no fewer than three members from each geographical group as established at the General Assembly of the United Nations.

Article 4

Nominations and elections

1. Each State Party may nominate not more than two persons having the qualifications prescribed in article 2 of this Annex. The members of the Tribunal shall be elected from the list of persons thus nominated.

2. At least three months before the date of the election, the Secretary-General of the United Nations in the case of the first election and the Registrar of the Tribunal in the case of subsequent elections shall address a written invitation to the States Parties to submit their nominations for members of the Tribunal within two months. He shall prepare a list in alphabetical order of all the persons thus nominated, with an indication of the States Parties which have nominated them, and shall submit it to the States Parties before the seventh day of the last month before the date of each election.

3. The first election shall be held within six months of the date of entry into force of this Convention.

4. The members of the Tribunal shall be elected by secret ballot. Elections shall be held at a meeting of the State Parties convened by the Secretary-General of the United Nations in the case of the first election and by a procedure agreed to by the States Parties in the case of subsequent elections. Two thirds of the States Parties shall constitute a quorum at that meeting. The persons elected to the Tribunal shall be those nominees who obtain the largest number of votes and a two-thirds majority of the States Parties present and voting, provided that such majority includes a majority of States Parties.

Article 5

Term of office

1. The members of the Tribunal shall be elected for nine years and may be re-elected; provided, however, that of the members elected at the first election, the terms of seven members shall expire at the end of three years and the terms of seven more members shall expire at the end of six years.

2. The members of the Tribunal whose terms are to expire at the end of the above-mentioned initial periods of three and six years shall be chosen by lot to be drawn by the Secretary-General of the United Nations immediately after the first election.

3. The members of the Tribunal shall continue to discharge their duties until their places have been filled. Though replaced, they shall finish any proceedings which they may have begun before the date of their replacement.

4. In the case of the resignation of a member of the Tribunal, the letter of resignation shall be addressed to the President of the Tribunal. The place becomes vacant on the receipt of that letter.

Article 6

Vacancies

1. Vacancies shall be filled by the same method as that laid down for the first election, subject to the following provision: the Registrar shall, within one month of the occurrence of the vacancy, proceed to issue the invitations provided for in article 4 of this Annex, and the date of the election shall

be fixed by the President of the Tribunal after consultation with the States Parties.

2. A member of the Tribunal elected to replace a member whose term of office has not expired shall hold office for the remainder of his predecessor's term.

Article 7

Incompatible activities

1. No member of the Tribunal may exercise any political or administrative function, or associate actively with or be financially interested in any of the operations of any enterprise concerned with the exploration for of exploitation of the resources of the sea or the sea-bed or other commercial use of the sea or the sea-bed.

2. No member of the Tribunal may act as agent, counsel or advocate in any case.

3. Any doubt on these points shall be resolved by decision of the majority of the other members of the Tribunal present.

Article 8

Conditions relating to participation of members in a particular case

1. No member of the Tribunal may participate in the decision of any case which he has previously taken part as agent, counsel or advocate for one of the parties, or as a member of a national or international court or tribunal, or in any other capactity.

2. If, for some special reason, a member of the Tribunal considers that he should not take part in the decision of a particular case, he shall so inform the President of the Tribunal.

3. If the President considers that for some special reason one of the members of the Tribunal should not sit in a particular case, he shall give him notice accordingly.

4. Any doubt on these points shall be resolved by a decision of the majority of the other members of the Tribunal present.

Article 9

Consequence of ceasing to fulfil required conditions

If, in the unanimous opinion of the other members of the Tribunal, a member has ceased to fulfil the required conditions, the President shall declare the seat vacant.

Article 10

Privileges and immunities

The members of the Tribunal, when engaged on the business of the Tribunal, shall enjoy diplomatic privileges and immunities.

Article 11

Solemn declaration by members

Every member of the Tribunal shall, before taking up his duties, make a solemn declaration in open session that he will exercise his powers impartially and conscientiously.

Article 12

President, Vice-President and Registrar

1. The Tribunal shall elect its President and Vice-President for three years; they may be re-elected.

2. The Tribunal shall appoint its Registrar and may provide for the appointment of such other officers as may be necessary.

3. The President and Registrar shall reside at the seat of the Tribunal.

Article 13

Quorum

1. All available members of the Tribunal shall sit; a quorum of elected members shall be required to constitute the Tribunal.

2. Subject to article 17 of this Annex, the Tribunal shall determine which members are available to constitute the Tribunal for the consideration of a particular dispute, having regard to the effective functioning of the chambers as provided for in articles 14 and 15 of this Annex.

3. All disputes and applications submitted to the Tribunal shall be heard and determined by the Tribunal, unless article 14 of this Annex applies, or the parties request that it shall be dealt with in accordance with article 15 of this Annex.

Article 14

Sea-Bed Disputes Chamber

A Sea-Bed Disputes Chamber shall be established in accordance with the provisions of section 4 of this Annex. Its jurisdiction, powers and functions shall be as provided for in Part XI, section 5.

Article 15

Special chambers

1. The Tribunal may form such chambers, composed of three or more of its elected members, as it considers necessary for dealing with particular categories of disputes.

2. The Tribunal shall form a chamber for dealing with a particular dispute submitted to it if the parties so request. The composition of such a chamber shall be determined by the Tribunal with the approval of the parties.

3. With a view to the speedy dispatch of business, the Tribunal shall form annually a chamber composed of five of its elected members which may hear and determine disputes by summary procedure. Two alternative members shall be selected for the purpose of replacing members who are unable to participate in a particular proceeding.

4. Disputes shall be heard and determined by the chambers provided for in this article if the parties so request.

5. A judgment given by any of the chambers provided for in this article and in article 14 of this Annex shall be considered as rendered by the Tribunal.

Article 16

Rules of the Tribunal

The Tribunal shall frame rules for carrying out its functions. In particular it shall lay down rules of procedure.

Article 17

Nationality of members

1. Members of the Tribunal of the nationality of any of the parties to a dispute shall retain their right to participate as members of the Tribunal.

2. If the Tribunal, when hearing a dispute, includes upon the bench a member of the nationality of one of the parties, any other party may choose a person to participate as a member of the Tribunal.

3. If the Tribunal, when hearing a dispute, does not include upon the bench a member of the nationality of the parties, each of those parties may choose a person to participate as a member of the Tribunal.

4. This article applies to the chambers referred to in articles 14 and 15 of this Annex. In such cases, the President, in consultation with the parties, shall request specified members of the Tribunal forming the chamber, as many as necessary to give place to the members of the Tribunal of the nationality of the parties concerned, and, failing such, or if they are unable to be present, to the members specially chosen by the parties.

5. Should there be several parties in the same interest, they shall, for the purpose of the preceding provisions, be considered as one party only. Any doubt on this point shall be settled by the decision of the Tribunal.

6. Members chosen in accordance with paragraphs 2, 3 and 4 shall fulfil the conditions required by articles 2, 8 and 11 of this Annex. They shall participate in the decision on terms of complete equality with their colleagues.

Article 18

Remuneration of members

1. Each elected member of the Tribunal shall receive an annual allowance and, for each day on

which he exercises his functions, a special allowance, provided that in any year the total sum payable to any member as special allowance shall not exceed the amount of the annual allowance.

2. The President shall receive a special annual allowance.

3. The Vice-President shall receive a special allowance for each day on which he acts as President.

4. The members chosen under article 17 of this Annex, other than elected members of the Tribunal, shall receive compensation for each day on which they exercise their functions.

5. The salaries, allowances and compensation shall be determined from time to time at meetings of the States Parties, taking into account the work load of the Tribunal. They may not be decreased during the term of office.

6. The salary of the Registrar shall be determined at meetings of the States Parties, on the proposal of the Tribunal.

7. Regulations adopted at meetings of the States Parties shall determine the conditions under which retirement pensions may be given to members of the Tribunal and to the Registrar, and the conditions under which members of the Tribunal and the Registrar shall have their travelling expenses refunded.

8. The salaries, allowances, and compensation shall be free of all taxation.

Article 19

Expenses of the Tribunal

1. The expenses of the Tribunal shall be borne by the States Parties and by the Authority on such terms and in such manner as shall be decided at meetings of the States Parties.

2. When an entity other than a State Party or the Authority is a party to a case submitted to it, the Tribunal shall fix the amount which that party is to contribute toward the expenses of the Tribunal.

SECTION 2. COMPETENCE

Article 20

Access to the Tribunal

1. The Tribunal shall be open to States Parties.

2. The Tribunal shall be open to entities other than States Parties in any case expressly provided for in Part XI or in any case submitted pursuant to any other agreement conferring jurisdiction on the Tribunal which is accepted by all the parties to that case.

Article 21

Jurisdiction

The jurisdiction of the Tribunal comprises all disputes and all applications submitted to it in accordance with this Convention and all matters specifically provided for in any other agreement which confers jursidiction on the Tribunal.

Article 22

Reference of disputes subject to other agreements

If all the parties to a treaty or convention already in force and concerning the subject-matter covered by this Convention so agree, any disputes concerning the interpretation or application of such treaty or convention may, in accordance with such agreement, be submitted to the Tribunal.

Article 23

Applicable law

The Tribunal shall decide all disputes and applications in accordance with article 293.

SECTION 3. PROCEDURE

Article 24

Institution of proceedings

1. Disputes are submitted to the Tribunal, as the case may be, either by notification of a special agreement or by written application, addressed to the Registrar. In either case, the subject of the dispute and the parties shall be indicated.

2. The Registrar shall forthwith notify the special agreement or the application to all concerned.

3. The Registrar shall also notify all States Parties.

Article 25

Provisional measures

1. In accordance with article 290, the Tribunal and its Sea-Bed Disputes Chamber shall have the power to prescribe provisional measures.

2. If the Tribunal is not in session or a sufficient number of members is not available to constitute a quorum, the provisional measures shall be prescribed by the chamber of summary procedure formed under article 15, paragraph 3 of this Annex. Notwithstanding article 15, paragraph 4, of this Annex, such provisional measures may be adopted at the request of any party to the dispute. They shall be subject to review and revision by the Tribunal.

Article 26

Hearing

1. The hearing shall be held under the control of the President or, if he is unable to preside, of the Vice-President. If neither is able to preside, the senior judge present of the Tribunal shall preside.

2. The hearing shall be public, unless the Tribunal decides otherwise or unless the parties demand that the public be not admitted.

Article 27

Conduct of case

The Tribunal shall make orders for the conduct of the case, decide the form and time in which each party must conclude its arguments, and make all arrangements connected with the taking of evidence.

Article 28

Default

When one of the parties does not appear before the Tribunal or fails to defend its case, the other party may request the Tribunal to continue the proceedings and make its decision. Absence of a party or failure of a party to defend its case shall not constitute a bar to the proceedings. Before making its decision, the Tribunal must satisfy itself not only that it has jurisdiction over the dispute, but also that the claim is well founded in fact and law.

Article 29

Majority for decision

1. All questions shall be decided by a majority of the members of the Tribunal who are present.

2. In the event of an equality of votes, the President or the member of the Tribunal who acts in his place shall have a casting vote.

Article 30

Judgment

1. The judgment shall state the reasons on which it is based.

2. It shall contain the names of the members of the Tribunal who have taken part in the decision.

3. If the judgment does not represent in whole or in part the unanimous opinion of the members of the Tribunal, any member shall be entitled to deliver a separate opinion.

3. The judgment shall be signed by the President and by the Registrar. It shall be read in open court, due notice having been given to the parties to the dispute.

Article 31

Request to intervene

1. Should a State Party consider that it has an interest of a legal nature which may be affected by the decision in any dispute, it may submit a request to the Tribunal to be permitted to intervene.

2. It shall be for the Tribunal to decide upon this request.

3. If a request to intervene is granted, the decision of the Tribunal in respect of the dispute shall be binding upon the intervening State Party in so far as it relates to matters in respect of which that State Party intervened.

Article 32

Right to intervene in cases of interpretation or application

1. Whenever the interpretation or application of this Convention is in question, the Registrar shall notify all States Parties forthwith.

2. Whenever pursuant to article 21 or 22 of this Annex the interpretation or application of an international agreement is in question, the Registrar shall notify all the parties to the agreement.

3. Every party referred to in paragraphs 1 and 2 has the right to intervene in the proceedings; if it uses this right, the interpretation given by the judgment will be equally binding upon it.

Article 33

Finality and binding force of decisions

1. The decision of the Tribunal is final and shall be complied with by all the parties to the dispute.

2. The decision shall have no binding force except between the parties in respect of that particular dispute.

3. In the event of a dispute as to the meaning or scope of the decision, the Tribunal shall construe it upon the request of any party.

Article 34

Costs

Unless otherwise decided by the Tribunal, each party shall bear its own costs.

SECTION 4. SEA-BED DISPUTES CHAMBER

Article 35

Composition

1. The Sea-Bed Disputes Chamber referred to in article 14 of this Annex shall be composed of 11 members, selected by a majority of the elected members of the Tribunal from among them.

2.In the selection of the members of the Chamber, the representation of the principal legal systems of the world and equitable geographical distribution shall be assured. The Assembly of the Authority may adopt recommendations of a general nature relating to such representation and distribution.

3. The members of the Chamber shall be selected every three years and may be selected for a second term.

4. The Chamber shall elect its President from among its members, who shall serve for the term for which the Chamber has been selected.

5. If any proceedings are still pending at the end of any three-year period for which the Chamber has been selected, the Chamber shall complete the proceedings in its original composition.

6. If a vacancy occurs in the Chamber, the Tribunal shall select a successor from among its elected members, who shall hold office for the remainder of his predecessor's term.

7. A quorum of seven of the members selected by the Tribunal shall be required to constitute the Chamber.

Article 36

Ad hoc chambers

1. The Sea-Bed Disputes Chamber shall form an *ad hoc* chamber, composed of three of its members, for dealing with a particular dispute submitted to it in accordance with article 188, paragraph 1(b). The composition of such a chamber shall be determined by the Sea-Bed Disputes Chamber with the approval of the parties.

2. If the parties do not agree on the composition of an *ad hoc* chamber, each party to the dispute shall appoint one member, and the third member shall be appointed by them in agreement. If they disagree, or if any party fails to make an appointment, the President of the Sea-Bed Disputes Chamber shall promptly make the appointment or appointments from among its members, after consultation with the parties.

3. Members of the *ad hoc* chamber must not be in the service of, or nationals of, any of the parties to the dispute.

Article 37

Access

The Chamber shall be open to all States Parties, the Authority and the other entities referred to inPart XI, section 5.

Article 38

Applicable law

In addition to the provisions of article 293, the Chamber shall apply:

(a) the rules, regulations and procedures of the Authority adopted in accordance with this Convention; and

(b) the terms of contracts concerning activities in the Area in matters relating to those contracts.

Article 39

Enforcement of decisions of the Chamber

The decisions of the Chamber shall be enforceable in the territories of the States Parties in the same manner as judgments or orders of the highest court of the State Party in whose territory the enforcement is sought.

Article 40

Applicability of other sections of this Annex

1. The other sections of this Annex which are not incompatible with this section apply to the Chamber.

2. In the exercise of its functions relating to advisory opinions, the Chamber shall be guided by the provisions of this Annex relating to procedure before the Tribunal to the extent to which it recognizes them to be applicable.

SECTION 5. AMENDMENTS

Article 41

Amendments

1. Amendments to this Annex, other than amendments to section 4, may be adopted only in accordance with article 313 or by consensus at a conference convened in accordance with this Convention.

2. Amendments to section 4 may be adopted only in accordance with article 314.

3. The Tribunal may propose such amendments to this Statute as it may consider necessary, by written communications to the States Parties for their consideration in conformity with paragraphs 1 and 2.

ANNEX VII. ARBITRATION

Article 1

Institution of proceedings

Subject to the provisions of Part XV, any party to a dispute may submit the dispute to the arbitral procedure provided for in this Annex by written notification addressed to the other party or parties to the dispute. The notification shall be accompanied by a statement of the claim and the grounds on which it is based.

Article 2

List of arbitrators

1. A list of arbitrators shall be drawn up and maintained by the Secretary-General of the United Nations. Every State Party shall be entitled to nominate four arbitrators, each of whom shall be

a person experienced in maritime affairs and enjoying the highest reputation for fairness, competence and integrity. The names of the persons so nominated shall constitute the list.

2. If at any time the arbitrators nominated by a State Party in the list so constituted shall be fewer than four, that State Party shall be entitled to make further nominations as necessary.

3. The name of an arbitrator shall remain on the list until withdrawn by the State Party which made the nomination, provided that such arbitrator shall continue to serve on any arbitral tribunal to which that arbitrator has been appointed until the completion of the proceedings before that arbitral tribunal.

Article 3

Constitution of arbitral tribunal

For the purpose of proceedings under this Annex, the arbitral tribunal shall, unless the parties otherwise agree, be constituted as follows:

(a) Subject to subparagraph (g), the arbitral tribunal shall consist of five members.

(b) The party instituting the proceedings shall appoint one member to be chosen preferably from the list referred to in article 2 of this Annex, who may be its national. The appointment shall be included in the notification referred to in article 1 of this Annex.

(c) The other party to the dispute shall, within 30 days of receipt of the notification referred to in article 1 of this Annex, appoint one member to be chosen preferably from the list, who may be its national. If the appointment is not made within that period, the party instituting the proceedings may, within two weeks of the expiration of that period, request that the appointment be made in accordance with subparagraph (e).

(d) The other three members shall be appointed by agreement between the parties. They shall be chosen preferably from the list and shall be nationals of third States unless the parties otherwise agree. The parties to the dispute shall appoint the President of the arbitral tribunal from among those three members. If, within 60 days of receipt of the notification referred to in article 1 of this Annex, the parties are unable to reach agreement on the appointment of one or more members of the tribunal to be appointed by agreement, or on the appointment of the President, the remaining appointment or appointments shall be made in accordance with subparagraph (e), at the request of a party to the dispute. Such request shall be made within two weeks of the expiration of the aforementioned 60-day period.

(e) Unless the parties agree that any appointment under subparagraphs (c) and (d) be made by a person or a third State chosen by the parties, the President of the International Tribunal for the Law of the Sea shall make the necessary appointments. If the President is unable to act under this subparagraph or is a national of one of the parties to the dispute, the appointment shall be made by the next senior member of the International Tribunal for the Law of the Sea who is available and is not a national of one of the parties. The appointments referred to in this subparagraph shall be made from the list referred to in article 2 of this Annex within a period of 30 days from the receipt of the request and in consultation with the parties. The members so appointed shall be of different nationalities and may not be in the service of , ordinarily resident in the territory of, or nationals of, any of the parties to the dispute.

(f) Any vacancy shall be filled in the manner prescribed for the initial appointment.

(g) Parties in the same interest shall appoint one member of the tribunal jointly by agreement. Where there are several parties having separate interests or where there is disagreement as to whether they are of the same interest, each of them shall appoint one member of the tribunal. The number of members of the tribunal appointed separately by the parties shall always be smaller by one than the number of members of the tribunal to be appointed jointly by the parties.

(h) In disputes involving more than two parties, the provisions of subparagraphs (a) to (f) shall apply to the maximum extent possible.

Article 4

Functions of arbitral tribunal

An arbitral tribunal constituted under article 3 of this Annex shall function in accordance with this Annex and the other provisions of this Convention.

Article 5

Procedure

Unless the parties to the dispute otherwise agree, the arbitral tribunal shall determine its own procedure, assuring to each party a full opportunity to be heard and to present its case.

Article 6

Duties of parties to a dispute

The parties to the dispute shall facilitate the work of the arbitral tribunal and, in particular, in accordance with their law and using all means at their disposal, shall:

(a) provide it with all relevant documents, facilities and information; and

(b) enable it when necessary to call witnesses or experts and receive their evidence and to visit the localities to which the case relates.

Article 7

Expenses

Unless the arbitral tribunal decides otherwise because of the peculiar circumstances of the case, the expenses of the tribunal, including the remuneration of its members, shall be borne by the parties to the dispute in equal shares.

Article 8

Required majority for decisions

Decisions of the arbitral tribunal shall be taken by a majority vote of its members. The absence or abstention of less than half of the members shall not constitute a bar to the tribunal reaching a decision. In the event of an equality of votes, the President shall have the casting vote.

Article 9

Default of appearance

If one of the parties to the dispute does not appear before the tribunal or fails to defend its case, the other party may request the tribunal to continue the proceedings and to make its award. Absence of a party or failure of a party to defend its case shall not constitute a bar to the proceedings. Before making its award, the arbitral tribunal must satisfy itself not only that it has jurisdiction over the dispute but also that the claim is well founded in fact and law.

Article 10

Award

The award of the arbitral tribunal shall be confined to the subject-matter of the dispute and state the reasons on which it is based. It shall contain the names of the members who have participated and the date of the award. Any member of the tribunal may attach a separate or dissenting opinion to the award.

Article 11

Finality of award

The award shall be final and without appeal, unless the parties to the dispute have agreed in advance to an appellate procedure. It shall be complied with by the parties to the dispute.

Article 12

Interpretation or implementation of the award

1. Any controversy which may arise between the parties to the dispute as regards the interpretation or manner of implementation of the award may be submitted by either party for decision to the arbitral tribunal which made the award. For this purpose, any vacancy in the tribunal shall be filled in the manner provided for in the original appointments of the members of the tribunal.

2. Any such controversy may be submitted to another court or tribunal under article 287 by agreement of the parties to the dispute.

Article 13

Application to entities other than States Parties

The provisions of this Annex shall apply *mutatis mutandis* to any dispute involving entities other than States Parties.

ANNEX VIII. SPECIAL ARBITRATION

Article 1

Institution of proceedings

Subject to Part XV, any party to a dispute concerning the interpretation or application of the articles of this Convention relating to (1) fisheries, (2) protection and preservation of the marine environment, (3) marine scientific research, or (4) navigation, including pollution from vessels and by dumping, may submit the dispute to the special arbitral tribunal provided for in this Annex by written notification addressed to the other party or parties to the dispute. The notification shall be accompanied by a statement of the claim and the grounds on which it is based.

Article 2

Lists of experts

1. A list of experts shall be established and maintained in respect of each of the fields of (1) fisheries, (2) protection and preservation of the marine environment, (3) marine scientific research, and (4) navigation, including pollution from vessels and by dumping.

2. The lists of experts shall be drawn up and maintained, in the field of fisheries by the Food and Agriculture Organization of the United Nations, in the field of protection and preservation of the marine environment by the United Nations Environment Programme, in the field of marine scientific research by the Inter-Governmental Oceanographic Commission, in the field of navigation, including pollution from vessels and by dumping, by the International Maritime Organization, or in each case by the appropriate subsidiary body concerned to which such organization, programme or commission has delegated this function.

3. Every State Party shall be entitled to nominate two experts in each field whose competence in legal, scientific or technical aspects of such field is established and generally recognized and who enjoy the highest reputation for fairness and integrity. The names of the persons so nominated in each field shall constitute the appropriate list.

4. If at any time the experts nominated by a State Party in the list so constituted shall be fewer than two, that State Party shall be entitled to make further nominations as necessary.

5. The name of an expert shall remain on the list until withdrawn by the State Party which made the nomination, provided that such expert shall continue to serve on any special arbitral tribunal to which that expert has been appointed until the completion of the proceedings before that special arbitral tribunal.

Article 3

Constitution of special arbitral tribunal

For the purpose of proceedings under this Annex, the special arbitral tribunal shall, unless the parties otherwise agree, be constituted as follows:

(a) Subject to subparagraph (g), the special arbitral tribunal shall consist of five members.

(b) The party instituting the proceedings shall appoint two members to be chosen preferably from the appropriate list or lists referred to in article 2 of this Annex relating to the matters in dispute, one of whom may be its national. The appointments shall be included in the notification referred to in article 1 of this Annex.

(c) The other party to the dispute shall, within 30 days of the receipt of the notification referred to in article 1 of this Annex, appoint two members to be chosen prefereably from the appropriate list or lists relating to the matters in dispute, one of whom may be its national. If the appointments are not made within that period, the party instituting the proceedings may, within two weeks of the expiration of that period, request that the appointments be made in accordance with subparagraph (e).

(d) The parties to the dispute shall by agreement appoint the President of the special arbitral tribunal, chosen preferably from the appropriate list, who shall be a national of a third State, unless the parties otherwise agree. If, within 30 days of receipt of the notification referred to in article 1 of this Annex, the parties are unable to reach agreement on the appointment of the President, the appointment shall be made in accordance with subparagraph (e), at the request of a party to the dispute. Such request shall be made within two weeks of the expiration of the aforementioned 30-day period.

(e) Unless the parties agree that the appointment be made by a person or third State chosen by the parties, the Secretary=General of the United Nations shall make the necessary appointments within 30 days of receipt of a request under subparagraphs (c) and (d). The appointments referred to in this subparagraph shall be made from the appropriate list or lists of experts referred to in article 2 of this Annex and in consultation with the parties to the dispute and the appropriate international organization. The members so appointed shall be of different nationalities and may not be in the service of, ordinarily reside in the territory of, or nationals of, any parties to the dispute.

(f) Any vacancy shall be filled in the manner prescribed for the initial appointment.

(g) Parties in the same interest shall appoint two members of the tribunal jointly by agreement. Where there are several parties having separate interests or where there is disagreement as to whether they are of the same interest, each of them shall appoint one member of the tribunal.

(h) In disputes involving more than two parties, the provisions of subparagraphs (a) to (f) shall apply to the maximum extent possible.

Article 4

General provisions

Annex VII, articles 4 to 13, apply *mutatis mutandis* to the special arbitration proceedings in accordance with this Annex.

Article 5

Fact finding

1. The parties to a dispute concerning the interpretation and application of the provisions of this Convention relating to (1) fisheries, (2) protection and preservation of the marine environment, (3) marine scientific research, or (4) navigation, including pollution from vessels and by dumping, may at any time agree to request a special arbitral tribunal constituted in accordance with article 1 of this Annex to carry out an inquiry and establish the facts giving rise to the dispute.

2. Unless the parties otherwise agree, the findings of fact of the special arbitral tribunal acting in accordance with subparagraph 1, shall be considered as conclusive as between the parties.

3. If all the parties to the dispute so request, the special arbitral tribunal may formulate recommendations which, without having the force of a decision, shall only constitute the basis for review by the parties of the questions giving rise to the dispute.

4. Subject to paragraph 2, the special arbitral tribunal shall act in accordance with the provisions of this Annex, unless the parties otherwise agree.

ED. NOTE: The above provisions constitute useful reference materials from more than one standpoint. First, they constitute a useful list of the kinds of issues that need to be resolved in any negotiation establishing other dispute settlement procedures on other subjects. In addition, they provide solutions to those issues that could be considered in establishing other fora. These provisions reflect a careful study of a great number of existing procedures already being utilized.

Sohn & Gustafson, THE LAW OF THE SEA (1984) 238-246[2]

A state is not bound to go to an international tribunal unless it has accepted previously that tribunal's jurisdiction or agrees by a special agreement (so-called "compromise") to submit a particular dispute to the tribunal. Consequently, when a state has a dispute with another state about an alleged violation of a law of the sea rule, in most cases there is no international tribunal having jurisdiction to decide the issue. If negotiations between the two governments do not lead to a settlement of the dispute, and if the other state cannot be persuaded to submit the dispute to a tribunal by special agreement, then there is no way to resolve the dispute, and it may disturb relations between the two states for a long time.

To avoid this, many treaties relating to law of the sea problems contain a so-called compromissory clause by which the parties to the treaty agree to submit to an international tribunal any dispute relating to the interpretation or application of that treaty. Several conventions concluded under the auspices of the International Maritime Consultative Organization (now International Maritime Organization) contain provisions authorizing the submission of such disputes to the International Court of Justice or to an arbitral tribunal. See, e.g., 1954 Oil Pollution Prevention Convention, Article 18; 1969 Convention on Intervention on the High Seas, Article 8 and Annex, Articles 13-19. At the 1958 Conference on the Law of the Sea, no agreement could be reached on an obligatory submission of disputes to adjudication; instead and optional protocol was prepared allowing states to accept the jurisdiction of the International Court of Justice for the purpose of deciding any dispute relating to the interpretation or application of the four conventions adopted by the Conference. This protocol was accepted by less than forty states. In the United States, the Senate vote for it was only 49 to 30, thus falling short of the necessary two-thirds. 12 Whiteman Digest of International Law 1333 (1971). Consequently, when disputes arose between the United States and Canada concerning pollution jurisdiction in the Arctic Ocean, the United States was not able to submit them to the Court.

The United States is further handicapped by the fact that its earlier acceptance of the jurisdiction of the International Court of Justice under the optional clause in Article 36 of the Statute of the Court was limited by two broad reservations: the so-called Connally Amendment (an amendment presented by the Senator from Texas, Chairman of the Committee on Foreign Relations, to the Senate resolution consenting to U.S. acceptance of jurisdiction), which excluded from the Court's jurisdiction all "disputes with regard to matters which are essentially within the domestic jurisdiction of the United States of America as determined by the United States of America"; and a reservation excluding from the Court's jurisdiction all "disputes arising under a multilateral treaty, unless (1) all parties to the treaty affected by the decision are also parties to the case before the Court, or (2) the United States of America specially agrees to jurisdiction." Declaration of August 14, 1946, 61 Stat. 1218 (1946). Under both clauses, the acceptance of the jurisdiction of the Court is in fact left to the discretion of the United States and, as the declarations under the optional clause are based on

---

2. Sohn & Gustafson, The Law of the Sea in a Nutshell, 1st. ed. copyright 1984. Reprinted by permission of the West Publishing Co.

reciprocity, any other state may invoke these reservations against the United States at that state's discretion. This actually happened in a case between the United States and Bulgaria, where Bulgaria invoked the domestic jurisdiction clause though the issue -- shooting down and Israeli airplane, with U.S. passengers on board -- was clearly an international law matter. See Gross, "Bulgaria Invokes the Connally Amendment," 56 A.J.I.L. 357 (1962).

Taking this experience into account, from the very beginning of the negotiations leading to the LOS Convention, several states (including the United States) have insisted that effective means be provided for settling law of the sea disputes. It was recognized that in such a complex document there will be many ambiguous compromises and conflicting provisions, which will require clarification and reconciliation through future decision-making. After difficult negotiations an intricate system for the settlement of law of the sea disputes was devised, which was spelled out in more than 100 articles scattered throughout the Convention and several annexes.

The guiding principle is that the will of the parties must prevail and that the parties may by agreement select the dispute settlement method they wish. They can bypass the provisions of the Convention by agreeing in advance to use some other bilateral, regional or general dispute settlement system. LOS Convention, Article 282. Even after a dispute has arisen and has been submitted to a procedure provided for in the Convention, the parties can agree "at any time" to settle it by a different procedure. Id., Article 280. Flexibility does not stop at this stage. Unlike most other international instruments, the LOS Convention does not provide for a unitary system of dispute settlement. As different groups of states desired different procedures, it was agreed that a state can chose one of four main systems of dispute settlement: the International Court of Justice, a special International Tribunal for the Law of the Sea, an international arbitral tribunal or a special technical arbitral tribunal. If the parties to a dispute have not accepted the same procedure, they are obliged to submit it to arbitration (id., Article 287(5)), and Annex VII to the Convention provides a fool-proof method for selecting an arbitral tribunal. This dispute settlement system applies without any exception to the vast majority of the provisions of the Convention, but in order to obtain general consensus on this part of the Convention, three categories of disputes had to be subjected to different procedures.

First, some coastal states were not willing to accept strict dispute settlement provisions with respect to all disputes relating the the exercise by a coastal state of its sovereign rights or jurisdiction in the exclusive economic zone. It became necessary to subdivide these disputes into three groups: (a) disputes relating to violations by either the coastal state or any other state of the provisions of the Convention in regard to the freedoms and rights of navigation, overflight, the laying of submarine cables and pipelines, or other internationally lawful uses of the sea, as well as disputes relating to violations by the coastal state of international rules and standards for the protection of the marine environment, remain subject to the general system for the settlement of disputes (id., Article 297(1)); (b) certain disputes relating to fisheries will be completely excluded from the dispute settlement system due to the broad discretionary powers of the coastal state with respect to several aspects of coastal fisheries; some other fishery disputes which involve the possibility of arbitrary actions of the coastal state will be subject to compulsory conciliation (resort to an international commission which can present a report on the facts and the law, which is not binding on the parties to the dispute but with which the parties usually comply); the remaining disputes will continue to be subject to the general system of dispute settlement (id., Article 297(3)); and (c) disputes relating to scientific research which are also subdivided into three subcategories, paralleling those relating to fishing (id., Article 297(2)).

Second, while the disputes relating to the exclusive economic zone discussed above are automatically exempt from dispute settlement procedures, another group of disputes may be excluded from dispute settlement procedures by filing a special optional declaration. The most complicated provisions relate to disputes concerning boundary delimitation or involving historical bays; old disputes, i.e., those which arose before the entry into force of the Convention, are totally exempt from dispute settlement under the Convention; new disputes, i.e., those which may arise after entry into force of the Convention, will be subject to compulsory conciliation similar to that used for fishery and scientific research disputes; mixed disputes, i.e., disputes involving the concurrent resolution of sea boundaries and of any unsettled dispute concerning sovereignty over a part of the mainland or over an island or group of islands, will be totally exempt from dispute settlement under the Convention; and sea boundary disputes, which have been finally settled by an arrangement between the parties or which are settled in accordance with an agreement between them, will also be totally exemmpt from dispute settlement under the Convention. Id., Article 298(1)(a). There is also the possibility of a total exemption of disputes relating to two parallel military activities; military activities (including military activities by government vessels and aircraft engaged in noncommercial service) and law enforcement activities by coastal states (if these activities are connected with those disputes involving fishing or marine scientific research which are themselves exempt from dispute settlement under Article 297(2) and (3). Id., Article 298(1)(b). Finally, in order to avoid discrepant decisions by different international authorities, disputes which are being dealt with by the Security Council of the United Nations may be exempted (by an optional declaration) from dispute settlement under the Convention, but they will become again subject to the Convention procedures if the Security Council should cease to deal with the matter. Id., Article 297(1)(c).

Third, most disputes relating to sea-bed mining are to be submitted to a special Sea-Bed Disputes Chamber of the International Tribunal for the Law of the Sea in order to provide a uniform system of interpretation for the part of the Convention which establishes a seabed mining regime. That Chamber will be composed of eleven members to by chosen from the 21-member Tribunal from among its membership. Id., Annex VI, Article 35. While the general dispute settlement system applies only to disputes between states, the Sea-Bed Disputes Chamber has jurisdiction also over disputes between states and the International Sea-Bed Authority, and in contractual matters, even between the Authority and both state and private enterprises. Id., Article 187. Some technical disputes relating to contracts may be submitted, however, to binding commercial arbitration. Id., Article 188(2). Similarly, commercial arbitration may be resorted to in disputes regarding transfer of seabed mining technology or to financial terms of mining contracts. Id., Annex III, Articles 5(4) and 13(5).

As the United States has announced that it will not ratify the LOS Convention, it will not be able to resort to the dispute settlement procedures provided for in the Convention even with respect to those parts of the Convention which it considers as reflecting customary international law. The United States could perhaps file a supplementary declaration (in addition to that filed in 1946, discussed supra), by which it would accept the jurisdiction of the Court with respect to those rules of customary international law which have been codified by the LOS Convention, with the exception of parts dealing with deep seabed mining. Such a declaration would confer jurisdiction on the Court with respect to any dispute concerning these law of the sea matters with respect to any state which has accepted the jurisdiction of the Court under the optional clause without crippling reservations, i.e., some forty states. See 36 I.C.J.Y.B. 59-93 (1982). In this way the United States might be able to make its contribution to the subjection of the law of the sea disputes to the rule of law, thus avoiding the danger of escalation of law of the sea disputes into threats to international peace and the security of the United States.

CHAPTER 13

MILITARY USE OF THE MARINE ENVIRONMENT

A. INTRODUCTION.

Military uses of the ocean involve many of the law of the sea issues already covered in this casebook, such as freedom of navigation, the doctrine of the continental shelf, and oceanogaphic research. The needs of military establishments are sufficiently different from other users of the marine environment, however, to warrant at least a cursory examination of those needs in relation to the existing and future law of the sea.

Most of the following materials were written prior to recent developments in Eastern Europe and the so-called Commonwealth of Republics, the successor to the Soviet Union. You may wish, as you read these more traditional concerns, to consider how, if at all, U.S. strategies may now be altered.

According to United States naval strategists, American naval missions include:

(1) Strategic deterrence -- the maintenance of a secure second nuclear weapon strike capability designed to deter any foreign power from launching a pre-emptive nuclear attack on the United States. Strategic deterrence has three components -- the sea-based nuclear submarine, carrier based bombers, and the Strategic Air Command. Nuclear submarines utilize the concept of freedom of the high seas in maintaining their security, but are also subject to the rule of surface navigation when in territorial waters of another nation even if those waters comprise international straits. Carrier based deterrent forces also utilize the principle of free navigation on the high seas for positioning.

(2) Sea control -- the control of limited areas of the sea for limited periods of time. This mission is often coupled with the projection of power ashore (e.g., the landing of Marines) and the resupply of overseas operations (e.g., Israel). Although its wartime objective is to terminate freedom of navigation and action for enemy forces, it must utilize the principle of freedom of the high seas to achieve this goal.

(3) Projection of power ashore -- a euphemism for amphibious assault, requiring sea control as a prerequisite.

(4) Naval presence -- the most important peacetime mission, viz., the achievement of political objectives short of war by the strategic and tactical deployment of naval forces. Included in this category is the navy's program for the exercise of rights, under which the navy will challenge any claim that interferes with its traditional ocean usage by exercising its rights in the area concerned.

ED. NOTE: These United States naval missions must be viewed in the light of the role of the Soviet Union as it was perceived at the time. Experts differed on the role of the Soviet navy, some seeing an essentially defensive posture, others perceiving an offensive mission. Among the missions often cited are the following: (1) defense against the United States ballistic missile submarines and carrier-based nuclear forces; (2) maintenance of a secure second nuclear weapon strike capability; (3) deterrence of a conventional U.S.-NATO attack on Soviet allies and clients; (4) expansion of Soviet influence in the third world; (5) exertion of pressure on raw material supply lines to the United States and Western Europe.

In the confusion created by the breakup of the Soviet Union in the 1990's, it is difficult to predict how either of these major navies will perceive their roles in the future. That perception will also be altered by the development of new technologies. Clearly, the development and use of the Cruise missile in the Gulf War in 1991 opens up many new possibilities. One thing is fairly certain, however. The U.S. Navy will be much "leaner and meaner" with substantial emphasis on speed and mobility. With superpower confrontation, at least for the present, no longer a major threat, the emphasis will be placed upon the capacity to move ships, supplies and troops rapidly to the scene of a regional conflict, if need be.

B. MILITARY USE OF THE SEABED.

1. DENUCLEARIZATION.

TREATY ON THE PROHIBITION OF THE EMPLACEMENT OF NUCLEAR WEAPONS AND OTHER WEAPONS OF MASS DESTRUCTION ON THE SEA-BED AND THE OCEAN FLOOR AND IN THE SUBSOIL THEREOF

The States Parties to this Treaty,

Recognizing the common interest of mankind in the progress of the exploration and use of the sea-bed and the ocean floor for peaceful purposes,

Considering that the prevention of a nuclear arms race on the sea-bed and the ocean floor serves the interests of maintaining world peace, reduces international tensions, and strengthens friendly relations among States,

Convinced that this Treaty constitutes a step towards the exclusion of the sea-bed, the ocean floor and the subsoil thereof from the arms race,

Convinced that this Treaty constitutes a step towards a treaty on general and complete disarmament under strict and effective international control, and determined to continue negotiations to this end,

Convinced that this Treaty will further the purposes and principles of the Charter of the United Nations, in a manner consistent with the principles of international law and without infringing the freedoms of the high seas,

Have agreed as follows:

Article I

1. The States Parties to this Treaty undertake not to emplant or emplace on the sea-bed and the ocean floor and in the subsoil thereof beyond the outer limit of a sea-bed zone as defined in Article II any nuclear weapons or any other type of weapons of mass destruction as well as structures, launching installations or any other facilities specifically designed for storing, testing or using such weapons.

2. The undertakings of paragraph 1 of this Article shall also apply to the sea-bed zone referred to in the same paragraph, except that within such sea-bed zone, they shall not apply either to the coastal State or to the sea-bed beneath its territorial waters.

3. The States Parties to this Treaty undertake not to assist, encourage or induce any State to carry out activities referred to in paragraph 1 of this Article and not to participate in any other way in such actions.

Article II

For the purpose of this Treaty the outer limit of the sea-bed zone referred to in Article I shall be coterminus with the twelve-mile outer limit of the zone referred to in Part II of the Convention on the Territorial Sea and the Contiguous Zone, signed in Geneva on 29 April 1958, and shall be measured in accordance with the provisions of Part I, Section II, of this Convention and in accordance with international law.

Article III

1. In order to promote the objectives of and ensure compliance with the provisions of this Treaty, each State Party to the Treaty shall have the right to verify through observation the activities of other States Parties to the Treaty on the sea-bed and the ocean floor and in the subsoil thereof beyond the zone referred to in Article I, provided that observation does not interfere with such activities.

2. If after such observation reasonable doubts remain concerning the fulfilment of the obligations assumed under the Treaty, the State Party having such doubts and the State Party that is responsible for the activities giving rise to the doubts shall consult with a view to removing the doubts. If the doubts persist, the State Party having such doubts shall notify the other States Parties, and the Parties concerned shall co-operate on such further procedures for verification as may be agreed, including appropriate inspection of objects, structures, installations or other facilities that reasonably may be expected to be of a kind described in Article I. The Parties in the region of the activities, including any coastal State, and any other Party so requesting, shall be entitled to participate in such consultation and co-operation. After completion of the further procedures for verification, an appropriate report shall be circulated to other Parties by the Party that initiated the proceedures.

3. If the State responsible for the activities giving rise to the reasonable doubts is not identifiable by observation of the object, structure, installation or other facility, the State Party having such doubts shall notify and make appropriate inquiries of States Parties in the region of the activities and of any other State Party. If it is ascertained through these inquiries that a particular State Party is responsible for the activities, that State Party shall consult and co-operate with other Parties as provided in paragraph 2 of this Article. If the identity of the State responsible for the activities cannot be ascertained through these inquiries, then further verification procedures, including inspection, may be undertaken by the inquiring State Party, which shall invite the participation of the Parties in the region of the activities, including any coastal State, and of any other Party desiring to co-operate.

4. If consultation and co-operation pursuant to paragraphs 2 and 3 of this Article have not removed the doubts concerning the activities and there remains a serious question concerning fulfilment of the obligations assumed under this Treaty, a State Party may, in accordance with the provisions of the Charter of the United Nations, refer the matter to the Security Council, which may take action in accordance with the Charter.

5. Verification pursuant to this Article may be undertaken by any State Party using its own means, or with the full or partial assistance of any other State Party, or through appropriate international procedures within the framework of the United Nations and in accordance with its Charter.

6. Verification activities pursuant to this Treaty shall not interfere with activities of other

States Parties and shall be conducted with due regard for rights recognized under international law including the freedoms of the high seas and the rights of coastal States with respect to the exploration and exploitation of their continental shelves.

Article IV

Nothing in this Treaty shall be interpreted as supporting or prejudicing the position of any State Party with respect to existing international conventions, including the 1958 Convention on the Territorial Sea and the Contiguous Zone, or with respect to the rights or claims which such State Party may assert, or with respect to the recognition or non-recognition of rights or claims asserted by any other State, related to waters off its coasts; including *inter alia* territorial seas and contiguous zones, or to the sea-bed and the ocean floor, including continental shelves.

Article V

The Parties to this Treaty undertake to continue negotiations in good faith concerning further measures in the field of disarmament for the prevention of an arms race on the sea-bed, the ocean floor and the subsoil thereof.

....

Article VIII

Each State Party to this Treaty shall in exercising its national sovereignty have the right to withdraw from this Treaty if it decides that extraordinary events related to the subject matter of this Treaty have jeopardized the supreme interests of its country. It shall give notice of such withdrawal to all other States Parties to the Treaty and to the United Nations Security Council three months in advance. Such notice shall include a statement of the extraordinary events it considers to have jeopardized its supreme interests.

Article IX

The provisions of this Treaty shall in no way affect the obligations assumed by States Parties to the Treaty under international instruments establishing zones free from nuclear weapons.

....

CONTEMPORARY PRACTICE OF THE UNITED STATES RELATING TO INTERNATIONAL LAW, 69 A.J.I.L.641, 666-667 (1975)[1]

On October 25, 1973, the Socialist Federal Republic of Yugoslavia deposited with the Department of State its instrument of ratification of the Teaty on the Prohibition of the Emplacement of Nuclear Weapons and Other Weapons of Mass Destruction on the Seabed and the Ocean Floor and in the subsoil thereof. Four months later, in a note dated February 25, 1974, the Yugoslav Ambassador at Washinton transmitted to the Secretary of State an interpretive statement with respect to Article III, paragraph 1 of the treaty reading as follows:

---

[1]. Reprinted with permission from 69 A.J.I.L. 666-667 (1975), published by the American Society of International Law.

In depositing this instrument of ratification, the Government of the Socialist Federal Republic of Yugoslavia wishes to declare the following:

In the view of the Government of the Socialist Federal Republic of Yugoslavia, Article 3, Paragraph 1, should be interpreted to the effect that a state exercising the right under this article shall be obliged to notify in advance the coastal state, insofar as its observations are to be carried out within the stretch of the sea extending above the continental shelf of the said state.

The Ambassador stated that the above statement had been accepted by the Federal Assembly at the time of the ratification of the treaty, and he requested that, in accordance with the pertinent provisions of the treaty, it be forwarded to the governments of the states signatory and acceding at Washington to the treaty.

In performance of the depositary duties of the Government of the United States under the treaty, the Secretary of State tranmitted the Yugoslav statement in a circular note of January 15, 1975, addressed to the Chiefs of Mission of the governments of the states signatory and acceding at Washington to the treaty. In a separate note dated January 16, 1975, addressed to the same states, the Secretary of State presented the views of the United States concerning the Yugoslav note. Those views read in pertinent part as follows:

> Insofar as the note is intended to be interpretive of the Treaty, the United States cannot accept it as a valid interpretation. In addition, the United States does not consider that it can have any effect on the existing law of the sea.
>
> Insofar as the note is intended to be a reservation to the Treaty, the United States places on record its formal objection to it on the grounds that it is incompatible with the object and purpose of the Treaty. The United States also draws attention to the fact that the note was submitted too late to be legally effective as a reservation.

ED. NOTE: The United States has considered deployment of an anti-submarine device known as "Captor." Captor consists of a torpedo encased in a cannister which contains its own acoustic detection and classification system. The passage of an enemy sub triggers the mine-cannister, which then fires the torpedo. The torpedo's own sensors take over and it homes on the submarine. It may be effective at a range of over one mile. See *Ocean Science News*, Vol. 17, No. 37 (September 12, 1975) at 1 for more details. Since Captor uses a TNT warhead rather than a nuclear device, is its deployment in compliance with the Seabed Denuclearization Treaty?

TREATY BANNING NUCLEAR WEAPON TESTS IN THE ATMOSPHERE, IN OUTER SPACE AND UNDER WATER, 480 U.N.T.S. 43, 14 U.S.T. 1313.

The Governments of the United States of America, the United Kingdom of Great Britain and Northern Ireland, and the Union of Soviet Socialist Republics, hereinafter referred to as the "Original Parties",

Proclaiming as their principal aim the speediest possible achievement of an agreement on general and complete disarmament under strict international control in accordance with the objectives of the United Nations which would put an end to the armaments race and eliminate the incentive to the production and testing of all kinds of weapons, including nuclear weapons,

Seeking to achieve the discontinuance of all test explosions of nuclear weapons for all time, determined to continue negotiations to this end, and desiring to put an end to the contamination of man's environment by radio-active substances,

Have agreed as follows:

Article I

1. Each of the Parties to this Treaty undertakes to prohibit, to prevent, and not to carry out any nuclear weapon test explosion, or any other nuclear explosion, at any place under its jurisdiction or control:

(a) in the atmosphere; beyond its limits, including outer space; or underwater, including territorial waters or high seas; or

(b) in any other environment if such explosion causes radioactive debris to be present outside the territorial limits of the State under whose jurisdiction or control such explosion is conducted. It is understood in this connection that the provisions of this subparagraph are without prejudice to the conclusion of a treaty resulting in the permanent banning of all nuclear test explosions, including all such explosions underground, the conclusion of which, as the Parties have stated in the Preamble to this Treaty, they seek to achieve.

2. Each of the Parties to this Treaty undertakes furthermore to refrain from causing, encouraging, or in any way participating in, the carrying out of any nuclear weapon test explosion, or any other nuclear explosion, anywhere which would take place in any of the environments described, or have the effect referred to, in paragraph 1 of this Article.

....

Article III

1. This Treaty shall be open to all States for signature. Any State which does not sign this Treaty before its entry into force in accordance with paragraph 3 of this Article may accede to it at any time.

....

Article IV

This Treaty shall be of unlimited duration

Each Party shall in exercising its national sovereignty have the right to withdraw from the Treaty if it decides that extraordinary events, related to the subject matter of this Treaty, have jeopardized the supreme interests of its country. It shall give notice of such withdrawal to all other Parties to the Treaty three months in advance.

....

ED. NOTE: In 1974, Australia and New Zealand brought suit in the International Court of Justice against France in response to the latter's conduct of nuclear weapons tests in the South Pacific Ocean. France has not ratified the Test Ban Treaty, but Australia and New Zealand argued that its principles had become customary international law (over 100 nations have ratified it; among nuclear powers, only France and the People's Republic of China have not done so). The Court did not render a judgment on the merits, however, stating in 1975 that the issue was moot as a result of France's indication that it would conduct no further tests in the South Pacific.

During the 1950's, United States testing of hydrogen bombs in the South Pacific was a major legal and diplomatic issue. For details, see Volume 4 of Whiteman, Digest of International Law.

2. ANTI-SUBMARINE WARFARE

The emplantation of anti-submarine warfare (ASW) tracking and detection devices on the seabed is an integral part of the theory and practice of nuclear deterence. The United States and the Soviet Union each maintain a fleet of sophisticated nuclear powered, nuclear armed submarines at sea to secure second strike capability in response to any first strike launched by the other power. The theory is that if the second strike capability is immune from destruction prior to or simultaneously with a first strike, no power will launch such a first strike because its own destruction would thereby be ensured. The key to this "balance of terror," then, is keeping the submarine based second strike capability secure from detection and destruction.

Obviously, however, neither power can rest assured that the other has not developed or perfected ASW systems which will immobilize its own second strike capability. Thus both powers continue to work on ASW systems, attempting to ensure that neither side has at any time a greater capability to destroy the second strike capability of the other.

A *sine quo non* to any system designed to neutralize a submarine based second strike capability is the ability to locate and track nuclear submarines. Though early systems were not very accurate, it was possible to detect the movement of submarines through straits and along coastal areas. More modern systems, though the precise details are highly classified, have the capability of tracking submarines at great distances with a high degree of accuracy. Not only can they track submarines, in many instances they are able to identify the exact vessel being tracked. To effect such a system, however, requires the emplacement of ASW tracking and detection devices on the seabed -- on the continental shelf, slope and rise, and on the deep ocean floor. A legal question is presented concerning the legality of placing such listening devices on the continental shelves of other nations. The documents which follow amplify this problem.

CONVENTION ON THE CONTINENTAL SHELF

Article 1

For the purpose of these articles, the term "continental shelf" is used as referring to (a) the seabed and subsoil of the submarine areas adjacent to the coast but outside the area of the territorial sea, to a depth of 200 metres or, beyond that limit, to where the depth admits of the exploitation of the natural resources of the said areas; (b) to the seabed and subsoil of similar submarine areas adjacent to the coasts of islands.

Article 2

1. The coastal State exercises over its continental shelf sovereign rights for the purpose of

exploring it and exploiting its natural resources.

2. The rights referred to in paragraph 1 of this article are exclusive in the sense that if the coastal State does not explore the continental shelf or exploit its natural resources, no one may undertake these activities, or make a claim to the continental shelf, without the express consent of the coastal State.

3. The rights of the coastal State over the continental shelf do not depend on occupation, effective or notional, or on any express proclamation.

4. The natural resources referred to in these articles consist of the mineral and other non-living resources of the seabed and subsoil together with living organisms belonging to sedentary species, that is to say , organisms which, at the harvestable stage, either are immobile on or under the seabed or are unable to move except in constant physical contact with the seabed or subsoil.

....

Article 4

Subject to its right to take reasonable measures for the exploration of the continental shelf and the exploitation of its natural resources, the coastal State may not impede the laying or maintenance of submarine cables and pipelines on the continental shelf.

ED. NOTE: The need to protect antisubmarine activities has been a consistent objective of the United States. This includes the ability to implant submarine detection devices on the seabed and ocean floor. The Defense Department of the United States has not objected to giving to coastal States or an international regime the right to explore for and exploit the natural resources of the seabeds or on the continental shelf, provided that all other activities remain unaffected. With respect to the unaccepted draft convention tabled by the United States in 1970, John R. Stevenson, then head of the U.S. Delegation, noted that "The right of states to conduct activities other than exploration and exploitation of natural resources in the International Trusteeship Area and beyond would be expressly protected by the Convention and the International Seabed Resource Authority would be empowered to adopt the additional rules necessary to protect these other uses of the marine environment." This is a reference to a draft proposal presented by the United States in the Seabed Committee for a regime governing the deep seabeds. The proposal did not receive support, but it is indicative of the fact that at least some were of the view that the continental shelf jurisdiction of the coastal State was limited to resource management..

You will recall that article 76 of the 1982 United Nations Convention on the Law of the Sea provides a detailed new definition of the outer limit of the shelf that eliminates the exploitability test. Article 76 incorporates the earlier definition of natural resources. Article 80 incorporates article 60 by cross-reference. Article 60 defines the jurisdiction of a coastal State in its exclusive economic zone, and article 80 applies that jurisdiction to the extent that it is viable. The jurisdiction extends to (a) artificial islands; (b) installations and structures for the purposes provided for in article 56 and other economic purposes; (c) installations and structures which may interfere with the exercise of the rights of the coastal State in the zone. Some countries, such as India and Brazil have interpreted the third category as giving them jurisdiction to deny any country the right to emplant any kind of device on their continental shelf. Certainly, the ambiguity of that provision creates room for such arguments. During the recent conference, some States made explicit proposals, such as the following:

KENYA AND MEXICO: DRAFT ARTICLE ON ITEM 5 -- CONTINENTAL SHELF, U.N. Doc. A/CONF.62/C.2/L.42/Rev. 1 (13 August 1974)

No State shall be entitled to construct, maintain, deploy or operate on or over the continental shelf of another State any military installations or devices or any other installations for whatever purposes without the consent of the coastal State.

C. PROBLEMS OF NAVAL MOBILITY

1. GENERALLY.

Clingan, THE NEXT TWENTY YEARS OF NAVAL MOBILITY, U.S. Naval Institute Proceedings, May, 1980, pp. 82-93[2]

I.

Before one embarks upon a discussion of naval mobility two decades in the future, a seductive subject with a highly presumptuous title, he ought to define his terms. While the term "naval mobility" tends toward self-definition, it can, like the ubiquitous popsicle, take on various colors depending upon the flavor of the ingredients. Here, let me define it as all of those activities, presently in place or rationally perceived, which naval forces might wish to utilize in the conduct of global peace-keeping operations. By its very breadth, this avoids an exercise in speculation concerning the shape of the navy of the future, which is an entirely different matter.

This definition will permit me to examine the forseeable legal constraints for the impacts they may have in shaping the kind of naval forces that might be most effective. Since war is already excluded by the definition, I will focus upon the degree to which international law and domestic constraints might affect naval forces in the conduct of their missions. As a corollary, I will consider naval forces as an arm of U.S. foreign policy rather than in their purely military role. I shall presume that naval mobility remains desirable, and that we should continue to pursue policies that would lead to its maximization. We can then examine the impact of law on ships' movements, with emphasis on those of warships. We must keep in mind that the issues to be addressed are still under discussion at the Third United Nations Conference on the Law of the Sea, and it is not now at all clear whether that exercise will be a success.

Success could be defined as a treaty signed and ratified by substantially all nations, particularly the major maritime powers. But that would be a superficial definition. The genuine success of the Conference will be measured by the degree to which the substantive norms relfected in the results of the negotiations find their way into universal state practice. A treaty followed by a few, ignored by some, and flouted by others, would be, not a success, but a compounding of chaos. Without knowing that a meaningful set of norms can be put in writing, we shall have to consider the movement of naval vessels both without a treaty ("ex-treaty) and under the rules that appear to be evolving in the Law of the Sea Conference. In the former case, not all of the results of the recent Law of the Sea (LOS) negotiations would survive.

Since mobility on the oceans necessarily involves navigation, we shall devote most of our attention to those rules affecting it either directly or indirectly. The areas which seem most critical to

---

[2]. Copyright U.S. Naval Institute Proceedings, Naval Review Issue; May, 1980; Annapolis, Maryland. Reprinted with permission.

naval mobility are three in number. These are the economic zone, reflecting coastal states' desires to exert greater economic influence in the belts of seas adjacent to their coasts; the straits problem; and the archipelagic principle.

....

[W]hile the freedoms of the high seas are often viewed in an attitude of doctrinal rigidity, there is in fact more flexibility than meets the eye. The freedoms are not restricted to those listed in the Geneva Convention; others are permitted so long as they meet the standard of reasonableness. Furthermore, conflicting uses, even exclusive ones, may be acceptable provided that there are overriding national security interests, that the uses are of a temporary nature, and that they achieve minimal international acceptance. Even permanent restrictions on how the oceans may be used can be deemed acceptable if agreed to by all the significantly affected states. This, then, is the gloss that lay upon the doctrine of the freedom of the high seas going in to the Third United Nations Law of the Sea Conference in 1974. It remains to be seen how that conference is affecting the basic doctrine, if at all. Lurking in potential opposition to the doctrine is the importance attached by many states to the need to conserve or to exploit resources of the sea. This need has produced different approaches to the whole question.

II.

....

The economic zone solution, as it now appears to emerge, evolved from the necessity to balance the rights of the coastal state for resources and other economic purposes (such, for example, as building a floating airport, as has been proposed far off the coast of New York), and the navigational interests in one and the same area. This conceptual balancing job has not been easy, and has been the subject of long and difficult negotiations.

To be acceptable from the standpoint of naval mobility, the formula would have to protect preexisting navigational and military interests in a zone extending to as far as 200 nautical miles from the coast, both qualitatively and quantitatively. The initial arguments, loaded with rhetoric on both sides, reflected this fact. The maritime powers, for their part, couched debate in terms of maintaining the "high seas status" of the waters beyond the territorial limits. The coastal states, on the other hand, insisted that the EEZ was neither high seas nor territorial seas, but a zone sui generis in nature. Neither side could accept the characterization of the other, and for some time it appeared that the effort might be doomed. But, as in all international negotiations, timing is everything, and in due course the conference delegates reached the point where they were ready to come to grips with the difficult job of compromise.

As a result of intensive negotiations at the head of delegation level, a set of economic zone articles has emerged designed to strike the balance without prejudice to either side. It was not easy. Initially, coastal states suggested a zone in which the rights of navigation, overflight, and the laying of submarine cables and pipelines would be preserved, but all other rights would be assigned to the coastal state, i.e., they would nearly accomplish the territorialization of the economic zone. The maritimes, on the other hand, argued for assignment to the coastal state of those rights appertaining to resources, but reserving all other interests to the international community in general. This was unacceptable to the Coastal States Group.

At stake was the wide range of possible ocean uses lying between resource rights and simple rights of navigation. Within this broad range could be identified many that would affect naval mobility because they would have influence on the ability of maritime powers to deploy certain classes of vessels, or would permit others to detect their presence. It can be no secret that decisions regarding the conduct of undersea missions would have to fator in the degree to which similar missions undertaken by a potential opponent might be ascertained. Any regime for the economic zone, therefore, would have to be of such quality that needs of this nature would be satisfied.

Language was sought to accommodate both sides on these unspoken or unidentified "residual" rights, or rights not specifically assigned to one side or the other by the draft articles. Clearly it would not be possible to identify and list each "right" and allocate it to the appropriate side of the debate. Some of this, of course, could be done, and it was. Coastal states were allocated "sovereign rights for the purpose of exploiting, conserving and managing the natural resources...and...other activities for the economic exploitation and exploration of the zone, such as the production of energy from the water currents and winds." They also received rights with regard to the conduct of marine scientific research and to the control of pollution, as provided for in other parts of the convention. These rights were balanced, and the question of residual rights addressed, by guaranteeing to all states "the rights of navigation and overflight and of the laying of submarine cables and pipelines, and other internationally lawful uses of the sea related to these freedoms such as those associated with the operation of ships, aircraft and submarine cables and pipelines," and compatible with other provisions of the Convention.

This language was carefully constructed to address the question of how closely a prospective use must relate to navigation before it is viewed as a freedom within the economic zone. The fact that the prospective use must be compatible with "other provisions" of the Convention has been the focus of some concern, but it is not expected that there will be any incompatibility. The language used in identifying the rights of other states within the zone is believed to be broad enough to accommodate all of the uses which in this discussion we are including under the heading of "naval mobility," and it excludes none foreseeable. These rights are reinforced by the fact that, should a dispute arise over a coastal state's navigational rules, the aggrieved party could take the dispute to compulsory settlement. They are further enahnced by the doctrine of sovereign immunity for both warships and non-commercial naval vessels.

At this point we should pause and ask what we might gain by giving up the three-mile limit in exchange for such a delicate balance. The question, while legitimate, should not be addressed in a vacuum. More appropriately, we should inquire what rules will apply if there should be no law of the sea treaty embodying the economic zone principles.

The advantage of the exiting EEZ formulations over the ex-treaty situation are, as I see it, two-fold. First, they establish a precise limit for EEZ jurisdiction by a treaty which when accepted will have global application. Second, they spell out with some precision the rights of the parties in that zone. Lacking a treaty, of course, we probably would also lack both these advantages.

At present there are more than 90 claims to extended jurisdiction beyond 12 nautical miles, incorporating various legal regimes ranging from simple fisheries conservation zones (like that of the United States), to various kinds of economic zones up to and including full territorial sea claims to a belt out to 200 nautical miles. The rich variety of such claims, lacking any kind of standardized practice on the subject, would create a chaotic basis good for nothing but common misunderstanding.

In addition, without a global agreement, there would be no assurance whatsoever that the line would remain at 200 nautical miles. On the contrary there is already reason to fear that some countries have aspirations on that subject, and one could imagine legitimate forces in play that could trigger action on them. For instance, consider a situation where coastal state A has declared jurisdiction over all fisheries, including highly migratory species (such as tuna), within 200 miles of its coast. The fishing trawlers of state B, excluded from the zone by exhorbitant license fees, begin to fish heavily outside the zone with the result that the entire stock of fish, both in and out of the zone, is being seriously depleted.

What would be the reaction of the foreign office of state A?

In this light, the choice, it appears, is between the creation of a legal concept embodying a zone which, while distasteful in principle, is of known limits and substantive content and is universally accepted as part of a global law of the sea treaty; or a hotch-pot of dissimilar unilateral assertions of authority which would require a united and uniform response from the maritime powers to achieve even a semblance of global uniformity. In that context, the draft provisions in the present negotiating text appear to be the preferable route.

III.

Along with the economic zone issue, the present text proposes an extension of the territorial sea to a distance of 12 nautical miles, up substantially from the three miles presently asserted by the United States. This would create another kind of navigational difficulty. It involves straits. It has long been recognized that because of their importance to maritime powers, straits connecting one part of the high seas with another, and used for international navigation, were subject to special consideration in the law. In 1958 special mention was made in the Geneva Conventions insuring that innocent passage through them could not be suspended in the same manner as it could in territorial waters when the security of the littoral state was threatened.

The concept of innocent passage lacked somthing in this connection, however. In the first place, the concept was rather open-ended. What is innocent and who decides the question? Secondly, innocent passage never applied to the overflight of aircraft or the submerged movement of submarines. For these reasons, the maritime states in general and the United States in particular were uncomfortable in extending that same principle to straits which would now be included if the territorial sea were to be 12 miles. It is estimated that more than 100 straits, previously high seas beyond three nautical miles, would become part of the territorial sea of one or more states if the greater limit is adopted. The result would be a drastic diminution of available air routes, and a new potential for containing the movement of naval vessels, perhaps forcing each naval power to seek to negotiate special arrangements with important littoral states, much as was done in the case of the Dardanelles. In today's political milieu, the prospect of doing so, or in being able to rely long on the arrangements thus achieved, does not appear to be especially good.

As a result of hard bargaining, the principles evolving in the Law of the Sea Conference would assure the exercise of "transit passage" in straits used for international navigation. This right is defined as that to be enjoyed by all ships and aircraft, and which shall not be impeded. it is the continuous and expeditious passage of vessels during which they must refrain from any activities other than those incident to their normal mode of transit. The term "normal mode" is a new one, and important to the concept of naval mobility. It assumes that naval fleets would be able to transit straits in any way that it is normal for such fleets to do so. Thus, for example, carriers would be able to deploy air cover and submarines, contrary to the case under the 1958 conventions, would be able to transit straits submerged, providing of course that it would be safe to do so.

This set of draft articles, if accepted, will constitute a major improvement in the legal regime of the oceans for maritime powers. The new concept represents a protection of a much higher order than the presently applicable principle of non-suspendable innocent passage. This leaves us with the question whether, should there be no treaty, this principle is imbedded deeply enough in the thinking of participating states that it could be claimed to be a universal principle of customary international law.

The answer, unlike the case of the economic zone, would probably be in the negative, since we could not point to state practice in support of the new rule. In the development of international law, the practice of states is important because it is evidence that those states respect a claimed rule in a certain fashion; that they are exercising with regard to it in such a way that suggests they believe they are bound by law to do so. Many states have already adopted some variation of 200-mile zones, and the only questions would be as to what kind of zone state practice would support. The practice with respect to straits is, if anything, negative, as is reflected in Indonesia's announcement toward the end of 1978 that she intended to close three straits (later reduced to only one strait) in her area. In the absence of a treaty, therefore, we would at best be thrown back upon the 1958 principle. But the problem would be that in addition to the economic zone, state practice could be claimed to support a universal territorial sea of 12 nautical miles, leaving maritime powers with inadequate assurances for passage of their ships and aircraft through straits.

The foregoing is not meant to suggest that the littoral straits states have "caved" to the maritime powers in this matter to the extent that they have sacrificed some of their own national interests. That is not the case. There are major protections for them as well, particularly in areas of great interest to them. For example, states bordering straits may designate sea lanes in them and prescribe traffic separation schemes where necessary to promote the safe passage of ships. Before doing so, they must refer their proposals to IMCO for adoption, and the latter may only adopt such schemes as agreed to with the straits states. These states may also make appropriate laws relating to transit passage for the safety of navigation, the control of pollution, the prevention of fishing, and taking on or discharging of persons or cargo in violation of customs and immigration laws. Furthermore, except for warships, which are protected by the sovereign immunity concept, if a ship commits a violation of safety or pollution laws or regulations, the straits states may take appropriate enforcement measures.

In one special respect, the straits states may have a choice to make. If the concept of transit passage is incorporated into law through the adoption of the law of the sea treaty, it will apply in all international straits, and the right will extend from shore to shore. This would mean that foreign aircraft, while transiting straits connecting high seas to economic zones, would acquire the right of overflight up to the littoral coast. The thought has proved discomforting to a number of states whose straits have customarily been used by certain maritime powers. Under existing law, those states have the protection of their territorial seas. To adjust to this situation, it could be more attractive for them to avoid the straits regime for such problem areas by retaining the three-mile territorial sea and leaving a high seas passage in the middle. In this way, aircraft would be kept further away from the coast.

The automatic nature of the straits regime would in a real sense constitute a political safeguard for many small, developing littoral states. Without an internationally agreed straits regime, such states would be forced to assess for themselves the threat posed by the passage of major maritime powers, and be forced into making a political choice which might put them in an awkward postions vis-a-vis the maritimes or their neighbors. Thus they could find themselves at the mercy of the maritimes who could, if they wished, engage in political or economic pressures to force these smaller states to favor their vessels at the expense of others, or at cost to their neighbors. Under the regime, straits states would have no such tough choices to make.

All told, the regime being evolved is a substantial gain for the cause of naval mobility. In view of the fact that it would most likely not be accepted in the absence of a treaty, it alone constitutes one major reason for U.S. interest in the completion of successful negotiations.

IV.

An area of negotiation having a like impact upon navigation stems from claims by archipelagic states. An archipelago is a group of islands, including parts of islands, interconnecting waters, and other natural features so closely interrelated that they form an intrinsic geographical, economic, and political entity, or which historically have been regarded as such.

Certain states constituted wholly by one or more groups of such islands have argued that because they are as much a political entity as a continental state, they should be entitled to encircle the outermost fringes of their islands, and to designate the waters thus contained as internal waters or territorial seas. These arguments, naturally, have been summarily dismissed by the maritime powers. Legalization of such an archipelago concept, without appropriate safeguards, would result in the internalization of large bodies of waters. Should these waters be regarded as the internal waters of the archipelagic state, even the movement of warships would be drastically affected, for sovereign states have sovereign rights in internal waters. One example of where this would have a drastic impact is Indonesia. Astride the Lombok Strait and bordering the ctical Singapore and Malacca Straits, she could arguably enclose and internalize a vast body of water, eliminating overflight and destroying even the right of innocent passage in the straits.

The United States has now indicated her willingness, in the law of the sea context, to consider acceptance of the archipelagic principle, but only with appropriate navigational safeguards. In exchange for recognition of their long-sought claim to sovereignty over archipelagic waters, the archipelagic states are also prepared to make the appropriate guarantees.

First, only a limited number of states, having the appropriate land-to-water ratios, could qualify to assert an archipelagic claim, and then, if they elected to draw archipelagic baselines, the enclosed waters would be designated as archipelagic waters. This new concept would utilize, as a general rule, the traditional regime of innocent passage within the archipelagic envelope. However, the archipelagic state may designate certain sea lanes, and air routes above those sea lanes, for traffic through the archipelago, and they must do so for all normal routes used for international navigation or overflight. In those lanes, ships and aircraft would enjoy the right of "archipelagic sealanes passage," defined as "the exercise...of the rights of navigation and overflight in the normal mode solely for the purpose of continuous, expeditious and unobstructed transit."

In a period when unilateral extensions are the custom, to have in place a well-defined and agreed-upon regime governing passage in archipelagoes seems preferable to facing and countering a plethora of claims of variable legal content on the part of groups of nations astride critical sea and air lanes. Countering such extensive claims is not as easy as it once was. At the very least, such claims would have to be protested. If such protests did not produce negotiations adequate to achieve a workable solution to the particular problem, then painful decisions would have to be made as to the level and degree of response to be undertaken so as to assure that passage was not impeded. This would involve, necessarily, elements of the Navy operating as an arm of U.S. foreign policy. Given the international political climate, such decisions are extremely difficult, and they might have to be made with embarrassing frequency, raising all of the problems faced by the flexing of major maritime muscles in today's world. Such decisions would necessarily have to be made at a high level, and a question is raised whether, from that perspective alone, this is a prudent or desirable course of action.

Taking into account the economic zone, the straits problem, the archipelagic principle, and any other restrictions possibly imagined, decision-makers may select from three possible outcomes with respect to the conduct of navigation for the next twenty years.

Assuming the failure of the Law of the Sea Conference, the United States could take the position that we now go back to square one: that nothing has changed. This argument would assert that the existing law of the sea on navigational issues, as embodied in the 1958 Geneva conventions, supplemented by rules of customary international law evolved through and supported by state practice, would apply. If such thinking were valid, we could conclude that we were entitled to continue to claim a narrow territorial sea, preferably three nautical miles, with high seas beyond, except for contiguous zones in which coastal states could exercise special competence for customs, immigration, fiscal, and sanitary purposes. The archipelago concept, not being supported by widespread state practice or recognized by the major maritimes, would not exist. Passage through straits would be non-suspendable innocent passage. Do these sound commendable? Perhaps so, but they are not attainable. That, in my opinion, is a world long past. This introduces model number two.

Model two is a modified model one. While relying on the Geneva conventions, it would recognize that customary law, supported by state practice, has already modified the conventional law. The idea of a zone of coastal juridiction to an extended distance (200 miles) from shore would have to be considered. In this view, it would be unrealistic to believe that the large number of states that have already moved in this direction would be persuaded to roll back their claims. Surely, there would be no way the Congress of the United States could be persuaded to give up the advantages of the 200-mile fisheries conservation and management zone now in place, to say nothing of persuading other states to do so as well. Under this modified scenario, it would also not be realistic to expect that the United States could long successfully maintain that the territorial seas should be retained at three nautical miles, or that we might be able to negotiate, bilateraly, straits regimes as advantageous as the one appearing to emerge from the Law of the Sea Conference. Without clearly ascertainable parameters, the model is necessarily indefinite. It stands for the proposition that there would be broader territorial seas, but not how broad; it offers continuation of the 200-mile zone concept, but without ascertainable juridical content on the global scale; and it projects uncertainty for straits and the claims of archipelagic states.

Model three consists of the draft articles being prepared in the Law of the Sea Conference. These postulate a 12-mile territorial sea, an economic zone with specified rights and duties, and clear, special regimes for transit through straits and archepelagoes more adequate to protect our vital transporation and military interests.

There are, of course, many variations on the models, but the fundamental options are these. Of the three, it is submitted that the first is inconceivable because history has simply passed it by. That regime cannot be recovered either by force or through negotiation. It will be rejected out of hand by the large majority of coastal states who will be stimulated to far more extensive territorial sea claims leading to conflict between nations in an atmosphere and arena where there will be no adequate peaceful means for the settlement of disputes.

Of the second and third models, it appears as if either is workable and could be made to fit the projected needs of the Navy. Before model two could work, however, there would have to be some serious decisions made and planning undertaken by those responsible for maintaining the viability of a strong and effective naval presence in the world. The planning would have to include a careful assessment of the variety of situations that conceivably could arise with respect to coastal state claims for the future, their implementation, and the range of responses the United States would assert. This would involve the contemplation of a substantial series of important scenarios with a careful assessment of the economic, political, and military costs, for each. We are speaking of a potentially large number of Mayaguez incidents. The seizure by Combodian gunboats of the Mayaguez, a U.S.-flag steamer, passing about six miles from the Wai Islands in the Gulf of Thailand, triggered the taking of military action by the United States with a view to recovering the ship and her people. While the United States was on firm legal grounds, using the dual arguments of high seas and innocent passage as alternatives, that alone was not sufficient to protect perceived U.S. interests. Under the law of reprisal, therefore, the decision was taken to employ force of a limited nature in proportion only sufficient to redress the international wrong.

With that as an example to consider, what would be our response, I wonder, to unilateral declarations by certain coastal states of "zones of peace" that amount to the exclusion of warships from large or strategically important areas? In this respect, the 1977 declaration of North Korea claiming a

50-mile demilitarized zone is in point. Lacking a universal treaty, by what magic measuring device does one balance the costs against the benefits of action or inaction? Perhaps they cannot be measured at all. Thus, without a treaty, the Navy's role as an arm of foreign policy would be increased drastically in a way that would involve some extremely difficult and unpleasant decisions. A universal law of the sea treaty, agreed upon globally, could reduce such tensions significantly and provide the means to bring massive public pressure to bear around the world against significant violators.

Before concluding, at least passing mention should be made with respect to those sets of rules being negotiated that do not bear directly upon navigation, but that have their impact nonetheless. These are the rules that do not regulate navigation as such, but might create limitations on the times, manner, and places that navigation might be conducted, or that might pose the threat of expanding into more dangerous regimes. This last-named problem is normally referred to as creeping jurisdiction.

As with the economic zone, problems of the high seas beyond this zone are both quantitative and qualitiative. The more worrisome aspect it the qualitative side. While warships are protected from restrictive rules regarding marine pollution by the doctrine of sovereign immunity and by explicit exceptions in appropriate parts of treaties, the question must be considered whether the quality of the high seas regime would be affected by a combination of restrictions on pollution and on marine scientific research, and the presence of an international seabeds authority having substantial competence over the area. The underlying issue is whether a generalized shift in the perception of high seas uses would not create new patterns in the area of navigation as well as resource extraction that in time would have an effect on the shape of future naval needs.

The question is more directly stated: How are national attitudes being shaped with regard to future uses of the high seas? Are they being changed in a way that will necessarily affect the fabric of the freedom of the high seas doctrine even though no specific rules are being written in that respect?

The creation of an international seabeds authority may well raise this question in its most interesting aspect. Basic questions about the size of the area under its jurisdiction and the influence of the authority are involved.

The initial questions involve a look at the extent of coastal-state offshore jurisdiction. As we have seen, the economic zone, if adopted, would increase certain coastal state competences to 200 nautical miles. Beyond that, however, jurisdiction also extends over the continental margin. In some areas continental shelves extend substantially beyond the economic zone. The definition of the line where the continental margin would legally terminate divides the competence of the coastal state from that of the seabeds authority, and thus it would be important to know where this would be. Underlying the debates on this issue is the policy decision whether one wishes to maximize coastal state jurisdiction, or that of the international authority in the area. Aside from potential oil and gas deposits on the shelf, there is the question of whether, from a naval point of view, it would be better to have a sovereign state presence in the area or that of a broadly-based international authority, possibly controlled by the developing countries.

With respect to the character of the hypothetical authority's jurisdiction, equally important decisions must be considered. What are the broad implications for the presence of such an entity, even if the rules for extraction of hard minerals from the deep seabed are framed in such a way as not to impact directly on naval operations in any significant manner? If, as has been claimed, the creation of an international seabed authority, with powers and functions restricting the exercise of free enterprise in the seabeds, is the first major shot in the creation of a new economic order, what are the implications of a victory for that order to future regimes affecting the Navy?

At this point, it is time to summarize and conclude. First of all, I must conclude that the overall picture for future naval mobility for the next twenty years is, while uncertain, displaying more positive signs than negative. This is particularly so if the law of the sea treaty should become a reality. If not, however, all is not lost. More hard work and particularized negotiations would have to be undertaken, sometimes at consideraable political and economic cost, to achieve necessary protections in critical areas of the world. It could be done only if the Navy could persuade the Congress to foot the immense bill attached. This would involve a potentially massive reordering of priorities. Of course, wartime operations would not be affected one way or the other, since the United States presumeably would protect its interests at all costs. Nor, in my judgment, would limited operations of a national defense nature, such as the Cuban quarantine, be affected. The historical pattern of national responses to such limited assertions by maritime states has been good, and there is no reason to believe that they would change. Such actions, of course, would have to be limited to clearly identified threats to important national interests close to home.

In the area of routine peacetime operations and missions of tactical or strategic military value, or of political significance, I believe we would be better off with the treaty than without, extending a caveat that we would have to watch closely and counter quickly and effectively any variations on coastal state competence or the nature of influence of the seabeds authority that would tend to change the basic qualitative nature of the seas, that is their legal status, as negotiated in the law of the sea treaty. In this regard, the Navy must be ready to play a diplomatic role where and when necessary.

Given these factors, however, I believe that the United States has been successful beyond expectation in doing what is necessary for the effective peacetime use of its naval forces, and new guarantees being evolved stand every chance of outlasting even the next two decades.

ED. NOTE: Events, of course, took a bad turn after the above was written. The attitude of the Reagan administration was distinctly hostile to the tready. The defense department shifted its emphasis from questions of naval mobility to deep seabed mining in order to guarantee assured access to strategic metals that could be extracted from the deep seabed. Attempts to achieve treaty language that incorporate such assurances were not successful, and, in the end, the Reagan administration rejected the treaty, as did some of our allies. These events make the comments written above seem extremely naive, and we are now in the position of having to claim that treaty principles have become customary international law.

2. TERRITORIAL SEA BREADTH.

H. Gary Knight, SPECIAL DOMESTIC INTERESTS AND UNITED STATES OCEANS POLICY, in Wirsing, ed., INTERNATIONAL RELATIONS AND THE FUTURE OF OCEAN SPACE (1974) at 10, 23-24.[3]

Obviously, operators of intelligence gathering vessels would prefer the narrowest possible territorial sea, for there is a marked increase in the resolution of electronically and visually gathered data as one moves closer to the source being investigated (of course, narrow territorial sea limits also make one's own shore based security installations more vulnerable to hostile surveillance). Further, traditional uses of naval power, including "gun-boat diplomacy," also dictate the narrowest possible territorial sea. Finally, any restriction which might be placed on warships under a subjective interpretation by the coastal state of the standard of innocent passage under present international law (which would be applicable to an increased number of straits if the territorial sea were expanded from

---

[3]. Reprinted From International Relations and the Future of Ocean Space, pages 23-24, edited by Robert G. Wirsing, by permission of the University of South Carolina Press. Copyright of South Carolina Press 1974.

three to twelve miles) might hamper traditional naval mobility. Thus, on the basis of these interests as well as the Polaris/Poseidon situation, the military establishment is interested in a relatively narrow territorial sea and a system of free transit through international straits.

Harlow, FREEDOM OF NAVIGATION, in Alexander, ed., THE LAW OF THE SEA: OFFSHORE BOUNDARIES AND ZONES (1967) at 188, 193.[4]

On the one hand, there is impetus to expand our territorial sea claims because of domestic concern for security and fear of oceanic resource depletion in areas adjacent to our shores. And on the other hand, there is a military need to preserve freedom of navigation by maintaining a narrow territorial sea; for if the United States were to unilaterally declare an expanded territorial sea, it could no longer refuse to recognize foreign claims to a like or larger amount. Such action would, furthermore, encourage other states claiming only three miles to increase the breadth of their own territorial seas.

Claims to expanded territorial seas would have a marked effect on the mobility of United States military forces; for the passage of the ships of one nation over the territorial sea of another must be "innocent".

ED NOTE: The United States, by Presidential decree, has in fact expanded its territorial sea to 12 nautical miles for international, but not domestic purposes. Allegedly, the expansion was made for security reasons.

3. PASSAGE THROUGH STRAITS

ED. NOTE: We have considered the issue of passage through straits earlier in these materials. Those materials should be considered incorporated by reference here.

4. ZONES OF PEACE AND SECURITY

UNITED NATIONS GENERAL ASSEMBLY RESOLUTION 2832 (XXVI) December 16, 1971 (Adopted by 61-0-55)

The General Assembly,

Conscious of the determination of the peoples of the littoral and hinterland States of the Indian Ocean to preserve their independence, sovereignty and territorial integrity, and to resolve their political, economic and social problems under conditions of peace and tranquility,

Recalling the Declaration of the Third Conference of Heads of State or Government of Non-Aligned Countries, held at Lusaka in September 1970, calling upon all States to consider and respect the Indian Ocean as a zone of peace from which great Power rivalries and competition as well as bases

[4]. Reprinted by permission of the Law of the Sea Institute.

conceived in the context of such rivalries and competition should be excluded, and declaring that the area should also be free of nuclear weapons,

Convinced of the desirability of ensuring the maintenance of such conditions in the area by means other than military alliances, as such alliances entail financial and other obligations that call for the diversion of the limited resources of these States from the more compelling and productive task of economic and social reconstruction and could further involve them in the rivalries of power blocs in a manner prejudicial to their independence and freedom of action, thereby increasing international tensions,

Concerned at recent developments that portend the extension of the arms race into the Indian Ocean area, thereby posing a serious threat to the maintenance of such conditions in the area,

Convinced that the establishment of a zone of peace in the Indian Ocean would contribute towards arresting such developments, relaxing international tensions and strengthening international peace and security,

Convinced further that the establishment of a zone of peace in an extensive geographical area in one region could have a beneficial influence on the establishment of permanent universal peace based on equal rights and justice for all, in accordance with the purposes and principles of the Charter of the United Nations,

1. Solemnly declares that the Indian Ocean, within limits to be determined, together with the air space above and the ocean floor subjacent thereto, is hereby designated for all time as a zone of peace;

2. Calls upon the great Powers, in conformity with this Declaration, to enter into immediate consultations with the littoral States of the Indian Ocean with a view to:

(a) Halting the further escalation and expansion of their military presence in the Indian Ocean;

(b) Eliminating from the Indian Ocean all bases, military installations, logistical supply facilities, the disposition of nuclear weapons and weapons of mass destruction and any manifestation of great Power military presence in the Indian Ocean conceived in the context of great Power rivalry;

3. Calls upon the littoral and hinterland States of the Indian Ocean, the permanent members of the Security Council and other major maritime users of the Indian Ocean, in pursuit of the objectives of establishing a system of universal collective security without military alliances and other co-operation, to enter into consultations with a view to the implementation of this Declaration and such action as may be necessary to ensure that:

(a) Warships and military aircraft may not use the Indian Ocean for any threat or use of force against the sovereignty, territorial integrity or independence of any littoral or hinterland State of the Indian Ocean in contravention of the purposes and principles of the Charter of the United Nations;

(b) Subject to the foregoing and to the norms and principles of international law, the right to free and unimpeded use of the zone by the vessels of all nations is unaffected;

(c) Appropriate arrangements are made to give effect to any international agreement that may ultimately be reached for the maintenance of the Indian Ocean as a zone of peace;

4. Requests the Secretary-General to report to the General Assembly at its twenty-seventh session on the progress that has been made with regard to the implementation of this Declaration;

5. Decides to include the item "Declaration of the Indian Ocean as a zone of peace" in the provisional agenda of its twenty-seventh session.

BRIEFINGS ON DIEGO GARCIA AND PATROL FRIGATE, HEARINGS BEFORE THE SENATE COMMITTEE ON FOREIGH RELATIONS (93d CONG., 2d SESS., APRIL 11, 1974) at 10.

Senator Pell. [W]hy is it that you believe, as you say, that the Indian concept primarily, but other nations in the area too, of a zone of peace in the area is a very dangerous concept. Why do you believe to have the Indian Ocean area basically peaceful, relatively weapon free, is not a good thing or is dangerous?

Admiral Zumwalt. The concept of abandoning an area of international ocean we think can play into the asymmetry of power that favors the Soviets with their land and air forces north of those littoral nations. If I were the Soviets I would think that would be a very wonderful deal.

5. THE "HIGH SEAS" STATUS OF THE EXCLUSIVE ECONOMIC ZONE

This material was covered earlier. Consult earlier chapters for problems of this nature.

Having read the above materials, once again consider whether, and in which way, naval operations might be much different in the light of the recent changes in Europe and the demise of the Soviet Union as it was once seen. Would existing treaty provisions be adequate to this new situation? Furthermore, given the importance of the Indian Ocean during the recent Gulf War, do you think the littoral States bordering that ocean would be more or less enthusiastic about the zone of peace? Would they be more or less insistent that the U.S. remove its base from Diego Garcia?

D. NATIONAL SECURITY, GENERALLY

Schachte, NATIONAL SECURITY INTERESTS IN THE 1982 U.N. CONVENTION ON THE LAW OF THE SEA (1993)[5]

. . . .

A View to the Future

We are living in a world transformed. The fundamental changes under way in Eastern Europe and the former Soviet Union offer great hope. Recent events, however, serve as important reminders that this hope must be tempered by the reality that we still live in an uncertain world, a potentially dangerous world. Threats to world order and U.S. interests in the post-Cold War era could include:

* Ethnic rivalry and separatist violence within national borders, resulting in crises within and perhaps beyond those borders;

5. Paper delivered by RADM William L. Schachte, Jr., DoD Representative for Ocean Policy Affairs at a public forum sponsored by the Council on Ocean Law and the American Society of International Law.

* Long-existing regional tensions in areas such as the Middle East and Northeast Asia;

* Humanitarian crises, caused perhaps by natural disasters or collapse of governments, resulting in widespread human misery, starvation or mass migration;

* Armed conflict between the new republics of the former Soviet Union;

* Conflict over resources, including those that straddle territorial boundaries or maritime zones (such as the exclusive economic zone of a coastal state and the adjacent high seas);

* Maritime environmental pollution, impacting sustainable yield and use of marine resources;

* Terrorist attacks against Americans travelling or working overseas; and

* Attacks on merchant shipping by private parties (pirates).

While the specific threats and challenges the U.S. will face in the years ahead undoubtedly will differ from those that have dominated our thinking over the past forty years, capable vigilant forces will continue to be required to deter agression, and, if deterrance fails, to take necessary action. The end of the Cold War has not changed the fact that many of our economic, political, and military interests are located far away from the United States. Budget reductions and the changed geopolitical landscape will result in reduced forward basing of forces, meaning that we must have substantial air and sealift capabilities to enable our forces to be where needed, when needed. This will require a stronger focus on versatility and flexibility. An essential element of this requirement is the assurance that key sea and air lines of communication will remain open as a matter of international legal right -- not contingent upon approval by coastal and island nations along the route or in the area of operations.

Without international respect for the freedoms of navigation and overflight set forth in the LOS Convention, exercise of our forces' mobility rights could be jeopardized. Disputes with littoral states could delay action and be resolved only by protracted political discussions. The response time for U.S. and allied/coalition forces based away from potential areas of conflict could lengthen. Deterrence could be weakened. Forces may arive on the scene too late to make a difference, affecting our ability to influence the course of events consistent with our interests and obligations.

While the LOS Convention has not entered into force, it continues to serve important functions impacting our national security interests. By serving as a source of authority, the Convention guides the behavior of nations, promoting stability of expectations, and providing a framework for issue resolution. It is widely recognized by the international community that the LOS Convention provides a fair balance between coastal and maritime interests. This balance includes the preservation of vital navigational freedoms relied upon by our naval and air forces and much of our commerce. Just as importantly, since the close of the Conference that produced the LOS Convention, the Convention has served as a basis for discussing and resolving difficult issues between nations. For example, the Convention has been invaluable in:

* U.S.-Canada discussions regarding transit through the Northwest Passage;

* bilateral discussions with the former Soviet Union leading to the U.S.-U.S.S.R. Uniform Interpretation of the Rules of International Law Governing Innocent Passage Through the Territorial SEa, signed at Jackson Hole, Wyoming, on September 23, 1989; and

* ongoing technical-level discussions with representatives from the Government of Indonesia concerning archipelagic sealanes passage.

Also, the Convention has been relied upon in multilateral discussions to work towards a common understanding of significant maritime issues. A recent example is the meeting, hosted by the U.S. Department of State, where law of the sea experts from France, Germany, Japan, Russia, the United Kingdom, and the United States discussed a variety of current LOS issues.

Thus, upholding the integrity of the Convention (aside from Part XI) is in the interest of both maritime and littoral nations.

National Security, Economics and the Convention

To be secure and influential in the international arena, the U.S. also must be strong economically. The dynamics of international trade and finance and their impact on economic growth have added new dimenstions to national security. U.S. economic growth is closely linked to the world economy, an important element of which is trade carried on and over the world's oceans. International seaborne commerce exceeds 3.5 billion tons annually and accounts for 80 percent of trade among nations. Manufacturing is increasingly a multinational enterprise. The cost of carrying excessive inventories, coupled with advanced production facilities, dictates that processed materials and finished parts arrive at the time and place specified.

This economic reality underscores the need to ensure transit rights under a widely agreed and comprehensive international legal regime. While such a regime may not preclude all attempts to suspend these rights by coastal and archipelagic states, it would signal to the world community that these rights have a solid legal basis.

The Convention and National Security

There is a close linkage between the LOS Convention and national security. A case in point is how the exercise of the navigational rights and freedoms embodied in the Convention are used by naval forces. In many states, these rights and responsibilities are a prominent part of operating guidance and orders issued by forces at all levels, who look to the Convention as an authoritative embodiment of rules for the maritime environment. For the United States, an example of the Convention's influence and impact is the Commander's Handbook on the Law of Naval Operations, NWP 9/FMEM 1-10, a U.S. Navy and U.S. Marine Corps warfare publication, which addresses both the law of the sea and law of naval warfare. From an operational perspective, the Handbook has had the practical effect of implementing the navigational articles of the Convention for the United States. For military lawyers, an Annotated version has been developed, containing legal analyses, citations, and supplementary annexes.

Turning to specifics, if one were to catalogue the Convention's primary contributions towards national security, such a list would include the following:

1. The right of innocent passage. This right of ships to continuous and expeditious transit, which is not prejudicial to the peace, good order, or security of the coastal state, is the principal right of nations in foreign territorial seas. Naval vessels need this right to be able to conduct their transits efficiently and effectively. As you will recall, in 1989, the United States and the former Soviet Union agreed upon a Joint Statement on the Uniform Interpretation Governing Innocent Passage Through the Territorial Sea. Of importance is the assertion therein that the relevant rules of international law governing innocent passage are set forth in the LOS Convention. Also of particular note are the following:

* all ships, including warships, regardless of cargo, armament or means of propulsion, enjoy the right of innocent passage through the territorial sea in accordance with international law, for which neither prior notification nor authorization is required.

* paragraph 2 of Article 19 of the LOS Convention is an exhaustive list of activities that would render passage not innocent; and

* the coastal state may not prescribe laws or regulations which have the practical effect of denying or impairing the exercise of the right of innocent passage.

2. The right of transit passage. The establishment of a regime to preserve historic rights of free passage through international straits, called transit passage, resulted from the needs of major maritime states who were unable to accept the extension of the breadth of the territorial sea to 12nm without a guarantee of unimpeded passage through all international straits. Under a 3nm territorial sea regime, all but a few international straits were traversed by a high seas corridor, beyond the national jurisdiction of coastal states. However, with a 12nm territorial sea, more than 100 straits used for international navigation are overlapped by territorial seas. The solution to preserving free passage through international straits is the regime of transit passage. Transit passage is similar to innocent passage in one regard -- no prior notice or permission can be imposed by the coastal states bordering the strait. Unlike innocent passage, transit passage permits overflight and submerged transit. Under transit passage, ships and aircraft are to conduct a continuous and expeditious transit through the strait in the normal mode; that is, units may undertake activities necessary for the security of the unit or force such as formation steaming, launch and recovery of aircraft, and flight operations.

Besides continuing previously existing transit rights, the regime of transit passage also serves important conflict limitation objectives. Since transit of straits by ships and aircraft is a matter of right rather than of consent by the straits states, international straits are depoliticized. Strait states, by not having the right to deny passage to a particular nation's or coalition's ships and aircraft, need not be drawn into a conflict that may be occurring thousands of miles away.

3. Archipelagic sea lanes passage. The right of transit by naval and air units through archipelagoes, such as the Philippines and Indonesia, can have a significant impact on the ability of forces to proceed to their area of operations in a timely and secure manner. Similar to transit passage, archipelagic sealanes passage (ASLP) is the right of navigation and overflight in the normal mode, solely for the purpose of continuous and expeditious transit, between one part of the high seas or EEZ and another. Thus, submarines may transit submerged and aircraft may overfly such sea lanes. ASLP may be conducted through all normal routes of international navigation whether or not designated by the archipelagic state (and approved by the International Maritime Organization). Apart from ASLP, there is the right of innocent passage through archipelagic waters beyond internal waters.

4. High sea freedoms. The LOS Convention provides far more than just rights of passage. Effective operations of military ships and aircraft involve more than transiting of ocean spaces. For warships beyond the territorial sea, this includes task force maneuvering, flight operations, military exercises, surveillance, intelligence gathering activities, and ordnance testing and firing. These operations also entail continual practice and exercises -- activities long recognized as high seas freedoms, and that all nations may conduct worldwide, in all ocean areas beyond the territorial sea and archipelagic waters, such as within the EEZ. Of course, these activities must be conducted with due regard for the rights of other nations and the safe conduct and operation of other ships and aircraft.

5. Maritime claims. The Convention provides limitations concerning the maximum permissible breadth of a coastal state's territorial sea and exclusive economic zone. By establishing limitations of 12 nm for the territorial sea and 200 nm for the exclusive economic zone, the Convention provides for coastal state interests as well as permitting maritime states to pursue their interests, including activities related to national security. State practice has demonstrated widespread acceptance of the Convention's regime. For example, as of January, 1993, of the 140+ littoral states, 127 states had established a territorial sea with a 12nm limit, and 86 states claimed a 200nm EEZ.

6. Marine environmental protection. Many nations, including the United States, believe that the LOS Convention provides an effective framework for protecting and preserving the marine environment. It is the first and, by far the most comprehensive approach to addressing this important area. The Convention is comprehensive in that it: (a) addresses state responsibiltiy to curb all sources of marine pollution, and (b) requires that those efforts give due regard to important maritime uses such as navigation and marine scientific research. Environmental regimes must be consistent with those rights. The Convention thus recognizes the delicate balance between protecting and preserving the environment and other competing interests, and provides the balanced framework for environmental norms that are being further developed.

From a national security perspective, an important example of this balancing of interests is the special nature of sovereign immune vessels and aircraft set forth in Article 236. While this article excludes sovereign immune vessels and aircraft from the Convention's environmental provisions, it requires that each flag state ensure that such ships and aircraft act in a manner consistent with those provisions "so far as is reasonable and practicable" without impairing their operations or operational capabilities.

States cannot use or construe the sovereign immunity provision to avoid the responsibility for protecting the environment. In fact, the U.S. Department of Defense views Part XII and Article 236 of the Convention as a mandate to ensure continued responsibility for environmentally sound practices. To this end, the Department has emphasized that protection of the marine environment is an integral component of the national security mission. Examples include incorporating hardware on board our ships to remove oil from bilge discharges, installing shipboard trash compactors, using recycled steel grit and plastic beads to remove old paint (instead of toxic chemical methods), replacing plastic products with biodegradable materials, and revising procurement practices to reduce waste and facilitate recylcling.

Challenges of Reform

The 1983 Presidential Statement on U.S. Oceans Policy announced that the U.S. would not sign the LOS Convention because some of the Convention's provisions on deep seabed mining were inimical to U.S. interests, but that the U.S. would observe and support the remaining provisions, particularly those dealing with navigation and overflight rights. This was based on the belief that the rights and responsibilities set forth in the navigational articles of the Convention embody principles reflecting international law, and therefore would be binding on all states whether or not the Convention entered into force.

Over the past two years, Secretary-General Boutros Boutros-Ghali and his predecessor, Javier Perez de Cuellar, have sought to explore the possibility of making necessary changes to the deep seabed mining regime to enable the Convention to have widespread acceptance. They, and many others, believe that the Convention's entry into force may occur in the near term and that efforts to amend the seabed mining provisions should precede this event. In a series of informal meetings in New York beginning in 1990, attended by key represenatatives from both developing and developed countries (including the U.S. Ambassador to the U.N. and other U.S. Department of State representatives), the Secretary-General has discussed tentative options for moving ahead with seabed mining reform.

Regarding national security, what is in the best interests of the United States? One certainly could argue that we could continue relying on the protection of U.S. national security interests based on customary international law. The U.S., as a maritime power, could press its rights unequivocally and, if necessary, unilaterally, when obstacles to traditional ocean freedoms are encountered. We have done so, thus far, with reasonable success. Claims inconsistent with the Convention would continue to be contested by diplomatic protest and by operational challenges under the Freedom of Navigation Program.

Although this may be our final posture regarding the Convention, it is submitted that it is problematic for the following reasons:

* First, a principal U.S. objective in the nine years of negotiations under Democratic and Republican administrations leading to the LOS Convention was to establish a stable, widely accepted, and comprehensive legal regime for the oceans. To date, without a widely accepted Convention in force, this objective has yet to be achieved. Even with a universal Convention in force, we all will need to remain vigilant against excessive claims, but ensuring compliance with the Convention should be more successful with everyone subject to the Convention.

* Second, some Convention signatories, a number of whom are nearby or adjacent to important waterways used for international transit, assert that the Convention is a legal contract -- and therefore its rights and benefits, such as transit passage and arichipelagic sea lanes passage, are not necessarily available to non-parties. We do not accept these claimed restrictions on international transit rights, but such questions would be mooted under a universal Convention.

* Third, while the U.S. has, since 1979, formally contested excessive coastal state claims, both operationally and diplomatically through the Freedom of Navigation Program, the political costs and military risks of such actions may increase in the changing world order.

* Fourth, there is the risk of losing the structural outline which the Convention provides in dealing with emerging issues of importance, including environmental protection and resource conservation, if the Convention enters into force without the major maritime powers as parties. The Convention provides an excellent framework for progress in addressing and resolving issues which, if left unattended and allowed to unravel, would give rise to increased tensions and conflict in the future. The U.S. and other major maritime powers would be more effective in influencing the continued viability of this legal framework as insiders rather than outsiders.

* Fifth, the long-standing leadership role of the U.S. in international ocean affairs could be eroded if the U.S. declines to become actively involved in bona fide efforts to achieve a Convention that will enjoy wide acceptance -- particularly when there is significant and growing interest in engaging in a serious dialogue with a view to making those changes that would overcome U.S. objections to the Convention's seabed mining regime.

As indicated during the Senate confirmation hearings for Secretary of State Christopher and Ambassador Albright, the is interest in assessing whether deep seabed mining provisions of the Convention can be reformed to be made compatible with U.S. concerns. This would be consistent with DoD's longstanding interest in achieving a stable, world-wide regime that would protect navigational freedoms essential to international maritime commerce and the mobility of U.S. naval and air forces.

A Time for Leadership

With 54 states having ratified or acceded to the Convention, it must be stressed that time is of the essence. There is an opportunity to achieve a Convention that will have widespread acceptance, with Part XI amended in a way that meets our needs -- but meaningful reform will become more difficult to achieve once the Convention has the threshold number of parties (60) necessary for it to come into force.

While the new Administration has numerous important issues to confront early on, I believe that we are rapidly approaching the time when a decision regarding U.S. leadership to seek amendments should be made. Viewed as one of the most ambitious and comprehensive legal documents negotiated by the world community to date, the Convention -- with a deep seabed mining regime modified to permit widespread acceptance and support -- could play a significant role in achieving U.S. national security objectives and economic growth in the years ahead. We are, as I've said, prepared to go it alone if we must. But as the prominent global power in the 1990's and beyond, the U.S. is uniquely positioned to assume a more visible leadership role in the ongoing U.N. effort to achieve a widely accepted international order to regulate and safeguard the many diverse activies and interests of nations regarding the world's oceans.

CHAPTER 14

UNITED STATES OCEANS POLICY

The objective of this chapter is to consider the historical development of U.S. Oceans policy, which has shifted dramatically over the years. At the time of the present writing, it could be said that there is almost literally no policy and no effective mechanism for its development within the U.S. government. Such policy as exists is reflected in national legislation, such as the Fishery Conservation and Management Act, previously considered, or the Hard Minerals Act. But policy does not depend upon past acts. Policy development for the future is essential, and that development seems to be completely lacking. The Department of State, the lead agency during the years of the Law of the Sea Conference, has fallen into lethargy on the subject, and no single agency has stepped in to fill the void. U.S. oceans policy lacks the impetus given to it by the report of the Stratton Commission, Our Nation and the Sea, in 1969. Some of the stages in the development of policy follow.

Lyndon B. Johnson, REMARKS OF THE PRESIDENT OF THE UNITED STATES AT THE COMMISSIONING OF THE OCEANOGRAPHIC RESEARCH SHIP "THE OCEANOGRAPHER", July 13, 1966

...I am happy to announce that one of the first long voyages of the Oceanographer will be a six-month expedition in which the scientists from a number of our great nations will participate. It is our intention to invite Great Britain, West Germany, France, the U.S.S.R., India, Malaysia, Australia, New Zealand, Chile and Peru to participate in the first round the world voyage of the Oceanographer.

We greatly welcome this type of international participation. Under no circumstances, we believe, must we ever allow the prospects of rich harvest and mineral wealth to create a new form of colonial competition among the maritime nations. We must be careful to avoid a race to grab and to hold the lands under the high seas. We must ensure that the deep seas and the ocean bottoms are, and remain, the legacy of all human beings.

The sea, in the words of Longfellow, `divides and yet unites mankind.'

ED. NOTE: This early policy statement, you will note, bears a striking similarity to the principle of the common heritage of mankind upon which the Law of the Sea Conference eventually foundered.

An important stage in the development of U.S. maritime policy began with the enactment, in 1966, of legislation creating the Commission on Marine Science, Engineering and Resources (known as the Stratton Commission after its chairman). Its 1969 report is one of the most thorough national commission reports ever written, titled "Our Nation and the Sea". This report became the blueprint for national policy for many years. The introduction to this report reveals the Commission's priorities.

OUR NATION AND THE SEA, Report of the Commission on Marine Science, Engineering and Resources (1969)

AN INTRODUCTION AND A SUMMARY

Our Stake in the Uses of the Sea

How fully and wisely the United States uses the sea in the decades ahead will affect profoundly its security, its economy, its ability to meet increasing demands for food and raw materials, its position and influence in the world community, and the quality of the environment in which its people live.

The need to develop an adequate national ocean program arises from a combination of rapidly converging and interacting forces.

The world population is expected to approximately double by the year 2000, but even a lesser rate of growth would intensify the already serious food problem. The need for supplemental animal protein sources is critical and growing daily. The sea is not the only source of additional protein but it is an extremely important one.

The United States itself faces no serious protein shortage, and its rate of population growth shows a promising decline. Nevertheless, it is expected that by the end of the century the population of our country will reach 300 to 350 million people and that the Nation will rely increasingly on food from the sea.

As the population grows, new means must be developed to expand the economy, to generate new jobs and products, and to pay the costs of publicly rendered services. Although land-based activities will continue to dominate the economy for many years to come, new and expanded ocean industries offer some of the Nation's most inviting opportunities for economic growth.

....

Vital though marine economic development is, it must be tempered by other considerations. There is increasing concern over the need to understand our physical environment, of which the oceans are but one part. This concern is based on growing appreciation that the environment is being affected by man himself, in many cases adversely. It is critical to protect man from the vicissitudes of the environment and the environment, in turn, from the works of man.

Today, man's damage to the environment too often is ignored because of immediate economic advantage. To maximize the present economy at the expense of the future is to perpetuate the pattern of previous generations, whose sins against the planet we have inherited.

If adequately protected, the sea and shoreline can provide unique and valuable opportunities for recreation. The growth of the country's population, most pronounced in urban areas along the shoreline, and the increased wealth and leisure of many of our people, are creating inexorable pressures for access to the sea. Contamination or destruction of beach, marsh, waterway, and shoreline aggravates these pressures by denying the use of the sea and shore to a growing population.

....

The oceans and marine-related activities must be viewed in the context of the total land-air-sea environment. In many ways the oceans are the dominant factor in the total environment. However, intervention by man in any one element produces effects on the others, frequently through processes we do not yet understand. Mankind is fast approaching a stage when the total planetary environment can be influence, modified, and perhaps controlled by human activities. The Nation's stake in the oceans is therefore an important part in its stake in the very future of man's world.

....

ED. NOTE: The report contains several chapters, backed up by extensive panel reports. These include comments on the national capability in the sea, the management of the coastal zone, marine resources, the global environment, technical and operating services, and organizing a national ocean effort.

Among the most significant legislative responses to this report was the Coastal Zone Management Act, and the creation, by executive order, the National Oceanic and Atmospheric Administration (NOAA) within the Department of Commerce. The report still has vitality, although the passage of the years, and the changes unforseen by the Commission, creates a need for a new look.

H. Gary Knight, UNITED STATES OCEANS POLICY: PERSPECTIVE 1974, 49 Notre Dame Lawyer 241, 242-246 (1973)1

The development and exposition of United States foreign policy are a complex process which seldom adheres to textbook methods or established lines of executive authority....

At the highest level presidential statements must be considered national policy (at least in foreign affairs, and that is the area with which we are dealing in the law of the sea negotiations). The principal presidential pronouncements on the topic of the law of the sea have been President Johnson's statement at the commissioning of the research vessel The Oceanographer, in 1966 and President Nixon's later, more comprehensive statement of May 23, 1970,.... Unfortunately, lawyers, scientists, bureaucrats, and others are still quibbling about precisely what the latter statement means in certain passages or why the federal government has or has not (depending on who is speaking) emphasized certain aspects of the statement. Thus, even at the highest level there appears to be some ambiguity on policy, although in fairness it must be admitted that a certain amount of flexibility is always required in such policy positions. Additional expositions on United States oceans policy have been made by President Nixon in each of his annual foreign policy reports to Congress.

A second source of policy is the draft treaty articles which have been submitted from time to time to the Seabed Committee by the United States. In August, 1970, the United States submitted a comprehensive draft seabed treaty. This was followed a year later by a three-part proposal on the breadth of the territorial sea, passage through straits, and fisheries. A revised draft treaty article on fisheries was introduced at the July-August, 1972, meeting of the Seabed Committee. During the July-August, 1973 Seabed Committee meeting, draft treaty articles were introduced on the subjects of the protection of the marine environment, rights and duties in coastal seabed economic areas, marine scientific research, and compulsory dispute settlement. These must be regarded as having the highest clearance by the National Security Council. Of equal value in assessing United States policy provisions

---

[1]. Volume 9, issue 2 The Notre Dame Lawyer (1973) 241-275. Reprinted with permission. copyright by Notre Dame Law Review, University of Notre Dame.

The publisher bears responsibility for any errors which have occurred in reprinting or editing.

are working papers submitted to the Seabed Committee. Two such papers have been submitted: one dealing with fisheries and the other with pollution.

Congressional resolutions, though not carrying the force of law, must also be considered as evidence of United States oceans policy, especially if they endorse the policies being supported by the Executive Branch of government. In 1973 both the Senate and the House of Representatives adopted resolutions supporting the basic outlines of United States oceans policy as reflected in presidential statements and subsequent draft treaty articles.

Ranking perhaps below official draft articles, but extremely valuable for their explanations and justifications of policy, are the formal statements made by representatives of the United States to the Seabed Committee during its semiannual sessions. Although the general principles contained in such messages are cleared through the negotiating instructions approved by the National Security Council, specific wording is generally left to the negotiating team -- the Inter-Agency Law of the Sea Task Force ("Task Force" hereinafter) -- and its executive committee. Also in this category are briefings and testimony given by members of the Task Force in open congressional committee and subcommittee sessions, and similar unclassified statements to the State Department's Advisory Committee on the Law of the Sea. Finally, there are the miscellaneous negotiating, educational, and other activities in which members of the Task Force and the United States delegation to the Seabed Committee must engage, whether the Seabed Committee is in or out of session. These include impromptu responses to policy statements by other nations (some made with more consultation and preparation than others), unofficial conversations with representatives of other nations, and speeches and papers before private and unofficial gatherings on the subject.

The policy picture is complicated by the fact that national positions tend to change over the course of negotiations. Clearly, all that our negotiating team does should remain essentially consistent with President Nixon's statement of May 23, 1970 (at least until a new oceans policy statement is issued); yet even within that seemingly limited framework substantial flexibility has been evident. The reader is thus cautioned that what follows is only one derivation of United States oceans policy from among all the sources listed above.

Although the agenda of issues being considered in the current law of the sea negotiations are quite lengthy, there appear to be five basic subject matter areas which this nation is presently emphasizing through its policy proposals. Two of these relate to the exploitation of resources of the marine environment, while the other three relate to general uses of ocean space. They may briefly be summarized as follows:

1. The question of the regime to govern exploration for and exploitation of the nonliving resources of the seabed and subsoil. This issue is divided into two subparts: one concerns the regime applicable to the area under adjacent coastal state jurisdiction, including the questions of the extent of such national jurisdiction and the coastal state's rights and duties with respect to activities conducted therein; the other concerns the area beyond such national control, generally referred to as the "deep seabed."

2. The question of management of living marine resources, wherever situated. In some proposals, but not that of the United States, the issue of the limits of national jurisdiction arises here, too.

3. The question of the breadth of the territorial sea and the concomittant right of navigation and overflight on the high seas and through international straits.

4. The question of freedom of scientific research in the ocean.

5. The question of protection of the marine environment.

The underlying premises behind the various policy positions taken on these issues were set forth in Presdient Nixon's Third Annual Report on United States Foreign Policy as follows:

> First, mulitlateral agreement is essential....
>
> Second, freedom of navigation and overflight must be protected....
>
> Third, an equitable system must be established for regulating the exploitation of the resources of the ocean and seabeds beyond national jurisdiction.
>
> Fourth, it is not possible for any nation, acting unilaterally, to ensure adequate protection of the marine environment.

Richard M. Nixon, UNITED STATES POLICY FOR THE SEABED, 62 STATE DEP'T BULL. 737 (1970)

The nations of the world are now facing decisions of momentous importance to man's use of the oceans for decades ahead. At issue is whether the oceans will be used rationally and equitably and for the benefit of mankind or whether they will become an arena of unrestrained exploitation and conflicting jurisdictional claims in which even the most advantaged states will be losers.

The issue arises now -- and with urgency -- because nations have grown increasingly suspicious of the wealth to be exploited from the seabeds and throughout the waters above and because they are also becoming apprehensive about ecological hazards of unregulated use of the oceans and seabeds. The stark fact is that the law of the sea is inadequate to meet the needs of modern technology and the concerns of the international community. If it is not modernized multilaterally, unilateral action and international conflict are inevitable.

This is the time, then for all nations to set about resolving the basic issues of the future regime for the oceans -- and to resolve it in a way that redounds to the general benefit in the era of intensive exploitation that lies ahead. The United States, as a major maritime power and a leader in ocean technology to unlock the riches of the ocean, has a special responsibility to move this effort forward.

Therefore, I am today proposing that all nations adopt as soon as possible a treaty under which they would renounce all national claims over the natural resources of the seabed beyond the point where the high seas reach a depth of 200 meters (218.8 yards) and would agree to regard those resources as the common heritage of mankind.

The treaty should establish an international regime for the exploitation of seabed resources beyond this limit. The regime should provide for the collection of substantial mineral royalties to be used for international community purposes, particularly economic assistance to developing countries. It should also establish general rules to prevent unreasonable interference with other uses of the ocean, to protect the sea from pollution, to assure the integrity of the investment necessary for such exploitation, and to provide for peaceful and compulsory settlement of disputes.

I propose two types of machinery for authorizing exploitation of seabed resources beyond a depth of 200 meters.

First, I propose that the coastal nations act as trustees for the international community in an international trusteeship zone comprised of the continental margins beyond a depth of 200 meters off their coasts. In return, each coastal state would receive a share of the international revenues from the zone in which it acts as trustee and could impose additional taxes if these were deemed desirable.

As a second step, agreed international machinery would authorize and regulate exploration and use of seabed resources beyond the continental margins.

The United States will introduce specific proposals at the next meeting of the United Nations Seabeds Committee to carry out these objectives.

Although I hope agreement on such steps can be reached quickly, the negotiation of such a complex treaty may take some time. I do not, however, believe it is either necessary or desirable to try to halt exploration and exploitation of the seabeds beyond a depth of 200 meters during the negotiating process.

Accordingly, I call on other nations to join the United States in an interim policy. I suggest that all permits for exploration and exploitation of the seabeds beyond 200 meters be issued subject to the international regime to be agreed upon. The regime should accordingly include due protection for the integrity of investments made in the interim period. A substantial portion of the revenues derived by a state from exploitation beyond 200 meters during this interim period should be turned over to an appropriate international development agency for assistance to developing countries. I would plan to seek appropriate congressional action to make such funds available as soon as a sufficient number of other states also indicate their willingness to join this interim policy.

I will propose necessary changes in the domestic import and tax laws and regulations of the United States to assure that our own laws and regulations do not discriminate against U.S. nationals operating in the trusteeship zone off our coast or under the authority of the international machinery to be established.

It is equally important to assure unfettered and harmonious use of the oceans as an avenue of commerce and transportation and as a source of food. For this reason the United States is currently engaged with other states in an effort to obtain a new law-of-the-sea treaty. This treaty would establish a 12-mile limit for territorial seas and provide for free transit through international straits. It would also accommodate the problems of developing countries and other nations regarding the conservation and use of the living resources of the high seas.

I believe that these proposals are essential to the interests of all nations, rich and poor, coastal and landlocked, regardless of their political systems. If they result in international agreements, we can save over two-thirds of the earth's surface from national conflict and rivalry, protect it from pollution, and put it to use for the benefit of all. This would be a fitting achievement for this 25th anniversary year of the United Nations.

Ann L. Hollick, UNITED STATES OCEANS POLITICS, 10 San Diego Law Review 467, 471-490 (1973)2

The Policy Participants

Of the domestic interests affected by the disposition of the seabed and its mineral resources, only four have had a significant influence on or involvement in policy formulation through 1972 -- the petroleum industry, the military, the hard minerals industry, and the marine science community. While the military and the scientist use the oceans for the more traditional purposes of mobility, the petroleum and hard minerals industries share a more recent interest in the exploitation of fixed mineral resources. The resulting clash between these new and traditional ocean uses has been a central element in the formulation of U.S. seabed policy.

Seabed policy has two major aspects: (1) the delimitation of national jurisdiction over seabed minerals and (2) the nature of the seabed regime to be established beyond national jurisdiction. Each of the four interest groups is concerned with different aspects of seabed policy. While the petroleum industry is primarily intent upon determining the location of the boundary of national jurisdiction, the hard minerals industry is concerned with the seabed regime to be established beyond that boundary. The military and the marine scientists are affected by both of these questions insofar as they might restrict their mobility on the oceans. Conflict has therefore arisen over both the national boundary and the international regime issues -- betweeen Defense and the petroleum industry in the former case and between Defense and the hard minerals industry in the latter. The clash over the boundary issue began earlier than that over the regime and was much more virulent, due in no small measure to the relative power parity of defense and petroleum interests. Only in 1972 did the Department of Defense withdraw from active involvment in the boundary issue to concentrate on the straits question.

The policy dispute over the boundary found its origin in the 1968 discovery that seabed petroleum deposits are generally limited to the continental margin. Although offshore petroleum operations had been underway for two decades, they were confined to the shallow areas of the continental shelf and knowledge of the area beyond was at best vague. In 1967 and early 1968, new discoveries and developments led the petroleum indusry to reevaluate its interest in the deeper offshore areas. The Malta proposal at the United Nations raised worldwide hopes of boundless seabed treasure while simultaneously threatening to jeopardize access to them. In the same period, estimates of the magnitude of offshore petroleum resources were skyrocketing as technological advances were lowering the cost of deep water operations.

Important in unifying the entire petroleum industry around a single position on offshore jurisdiction were two reports emanating from the U.S. Geological Survey in 1968. In the first, the Director of the Geological Survey indicated that commercial petroleum deposits would be restricted to the continental margin and suggested that the legal definition of the Continental Shelf should be adapted to correspond with the geological boundary. The impact of this statement on subsequent petroleum policy was reinforced by new and substantially increased estimates of offshore petroleum resources. The Geological Survey reported recoverable reserves on the U.S. continental margins ranging from 180 to 220 billion barrels of petroleum liquids and from 820 to 1,100 trillion cubic feet of gas.

On the basis of these findings, major segments of the U.S. petroleum industry moved quickly to stake out a policy position on the location of the Continental Shelf boundary. The National Petroleum Council offered a definitive policy formulation in the interim report entitled Petroleum

Resources under the Ocean Floor. The NPC's argumentation combined an ingenious earlier version of a national "energy crisis" with elaborate legal reasoning. Using the Interior Department's estimates, the NPC pointed to the substantial resources off the U.S. shores and advanced the view that it was vital to the nation's security to guarantee national control of all the energy resources of the continental margin. The alternative, it was suggested, would be a dangerous dependence on foreign supplies of petroleum.

To secure national control of these offshore petroleum resources, the U.S. Government was urged to unilaterally assert sovereign rights over offshore seabed resources to the outer edge of the continental margin. Such a move, the petroleum industry argued, would be consistent with the intent of the Geneva Convention on the Continental Shelf and would in no way impair high seas freedoms in the area. According to Article 1 of the 1958 Convention, coastal state jurisdiction over seabed resources, or the limit of the legal Continental Shelf extends to the 200 meter (656 feet) isobath or beyond that to the depth that admits of exploitation. Although in 1969 producing wells were operating well within the 200 meter isobath (340 feet), exploratory wells were being drilled at depths far exceeding this limit (1,300 feet). Adding the expected advance of recovery capabilities to the geological break between the margin and the deep seabed, the industry contended that the intent of the Geneva Convention was to advance the Continental Shelf boundary to the outer limit of the continental margin. Underlying the early petroleum position was the traditional belief shared by both the domestic and overseas branches of the petroleum industry that in gaining access to resources off the U.S. coasts as well as off those of other nations it was safer and more profitable for American firms to deal bilaterally with coastal nations rather than with an unfamiliar international regime possibly weighted against U.S. interests.

As the petroleum industry began to advance this position within the Government, the Defense Department position on the boundary moved in the opposite direction. The military observed that the Interior Department's issuing of leases at depths far greater than the 200 meter isobath constituted de facto extension of the U.S. continental shelf based on the exploitability clause of the Geneva Convention. Although under the terms of the Continental Shelf Convention resource jurisdiction was not to affect other uses of the area, the military came increasingly to fear that such would not be the case. Not only was it concerned about the effect of such extensions on the placement of ASW detection devices, but Defense was equally fearful that the limited resource sovereignty delegated to a coastal state would gradually expand, through the phenomenon of "creeping jurisdiction," to claims of total territorial sovereignty. Thus the military came to the view that the seaward extension of the Continental Shelf boundary as exploitation proceeded, together with the expansion of coastal state sovereignty over superjacent waters, would ultimately close off U.S. military access to coastal areas around the world.

At that time the Defense Department solution to the threat of creeping jurisdiction was to attempt to limit the size of special purpose or resource zones in the oceans. Constrained from a resort to force to protect its navigational rights from coastal state encroachment, Defense Department representatives opted for a broad international agreement through a formal conference. With regard to seabed minerals, the Defense Department sought international agreement on a Continental Shelf extending no farther than the 200 meter isobath. To sell such a scheme to governments of developing nations the Defense Department proposed the establishment of a generous and powerful seabed mineral regime in the area beyond the narrow Continental Shelf. In an unsuccessful effort to convince the skeptical petroleum industry of the merits of such a boundary, the Defense Department pointed out that 92% of the world's continental margins were off foreign shores. To gain access to these, it was far better for the petroleum industry to deal with an impartial international seabed authority than to deal bilaterally with unpredictable national governments that might resort to harassment, profit squeezing or outright expropriation. The technological superiority of the American petroleum industry and the dominant role that the U.S. Government would presumably assure favorable treatment for U.S. companies.

Inherent in the policy question that Defense was advancing within the Government was a readiness to risk the petroleum industry's resource interests, as industry saw them, in return for internationally agreed rights of transit. The industry was predictably opposed to such a tradeoff and fought it vigorously through the Interior Department. The petroleum industry's ready access to information and to policy makers within the Government contributed to its effective and early input into the policy process.

The hard minerals and marine science interests were less fortunate. Throughout 1969 and 1970 neither hard minerals nor science was adequately represented in the closely-held policy deliberations within the Government. The primary concern of the hard minerals industry with seabed policy has been the nature of the regime rather than with the location of the Continental Shelf boundary.... Because nodules of commercial value are rarely found on the continental margin, locating the Continental Shelf boundary at any point up to the outer edge of the margin will not significantly affect the miner of nodules.

First discovered in the 1870's, the manganese nodule came to be considered as a potential resource only recently. As information about nodules has increased, mining industry policy has undergone several transitions -- from early support for a broad Continental Shelf, to a policy of a moving Shelf boundary, to a total disregard of the boundary issue and a strong position on the regime beyond national jurisdiction. In August 1968 the petroleum and hard minerals industries were in substantial agreement on the boundary question as was reflected in a Joint Report sent to the American Bar Association House of Delegates by Sections of Natural Resources Law, International and Comparative Law, International Peace and Law through the United Nations. The Joint Report supported the National Petroleum Council view that the rights of coastal states to the minerals of the seabed already extended to the foot of the continental margin. The Report also considered it premature to consider establishing a regime for the seabed beyond that boundary.

By 1969 the hard mineral interest group began to move away from this position. In an August 1969 Joint Report by the same section of the American Bar Association, the split was evident. The new Joint Report explicitly stated that some members no longer supported the interpretation of the Continental Shelf boundary that had been advocated a year before. Instead these members urged that the Geneva Convention on the Continental Shelf "extends sovereign rights over the seabed beyond the 200 meter line only as technological progress makes exploitation in that area possible in fact."

This diverging position on the Continental Shelf boundary coincided with increased industry interest in the recovery of manganese nodules and increased knowledge of the location of commercially attractive deposits. Although the mineral industry shared the petroleum industry's aversion to international administrative organizations, it came gradually to realize that mining companies would be operating in areas beyond the limits of national jurisdiction, no matter where the Continental Shelf boundary was drawn. Ocean miners became increasingly concerned, therefore, with the nature of the seabed regime which would govern deep sea exploitation -- a concern which was not shared by the petroleum interest group given petroleum's stand on the extent of national seabed jurisdiction.

Despite the lack of direct interest in the boundary issue, the hard minerals industry continued to involve itself in the boundary dispute for tactical purposes in 1969 and 1970. The industry was willing to support a narrow but outward moving boundary, if such a boundary could be used to buy a satisfactory seabed regime. By a "satisfactory regime," the hard minerals industry meant a system of freedom to explore the seabed, to stake a claim and to receive an exclusive license to exploit the claimed area. An international authority, in this view, should be no more than a registry agency, and its financial exactions should be minimal. Although the mining industry was willing to trade the petroleum industry's interest in the boundary for a favorable seabed authority, it soon found the Defense Department to be a dangerous ally. To induce other nations to agree to a narrow Continental Sehlf, Defense was urging the establishment of a generous and powerful seabed regime to administer the exploration and exploitation of seabed resources and to allocate substantial revenues from these activities to an international development fund. Despite its opposition to the Defense Department position, the hard minerals industry was not particularly successful in blocking it. Due to its position on the boundary, the hard minerals industry had lost the support of the petroleum industry. And within the Interior Department, hard minerals had to compete with petroleum for the time and energy of government bureaucrats responsible for seabed policy.

The problems of the marine science interest were somewhat different. Because the marine scientist shares the military's interest in unrestricted access to the world's oceans, he is concerned both with the boundary and with the regime. However, the scientific community believes it can and should distinguish its research in the oceans from commercial and military investigations. In all ocean policy efforts, therefore, the scientist has sought to include explicit guarantees for open scientific research. Such guarantees, however, necessarily imply the absence of a similiar freedom of military access for research, monitoring and even transit. They were, therefore, strongly resisted by the military.

The policy position advocated by the United States in 1970, with its strong emphasis on maintaining ocean freedoms, was consonant with the scientific interest. While State Department officials representing science and, to a lesser extent, the National Science Foundation were in substantial agreement on the needs of science, they were unable to override military opposition to explicit guarantees for freedom of scientific research. The scientific community, therefore, failed to secure inclusion of the coveted guarantees for scientific freedom in the U.S. Draft Seabed Treaty of 1970.

An additional interest which has not been mentioned, and one with limited influence on ocean policy until 1970, was that of the Department of State itself -- the Government's official foreign policy arm. The State Department's guiding purpose has been to advance U.S. ocean interest in international negotiations while maintaining ordered and harmonious relations with other nations on a broad range of ocean issues. Its overriding bias is toward reaching an international agreement. To achieve these objectives the Department of State seeks to maintain control over the formulation of ocean policy. This in turn has required strenuous efforts to resolve domestic contention over ocean policy issues to arrive at a policy position acceptable to all parties. When the seabed issue was first introduced in the United Nations in 1967, the State Department encountered a series of obstacles to the achievement of its objectives. These impediments placed the Department in the unenviable position of having to stall in the face of growing international pressures. The first difficulty was that of resolving internal bureaucratic contention over the control of ocean policy. This was temporarily resolved in February 1970 when the then Legal Advisor, John R. Sevenson, became the head of a consolidated Law of the Sea Task Force. With Mr. Stevenson's retirement from government in January 1973, the issue of direct overall U.S. ocean policy has been once again raised.

A second difficulty in formulating early seabed policy was the growing dispute between the Departments of Interior and Defense. In a successful effort to forestall the imposition of a boundary policy by the State Department, the Department of Defense requested an Under Secretaries Committee review of the seabed boundary question. In response to this request, the White House issued a National Security Study Memorandum in April 1969 proposing that, in the absence of inter-agency agreement, the Under Secretaries Committee meet to consider the position that the United States should take in the United Nations regarding the location of the Continental Shelf boundary. The NSSM further proposed that the Under Secretaries Committee attempt to reconcile the U.S. position on the Continental Shelf boundary with that on the territorial sea and related issues.

Between the April, 1969 NSSM and the January, 1970 meeting of the Under Secretaries Committee, the State Department intensified its efforts to reach a compromise acceptable to both sides. To accomodate the interests of both the Department of Defense and the Department of the Interior, the State Department proposed the adoption of an intermediate zone in the disputed area between the 200 meter isobath and the edge of the continental margin. In this zone, the coastal nation would enjoy control over the exploration and exploitation of seabed resources. While responsible for enforcing standards to protect against pollution and navigation hazards, the coastal nation would not have the right to exclude other nations from conducting scientific research or military activities on the continental margin beyond the 200 meter isobath. The State Department compromise further stipulated that a small royalty of 2% based on the value of the resources exploited in the zone would be paid to an international community fund.

The State Department compromise proposal received a mixed reaction. While Interior did not object to it strenuously, the Defense Department rejected it flatly. Defense argued that an intermediate zone would be temporary at best and that giving the coastal state exlcusive jurisdiction over resource exploitation on the continental margin would jeopardize the freedom of other nations to use that area for other purposes. Explicit guarantees of access for military or scientific purposes, Defense argued, would simply not be acceptable to coastal nations. Only by combining a narrow Continental Shelf with a satisfactory international regime would there be any chance of halting the proliferation of unilateral national claims.

The NSC System

With this final failure to reach agreement, the Under Secretaries Committee meeting was scheduled for January 29, 1970, and the major contenders assiduously recruited allies within the bureaucracy. Interior consolidated the backing of the Commerce Department and won the added support of the Bureau of the Budget and John Ehrlichman's White House staff. The Defense Department found backing within the Justice Department and the National Security Council (while continuing to lobby the State Department for a revision of its proposal). And, in back of its intermediate zone proposal, the State Department lined up the Transportation Department and the National Science Foundation. Given the obvious power of the major antagonists -- the petroleum industry and the military -- allies seemed scarcely necessary to ensure that the Under Secretaries Committee would not render a judgment adverse to either interest. In any case, under the NSC options system the Committee did not have the power to impose a decision. Chaired by then Under Secretary of State Elliott Richardson, the Committee's mandate was limited to submitting a report to Presidential Assistant Henry Kissinger, for review and consideration by the President. The result of the meeting, therefore, was a foregone conclusion. While the pros and cons of the State, Interior and Defense positions were heatedly discussed, they were not resolved. The only decision taken was to send the policy dispute further up the NSC ladder with Under Secretary Richardson's recommendation accompanied by position papers from the dissenting agencies.

In the month and a half immediately after the Under Secretaries Committee meeting, the Defense Department and its supporters mounted a particularly vigorous campaign against the State Department position. In response to these objections and in his capacity as Chairman of the Under Secretaries Committee, Elliott Richardson proposed a fourth policy position on the Continental Shelf boundary and the seabed regime. The new position was an obvious compromise between the State Department position on an intermediate zone and the Defense Department position in favor of a narrow Continental Shelf. In his proposal Richardson suggested that the concept of the intermediate zone be retained but that the zone be expressly incorporated into the international regime. The proposal went on to stipulate that, within the intermediate zone, the coastal state would have the exclusive right to grant concessions and to collect royalties as a "trustee" of the international community. Substantial royalties from exploitation in the zone would be allocated to international economic development. Richardson's proposal differed from the original State Department position on the outer limit of the national Continental Shelf boundary and the size of royalties to be allocated to the international community. It promptly superceded the earlier State Department proposal as the new official State Department position.

The reactions of both Defense and Interior to the revised State Department position were revealing. The Defense Department continued to prefer its own concept of preferential bidding rights for coastal nations, but it deemed the new proposal acceptable as a "fall-back" position since it explicitly stipulated that national sovereignty would end at the 200 meter isobath and concentrated its efforts on assuring the international character of the trusteeship zone. The Interior Department was far less sanguine about Mr. Richardson's proposal. Interior's main objection was to the provisions that would give the international community discretionary authority in the intermediate zone and would only allow the coastal state to act as "trustee." Such authority would mean that the international community, of which developing nations constitute a majority, would have the power to decide upon and to impose production controls, to fix high royalty payments, to impose other onerous restrictions upon the coastal state, or to exclude the coastal state altogether from its trusteeship zone. Finally, the Interior Department expressed concern that the Richardson proposal, unlike its predecessor in the State Department, called for a large amount of royalties to be paid to an international fund. The Interior Department urged, therefore, a return to the abandoned State Department's position on the Shelf boundary and a seabed regime.

With the formulation of the Richardson proposal and the retention of the original State Department proposal at the insistence of Interior, there were four policy options to be considered by the White House. Although these were sent to the President in March, no decision on the options was forthcoming until the end of May. An obvious cause of the delay was the fact that the Continental Shelf/seabed regime issue had to compete with more urgent matters for the time and attention of busy presidential advisors. The invasion of Cambodia is a case in point. A more fundamental source of delay, however, was the difficulty for White House officials of mastering the complex technical and legal issues of the seabed question. Mr. Kissinger was particularly reluctant to involve himself in a subject with which he had little experience. Hence the problem was shoved aside.

This state of affairs might have persisted indefinitely had not other parts of the White House intervened in the agency dispute. Because the Continental Shelf/seabed regime problem spans domestic as well as foreign policy considerations, Interior Department officials directly solicited the support of John Ehrlichman, the President's advisor for domestic affairs. Unlike Mr. Kissinger, Mr. Ehrlichman was quite prepared to take a position on this question after an initial briefing by Interior Department officials. Mr. Ehrlichman was concerned that an Executive branch policy in support of a narrow Continental Shelf would expose the President to the politically damaging claim of "giving away" the nation's mineral estate. Therefore, Ehrlichman opted for either the Interior Department or the original State Department position. Officials of the National Security Council received Mr. Ehrlichman's intervention in a matter of foreign policy with less than complete enthusiasm. NSC officials were concerned that American strategic interests would be gravely endangered by the wide Continental Shelf policies of the Interior and original State Department positions. Thus the lines were firmly drawn between the President's foreign and domestic affairs advisors and the issue was once again stalled.

External events, however, continued to force strenuous efforts within the White House to negotiate a mutually acceptable options paper for the the President. While the U.N. Seabed Committee was pressing ahead with deliberations, a growing number of countries were laying claim to extensive offshore jurisdiction -- Brazil to a 200 mile territorial sea and Canada to a 100 mile pollution safety zone. At the same time, news of the interagency dispute was leaking to Congress and the press. The Senate Interior and Insular Affairs Committee was threatening to hold hearings which would have exposed the interagency dispute and to issue a report on its own in the absence of a prompt Presidential decision.

The challenge, therefore, was to prepare an options memorandum for the President that was acceptable both to Ehrlichman and Kissinger. The NSC staff drafted a series of memorandums for review and comment by the domestic affairs staff. Of paramount concern to Mr. Ehrlichman in the first drafts was the NSC's ommission of the original State Department position as one of the options to go to the President. It was that position, in Mr. Ehrlichman's view, that offered the best compromise between domestic and foreign policy considerations. The Defense Department position did not ensure the national control over the valuable petroleum resources of the U.S. continental margin. The Interior Department position, on the other hand, ignored the problem of creeping jurisdiction. And, in a contest between the Richardson and the first State Department positions, Mr. Ehrlichman preferred the latter since it recognized the inherent legal rights of states to the resources of their continental margins.

The Ehrlichman views were taken into account in the final version of the option paper that was sent to the President over Mr. Kissinger's signature at the end of April. The NSC staff, however, was responsible for structuring the memorandum, giving it an obvious advantage in determining the President's decision. After setting out the four agency positions and their rationales and after explaining Mr. Ehrlichman's support for the original State Department, the Kissinger memorandum concluded with the recommendation that the President choose the Defense or the Richardson option. The Richardson position thereby became the obvious middle position, and it was that policy that was ultimately adopted by the President.

Following months of delay while the issue made its way to the White House, the President's decision was taken after only brief consideration and on the basis of a carefully constructed set of options. Once President Nixon selected the Richardson option, the "NSC system" again took over. In cooperation with the State Department, the victorious agency, the NSC staff drafted a National Security Decision Memorandum conveying the President's decision to the heads of all interested federal agencies. The NSDM not only outlined the principles that were to govern a prospective treaty to be submitted to the United Nations Seabed Committee, but it also specified that the State Department would be responsible for preparing the treaty, the U.S. negotiating position, and the necessary legislative measures in coordination with the Departments of Defense and Interior.

The stipulation that the State Department coordinate its efforts to negotiate a Seabed Treaty with both Interior and Defense merely confirmed the fact that the NSC system reserved all critical foreign policy issues for White House decision. From the time of the June 1969 National Security Study Memorandum, the State Department had been effectively precluded from making an independent decision on the seabed regime without the agreement of all affected agencies. The January 1970 meeting of the Under Secretaries Committee was simply one further step in the progress of the decision to the White House. Elliott Richardson, Chairman of the Committee, did not have the authority under the NSC system to impose a decision. His recommendation simply went to the President as one of several options advanced by the dissenting agencies. The options as they reached the President were carefully structured and articulated by Mr. Kissinger and his staff, with the intervention in this instance of Mr. Ehrlichman. At the top of the pyramid was the President, advised by Mr. Kissinger to adopt the Richardson or the Defense option. The success of the Richardson position lay as much in its presentation as in its intrinsic merit or persuasiveness. No doubt Mr. Kissinger's and Mr. Nixon's personal rapport with Mr. Richardson also played an important role in their choice.

While the NSC options system reserved the key for disputed ocean policy decisions for the White House, the implementation of those decisions was left to lower level bureaucrats. Important power, thereby, remained in the hands of the technicians who had mastered the complex legal, geological, strategic and economic ocean issues.

The President's Seabed Policy

With the issuance of the May 22 NSDM, the task of announcing and implementing the President's decision returned to the bureaucracy. The "President's seabed policy" was announced by John Stevenson, the Legal Advisor, and Ronald Zeigler at a White House press conference on May 23. The public was told that the President was calling for the renunciation of national claims to seabed resources beyond the depth of 200 meters and for the establishment, beyond this point, of an international regime to govern the exploitation of seabed resources. Two types of machinery would be created to authorize resource exploitation in this international seabed area. To the edge of the continental margin, an area called the "trusteeship zone," the coastal state would administer exploitation as a trustee for the international community. In return the "coastal state would receive a share of the international revenues from the zone in which it acts as a trustee." Beyond the continental margin, the international machinery would authorize and regulate exploitation and would collect "substantial mineral royalties" to be used for economic assistance to developing countries. In addition the international regime would formulate "rules to prevent unreasonable inteference with other uses of the oceans, to protect the ocean from pollution, to assure the integrity of the investment necessary for such exploitation, and to provide for peaceful and compulsory settlement of disputes."

The May 23 statement, Elliot Richardson informed the Congress, represented only an initial "approach to dealing with the exploitation of the continental margin." The President promised that the Executive would introduce more specific proposals at the U.N. Seabed Committee scheduled in August 1970. On August 3, the first day of the session, the United States presented a "United Nations Draft Convention on the International Seabed Area." Five officials from the Departments of State, Defense and Interior had drafted the seventy-eight articles and five appendices of the Convention. The ad hoc drafting committee included Bernard Oxman, of the Legal Advisor's office, chairman, Louis Sohn and Stuart McIntyre of the State Department, Leigh Ratiner of the Defense Department, and Vincent McKelvey of the Interior Department. This lengthy and complex document, rather than the President's May 23 statement, quickly became the focus of domestic opposition to a narrow offshore resource zone. While the President's announced decision was not considered a legitimate object of attack, its implementation in the draft Convention was.

Even before its presentation at the Seabed Committee, private industry, the Congress and the Interior Department had strenously opposed many of the draft treaty's provisions and had succeeded in securing some modifications. Then with the draft treaty's tabling at the Geneva meeting, the domestic contention over the extent of the Continental Shelf merged with United Nations debate over the breadth of an economic resource zone.

U.S. Territorial Sea, Straits and Fisheries Policy

The principle strategy behind the U.S. seabed proposal was to encourage other nations to adopt a narrow Continental Shelf policy. It was also hoped, at least by Defense Department officials, that the seabed proposal would have a positive effect on separate negotiations then underway regarding the breadth of the territorial sea, international straits and fisheries. The territorial sea, straits and fisheries issues had been linked together since 1967 and 1968 when they were first discussed with the Soviet Government and then with U.S. and Soviet allies. Within each Government agency the issues had been handled as a package by a group of officials distinct from that dealing with seabed policy.

Among the three issues, those of strategic importance--straits and the territorial sea -- were accorded primacy. Fisheries was incorporated within the policy package as a tradeoff for concessions on straits and territorial sea because there was no policy objection raised by the fishing industry. The United States position announced in 1970 was that it was prepared to recognize a twelve mile territorial sea only if freedom of transit through and over international straits were to be guaranteed by international agreement. If the breadth of the territorial sea were universally extended to twelve miles, 116 international straits would be covered by territorial waters. In these straits high seas corridors would cease to exist and transit would be subject to the regime of innocent passage. To avoid the application of coastal state discretion to these vessels, it was necessary to guarantee the right of freedom of transit.

Although the Soviets adopted a twelve mile territorial sea in 1927, they have since become a maritime power with global interests. They have therefore fully supported the U.S. position on freedom of transit through and over international straits. The interests of the Japanese and the Soviets, however, diverge from those of the United States over fisheries. The second and third largest fishing nations of the world, respectively, the Japanese and Soviets were not in accord with the preferential fishing rights the United States was prepared to grant to coastal nations dependent on their coastal fisheries. By the late 1960's nine Latin American nations had claimed zones of 200 miles to protect fishery resources off their shores. To halt the trend toward such claims and to induce these nations to roll back established claims, the United States proposed that special preferential rights over offshore living resources be granted to coastal nations. According to the concept of preferential rights, a coastal fishing nation would be able to reserve a portion of the catch off its shores for its own fishermen. The amount would be determined by the coastal State's economic dependence on or extent of investment in offshore fisheries. At the insistence of the Department of Defense, this proposal deliberately avoided the concept of a fishing zone that might subsequently evolve into a fixed area of expanded coastal state jurisdiction.

Among fishing nations, the United States ranks sixth, and it fishes off its own coasts as well as those of other nations. U.S. proposals with regard to preferential rights, therefore, were not detrimental to all U.S. fishing interests. They were, however, primarily determined by external rather than domestic considerations -- by the need to balance Soviet and Japanese distant water fishing interests with the coastal interests of developing countries and by the need to persuade the latter to accept a twelve mile territorial sea and freedom of transit through straits.

Reasons for the early lack of policy input by the U.S. fishing industry were twofold. First, the fishing industry, unlike the petroleum industry, simply lacked the knowledge that discussions were underway within and between governments and that the Department of Defense was determining the fisheries position in exchange for concessions on straits and the territorial sea. The second problem hampering industry policy input was that of internal differences within the industry between coastal and distant water fishing interests. With the public announcement of U.S. policy on straits, territorial seas, and fisheries of February 18, 1970, the industry was first apprised of governmental discussions. Although the Stevenson reference to preferential rights was quite sketchy in his speech to the Philadelphia Bar Association, it was sufficient to alarm the distant water fishing segments of the U.S. fishing industry. The reaction of the distant water fishermen to the preferential rights aproach was analogous to that of the Soviet Union and Japan. The U.S. coastal fishermen, on the other hand, shared the interests of developing coastal countries in preferential rights to offshore resources. Neither segment of the industry, however, appreciated being excluded from the policy deliberations. Despite intra-industry differences, they recognized that if they were to have a say in determining U.S. fisheries policy, they would have to act in concert.

The first sign of a tenuous resolution of industry differences was visible in the adoption of the "species approach" presented by the U.S. Government to the U.N. Seabed Committee on August 3, 1971. In this approach, the concept of preferential rights for the coastal state was applied only to stocks that were adjacent to the coast or that spawned in fresh water. Highly migratory oceanic stocks were excluded, thereby protecting the U.S. tuna fleets fishing off the west coast of Latin America. The U.S. proposed that the actual fishing capacity of a coastal state be used to determine the extent of its preferential rights in an offshore fishery. As that capacity expanded, so would its preferential rights. This posed an obvious problem with regard to phasing out other national fishing efforts in the area. In its approach to historic fishing rights, the U.S. "species approach" of 1971 resembled the 1970 U.S. seabed proposal. Both envisioned a strong role for international and regional organizations in the regulation of high seas resources in order to reduce pressure for unilateral extension of coastal state control over offshore resources. Provisions for international cooperation in the U.S. fishing proposal included inspection and dispute settlement as well as joint conservation measures to prevent overfishing. Only if all other measures failed was unilateral state action deemed acceptable.

The elaboration of the species approach in the U.S. August 1971 statement was one facet of a speech dealing with international straits and territorial seas as well. Whereas the fisheries segment of the speech showed an evolution from previous statements and reflected an increased industry input, the straits and territorial waters position remained essentially unchanged reflecting a consistent Defense Department support for these policies. The United States was prepared to accept a twelve mile limit if the right of free transit were provided for all vessels and aircraft through and over international straits overlapped by territorial seas. Mr. Stevenson stressed that free transit was a "limited but vital right" and added that the right was merely one of "transiting the straits, not of conducting any other activities." In a further elaboration of U.S. views, Stevenson stipulated that the coastal state could designate corridors suitable for transit, and international safety regulations would be agreed upon. The right of a vessel to transit, however, could not be left to the discretion of a coastal state.

ED. NOTE: The United States subsequently abandoned both its "trusteeship" concept for the seabed and its "species approach" for fisheries management in the face of overwhelming international support for the idea of a 200 mile economic resource zone, which emerged in the treaty as the exclusive economic zone.

Comptroller General of the U.S., INFORMATION ON UNITED STATES OCEANS INTERESTS TOGETHER WITH POSITIONS AND RESULTS, LAW OF THE SEA CONFERENCE AT CARACAS (ID-75-46; March 6, 1975) 5-9.

The United States is a seagoing nation, dependent on the oceans. Proper use and development of oceans is essential to the United States and to other countries of the world. U.S. Presidents have recognized the inadequacy of existing ocean law to prevent confict and have urged its modernization to insure orderly and peaceful development for the benefit of all mankind.

Organizations Responsible for Establishing and Implementing Policy

The President has overall responsibility for formulating and executing U.S. oceans policy. The National Security Council, composed of the President, Vice President, Secretaries of State and Defense, and Director of the Office of Emergency Preparedness, is the principal forum for Presidential consideration of this policy. This organization includes the National

Security Council Under Secretaries Committee, whose Chairman is the Deputy Secretary of State. Under his direction are the (1) Chairman of the National Security Council Interagency Task Force on the Law of the Sea to propose oceans policy alternatives, (2) Special and Deputy Representatives of the President for the Law of the Sea Conference to implement oceans policy, and (3) Office of the Law of the Sea Negotiations within the Department of State, which supports both the Chairman of the National Security Council Interagency Task Force on the Law of the Sea and the Special Representative of the President for the Law of the Sea Conference.

The National Security Council Interagency Task Force on the Law of the Sea evolved from an ad hoc Law of the Sea Task Force established in 1969 within the State Department. In 1973 this ad hoc

Task Force was formally placed under the direction of the National Security Council. The National Security Council Interagency Task Force on the Law of the Sea analyzes the pros and cons of different courses of action and formulates policy choices. These choices are reviewed by the National Security Council Under Secretaries Committee, then sent to the President, who ultimately decides U.S. oceans policy and positions. The executive group of the Task Force consists of representatives of the Departments of State, Defense, Interior, Commerce, Justice, Treasury, and Transportation; Federal Energy Office; Office of Management and Budget; Council on Environmental Quality; National Science Foundation; and Environmental Protection Agency.

The delegation to the third Law of the Sea Conference is responsible for implementing U.S. oceans policy and positions. The Special Representative of the President for the Law of the Sea Conference is the chairman of the delegation. The Chairman of the National Security Council Interagency Task Force on the Law of the Sea who is also the Deputy Special Representative of the President for the Law of the Sea Conference is vice chairman and a U.S. delegation representative. There were 15 alternates to the Caracas session, including representatives from the Executive Office of the President; Departments of State (3), Defense (2), Interior, Commerce, Treasury, and Transportation; Ambassador to Venezuela; Federal Energy Office; Environmental Protection Agency; National Science Foundation; and United States Mission to the United Nations. In addition to the representatives and alternates, there are a number of governmental staff advisers and other special advisers. Eight Senators and seven Members of the House of Representatives have been designated as advisers.

The Office of the Law of the Sea Negotiations was established in September 1973 and supports both the Special Representative of the President for the Law of the Sea Conference and the Chairman of the National Security Council Task Force on the Law of the Sea. On matters relating to the Law of the Sea negotiations, the Office of the Law of the Sea Negotiations supervises and coordinates positions within the executive branch, is responsible for action within the Department of State and for liason between the Congress and the interested public, and acts as the interagency and Department of State backstopping office.

Current Policy

President Johnson established the general direction of U.S. oceans policy when he stated in 1966 that:

> "Under no circumstances, we believe, must we ever allow the prospects of rich harvest and mineral wealth to create a new form of colonial competition among maritime nations. We must be careful to avoid a race to grab and hold the lands under the high seas. We must ensure that the deep seas and ocean bottoms are, and remain, the legacy of all human beings."

In the same year, the Marine Resources and Engineering Development Act became law (Public Law 89-454). This act declared U.S. policy to be to develop, encourage, and maintain a coordinated, comprehensive, and long-range program in marine science for the benefit of mankind and to assist in (1) protecting health and property, (2) enhancing commerce, transportation, and national security, (3) rehabilitating commercial fisheries, and (4) increasing use of these and other resources. The act also established the cabinet-level National Council on Marine Resources and Engineering Development and created a Commission on Marine Science, Engineering, and Resources. The work of the Council and the Commission helped the Government move from a narrow scientific approach to the oceans to a broad program of activities blending engineering, educational, legal, economic, and political considerations.

On May 23, 1970, President Nixon announced a new oceans policy designed to accomodate a wide variety of interests. He emphasized the inadequacy of the present law of the sea to meet the needs of modern technology and the concerns of the international community. He noted the (1) threat of unrestricted exploitation and conflicting jurisdiction if the law of the sea were not modernized on a multilateral basis, (2) ecological hazards of unregulated use of seabeds, and (3) special responsibility of major maritime powers, which have technological capacity to exploit seabeds, to provide leadership in working out an equitable international solution.

The new policy proposed that all national claims to natural resources of the seabeds beyond 200 meters in depth be renounced and that these resources be regarded as the common heritage of mankind under the jurisdiction of a new international agency. The President urged all nations to adopt a treaty embodying these principles as soon as possible. He indicated, however, that it was neither necessary nor desirable to try to halt exploration and exploitation of the seabeds beyond the depth of 200 meters during negotiations, if activities were subject to the international regime to be agreed upon and if the international regime included due protection of the integrity of investments made in the interim. In addition, President Nixon proposed that the treaty establish rules to prevent unreasonable interference with other sea uses, protect the seas from pollution, and provide for peaceful and compulsory settlement of disputes.

A central goal of the oceans policy is to achieve an agreement that accommodates rather than compromises basic interests of the United States and other nations.

To this end, U.S. objectives at the third U.N. Law of the Sea Conference are to negotiate a comprehensive treaty which would provide for

-- internationally agreed territorial sea limits not to exceed 12 nautical miles;

-- unimpeded transit on, over, and under straits used for international navigation;

-- full use and conservation of fishing resources;

-- international standards defining rights and duties of states on exploiting marine resources;

-- a satisfactory international legal system for rational and efficient development of deep seabed marine resources which guarantee access to U.S. firms on reasonable terms for development to occur;

-- protecting marine scientific research rights;

-- preserving and protecting the marine environment; and

-- agreement on compulsory settlement of disputes.

ED. NOTE: The foregoing materials indicate the development of U.S. oceans policy in the years leading up to the third U.N. Conference on the Law of the Sea. The policy remained relatively stable until the inauguration of the Reagan administration. As he had promised during his campaign, he immediately ordered a complete review of the texts then in existence at that Conference. The review, once completed, concluded that the emerging treaty did not meet U.S. national interests. As indicated elsewhere, the President subsequently decided that the U.S. would not sign or become a party to the treaty. That policy remains in place at the time of this writing.

For a complete picture of the development and implementation of oceans policy between the time that the Conference began, and its conclusion, see the reports of the U.S. delegation to the conference contained in <u>Occasional Paper No. 33 of the Law of the Sea Institute (1983).</u>

In December, 1992, the Panel on the Law of Ocean Uses,[3] a group sponsored by the Council on Ocean Law, met at Columbia University and prepared a report setting forth U.S. interests in the Law of the Sea Convention for transmission to the incoming Clinton administration and other policy-makers. The report follows.

UNITED STATES INTERESTS IN THE LAW OF THE SEA CONVENTION

Fundamental United States interests would be served by removing the obstacles to widespread ratification of the 1982 United Nations Convention on the Law of the Sea. U.S. interests in the Convention include those related to the use and protection of the oceans, international trade and economic growth, as well as national interests in order, stability, and orderly change in international relations.

<u>Fundamental U.S. Interests</u>

The Convention would protect and advance U.S. interests in the following ways:

1. <u>Security</u>: The provisions regarding free transit of straits and archipelagoes, and free navigation and overflight beyond the territorial sea of any state, protect the global mobility of our armed forces, including our capacity to "show the flag" without introducing U.S. forces into foreign territory. These provisions also enhance our ability to help implement decisions of the UN Security Council and other international organs.

2. <u>Economic</u>: The same provisions protect our historic interests in free movement of trade and communications on, under, and over the sea, and thereby promote economic growth in the U.S. and throughout the world. The provisions on resources give us virtually complete control over fisheries, oil, and other natural resources in vast areas off our coasts.

3. <u>Environment</u>: The Convention introduces into the Law of the Sea a comprehensive new code of environmental rights and duties. It provides a legal and institutional framework for concrete national and international measures to protect the marine environment from activities conducted on (or permitted by) any government anywhere in the oceans, in a manner that balances the various interests at stake.

4. <u>Dispute Resolution</u>: The arbitration and adjudication provisions of the Convention would promote not only the peaceful resolution of international, political, and commercial disputes, but more broadly, the rule of law. They would also provide a stronger basis for responding to excessive claims by other coastal states that impair U.S. rights to freedom of navigation and other interests.

U.S. policy during the last decade has been based on the assumption that, notwithstanding the absence of widespread ratification of the Convention and of compulsory arbitration, the U.S. can achieve equivalent restraints on national behavior by treating the provisions of the Convention (except for the deep seabed provisions) as declaratory of customary international law. That assumption has already been proved incorrect by the erosion of important terms of the Convention that has already

---

3. The panel consists of fourteen members, mostly academic, primarily lawyers, but other disciplines such as economics and political science are represented. Three of the panel members were also chief negotiators at the Third United Nations Law of the Sea Conference, and others served as advisors.

taken place, and further erosions are likely to accelerate with time. The basic need is to establish compelling legal restraints on other governments (and on our own policy makers) in responding to domestic political pressures. Binding treaty texts are more likely than customary law to induce self-restraint by politicians and national courts, and the dispute resolution provisions of the Convention can mitigate the precedential effects of unrestrained behavior.

The Changed Political Context

During the negotiation of the Convention, conflict emerged over the provisions establishing a regime for seabed mining of hard minerals beyond coastal state jurisdiction (Part XI of the Convention and related Annexes). As a result of the ideological struggle between the industrial countries and developing countries, and an overly optimistic view of the economic prospects for deep seabed mining, deep seabed mining came to be seen as the most important issue. That is a dangerously false view, given the fundamental U.S. interests which have been identified above. As a result of political dynamics, deep seabed mining was pushed far beyond its real significance and obscured more important matters.

Although few, if any, states have significant interests in deep seabed mining today, the political consequences of the ideological conflict of more than 10 years ago surrounding Part XI continue to inhibit widespread ratification of the Convention, particularly by industrialized countries. It now appears possible, however, to remove those obstacles because the large political context has changed in three important ways.

First, the end of the Cold War is transforming the international system as a whole with important implications for U.S. military policy. Today, small, rapidly developing crises in different parts of the globe respresent an increasing challenge to U.S. interests and international order. These kinds of conflicts highlight the importance of highly mobile forces that can be brought to bear decisively where needed, and newly enunciated U.S. defense strategies reflect this change of focus. Therefore, U.S. interests -- and the potential effectiveness of collective security operations -- require that the rules regarding navigation and overflight, particularly through strategic straits and confined seas, be solidified and confirmed in clear international law.

Secondly, there is a new interest among developing countries on responding to market forces in formulating economic policy, along with the realization that viable mining of the seabeds is several decades away.

Thirdly, there is increased global concern with and awareness of the difficulties of achieving effective protection of the environment and the need for international arrangements in this regard.

The 1992 Earth Summit in Rio de Janeiro effectively recognized the major contribution of the Law of the Sea Convention to protection of the environment. In our view, the Convention remains the strongest and most ambitious treaty regime for environmental protection ever negotiated. All marine-based sources of pollution anywhere in the world, whether from ships, oil rigs, or offshore terminals, are made subject to existing and emerging international standards. The duty of all states to respect those standards is subject to arbitration under the Convention. The full enjoyment of these benefits cannot be achieved without widespread ratification.

The developing country coalition has recognized that circumstances have changed. For the past two years, its members have been willing to engage in a dialogue with industrial countries to consider ways of removing the obstacles to widespread ratification of the Convention represented by Part XI. Developing countries and almost all industrialized countries are now fully engaged in informal consultations convened by the UN Secretary-General for these purposes. But the U.S. is not fully engaged in those consultations. It is important that the U.S. urgently become so engaged since two potential developments threaten to foreclose U.S. options to make desired changes in the Convention. These developments are the growing unwillingness of the developing country coalition to remain flexible and the possible entry into force of the Convention with the participation of our allies. (54 of the required 60 ratifications have been completed.)

The interests in effective security arrangements, in economic development through free markets, and in protecting the environment, together create a new opportunity to remove the obstacles to widespread ratification of the Convention posed by political objections to the deep seabed mining regime.

RECOMMENDATIONS

The United States should take steps to remove obstacles to widespread ratification of the Convention, including ratification by the U.S. As soon as possible, a study with recommendations and options for the new President, should:

* analyze the range of U.S. interests in the law of the sea and in the coming into force of the UN Convention on the Law of the Sea;

* propose strategies, including full participation in the informal consultations convened by the Secretary-General, to maximize the chances of achieving widespread ratification of the Convention both by industrial nations and by developing countries, by removing the obstacles to general acceptance posed by the Convention's deep seabed mining provisions;

* propose strategies to maintain, pending widespread ratification, domestic and international respect for the Convention's provisions on freedom of transit, on coastal state rights, environmental protection, and other freedoms of the sea;

*recommend an internal U.S. oceans policy-making structure to implement these strategies.

ANNEX A

CONVENTION ON THE HIGH SEAS

450 U.N.T.S. 82, 13 U.S.T. 2312. T.I.A.S. No. 5200, In force Sept. 30, 1962

The States Parties to this Convention,

Desiring to codify the rules of international law relating to the high seas,

Recognizing that the United Nations Conference on the Law of the Sea, held at Geneva from 24 February to 27 April 1958, adopted the following provisions as generally declaratory of established principles of international law.

Have agreed as follows:

Article 1

The term "high seas" means all parts of the sea that are not included in the territorial sea or in the internal waters of a State.

Article 2

The high seas being open to all nations, no State may validly purport to subject any part of them to its sovereignty. Freedom of the high seas is exercised under the conditions laid down by these articles and by the other rules of international law. It comprises, inter alia, both for coastal and non-coastal States:

(1) Freedom of navigation;

(2) Freedom of fishing;

(3) Freedom to lay submarine cables and pipelines:

(4) Freedom to fly over the high seas.

These freedoms, and others which are recognized by the general principles of international law, shall be exercised by all States with reasonable regard to the interests of other States in their exercise of the freedom of the high seas.

Article 3

1. In order to enjoy the freedom of the seas on equal terms with coastal States, States having no sea-coast should have free access to the sea. To this end States situated between the sea and a State having no sea-coast shall by common agreement with the latter and in conformity with existing international convention accord:

(a) To the State having no sea-coast, on a basis of reciprocity, free transit through their territory; and

(b) To ships flying the flag of that State treatment equal to that accorded their own ships, or to the ships of other States, as regards access to seaports and the use of such ports.

2. States situated between the sea and a State having no sea-coast shall settle, by mutual

agreement with the latter, and taking into account the rights of the coastal State or State of transit and the special conditions of the State having no sea-coast, all matters relating to freedom of transit and equal treatment in ports, in case such States are not already parties to existing international conventions.

Article 4

Every State, whether coastal or not, has the right to sail ships under its flag on the high seas.

Article 5

1. Each State shall fix the conditions for the grant of its nationality to ships, for the registration of ships in its territory, and for the right to fly its flag. Ships have the nationality of the State whose flag they are entitled to fly. There must exist a genuine link between the State and the ship; in particular, the State must effectively exercise its jurisdiction and control in administrative, technical and social matters over ships flying its flag.

2. Each State shall issue to ships to which it has granted the right to fly its flag documents to that effect.

Article 6

1. Ships shall sail under the flag of one State only and, save in exceptional cases expressly provided for in international treaties or in these articles, shall be subject to its exclusive jurisdiction on the high seas. A ship may not change its flag during a voyage or while in a port of call save in the case of a real transfer of ownershp or change of registry.

2. A ship which sails under the flags of two or more States, using them according to convenience, may not claim any of the nationalities in question with respect to any other State, and may be assimilated to a ship without nationality.

Article 7

The provisions of the preceding articles do not prejudice the question of ships employed on official service of an inter-governmental organization flying the flag of the organization.

Artice 8

1. Warships on the high seas have complete immunity from the jurisdiction of any State other than the flag State.

2. For the purposes of these articles, the term "warship" means a ship belonging to the naval forces of a State and bearing the external marks distinguishing warships of its nationality, under the command of an officer duly commissioned by the government and whose name apppears in the Navy list, and manned by a crew who are under regular naval discipline.

Article 9

Ships owned or operated by a State and used only on government non-commercial service shall, on the high seas, have complete immunity from the jurisdiction of any State other than the flag State.

Article 10

1. Every State shall take such measures for ships under its flag as are necessary to ensure safety at sea with regard inter alia to:

(a) The use of signals, the maintenance of communications and the prevention of collisions;

(b) The manning of shps and labour conditions for crews taking into account the applicable international labour instruments;

(c) The construction, equipment and seaworthiness of ships.

2. In taking such measures each State is required to conform to generally accepted international standards and to take any steps which may be necessary to ensure their observance.

Article 11

1. In the event of a collision or of any other incident of navigation concerning a ship on the high seas, involving the penal or disciplinary responsibility of the master or of any other person in the service of the ship, no penal or disciplinary proceedings may be instituted against such persons except before the judicial or administrative authorities either of the flag State or of the State of which such person is a national.

2. In disciplinary matters, the State which has issued a master's certificate or a certificate of competence or license shall alone be competent, after due legal process, to pronoumce the withdrawal of such certificates, even if the holder is not a national of the State which issued them.

3. No arrest or detention of the ship, even as a measure of investigation, shall be ordered by any authorities other than those of the flag State.

Article 12

1. Every State shall require the master of a ship sailing under its flag, in so far as he can do so without serious danger to the ship, the crew or the passengers,

(a) To render assistance to any person found at sea in danger of being lost;

(b) To proceed with all possible speed to the rescue of persons in distress if informed of their need for assistance, in so far as such action may reasonably be expected of him;

(c) After a collision, to render assistance to the other ship, her crew or her passengers and, where possible, to inform the other ships of the name of his own ship, her port of registry and the nearest port at which she will call.

2 Every coastal State shall promote the establishment and maintenance of an adequate and effective search and rescue service regarding safety on and over the sea and -- where circumstances so require -- by way of mutual regional arrangements co-operate with neighbouring States for this purpose.

Article 13

Every State shall adopt effective measures to prevent and punish the transport of slaves in ships authorized to fly its flag, and to prevent the unlawful use of its flag for that purpose. Any slave taking refuge on board any ship, whatever its flag, shall ipso facto be free.

Article 14

All States shall co-operate to the fullest possible extent in the repression of piracy on the high seas or in any other place outside the jurisdiction of any State.

Article 15

Piracy consists of any of the following acts:

(1) Any illegal acts of violence, detention or any act of depradation, committed for private ends by the crew or the passengers of a private ship or a private aircraft, and directed:

(a) On the high seas, against another ship or aircraft, or against persons or property on board such ship or aircraft;

(b) Against a ship, aircraft, persons or property in a place outside the jurisdiction of any State;

(2) Any act of voluntary participation in the operation of a ship or of an aircraft with knowledge of facts making it a pirate ship or aircraft;

(3) Any act of inciting or of intentionally facilitating an act described in sub-paragraph 1 or sub-paragraph 2 of this article.

Article 16

The acts of piracy, as defined in article 15, committed by a warship, government ship or government aircraft whose crew has mutinied and taken control of the ship or aircraft are assimilated to acts committed by a private ship.

Aricle 17

A ship or aircraft is considered a pirate ship or aircraft if it is intended by the person in dominant control to be used for the purpose of committing one of the acts referred to in article 15. The same applies if the ship or aircraft has been used to commit any such act, so long as it remains under the control of the persons guilty of that act.

Article 18

A ship or aircraft may retain its nationality although it has become a pirate ship or aircraft. The retention or loss of nationality is determined by the law of the State from which such nationality was derived.

Article 19

On the high seas, or in any place outside the jurisdiction of any State, every State may seize a pirate ship or aircraft, or a ship taken by piracy and under the control of pirates, and arrest the persons and seize the property on board. The courts of the State which carried out the seizure may decide upon the penalties to be imposed, and may also determine the action to be taken with regard to the ships, aircraft or property, subject to the rights of third parties acting in good faith.

Article 20

Where the seizure of a ship or aircraft on suspicion of piracy has been effected without adequate grounds, the State making the seizure shall be liable to the State the nationality of which is possessed by the ship or aircraft, for any loss or damage caused by the seizure.

Article 21

A seizure on account of piracy may only be carried out by warships or military aircraft, or other ships or aircraft on government service authorized to that effect.

Article 22

1. Except where acts of interference derive from powers conferred by treaty, a warship which encounters a foreign merchant ship on the high seas is not justified in boarding her unless there is reasonable ground for suspecting:

(a) That the ship is engaged in piracy; or

(b) That the ship is engaged in the slave trade; or

(c) That, though flying a foreign flag or refusing to show its flag, the ship is, in reality, of the same nationality as the warship.

2. In the cases provided for in sub-paragraphs (a), (b), and (c) above, the warship may proceed to verify the ship's right to fly its flag. To this end, it may send a boat under the command of an officer to the suspected ship. If suspicion remains after the documents have been checked, it may proceed to a further examination on board the ship, which must be carried out with all possible consideration.

3. If the suspicions prove to be unfounded, and provided that the ship boarded has not committed any act justifying them, it shall be compensated for any loss or damage that may have been sustained.

Article 23

1. The hot pursuit of a foreign ship may be undertaken when the competent authorities of the coastal State have good reason to believe that the ship has violated the laws and regulations of that State. Such pursuit must be commenced when the foreign ship or one of its boats is within the internal waters or the territorial sea or the contiguous zone of the pursuing State, and may only be continued outside the territorial sea or the contiguous zone if the pursuit has not been interrupted. It is not necessary that, at the time when the foreign ship within the territorial sea or the contiguous zone receives the order to stop, the ship giving the order should likewise be within the territorial sea or the contiguous zone. If the foreign ship is within a contiguous zone, as defined in article 24 of the Convention on the Territorial Sea and the Contiguous Zone, the pursuit may only be undertaken if there has been a violation of the rights for the protection of which the zone was established.

2. The right of hot pursuit ceases as soon as the ship pursued enters the territorial sea of its own country or of a third State.

3. Hot pursuit is not deemed to have begun unless the pursuing ship has satisfied itself by such practicable means as may be available that the ship pursued or one of its boats or other craft working

as a team and using the ship pursued as a mother ship are within the limits of the territorial sea, or as the case may be within the contiguous zone. The pursuit may only be commenced after a visual or auditory signal to stop has been given at a distance which enables it to be seen or heard by the foreign ship.

4. The right of hot pursuit may be exercised only by warships or military aircraft, or other ships or aircraft on government service specially authorized to that effect.

5. Where hot pursuit is effected by aircraft:

(a) The provisions of paragraph 1 to 3 of this article shall apply mutatis mutandis;

(b) The aircraft giving the order to stop must itself actively pursue the ship until a ship or aircraft of the coastal State, summoned by the aircraft, arrives to take over the pursuit, unless the aircraft is itself able to arrest the ship. It does not suffice to justify an arrest on the high seas that the ship was merely sighted by the aircraft as an offender or suspected offender, if it was not both ordered to stop and pursued by the aircraft itself or other aircraft or ships which continue the pursuit without interruption.

6. The release of a ship arrested within the jurisdiction of a State and escorted to a port of that State for the purpose of an enquiry before the competent authorities may not be claimed solely on the ground that the ship, in the course of its voyage, was escorted across a portion of the high seas, if the circumstances rendered this necessary.

7. Where a ship has been stopped or arrested on the high seas in circumstances which do not justify the exercise of the right of hot pursuit, it shall be compensated for any loss or damage that may have been thereby sustained.

Article 24

Every State shall draw up regulations to prevent pollution of the seas by discharge of oil from ships or pipelines or resulting from the exploitation and exploration of the seabed and its subsoil, taking account of existing treaty provisions on the subject.

Article 25

1. Every State shall take measures to prevent pollution of the seas from the dumping of radio-active waste, taking into account any standards and regulations which may be formulated by the competent international organizations.

2. All States shall co-operate with the competent international organizations in taking measures for the prevention of the pollution of the seas or air space above, resulting from any activities with radio-active materials or other harmful agents.

Article 26

1. All States shall be entitled to lay submarine cables and pipelines on the bed of the high seas.

2. Subject to its right to take reasonable measures for exploration of the continental shelf and the exploitation of its natural resources, the coastal State may not impede the laying or maintenance of such cables and pipelines.

3. When laying such cables and pipelines the State in question shall pay due regard to cables or pipelines already in position on the seabed. In particular, possibilities of repairing existing cables or pipelines shall not be prejudiced.

Article 27

Every State shall take the necessary legislative measures to provide that the breaking or injury by a ship flying its flag or by a person subject to its jurisdiction of a submarine cable beneath the high seas done wilfully or through culpable negligence, in such a manner as to be liable to interrupt or obstruct telegraphic or telephonic communications, and similarly the breaking or injury of a submarine pipeline or high-voltage power cable shall be a punishable offense. This provision shall not apply to any break or injury caused by persons who acted merely with the legitimate object of saving their lives or their ships, after having taken all necessary precautions to avoid such break or injury.

Article 28

Every State shall take the necessary legislative measures to provide that, if persons subject to its jurisdiction who are the owners of a cable or pipeline beneath the high seas, in laying or reparing that cable or pipeline, cause a break in or injury to another cable or pipeline, they shall bear the cost of the repairs.

Article 29

Every State shall take the necessary legislative measures to ensure that the owners of ships who can prove that they have sacrificed an anchor, a net or any other fishing gear, in order to avoid injuring a submarine cable or pipeline, shall be indemnified by the owner of the cable or pipeline, provided that the owner of the ship has taken all reasonable precautionary measures beforehand.

Article 30

The provisions of this Convention do not affect other conventions or other international agreements already in force, as between States Parties to them.

Article 31

This Convention shall, until October 1958, be open for signature by all States Members of the United Nations or of any of the specialized agencies, and by any other State invited by the General Assembly of the United Nations to become a Party to the Convention.

Articl 32

This Convention is subject to ratification. The instruments of ratification shall be deposited with the Secretary-General of the United Nations.

Article 33

This Convention shall be open for accession by any States belonging to any of the categories mentioned in article 31. The instruments of accession shall be deposited with the Secretary-General of the United Nations.

Article 34

1. This Convention shall come into force on the thirtieth day following the date of deposit of the twenty-second instrument of ratification or accession with the Secretary-General of the United

Nations.

2. For each State ratifying or acceding to the Convention after the deposit of the twenty-second instrument of ratification or accession, the Convention shall enter into force on the thirtieth day after deposit by such State of its instrument of ratification or accession.

Article 35

1. After the expiration of a period of five years from the date on which this Convention shall enter into force, a request for the revision of this Convention may be made at any time by any Contracting Party by means of a notification in writing addressed to the Secretary-General of the United Nations.

2. The General Assembly of the United Nations shall decide upon the steps, if any, to be taken in respect of such request.

Article 36

The Secretary-General of the United Nations shall inform all States Members of the United Nations and the other States referred to in article 31:

(a) Of signatures to this Convention and of the deposit of instruments of ratification or accession, in accordance with article 31, 32 and 33;

(b) Of the date on which this Convention will come into force, in accordance with article 34;

(c) Of requests for revision in accordance with article 35.

Article 37

The original of this Convention, of which the Chinese, English, French, Russian and Spanish texts are equally authentic, shall be deposited with the Secretary-General of the United Nations, who shall send certified copies thereof to all States referred to in article 31.

ANNEX B

CONVENTION ON THE TERRITORIAL SEA AND THE CONTIGUOUS ZONE
516 U.N.T.S. 205, 15 U.S.T. 1606, T.I.A.S. No. 5639, In force Sept. 10, 1964

The States Parties to this Convention have agreed as follows:

Part I

Territorial Sea

Section I. General

Article 1

1. The sovereignty of a State extends, beyond its land territory and its internal waters, to a belt of sea adjacent to its coast, described as the territorial sea.

2. This sovereignty is exercised subject to the provisions of these articles and to other rules of international law.

Article 2

The sovereignty of a coastal State extends to the air space over the territorial sea as well as to its bed and subsoil.

Section II. Limits of the Territorial Sea

Article 3

Except as otherwise provided in these articles, the normal baseline for measuring the breadth of the territorial sea is the low-water line along the coast as marked on large-scale charts officially recognized by the coastal State.

Article 4

1. In localities where the coast line is deeply indented and cut into, or if there is a fringe of islands along the coast in its immediate vicinity, the method of straight baselines joining appropriate points may be employed in drawing the baseline from which the breadth of the territorial sea is measured.

2. The drawing of such baselines must not depart to any appreciable extent from the general direction of the coast, and the sea areas lying within the lines must be sufficiently closely linked to the land domain to be subject to the regime of internal waters.

3. Baselines shall not be drawn to and from low-tide elevations, unless lighthouses or similar installations which are permanently above sea level have been built on them.

4. Where the method of straight baselines is applicable under the provisions of paragraph 1, account may be taken, in determining particular baselines, of economic interests peculiar to the region concerned, the reality and the importance of which are clearly evidenced by long usage.

5. The system of straight baselines may not be applied in such a manner a to cut off from the high seas the territorial sea of another State.

6. The coastal State must clearly indicate straight baselines on charts, to which due publicity must be given.

Article 5

1. Waters on the landward side of the baseline of the territorial sea form part of the internal waters of the State.

2. Where the establishment of a straight baseline in accordance with article 4 has the effect of enclosing as internal waters areas which previously had been considered as part of the territorial sea or of the high seas, a right of innocent passage, as provided in article 14 to 23, shall exist in those waters.

Article 6

The outer limit of the territorial sea is the line every point of which is at a distance from the nearest point of the baseline equal to the breadth of the territorial sea.

Article 7

1. This article relates only to bays the coasts of which belong to a single State.

2. For the purposes of these articles, a bay is a well-marked indentation whose penetration is in such proportion to the width of its mouth as to contain landlocked waters and constitutes more than a mere curvature of the coast. An indentation shall not, however, be regarded as a bay unless its area is as large as, or larger than, that of the semi-circle whose diameter is a line drawn across the mouth of that indentation.

3. For the purpose of measurement, the area of an indentation is that lying beteen the low-water mark around the shore of the indentation and a line joining the low-water marks of its natural entrance points. Where, because of the presence of islands, an indentation has more than one mouth, the semi-circle shall be drawn on a line as long as the sum total of the lengths of the lines across the different mouths. Islands within an indentation shall be included as if they were part of the water areas of the indentation.

4. If the distance between the low-water marks of the natural entrance points of a bay does not exceed twenty-four miles, a closing line may be drawn between these two low-water marks, and the waters enclosed thereby shall be considered as internal waters.

5. Where the distance between the low-water marks of the natural entrance points of a bay exceeds twenty-four miles, a straight baseline of twenty-four miles shall be drawn within the bay in such a manner as to enclose the maximum area of water that is possible with a line of that length.

6. The foegoing provisions shall not apply to so-called "historic" bays, or in any case where the straight baseline system provided for in article 4 is applied.

Article 8

For the purpose of delimiting the territorial sea, the outermost permanent harbour works which form an integral part of the harbour system shall be regarded as forming part of the coast.

Article 9

Roadsteads which are normally used for the loading, unloading and anchoring of ships, and which would otherwise be situated wholly or partly outside the outer limit of the territorial sea, are included in the territorial sea. The coastal State must clearly demarcate such roadsteads and indicate them on their charts together with their boundaries, to which due publicity must be given.

Article 10

1. An island is a naturally-formed area of land, surrounded by water, which is above water at high-tide.

2. The territorial sea of an island is measured in accordance with the provisions of these articles.

Article 11

1. A low-tide elevation is a naturally-formed area of land which is surrounded by and above water at low-tide but submerged at high-tide. Where a low-tide elevation is situated wholly or partly at a distance not exceeding the breadth of the territorial sea from the mainland or an island, the low-water line on that elevation may be used for the baseline for measuring the breadth of the territorial sea.

2. Where a low-tide elevation is wholly situated at a distance exceeding the breadth of the territorial sea from the mainland or an island, it has no territorial sea of its own.

Article 12

1. Where the coasts of two States are opposite or adjacent to each other, neither of the two States is entitled, failing agreement between them to the contrary, to extend its territorial sea beyond the median line every point of which is equidistant from the nearest points of the baselines from which the breadth of the territorial seas of each of the two States is measured. The provisions of this paragraph shall not apply, however, where it is necessary by reason of historic title or other special circumstances to delimit the territorial seas of two States in a way which is at variance with this provision.

2. The line of delimitation between the territorial seas of two States lying opposite to each other or adjacent to each other shall be marked on large-scale charts officially recognized by the coastal States.

Article 13

If a river flows directly into the sea, the baseline shall be a straight line across the mouth of the river between two points on the low-tide line of its banks.

Section III. Right of Innocent Passage

Sub-Section A. Rules Applicable to All Ships

Article 14

1. Subject to the provisions of these articles, ships of all States, whether coastal or not, shall enjoy the right of innocent passage through the territorial sea.

2. Passage means navigation through the territorial sea for the purpose either of traversing that sea without entering internal waters, or of proceeding to internal waters, or of making for the high seas from internal waters.

3. Passage includes stopping and anchoring, but only in so far as the same are incidental to ordinary navigation or are rendered necessary by force majeure or by distress.

4. Passage is innocent so long as it is not prejudical to the peace, good order or security of the coastal State. Such passage shall take place in conformity with these articles and with other rules of international law.

5. Passage of foreign fishing vessels shall not be considered innocent if they do not observe such laws and regulations as the coastal State may make and publish in order to prevent these vessels from fishing in their territorial sea.

6. Submarines are required to navigate on the surface and to show their flag.

Article 15

1. The coastal State must not hamper innocent passage through the territorial sea.

2. The coastal State is required to give appropriate publicity to any dangers to navigation, of which it has knowledge, within its territorial sea.

Article 16

1. The coastal State may take the necessary steps in its territorial sea to prevent passage which is not innocent.

2. In the case of ships proceeding to internal waters, the coastal State shall have the right to take the necessary steps to prevent any breach of the conditions to which admission of those ships to those waters is subject.

3. Subject to the provisions of paragraph 4, the coastal State may, without discrimination amongst foreign ships, suspend temorarily in specified areas of its territorial sea the innocent passage of foreign ships if such suspension is essential for the protection of its security. Such suspension shall take effect only after having been duly published.

4. There shall be no suspension of innocent passage of foreign ships through straits which are used for international navigation between one part of the high seas and another part of the high seas or the territorial sea of a foreign State.

Article 17

Foreign ships exercising the right of innocent passage shall comply with the laws and regulations enacted by the coastal State in conformity with these articles and other rules of international law and, in particular, with such laws and regulations relating to transport and navigation.

Sub-Section B. Rules Applicable to Merchant Ships

Article 18

1. No charge may be levied upon foreign ships by reason only of their passage through the territorial sea.

2. Charges may be levied upon a foreign ship passing through the territorial sea as payment only for specific services rendered to the ship. These charges shall be levied without discrimination.

Article 19

1. The criminal jurisdiction of the coastal State should not be exercised on board a foreign ship passing through the territorial sea to arrest any person or to conduct any investigation in connexion with any crime committed on board the ship during its passage, save only in the following cases:

(a) If the consequences of the crime extend to the coastal State; or

(b) If the crime is of a kind to disturb the peace of the country or the good order of its territorial sea; or

(c) If the assistance of the local authorities has been requested by the captain of the ship or by the consul of the country whose flag the ship flies; or

(d) If it is necessary for the suppression of illicit traffic in narcotic drugs.

2. The above provisions do not affect the right of the coastal State to take any steps authorized by its law for the purpose of making an arrest or investigation on board a foreign ship passing through the territorial sea after leaving internal waters.

3. In the cases provided for in paragraphs 1 and 2 of this article, the coastal State shall, if the captain so requests, advise the consular authority of the flag State before taking any steps, and shall facilitate contact between such authority and the ship's crew. In cases of emergency this notification may be communicated while the measures are being taken.

4. In considering whether or how an arrest should be made, the local authorities shall pay due regard to the interests of navigation.

5. The coastal State may not take any steps on board a foreign ship passing through the territorial sea to arrest any person or to conduct any investigation in connexion with any crime committed before the ship entered the territorial sea, if the ship, proceeding from a foreign port, is only passing through the territorial sea without entering internal waters.

Article 20

1. The coastal State should not stop or divert a foreign ship passing through the territoriaol sea

for the purpose of exercising civil jurisdiction in relation to a person on board the ship.

2. The coastal State may not levy execution against or arrest the ship for the purpose of any civil proceedings, save only in respect of obligations or liabilities assumed or incurred by the ship itself in the course or for the purpose of its voyage through the waters of the coastal State.

3. The provisions of the previous paragraph are without prejudice to the right of the coastal State, in accordance with its laws, to levy execution against or to arrest, for the purpose of any civil proceedings, a foreign ship lying in the territorial sea, or passing through the territorial sea after leaving internal waters.

Sub-Section C. Rules Applicable to Government Ships Other Than Warships

Article 21

The rules contained in sub-sections A and B shall also apply to government ships operated for commercial purposes.

Article 22

1. The rules contained in sub-sections A and in article 18 shall apply to government ships operated for non-commercial purposes.

2. With the exceptions as are contained in the provisions referred to in the preceding paragraph, nothing in these articles affects the immunities which such ships enjoy under these articles or other rules of international law.

Sub-Section D. Rule Applicable to Warships

Article 23

If any warship does not comply with the regulations of the coastal State concerning passage through the territorial sea and disregards any request for compliance which is made to it, the coastal State may require the warship to leave the territorial sea.

Part II

CONTIGUOUS ZONE

Article 24

1. In a zone of the high seas contiguous to its territorial sea, the coastal State may exercise the control necessary to:

(a) Prevent infringment of its customs, fiscal, immigration or sanitary regulations within its territory or territorial sea;

(b) Punish infringement of the above regulations committed within its territory or territorial sea.

2. The contiguous zone may not extend beyond twelve miles from the baseline from which the breadth of the territorial sea is measured.

3. Where the coasts of two States are opposite or adjacent to each other, neither of the two States, failing agreement between them to the contrary, to extend its contiguous zone beyond the median line every point of which is equidistant from the nearest points on the baselines from which the breadth of the territorial sea of the two States is measured.

Part III

FINAL ARTICLES

Article 25

The provisions of this Convention shall not affect conventions or other international agreements already in force, as between States Parties to them.

Article 26

This Convention shall, until 31 October 1958, be open for signature by all States Members of the United Nations or of any of the specialized agencies, and by any other State invited by the General Assembly of the United Nations to become a Party to the Convention.

Article 27

This Convention is subject to ratification. The instruments of ratification shall be deposited with the Secretary-General of the United Nations.

Article 28

This Convention shall be open for accession by any States belonging to any of the categories mentioned in article 26. The instruments of accession shall be deposited with the Secretary-General of the United Nations.

Article 29

1. This Convention shall come into force on the thirtieth day following the date of deposit of the twenty-second instrument of ratification or accession with the Secretary-General of the United Nations.

2. For each State ratifying or acceding to the Convention after the deposit of the twenty-second instrument of ratification or accession, the Convention shall enter into force on the thirteenth day after deposit by such State of its instrument of ratification or accession.

Article 30

1. After the expiration of five years from the date on which this Convention shall enter into force, a request for the revision of this Convention may be made at any time by any Contracting Party by means of a notification in writing addressed to the Secretary-General of the United Nations.

2. The General Assembly of the United Nations shall decide upon the steps, if any, to be taken in respect of such request.

Article 31

The Secretary-General of the United Nations shall inform all States Members of the United Nations and the other States referred to in article 26:

(a) Of signatures to this Convention and of the deposit of instruments of ratification or accession, in accordance with articles 26, 27 and 28;

(b) Of the date on which this Convention will come into force, in accordance with article 29;

(c) Of requests for revision in accordance with article 30.

Article 32

The origninal of this Convention, of which the Chinese, English, French, Russian, and Spanish texts are equally authentic, shall be deposited with the Secretary-General of the United Nations, who shall send certified copies thereof to all States referred to in article 26.

ANNEX C

CONVENTION ON THE CONTINENTAL SHELF
499 U.N.T.S.311, 15 U.S.T. 471, T.I.A.S. No. 5578, In force June 10, 1964

The States Parties to this Convention

Have agreed as follows:

Article 1

For the purposes of these articles, the term "continental shelf" is used as referring (a) to the seabed and subsoil of the submarine areas adjacent to the coast but outside the area of the territorial sea, to a depth of 200 metres or, beyond that limit, to where the depth of the superjacent waters admits of the exploitation of the natural resources of the said areas; (b) to the seabed and subsoil of similar submarine areas adjacent to the coasts of islands.

Article 2

1. The coastal State exercises over the continental shelf sovereign rights for the purpose of exploring it and exploiting its natural resources.

2. The rights referred to in paragraph 1 of this article are exclusive in the sense that if the coastal State does not explore the continental shelf or exploit its natural resources, no one may undertake these activities, or make a claim to the continental shelf, without the express consent of the coastal State.

3. The rights of the coastal State over the continental shelf do not depend on occupation, effective or notional, or on any express proclamation.

4. The natural resources referred to in these articles consist of the mineral and other non-living resources of the seabed and subsoil together with living organisms belonging to sedentary species, that is to say, organisms which, at the harvestable stage, either are immobile on or under the seabed or are unable to move except in constant physical contact with the seabed or the subsoil.

Article 3

The rights of the coastal State over the continental shelf do not affect the legal status of the superjacent waters as high seas, or that of the airspace above those waters.

Aricle 4

Subject to its right to take reasonable measures for the exploration of the continental shelf and the exploitation of its natural resources, the coastal State may not impede the laying or maintenance of submarine cables or pipelines on the continental shelf.

Article 5

1. The exploration of the continental shelf and the exploitation of its natural resources must not result in any unjustifiable interference with navigation, fishing or the conservation of the living resources of the sea, nor result in any interference with fundamental oceanographic or other scientific

research carried out with the intention of open publication.

2. Subject to the provisions of paragraphs 1 and 6 of this article, the coastal State is entitled to construct and maintain or operate on the continental shelf installations and other devices necessary for its exploration and the exploitation of its natural resources, and to establish safety zones around such installations and devices and to take in those zones measures necessary for their protection.

3. The safety zones referred to in paragraph 2 of this article may extend to a distance of 500 metres around the installations and other devices which have been erected, measured from each point of their outer edge. Ships of all nationalities must respect these safety zones.

4. Such installations and devices, though under the jurisdiction of the coastal State, do not possess the status of islands. They have no territorial sea of their own, and their presence does not affect the delimitation of the territorial sea of the coastal State.

5. Due notice must be given of the construction of any such installations, and permanent means for giving warning of their presence must be maintained. Any installations which are abandoned or disused must be entirely removed.

6. Neither the installations or devices, nor the safety zones around them, may be established where interference may be caused to the use of recognized sea lanes essential to international navigation.

7. The coastal State is obliged to undertake, in the safety zones, all appropriate measures for the protection of the living resources of the sea from harmful agents.

8. The consent of the coastal State shall be obtained in respect of any research concerning the continental shelf and undertaken there. Nevertheless the coastal State shall not normally withhold its consent if the request is submitted by a qualified institution with a view to purely scientific research into the physical or biological characteristics of the continental shelf, subject to the proviso that the coastal State shall have the right, if it so desires, to participate or to be represented in the research, and that in any event the results should be published.

Article 6

1. Where the same continental shelf is adjacent to the territories of two or more States whose coasts are opposite to each other, the boundary of the continental shelf appertaining to such States shall be determined by agreement between them. In the absence of agreement, and unless another boundary line is justified by special circumstances, the boundary is the median line, every point of which is equidistant from the nearest points of the baselines from which the territorial sea of each State is measured.

2. Where the same continental shelf is adjacent to the territories of two adjacent States, the boundary of the continental shelf shall be determined by agreement between them. In the absence of agreement, and unless another boundary line is justified by special circumstances, the boundary shall be determined by application of the principle of equidistance from the nearest points of the baselines from which the breadth of the territorial sea of each State is measured.

3. In delimiting the boundaries of the continental shelf, any lines which are drawn in accordance with the principles set out in paragraphs 1 and 2 of this article should be defined with reference to charts and geographical features as they exist at a particular date, and reference should be made to fixed permanent identifiable points on the land.

Article 7

The provisions of these articles shall not prejudice the right of the coastal State to exploit the subsoil by means of tunnelling irrespective of the depth of water above the subsoil.

Article 8

This Convention shall, until 31 October 1958, be open for signature by all States Members of the United Nations or any of the specialized agencies, and by any other State invited by the General Assembly of the United Nations to become a Party to the Convention.

Article 9

This Convention is subject to ratification. The instruments of ratification shall be deposited with the Secretary-General of the United Nations.

Article 10

This Convention shall be open for accession by any States belonging to any of the categories mentioned in article 8. The instruments of accession shall be deposited with the Secretary-General of the United Nations.

Article 11

1. This Convention shall come into force on the thirtieth day following the date of desposit of the twenty-second instrument of ratification or accession with the Secretary-General of the United Nations.

2. For each State ratifying or acceding to the Convention after the twenty-second instrument of ratification or accession, the Convention shall enter into force on the thirtieth day after deposit by such State of its instrument of ratification or accession.

Article 12

1. At the time of signature, ratification or accession, any State may make reservations to articles of the Convention other than to article 1 to 3 inclusive.

2. any Contracting State making a reservation in accordance with the preceding paragraph may at any time withdraw the reservation by a communication to that effect addressed to the Secretary-General of the United Nations.

Article 13

1. After the expiration of five years from the date on which this Convention shall enter into force, a request for the revision of this Convention may be made at any time by any Contracting Party by means of a notification in writing addressed to the Secretary-General of the United Nations.

2. The General Assembly of the United Nations shall decide upon the steps, if any, to be taken in respect of such request.

Article 14

The Secretary-General of the United Nations shall inform all States Members of the United Nations and the other States referred to in article 8:

(a) Of signatures to this Convention and of the deposit of instruments or ratification or accession, in accordance with article 8, 9 and 10;

(b) Of the date on which this Convention will come into force, in accordance with article 22;

(c) Of requests for revision in accordance with article 13;

(d) Of reservations to this Convention, in accordance with article 12.

Article 15

The original of this Convention, of which the Chinese, English, French, Russian and Spanish texts are equally authentic, shall be deposited with the Secretary-General of the United Nations, who shall send certified copies thereof to all States referred to in article 8.

ANNEX D

CONVENTION ON FISHING AND CONSERVATION OF THE LIVING RESOURCES OF THE HIGH SEAS

559 U.N.T.S. 285, 17 U.S.T. 138, T.I.A.S. No. 5969, In force March 20, 1966

The States Parties to this Convention,

Considering that the development of modern techniques for the exploitation of the living resource of the sea, increasing man's ability to meet the need of the world's expanding population for food, has exposed some of these resources to the danger of being over-exploited,

Considering also that the nature of the problems involved in the conservation of the living resources of the high seas is such that there is a clear necessity that they be solved, whenever possible, on the basis of international co-operation through the concerted action of all the States concerned,

Have agreed as follows:

Article 1

1. All States have the right for their nationals to engage in fishing on the high seas, subject (a) to their treaty obligations, (b) to the interests and rights of coastal States as provided for in this Convention, and (c) to the provisions contained in the following articles concerning conservation of the living resources of the high seas.

2. All States have the duty to adopt, or to co-operate with other States in adopting, such measures for their respective nationals as may be necessary for the conservation of the living resources of the high seas.

Article 2

As employed in this Convention, the expression "conservation of the living resources of the high seas," means the aggregate of the measures rendering possible the optimum sustainable yield from those resources so as to secure a maximum supply of food and other marine products. Conservation programmes should be formulated with a view to securing in the first place a supply of food for human consumption.

Article 3

A State whose nationals are engaged in fishing any stock or stocks of fish or other living marine resources in any area of the high seas where the nationals of other States are not thus engaged shall adopt, for its own nationals, measures in that area when necessary for the purpose of the conservation of the living resources affected.

Article 4

1. If the nationals of two or more States are engaged in fishing the same stock or stocks of fish or other living marine resources in any area or areas of the high seas, these States shall, at the request of any of them, enter into negotiations with a view to prescribing by agreement for their nationals the necessary measures for the conservation of the living resources affected.

2. If the States concerned do not reach agreement within twelve months, any of the parties may initiate the procedure contemplated by article 9.

Article 5

1. If, subsequent to the adoption of the measures referred to in article 3 and 4, nationals of other States engage in fishing the same stock or stocks of fish or other living marine resources in any area or areas of the high seas, the other States shall apply the measures, which shall not be discriminatory in form, to their own nationals not later than seven months after the date on which the measures shall have been notified to the Director-General of the Food and Agriculture Organization of the United Nations. The Director-General shall notify such measures to any State which so requests and, in any case, to any State specified by the State initiating the measure.

2. If these other States do not accept the measures so adopted and if no agreement can be reached within twelve months, any of the interested parties may initiate the procedure contemplated by article 9. Subject to paragraph 2 of article 10, the measures adopted shall remain obligatory pending the decision of the special commission.

Article 6

1. A coastal State has a special interest in the maintenance of the productivity of the living resources in any area of the high seas adjacent to its territorial sea.

2. A coastal State is entitled to take part on an equal footing in any system of research and regulation for purposes of conservation of the living resources of the high seas in that area, even though its nationals do not carry on fishing there.

3. A State whose nationals are engaged in fishing in any area of the high seas adjacent to the territorial sea of a State shall, at the request of that coastal State, enter into negotiations with a view to prescribing by agreement the measures necessary for the conservation of the living resources of the high seas in that area.

4. A State whose nationals are engaged in fishing in any area of the high seas adjacent to the territorial sea of a coastal State shall not enforce conservation measures in that area which are opposed to those which have been adopted by the coastal State, but may enter into negotiations with the coastal State with a view to prescribing by agreement the measures necessary for the conservation of the living resources in that area.

5. If the States concerned do not reach agreement with respect to conservation measures within twelve months, any of the parties may initiate the procedure contemplated by article 9.

Article 7

1. Having regard to the provisions of paragraph 1 of article 6, any coastal State may, with a view to the maintenance of the productivity of the living resources of the sea, adopt unilateral measures of conservation appropriate to any stock of fish or other marine resources in any area of the high seas adjacent to its territorial sea, provided that negotiations to that effect with other States concerned have not led to an agreement within six months.

2. The measures which the coastal State adopts under the previous paragraph shall be valid as to other States only if the following requirements are fulfilled:

(a) That there is a need for urgent application of conservation measures in the light of the existing knowledge of the fishery;

(b) That the measures adopted are based on appropriate scientific findings;

(c) That such measures do not discriminate in form or in fact against foreign fishermen.

3. These measures shall remain in force pending the settlement, in accordance with the relevant provisions of this Convention, of any disagreement as to their validity.

4. If the measures are not accepted by other States concerned, any of the parties may initiate the procedure contemplated by article 9. Subject to paragraph 2 of article 10, the measures adopted shall remain obligatory pending the decision of the special commission.

5. The principles of geographical demarcation as defined in article 12 of the Convention on the Territorial Sea and the Contiguous Zone shall be adopted when coasts of different States are involved.

Article 8

1. Any State which, even if its nationals are not engaged in fishing in an area of the high seas not adjacent to its coast, has a special interest in the conservation of the living resources of the high seas in that area, may request the State or States whose nationals are engaged in fishing there to take the necessary measures of conservation under article 3 and 4 respectively, at the same time mentioning the scientific reasons which in its opinion make such measures necessary, and indicating its special interest.

2. If no agreement is reached within twelve months, such State may initiate the procedure contemplated by article 9.

Article 9

1. Any dispute which may arise between States under articles 4, 5, 6, 7 and 8 shall, at the request of any of the parties, be submitted for settlement to a special commission of five members, unless the parties agree to seek a solution by another method of peaceful settlement, as provided for in Article 33 of the Charter of the United Nations.

2. The members of the commission, one of whom shall be designated as chairman, shall be named by agreement between the States in dispute within three months of the request for settlement in accordance with the provisions of this article. Failing agreement they shall, upon the request of any State party, be named by the Secretary-General of the United Nations, within a further three-month period, in consultation with the States in dispute and with the President of the International Court of Justice and the Director-General of the Food and Agriculture Organization of the United Nations, from amongst well-qualified persons being nationals of States not involved in the dispute and specializing in legal, adminstrative or scientific questions relating to fisheries, depending upon the nature of the dispute to be settled. Any vacancy arising after the original appointment shall be filled in the same manner as provided for the initial selection.

3. Any State party to proceedings under these articles shall have the right to name one of its nationals to the special commission, with the right to participate fully in the proceedings on the same footing as a member of the commission, but without the right to vote or to take part in the writing of the commission's decision.

Article 19

1. at the time of signature, ratification or accession, any State may make reservations to articles of the Convention other than to articles 6, 7, 9, 10, 11 and 12.

2. Any contracting State making a reservation in accordance with the preceding paragraph may at any time withdraw the reservation by a communication to that effect addressed to the Secretary-General of the United Nations.

Article 20

1. After the expiration of five years from the date on which this Convention shall enter into force, a request for the revision of this Convention may be made at any time by any contracting party by means of a notification in writing addressed to the Secretary-General of the United Nations.

2. The General Assembly of the United Nations shall decide upon the steps, if any, to be taken in respect of such request.

Article 21

The Secretary-General of the United Nations shall inform all States Members of the United Nations and the other States referred to in article 15:

(a) Of signatures to this Convention and of the deposit of instruments of ratification or accession, in accordance with article 15, 16 and 17;

(b) Of the date on which this Convention will come into force, in accordance with article 18;

(c) Of requests for revision in accordance with article 20;
(d) Of reservations to this Convention, in accordance with article 19.

Article 22

The original of this Convention, of which the Chinese, English, French, Russian and Spanish texts are equally authentic, shall be deposited with the Secretary-General of the United Nations, who shall send certified copies thereof to all States referred to in article 15.

ANNEX E

OPTIONAL PROTOCOL OF SIGNATURE

The States Parties to this Protocol and to any one or more of the Conventions on the Law of the Sea adopted by the United Nations Conference on the Law of the Sea held at Geneva from 24 February to 27 April 1958,

Expressing their wish to resort, in all matters concerning them in respect of any dispute arising out of the interpretation or application of any article of any Convention on the Law of the Sea of 29 April 1958, to the compulsory jurisdiction of the International Court of Justice, unless some other form of settlement is provided in the Convention or has been agreed upon by the Parties within a reasonable period,

Have agreed as follows:

Article I

Disputes arising out of the interpretation or application of any Convention on the Law of the Sea shall lie within the compulsory jursidiction of the International Court of Justice, and may accordingly be brought before the Court by an application made by any party to the dispute being a Party to this Protocol.

Article II

This undertaking relates to all the provisions of any Convention on the Law of the Sea except, in the Convention on Fishing and Conservation of the Living Resources of the High Seas, articles 4, 5, 6, 7, and 8, to which articles 9, 10, 11 and 12 of that Convention remain applicable.

Article III

The Parties may agree, within a period of two months after one party has described its opinion to the other that a dispute exists, to resort not to the International Court of Justice but to an arbitral tribunal. After the expiry of the said period, either Party to this Protocol may bring the dispute before the Court by an application.

Article IV

1. Within the same period of two months, the Parties to this Protocol may agree to adopt a conciliation procedure before resorting to the International Court of Justice.

2. The conciliation commission shall make its recommendations within five months after its appointment. If its recommendations are not adopted by the parties to the dispute within two months after they have been delivered, either party may bring the dispute before the Court by an application.

Article V

This Protocol shall remain open for signature by all States who become Parties to any Convention on the Law of the Sea adopted by the United Nations Conference on the Law of the Sea and is subject to ratification, where neccessary, according to the constitutional requirements of the signatory States.

Article VI

The Secretary-General of the United Nations shall inform all States who become Parties to any Convention on the Law of the Sea adopted by the United Nations Conference on the Law of the Sea and is subject to ratification, where necessary, according to the constitutional requirements of the signatory States.

Article VII

The original of this Protocol, of which the Chinese, English, French, Russian and Spanish texts are equally authentic, shall be deposited with the Secretary-General of the United Nations, who shall send certified copies to all States referred to in Article 4.

INDEX

Agreement for Implementation, the "Boat Paper" 344
Alexander, L.M. 455
Anti-Smuggling Act of 1935 128
Archipelagic Sealanes Passage 121
Barros and Johnson 471
Baselines, Islands 147
Baselines, Normal 145
Baselines, Permanent Harbor Works 173
Baselines, Straight 151
Bays, Bounded by Two or more States 172
Bays, Historic 162
Bays, Juridical 160
Boundary Delimitation, Continental Shelf 218
Boundary Delimitation, Exclusive Economic Zone 220
Boundary Delimitation, Territorial Sea 216
Canada v. France, Maritime Boundary 247
Christy, Francis T. 272
Churchill and Lowe 76, 81, 125, 137, 151, 172. 175
Clingan, Thomas A., Jr. 35, 466, 517, 568
Collision Jurisdiction
Continental Shelf Doctrine, Evolution of 183
Continental Shelf, and Federalism 213
Continental Shelf, Geology of 177
Continental Shelf, Oil and Gas Technology 181
Continental Shelf, Resources of 179
Continental Shelf, Resoures Included 190
Continental Shelf, Rights Exercisable 190
Continental Shelf, Seaward Extent 200
Continental Shelf, Structures Permitted 208
Convention Concerning Regime of Straits, Dardanelles 113
Convention on Civil Liability, Oil Pollution 476
Convention on Compensation, Oil Pollution 477
Convention on Ocean Dumping 506
Convention on the Prevention of Pollution by Oil 479
Convention Relating to Intervention 485
Corfu Channel Case 110, 472
Dean, Arthur H. 89
Declaration of Panama - Mutual Security 131
Deep Seabed Hard Minerals Act 321
Deep Seabed Mining, The Moratorium Resolution 275
Deep Seabed Mining, The Principles Resolution 278
Deep Seabed Mining, the UNCLOS III Regime, Policies 282
Deep Seabed Mining, the UNCLOS III Regime, Powers of the Assembly 285
Deep Seabed Mining, the UNCLOS III Regime, Principles 282
Deep Seabed Mining, the UNCLOS III Regime, Production Limitations 302
Deep Seabed Mining, the UNCLOS III Regime, Qualification of Applicants 298
Deep Seabed Mining, the UNCLOS III Regime, Subsidiary Organs 292
Deep Seabed Mining, the UNCLOS III Regime, the Authority 283
Deep Seabed Mining, the UNCLOS III Regime, the Banking System 296
Deep Seabed MIning, the UNCLOS III Regime, the Council 287

Deep Seabed Mining, the UNCLOS III Regime, the Parallel System 296
Deep Seabed Mining, UNCLOS III Regime, Amendments 313
Deep Seabed Mining, UNCLOS III Regime, Financial Implications 304
Deep Seabed Mining, UNCLOS III Regime, Investment Protection 315
Deep Seabed Mining, UNCLOS III Regime, Plans of Work 297, 299
Deep Seabed Mining, UNCLOS III Regime, Production Authorizations 301
Deep Seabed Mining, UNCLOS III Regime, Review Conference 311
Deep Seabed Mining, UNCLOS III Regime, Transfer of Technology 309
Deep Seabed, Geology and Technology 264
Deep Seabed, in the United Nations 269
Deep Seabed, the Seabed Committee 269
Dispute Settlement, Procedures for, Generally 517
Dispute Settlement, Procedures under the Convention 527
Enclosed and Semi-enclosed Seas 39
Exclusive Economic Zone 24
Fisheries Case (U.K. v. Norway) 152
Fisheries, Bilateral Agreements 368
Fisheries, Domestic Fisheries Management 395
Fisheries, Exclusive Fishing Zones 378, 387
Fisheries, International Enforcement Problems 427
Fisheries, Limited Entry 363
Fisheries, Management Objectives 359
Fisheries, Management Options 361
Fisheries, Marine Mammals and GATT 432
Fisheries, Multilateral Agreements 373
Fishery Conservation and Management Act (Magnusson Act) 396
Freedom of the High Seas, Early History and Evolution of Doctrine 10
Freedom of the High Seas, Treaty Provisions 21, 49
Gillam v. United States 68
Gulf of Maine Case 237
Harlow, Bruce 577
High Seas, Cables and Pipelines 71
High Seas, Collision Jurisdiction 56
High Seas, Hot Pursuit 62
High Seas, Immunity of Vessels 54
High Seas, Narcotic Drugs 61
High Seas, Piracy 58
High Seas, Rules Pertaining to Flags and Nationality 49
High Seas, Slavery 57
Hodgson, Robert 145, 261
Hollick, A. 269, 592
Hugo Grotius 12
I'm Alone, The 65
Innocent Passage, Generally 98
Innocent Passage, UNCLOS III 101
Innocent Passage, Warships 101
Internal Waters, Access to 76
Internal Waters, Coastal State Authority 79
Internal Waters, Definition 75
Islands, Problems of 260
John Selden 18
Johnston, Douglas 359

Jones, G. Kevin 179
Kindt, J.W. 504
Knight, H. Gary 177, 490, 576, 588
Landlocked States 42
Lansford (Water Log) 363
Low Tide Elevations 174
Mare Clausum 18
Mare Liberum 12
Marine Environment, Ocean Dumping 504
Marine Environment, Responsibilty and Liability 471
Marine Environment, Sources of Pollution 466
Marine Environment, UNCED 515
Marine Environment, UNCLOS Provisions 492
Marine Sanctuaries Act 513
Marine Scientific Research, Conduct of under the Convention 442
Marine Scientific Research, Goals of 435
Marine Scientific Research, International Cooperation 452
Marine Scientific Research, Transfer of Technology 460
Maritime Boundary, Mexico - United States 220
McConnell, Moira 49
McDougal and Burke 142
McKelvey and Wang 264
Miles and Burke 428
Military Use of the Environment, Generally 460
Military Use of the Seabed 561
Military Use, Anti-Submarine Warfare 566
Military Use, National Security Issues 579
Military Use, Problems of Naval Mobility 568
Military Use, Zones of Peace and Security 577
Nandan, Satya 337
Narcotic Drugs
Newton, W. Frank 19
North Sea Continental Shelf Cases 189, 222
Note from Thomas Jefferson to the British Minister 84
Nuclear Test Ban Treaty 564
Oil Pollution Liability under Treaties Other Than UNCLOS 475
Orrego, Francisco 27
Outer Continental Shelf Lands Act 211
Pardo, Arvid 10
Petroleum Development Ltd. v. Sheik of Abu Dhabi 186
Pharand, Donat 162
Piracy 58
Presential Sea 27
Presidential Proclamation, Continental Shelf 184
Presidential Proclamation, Exclusive Economic Zone 395
Presidential Proclamation, Fisheries 379
Presidential Proclamation, Territorial Sea 97
Report of Panel on Oceanography, PSAC 435
Report of the Comptroller General, 1975 601
Report of the Marine Science Commission 177, 587
Report of the Merchant Marine and Fisheries Committee 372
Rivers Emptying into the Sea 175

Roadsteads 169
Santiago Declaration 380
Schachte, William 119, 579
Seabed Interim Arrangements (Mini-treaty) 330
Shalowitz, Aaron 147, 148, 161
Sinjela, Mpazi 43
Slavery 57
Sohn and Gustafson 557
Soons, A. 452
Stevenson, John R. 96
Stockholm Declaration 473
Straits Used for International Navigation 110
Study, U.N. Secretariate, Economic Implications of Mining 266
Study, U.N.Secretariate, Continental Shelf 201
Territorial Sea, Breadth, UNCLOS I and II 86
Territorial Sea, Breadth, UNCLOS III 97
Territorial Sea, Legal Regime 81
Territorial Sea, Presidential Proclamation on 97
Trail Smelter Arbitration 472
Treasure Salvors v. Unidentified Wreck 193
Tunisia/Libya Case, Continental Shelf 229
U.K./France Arbitration, Maritime Boundary 225
U.S./Great Britain - Smuggling 127
U.S./USSR Agreement, Cooperative MSR Studies 457
UN Resolution, General Principles 278
UN Resolution, The Moratorium 275
UNCLOS III, Drafting Committee 8
UNCLOS III, Negotiations 5
UNCLOS III, Rules of Procedure 3
UNCLOS III, Structure 1
United Kingdom v. Iceland, Fisheries Case 381
United States Ocean Pollicy, Generally
United States v. Alaska 167
United States v. Alexander 199
United States v. California 159
United States v. Conroy 104
United States v. F/V Taiyo Maru 68
United States v. Louisiana 160
United States v. Mexico (Kate A. Hoff Claim) 78
United States v. Ray 196
Wildenhus's Case 80
Wooster, Warren 451
Wulfrom, R. 118
Zones, Article 24 134
Zones, Contiguous 125
Zones, Customs 127
Zones, Environmental Protection 139
Zones, Neutrality 130
Zones, Pirate Broadcasting 137

